RURAL MARKETING

Text and Cases

Second Edition

C. S. G. Krishnamacharyulu

Professor (Retd.), Department of Management Studies
Sri Venkateswara University
Tirupati

Lalitha Ramakrishnan

Professor, Department of Management Studies and
Centre Head, Pondicherry University P. G. Centre
Karaikal

Pearson

ISBN 9788131732632
First Impression, 2011
Seventeenth Impression, 2023
Eighteenth Impression, 2025

Published by Pearson India Education Services Pvt. Ltd, CIN: U72200TN2005PTC057128.

Head Office: 1st Floor, Berger Tower, Plot No. C-001A/2, Sector 16B, Noida - 201 301, Uttar Pradesh, India.
Registered Office: Featherlite, 'The Address' 5th Floor, Survey No 203/10B, 200 Ft MMRD Road, Zamin Pallavaram, Chennai – 600 044.
Website: in.pearson.com; Email: companysecretary.india@pearson.com

Printed in India at: Manipal Technologies Limited, Manipal

To our parents,

Smt. C. Atchyutavalli and
Late Sri. C. S. Lakshmanacharyulu

and

Smt. R. Rajeswari and
Late Thiru R. Ramakrishnan

with

love and gratitude

About the Authors

C. S. G. Krishnamacharyulu retired as Professor and Head of the Department of Management Studies, Sri Venkateswara University, Tirupati. A graduate in electrical engineering and a postgraduate in management from Andhra University, he did his doctoral research in business policy at Nagarjuna University. He was awarded a gold medal by the Andhra University for outstanding performance in MBA.

Dr Krishnamacharyulu has been actively engaged in teaching, research and consultancy in a distinguished career spanning more than 36 years. An active academician, he is also the author of *Cases in Rural Marketing* (Pearson Education, 2003), *Industrial Marketing* (Jaico Publishing House, 2006) and *Management of Technology* (Himalaya Publishing House, 2008). He is engaged in research in the areas of human resources and marketing.

Lalitha Ramakrishnan is Professor of marketing management, Department of Management Studies and Head of the Pondicherry University Campus at Karaikal. She specialized in marketing for obtaining her MBA degree and did research in business policy for her Ph.D. at Sri Venkateswara University, Tirupati.

Dr Lalitha has worked for the TVS group, IGGI Resorts International and Moneta Resorts before being appointed as Head, Department of Business Management, Sri. Padmavati Mahila University, Tirupati where she contributed significantly to its development. She has been teaching postgraduate management students for the past 18 years. She received the Best Teacher award from the Government of Andhra Pradesh in 2007.

She has co-authored six text books with Dr C. S. G. Krishnamacharyulu and published 18 research papers. She has been a prominent resource person at several training programmes, seminars and workshops. Her areas of interest include marketing, strategic management and women in management.

Brief Contents

Brief Contents

PART I NEW HORIZONS

PART II INSIGHTS

PART III DESIGNING STRATEGIES

PART IV APPLICATIONS

PART V LOOKING INTO THE FUTURE

PART VI CASES

Contents

Preface

Though change is common, some changes seem peculiar and paradoxical. Today, in the Indian economy, we witness one such bi-faceted change—a change from national to global on one side, and urban to rural on the other. Though the change is evolutionary and characteristic of a developing nation with a huge population and vast resources, one requires visionary entrepreneurship to respond proactively to it.

FMCG companies such as HUL, P&G and Colgate–Palmolive and consumer durables companies such as LG, Samsung and Philips, along with agri-input marketers, social workers and government agencies have exhibited visionary leadership in nurturing the rural markets. Rural markets have become sought-after destinations for corporations by compulsion as well as choice. Compulsion, because markets are saturated and there is nowhere to go and choice, because they are attractive and viable. Many experiments are being conducted to find the best way of reaching, attracting and retaining rural customers. Further, having survived the recent recession, the rural markets hold the promise of a bright future for intelligent and innovative marketers.

WHY STUDY RURAL MARKETING?

The study of rural marketing has become significant because of the saturation of the urban markets and the increase in the purchasing power of the rural population. The rural market is a tough place to explore with many differences, difficulties and vagaries. The sector poses a variety of challenges, including understanding the strategies to supply and satisfy the rural consumers.

The expanding interest of business managers in rural marketing has led to the formation of the Rural Marketing Association of India (RMAI), which has become a knowledge bank and training forum for young, budding marketers. These developments have produced a considerable academic response in the form of courses, seminars, research papers and text books. This is enough to stimulate interest in documenting the philosophy, concepts and techniques in a more systematic way for the benefit of readers.

The first edition of *Rural Marketing: Text and Cases* was written to fill the need for a comprehensive book on rural marketing that discusses strategies specific to the rural markets within the framework of general marketing. The second revised and enlarged edition of the book, while retaining the popular features of the first edition, provides a more comprehensive coverage of the changing profiles, issues and practices in the context of rural marketing. *Rural Marketing: Text and Cases* now covers a wider spectrum of products and services, with a decision-oriented and strategic outlook, and attempts to capture the rapidly changing profile of the rural market.

NEW TO THE SECOND EDITION

The second edition has been written after taking into account the feedback provided by students, reviewers and the numerous instructors who have used the first edition of the book. Besides discussing the traditional 4 P's of marketing in the rural context, extensive coverage of the applications of the rural marketing mix for promoting consumer products and services as well as agri-inputs and outputs has been provided. Emphasis has been laid on decision making by questioning and explaining the implications of the different situations and behaviours. The experiences of marketers and leading companies have been codified as examples and cases throughout the book.

Some of the major changes you will find in this edition are:

- **Addition of eight new chapters:** The second edition comprises 18 chapters that examine the expanded field of operations of rural marketers and the innovations in approaches and techniques.
- **Increased coverage of the agri-input and service sectors:** The agri-input and service sectors have been covered in great detail.
- **New chapter on social marketing:** An exclusive chapter that focuses on the concept of societal marketing in rural areas.
- **Additions to the end-of-chapter exercises:** Short answer questions, essay questions, mini projects and Internet exercises test students' understanding of concepts and promote critical thinking.
- **Forty-six new case studies:** Thirty-six end-of-chapter cases and ten comprehensive cases at the end of the book highlight the best practices followed by leading companies and provide conceptual clarity to the unique integrities of the rural market.
- **Complete supplement package:** A comprehensive supplement package comprising an instructors' manual, PowerPoint lecture slides and multiple choice questions support interactive teaching and learning.

STRUCTURE OF THE BOOK

Rural Marketing: Text and Cases comprises 18 chapters divided into six parts—new horizons, insights, designing strategies, applications, looking into the future and cases.

Part I—New Horizons explores the new horizons of rural marketing. Chapters 1, 2 and 3 examine the opportunities provided by the rural markets and establish a foundation for the study of rural marketing.

Part II—Insights discusses the important aspects that provide insights to marketers interested in designing strategies. Chapter 4 examines the intricacies of rural consumer behaviour and their implications on marketers. Chapter 5 discusses the methods and tools useful for researching the rural markets, while Chapter 6 evolves the guidelines for target marketing and positioning.

Part III—Designing Strategies elaborates on the 4 P's of the marketing mix in the context of rural markets. Chapters 7, 8, 9, 10 and 11 deal with product, price, promotion, communication, and sales and distribution strategies. The chapters in this part examine the application of the marketing framework for the different products and services in the rural markets.

Part IV—Applications offers an insight into how marketers make use of the marketing mix framework for different products and services. Chapter 12 explains the marketing practices of companies dealing with FMCGs and consumer durables. Chapter 13 elaborates the approaches adopted by agri-input companies to promote their products and services. Chapters 14 and 15 discuss the marketing of services such as banking, insurance and telecommunications as well as social marketing. Chapter 16 and 17 present the problems faced by farmers and artisans in marketing their products and examine the roles played by the government, corporate enterprises and NGOs.

Part V—Looking into the Future focuses on the future trends of rural marketing. The final chapter of the book establishes that cultural differences, emotional attachments, ICT developments, and grass-roots level innovations are the future drivers of rural marketing.

Part VI—Cases presents ten comprehensive cases that provide an insight into the application of rural marketing knowledge, skills and techniques with respect to different products and services in divergent marketing situations.

KEY FEATURES

Learning Objectives outline the learning goals of each chapter.

2

Understanding the Rural Economy

LEARNING OBJECTIVES

Upon completion of this chapter, you will be able to:

- Understand the socio-economic characteristics of rural areas in India
- Know the infrastructural facilities available for rural people
- Appreciate the technological developments and innovations that transformed rural life
- Recognize the role played by the government and other agencies in promoting rural development
- Identify the potential rural markets can offer in the future years

Opening Vignettes correlate the theories discussed in the chapters to real-world examples.

The life of a farmer, K. T. Srinivasa, has changed recently, though the two dirt roads near his home about 40 miles from India's high-tech capital of Bengaluru, his house without toilet facility, farm without tractor support and the way in which his family threshes rice by crushing it with a massive stone roller, have remained the same. How?

The change has been brought about by a cell phone. The little, attractive gadget is helping him make decisions related to farming. When to plant and harvest, at what price to sell the produce (rice, coconuts and jasmine), and how and when to transport and sell—all these intriguing questions are now resolved intelligently. Idea Cellular, Mr Srinivasa's service provider, has effectively utilized its first-mover advantages. Close to half the 800 people in the village, including Mr Srinivasa, have become its subscribers. Most of the villagers make voice calls as they don't know how to text message or download e-mails. On an average, rural Indians use their phones around 8.5 hours a month, up by 10 per cent over the past year.

The villagers are very amused with their new found connectivity with the world. They are now aware of the people and events affecting the rest of India and the world. They can answer quiz questions such as who is America's President and why there is an economic slowdown. The recession is not bullying them. They have understood that it is hurting their high-tech neighbours in Bengaluru much more and that the Indian economy is able to absorb the shocks much better than other developed nations. "After the global crises," says Mr Srinivasa, the farmer, "I think we are in better shape."[1]

This is an example of one of the many changes in the rural environment that have had a profound impact on rural lives. Every change brings with it an opportunity and a challenge. This chapter deals with environmental changes and their implications on marketers.

Each chapter contains several **boxes** that highlight innovative practices and examples from the rural marketing arena.

Box 1.3 Sustainable Partnership Models of Corporate Organizations

HUL-Vindhya Valley Project: In 2000, HUL helped the state-owned *Khadi* Board through an advisory relationship with the government of Madhya Pradesh. It helped the board to brand local produce from villages and tribal areas, such as natural honey collected from forests, in the state under the brand name Vindhya Valley. The product range includes edible products like *papads*, pickles, *masala* and turmeric. HUL provided the corporate expertise, marketing acumen and quality parameters, while the state government bore the marketing expenses for the brand building.

CFCL: *Uttam Bandhan* is the community welfare initiative launched in Rajasthan in 2000 by Chambal Fertilisers and Chemicals Ltd, the flagship company of the K. K. Birla group. Under this programme, CFCL trains unemployed rural youths as extension workers known as *krishi sewaks*, who interact with the farmers and advice them.

Canara Bank: The bank's main thrust is on imparting vocational skills to unemployed people. The bank has partnered with the Syndicate Bank and the Dharmastala Manjunatheshwara Educational Trust to set up 20 Rural Entrepreneurship Institutes across India. Then there are the projects it undertakes alone, such as artisans' training and computer literacy initiatives.

HUL: Project *Shakti* was piloted in 2001 in 50 villages in the state of Andhra Pradesh by involving members of Self-help groups (SHG). They are trained and provided micro credit to buy and sell HUL's products. On average, each *Shakti* entrepreneur earns enough each month to approximately double their previous household income—this makes a significant difference to family living standards. Through the nature of the products sold, the project is helping to increase awareness on health, hygiene and nutrition, thus improving the standard of living of the rural community. In addition, health educators known as *"Shakti Vanis"*, talk to self-help groups about HUL's brands and the importance of good nutrition and hygiene practices in combating diseases. In 2003, HUL piloted I-*Shakti*, an IT-based rural information service providing access to these key rural information needs in areas such as agriculture, education, health and hygiene, veterinary, etc.

The **Summary** recapitulates the main points discussed in the chapter.

Summary

Rural marketing is gaining recognition as a growing profession, distinct academic discipline and rewarding career for young management students and executives. A rural area can be defined at the convenience of companies, based on market potential. Rural demand exists for several products and services required for household consumption and occupational needs. Rural market entry decisions are influenced by three types of factors—urban push, rural pull and rural inhibiting. Urban push factors include saturated market, fierce competition and changing life-styles of urban people. Rural pull factors comprise rising affordability due to changes in population size, occupations, incomes, consumption and disposable incomes, growing acceptance for new products and services owing to increasing literacy, life-style changes and shifts in decision making, increasing availability needs due to growing usage and demand for products, upgrading of purchases and growing brand consciousness and improving accessibility by road and communication connectivity. The success of several companies is an important motivator. However, there are certain inhibiting factors too. Uneven development, fragmented markets, diversity in occupations, heterogeneity in life-styles, low income streams, lack of steady and sustainable consumption, poor marketing skills of promotional agencies, difficulty in accessing, less acceptance for urban life-style products (this is due to low education levels and few creative efforts of corporations in changing traditional thinking), intensifying competition and failure of some companies.

Four distinct approaches are identified to operate in rural markets. They are the trickle-down approach, the undifferentiated approach, the differentiated approach and the Integrated-Innovative-and-Inclusive (3-I) approach based on the bottom-of-the-pyramid theory.

The following guidelines help implement the 3-I approach.

Discussion Questions at the end of chapters stimulate classroom debates and discussions.

Discussion Questions

1. "Rural India is a less developed countryside where the infrastructure is primitive, houses are of mud or brick but rarely painted well, the primary source of livelihood is agriculture, employment opportunities in the organized sector are negligible, eating choices are restricted to home-cooked, simple food, schools are far away, health facilities are rudimentary and—importantly—the youth, while energetic and ambitious, are to be seen playing cards the whole day," says Ajit Gupta of www.ruralnaukri.com. Do you agree?
2. "While mobile phones are widely seen merely as a communications medium, they should really be seen as a new and essential form of infrastructure that will transform a host of other service sectors in rural economies around the world," Discuss.

Short Answer Questions facilitate a review of the concepts discussed in the chapters.

Short Answer Questions

1. Discuss the impact of environmental variables on the selection of markets by a firm.
2. Briefly describe the changes in the economic scenario of rural areas.
3. Examine the improvements in rural life-style and media habits.
4. Elucidate the role of technology in the development of rural areas.
5. Explain how the urban–rural divide is challenged by ICT projects in rural areas.
6. What do you understand by appropriate technology for rural people? Give examples.
7. What is micro-financing? How does it help improve the lot of women in rural areas?
8. Generate a list of rural development schemes and identify their key achievements.

Essay Questions at the end of each chapter help students gauge their understanding of the concepts covered in the chapter.

Essay Questions

1. Explain the factors that have made rural markets attractive.
2. Explain the approaches to rural marketing and decide which one is suitable for the following: (a) Jewellery: Nakshatra (b) Surf-Excel (c) Tractors of M&M (d) Nirma washing powder.
3. How does rural marketing differ from urban marketing? What qualities should a rural marketer possess?
4. Explain the Integrated–Innovative–Inclusive marketing model. Provide suitable guidelines for companies planning to go rural.

Mini Projects are analysis-oriented assignments that help students' correlate theoretical concepts to reality.

Mini Projects

1. Design a questionnaire and conduct a survey in rural areas to understand consumer behaviour with respect to one consumer durable of your choice.
2. Conduct a focus group study to know the purchase preferences of housewives with respect to detergents.
3. Interview young men and women to know about their lifestyles and aspirations.
4. Visit households in villages, close to the towns and remote ones, and prepare a report on purchases for children (below 6 years) in households of different income groups.

Internet Exercises stimulate data collection and further research into the rural hinterland.

Internet Exercise

Obtain information about the detailed methodology and data employed for constructing Household Premiumness Index (HPI). Contact the IRS team of Hansa Research. The e-mail addresses that can be used are irsinfo@hansaresearch.com and Vineet.Sodhani@hansaresearch.com.

Two **cases** at the end of each chapter highlight the practical applications of the theories discussed in the chapter.

Case 1.1 Trials of a Rural Sales Trainee

When choosing to be a rural sales trainee in the largest consumer durables company of India, Bhalla did not size up the challenges a woman sales trainee might face, perhaps overwhelmed by the enthusiasm of going rural and serving the nation. As she battles to find a foothold in the male-dominated distribution chain and retail world, one question that looms large in her mind is—Is India liberated?

Encountering the prejudiced and patronizing attitude of distributors and shopkeepers on a daily basis, handling questions like "why didn't you join Citibank?", listening to her superiors proclaim that the "single-most definitive thing about sales is that it is a man's world," Bhalla learns to take it in her stride as she goes through bumpy rides on delivery vans, assignments with no basic amenities, and junior sales managers who watch porn movies in conference rooms.

In the "real" India, the girl-child is routinely used to serve the father, the brother and the husband even today. Even meritorious girls have to forego their dreams at the altar of tradition and marriage, the lines of religious divide are sacrosanct and a poor village girl can get her nose chopped off for talking to a strange man.

Bhalla counsels, "You certainly need a strong positive attitude for facing life head-on, as you often land in weird adventures—dealing with eve-teasers, floods and crocodiles, getting stranded with a much touted stain-removing detergent that fails to work its magic in front of a crowd, dealing with a black-mailing policeman or a bus ride with a goat—all in the daily life of a sales trainee!"

Bhalla further observes, "I learnt the rules of survival when after trying hard for a year "to be one of the boys" and "to feel comfortable in the Martian territory", I discovered how to turn my handicap of being a woman into an advantage. Though frustrated at being designated either a sister or a daughter by sundry distributors and shopkeepers, I later found that these very roles allowed me access into their family and to their womenfolk (how many males can manage that) and thus, I understood not only the efficacy of my company's products but also I indulged in some smart bonding, a factor that provided the much-needed edge over my male colleagues."

Bhalla goes back to Mumbai with the pleasure of doing what others said "I could not do" and says, "The lesson I learnt is—in rural India, it's best to stick to popular wisdom."

For discussion

1. Identify the problems and challenges faced by sales trainees of both genders.
2. Suggest steps to be taken by (i) educational institutions, (ii) recruiting companies and (iii) career aspirants in developing effective rural sales skills.

Source: Debasree Bhattacharjee, "Retail's Tryst with Rural India," *The Financial Express*, 1 December 2007.

Ten **Comprehensive Cases** at the end of the book offer an insight into the actual application of rural marketing theories and skills in dynamic markets.

CASE 5 AN ALL-WEATHER FRIENDSHIP

The Nagarjuna group was founded by the late K. V. K. Raju, a professional technocrat in 1973. It is one of the rapidly growing business houses in India. The group's asset base will cross USD 5 billion in the next five years. The group has significant presence in the steel, fertilizers, chemicals and financial services sectors of the country.

Nagarjuna Fertilizers and Chemicals Limited (NFCL), the flagship company, is the first gas-based fertilizer factory in South India. Construction began in 1988 in Kakinada in Andhra Pradesh and commercial production commenced from 1 August 1992. In 1998, it doubled the capacity of urea to 1.4 million tonnes. The other companies of the group offering agricultural solutions are Vijayalakshmi Insecticides and Pesticides, Nagarjuna Agri-chem Ltd, Nagarjuna Agricultural Research and Development Institute and Nagarjuna Haifa India Ltd (Vietnam).

The new logo of the group symbolizes a dynamic and value-based organization actuating the concept of trusteeship. The logo exemplies the group's inner strength through the core values of organizational concern, commitment, quality and integrity towards its stockholders and customers. The central circle symbolises the sun, the source of prime energy of the solar system. The five circles also symbolize the five elements of the universe and spirit of continuity. The triangle represents the planet Mars, which from time immemorial has symbolized prosperity, success and an abundance of energy. Therefore, it represents the upward flow of perennial energy towards the mission of the group.

The Company's Mission

The company visualizes itself as a highly trusted business partner of Indian farmers and seeks to serve society through its business. It is ambitious of becoming the leading agri–input supplier in the country meeting the farmers' need of quality inputs for improving their productivity through latest technologies and services of committed and knowledgeable team of people.

Marketing Organization

The marketing head office of the company is located at Hyderabad. The organizational structure is depicted in Exhibit 5.1. With more than 3,000 dealers over 11 states across the country, the department handles a turnover above Rs 8 billion for its product range comprising 25 to 30 products.

It has six marketing zones across the country—two in Andhra Pradesh (one at Vishakhapatnam and the other at Hyderabad) and one each in West Bengal, Orissa, Maharashtra and Karnataka.

Market Share

NFCL is the leader with a share of 50 per cent in the 4 million tonne urea market, which is growing at a rate of 10 per cent. The primary competitors in the urea market are:

State	Competitors
Andhra Pradesh	Kribhco, RCF, SPIC, MFL, NFL & ZACL
Orissa	IFFCO, NFL, Oswal & DIL
West Bengal	IFFCO, TCL, IG, NFL, Oswal & DIL
Maharashtra	RCF, Kribhco, IFFCO, GIWFC & GSFC
Karnataka	MFL, RCF, ZACL, Kribhco & SPIL

Product Portfolio

The company has a range of products that includes:

- Fertilizers
  - Manufactured urea (1.4 million MTs p.a.)
  - Traded fertilizers (0.2 million MTs p.a.) (MOP, DAP, Urea, AS, ZSSP).

THE TEACHING AND LEARNING PACKAGE

The student and instructor support resources provided with this book make learning and teaching a pleasurable experience. They include:

- An Instructors' Resource Manual that provides an analysis of all the case studies and answers to all the chapter-ending exercises in the book.
- PowerPoint lecture slides that outline the main theories discussed in the chapters and enable instructors to make effective presentations.
- The *mQuest* application that enables students to revise concepts, search for or find definitions, take quizzes and get instant feedback on their cell phones.

The instructors' manual and the PowerPoint slides are available at www.pearsoned.co.in/csgkrishnamacharyulu.

WHO MADE THE REVISION POSSIBLE?

The book has drawn information and inspiration from several executives, writers and researchers. We are highly indebted to them for their path-breaking and thought-provoking contributions. The sources of information are carefully acknowledged to facilitate further references.

Special thanks are due to researchers, management students and teachers in different colleges and academic institutions and marketing executives, who have appreciated the first edition of the book and offered ideas for updating the book with contemporary information. We are obliged to R. Seshadri, Managing Director of Anugrah Madison Advertising Pvt. Ltd for his encouragement and support. We are grateful to Professor T. Siddaiah, Principal, SVU College of Commerce, Management and Computer Science, for his interest in the revision of the book.

We are indebted to Pearson Education for encouraging us to revise the book. Rajesh Shetty coordinated the reviews at the time of preparing the revision plan. We are thankful to our reviewers for their frank opinions, critical evaluation and constructive suggestions. A major credit for the book coming out in its present form goes to Priya Christopher, who inspired us from time to time by setting deadlines, suggesting ideas and promising support. We are grateful to her for her analytical feedback. We also express our thanks to M. E. Sethurajan, M. R. Ramesh and A. Maran who worked hard to bring the book out in time.

Finally, our gratitude and appreciation to the light of our lives—C. Sri Krishna and C. Srivalli—who are adept at selling their ideas using innovative marketing techniques.

HOPES AND EXPECTATIONS

The book is targeted at post graduate management students, researchers, teachers and industry executives. We hope that it benefits marketers interested in rural conquest and teachers engaged in training young management students for marketing careers. Students pursuing distance education programmes will also find the book useful as it is written in a lucid style with numerous examples and interesting case studies. The book is also intended to stimulate research scholars to undertake projects in this burgeoning field. We welcome feedback and suggestions for further improvements.

C. S. G. Krishnamacharyulu
Lalitha Ramakrishnan

Reviewers

Rural Marketing: Text and Cases has benefited from an extensive development process, which involved faculty reviewers providing feedback about the accuracy and relevance of the content as well as suggestions for its improvement. While we could not incorporate every suggestion from everyone, we do acknowledge that their feedback was invaluable in our attempt at creating the best possible rural marketing textbook. We would like to thank the following for their time and commitment:

Ramana Acharyulu
Pioneer Institute of Management, Udaipur

Biswajit Das
KIIT School of Management, Bhubaneshwar

Rajat Gera
Institute of Management Technology, Ghaziabad

Somiyajulu Gharimella
International Management Institute, New Delhi

Sunil Kulkarni
Future Institute of Management, Mumbai

Milind Trivikram Phadtare
National Institute of Construction Management and Research, Pune

Satya Prasad
Vishwa Vishwani Institute of Systems and Management, Hyderabad

A. M. Sakkthivel
Loyola Institute of Business Administration, Chennai

Part I New Horizons

1

Rural Marketing Opportunities

LEARNING OBJECTIVES

Upon completion of this chapter, you will be able to:

- Understand the meaning of rural marketing, its scope and nature
- Analyse the emergence of rural markets and classify them
- Use the 4 A's and 4 P's frameworks and the bottom-of-the-pyramid theory to take three important decisions—(i) going rural, (ii) adopting a suitable approach and implementing it and (iii) becoming a rural marketer
- Test whether you have the potential to become a rural marketer

Seventy per cent of India's population, 56 per cent of its income, 64 per cent of its expenditure and 33 per cent of its savings come from rural India. A recent study on rural marketing by the Confederation of Indian Industry (CII) points out that the consumption trend in rural areas has shown a paradigm shift from price-driven to quality-driven products. The winds of liberalization removed barriers and presently, many national as well as international manufacturers have made a foray into different markets. Each of the companies has products in several categories, for example, Hindustan Unilever Limited (HUL) is in hair care (shampoos, hair oil, and creams), skin care, fabric care, home care, food and beverages, etc. Similarly, in the durables category there are players such as Philips which has products such as TVs, audio systems, DVD players, etc.

New companies are fighting an intense battle to get a foothold while the existing players are putting in all their counter strategies in this battle for survival. The battle is on across all the product categories—be it consumer non-durables, consumer durables or the service industry—though the degree or nature of battle may vary in each case. According to Pradeep Lokhande, head of Rural Relations, "Marketing a product or service in a rural centre is like sowing a seed. You have to wait for it to take root." Indeed, the seeds of some of the foremost innovations in rural marketing were sown by FMCG companies, such as HUL, that were looking for new ways to reach out to rural consumers.[1]

What kind of marketing strategies are required in the present marketing environment characterized by dynamic changes and challenges? What kind of innovations have companies such as HUL, ITC, LG and HPCL introduced to become successful? Are they sustainable? Do they have to look in new directions?

The questions raised above are indicative of the fascinating subject matter this book deals with. Chapter 1 serves as an introduction to this intriguing area. It introduces the concepts and approaches that a marketer can consider for designing appropriate strategies.

INTRODUCTION

Rural marketing has gained recognition as a growing profession, a distinct academic discipline and a rewarding career for young management students and executives. The predictions of eminent business persons that rural markets would outstrip urban markets have proved right. Today, rural markets are not only attractive but also responsive. With this new opportunity the marketing battlefield has expanded from the cities to the villages. "Go rural and be rural" seems to be the guiding principle of marketing.

All smart marketers, Indian as well as MNCs, seem to have embraced this tenet. Companies such as Asian Paints, HUL, ITC, Colgate–Palmolive, Godrej, Philips, LG, Nokia and Dabur have made inroads into the countryside. New approaches, new strategic alternatives and new operational techniques are being evolved to gain competitive advantage.

WHAT IS RURAL?

The different definitions of the term "rural" may be classified under three perspectives—public administration, action oriented and marketing oriented.

The public administration perspective considers urbanization as a sign of development and focuses on the urban concept to move from a *panchayat* set up to a corporation.

The census of India (2001) defines rural as that which is not urban. Urban is defined as:

- All locations within a municipality/corporation, cantonment board or a notified town area committee.
- All other locations that satisfy the following criteria:
  1. Minimum population of 5,000.
  2. At least 75 per cent of the male workforce engaged in non-agricultural activities, and
  3. A population density of over 400 persons per sq. km.

This definition is not useful when you consider the marketing-oriented perspective because of the following paradoxes:

- A city may be classified as a mini-metro on the basis of its population, the occupation of its residents, population density. However, some of its other characteristics may be that of a rural market even though the administrative setup may be that of a corporation.
- Similarly, a slum in a metro could have the attributes of a rural market for some products and the attributes of an urban market for some others.
- Many towns are actually overgrown villages and are classified as towns only because they have a municipality. On the other hand, many administratively-defined villages that are surrounded by cities, are more like urban centres.

As such, the census of India (2001) definition is not appealing to rural marketers. They need a definition that signifies market potential or lifestyles for initiating action. Consider the following case that shows how an action-oriented definition is provided by the Insurance Regulatory Development Authority (IRDA).[2]

> The IRDA definition of rural areas included all areas with a population of less than 5,000, with a density of population less than 400 per sq.km and where at least 75 per cent of the male working population was engaged in agricultural pursuits. The IRDA had amended the definition earlier in 2002 to bring down the required stipulated percentage of the population that had to be engaged in agricultural pursuits to at least 25. The revised definition has widened the market. Mr Vivek Khanna, Director of Marketing, Aviva Life Insurance Company, said, "A couple of thousand villages would now be brought under the fold. The earlier definition meant that only some remote villages could be tapped. And there is no ambiguity now." Ms Anjana Grewal, Vice-President of Marketing at Birla Sun Life Insurance Company, said, "The revised definition brings a larger part of the population under 'rural', almost 72 per cent compared to 42 per cent under the earlier definition. What this would do is make it possible for insurance companies to introduce different products with higher premiums."

Innovation-focused marketers may like the following definition from the sociological point of view:

> Rural is defined as a group of people who are traditionalists in outlook, rooted in the land, and who resist change.

Action-based definitions aim at providing specifications of the target markets that remove ambiguity and improve decision making. In doing so, they enable decision makers to define possible areas of action, help focus on variables in the decision situation, assist in information search and guide decision making and implementation. They are generally based on the calculation of market potential value (MPV) of a particular area. They differ from one product group to another as given here:

- Most companies in the FMCG and agri-input sector would define rural as a place with a population of up to 20,000.
- Durable goods' companies would consider any town with a population of below 50,000 as a rural market.

TAXONOMY OF THE RURAL MARKET

Rural markets can be classified in a manner similar to urban markets. They can be classified into consumer markets, industrial markets, and services markets.

Consumer markets

Constituents: Individuals and households
Products: Consumables—Food products, toiletries, cosmetics, textiles and garments, foot wear, etc.
Durables: Watches, bicycles, radios, TVs, kitchen appliances, furniture, sewing machines, two-wheelers, etc.

Industrial markets

Constituents: Agricultural and allied activities, poultry farming, fishing, animal husbandry, cottage industries, health centres, schools, co-operatives, *Panchayat* offices, etc.
Products: Consumables—Seeds, fertilizers, pesticides, animal feed, fishnets, medicines, petrol/diesel, etc.
Durables: Tillers, tractors, pump sets, generators, harvesters, boats, etc.

Services markets

Constituents: Individuals, households, offices, and production firms
Services: Repairs, transport, banking, credit, insurance, health care, education, communication, power, etc.

GO RURAL DECISION

The factors influencing the decision to enter a rural market can be divided into three categories as given below. The first two factors have a positive influence whereas the third one exercises a negative influence on the "go rural" decision.

- Urban push factors
- Rural pull factors
- Rural inhibiting factors

Urban push factors

Companies that have so far successfully operated in the urban markets have found them no longer attractive for the following reasons:

Saturation stage

Many products such as soaps, detergents, shampoos, fairness products and consumer durables such as refrigerators, TVs and air coolers/conditioners have achieved maturity in the urban market on account of their high penetration levels.

Fierce competition

Urban markets have become congested with too many competitors. Heavy expenditure on marketing has become necessary as there are too many brands, both domestic and foreign, fighting for a justifiable share. Sustaining brand image and growth in sales have become difficult and challenging tasks.

Changing lifestyles

The market is now dominated by the youth. According to MindShare Insights, the research division of a media buying agency MindShare, 65 per cent or over 700 million Indians are younger than 35 years. They are "trysumers"—open to risk and are willing to try anything that is trendsetting, an attribute that has been accentuated by their growing purchasing power. As a result, marketers are forced to try innovative strategies.

Rural pull factors

The rural pull factors or the factors that make rural markets attractive are as follows:

(i) Rising affordability
(ii) Growing acceptance
(iii) Increasing availability needs
(iv) Improving accessibility
(v) Success stories of corporations

Rising affordability

Rural markets are now dominating the urban markets in terms of demand and potential. According to McKinsey & Company[3]:

"In 20 years the rural Indian market will be larger than the total consumer markets in countries such as South Korea or Canada today, and almost four times the size of today's urban Indian market. The estimated size of the rural market will be USD 577 billion."

Rural India is a major part of India's domestic consumption story not just because it is home to 70 per cent of India's population, but because of its growth potential. The purchasing power of the rural population is on the rise on account of the good monsoon and development programmes by the government. There is also a shift from total dependence on farm income to non-farm incomes.

We will now examine the key parameters of the rural economy to know why rural markets have become attractive.[4–6]

(i) *Population:* The rural market is attractive because of its size and growth of population and households despite the exodus by migration to urban areas. About 70 per cent of the more than 1.1 billion people in India live in rural areas. Approximately 70 per cent of the households in India are in the rural regions. The number is expected to rise from 135 million in 2001–02 to 153 million in 2009–10.

(ii) *Occupation:* The country has 235 million farmers and agriculture accounts for about a fifth of the USD 775 billion economy. About 4 per cent of rural Indian households comprise large farmers with landholdings of more than 10 acres. 30 per cent of rural households are marginal farmers with less than two acres, and another 15 per cent have 2–4 acres. Half of the rural Indian economy is non-agriculture-based and a third of the households—around 50 million—are engaged in non-agricultural activities with people working in manufacturing, or as traders, shopkeepers, providing services such as electricity generation, construction, mining and quarrying, transportation and haulage.

(iii) *Income:* As per current estimates, the annual household income of urbanites is Rs 95,827 against Rs 5,19,222 of ruralites. The per capita income among semi-urban folks is around Rs 14,000 to 15,000 per annum while for rural folks it is less than Rs 7,000 per annum. The per capita income of rural and semi-urban people would double by 2012 thereby leading to an increase in demand. It is estimated that if rural incomes rise by one per cent, buying power would increase by Rs 100 billion.

(iv) *Consumption:* Expenditure as a percentage of income is 78 per cent in rural areas and 72 per cent in urban areas. The rural share of popular consumer goods and durables ranges from 30 per cent to 60 per cent of sales. The expenditure as a percentage of income of rural areas is higher for many categories.

- On food, it is 36.6 per cent as against 24.6 per cent in urban areas
- On FMCGs, it is 5.6 per cent as against 4.9 per cent in urban areas
- On clothing and footwear, it is 5 per cent as against 4 per cent in urban areas
- On durables, it is 3.8 per cent as against 3.7 per cent in urban areas

The only exception is miscellaneous goods. On miscellaneous goods and services, it is 48.7 per cent as against 62.8 per cent in urban areas.

(v) *Disposable income:* The disposable surplus is 22 per cent of total income in rural and 28 per cent in urban areas. The marginal difference is positive news to marketers as it leads to an increase in purchases in many categories including construction materials, apparel and durables.

Growing acceptance

The rural society is also urbanizing gradually with the increase in literacy rates and exposure to global trends. It is showing interest in branded products and services.

Increasing literacy

The literacy in urban areas was 80.3 per cent and that in rural areas 59.4 per cent. The encouraging point is that the literacy growth rate in the decade ending 2001 has been higher in the rural areas, at 14.75 per cent as compared to the 7.2 per cent increase in urban areas. The total literacy goal is not far off. There is progress in e-learning opportunities and community development projects of universities and corporations that are focusing on this.[7]

Lifestyle changes

Many lifestyle changes have been witnessed in the rural areas. These can be attributed to three sources of influence.

(i) *Increasing literacy levels and education:* Most of the elders in rural areas can now read newspapers and magazines and understand the changing trends in the country. The sons of the rural soil are now benefited by charitable foundations of IT companies that are imparting computer education in villages. The young go to urban areas for higher education and bring home urban lifestyles.

(ii) *Media explosion:* With the advent of satellite television, the rural populace has been exposed to the rich lifestyle of urban households. This has created awareness about branded products and also induced an attraction for premium products such as Surf, Ariel, Pantene and Denim.

(iii) *Cinemas:* The portrayal of heroes growing from rags to riches and challenging the rich has an impact on the psyche of rural people.

Shifts in decision making

Decision making is no longer dominated by the male head of the family. The self-help group (SHG) movement is empowering women. Education is empowering rural youth. The youth are emerging as key decision makers in the family. Since women are more home-oriented, they buy related products. As the youth are more open to fresh concepts, they become innovation adopters and prefer lifestyle products. Thus, some rural households possess a range of products comparable to urban households. Surprisingly, the experimenting households are more or less evenly spread across the various socio-economic clusters of the rural market.

Increasing demand

The entry into rural market is encouraged by two factors—growing usage and demand for branded products.

Growing usage and demand for products

According to Indicus Analytics, the rural market is almost equal to the urban market in size, being worth Rs 13,170 vis-à-vis the Rs 13,650 billion worth of the urban market. According to a study by the Chennai-based Francis Kanoi Marketing Planning Services,[8] the estimated annual size of the rural market is as follows (Table 1.1):

Table 1.1 Size of the Rural Market

FMCGs	Rs 650 billion
Consumer Durables	Rs 50 billion
Agri-inputs (e.g., tractors)	Rs 450 billion
2/4 Wheelers	Rs 80 billion
Total	Rs 1,230 billion

Information from various agencies indicates growth in rural demand:

(i) The FMCG sector continues to grow at 20 per cent (urban growth 17 per cent) with no downgrading of brands despite price increase in some categories, durables at around 15 per cent with upgrading from regular to flat screen colour TVs and a sharp rise in DVD sales and DTH connections.[5]

(ii) The insurance sector was estimated to be worth USD 2.8 billion and it is likely to grow by 200 per cent, reaching USD 51.2 billion by 2009–10. Rural India is expected to provide business opportunities worth USD 23 billion for insurance companies providing them with the right product mix.[9]

(iii) The service sector is also growing.[6]

- From 2008 to 2009, there was a steep increase in sales of DTH connections. In case of telecom services, 71 per cent of new subscribers are from rural areas as against 29 per cent in urban areas. Of the two million BSNL mobile connections, 50 per cent are in rural areas. Of the 0.6 million villages, 0.522 million villages have a Village Public Telephone (VPT).
- Villagers hold 41 million *kisan* credit cards with a cumulative credit of Rs 977 billion. About 42 million households are availing banking services in comparison to 27 million households in urban areas. About 6.6 million households have invested in savings schemes in rural areas. This is close to the urban count of 6.7 million households.

Upgrading of purchases

In rural households, there is an upgradation in the form of the product used. For example, households are upgrading from traditional mosquito repellants such as *gober* to coils and mats. There is also an upgradation from local or unbranded products to national brands and from low-priced brands to premium brands. This is primarily due to the influence of the youth in households. This has resulted in the use of products of more than one brand for the same purpose in the household. This phenomenon was noticed way back in 1999. An interesting insight made by the R-panel of ORG-MARG (June 1999) was that trials for premium products were not restricted to the more affluent classes of rural India.

For instance, 20 per cent of the households using toothpowder also use toothpaste. The difference in choice of products has thus led to dual usage of product categories. Many of the households using premium brands also use mass-market washing powders.

Growing brand consciousness

The rural market is flooded with local brands and fake products. The view that rural people don't use quality brands is based on a wrong understanding of the rural mindset. Rural people have readily accepted several brands when they have been offered in small pack sizes and at low price points.

Improving accessibility

Infrastructure is improving rapidly in rural India. The government is spending more to build roads to connect villages, expand irrigation networks and supply electricity to improve productivity and raise incomes. Prime Minister Manmohan Singh started the *Bharat Nirman*, or Building India, project with a plan to spend Rs 1.76 trillion by 2009 to build roads, provide electricity to 100,000 villages, extend irrigation to 10 million hectares, or 24.7 million acres, and build 6 million houses.[10] The important highlights are:

- There has been a steep change in rural road connectivity from less than 40 per cent connectivity in 2004 to at least 70 per cent connectivity at the end of 2008, according to an IIFL (India Infoline) research report.
- There has been real improvement in phone connectivity as well. The growth in rural teledensity from 2000 to 2008 is significant as it rose to 9.43 per 100 population from 0.68. Every 1000+ population is connected by STD.

Table 1.2 Retail Distribution Facilities

Post offices	1,38,000
Haats	42,000
Melas	25,000
Mandis	7,000
Public distribution shops	3,80,000
Bank branches	32,000
Cooperative societies	5,00,000

- More than 90 per cent of villages have electricity and investments in the power sector are being made to make them functional.
- PC penetration in rural homes grew by 24 per cent in 2008 as compared to 7 per cent in urban areas. With IT companies partnering with government projects, every student will have a laptop and many more rural homes will have PCs.
- Rural retail distribution has been made less complex by several available facilities (Table 1.2).
- Corporations have invested in their own retail chains that other companies can make use of by arriving at a mutual agreement. For instance, DCM Shriram Consolidated Limited (DSCL) started *Haryali* Stores, M&M opened *Subhlabh* stores, and IOC set up *Kisan Seva Kendras* (KSK).

Success stories

Companies like HUL, ITC, Nirma, Dabur, Godrej, Coca-Cola, Pepsi, LG, Samsung, Maruti, Hyundai Bharti Airtel, Idea Cellular and many others have succeeded by using innovative strategies. Some of the success stories are as follows:

- Hindustan Unilever, the Mumbai-based local unit of Unilever, sells its products through 6.3 million shops, reaching eight out of 10 households in India. Its Project *Shakti* is a resounding success.
- ITC revolutionized village life by starting e-*choupals*.
- Reader's Digest has 0.6 million customers in rural and semi-urban areas.
- Bharti Airtel started focusing on rural markets in 2007 and gained 60 per cent of its customer base in rural areas within two years.
- Hero Honda launched its rural vertical "*Har gaon, Har Angan*" and its sales went up.

RURAL INHIBITING FACTORS

Companies entering rural markets need to prepare themselves for some surprises and shocks. The media reports are contradictory—some report stark poverty in rural areas and others showcase the urban style of living. The truth obviously lies somewhere in between. This is why companies should exercise caution while taking entry decisions. We will now identify some of the problems that inhibit the successful operations of corporations in the rural market.

Uneven development

Anecdotal evidence shows very visible signs of marked modernity and progress, yet census data corroborates the "stuck in the dark ages" description of rural India. Only 25 per cent of rural households have access to tap water (compared with 70 per cent in urban India); 30 per cent do not have road connectivity; 40 per cent do not have electricity in households; and only 52 per cent have semi-*pucca* houses (compared with 80 per cent in urban areas). There are remote villages which are not touched by the economic and social reforms. There are many below poverty line (BPL) households. Occasionally, we see media reports on suicides of farmers and weavers. The development programmes of the government are subverted by corrupt officials. The poor villager continues to be ignored. He suffers from lack of proper information and awareness. Inadequate infrastructure such as the non-availability of gas supply, frequent power cuts, improper sanitary conditions, etc. are common problems in many villages.

Fragmented market

The average population in the villages of India is 100 for 15 per cent of villages, 345 for 21 per cent of villages, 724 for 24 per cent of villages, and 2,974 for 32 per cent of villages. Thus, about 96 per cent of the villages have a population that is less than 5,000 people. Thus, we are dealing with extremely fragmented markets where the population density is extremely low. This is vastly different from urban markets where population density is high and distribution is standardized.

Diversity in occupations

The rural consumer could be a bank clerk commuting to the nearest town or an agricultural labourer in a thatched-roof hut. Employees in government, business, industry and service organizations, people engaged in farming and animal husbandry, traditional artisans and contract or daily labourers in organized and unorganized sector all constitute the rural market. They may be engaged in more than one business or occupation. For instance, a farmer may be engaged in land cultivation, poultry farming, a chit fund business and money lending.

Heterogeneity in lifestyles

The heterogeneity in lifestyles is mainly on account of the geography, varied income levels and cultural differences of the consumers.

> The Punjabi farmer has a better standard of living as compared to farmers in Bihar and UP. The villagers in South India are better educated than those in North India. Women occupy an important role in the society and more often than not, are responsible for a number of product decisions.[11]

Low-income streams

Rural consumers have small disposable incomes and very little storage space. Rural India has an average per capita income that is half of that of urban India. Extrapolating from income data from the National Council for Applied Economic Research (NCAER), we know that 21.7 per cent of the rural population is below the poverty line; for urban populations, the incidence of poverty is 20.8 per cent, not much lower.

Lack of steady and sustainable consumption

Even today, agriculture accounts for half of rural income. The Green Revolution and other reforms have encouraged productivity-driven income growth (as opposed to price-driven growth) in the agricultural sector on a sustained basis. In some states like Punjab and Haryana we may see better crops, captive buyers, export-focused higher price. However, in other places, the income growth is because of better prices (either market or support prices). The popular view is that non-agricultural income, which accounts for a hefty 50 per cent of rural income, is far more stable than agricultural income. Data from the National Service Schemes (NSS) show that rural households with non-agriculture as the main source of income are far higher spenders than agricultural households and are more urban-like in their proportion of food expenditure. Non-agricultural income is widespread, and of different kinds. Research from IIFL indicates that of the 54 per cent of non-farm rural income, 12 per cent is dependent on the urban or overseas markets while 42 per cent is dependent on farming or hunting. This is worrying indeed.

Promotional agencies lack marketing skills

The promotional agencies (*Khadi* Commission, Handicrafts, Handlooms, etc.) and NGOs that are engaged in the non-farm sector lack professional marketing support and hence are unable to help the poor get better value for products made by them. This affects the purchasing power of rural consumers.

Access difficulty

Reach and penetration of most companies, other than the likes of HUL, is poor. Almost 25 per cent of the villages with less than 500 people have no access to a shop.

Limited awareness and acceptance

The awareness as well as acceptance levels for branded products and services have been low among rural consumers. This is due to the low level of education of the rural people on the one hand and less focused and less creative educative campaigns of corporations on the other.

Low level of education

Rural India still has a low level of traditional education, making rural Indians different kind of consumers. 26 per cent of rural India's chief wage earners (CWEs) are illiterate compared to eight per cent in urban India. Seven per cent of rural CWEs are graduates compared to 29 per cent in urban India.

Low budget for promotion

According to estimates by the Rural Marketing Agencies Association of India, the total budget for rural marketing is only about Rs 5 billion, compared to the over Rs 130 billion allotted to mass media. This is grossly inadequate to cover the huge marketing potential for different products in the rural markets.

Intensifying competition

Cut-throat competition pressurizes the margins of big firms such as Nirma, Hindustan Unilever, Dabur, ITC, Godrej, Britannia, Coca-Cola and Pepsi. Competition is found at three levels: foreign and national brands, regional brands and fake products.

Bhag Bakri tea, *Ghadi* detergent powder and Power soap are proofs that regional brands can become brands to reckon with at the national level. Similarly, Nirma began as a regional player and is now a national giant. They all started in small, concentrated markets, appealing to the local ethos and aspirations of the targeted area.

Brands such as "Jifebuoy", "Bonds Talcum" and "Funny & Lovely" are counterfeit products. It is estimated that FMCG companies lose more than Rs 100 billion to spurious products every year, mostly sold through local *haats* and bazaars.

Failure of some companies

It is true that some companies had earlier failed to make a dent in rural markets. This can be attributed to their half-hearted efforts and faulty tactical approaches.

Many FMCG companies had applied faulty tactical approaches. They appointed vendors who implemented the company's ideas blindly, whether they were van campaigns or below-the-line activities. Very little effort to tailor the communication to suit the local audience or fit it with the overall campaign initiatives in the mass media was made. This invariably led to less than satisfactory results in terms of awareness of the brands and long-term impact of the efforts in the targeted markets.

APPROACH DECISION: RURAL MARKETING MODELS

What are the different approaches to rural marketing? What are the philosophical orientations of the companies operating in the rural hinterland? Do they consider rural marketing as a part of their corporate social responsibility? Are they entering rural markets guided by their business growth philosophy? Are they inspired by the bottom-of-the-pyramid theory proposed by Dr C. K. Prahalad? We will now examine the rural marketing approaches in relation to urban marketing and philosophical orientations of business organizations.

There are four rural marketing approaches found in practice and they are:

- Trickle-down approach
- Undifferentiated approach
- Differentiated approach
- Bottom-of-the-pyramid marketing

Trickle-down approach

Companies that focused mainly on urban areas for sales and experienced growth in urban sales relied only on the "trickle-down approach" for the rural market. They believe that there is absolutely no need for designing marketing programmes to reach rural areas (See Figure 1.1).

Assumptions

This approach is based on the following premises.

First, the rural market can be conveniently ignored. The top-end rural market is small in size and the sales from rural areas are only a bonus.

Second, the top-end, urban-society culture approximates the culture of the West at the aspirational level. Similarly, the top-end, rural-society culture comes close to the top-end urban one.

Third, the rural householder buys his wares from the nearby "feeder town" either on a special visit or when he is there on work.

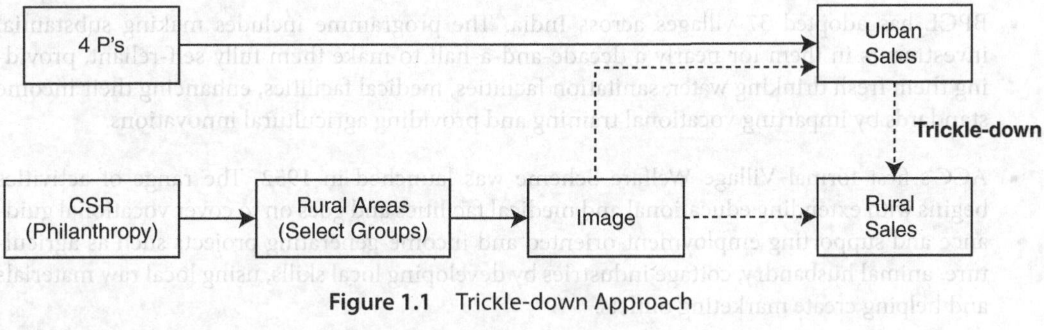

Figure 1.1 Trickle-down Approach

Suitability

Companies offering top-end, urban-centric premium and luxury products do not have any concern for rural markets.

Luxury-products market in India is estimated to be in excess of USD 500 million and is likely to grow at a Compound Annual Growth Rate (CAGR) of 28 per cent to reach USD 1.2 billion by 2010. The market is expected to double by 2015, touching USD 2.5 billion. Brands like Damro, ETAM, Zegna, Fendi, Nike, Llardo, Rino Greggio and Lee Cooper, high-end LCD TVs and plasma TVs, "dual-tech" larger-capacity (two-door, four-door and six-door) refrigerators, luxury cars like Mercedes-Benz India, BMW and Audi are essentially urban market products.

Rural focus

Many companies operating in the urban markets are engaged in rural development activities as a part of their corporate social responsibility (CSR).

The World Business Council for Sustainable Development states,

> Corporate social responsibility is the continuing commitment by business to behave ethically and contribute to economic development while improving the quality of life of the workforce and their families as well as of the local community and society at large.[12]

CSR has a long history in India and the Tatas have been the role models in this regard. Commitment to CSR has been displayed by several corporations in India. Box 1.1 discusses the initiatives undertaken by some companies that are not directly related to their business.

The drivers of CSR

Why do corporations undertake social responsibility? Is it a philanthropic gesture or a business development initiative?

Box 1.1 CSR Initiatives Undertaken by Some Prominent Organizations

- The Malanpur plant of Godrej Consumer Products Ltd has adopted a school at a village 'Singwari' and granted financial help by way of scholarships to the best performing child belonging to SC/ST from the fifth to the eighth standard.
- Dabur India Ltd established Sustainable Development Society, or *Sundesh*, in 1993—a non-profit organization to promote research and welfare activities in rural areas.
- Lafarge Cement worldwide gives prime importance to sustainable development for sustainable economic performance. Their major initiatives in India are: Project Employability, Project Low Cost Housing, and Project Education.
- BPCL has adopted 37 villages across India. The programme includes making substantial investments in them for nearly a decade-and-a-half to make them fully self-reliant, providing them fresh drinking water, sanitation facilities, medical facilities, enhancing their income standards by imparting vocational training and providing agricultural innovations.
- ACC's first formal Village Welfare Scheme was launched in 1952. The range of activities begins with extending educational and medical facilities and goes on to cover vocational guidance and supporting employment-oriented and income-generating projects such as agriculture, animal husbandry, cottage industries by developing local skills, using local raw materials and helping create marketing outlets.

Ratan N. Tata, the chairman of the Tata Group, maintains:

> We do not do it for propaganda. We do not do it for publicity. We do it for the satisfaction of having really achieved something worthwhile.

The key drivers of corporate social responsibility in India were diverse, ranging from stated philosophy of founding fathers to improving the relationship with local communities to availing of tax benefits.

Private-sector companies have been encouraged by the government to undertake rural development programmes over the years through fiscal incentives. For instance, special benefits are offered in the industrial policy to companies that set up industries in backward areas and tax incentives are also offered to companies that set up water purification projects.

Role of marketing

Marketing is, at best, public relations and publicity under this model. Its twin objectives are:

(i) Educating the target beneficiary groups in order to encourage and engage them in the development process.

(ii) Building the image of the corporate enterprise as a good citizen and promoting sales of the company's products and services in the urban and, to some extent, in rural areas by adopting a trickle-down approach (see Figure 1.1).

Undifferentiated approach

When the rural markets started growing, some FMCG and consumer durables companies found the trickle-down approach and its assumptions inappropriate. They felt that it was high time that the largely ignored but valuable rural population was paid attention to. However, they believed that to reach rural markets urban market strategies with minor modifications to suit rural conditions would serve the need. They sought to benefit from corporate social responsibility programmes that promote cause branding (See Figure 1.2).

Assumptions

This belief is based on the following assumptions:

(i) *Affordability:* The top- and upper-middle income holders in rural markets are fewer in number. The poor, who form a large chunk of the rural market, cannot afford to buy the products. For the middle-income holders, incomes are less stable as they are derived mostly from agriculture that is subject to the vagaries of monsoon. Thus, affordability is low. A typical view for achieving scalability is: The richest quintile of urban India and the poorest of rural India

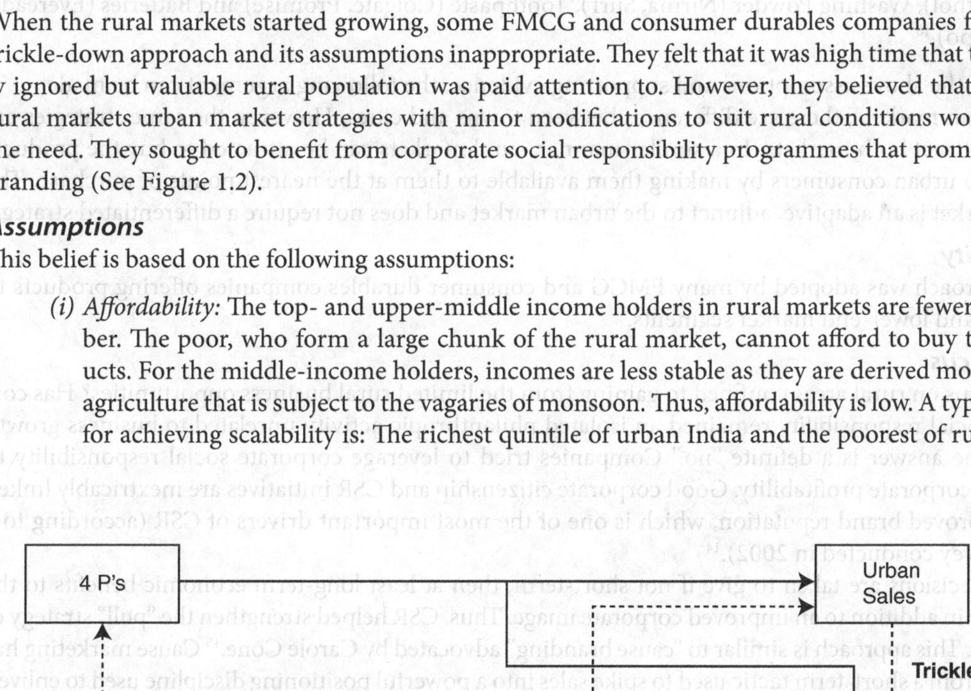

Figure 1.2 Undifferentiated Approach

are the outliers. The rest are fairly comparable showing that scaling is possible by skillfully combining urban and rural consumers, especially in geographies connected by good roads.

(ii) Accessibility: Poor road connectivity and lack of proper transport facilities make it difficult to reach rural areas. Logistics and supply-chain management are not only expensive, but also inconvenient.

(iii) Acceptance: Rural people are also like urban people and have the same needs, desires and aspirations. The "rural–urban," construct is born of convenience. The rural consumer moulds his aspirations to mach those of his urban cousin. The urbanization of rural India is a reality of the 1990s. Rural India is catching up when it comes to attitudes and aspirations.

(iv) Availability: The availability of branded products of FMCG companies is insignificant. The only players in the rural market are the agri-business companies.

Companies employing the undifferentiated approach found evidence that supported their assumptions.

For instance, the NCAER Survey conducted in 1994 showed that the variations in asset preferences of rural and urban consumers are minor.

> Fans and wrist watches are preferred by all income groups of urban and rural areas. TVs are preferred by all income groups. The exceptions are the rural upper middle- and low-income groups. They preferred two-in-ones. Two-wheelers are preferred by all income groups. The refrigerator is preferred by all income groups except the middle-income group in rural and low-income group in urban areas. The brand choices of rural consumers are not that different from their urban counterparts. The brand leaders are the same: Popular soaps (Lifebuoy, Lux), Premium Soaps (Liril, Cinthol), Washing Powder (Nirma, Surf), Toothpaste (Colgate, Promise) and Batteries (Eveready, Nippo).[13]

Based on the above assumptions and supporting evidence, the following argument can be made.

In urban markets, there are differences between towns and cities. However, the same strategies are used to attract both markets. In a similar manner, rural markets can be attracted to buy the products offered to urban consumers by making them available to them at the nearest points of purchase. The rural market is an adaptive, adjunct to the urban market and does not require a differentiated strategy.

Suitability

This approach was adopted by many FMCG and consumer durables companies offering products to middle- and lower-end market segments.

Rural focus

Is the focus on rural areas confined to gaining from the limited rural business opportunities? Has corporate social responsibility remained an isolated philanthropic activity unrelated to business growth goals? The answer is a definite "no." Companies tried to leverage corporate social responsibility to enhance corporate profitability. Good corporate citizenship and CSR initiatives are inextricably linked with improved brand reputation, which is one of the most important drivers of CSR (according to a CSR Survey conducted in 2002).[14]

CSR decisions are taken to give if not short-term, then at least long-term economic benefits to the company in addition to an improved corporate image. Thus, CSR helped strengthen the "pull" strategy of the firms. This approach is similar to "cause branding" advocated by Carole Cone.[15] Cause marketing has evolved from a short-term tactic used to spike sales into a powerful positioning discipline used to enliven brand equity and enhance corporate image with significant bottom-line and community impacts.

Many Indian companies are now employing CSR with a rural focus to further their business. Box 1.2 showcases the initiatives of three leading companies.

The experiences of these companies reinforce the fact that the rural market can become viable for corporations, which practice the developmental approach of social marketing. Organizations can launch

Box 1.2 Cause-branding CSR Initiatives

- **ITC:** ITC focuses on social forestry related to its paper boards business and also on primary education, livestock development, and integrated watershed development in states.
- **HUL:** The Fair & Lovely Foundation seeks to encourage economic empowerment of Indian women through information and resources in the areas of career and enterprise. Other projects are: Project Saraswati (scholarships for girls), Project *Disha* (career guidance for young girls) Project *Kaladarshan* (skill development in embroidery and garment designing) and Project *Sanjivini* (3-month nurse training in collaboration with Dr Reddy's Labs).
- **Colgate:** In 1998, Colgate started project *Jagruti*, a rural hygiene drive along with the Indian Dental Association. This project covers 6 million people in 20,000 villages out of which 15,000 villages had no access to toothpaste and tooth powder. The aim of the drive is to promote the brand in rural areas but the overall strategy is also to spread the vital information of oral hygiene among the less aware rural people.

social responsibility initiatives in order to build brands in the rural areas. The social responsibility initiatives are far more effective in building brands in rural markets than commercial advertisements.

Rural marketing

Its main focus is on distribution and less on the adaptation of the other 3 P's (Product, Price and Promotion) to rural markets supported by limited rural communication and promotion. Communication is disseminated through CSR activities and limited media channels, depending upon sales. Advertisements are not specially designed. Radio advertisements, van campaigns, cinema commercials, and wall paintings make up the media mix. The urban messages are dubbed into the local languages. The distribution pattern can be as follows.

FMCG companies cover as many as 0.1 million villages by appointing 2,000 stockists in towns with a population of 20,000. Even stockists can conveniently redistribute products to 50 locations around the towns. For durables, 90 per cent of products are bought in the 2,000 small town markets. Yet another of way selling products to people in villages below a population of 5,000 is by generating a consumer pull. It obviates the necessity to personally distribute it in the remotest villages.

Differentiated approach

The differentiated approach has more proponents now as the untapped rural markets are found to have huge and stable potential. The emergence of rural markets as the business targets for corporations is a new turn in the history of the economic development of our nation. In this approach, marketers design separate marketing programmes for rural markets and leverage on cause branding.

Assumptions

This approach is based on the following assumptions.

(i) *Affordability:* The incomes of the rural people have substantially increased and become stable with increase in the income from non-farming occupations. Government schemes of employment, subsidies, loan waivers, microfinance, free meal and education schemes have boosted rural buying power. IT and mobile telephony have enabled farmers and rural entrepreneurs to produce more and sell at better prices. There is latent purchasing power that can be tapped by suitable promotion and distribution.

(ii) Accessibility: Infrastructure development programmes by Central and State governments have improved road connectivity to a large extent. Government and private transport facilities have improved with the rise in the production of automobiles. There are many villages cut off from towns and cities but their numbers are decreasing. Farmers today keep abreast of the latest information and maximize gains at both ends—the input as well as output and sales. They search Web sites and use their cell phones to stay constantly connected to the global markets. The market information (like price, products and demand) seems to drive their local business strategies.

(iii) Acceptance: IT and telephone services have brought in new connectivity. The rural and the urban divide is shrinking. Rural people, especially the youth, share the same visions as their urban cousins and are adopting similar lifestyles. About 40 per cent of graduates passing out of Indian universities are from rural areas. They are the decision makers and are not very different in education, exposure, attitudes and aspirations from their urban counterparts. The effects of globalization are percolating to rural areas. The availability of satellite channels in rural India provided the required exposure to enhance acceptance of new brands.

(iv) Availability: The reforms adopted by corporations are now reaching the rural hinterlands. Many Indian firms and MNCs have become suppliers to rural markets and there is scope for other players to enter this market.

Differentiators identified

With substantial improvements in villages in terms of affordability, accessibility and acceptance, companies have started giving rural business a separate status. At the same time they have found that rural markets comprising middle- and lower-income groups have certain peculiar features that warrant a differentiated approach in marketing. The differences are both in the environment and lifestyles. Some of them are:

(i) They have infrastructural constraints. Electric power supply is interrupted frequently. Drinking water is not available in many villages. Therefore, they need products that are not based on power supply and water consumption.

(ii) They are value conscious. They prefer solid and functional products. No-frills products with good quality are preferred. An innovation that speaks of finer points like—"now with calcium"—may not appeal to them.

(iii) They are price sensitive since their income streams are small. They cannot purchase large packs. That is why sachets with low price points brought about a revolution in rural marketing.

(iv) They value relationships and respect elders, the educated and the administrative heads. They don't take decisions independently. They take the opinion of the persons whom they consider competent to give advice.

(v) They are adoptive. When they don't find a product, they invent intelligent ways of using available products. This is the reason for peculiar uses of some products (hair dye make up for buffaloes, Iodex application for pain management of animals, Horlicks nourishment for cattle and lassi making in washing machines and so on).

(vi) They are slow in processing information. It is difficult for them to understand complex and non-linear messages. Messages should be closely related to life and should be decent and pragmatic.

Suitability

Many FMCG and consumer durables companies that had ignored this segment considering it to be a heavy investment–low returns market have started foraying into it and have developed differentiated strategies.

Focus on rural market development

The focus is on rural market development as well as rural development. Accordingly, companies used CSR as a promoter of business and creator of good image. There is a tight integration of CSR with marketing strategy. CSR programmes are designed and implemented to subserve the marketing goals of enterprises. Consider the following examples.

Union Bank of India set apart one per cent of its annual public profits to undertake corporate social responsibility activities through its trust named "Union Bank Social Foundation." Its activities include: Rural Development and Self-Employment Training Institute (RUDSETI) to train rural youth for self employment, Farmers' clubs to encourage learning by discussion of issues, Village Knowledge Centres (VKC) to provide information related to farming and marketing of produce, and Union *Mitr* to provide counselling on financial issues like savings and investments. Its financial product innovations include: *Bhumiheen* Green Card (loans without security), Joint Liability Groups (group financing), "No Frills" accounts (for the poor) and its campaign for "100 per cent Banking Habit Villages."

Rural Marketing

Rural marketing is now a full fledged and challenging function with an emphasis on marketing research to understand the rural market, segmentation, targeting and positioning for designing the marketing mix of 4 P's and evolving and implementing marketing strategies. It is supported by marketing-oriented CSR that is developmental in spirit and approach (See Figure 1.3).

BOTTOM-OF-THE-PYRAMID APPROACH

The differentiated approach is improved radically by injecting social entrepreneurship into the marketing philosophy by path-breaking companies such as HUL and ITC in India. They have rightly understood that development is not a CSR or philanthropic act but a business that benefits the company and the poor. Since business cannot succeed in a society that fails, a new win–win sustainable model is necessary. The key idea in this model is developing rural people into entrepreneurs or participants in business. This has resulted in the creation of opportunities for partnerships between companies and non-governmental organizations, not-for-profit organizations, governmental agencies and other

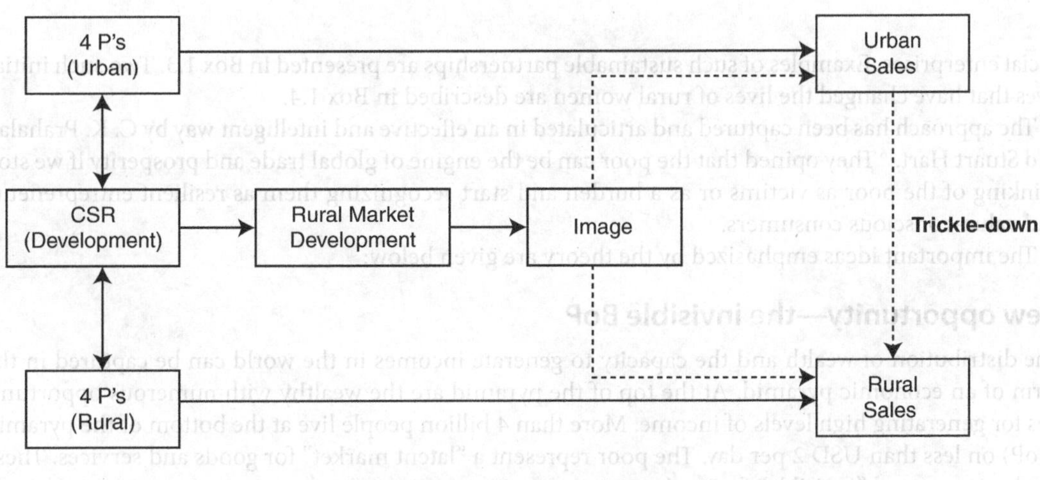

Figure 1.3 Differentiated Approach

Box 1.3 Sustainable Partnership Models of Corporate Organizations

HUL–Vindhya Valley Project: In 2000, HUL helped the state-owned *Khadi* Board through an advisory relationship with the government of Madhya Pradesh. It helped the board to brand local produce from villages and tribal areas, such as natural honey collected from forests, in the state under the brand name Vindhya Valley. The product range includes edible products like *papads*, pickles, *masala* and turmeric. HUL provided the corporate expertise, marketing acumen and quality parameters, while the state government bore the marketing expenses for the brand building.

CFCL: *Uttam Bandhan* is the community welfare initiative launched in Rajasthan in 2000 by Chambal Fertilisers and Chemicals Ltd, the flagship company of the K. K. Birla group. Under this programme, CFCL trains unemployed rural youths as extension workers known as *krishi sewaks*, who interact with the farmers and advice them.

Canara Bank: The bank's main thrust is on imparting vocational skills to unemployed people. The bank has partnered with the Syndicate Bank and the Dharmastala Manjunatheshwara Educational Trust to set up 20 Rural Entrepreneurship Institutes across India. Then there are the projects it undertakes alone, such as artisans' training and computer literacy initiatives.

HUL: Project *Shakti* was piloted in 2001 in 50 villages in the state of Andhra Pradesh by involving members of Self-help groups (SHG). They are trained and provided micro credit to buy and sell HUL's products. On average, each *Shakti* entrepreneur earns enough each month to approximately double their previous household income—this makes a significant difference to family living standards. Through the nature of the products sold, the project is helping to increase awareness on health, hygiene and nutrition, thus improving the standard of living of the rural community. In addition, health educators known as *"Shakti Vanis"*, talk to self-help groups about HUL's brands and the importance of good nutrition and hygiene practices in combating diseases. In 2003, HUL piloted I-*Shakti*, an IT-based rural information service providing access to these key rural information needs in areas such as agriculture, education, health and hygiene, veterinary, etc.

social enterprises. Examples of such sustainable partnerships are presented in Box 1.3. Two such initiatives that have changed the lives of rural women are described in Box 1.4.

The approach has been captured and articulated in an effective and intelligent way by C. K. Prahalad and Stuart Hart.[16] They opined that the poor can be the engine of global trade and prosperity if we stop thinking of the poor as victims or as a burden and start recognizing them as resilient entrepreneurs and value-conscious consumers.

The important ideas emphasized by the theory are given below:

New opportunity—the invisible BoP

The distribution of wealth and the capacity to generate incomes in the world can be captured in the form of an economic pyramid. At the top of the pyramid are the wealthy with numerous opportunities for generating high levels of income. More than 4 billion people live at the bottom of the pyramid (BoP) on less than USD 2 per day. The poor represent a "latent market" for goods and services. These markets remained "invisible" for too long.

Box 1.4 Project *Shakti*: Changing Lives in Rural India

HUL's *Shakti* Entrepreneur programme contributes by creating profitable micro-enterprise opportunities for rural women. Armed with micro-credit, rural women become *Shakti* entrepreneurs—direct-to-home distributors in rural markets. A *Shakti Amma* earns about Rs 1000 per month and the income is significant to them as most of them are from below the poverty line.

The project has been successfully implemented in fifteen states: Andhra Pradesh, Karnataka, Tamil Nadu, Gujarat, Madhya Pradesh, Chattisgarh, Maharashtra, Uttar Pradesh, Punjab, Haryana, Rajasthan, West Bengal, Bihar, Jharkhand and Orissa.

This model has been the growth driver for HUL and presently about half of HUL's FMCG sales come from the rural markets. The *Shakti* network at the end of 2008 was 45,000 *Ammas* covering 100,000+ villages across 15 states reaching 3 million homes. The long-term aim of the company is to have 100,000 *Ammas* covering 500,000 villages and reaching 600 million people.

Nagajyothi—An HUL *Shakti Amma*

Nagajyothi, a 35-year-old *Vysya* woman from the revenue village of Mannesamudram in Anantapur district of Andhra Pradesh, is a fine example of how Project *Shakti* has positively impacted the lives of rural women in India. She found it extremely difficult to make ends meet with her husband, the sole earning member, earning only a daily wage of Rs 100 and two young children to provide for. Nagajyothi heard about HUL after becoming a member of her local Development of Women and Children in Rural Areas (DWACRA) group, a self-employment scheme for rural women and children of the Andhra Pradesh government. She decided to join *Shakti* in 2004 after obtaining guidance from HUL officials. She started her dealership with an investment of Rs 10,000. With the support of the HUL rural sales promoter and her friends she has overcome the initial hiccups in selling her products and today her monthly turnover is approximately Rs 24,000.

She covers her own village comprising a population of about 3,800 by home-to-home sales and also covers retailers. She is confident of providing for her two children, a 15-year-old son who works as a labourer in a factory and a daughter who is interested in studies. Her confidence in facing the future is evident from what she often says to her new acquaintances, "*Shakti* not only gave me an additional source of income but also has introduced us to a number of people who help our family in promoting our business." She was also appreciated for her involvement in organizing a dental camp sponsored by HUL officials.

The *Shakti* initiative has been one of the main growth drivers for HUL and presently about half of HUL's FMCG sales come from rural markets.

Source: Field survey of authors and their research scholar Mrs V. Bhargavi Reddy in 2008.

Demands innovations

BoP, as a market, provides a new growth opportunity for the private sector and a forum for innovations. Innovations in technology, products and services, and business models will be needed to serve BoP consumers.

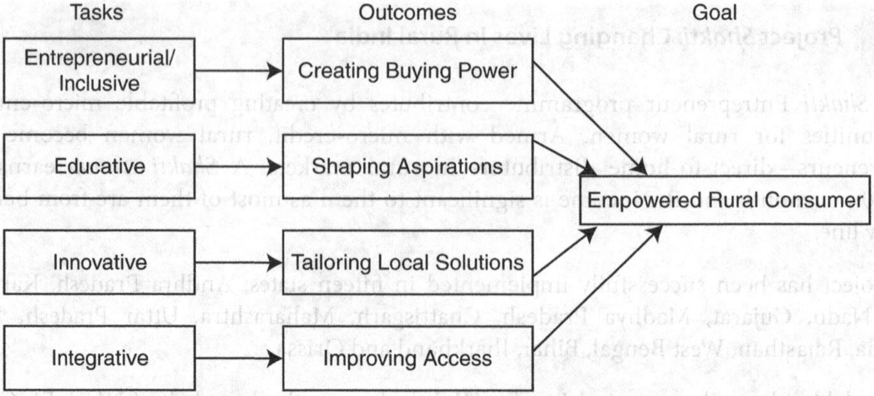

Figure 1.4 Bottom-of-the-pyramid Marketing

Requires partnerships

Large scale and wide spread entrepreneurship is at the heart of the solution to poverty. For this, there is a strong need for large organizations to collaborate with the poor, who are to be uplifted, and the supporting organizations that provide resources and counselling. The supporting organizations may include social organizations and government agencies. Through such public–private partnerships (PPPs) markets can be created at the bottom of the pyramid for eradicating poverty.

Promotes entrepreneurship

Free and transparent private-sector competition, unlike local village and shanty-town monopolies controlled by slum lords, can transform the "poor" into consumers. Market development at BoP level will also create millions of new entrepreneurs at the grass roots level—from women working as distributors and entrepreneurs to village level micro enterprises.

Core business, not social responsibility

BoP markets must become an integral part of the work of the private sector. They must become part of the firm's core businesses; they cannot merely be relegated to the realm of corporate social responsibility initiatives.

As shown in Figure 1.4, the four marketing tasks required to meet the challenge are: (i) Creating buyer power (entrepreneurial/inclusive), (ii) Shaping aspirations (educative), (iii) Tailoring local solutions (innovative) and (iv) Improving access (integrative).

INTEGRATED, INNOVATIVE AND INCLUSIVE GROWTH MODEL

The rural Indian market and consumer calls for sophisticated new marketing strategies and paradigms, not a transplantation of old ideas. The demand is for development not by charity but by entrepreneurship, and supply of goods and services not based on the convenience of the producer but based on innovation to meet consumer requirements. The new, comprehensive model should address the bottom of the pyramid with a commitment to uplift the masses and the company goals of profitability. Given this, the three elements that constitute the new model are: integrated marketing, innovative marketing and inclusive marketing (Figure 1.5).

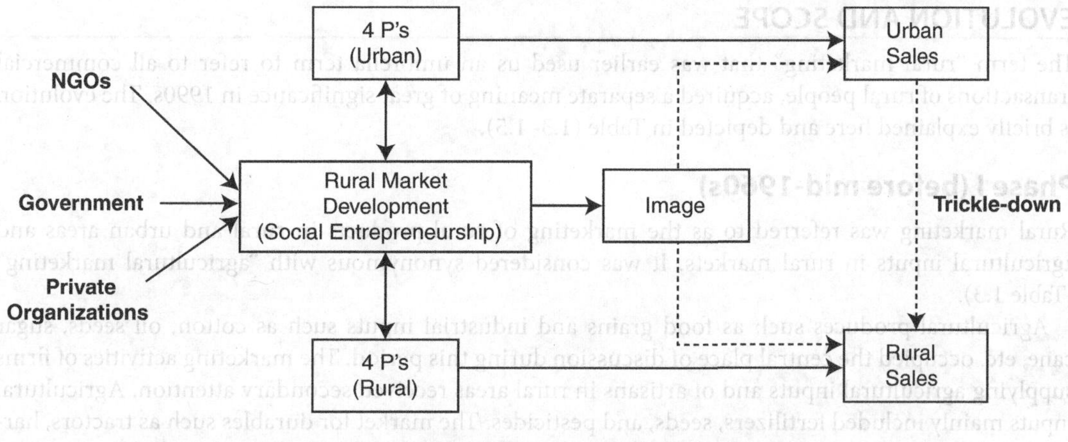

Figure 1.5 Integrated–Innovative–Inclusive Approach

Integrated marketing

It involves devising marketing activities, programmes and networking with other functional areas to create, communicate and deliver value for consumers with the goal of profitability along with consumer satisfaction. The two components of this approach are transactional marketing (4 P's) and relationship marketing. In this context linkages are necessary with research agencies, customer relationship management (CRM) agencies, and consumer groups.

Innovative marketing

This looks for breakthrough ideas in products and processes for continuously offering exciting experiences and values to the customers. One process innovation is developmental marketing. Developmental marketing refers to taking up marketing programmes keeping the development objective in mind and using various managerial and other inputs of marketing to achieve these objectives. Its aim in the present context is to develop the rural people by social entrepreneurship as advocated by the bottom-of-the-pyramid approach. For innovation, linkages are necessary with R&D institutions, public, consumers, NGOs, and competitors.

Inclusive marketing

Pradeep Kashyap (CEO, MART), advocated the adoption of inclusive marketing by corporations as an "enlightened strategy" to serve their own long-term interests in growing the mass market. It aims at triggering development at the bottom of the pyramid by partnering with change agents.[17]

If marketing skills of promotional agencies (*Khadi* Commission, Handicrafts, Handlooms, etc.) and NGOs that are engaged in the non-farm sector are enhanced, these agencies will then be able to help the poor get better value for their products and earn higher incomes. Public–private partnership is one such approach that can benefit the poor. However, it should be a win–win model that offers benefits to all stakeholders equally. Such equitable, market-based models are more likely to be sustainable as they utilize the best strengths of each partner. The microfinance model is one PPP initiative that has achieved scale and sustainability because of the active involvement of the different stakeholders—the poor themselves, NGOs, government and financial institutions.

EVOLUTION AND SCOPE

The term "rural marketing" that was earlier used us an umbrella term to refer to all commercial transactions of rural people, acquired a separate meaning of great significance in 1990s. The evolution is briefly explained here and depicted in Table (1.3–1.5).

Phase I (before mid-1960s)

Rural marketing was referred to as the marketing of rural products in rural and urban areas and agricultural inputs in rural markets. It was considered synonymous with "agricultural marketing" (Table 1.3).

Agricultural produces such as food grains and industrial inputs such as cotton, oil seeds, sugar cane, etc. occupied the central place of discussion during this period. The marketing activities of firms supplying agricultural inputs and of artisans in rural areas received secondary attention. Agricultural inputs mainly included fertilizers, seeds, and pesticides. The market for durables such as tractors, harvesters, threshers, power tillers, pump sets, oil engines, and electric motors was miniscule.

The local marketing of products such as bamboo baskets, ropes, window and door frames, household earthen and small agricultural tools such as ploughs, products by sellers like black smiths, carpenters, cobblers and pot makers were discussed in general. This was an unorganized market.

Phase II (mid-1960s–mid-1990s)

The green revolution ushered in scientific farming practices and transformed many of the poor villages into prosperous busy centres. As a result, the demand for agricultural inputs went up. Better irrigation facilities, soil testing, use of high-yield-variety seeds, fertilizers, pesticides and employment of machinery such as power tillers, harvesters, threshers, etc. changed the rural scenario.

In this context, marketing of agricultural inputs assumed significance. Two separate areas of activities had emerged—the new "marketing of agricultural inputs" and the conventional "agricultural marketing". Table 1.4 presents the overview of the marketing in this phase.

During this period, the marketing of rural products received considerable attention in the general marketing framework. The formation of agencies like *Khadi* and Village Industries Commission, *Girijan* Cooperative Societies and APCO Fabrics (in Andhra Pradesh) and the special attention paid by government to promote these products were responsible for this upsurge. Village industries

Table 1.3 Rural Marketing Before Mid-1990s

From/To	Rural	Urban
Urban	Agricultural inputs–consumables	Not relevant
Rural	Artisan services and products	Agricultural products

Table 1.4 Rural Marketing in Phase II

From/To	Rural	Urban
Urban	Agricultural inputs	Not relevant
Rural	Artisan services and products	Agricultural produce

Table 1.5 Rural Marketing—Phase III

From/To	Rural
Urban	Agri-inputs marketing (occupational inputs)
	Consumer marketing (products and services to households)
Rural	Products and services of rural origin.

flourished and products such as handicrafts, handloom textiles, soaps, safety matches, crackers, etc. hit the urban market on a large scale.

Phase III (after mid-1990s)

The marketing of household consumables and durables in the rural markets were not considered in the two earlier phases. The reasons are obvious:

First, there was no rural market as such. The existing rural markets for these products were not substantial—not large enough to attract the attention of the urban marketers.

Second, they were inaccessible. The small villages/hamlets were widely scattered making reach difficult and expensive.

Consequently, the rural market was seen as an adjunct of the urban market and was conveniently ignored.

However, India's industrial sector had gained in strength and maturity since the 1980s. Its contribution to the Gross National Product (GNP) increased substantially. A new service sector had emerged signifying the metamorphosis of the agricultural society into an industrial society. Meanwhile, due to the development programmes of the Central and State governments, service organizations and socially responsible business groups such as Mafatlal, Tata, Birla, Goenka and others, the rural areas witnessed an all round socio-economic progress. The economic reforms of 1991–92 further accelerated the process by introducing competition in the rural market. The rural market for household consumables and durables has also grown steadily.

Rural marketing represented the emergent distinct activity of attracting and serving rural markets to fulfill the needs and wants of persons, households and occupations of rural people. Table 1.5 depicts the present rural market structure.

Phase IV (around 2015)

Global rural marketing will emerge. Some of the key drivers for the emergence of global rural markets as an attractive business proposition are globalization, information revolution, the bottom-of-the-pyramid theory, growth in size of Indian organizations, ability to create appropriate technologies by our R&D institutions for the rural market, heavy competition in domestic rural markets and increasing urbanization promoted by the formation of greater cities and corporations leading to disappearance of many rural areas.

CONCEPT AND NATURE

How do you define rural marketing? We find that different writers have offered different definitions. The definitions may create some confusion for the following reasons.

(i) Time differences—They represent the scope of rural marketing of their times.

(ii) Approach differences—Some are process oriented and some are content based.

(iii) Target differences—The focus is on the market or people.

Now we will take a look at the definitions of rural marketing provided by some writers to appreciate the above argument.

The National Commission on Agriculture defined it as:

> Rural marketing is a process that starts with a decision to produce a saleable farm commodity and it involves all the aspects of market structure and system, both functional and institutional, based on technical and economic considerations and includes pre- and post-harvest operations, assembling, grading, storage, transportation and distribution.

T. P. Gopalaswamy[18] observed:

> Rural marketing is a two-way marketing process. Its content now encompasses inflow of products into rural areas for production and consumption purposes and also outflow of products to urban areas.

C. S. G. Krishnamacharyulu and Lalitha Ramakrishnan[19] and Pradeep Kashyap and Siddhartha Raut[20] defined corporate rural marketing in the following terms.

> Rural marketing can be defined as a function that manages all activities involved in assessing, stimulating and converting the purchasing power of rural consumers into an effective demand for specific products and services and moving these products and services to the people in rural areas to create satisfaction and a better standard of living and thereby achieving organizational goals.

Balaram Dogra and Karminder Ghuman[21] explained the concept as follows:

> Rural marketing is a distinct specialized field of the marketing discipline that encompasses a customized application of the marketing tools and strategies to understand the psyche of the rural consumer in terms of needs, tailoring the products to meet such needs and effectively delivering them to enable a profitable exchange of goods and services to and from the rural market.

An academician who does not subscribe to the "place" concept ("market is a place where exchanges take place between buyers and sellers") of marketing says, "Rural marketing is marketing to a rural 'mindset'; not a rural market."

Given the above definitions and views, we can identify the following important aspects about rural marketing:

- It is a function and a discipline.
- It is a process with two objectives—(i) customer satisfaction and enhancement of standard of living and (ii) reaching organizational goals.
- It is a process involving activities such as assessing, stimulating and converting the purchasing power of prospects.
- It involves application of strategies and tools based on understanding the consumer.
- It involves design of products and related components of the marketing mix.

A new dimension is to be added to the points discussed above to make the definition contemporary.

> Rural marketing involves creating purchasing power by partnering with consumers and other development agencies.

Therefore, rural marketing can be defined as follows.

> Rural marketing is an entrepreneurial process of developing rural people by partnering with development agencies and a business function that involves assessing, stimulating and satisfying demand for products and services through innovative approaches with a concern for customer satisfaction and corporate profitability.

Nature of Rural Marketing

What are the characteristics of rural marketing? From the definitions and observation about the evolution of rural marketing discussed in the previous sections, we can identify the following characteristics.

(i) *Elastic:* Rural marketing has broadened with changing times. It has changed in nature from being transactional to developmental and from going alone to partnerships. It has benefited from information technology developments to embrace virtual solutions to rural problems.

(ii) *Developmental:* The role of rural marketing is more developmental than transactional. It is more a process of delivering a better standard of living and quality of life to the rural consumers, taking into consideration the prevailing rural milieu.

(iii) *Innovation-driven:* Innovation is the essence of marketing. Innovative methods of social change for successful transformation of traditional society are vital. Such a change narrows the rural–urban divide.

(iv) *Social process:* Communication is the vital element of rural marketing. It should serve to resolve social conflicts, encourage cooperation and strengthen competitive spirit during interactions between rural and urban locations as well as within rural areas. Another critical point for communication is the point of conversion of a "ruralite" from an "induced beneficiary" to an "entrepreneur" and "intelligent buyer."

(v) *Strategy-based:* The process of transformation can only be evolutionary and not revolutionary. The growth of the rural market can be a planned evolutionary process based on strategic instruments of change rather than just constituting short-term opportunities for commercial gains.

(vi) *Win–win process:* Rural marketing process is both a catalyst as well as an outcome of the general rural development process. Initiation and management of social and economic change in the rural sector is the core of the rural marketing process. It becomes both the benefactor and beneficiary in this process.

(vii) *A discipline:* Rural marketing has emerged as a separate discipline and is offered as a subject of study in management programmes of institutes, universities and colleges. Several text books on the subject are available in the market. A large number of articles on different aspects of rural marketing highlighting experiments and experiences of different companies can be found in the print and electronic media. The subject has also caught the attention of researchers. Many researchers are investigating the rural marketing phenomenon. With all these efforts we find a new theory with concepts, principles, and tools developing.

(viii) *A growing profession:* In order to qualify as a profession, an occupation has to fulfill the following criteria also satisfied by rural marketing:

- *A distinct body of knowledge:* Rural marketing is a distinct theory with knowledge and techniques drawn from different fields such as marketing, sociology, psychology and information technology. Though basic frameworks are drawn from marketing, the theory is developed based on rural-oriented behavioural sciences. As such it differs from urban and international marketing applications.
- *Skills:* Rural marketing requires a different skill set. The rural marketer is a barefoot manager, having communication skills with working knowledge of local dialect. Patience, ability to convince and good technical knowledge of the product are important for the rural marketer.
- *Training:* Many institutes are offering rural marketing as a subject or course. Well known among them are the Indian Institute of Rural Management, Anand, National Institute of Rural Management, Ahmedabad, and Indian Institute of Management Ahmedabad. Xavier

Institute of Management, Bhubaneswar (XIMB) and Thiagarajar School of Management (TSM), Madurai have organized *Gramotsavs* as part of the training offered to students. The Indian Institute of Planning and Management (IIPM), Ahmedabad organized a "Rural Sensitization Drive" in a village called Upariyala in North Gujarat. The students were given a project to conduct a rural lifestyle and consumer behaviour survey.

- *Social status and remuneration:* The job opportunities in rural areas are increasing and there is good response to them from the youth. It is reported that the *Shakti Ammas* of HUL's Project *Shakti* have gained new respect in their areas. A survey revealed that rural retailers influence 35 per cent of purchases. The rural salaries are reasonable and they will soon catch up with the urban ones as scalability and sustainability of operations are established.
- *Association:* Every profession has an association that creates a forum for exchange of ideas and improvement of practices. Such associations lay out a code of conduct for its members to follow and also design standards for excellence. Though there is no such association, the formation of Rural Marketing Agencies Association of India (RMAAI) is a happy augury to this growing profession.

IMPLEMENTING THE DECISION

How do you implement the 3-I model (Integrated, Innovative and Inclusive growth model) of rural marketing? Some guidelines are given below:

Create a right organization

Rural marketing requires an organization that is innovative and organic. Based on the well known Mckinsey 7-S framework, we suggest the following guidelines.

Strategy

Rural marketing requires strategies for five reasons.

1. The projection of household income distribution for 2015 by NCAER holds a big promise for success in the long run. According to it, the consuming class will be 54 per cent of the rural population, followed by climbers who will be about 34 per cent. The market is growing at a rate of 3 to 4 per cent per annum adding more than one million new customers every year.
2. The experiences of many companies indicate that tactical approaches do not work.
3. A long-term approach for building a rural market is necessary.
4. It involves developing partnerships and coordinating their work.
5. Innovation is necessary for creating appropriate product distribution and communications.

A comprehensive brand building strategy, with both short-term and long-term goals, is a must to have sustainable growth in sales in rural India. Tactical approach leads to temporary and limited benefits.

Guideline 1: Define mission, vision and value statements. Develop an inclusive growth strategy, set goals and make proper resource allocation. Work out partnerships and alliances.

Structure

Obviously, structural arrangements for implementing rural marketing strategies are essential. Beginning with a task force, a company may go for a separate marketing and sales vertical supported by a field team. Many companies have started their rural retail chains.

Guideline 2: Consider setting up a task force, sales vertical and rural malls.

Systems
Marketers need marketing research systems and intelligence to make wise choices. An efficient human resource system is essential to recruit, train and reward people. Design planning and control systems are required to set objectives and monitor the progress.

Guideline 3: Establish appropriate systems covering the key operational areas.

Shared values
Total commitment from the top leadership is imperative and it should be communicated to all the employees. To establish enduring and effective teamwork, (i) formulate mission and vision statements and (ii) develop a description of values. The value statements may include recognition for the dignity and abilities of the poor, positive regard for entrepreneurship, a development gateway, thrust on innovation to achieve excellence, concern for quality, desire to build good image and provide better standard of living.

Guideline 4: Prepare a statement of values and communicate it to employees.

Staff
Rural marketing efforts need a special mindset that many of the urban-oriented management graduates do not possess. The best bet is to recruit students from specialized institutes such as the Indian Institute of Rural Management, or at least, management graduates who have studied the subject as an elective. Students from small towns, who want to prove themselves in big companies and have no issues about working in smaller markets, are ideal for rural jobs.

Guideline 5: Choose people with rural orientation and experience.

Skills
Social skills for understanding the rural market by interaction and participant observation techniques, technical skills to create products based on rural-appropriate technologies, entrepreneurial skills for innovation and risk management and design skills to formulate marketing programmes are essential. It is very important to create such skill sets.

Guideline 6: Train employees to gain relevant social, technical, entrepreneurial and design skills.

Style
The style suitable for leading the organization is participative as the organization functions in association with many other organizations—governments, NGOs, microfinance institutions, the rural poor who are channel or production partners.

Guideline 7: Encourage and employ participative style to educate, engage and empower people.

Understand, segment and target markets
A good understanding of rural markets is necessary to initiate action.

Consumer behaviour
Marketers often look for common points to simplify their decisions. However, strategic marketing calls for finding out differences and gaining competitive advantage by focusing on them. Rural markets are fragmented, scattered and thinly populated making the task of understanding complex.

Rural consumers are people living under the following conditions that are different from urban ones.

(i) Environment of constraints (poor road connectivity, irregular power supply, no drinking water, poor sanitary conditions, lack of health care and so on)

(ii) Traditional culture (respect for elders, saving for future, simple living, family orientation, regard for ceremonies and festivals, worship of gods, etc.)

(iii) Occupations that are temporary/seasonal and provide low incomes

(iv) Caste or political affiliations

(v) Small area with few households

As such their purchase preferences are likely to be shaped by five aspects: functionality (products that do not require electricity or that provide pure drinking water), economic considerations (simple and low priced), ease of use and maintenance (lack of support from service centres), sturdiness with longevity of life (saving for future) and decency (social acceptance). Their buying behaviour is characterized by the following features:

- Long process of inquiry and evaluation that involves many people to gain social acceptance and make rational choices.
- Domination of the father, influence of patriarchy and joint family (this of course is changing; women and youth are now playing important roles in decision making)
- Preference of cash purchases—habit of buying when farm proceeds are sold and money is available (but this is also changing with the increase in non-farming income)
- Weekly buying at weekly fairs and *haats* (this too, is alterring with availability of products)
- Collective decisions guided by village head or a dominating person—this is found in some villages where all villagers purchase products of the same brand.

Evidently, rural people face different situations and have different preferences compared to urban consumers. More significantly, a wind of change is sweeping the countryside.

Guideline 8: Understand that rural markets are different and changing. Get first-hand information from personal observation and get problem-specific information from rural research agencies. Also remember that any description made today cannot be comprehensive, definitive and enduring.

Marketing research

Spending time researching the rural Indian market before diving in can help prevent failures. Rural consumers, their living environment and product usage are different, leading to differences in usage patterns. Research has provided the following understanding of consumers and their needs.

The purchase decision is characterized by collective decision making and it is highly influenced and opinion driven. Rural choices are guided by quality–value paradigms and stress on the functionality of the products rather than on the frills attached with it. In general, it is a recognized fact that rural consumers are relatively more brand loyal than their urban counterparts. And here too, the collective principle works. That is why there are Nirma villages, Wheel villages, Escorts villages and Mahindra and Mahindra villages. Against this, there are reports that rural people are also exhibiting tendencies of disloyalty.

However, caution should also be exercised. Complexities such as recalibrating the scales and usage of the right dialect of language in research instruments must be taken care of for proper rural market research. Associations with colour and symbols work well. The individual-interview technique may suffer from some limitations as rural people believe in participatory approaches.

Guideline 9: Rural marketing research requires customization in terms of questions and research tools based on language, level of literacy, and style of participation of subjects.

Segmentation

Marketers have to find appropriate variables to segment the rural market. Rural markets are deceptively simple; segmentation is by no means an easy task. The heterogeneity in geographic locations, occupations, incomes and languages require attention. Here are some confusing variables:

(i) Family size, not income, determines the purchase of durables like TVs.

(ii) Land holdings and incomes are not strongly correlated. Factors like crop pattern, rainfall and method of farming make a difference.

(iii) Income of a family cannot be easily ascertained. There are multiple employments, differential wage structures and irregular receipts. Expenditures as such, are seasonally varied.

Guideline 10: Marketers have to choose multiple and relevant variables to segment the rural market.

Product decisions

Tailoring products, including packaging them and giving them brand names, to give them a rural image is the first mile in rural marketing strategy. This is possible when the products are related to the rural life and mindset.

(i) *Products based on resource constraints:* A refrigerator with standby power for 12 hours, pressure cookers with two handles and a radio with key-winding mechanism were developed keeping resource problems in view. Samsung introduced stabilizer free operations in its direct cool refrigerators to take care of voltage fluctuations.

(ii) *Products related to health and protection:* IFFCO Tokio General Insurance offered a free insurance cover worth Rs 40,000 with every fertilizer bag through its *Sankat Haran* policy. Nokia introduced pest-resistant covers for its mobiles. Cadbury launched a chocolate flavoured biscuit that is based on the consumer insight that rural mothers opt for biscuits rather than chocolates for their children.

(iii) *Products based on affordability:* Small-size packs with low price points are popular in the rural market. Chik Shampoo sachets at Re 1, Parle G *Tikki* packs at Rs 2, mini Amrutanjan satchets priced at Rs 2, Cinthol, Fair Glow and Godrej in 50 g packs priced at Rs 4–5 are some examples. Baron International ran a successful exchange for TVs in urban areas and sold old exchanged sets after reconditioning them in the rural market.

(iv) *Products packed for convenience in use:* Bubble pack (30 ml) Clinic Plus is offered at Rs 8 as there are more storage related problems in rural areas. It allows the use of the right quantity.

(v) *Products with simple packaging:* Nirma washing powder is an example of this.

(vi) *Products branded for easy recognition:* LG's *Sampoorna* TV, Meera shampoo and *Kuttihamam* soap can be mentioned here.

(vii) *Products with multiple uses:* Paints from Asian Paints are used for painting houses as well as the horns of buffalos.

Guideline 11: Innovate to create appropriate technology products ensuring utility and affordability.

Price decisions

Rural consumers are price sensitive in general. They prefer to buy low-priced, large packs of popular products or low-priced, small unit packs of premium products. However, they are willing to upgrade their purchases by buying branded, quality products priced at higher levels. In case of durables, they look for reasonably priced products. Therefore, pricing of routine buying products should be at lower levels. This can be achieved by taking advantage of packaging techniques. In case of durables, peg prices at affordable or at slightly higher levels by offering two variants—one with no frills and another with fascinating frills.

Guideline 12: Offer products at multiple price points to meet the expectations of the different segments of the market. Price low for repeat purchase items and provide small packs. Adopt value-pricing for low-end economy/popular products in regular pack sizes as well as consumer durables. Adopt high-priced, high-quality strategy for premium products in all categories to encourage upgrading by middle-income segment and to satisfy the top-end consumers.

Promotion decisions

The rural area is a market where large portions of the population are illiterate. Therefore, communication should depend on two important principles—simplicity and visibility.

Print and electronic media: One can make use of different media to promote products in the rural market. Coca-Cola uses a combination of TV, cinema and radio to reach 53.6 per cent of rural households. It doubled its spending on advertising on Doordarshan, which alone reached 41 per cent of rural households. It has also used banners, posters and tapped all the local forms of entertainment.

Mobile advertising: Marketers can make use of all moving modes of advertisement such as cycles, bikes, cars, buses, cattle, bullock carts, and T-shirts.

Fixed-location advertising

- *Point-of-purchase*: Loud, bright colours are typically used on packages to differentiate a product from the others on the shelf and to create a lasting impression in a consumer's mind.
- *Point-of-use*: Wall paintings, tin plates tied to trees, large sized rocks and so on could be used.
- *Traffic places*: Hoardings, wall paints, and so on are used.

Traditional oral media: They include *Burraktha*, *Harikatha*, puppetry, street theatre, drama and music programmes.

Distribution-related advertising: *Mandis,* fairs, *melas, haats, jataraas, gramotsavs,* and so on fall under this category.

Message choices: Rural people are less educated and are naïve when it comes to communication. They value functionality, decency, social acceptance and affiliation. Experience indicates that messages should be linear, address benefits, solve problems, involve people and be musical, and create an optimistic mood. Rural people may be simple but judge things based on common sense.

Rural brands are mostly recognized through symbols, logos and colours. They consider heavy watches to be high quality ones. They taste cement to determine its quality.

Opinion leadership and group relations can be effective approaches to promote products.

During a study conducted by Anugrah Madison Advertising Pvt. Ltd for Philips in Tamil Nadu, it was found that almost an entire village owned a single brand of TV such as BPL or Videocon.

Music, demonstration and intelligent advice will form the right combination to promote products in rural areas.

An award winning ad of Xpanse Asia, the rural marketing arm of Starcom MediaVest Group, shown at the Festival of Media Awards, Spain, 2009, illustrates how people and music can be employed to woo rural folk. Procter & Gamble wanted to increase penetration of hygiene essentials such as shampoos

(Head & Shoulders) and detergents (Tide) in villages. It engaged Xpanese Asia who created a character called Sangeeta Bhabhi, whom rural women could trust. Sangeeta Bhabhi was a semi-urban, educated woman, married into a typically rural family who wins appreciation by performing household chores using products of Procter & Gamble. The story was told by teams of two male communicators armed with kits that included games, signage and the products. They travelled on motorbikes through 100 villages. Visiting many locations, they gathered 20–30 households together, entertaining them with games and raffle draws to maximize participation before introducing Sangeeta Bhabhi's story.[22]

Guideline 13: Promotion should be innovative in choosing media and simple in communicating the messages to individuals and groups.

Distribution decisions

For a product to reach 0.6 million villages spread over 3.2 million sq. metres of area, it is important for the marketer to have a good distribution system. Limited transport facilities act as a constraint to marketing action. Innovations are required in three areas:

1. Physical transportation modes: These include existing ones like animals (bullocks, horses, donkeys, yaks, and zebras and carts driven by them), boats, cycles, and motor vehicles, tractors, light commercial vehicles, mini-lorries, and vans.
2. People involved: Sales persons, social workers, rural people (village heads, part-time business people and consumers (HUL's *Shakti ammas*). "Consumers as sellers" is the new trend in rural marketing.

   A new breed of consumers is emerging in the rural markets. A consumer can be an insurance agent, the intermediary for a financial product, and the person who acts as an intermediary distributor of a detergent or a cake of soap alike. This channel, uniquely, is not restricted to the efforts of multi-level channel marketers like Amway, but equally involved in selling products and services as a distributor on a direct mode of distribution. Self-help groups are another channel that are becoming micro-entrepreneurs assisted by corporations and micro-finance agencies.
3. Retail outlets: The traditional and innovative modes are these.
   - *Traditional selling points:* Retailers, cooperatives, *mandis*, *haats* and *melas*.
   - *Innovative initiatives:* Fair prices shops (becoming malls), NGOs, post offices, *anganwadis*, rural malls, van marketing and road shows.
   - *Innovative IT-based initiatives:* ITC-e *choupal*, i-*shakti* and others.

Marketers are on an innovation spree to overcome the hurdles of distribution. While state governments are expanding fair price shops to create malls, private entrepreneurs are venturing to start modernized retail outlets.

Nadeem Jafri's Hearty Mart chain of supermarkets, that targets business at the "bottom of the pyramid" in rural areas in Gujarat, is an example of this. Hearty Mart's *saral* is modelled on the neighbourhood *kirana* stores found in cities.

Guideline 14: Distribution should be innovative in leveraging a rural retail revolution, IT developments and people participation.

RURAL VERSUS URBAN MARKETING

Rural marketing is different from urban marketing for various reasons.

Let us make an attempt to highlight the differences between rural and urban marketing (Table 1.6).

Table 1.6 Urban Versus Rural Marketing.

Sl No.	Base	Urban Marketing	Rural Marketing
1	Philosophy	Integrated, innovative relationship orientation.	Additionally, development oriented with inclusive growth concept.
2	Views about customers	A buyer. An innovator who looks for style, novelty and quality.	A buyer and an entrepreneur, partner in the business growth model. As a buyer looks for quality products that offer value for money.
3	Marketing research	Sophisticated marketing research methods. Internet, TV channels and mobile SMS, etc. are being used.	Needs simple, interactive approaches (like interviews, discussions), observation (diary of farmer, a day in a *haat*, etc.). Simple methods of rating scale are required. Image of faces, colour wheel for rating, playing cards and carom coins for ranking are helpful.
4	Segmentation	Psychographic (lifestyle) and usage-based segmentation.	Demographic and geographic segmentation is the starting point. Research agencies have developed marketing potential studies that help in segmenting markets.
5	Targeting	Segment with relevant characteristics.	Segment with relevant characteristics with or without buying power.
6	Marketing goal	Sustainable market share, profitability and image.	Sustainable development of the poor, market share, profitability and image building.
7	Development strategy	Limited to CSR (philanthropy to cause marketing).	Partnering with government, NGOS and private organizations (for training, microfinance, and managerial assistance in entrepreneurial ventures of the poor).
8	Marketing mix	Innovative 4 P's to meet the customer's current and future expectations.	Innovative 4 P's to meet the customer's current and future expectations. Obviously different from urban ones.
9	Technology and innovations	Sophisticated technology to create luxury goods and convenience products/ services to simplify home and work life. Also focus can be on health, recreational and entertainment services.	Primarily appropriate technologies for rural innovations that remove basic bottlenecks in village life like shortage of transport, poor drinking water facility, power failures, etc.
10	Marketing evaluation	Economic standards relating to cost, revenue, profits, sales and brand equity. Social standards like customer satisfaction and image.	In addition, necessary criteria are: development related economic standards (like a rise in the incomes of people by social entrepreneurship action) and social standards (like quality-of-life improvements in partnering customers and achievements of a company in partnering with government and social agencies).

BECOMING A RURAL MARKETER

This is a mind-boggling proposition for two types of persons—one, the manager interested in expanding the business of his enterprise and the other, the management student aspiring for a rewarding career. The answer is simple—if you have motivation, ability and knowledge, you can perform well in rural markets and you can choose to be a rural marketer. However, assessing the three aspects is not as simple as one may think. Some of the important requirements to help you assess your potential are discussed below.

Motivation

Motivation to work in rural markets may have the following sources:

Accepting the challenging assignment to prove oneself, the desire to take up a different job, staying in rural areas (being a rural native), serving the nation (patriotic spirit), helping the poor to change their lives (service challenge) and expecting acceptable rewards (salary and benefits that are enough to lead a good life).

Knowledge

Strategies are made by top executives in board rooms. However, they are practised on the dusty roads of villages. Effective formulation and implementation of strategy requires understanding at the grass roots level. As such, the middle- to lower-level managers require exposure and experience relevant to rural markets. A deeper understanding of the rural milieu is needed to be successful and comfortable in rural operations. Knowledge of rural areas—the geographical spread of rural villages, demographics, culture and language, lifestyles and preferences, competition, political and caste affiliations and rivalries, administration and development plans and progresses and other related information is important.

Till recently, marketers had exposure mostly to urban markets and they chose people from urban areas to work in rural villages. They have to reorient themselves to be successful in their mission.

Skills

Rural people don't easily trust urban people. Establishing mutual trust is a big challenge for urban marketers. In view of this, it can be said that a rural marketer requires the following skills and attributes:

(i) *Social skills:* Rural marketers have to go beyond relationship marketing. Rather, they should include humour and recreation in their plan of action. Using an interactive approach, they may organize games and events that attract the attention of villagers of all professions uniformly. This would require local-level goodwill creation and social negotiation skills.

(ii) *Respect and humility:* Rural folk look up to the urbanites and hence, the behaviour of marketers, while conducting business in villages, should be respectful and humble.

(iii) *Patience:* Rural buyers take a long time to make up their mind to buy. Therefore, marketers need to learn to exercise more patience in dealing with the less educated rural traders and consumers.

(iv) *Courtesy and concern:* Rural India is a network of relationships. Marketers have to show courtesy and concern in dealing with rural consumers. The focus should be on "relationship" building and not mere product selling. Mobile traders selling a variety of products by visiting the same home for years have been practicing relationship marketing for centuries in India.

Box 1.5 Choosing a Career in Rural Marketing

Young men and women can now boldly choose rural marketing as their career option as it is exciting and rewarding.

Agri-business management, NGO management, natural resource management, rural infrastructure, micro-finance and corporate social responsibility (CSR) are just some of the emerging areas in rural management. FMCG companies, rural marketing agencies, non-governmental organizations, agencies under the United Nations, micro-finance companies, banking and insurance sectors, companies engaged in agro-based businesses and others foresee exponential growth in rural India.

ICICI Bank, HDFC Bank, Hindustan Unilever, ITC, Tata Chemicals, Maruti Udyog and Proctor & Gamble are hiring professionals with expertise in rural management to try and reach out into the untapped markets of Indian villages. The salaries offered to students have also boomed over the years.

Although the demand for rural managers is very high, the availability of competent human resources is rather limited. Institutions like the Xavier Institute of Management, Bhubaneswar (XIMB), Institute of Rural Management, Anand, S. P. Jain Institute of Management and Research (SPJIMR), Pune, Mudra Institute of Communications (MICA), Ahmedabad and National Institute of Rural Management, Jaipur also offer management programmes that are in great demand. Various universities in the country also offer rural marketing as a specialization in their MBA programmes. Witnessing the trends, Rural Marketing Agencies Association of India (RMAAI) has started organizing various activities to promote talent among youth.

One such initiative is the announcement of awards for the best summer projects in rural marketing by students from premier management schools across the country. A team of experts nominated by RMAAI will evaluate the projects and the top 10 entries will be invited to an awards event where each project team will make a presentation. The three best presentations receive the following awards:

- Gold Award (Rs 15,000)
- Silver Award (Rs 10,000)
- Bronze Award (Rs 5,000)

Source: N. Jojo Joy, "In Search of Rural Expertise," *Rural Marketing Association of India Journal* (March 2008).

TEST YOUR RURAL MARKETING POTENTIAL

Answer the following questions using one of the three following responses: Yes, No and Uncertain. If you have more number of "Yes" responses, you are a rural marketer.

1. Am I interested in working in rural areas?
2. Is my motivation factor strong?
3. Can I sustain my motivation for at least two years?

4. Have I travelled and visited rural villages so that I can say that "I know the rural areas" of a particular region?
5. Have I completed a project that gave me first-hand exposure to rural life?
6. Have I completed a rural marketing course that gave me conceptual and analytical understanding of rural marketing operations?
7. Have I undergone training in any institute to gain the knowledge and skills needed by a rural marketer?
8. Am I good at conversations in the local language of rural people?
9. Am I known to rural people?
10. Am I accepted and respected by rural people?
11. Can I negotiate well with simple people to convince them to agree with my points?
12. Can I use the demonstration method in making explanations?
13. Do I have a positive regard for people in rural areas irrespective of caste and income considerations?
14. Can I speak clearly with respect and consideration to my customers?
15. Do I have the patience to talk to less educated farmers and traders?
16. Do I show courtesy to people naturally?
17. Am I rated as a social person who cares for relationships?
18. Do I have good energy levels to move around the villages, scattered and unconnected by road?
19. Do I have robust health to stay in dusty and dirty village environments?
20. Do I have a feeling that I am the right person for a rural job?

You have interesting news if you have received a good score. For students engaged in rural marketing studies and looking for bright careers, opportunities to prove themselves start much early.

Box 1.5 discusses how you can win and gain recognition from prospective employers as a student.

Summary

Rural marketing is gaining recognition as a growing profession, distinct academic discipline and rewarding career for young management students and executives. A rural area can be defined at the convenience of companies, based on market potential. Rural demand exists for several products and services required for household consumption and occupational needs. Rural market entry decisions are influenced by three types of factors—urban push, rural pull and rural inhibiting. Urban push factors include saturated market, fierce competition and changing lifestyles of urban people. Rural pull factors comprise rising affordability due to changes in population size, occupations, incomes, consumption and disposable incomes, growing acceptance for new products and services owing to increasing literacy, lifestyle changes and shifts in decision making, increasing availability needs due to growing usage and demand for products, upgrading of purchases and growing brand consciousness and improving accessibility by road and communication connectivity. The success of several companies is an important motivator. However, there are certain inhibiting factors too. Uneven development, fragmented markets, diversity in occupations, heterogeneity in lifestyles, low income streams, lack of steady and sustainable consumption, poor marketing skills of promotional agencies, difficulty in accessing, less acceptance for urban lifestyle products (this is due to low education levels and few creative efforts of corporations in changing traditional thinking), intensifying competition and failure of some companies.

Four distinct approaches are identified to operate in rural markets. They are the trickle-down approach, the undifferentiated approach, the differentiated approach and the Integrated–Innovative–and–Inclusive (3-I) approach based on the bottom-of-the-pyramid theory.

The following guidelines help implement the 3-I approach.

1. Define mission, vision and value statements. Develop an inclusive growth strategy, set goals and make proper resource allocation. Work out partnerships and alliances.
2. Consider setting up a task force, sales verticals and rural malls.
3. Establish appropriate systems covering the key operational areas.
4. Prepare a value statement and circulate it among employees.
5. Choose people with rural orientation and experience.
6. Train employees to gain relevant skills in the skills set—social, technical, entrepreneurial and design.
7. Encourage and employ participative style to educate, engage and empower people.
8. Understand that rural markets are different and changing. Acquire first-hand information by personal observation and get problem-specific information from rural research agencies.
9. Rural marketing research requires customization in terms of questions and research tools based on language, level of literacy, and style of participation of subjects.
10. Marketers have to choose multiple and relevant variables to segment the rural market.
11. Innovate to create appropriate technology products ensuring utility and affordability.
12. Offer products at multiple price points to meet the expectations of different segments of the market. Price the products low for repeat purchase items and provide small packs. Adopt value-pricing for low-end economy/popular products in regular pack sizes as well as consumer durables. Adopt high-priced, high-quality strategy for premium products in all categories to encourage upgrading by the middle-income segment and satisfy the top-end consumers.
13. Promotion should be innovative in choosing media and simple in communicating the messages to individuals and groups.
14. Distribution should be innovative in leveraging rural retail revolution, IT developments and people participation.

One can be a rural marketer provided the person has the motivation, knowledge and skills necessary to function effectively.

Discussion Questions

1. Discuss the approaches to rural marketing and identify their suitability to companies offering FMCGs, services and agri-inputs.
2. There are two views on rural markets. One view is that "a market thriving on subsidies, loan waivers, migration to urban areas and the vagaries of the monsoon cannot be sustainable." Another view suggests that "the formation of SEZs, industrialization and BoP approach by companies are leading to sustainable rural markets." Discuss.

Short Answer Questions

1. Sketch the evolution of rural marketing.
2. Define rural marketing.
3. Explain the nature of rural marketing.
4. Make a classification of the rural market and identify the major players in each category.
5. Explain development marketing.
6. What is innovative marketing?
7. Elucidate the concept of inclusive marketing.
8. What do you understand by bottom-of-the-pyramid marketing?

Essay Questions

1. Explain the factors that have made rural markets attractive.
2. Explain the approaches to rural marketing and decide which one is suitable for the following: (a) Jewellery: Nakshatra (b) Surf-Excel (c) Tractors of M&M (d) Nirma washing powder.
3. How does rural marketing differ from urban marketing? What qualities should a rural marketer possess?
4. Explain the Integrated–Innovative–Inclusive marketing model. Provide suitable guidelines for companies planning to go rural.

Internet Exercise

Visit the Web sites of two companies of your choice and prepare a note on the rural marketing initiatives of the two companies.

Mini Project

Prepare a questionnaire to investigate the intentions of management students to become rural marketers and to accumulate data on their experience, exposure, abilities and efforts in that direction. Prepare a report and present it in the class room.

End Notes

1. CII study, "Paradigm Shift in Rural Buying Pattern," 13 November 2009.
2. Radhika Menon and N. S. Vageesh, "Private Insurers Reach Out to Rural Customers," *The Hindu Business Line*, 6 April 2005.
3. *The Bird of Gold: The Rise of Indian Consumer Market* (McKinsey Global Institute, McKinsey & Company, 2007).
4. "The Max-NCAER Study, 2005," *The Marketing Whitebook*, 2009–2010, (New Delhi: *Business-world*, 2009).
5. "The Indicus Analytics Survey, 2008," *Business Today*, 5 April 2009, p. 53.
6. "RMAAI/MART Study, 2008," cited in "Robust Rural," *The Hindu Business Line*, 2 April 2009.
7. "Literacy as Seen in the 2001 Census," available at http://indiabudget.nic.in/es2001-02/chapt2002/chap106.pdf.
8. Soumen Banerjee, "Rural Marketing: Challenges in Distribution and Channel Management," 21 March 2009, available at www.coolavenues.com/know/mktg/soumen-rural-1.php.
9. ASSOCHAM Report, cited in "In Need of an Overhaul," *The Hindu Business Line*, 2 April 2009.
10. Arvind Mayaram, "Rural Roads: Considering a New Paradigm," *The Financial Express*, 26 January 2010, available at www.financialexpress.com/news/rural-roads-considering-a-new-paradigm/571516/.
11. *The Marketing Whitebook*, 2009–2010.
12. World Business Council for Sustainable Development, 1999.
13. NCAER Survey, 1994.
14. The Corporate Social Responsibility (CSR) Survey 2002–India, jointly conducted by the United Nations Development Programme, the British Council, the Confederation of Industry and PricewaterhouseCoopers.
15. "The Role of Cause Branding," Cone Corporate Citizenship Study, 2002, available at www.coneinc.com.
16. C. K. Prahalad and Stuart Hart, *The Fortune at the Bottom of the Pyramid: Eradicating Poverty Through Profits* (Wharton University of Pennsylvania, 2004), pp. 1–5.
17. Pradeep Kashyap, "Inclusive Marketing: Innovative Strategies for the Development of Masses."
18. T. P. Gopalaswamy, *Rural Marketing Environment, Problems and Strategies* (Noida: Vikas Publishing House, 1997), p. 4.
19. C. S. G. Krishnamacharyulu and Lalitha Ramakrishnan, *Rural Marketing: Text and Cases* (New Delhi: Pearson Education, 2002), p. 62.
20. Pradeep Kashyap and Siddartha Raut, *The Rural Marketing Book* (New Delhi: Biztantra, 2007), p. 12.
21. Balaram Dogra and Karminder Ghuman, *Rural Marketing: Concepts and Practices* (New Delhi: Tata McGraw-Hill, 2008), p. 3.
22. NDTV Profit, 17 February 2009, available at www.ndtv.com.

Case 1.1 Trials of a Rural Sales Trainee

When choosing to be a rural sales trainee in the largest consumer durables company of India, Bhalla did not size up the challenges a woman sales trainee might face, perhaps overwhelmed by the enthusiasm of going rural and serving the nation. As she battles to find a foothold in the male-dominated distribution chain and retail world, one question that looms large in her mind is—Is India liberated?

Encountering the prejudiced and patronizing attitude of distributors and shopkeepers on a daily basis, handling questions like "why didn't you join Citibank?", listening to her superiors proclaim that the "single-most definitive thing about sales is that it is a man's world," Bhalla learns to take it in her stride as she goes through bumpy rides on delivery vans, assignments with no basic amenities, and junior sales managers who watch porn movies in conference rooms.

In the "real" India, the girl-child is routinely used to serve the father, the brother and the husband even today. Even meritorious girls have to forego their dreams at the altar of tradition and marriage, the lines of religious divide are sacrosanct and a poor village girl can get her nose chopped off for talking to a strange man.

Bhalla counsels, "You certainly need a strong positive attitude for facing life head-on, as you often land in weird adventures—dealing with eve-teasers, floods and crocodiles, getting stranded with a much touted stain-removing detergent that fails to work its magic in front of a crowd, dealing with a blackmailing policeman or a bus ride with a goat—all in the daily life of a sales trainee!"

Bhalla further observes, "I learnt the rules of survival when after trying hard for a year "to be one of the boys" and "to feel comfortable in the Martian territory", I discovered how to turn my handicap of being a woman into an advantage. Though frustrated at being designated either a sister or a daughter by sundry distributors and shopkeepers, I later found that these very roles allowed me access into their family and to their womenfolk (how many males can manage that) and thus, I understood not only the efficacy of my company's products but also I indulged in some smart bonding, a factor that provided the much-needed edge over my male colleagues."

Bhalla goes back to Mumbai with the pleasure of doing what others said "I could not do" and says, "The lesson I learnt is—in rural India, it's best to stick to popular wisdom."

For discussion

1. Identify the problems and challenges faced by sales trainees of both genders.
2. Suggest steps to be taken by (i) educational institutions, (ii) recruiting companies and (iii) career aspirants in developing effective rural sales skills.

Source: Debasree Bhattacharjee, "Retail's Tryst with Rural India," *The Financial Express,* 1 December 2007.

Case 1.2 Rural Entrepreneurship

Nadeem Jafri is beaming with joy as his dream of serving the rural folk by venturing into business in rural areas has become a reality. He set up "Hearty Mart," a chain of supermarkets, in little-known villages such as Pipodar, Kakoshi, Vadnagar and Idar in Madhya Pradesh.

"Previously the people of Illol village travelled to the nearest town of Himmatnagar, Gujarat, to buy a sachet of shampoo. But now they are able to buy it from the shop in the village," says Jafri. Hearty Mart provides a modern retail experience for rural folk aspiring for brands that television has introduced into their homes.

Jafri has made four important decisions in promoting his chain. They are:

- Adoption of a franchisee model
- Introduction of private labels in the stores
- Introduction of new brands
- Use of promotion

Franchisee Model

The stores are generally 500 to 800 sq. ft in size. A smaller format of stores of less than 300 sq. ft, have also been devised to enable villagers with limited space to tie-up with the chain. The small formats are known as "Hearty Mart *Saral*" shops and they are modelled after the neighbourhood *kirana* stores found in cities. Jafri and his team take care of the initial stocking for the store and claim 1.5 per cent of annual royalty from the franchisees. The first franchise was issued at Illol for a deposit of Rs 25,000. The chain intends to set up about 15 stores in a couple of years.

Private Labels

To reduce the risk of franchisees, Jafri allowed people to sell private labels to him. He observed, "In the event that we decide to pull out of the association, the shopkeeper should be able to operate on his own." *Sahyog*, Easy Shop and Tiny Shop are the second brand names chosen by the franchisees in Illol, Kakoshi and Pipodar, respectively. The stocking of private labels for products such as *papad*, pickle, *besan* and so on, that are not available locally, is done with an expectation to generate more revenue.

Introduction of New Brands

Jafri is innovative in the supply of his brands. Two latest introductions are Lutf, a homemade ketchup that is sold to hotels and other institutions and Good Time packaged spices.

Diversification

Jafri floated a wholesale partnership venture called Hearty Mart Enterprise to help sustain this model of business. The company supplies the grocery requirements of hotels and restaurants in and around Ahmedabad from its rented godown on the SG Highway. Besides the rural retail venture, he has floated an advertising firm with his friend and also gives guest lectures in colleges across Gujarat.

Promotion

"*Sabse khaas, ghar ke paas* (the best, closer home)" is the tagline of the Hearty Mart chain. Having worked in the advertising industry, Jafri knew only too well the impact of advertising on sales. Within a year the mart broke even and recorded an average sales of Rs 7,000 a day.

On its first anniversary, the mart sent a packet of sugar to all its customers along with a signed letter that acknowledged their support and expressed a desire to continue the "sweet relationship." He was aware of the importance attached to sugar in that region and the gesture did indeed impact footfalls tremendously.

A first-time entrepreneur, Jafri ventured into this business two years ago with an initial capital of Rs 4 million. Last year the venture clocked a retail turnover of Rs 6 million, which is expected to cross Rs 7.5 million this year.

Jafri's background has been quite useful to him in his venture. He did his MBA from IMS Indore and worked for companies such as The Bhaskar Group, AT&T, *Indian Express*, Grey Worldwide and Bennett Coleman.

He made a careful move from his family business to follow passion. Getting into the family's restaurant business would have been easy but he chose to become a retailer instead. With limited funds and resources, he set up the first Hearty Mart at Vishala Circle, Ahmedabad. "People from my community, Chiliya, are in the hotel business and I could leverage my family name to tap this network of hoteliers to supply groceries. Adding this bulk-buying capacity also allowed me to negotiate a better deal with vendors," he says.

For discussion

1. Identify the reasons for Jafri's success.
2. Evaluate the decisions taken by Jafri in setting and operating the chain.
3. Do you have ideas to help Jafri expand and strengthen his business?

Source: Divya Trivedi, "Mart with a Rural Heart," *The Hindu Business Line*, 3 April 2009.

2

Understanding the Rural Economy

LEARNING OBJECTIVES

Upon completion of this chapter, you will be able to:

- Understand the socio-economic characteristics of rural areas in India
- Know the infrastructural facilities available for rural people
- Appreciate the technological developments and innovations that transformed rural life
- Recognize the role played by the government and other agencies in promoting rural development
- Identify the potential rural markets can offer in the future years

The life of a farmer, K. T. Srinivasa, has changed recently, though the two dirt roads near his home about 40 miles from India's high-tech capital of Bengaluru, his house without toilet facility, farm without tractor support and the way in which his family threshes rice by crushing it with a massive stone roller, have remained the same. How?

The change has been brought about by a cell phone. The little, attractive gadget is helping him make decisions related to farming. When to plant and harvest, at what price to sell the produce (rice, coconuts and jasmine), and how and when to transport and sell—all these intriguing questions are now resolved intelligently. Idea Cellular, Mr Srinivasa's service provider, has effectively utilized its first-mover advantages. Close to half the 800 people in the village, including Mr Srinivasa, have become its subscribers. Most of the villagers make voice calls as they don't know how to text message or download e-mails. On an average, rural Indians use their phones around 8.5 hours a month, up by 10 per cent over the past year.

The villagers are very amused with their new found connectivity with the world. They are now aware of the people and events affecting the rest of India and the world. They can answer quiz questions such as who is America's President and why there is an economic slowdown. The recession is not bullying them. They have understood that it is hurting their high-tech neighbours in Bengaluru much more and that the Indian economy is able to absorb the shocks much better than other developed nations. "After the global crises," says Mr Srinivasa, the farmer, "I think we are in better shape."[1]

This is an example of one of the many changes in the rural environment that have had a profound impact on rural lives. Every change brings with it an opportunity and a challenge. This chapter deals with environmental changes and their implications on marketers.

INTRODUCTION

Rural marketing requires an understanding of the environment in which companies have to operate to deliver products and services. As successful marketing is customer-centric, it starts from understanding the consumers. Consumer decisions and actions can be properly comprehended only when the force field in which they are operating is understood. As such, a study of environmental factors is essential for marketers. It is also important for marketers to realize the developments and trends rather than know the static picture of the environment. Today's decisions are not only for current problems but also for future opportunities, performance and results.

RURAL MARKETING ENVIRONMENT

One of the standard ways of analysing the environment is by using the STEP model. The different factors that are relevant, directly or indirectly, to rural marketers in each of the environments are as given under.

- Social environment—Population and households, education and literacy levels, social groups, festivals and *melas,* entertainment and arts.
- Technological environment—Power and energy sources, postal services, telecommunications, information and communication technology, appropriate technology and innovations.
- Economic environment—Occupations, land distribution, land use pattern, irrigation, asset holding, income, consumption, savings, disposable incomes, rural lifestyles and sales potential, rural credit institutions, rural retail outlets, micro-financing and rural industry.
- Political environment—Development initiatives and administrative bodies.

How do these factors influence marketing decisions? Table 2.1 shows the four key decision areas of marketing and the relevant environmental factors.

Table 2.1 Marketing Decisions and Environment

Sl No.	Decision area	Environmental factors
1	Demand estimation	Demographics (size and distribution of population by age, gender, occupation, education, geographical areas, marital status and family size), income, consumption, savings and investment.
2	Segmentation and target marketing	Demographics, lifestyle indicators, purchase and usage of inventories, etc.
3	Product decision	Income, quality consciousness, brand awareness and preferences of consumers, competition, technology developments, etc.
4	Price decision	Disposable incomes, propensity to consume, competition, costs of input factors, demand, etc.
5	Place decision	Availability of trade channels, physical distribution facilities, technological developments, competition, location and participation of consumers, etc.
6	Promotion decision	Media availability and costs, media habits of target customers, competition, etc.

We will now discuss the key factors that influence the decision making of consumers and; hence, rural marketers.

SOCIAL ENVIRONMENT

Information about population, households and number of earning members in a family provides the starting point for understanding the rural economy.

Population and households

The country's population is 1,027 million and the share of rural population is about 73 per cent. There are 205.9 million households of which 30 per cent (61.4 million) are in urban areas and the rest, 70 per cent (144.5 million), in rural areas.

The average family in the country consists of five members. The rural family size is larger than the national average at 5.08. Obviously, the urban family size is smaller being 4.81. The MAX-NCAER survey of 2008 identified that less than one per cent of Indian households are single-member ones and around 10 per cent have more than seven members.

How many in a household are earning members? Table 2.2 gives the answer: an average of 1.43 in rural and 1.34 in urban areas. It implies that most of the families have a single earning member, both in urban and rural areas.

The MAX-NCAER survey has divided the states into three categories based on incomes as follows.

- Low-income (LI) states:

  Assam, Bihar, Madhya Pradesh, Meghalaya, Orissa, Rajasthan, Uttar Pradesh, Chattisgarh, Uttaranchal and Jharkhand
- Middle-income (MI) states:

  Andhra Pradesh, Himachal Pradesh, Karnataka, Kerala, Tamil Nadu and West Bengal
- High-income (HI) states:

  Goa, Gujarat, Haryana, Maharashtra, Punjab, Puducherry, Chandigarh and Delhi

The distribution of population across the three different categories of states is shown in Table 2.3. The income levels and population parameters are inversely related. The high-income states have lower estimated population and households. The percentage of rural population in the high-income states 54.5 per cent is less compared to 68.2 per cent in the middle-income states and 80.7 per cent in the low-income states. Therefore, it can be said that a larger proportion of the rural population is living in less developed areas of our nation.

Table 2.2 Distribution of Population (2004–05)

Factors	Rural	Urban	All India
Population (mn)	732	295	1,027
Households (mn)	144.5	61.4	205.9
Household size (number of members)	5.08	4.81	5.00
Number of earning members per household	1.43	1.34	1.40

Source: The MAX-NCAER India Financial Protection Survey, 2008.

Table 2.3 Distribution of Population Across States (2004–05)

Factors	LI States	MI States	HI States	All India
Estimated population (mn)	493	314	220	1,027
Estimated households (mn)	91.7	69.6	44.3	205.6
Average household size	5.38	4.51	4.97	5.00
Per capita income (Rs per annum)	9,749	14,543	18,172	13,018
Share of rural population (%)	80.7	68.2	54.5	71.2

Source: The MAX-NCAER India Financial Protection Survey, 2008.

Table 2.4 Household Size in Rural India

Size	Percentage
1 to 2	10.3
3 to 4	32
5 to 6	33.7
7 to 8	14.5
9 to 10	5.2
Above 11	4.1

Source: IRS 2007 R2 Hansa Research, *The Marketing Whitebook* (New Delhi: *Businessworld,* 2009–2010).

What is the average size of a household? The average size ranges from 4.51 to 5.38 across different categories of states. Table 2.4 provides the household sizes in rural India. The predominant sizes are 3 to 4 and 5 to 6. About 32 per cent and 33.7 per cent households, respectively, are found with these sizes in rural India.

Gender-wise distribution

Sex ratio (the number of females per 1,000 males) for India is 933 females per 1,000 males. Table 2.5 provides the gender-wise distribution of population in rural areas. Women and men are almost in equal numbers in many of the states. The male population is larger in union territories like Andaman and Nicobar Islands, Chandigarh, Dadra and Nagar Haveli, Daman and Diu, Delhi and most of the northern states such as Bihar, Gujarat, Haryana, Madhya Pradesh, Maharashtra, Nagaland, Punjab, Rajasthan, Uttar Pradesh and West Bengal. In almost all southern parts of the nation, males and females are almost equal in number, the exception being Kerala where the female population dominates the male population.

Literacy levels

What is the education level of chief earning members in rural households? The percentage of educated heads of households in rural areas is less compared to those in urban areas. The percentage

Table 2.5 Rural Population—Gender-wise Distribution

Sl No.	State/Union territory	Persons	Males	Females
1	India	742,490,639	381,602,674	360,887,965
2	Andaman and Nicobar Islands	239,954	128,961	110,993
3	Andhra Pradesh	55,401,067	27,937,204	27,463,863
4	Arunachal Pradesh	870,087	454,680	415,407
5	Assam	23,216,288	11,939,945	11,276,343
6	Bihar	74,316,709	38,594,996	35,721,713
7	Chandigarh	92,120	56,816	35,304
8	Chhattisgarh	16,648,056	8,307,443	8,340,613
9	Dadra and Nagar Haveli	170,027	91,832	78,195
10	Daman and Diu	100,856	63,606	37,250
11	Delhi	944,727	522,087	422,640
12	Goa	677,091	340,545	336,546
13	Gujarat	31,740,767	16,317,771	15,422,996
14	Haryana	15,029,260	8,052,988	6,976,272
15	Himachal Pradesh	5,482,319	2,756,073	2,726,246
16	Jammu and Kashmir	7,627,062	3,977,652	3,649,410
17	Jharkhand	20,952,088	10,679,596	10,272,492
18	Karnataka	34,889,033	17,648,958	17,240,075
19	Kerala	23,574,449	11,451,282	12,123,167
20	Lakshadweep	33,683	17,191	16,492
21	Madhya Pradesh	44,380,878	23,031,093	21,349,785
22	Maharashtra	55,777,647	28,458,677	27,318,970
23	Manipur	1,590,820	808,953	781,867
24	Meghalaya	1,864,711	946,999	917,712
25	Mizoram	447,567	232,726	214,841
26	Nagaland	1,647,249	859,716	787,533
27	Orissa	31,287,422	15,748,970	15,538,452
28	Puducherry	325,726	163,703	162,023
29	Punjab	16,096,488	8,516,596	7,579,892

(Continued)

Table 2.5 (Continued)

Sl No.	State/Union territory	Persons	Males	Females
30	Rajasthan	43,292,813	22,426,640	20,866,173
31	Sikkim	480,981	255,774	225,207
32	Tamil Nadu	34,921,681	17,531,494	17,390,187
33	Tripura	2,653,453	1,363,638	1,289,815
34	Uttar Pradesh	131,658,339	69,157,470	62,500,869
35	Uttaranchal	6,310,275	3,144,590	3,165,685
36	West Bengal	57,748,946	29,616,009	28,132,937

Source: Census of India, 2001.

Table 2.6 Education Levels of Chief Earners (per cent) (2004–05)

Education level	Rural	Urban	All India
Illiterate	26.0	7.9	20.6
Primary	22.5	11.5	19.2
Middle	19.2	14.1	17.7
High school	17.2	22.3	18.7
Higher secondary	8.1	15.0	10.1
Graduate	7.0	29.2	13.7
Total	100.0	100.0	100.0

Source: The MAX-NCAER India Financial Protection Survey, 2008.

of rural chief earners is less than the percentage of urban persons in all categories of educational levels, excepting middle school as given in Table 2.6. The illiterate and primary school educated in rural areas constitute 26 per cent and 22.5 per cent, respectively, as against 7.9 per cent and 11.5 per cent in urban areas. This means that half the chief earners in rural areas are less educated as against the one-fifth in urban areas. About 19.2 per cent of rural chief earners and 14.21 per cent of chief earners in urban areas have middle school-level training. This case is an exception, but at the next higher levels of education, we find the urban citizens dominating their counterparts in rural areas. At the graduate level, we find the statistic is only seven per cent in rural areas as against 29.2 per cent in urban areas.

Indicus Analytics provides data on the education levels of people above 20 years in rural areas. Table 2.7 shows that 37 per cent of rural persons above 20 years are illiterate. The number of people at higher education levels are low at 11 per cent. The happy news is that about 62.8 per cent of rural people are now literate.

Media habits and reach

The Media Guide, 2008 released by the Lintas Media Group, analyses the penetration and reach of each medium of communication. The population distribution shows that of the 1,028.7 million people in the country, 65.4 per cent are literate. Around 29.1 per cent live in urban areas and 70.9 per cent in rural areas. Males form 51.8 per cent of the total population and females, 48.2 per cent. Media analysts like Atul Phadnis proposed the idea of a two-in-one nation to signify the urban–rural divide. Table 2.8 supports the view.[2]

Television

Television continues to be the medium with the highest reach, but penetrates only 38 per cent of the huge rural population in the country. From six channels in 1991 to just under 300 TV stations by end of 2004, TV has come a long way. The last National Readership Study (NRS) (2003) puts TV ownership at only 86 million of the 202 million Indian homes, a meagre 42 per cent. In fact, TV ownership for urban India and rural India is 75 per cent and 30 per cent, respectively. Though there is an increase in the ownership numbers, an important concern is the kind of TV sets available in rural India. Of the 30 per cent that own TV sets in rural India, three-fourth have black-and-white sets, meaning that they probably receive less than 20 channels. India will have more than 500 channels in the next two years and may well become the largest television market in the world by 2015.

Table 2.7 Educational Distribution of Population Above 20 Years in Rural Areas (2004–05)

Education level	Rural
Illiterate	37.2
Less than Primary	11.2
Primary	12.1
Upper primary/Middle	13.3
Secondary	9.1
Higher secondary	6.1
Graduate and above	11.0
Total	100.0

Source: Indicus Analytics, available at www.indicus.net.

Table 2.8 Media Habits in Urban and Rural Areas

Media vehicle	All India	Urban (U)	Rural (R)	U:R
TV viewers	45	75	33	2.3:1
Press readership	35	58	24	2.3:1
Radio listenership	20	21	19	1.1:1
Cinema goers	19	29	15	2:1

Source: N. Bhaskara Rao and P. N. Vasanti, "Media Scene as India Globalises," September 2005, available at www.cmsindia.org.

Radio

Radio has overtaken the print media in rural India and has become the medium with the second largest reach. Radio channels reach 18 per cent of the rural population. The advent of community radios have opened up an easy-to-reach local channel. Box 2.1 describes one such community radio initiated by Development Alternatives.

Print

The penetration of the print media in the rural market is 15 per cent. Initiatives by social organizations to design and supply newspapers are generating new hopes of increasing rural readership. Box 2.2 describes how a group of women in UP, supported by a centre for gender and education, created infotainment for the villagers.

Cinema

Like in urban India, cinema has the lowest reach in rural India—it reaches a mere five per cent of the rural population.

Internet

According to a new report of the Internet and Mobile Association of India (IAMAI), rural India has 3.3 million active Internet users. The research report—part of the ongoing I-Cube, 2008 being jointly undertaken by IMRB International and IAMAI—also notes that there are 5.5 million people who claim to have used the Internet at some point. For the first time, rural India was mapped. The rural

Box 2.1 Bundelkhand Radio—Giving Voice to the Voiceless

The women in Azadpura village in Bundelkhand region are thankful to Radio Bundelkhand as it helped to solve the acute water scarcity problem of the village. The wheel of their only well was missing and their request to repair it was not given due attention by concerned authorities. They were able to get a respite when the problem was aired on the radio and the concerned authorities responded within four days.

Development Alternatives (DA) is the first among several NGOs to start community radio station in its project area under the Government of India scheme. The radio has service and entertainment purposes. It reaches about 15,000 people in 25 villages located in the range of approximately 5–10 kms. Its special focus groups are the poorest women and unemployed youth. The programmes provide information and encouragement to people to take part in local self-governance. The programmes are designed based on the requests and feedback from the community. The field work is organized by five community reporters and six community coordinators.

In fact, the community and DA, jointly manage the station. The management committee comprises the Sarpanch (elected village-head) of the village, doctors, farmers and self-help group members.

The communities prefer infotainment programmes with a focus on livelihood opportunities, development of women, girl's education, legal rights, farmer's issues, training, their culture and history, infrastructure problems such as water, energy and roads, development issues, etc. Entertainment programmes include traditional songs, folk music and *nataks*, discussions, reports, phone-ins, reports of events in villages, jokes, etc.

Source: Indira Mansingh, "Building Change-makers Through Community Radio," 19 August 2009, available at www.digitalopportunity.org.

Box 2.2 ***Khabar Lahariya*—A Weekly Newspaper in Bundeli**

A group of women from various sections of the society from the interiors of Chitrakoot and Banda in Uttar Pradesh were in the news for winning the prestigious Chameli Devi Jain Award for Outstanding Woman Media person. What was their outstanding contribution? Why did they attract the attention of leading national dailies including *The New Indian Express, The Hindu, Hindustan Times, Tehelka* and various other dailies and weeklies?

The recognition was given to them for running a weekly newspaper in Bundeli (the local dialect of Bundelkhand) that provided infotainment for the people in the nearby villages.

It was in the year 2008 that the *Khabar Lahariya* (KL) group registered themselves as an independent organization, Pahal drawing inspiration and support from Nirantar, an acclaimed centre for gender and education.

The eight-page newsletter focuses on issues of importance to the masses, youth and women. Accordingly it has sections presenting current affairs, national and international news, cases of violence against women, problems of Dalits, school education, marriage, health care and more.

The teamwork of the women is impressive. They divide the research and writing works among themselves and work to contribute to the different items of the paper. They go all the way to the nearest city of Allahabad for printing. The women are tech-savvy too. The offices of KL have computers with broadband connections.

They also added another feather in their caps when three members of the group received fellowships from the Dalit Foundation in 2004 for reporting on issues related to the rights of the Dalit community.

Source: Jheel Parekh, "Khabar Lahariya—A Weekly Newspaper in Bundeli," August 2009, available at www.thebetterindia.com.

market holds tremendous potential for any media. However, for the Internet to flourish in rural India, the applications need to be in vernacular languages, preferably with "Text to Speech" capabilities. It would be better if visual symbols, graphics and rich media applications are used. The key question is whether we have the right infrastructure to support these applications.

State-wise reach of different media

State-wise reach is highest for television in Goa, with 83 per cent penetration; it is the lowest in Bihar, with 11 per cent penetration. Radio, like in urban India, has the maximum reach in Tamil Nadu (40 per cent) and the minimum reach in Andhra Pradesh (3 per cent). Print is most effective as a medium in Kerala with 62 per cent reach, and least effective in Madhya Pradesh, with only 4 per cent reach. Cinema follows the same trend in rural India as in urban India and has the highest reach of 20 per cent in Andhra Pradesh. The medium has the lowest reach in the states of Bihar, Gujarat, Haryana, Chattisgarh, Orissa, Uttar Pradesh and West Bengal—with one per cent penetration in each of these states.

Gender-based analysis of different media

Looking at the reach of the various media on the basis of gender division, TVs penetration in rural areas is 39 per cent for men and 35 per cent for women. Radio reaches 22 per cent males and

13 per cent females. Print reaches 20 per cent males and seven per cent females. Cinema reaches four per cent males and one per cent females.

What does this mean for advertisers?

According to the Lintas Media Guide 2008, radio is estimated to provide 1.5 million hours of content for 300 channels at present. The medium accounts for three per cent of the total advertisement expenditure this year, and is expected to grow to five per cent in 2008–09. The Out-Of-Home (OOH) industry is growing at a rate of 17 per cent per year and is expected to grow from Rs 10 billion at present to Rs 21.5 billion by 2010. The Internet also shows a lot of promise and has grown by 43 per cent in terms of advertising revenue.[3]

ECONOMIC ENVIRONMENT

The economic variables that impact the decisions of marketers are explained here.

Occupation

What are the major occupations and incomes of the rural and urban households? Who earns most and how? Table 2.9 shows that the self-employed in agriculture, followed by labour, comprises the largest group in rural areas, accounting for 41.3 per cent and 34.6 per cent of the population, respectively. In other words, they are the average rural households. On the contrary, in urban areas, regular salaries and wages constitute the largest part of income—being 45.2 per cent of the total. The next predominant occupation in urban areas is self-employment in non-agricultural areas. From this, it is evident that rural occupations are agriculture related unlike urban ones.

The data provided by Indicus Analytics throws light on different categories of workers in rural areas as shown in Table 2.10. Obviously, 70 per cent of the workers are in agriculture and allied activities. The percentage of white collar workers is very less.

Land holding

Levels of land possessed (land possessed = land owned + land rented-in and land rented-out) have as much of an impact on earning levels as occupation. Table 2.11 shows that nearly 40 per cent of rural households in India do not possess any land while 30 per cent own 0.1 to 2 acres of land. The table shows that the average size of households as well as the per capita income is positively related to land holding. The average size of households and per capita income of the landless is 4.68 persons and Rs 8,409. In case of large-size holders, the figures are 6.42 persons and Rs 19,666, respectively.

Table 2.9 Distribution of Households by Occupation (Percentages), 2004–05

Source	Rural households	Urban households
Regular salary/wages	10.5	36.9
Self-employment in non-agricultural fields	11.5	32.5
Labour	34.6	22.9
Self-employment in agriculture	41.3	3.1
Others	2.1	4.6

Source: The MAX-NCAER India Financial Protection Survey, 2008.

Table 2.10 Distribution of Workers (2004–05)

Categories	Percentage
Farmers, fishermen, hunters, loggers and related workers	70
Production and related workers, transport equipment operators	17
Sales workers	5
Professional and technical workers	3
Service workers	2
Administration, executive and managerial workers	2
Clerical and related workers	1

Source: Indicus Analytics, available at www.indicus.net.

Table 2.11 Land Holding Patterns, 2004–05

Parameter	Landless (0 acre)	Marginal (up to 2 acres)	Small (2 to 4 acres)	Medium (4 to 10 acres)	Large (over 10 acres)	Rural (total)
Estimated households (in millions)	58.4	42.9	20.4	17.2	5.4	144.1
Estimated households (per cent)	40.5	29.7	14.1	11.9	3.7	100.0
Estimated population (in millions)	273.0	218.9	108.4	96.9	34.5	731.8
Average household size	4.68	5.10	5.33	5.65	6.42	5.08
Per capita income (Rs annum)	8,409	8,929	10,962	14,101	19,666	10,227

Source: The MAX-NCAER India Financial Protection Survey, 2008.

Income profile

Income levels vary significantly across rural and urban areas, as well as across occupation groups. Table 2.12 provides information about incomes. As already pointed out, the number of earning members in urban households (1.43) is slightly higher than in rural households (1.34). The average household in India had an annual income of Rs 65,041 in 2004–05. The rural household earnings are lower than that of urban households at Rs 51,922 per annum compared to Rs 95,827 of urban households. The per capita income of rural households (Rs 10,227) is about half of the urban households, whose per capita income is Rs 19,935. The poverty ratio (21.7%) as well as the population below the poverty line (159 million) is much higher in rural areas when compared to urban areas. The poverty ratio in urban areas is 18.7% and the population below the poverty line is 55.2 million.

Table 2.13 shows the income pyramid of rural and urban people. At the bottom of the pyramid, in the income bracket of less than Rs 75,000 per annum, we find 428 million people in rural areas as

Table 2.12 Estimates of Incomes (2004–05)

	Urban	Rural	All India
Number of earners per household	1.43	1.34	1.40
Income (Rs/annum/household)	95,827	51,922	65,041
Per capita income (Rs)	19,935	10,227	13,018
Poverty ratio (%)	18.7	21.7	20.8
Population below poverty line (in millions)	55.2	159.0	214.2

Source: The MAX-NCAER India Financial Protection Survey, 2008.

Table 2.13 Income Distribution Across Population (Population in millions)

Annual income size (Rs)	Urban	Rural
>1, 000 k	11	4
500 to1,000 k	18	10
300 k to 500 k	51	22
150 k to 300 k	119	111
75 k to 150 k	84	239
> 75 k	49	428

Source: Indicus Analytics, available at www.indicus.net.

against 49 million in urban areas. However, two interesting points emerge from the observation of the data:

- People in rural areas are also spread across different income categories like their urban counterparts.
- In all income categories, excepting the lowest two, the size of the rural population is less than the urban one.

The analysis of minimum household income in rural and urban areas helps us to understand the minimum earning potential in rural areas. The data in Table 2.14 confirms that the percentage of low-income groups is more in rural areas. Majority of households in rural areas are in the income range of below Rs 2,000 per month, whereas urban households are found mostly in different categories above Rs 2,000.

It is believed that education makes a big difference in earning levels. How far has it been proved true in rural and urban areas? Table 2.15 shows the average household earnings in relation to education level of chief earning members. The average income of households headed by illiterates is less, being Rs 36,028 per annum, compared to those who have higher educational levels. The average income of households headed by graduates is about 3 times that of the illiterate chief earning members. Another

Table 2.14 Minimum Household Income (MHI) (Percentages)

Levels of MHI (in Rs)	Urban	Rural
Upto 500	1.0	4.1
501 to 1,000	4.7	20.1
1,001 to 1,500	8.7	17.5
1,501 to 2,000	12.2	21.4
2,001 to 3,000	20.1	16.9
3,001 to 4000	12.7	8.2
4,001 to 5,000	12.0	5.0
5,001 to 6,000	7.6	2.4
6,001 to 8,000	8.8	2.2
8,001 to 10,000	5.7	0.4
10,001 to 12,000	1.8	0.3
Above 12,000 to 1,00,00	4.9	1.5

Source: IRS 2007 R2 Hansa Research, *The Marketing Whitebook* (New Delhi: *Businessworld*, 2009–2010).

Table 2.15 Education Levels of Chief Earning Members and Household Incomes (2004–05)

Education level	Rural	Urban	All India
Illiterate	36,028	49,464	37,574
Primary	41,900	58,721	44,900
Middle	46,393	63,599	50,473
High school	61,143	86,984	70,347
Higher secondary	74,518	99,719	85,691
Graduate	109,527	143,302	131,104
Total	51,922	95,827	65,041

Source: The MAX-NCAER India Financial Protection Survey, 2008.

important observation is that the urban households have higher incomes in all categories. This indicates that besides education there should be opportunities to make it big. Rural people have limited opportunities.

How confident are people in the urban and rural areas about the stability of their earnings? In most of the cases, it is the confidence level that determines the distribution of income among consumption, savings and investment. The confidence in the stability of household income is ascertained for this reason. Table 2.16 shows that confidence in stability of income is less in case of rural people. Only 50 per cent of rural people are confident as against 62.9 per cent of urbanites.

Consumption, savings and investment

Table 2.17 provides the consumption and savings statistics of rural, urban and overall India in detail. At the all India level, the annual household expenditure is Rs 48,902 leaving a surplus of Rs 16,139 to save and invest. Urban income levels are around 85 per cent more than rural ones (Rs 95,827 per annum in urban India versus Rs 51,922 per annum in rural areas). Since expenses in urban areas are substantially higher (Rs 69,065 per annum in urban areas versus Rs 40,309 per annum in rural ones), the difference in the surplus income (of urban and rural areas) that can be saved or invested is not all that huge in absolute terms.

The average urban household saves nearly double that of a rural household (Rs 26,762 per annum in urban areas versus Rs 11,613 for rural areas). What is the aggregate savings potential among different income groups? Table 2.18 shows the figures. The aggregate savings potential is larger in the income category of Rs 150 k to 300 k in both urban and rural areas. As already observed, lower income categories of the urban population save less than rural households.

Where does the surplus income go? Table 2.19 indicates that most of the savings in urban and rural areas are in the form of cash. The savings in cash are to the tune of Rs 65.2 per annum per household in rural areas. In rural areas, of the surplus income of Rs 11,613 about 34.8 per cent is invested, about 10.3 per cent of it in financial investments and 24.5 per cent in physical investments.

Table 2.16 Confidence in Stability of Household Income (% of Households)

	Urban	Rural
Confident	62.9	50.0
Less confident	15.3	20.9
Least confident	7.9	13.4
Can't say	13.9	15.7

Source: The MAX-NCAER India Financial Protection Survey, 2008.

Table 2.17 Estimate of Average Household Income Consumption and Surplus Income (Figures in Rs/Annum/Household) (2004–05)

	Urban		Rural		All India	
Income	95,827	100.0	51,922	100.0	65,041	100.0
Expenditure	69,065	72.1	40,309	77.6	48,902	75.2
Surplus income	26,762	27.9	11,613	22.4	16,139	24.8

Source: The MAX-NCAER India Financial Protection Survey, 2008.

Table 2.18 Savings Across Different Income Groups (Rs in million)

Annual income size (Rs)	Urban	Rural
>1,000 k	1,132,813	445,622
500 to 1,000 k	832,453	526,741
300 k to 500 k	1,094,092	521,032
150 k to 300 k	1,534,758	1,194,467
75 k to 150 k	445,191	989,910
> 75 k	92,050	430,322

Source: Indicus Analytics, available at www.indicus.net.

Table 2.19 Estimate of Investment and Savings (Figures in Rs/Annum/Household) (2004–05)

	Urban		Rural		All India	
Surplus income	26,762	100.0	11,613	100.0	16,139	100.0
Financial investment	3,757	14.1	1,198	10.3	1,961	12.2
Physical investment	5,754	21.5	2,841	24.5	3,713	23.0
Savings in cash	17,246	64.4	7,574	65.2	10,465	64.8

Source: The MAX-NCAER India Financial Protection Survey, 2008.

Table 2.20 Motivation to Save for the Future

Sl No.	Reasons	Rural (%)	Urban (%)
1	Emergencies	81.2	86.6
2	Education of children	79.0	85.3
3	Old age	66.7	73.9
4	Social ceremonies	63.9	60.1
5	Buying or building a house	44.8	51.5
6	Improving or expanding business	43.5	54.4
7	Buying large consumer goods	19.8	28.5
8	Gifts, donations and pilgrimages	17.5	20.4

Source: The MAX-NCAER India Financial Protection Survey, 2008.

The reasons for savings are similar in both urban and rural areas. Emergencies, education of children, old age and social ceremonies are among the top four reasons in both urban and rural areas. Table 2.20 provides the motives for savings of rural and urban people.

Consumption patterns

The spending patterns are not the same in rural and urban households as indicated in Table 2.21. Routine expenditure is 82.5 per cent of the total expenditure in rural areas as against 85.6 per cent in urban areas. Rural households spend an average of Rs 18,404 on food items in a year whereas urban households spend Rs 26,858. Also in case of non-food routine expenditure, it is lower for rural people being Rs 14,385 compared to Rs 32,272 of urban households.

Table 2.22 shows the distribution of routine expenditure. Food is the major item of expenditure in urban and rural areas. The expenditure on food is more in rural areas (55.4 per cent) compared to 45.4 per cent in urban areas. Another item on which money is spent is clothing. In case of clothing, rural expenditure is slightly higher (7.1 per cent) than the urban one (6.8 per cent). The opposite is true in respect of consumer durables. The expenditure on consumer durables is 4.9 per cent and 5 per cent in rural and urban areas, respectively. The rural expenditure is relatively on the lower side compared to the urban ones on all other items like housing (3.8 per cent), health care (4.7 per cent) transport (10 per cent) education (6.4 per cent), and others (7.7 per cent).

Table 2.21 Estimation of Routine and Non-routine Expenditure (Figures in Rs/Annum/Household), (2004–05) (Figures in Parentheses are Percentages)

	Rural	Urban	All India
Expenditure on food (routine)	18,404 (45.7)	26,858 (38.9)	20,930 (42.8)
Expenditure on non-food items (routine)	14,835 (36.8)	32,272 (46.7)	20,046 (40.9)
Non-routine expenditure	7,070 (17.5)	9,935 (14.4)	7,926 (16.3)
Expenditure	40,309 (100.0)	69,065 (100.0)	48,902 (100.0)

Source: The MAX-NCAER India Financial Protection Survey, 2008.

Table 2.22 Distribution of Routine Expenditure (2004–05)

Item	Rural (%)	Urban (%)	All India (%)
Food	55.4	45.4	51.1
Housing	3.8	4.6	4.7
Health care	4.7	5.9	4.7
Transport	10.0	11.1	10.5
Education	6.4	8.7	7.4
Clothing	7.1	6.8	6.9
Durables	4.9	5.0	5.0
Others	7.7	12.5	9.8

Source: The MAX-NCAER India Financial Protection Survey, 2008.

Table 2.23 Distribution of Non-routine Expenditure (2004–05)

Item	Rural (%)	Urban (%)	All India (%)
Ceremonies	55.4	44.9	51.5
Medical	28.8	25.1	27.4
Education	4.7	13.0	7.8
Travel	2.8	5.9	3.9
Others	8.2	11.2	9.3

Source: The MAX-NCAER India Financial Protection Survey, 2008.

When it comes to non-routine expenditure, as shown in Table 2.23, ceremonies and medicines make up the large chunk of it. The percentage spent on these two items is larger in rural areas being 55.4 per cent and 28.8 per cent, respectively, as against 44.9 per cent and 25.1 per cent in urban areas. The expenditure on education is more in urban areas (13 per cent) than in rural areas (4.7 per cent). In case of travel, the expenditure by rural people (2.8 per cent) is less than half of the expenditure by urbanites (5.6 per cent).

Rural credit and institutions

Public policy on rural credit in India has been focused on institutionalization as a means of providing cheaper credit to farmers. From the initial steps to provide *Takkavi* loans by the Government, co-operatives emerged as the first institutional arrangement to provide loans to farmers. Though the Co-operative Act came into effect in 1904, progress in terms of outreach by co-operatives was limited till the 1950s. This led to the nationalization of commercial banks in 1969 and again in 1980 to step up credit supply to rural people. Then came the Regional Rural Banks (RRBs) in the mid-1970s. Thus, the credit architecture consisted basically of co-operatives, commercial banks and regional rural banks. In terms of agency-wise share in rural credit, the progress of institutionalization was impressive.

Non-institutional sources remain significant

The share of private moneylenders had decreased substantially from 93 per cent in the early-1950s to 31 per cent by 1991. The share of institutional agencies in the borrowings of cultivator households increased from a mere 7.3 per cent in 1951 to 66.3 per cent in 1991. During the 1990s, the share of non-institutional agencies increased and reached 38.9 per cent in 2002. This may have been due to the increased role of dealers of various inputs in financing cultivators, diminished interest of commercial banks in rural finance after the financial sector reforms of 1991, deterioration of the health of the co-operative system, among others. Ironically, the states with higher degree of commercialization had higher share of non-institutional sources.[4]

Decline in the role of commercial banks

As a result of liberalization in branch licensing policy, rural branches dwindled in numbers after 1991, both in the absolute and relative senses. The proportion of rural branches declined from 57 per cent in 1990–91 to 44.5 per cent in 2005–06 (Table 2.24). On an average, the number of rural branches came down by 260 every year. As a result of the reduction in the number of branches and general relaxation in the emphasis on priority-sector lending, the involvement of commercial banks in rural credit declined.

The average population served by a bank branch is 15,000. If one includes rural co-operative banks, the average could be lower still—12,800. The numbers compare favourably with Indonesia and Mexico. The present target is to reach out to all 0.107 million unbanked villages, which have population over 2,000 by 2011.

Table 2.24 Decline of Rural Bank Branches (1991–2006)

Year	Number of rural branches	Percentage of total
1990 to 1991	35,134	56.9
1996 to 1997	32,909	50.5
2000 to 2001	32,640	48.3
2005 to 2006	30,750	44.5
Linear growth rate / year	(–) 260	(–) 0.77

Source: K. J. S. Satyasai and K. U. Viswanathan, "Persistence of Private Moneylenders in Rural Credit Markets," *National Bank News Review*, Volume 19, No. 4 (2003): 15–22.

Regional Rural Banks (RRBs) play key role

From a modest beginning of just 6 RRBs with 17 branches covering 12 districts in 1975, the numbers grew to 196 RRBs with 14,446 branches in 518 districts across the country in 2004. However, given the multi-agency shareholding and entailed restrictions, several RRBs failed to sustain viable operations and others merged vertically or horizontally, resulting in the total number of RRBs stabilizing at 91 in 2007, with over 14,000 branches, spread across 585 of the 622 identified districts. With 80% of RRBs in rural India, it serves the larger cause of financial inclusion as well.

Co-operative banks support rural people

Co-operative banks in India are registered under the Co-operative Societies Act. They fall under two categories based on the type of credit.

- Short-term co-operatives (District Central Co-operative Banks, State Co-operative Banks and Primary Agriculture Credit Co-operative Societies).
- Long-term co-operatives (State Agriculture and Rural Development Banks, Primary Agriculture and Rural Development Banks, Primary Agricultural Credit Societies (PACSs).

The 29 state co-operative banks and 92,000 primary agricultural credit societies are playing a key role in credit delivery to rural people.

Rural credit flow

Table 2.25 gives the quantum of credit flow to agriculture between the years 2003–2004 and 2007–2008. Total ground-level credit flow increased to 25 per cent annually during this period to peak at Rs 22,939.9 million in 2006–2007. The credit flow from the co-operative system grew at 13 per cent per annum, the lowest among the agencies. As a result, the share of co-operatives in the total credit flow declined from about 31 per cent to a bit below 22 per cent during the same period.

Micro-finance

The Self-help Group (SHG)Bank linkage programme started as a pilot project in 1992 with 500 SHGs. As of 31 March 2008 about 5,009,794 SHGs are credit linked to banks as shown in Table 2.25. For the 2007–2008, the data has been presented under two models of micro-finance involving credit linkage with banks:

1. *SHG-bank linkage model:* This model involves the SHGs financed directly by the banking agencies, i.e. commercial banks (public sector and private sector), RRBs and co-operative banks.
2. *MFI-bank linkage model:* This model covers financing of Micro-Finance Institutions (MFIs) by banking agencies for lending to SHGs and others small borrowers covered under the micro-finance sector.

Table 2.25 Agency-wise Credit Flow to Agriculture (in billion Rs) (Figures Within Brackets are Shares in Percentages)

Agency	2003–04	2007–08	Compound growth rate (2003–08)
Cooperatives	267.85 (30.4)	418.13 (21.7)	0.13
Regional rural banks	75.81 (8.7)	222.27 (11.5)	0.3
Cooperative banks	522.41 (60.3	1,284.95 (66.7)	0.28
Other agencies	0.84 (0.1)	–	–
Total	869.81(100.0)	1,925.35 (100.0)	0.25

Source: K. J. S. Satyasai, "Rural Credit Delivery in India: Structural Constraints and Some Corrective Measures," *Agricultural Economics Research Review* (2008): 387–394.

Table 2.26 Overall Progress Under Micro-finance (2006–08)

Particulars	Units	2006–07	2007–08	% growth
Savings A/c of SHGs with banks as on March 31	No. of SHGs	4,160,584	5,009,794	20.4
	Amount (Rs in billion)	3,512.71	378.54	0.78
Bank loans disbursed to SHGs	No. of SHGs	1,105,749	1,227,770	11.0
	Amount (Rs in billion)	6,570.39	8,849.26	3.47
Bank loans disbursed to MFIs	No. of MFIs	334	518	55.1
	Amount (Rs in billion)	1,151.56	1,910.95	7.71

Credit is a critical factor in the development of the agriculture and rural sectors as it enables investment in capital formation and technological upgradation. Hence, strengthening of rural financial institutions that deliver credit to these sectors has been identified as a thrust area.

Role of NABARD

In order to reinforce credit functions and to make credit more productive, the National Bank for Agriculture and Rural Development (NABARD) was established in 1982 by an Act of Parliament. It has a nationwide network of 28 regional offices in the state capitals, a sub-office at Port Blair and 391 district development offices. NABARD prepares a Potential Linked Credit Plan (PLP) annually for each district of the country by assessing potential of the agriculture and rural sectors. This serves as a guide for banks and government agencies to prepare their own investment and credit plans in the district and the state.

It re-finances commercial, co-operative and regional rural banks for lending to on-farm and non-farm activities. Re-finance is provided by NABARD for both long-term investment credit as well as short-term production credit for crop loans and for working capital for non-farm activities.

NABARD has effectively brought in a number of innovations in the rural credit domains as given below:

- Self-help groups and micro-finance
- Farmers clubs
- Rural Infrastructure Development Fund (RIDF)
- Watershed Development
- Tribal Development and WADI approach
- Women and development
- District Rural Industries Project (DRIP)
- Rural Entrepreneurship Development Programme (REDP)
- Rural marketing
- Revival of the Short-term Rural Co-operative Structure (STCCS)
- Co-financing

Rural lifestyle indicators

The urban lifestyle is marked by purchases of branded items that offer quality, convenience and comfort. Table 2.27 shows the FMCG consumption in 2008 in rural India. Tea, *vanaspati* and instant noodles in the food category, toothbrush, toothpowder, toilet soap, shampoo and hair oil in the personal care category, washing powder, blues and washing cakes in the wash category figured as the major items of consumption. They indicate the conservative, price conscious, economy-oriented lifestyle of the rural people.

In the process of development and changing lifestyles, it is evident that the rural market is opening up for durables.

Rural sales potential

What do the demographic and economic factors stated above mean to the rural marketer? The rural population is larger, households are more in number, people are less educated, and occupations

Table 2.27 FMCG Consumption in Rural India, 2008

Category	Item (%)
Food	*Vanaspati* (42.9), *Ghee/Desi ghee* (19.2), Instant noodles (21), Jam (0.7), Branded soup (0.1) and Tea (88.6)
Personal Care	Deodorant (0.6), Toothbrush (49.8), Toothpowder (38.8), Toilet soap (93.6), Shampoo (66.7), Hair oil (66.8), Edible oil as hair oil (26.1), and Hair dyes/Hair colour (1.4)
Durables	Wrist watch (20.6), TV (36), Refrigerators (5), Washing machine (1) and Air conditioners (1)
Health	*Chawanprash* (1.5), Digestive pills/tablets (16.7), Laxatives (1.6), Antacids (6.9), Cough syrups (2.9), and Health tonics (0.8)
Wash	Blues (45.2), Fabric bleaches (0.9), Washing cake/bar (26.1) and Washing powder/liquid (87.8)

Source: *The Marketing Whitebook* (New Delhi: *Businessworld*, 2009), pp. 308–19.

are less reliable from the earning point of view, being risk prone due to reliance on farming activities. Incomes are less but attractive in certain categories. Both consumption and savings are balanced to maintain a conservative lifestyle. Purchases of branded and contemporary products in food, personal care, wash and health categories have become common. All this means that rural India is catching upto urban India. Table 2.28 confirms this view. Rural India is as much a potential market as urban India by providing a sizeable market worth Rs 13,170 billion as against the Rs 13,650 billion share of urban India.

Ajay Gupta, founder and CEO of www.ruralnaukri.com presents an optimistic view.[5] "The purchasing power of rural India is more than half for fast moving consumer goods [USD 17 billion]," he says. "The durables and automobile sectors contribute USD 2.5 billion each, and agri-inputs (including tractors) about USD 1 billion. Some 42 million rural households [use] banking services against 27 million urban households. There are 41 million *Kisan* credit card holders [credit cards issued to farmers for purchase of agricultural goods] against some 22 million card users in urban markets. Be it automobile, telecom, insurance, retail, real estate or banking, the future drivers of growth are rural."

However, there seems to be a lot of action across product categories. Even in small villages, people who have seen the urban lifestyle on television seem to want similar goods and services.

Table 2.28 shows the state-wise rural market size. Uttar Pradesh, Andhra Pradesh, Maharashtra and West Bengal are the largest markets among the states in the country.

Table 2.28 Size of Market

Area	Amount (in billions)	%
Rural	13,170	49
Urban	13,650	51
All India	26,820	100

Source: Indicus Analytics, available at www.indicus.net.

Table 2.29 State-wise Rural Market Size

Sl No.	Market size (Rs in millions)	States
1	12 to 15 lakh	Uttar Pradesh, Andhra Pradesh, Maharashtra, and West Bengal
2	6 to 8 lakh	Gujarat, Karnataka, Rajasthan, Tamil Nadu, Kerala
3	5 to 6 lakh	Orissa, Bihar, Haryana, Madhya Pradesh
4	3 to 4 lakh	Punjab, Jharkhand, Assam and Chattisgarh
5	1to 2 lakh	Himachal Pradesh, Jammu & Kashmir and Uttaranchal
6	0.4 to 0.7 lakh	Tripura, Delhi, Goa, Meghalaya, Nagaland and Manipur
7	Below 0.2 lakh	Arunachal Pradesh, Sikkim, Pondicherry, Mizoram, Andaman and Nicobar Islands, Daman and Diu, Chandigarh, Dadra and Nagar Haveli and Lakshadweep

Source: Indicus Analytics, available at www.indicus.net.

Rural retailing

Rural retail is witnessing radical changes with marketers tapping every opportunity to reach rural consumers. Though traditional *kirana* shop, co-operative stores, *haats*, weekly market days, fairs, *melas*, vans and home-to-home campaigns continue to be attractive, there is a trend to utilize information technology (e-*choupal*), existing infrastructure (petrol bunks) and people (*Shakti* groups).

TECHNOLOGICAL ENVIRONMENT AND INNOVATIONS

In this section, let us examine the key infrastructural facilities such as power, IT, telecom, post office and innovative facilitators.

Power and energy

India shines when rural areas shine. As per the recent statistics shown in Table 2.30, about 83.1 per cent of villages in India have electricity.

Table 2.30 Villages that Received Electricity by 2009

Sl No.	States/Union Territories	Total inhabited villages as per 2001 census	Villages that received electricity as on 31.03.2009		Villages without electricity as on 30.03.2009
			Numbers	% age	
1	Andhra Pradesh	26,613	26,613	100.0	0
2	Arunachal Pradesh	3,863	2,195	56.8	1,668
3	Assam	25,124	19,741	78.6	5,383
4	Bihar	39,015	23,914	61.3	15,101
5	Delhi	158	158	100.0	0
6	Jharkhand	29,354	9,119	31.1	20,235
7	Goa	347	347	100.0	0
8	Gujarat	18,066	18,015	99.6	51
9	Haryana	6,764	6,764	100.0	0
10	Himachal Pradesh	17,495	17,183	98.2	312
11	Jammu and Kashmir	6,417	6,304	98.2	113
12	Karnataka	27,481	27,458	99.9	23
13	Kerala	1,364	1,364	100.0	0
14	Madhya Pradesh	52,117	50,226	96.4	1,891
15	Chattishgarh	19,744	18,877	95.6	867
16	Maharashtra	41,095	36,296	88.3	4,799
17	Manipur	2,315	1,984	85.7	331

(Continued)

Table 2.30 (Continued)

Sl No.	States/Union Territories	Total inhabited villages as per 2001 census	Villages that received electricity as on 31.03.2009		Villages without electricity as on 30.03.2009
			Numbers	(%)	
18	Meghalaya	5,782	3,428	59.3	2,354
19	Mizoram	707	570	80.6	137
20	Nagaland	1,278	823	64.4	455
21	Orissa	47,529	26,535	55.8	20,994
22	Punjab	12,278	12,278	100.0	0
23	Rajasthan	39,753	27,506	69.2	12,241
24	Sikkim	450	425	94.4	25
25	Tamil Nadu	15,400	15,400	100.0	0
26	Tripura	858	491	57.2	367
27	Uttar Pradesh	97,942	86,450	88.3	11,492
28	Uttaranchal	15,761	15,213	96.5	548
29	West Bengal	37,945	36,934	97.3	940
	Total (States)	593,015	492,611	83.1	100,327
	Union Territories				
1	Andaman and Nicobar Islands	501	336	67.1	165
2	Daman and Diu	23	23	100.0	0
3	Dadra and Nagar Haveli	70	70	100.0	0
4	Chandigarh	23	23	100.0	0
5	Lakshadweep	8	8	100.0	0
6	Pondicherry	92	92	100.0	0
	Total (UTs)	717	552	77.0	165
	Total (All India)	593,732	493,163	83.1	100,492

NA: Not Available.

Note: Andaman and Nicobar Islands stated that out of the 501 total inhabited villages, 81 villages are under encroached forest area and 72 villages were washed out during the tsunami of 2004.

Source: www.powermin.nic.in/, accessed April 2010.

The challenges for providing electricity to rural areas are in:

1. Expanding access of electricity to villages without electricity.
2. Increasing penetration rates in villages where electricity has been provided.
3. Strengthening technical and operational performance of the distribution network in villages.
4. Providing a sustainable model for rural electrification.

The Rural Electrification Corporation (REC), established as a public sector undertaking in July 1969 provided the impetus for the growth in rural electrification. It is the implementing agency of the Rajiv Gandhi Grameen Vidyutikaran Yojana (RGGVY). It builds on Kutir Jyoti Programme launched between 1988 and 1989 and the Rural Electricity Technology Mission initiated in 2002. The Kutir Jyoti Scheme, started in 1989, connected nearly 6 million households in 15 years, or approximately 400,000 households per year. With the new Electricity Act of 2003 and the Prime Minister's Rural Electricity Supply Technology (REST) Mission, the whole face of rural India can change in the coming years. A sustainable energy development programme envisages the following approaches.

- Production of electricity from biomass and agricultural residues. Box 2.3 describes how this source of energy can lead to rural development.
- Liquid fuel production from biomass that can be grown in arid regions and on wastelands and saline soils. Besides producing liquid fuels, this will also help in land reclamation.
- Creation of synergy between corporate sector, national government labs and institutions and NGOs so that energy technologies can be developed and disseminated in rural areas.

India is following the world trend of increasingly relying on liquid fuels. Last year, 75 per cent of all liquid fuels consumed were imported. By 2010, this figure might jump to 85 to 90 per cent. Presently, ethanol production in the country is mostly molasses based. However, with the expanded use of ethanol, both for transportation and as cooking and lighting fuel, there is a need for its production to have a broader biomass base. Thus, the use of alternative feedstock like sweet sorghum, sugar beet, cassava, etc. can help in its increased production. Besides, these crops require less water than sugarcane and

Box 2.3 Land-based Renewable Energy

Biomass power plants can create wealth by producing electrical energy and by providing employment to people. This is the finding of a study done by the Nimbkar Agricultural Research Institute (NARI) in Maharashtra. The institute found that agricultural residue in Phaltan *taluka* in Western Maharashtra could produce about 10–15 MW of power from biomass. This was sufficient to meet the electricity demands for one *taluka*.

With an investment of Rs 3 billion, each *taluka* can produce wealth of Rs 2–2.5 billion per year. About 30,000 people can be given full-time employment. India has 3,340 *talukas* and this business model promises to generate employment for about 100 million people and wealth of about Rs 700 billion per year.

The implications of this strategy for rural development are staggering and can create a quantum jump in the quality of life for the rural population.

Source: Anil K. Rajvanshi, "With Rural India Shining, India Will Shine!" *Project Monitor*, 22 October 2009.

some of them can be grown on saline soils. It is estimated that ethanol production itself can bring in about Rs 400 to 500 billion worth of wealth to rural India.

For the technology missions to succeed, it is necessary that very intensive R&D is carried out in agriculture, materials and renewable energy technologies. The Government of India should substantially increase the level of R&D funding in renewable energy and agricultural crops for liquid fuel production. It is necessary that a strong synergy is developed between the corporate sector, the Central Government R&D establishments and non-governmental organizations for the fruits of extensive R&D to reach the rural areas. Both the corporate sector and national labs can work together to research, produce and commercialize renewable energy technologies that can be disseminated through NGOs in rural areas. Finally, the development of rural India should be *taluka*-based, for it provides the critical mass for rural development.

Digital revolution

Bridging the digital divide through technology has been the focus of many initiatives worldwide. Some of these are:

- FarmNet (for agricultural workers in Uganda)
- Rural Multipurpose Community Telecentres (libraries and online centres in Benin, Mali, Mozambique, Tanzania and Uganda)
- MahilaWeb (for information sharing about women and gender in Nepal)
- Pakissan (for farmers in Pakistan)
- Grameen Phone (in Bangladesh)

Malaysia has come up with a number of "demonstration applications" such as Project Cybercare for providing Internet access and educational resources among 26 networked orphanages. A telecentre called e-Bario has also been set up for the Kelabit ethnic community in rural Sarawak.

The initiatives for taking the digital revolution to rural India have assumed urgency because there is a gradual realization that as the world switches to a highly interconnected information-intensive economy, communities left out of the network will suffer economic decline. The Government as such is supporting the development projects of administrative bodies and voluntary organizations. Box 2.4 describes two government projects. Some of the IT projects are listed here.

- *Tarahaat* (for e-marketing in rural areas)
- *AkashGanga* (for dairy cooperatives in Gujarat)
- Warna Wired Village Project (for sugarcane farmers in Maharashtra)
- HoneyBee Network (documenting grassroots innovations for knowledge on sustainable natural resource management)
- *Gyandoot* (community centre network in rural Madhya Pradesh)
- *Bhoomi* (for land records in Karnataka)
- "E-governance grid" (services to citizens in Kerala)
- Information Village Project (MS Swaminathan Research Foundation has set up a project in Pondicherry)

The National Informatics Centre is proposing a "Rural Studio" initiative for developing reusable software components and services for the rural development sector. The Indian Volunteers.org network provides volunteers interested in such initiatives.

There are several projects centred on education. These include Head Start (Madhya Pradesh), AP Schools (Andhra Pradesh), *Vidya Vahini* (an initiative of the Indian Government) and community learning centres (Azim Premji Foundation). Box 2.5 describes these initiatives.

Box 2.4 Citizen Service Projects

Samadhan Kendra

Village information centres (*Samadhan Kendras*) were introduced by the Ministry of Information Technology. A pilot project was set up in Ramanathapuram district of Tamil Nadu by a Pondicherry-based NGO—the Centre for Ecology and Rural Development (CERD). Two *Samadhan Kendras* to cater to around 60 villages were set up with computer facilities in Bogallur and Mudukalattur blocks of the district.

Block-level activists are trained in software for the successful functioning of the project. A True Type Font (TTF) called *Bamini* is being used for data entry. Data of villages were collected by a network of people and forms were designed involving local people.

A Decision Support System (DSS) has been put in place for facilitating analysis and decision making. Internet facility also has been provided.

E-seva

The credit for starting the first-of-its-kind integrated single-window citizen services system in the country goes to the Government of Andhra Pradesh. It provides a wide spectrum of citizen-friendly services of various departments in one place.

It is a one-stop-shop for G2C and B2C services without any jurisdiction limits. Services offered include the following:

- Utility bills/Tax payments (e-electricity bills, water and sewerage bills, telephone bills and property taxes), transfer of ownership of non-transport vehicles and reservation of APSRTC tickets.
- Certificates (registration of birth, issue of birth certificates, registration of death, issue of death certificates and encumbrance certificates.
- Permits/Licenses (trade licenses (MCH), issue of learners licenses, issue/renewal of driving licenses (non-transport vehicles only) and registration certificates of new vehicles (non-transport vehicles only).

Source: www.utlindia.com/utl/templates/services/egovernance_eseva.jsp, accessed February 2010.

Postal services

India has the largest postal network in the world with 155,618 post offices at the end of 2003 including 139,081 post offices in rural areas. At the time of independence, India had 23,344 post offices that were largely confined to urban areas and selected villages. During the last 50 years it has grown by almost seven times. As of 2008, post offices outnumbered bank branches in rural areas by a factor of four. In 2008, the scheduled commercial bank network in the rural sector was 30,977 branches strong. The number of rural post offices stood at 130,847.[6]

In the case of India Post, the retailing is limited to the sale of postal products like post cards, letter cards and small saving services like recurring deposits, savings bank deposits, monthly income schemes, etc. Moreover, the platform was predominantly manual. Because of the changing business scenario, the postal business, especially in the rural areas, has been shrinking over a period of time.

Box 2.5 Educational Projects

"We believe that technologically-enabled, modern classrooms have enormous potential to contribute to quality in all government schools, especially in rural India," said Azim Premji, chairman of Wipro and founder of the Azim Premji Foundation

Driven by the zeal to improve learning opportunities, the Azim Premji Foundation collaborated with Qualcomm and took up a project to provide wireless broadband access to rural and Government-run schools in India. There are 1.3 million Government-run schools in India.

To begin with, about 40 Government-run schools in underserved communities across four states—Gujarat, Karnataka, Orissa and Rajasthan—were selected.

Source: "Indian Rural Schools Get Broadband Connected," *EE Times*, 11 September 2009, available at www.eetindia.co.in/ART_8800583890_1800005_NT_804a9ddd.HTM.

Increasing penetration of mobile phones have adversely affected the personal mail service while relatively less attractive interest rates have affected the volumes of small scale saving schemes, NSCs, etc. In these circumstances, it is a compulsion for India Post to seek new avenues of business for the rural postal network. Rural retailing of products through vast networks is one of the strategies that will not only improve the viability of this network but also create a situation of profitability for India Post that will match the profitability of the Indian Railways today.

Project arrow

The Department of Posts in India has launched "Project Arrow," whereby it has adopted a new logo and new infrastructure to widen and innovate operations. Under the project, the Department of Posts has identified 50 post offices in Andhra Pradesh, Jharkhand, Maharashtra, the North East, Madhya Pradesh, Orissa, Rajasthan, Tamil Nadu, Uttar Pradesh and Uttarakhand covering 10 Postal Circles. By the end of the current year, 500 such post offices will be operational in the country.

The post offices are being given a thorough make-over both in terms of physical look and feel and upgrading service delivery through IT enabled procedures. Some new initiatives include e-payment, instant money transfers, *daknet*, online banking and a new look for rural post offices.[7] The post offices will also form an indispensable part of all social and civic initiatives such as the National Rural Employment Guarantee Act (NREGA) and the National Old Age Pension Scheme. Project Arrow is being seen as a significant step towards the realization of India Post's motto—*Dak Seva–Jan Seva.*

Telephones and rural connectivity

Promotion of rural telephone and accessibility of telephones in remote areas has been an important thrust area of the Government. Out of the more than 2.271 million Public Call Offices (PCOs) functioning in the country, 0.2 million are in rural areas. Box 2.5 discusses a project undertaken by the Azim Premji foundation to provide broadband access to government schools. The Mobile *Grameen Sanchar Sewak* Scheme, which provides telephones at the doorstep of villagers in about 12,000 villages, has also been put in place. More than 0.564 million villages have been covered by Village Public Telephones (VPTs) to provide universal access to telecom facilities in the rural areas. Under *Bharat Nirman*, a target of providing Village Public Telephones (VPTs) in 66,822 uncovered villages was visualized. Out of this, 52,342 VPTs have been provided till December 2007 and the remaining VPTs were scheduled to be provided by June 2008 in a phased manner. A scheme of Rural Community Phones

(RCPs) has been launched under the Universal Service Obligation Fund (USOF) to create infrastructure in rural and remote areas. Box 2.6 shows how BSNL is partnering with HCL to promote rural connectivity.

It is envisaged to provide support for setting up and managing 7,871 infrastructure sites spread over 500 districts in 27 states of the country for the provision of wireless phone services. The infrastructure so created will be used in the provision of wireless phone services in the specified rural and remote areas where there is no existing fixed wireless or mobile coverage. Wireless phone services through these shared towers were targeted to be made operational in a phased manner by May 2008.

By implementing the above efforts, the Eleventh Plan target of achieving rural tele-density of 25% by means of 200 million rural connections, seems feasible. Rural penetration has gone up from a mere 0.29% in 1995–96 to 9.43% in 2007–08 as shown in Table 2.31.

Mobiles have become a necessity in rural India today. According to the latest report of the Telecom Regulatory Authority of India (TRAI), 48 million rural consumers took a new mobile connection in the first six months of the calendar year 2009 when compared with just 32 million in the cities. There are now a total of 136 million mobile users residing in villages against the 329 million mobile consumers in the urban areas. It is predicted that the next 500 million mobile subscribers will come mostly from the hinterland.[8]

Table 2.31 Tele-density (Number of Telephones per 100 Population) (in %)

Year	Urban	Rural	Total
1995 to 1996	3.95	0.29	1.28
2000 to 2001	10.37	0.93	3.58
2005 to 2006	38.28	2.34	12.74
2006 to 2007	48.1	5.89	18.31
2007 to 2008	72.25	9.43	26.22

Source: Department of Telecommunications, Annual Report, 2007–08.

Box 2.6 BSNL and HCL Partner for Broadband Connectivity in Rural India

National Broadband Penetration Program (NBPP) is an initiative of the Government of India and USOF that aims at accelerating IT proliferation in rural India for inclusive growth. Korea, Singapore and Sweden attribute their inclusive economic growth to this model. In India, BSNL and HCL Infosystems have partnered together to power a million personal computers and broadband connections in India through its existing 27,789 rural and remote telephone exchanges of BSNL.

USOF will be providing a subsidy of Rs 4,500 per broadband connection. The programme is strengthened by the support provided by the "HCL Touch" network. The network has 14 remote support centres, 505 service offices, 390 warehouses and 150 repair centres. It reaches out to over 4,000 towns and delivers services in 11 regional languages.

Source: "BSNL, HCL to Bring Broadband Connectivity to Rural India," 22 September 2009, available at www.ectindia.co.in.

With the rural mobile market growing, there is a huge market for mobile Value Added Services (VAS). A few of the service providers have already taken the initiative for rural VAS.

- Thomson Reuters has been updating over 0.1 million farmers in the country with the latest market trends, weather forecast, and crop information via its SMS-based service.
- Tata Indicom launched a project in a district in Gujarat that allows farmers to operate their irrigation pumps from remote locations without them having to travel to the farm.
- Nokia on the other hand, launched their Life Tools Services, to offer agricultural information, educational information and more to people in both rural and urban areas.

The Government has decided to extend broadband connectivity in all villages in India by 2012. So far, the usage of VAS in rural areas is just 1% despite the huge network roll-out in rural areas and the intense low-tariff war among operators. Significant growth in the number of users in a rural market could facilitate players to plan services that can help both parties. Bharti Airtel, Reliance Communications, Vodafone and Idea Cellular have plans to increase their average revenue per user.[9]

Promotion of appropriate technologies

There is a need for creating appropriate technologies for rural people. Measures are being initiated by the Government and voluntary organizations to encourage creative thinking for problem solving and generating innovations.

Council for Advancement of People's Action and Rural Technology (CAPART)

The Council for Advancement of People's Action and Rural Technology (CAPART) was set up in September 1986 by the amalgamation of the People's Action for Development India (PADI) and Council for Advancement of Rural Technology (CART). It is a society registered under the Societies' Registration Act, 1980 and operates as an autonomous body under the aegis of the Ministry of Rural Development, Government of India, with headquarters in New Delhi. Today, this agency is a major promoter of rural development in India, assisting over 12,000 voluntary organizations across the country in implementing a wide range of sustainable development initiatives.

Rural Innovation Fund

In association with the Swiss Agency for Development and Cooperation (SDC), NABARD has constituted the "NABARD SDC Rural Innovation Fund (RIF)" to support innovative projects in farm, non-farm and micro-finance sectors leading to the creation of livelihood opportunities for the poor. Government and non-government institutions, corporate bodies, financial institutions and individuals can avail funding support for activities involved in development of new products, processes, prototypes, technology, etc. that have the poor as their focus.

Voluntary organizations

In the rural hinterland many voluntary organizations are engaged in native innovations to find appropriate solutions to nagging problems. For example, the Appropriate Rural Technology Institute (ARTI) in Pune has developed a biogas plant that uses food waste rather than manure as feedstock and supplies biogas for cooking. The plant is sufficiently compact even to be used by urban households, and over 700 are currently in use.

POLITICAL ENVIRONMENT AND DEVELOPMENT INITIATIVES

Since the dawn of independence, concerted efforts have been made to improve the living standard of the rural masses. So, rural development as an integrated concept of growth and poverty elimination has been of paramount concern in all the consequent five year plans. The Government of India has set up the following departments to undertake rural development activities:

- Department of Drinking Water Supply (DDWS)
- Department of Land Resources (DLR)
- Department of Rural Development (DRD)

In addition to the departments, the following autonomous bodies have also been established.

- Council for Advancement of People's Action and Rural Technology (CAPART)
- National Institute of Rural Development (NIRD)

Rural Development (RD) programmes comprise the following:

- Provision of basic infrastructure facilities in rural areas, for example, schools, health facilities, roads, drinking water, electrification, etc.
- Improving agricultural productivity in the rural areas.
- Provision of social services like health and education for socio-economic development.
- Implementing schemes for the promotion of rural industry to increase agriculture productivity, providing rural employment, etc.
- Assistance to individual families and their Self-Help Groups (SHG) who are living below the poverty line by providing productive resources through credit and subsidy.

The increase in the allocation of resources for the implementation of poverty alleviation programmes indicates the renewed emphasis on rural development. The allocation of funds for rural development programmes in the Tenth Five Year Plan has been enhanced to Rs 767.74 billion as against the Rs 428.74 billion allocated in the Ninth Plan.

Addressing the challenge of unemployment in the rural areas of the country is central to the development of the rural sector for ameliorating the economic condition of the people. Wage employment is provided in rural areas under the National Rural Employment Guarantee Act (NREGA).

Role of DDWS

Providing water supply, sanitation and hygiene education in schools and *anganwadis* are the important concerns of the Government of India. The Department of Drinking Water Supply (DDWS) is implementing programmes involving many cross-cutting issues such as water supply and sanitation, heath and family welfare, *Panchayati Raj* and rural development, public health engineering, women and child development, education, tribal welfare, social justice, etc.

School and *anganwadi* sanitation programmes have been initiated and DDWS has taken several initiatives to ensure a strong coordination. It has also initiated Secretary and Joint Secretary level meetings with the concerned departments to ensure priority of this programme and its overall implementation. A Central Coordination Panel has been constituted under the Chairmanship of the Secretary, DDWS.

To ensure inter-sectoral coordination at all the levels—from the centre, state, district, block and village to school level—the department has taken several initiatives to ensure a strong coordination between the concerned departments.

- Coordination with the Ministry of Water Resources
- Coordination with the Department of Elementary Education and Literacy, MoHRD, Government of India
- Coordination with the Department of Women and Child Development, MoHFW, Government of India
- Coordination with the Ministry of Tribal Affairs

Role of the Department of Land Resources

Starting as the National Wasteland Development Board in 1985 in the Ministry of Environment and Forests, a separate Department of Wasteland Development was created in the Ministry of Rural Development in 1992 and renamed the Department of Land Resources in 1999. A separate Secretary was posted in the Department for the first time in January 2008. The major programmes of the department are:

- Integrated Watershed Management Programme (IWMP)
- National Land Records Modernization Programme (NLRMP)
- Bio-diesel programme
- Agrarian reforms
- Technology Development Extension and Training

Role of the Department of Rural Development

The department is implementing a number of programmes in rural areas through the state governments for poverty reduction, employment generation, rural infrastructure habitat development, provision of basic minimum services, etc. The important programmes presently being implemented by the department are:

1. *Pradhan Mantri Gram Sadak Yojana* (PMGSY)
2. *Swarnjayanti Gram Swarozgar Yojana* (SGSY)
3. *Sampoorna Gramin Rozgar Yojana* (SGRY)
4. Rural Housing (*Indira Awaas Yojana*)
5. Training Schemes
6. Promotion of Voluntary Schemes and Social Action Programme, organization of beneficiaries, advancement and dissemination of rural technology through CAPART.

Pradhan Mantri Gram Sadak Yojana (PMGSY)

The Government of India launched the *Pradhan Mantri Gram Sadak Yojana* (PMGSY) on 25 December 2000 to provide all-weather access to unconnected habitations. The programme sought to provide connectivity to all unconnected habitations in rural areas with a population of more than 500 persons through good all-weather roads by the end of the Tenth Plan Period. In respect to the hill states (the North-East, Sikkim, Himachal Pradesh, Jammu and Kashmir and Uttaranchal) and the desert areas, the objective was to connect habitations with a population of 250 persons and above.

Swarnjayanti Gram Swarozgar Yojana (SGSY)

This is the only self-employment programme for the rural poor. The *Yojana*, which came in to effect from April 1999, was conceived as a holistic programme covering all aspects of self-employment like organization of the rural poor into self help groups (SHGs) and their capacity building, training, planning of activity clusters, infrastructure development, financial assistance through bank credit and subsidy and marketing support, etc.

Sampoorna Gramin Rozgar Yojana (SGRY) scheme

The scheme was launched with effect from 25 September 2001 after merging the Employment Assurance Scheme and the *Jawahar Gram Smridhi Yojana*. This is being implemented as a centrally sponsored scheme on cost sharing basis between the Centre and the States. The cash component of the programme is shared between the Centre and State in the ratio of 75:25. Food grains are provided free of cost to the States/Union Territories. The cost of transportation of the food grains is borne by the concerned States/UTs. The special component of SGRY aims at augmenting food security through additional wage employment in calamity affected rural areas after due notification by the State governments and its acceptance by the Ministry of Agriculture.

Indira Awaas Yojana (IAY)

Construction of houses was included as one of the major activities under the National Rural Employment Programme that began in 1980. Rural Landless Employment Guarantee Programme (RLEGP) began in 1983. *Indira Awaas Yojana* (IAY) was launched during 1985–1986 as a sub-scheme of RLEGP and thereafter it continued as a sub-scheme of *Jawahar Rozgar Yojana* (JRY). From 1 January 1986, IAY was delinked from JRY and made an independent scheme. In 1998, the Government of India announced a National Housing and Habitat policy that aims at providing "housing for all" and facilitating the construction of 2 million additional housing units (1.3 million in rural areas and 0.7 million in urban areas), with emphasis on standing benefits to the poor and the deprived. The intention is to end shelterlessness and ensure the conversion of all unserviceable *kuchcha* houses into *pucca* houses by the end of the Eleventh Plan Period. The Action Plan is being implemented through various programmes such as *Indira Awaas Yojana* (IAY), Credit cum Subsidy Scheme for Rural Housing, Innovative Scheme for Rural Housing and Habitat Development, through rural building centres, equity contribution by the Ministry of Rural Development to HUDCO and the National Mission for Rural Housing and Habitat.

Administration and monitoring

The overall monitoring of the programmes at the national level is carried out by the monitoring division of the ministry. The programme divisions monitor the respective programmes implemented by them. The programmes of the ministry are implemented by the state implementing agencies. At the State level, the Secretary/Commissioner dealing with the programme monitors its implementation. The actual execution of the programmes take place at the district/village level through DRDAs, Panchayati Raj Institutions (PRIs) and other implementing agencies, which monitor the execution of the programmes at the grassroots level.

The *Panchayati Raj* Institutions are considered to be an important tool for the implementation of the programmes of the ministry. They make sure that the programme implementation reflects the needs and aspirations of the local people. As a step toward decentralization of the planning process and implementation of the programmes, strengthening of the *Panchayati Raj* Institutions has been envisaged through the Constitutional (73rd) Amendment Act, 1992. Constitutional Status has been provided to the *Panchayati Raj* Institutions (PRIs) with the passing of this Act. Therefore, in most of the rural development programmes, a crucial role has been assigned to PRIs for programme implementation. Sustained efforts are being made to strengthen local governance, institutionalize people's participation and empower women through PRIs.

Autonomous bodies

There are three autonomous bodies under the department of rural development—the Council of Advancement of People's Action and Rural Technology (CAPART), the National Institute of Rural Development (NIRD) and the National Rural Road Development Agency (NRRDA).

- The Council of Advancement of People's Action and Rural Technology (CAPART) has been set up to encourage participation of voluntary agencies in rural development and also to provide financial assistance to them in their rural development projects. CAPART directly deals with voluntary agencies and their projects.
- The National Institute of Rural Development (NIRD) is engaged in planning and coordination of national level training. For state and district level training, assistance is given to State Institutes of Rural Development (SIRD) and Extension Training Centres (ETC), respectively.

- The National Rural Road Development Agency (NRRDA) registered under the Societies Registration Act, 1860 extends support to the *Pradhan Mantri Gram Sadak Yojana* (PMGSY). It provides advice on technical specifications, project appraisal, appointment of part-time quality control monitors, management of monitoring systems. It also submits periodic reports to the ministry.

IMPLICATIONS ON RURAL MARKETERS

The growing rural economy presents a wide range of opportunities to consumer and industrial marketers. Table 2.32 presents the opportunities and limitations that these marketers face.

In this kind of scenario, what kind of marketing opportunities are there and for whom? The TV industry can look to sell colour TVs; financial institutions can think of new savings scheme; agri-input sellers can try innovations in farming practices and input products. The following specific examples will drive the point home.

- Low-incomes, small savings and low literacy levels in villages prompted the State Bank of India (SBI) to start a zero-balance bank account programme for villagers. Called the SBI Tiny account, there are no physical branches or officials for this, just a paid volunteer who is equipped with a small box and a cell phone. The box enables biometric measurements (fingerprints) at the time of opening the account to confirm the account holder's identity. The cell phone enables communication with the zonal office to check on the available balance. Payments under programmes such as the NREGA and pensions are made directly to these accounts. The advantage for the villagers in this system is

Table 2.32 Marketing Environment and Challenges

Sl No.	Decision area	Opportunities	Limitations
1	Social environment	Rural population is large. Household sizes are larger. Sex ratio is comparable to all India standards.	Per capita income is lower. Literacy levels are lower. Awareness of products and services will be lower.
2	Economic environment	Self-employment and labour constitutes the major avenues of earning money. About 40 per cent of the people are landless. Lifestyle changes are progressive. Rural credit flow has improved. New retailing opportunities are in the offing.	Income earners are many but incomes are low. A large proportion of the population is in the bracket that earns below Rs 75,000 per annum. In the credit scenario, role of non-institutional agencies is increasing.
3	Technological environment	Power, postal and telecommunication services showed significant improvement. Innovative measures are in the offing.	Media reach is not extensive.
4	Political environment	The Government promotes many schemes. Self-help groups and voluntary organizations are also helping actively.	Low levels of education and lack of motivation.

that they can withdraw money from their accounts at any time of the day or night. SBI hopes to cover 100,000 villages under this scheme by 2012.

- "GoldPlus" is an interesting example of a brand addressing the non-metro jewellery culture by giving an ethnic touch to the designs and retailing of ornaments. In rural areas, gold jewellery is not used for ornamentation alone; it is also regarded as a safety net for emergency situations. Keeping this in mind, the Tatas have introduced their mass-market jewellery brand—GoldPlus. The Tatas train unemployed youth and send them to the villages as brand ambassadors.

Summary

Rural marketing requires an understanding of the environment in which companies have to operate to deliver products and services. Various environmental factors impact marketing decisions related to demand estimation, segmentation and targeting, and also the design of the marketing mix of the 4 P's.

When we examine the social environment, we find 732 million people living in 144.5 million households, most with 5–6 members, with 1.43 earning members per household, in rural areas. More than half the population (493 million) is in low-income states with per capita income below Rs 10,000 per annum. Males form 51.8 per cent of the total population and females, 48.2 per cent. However, in south India, males and females are almost equal in number. In fact, the female population is larger in Kerala. The percentage of illiterate heads of households is about 37.2. Among the 62.8 per cent educated population, only 7 per cent are graduates. Media-reach analysis indicates that television has a low reach at 38 per cent. The radio has a reach of 18 per cent, print of 15 per cent and cinema of 5 per cent. There are 3.3 million active Internet users.

Self-employed in agriculture (41.3 per cent) and labour (34.6 per cent) constitute the majority of earners in rural areas. About 70 per cent of workers are farmers, fishermen, hunters, loggers and related workers. About 40 per cent of households are landless with family size of 4.68 persons and per capita income of Rs 8,000. At the bottom of the pyramid, in the income bracket of less than Rs 75,000 per annum, we find 428 million people. Educated rural people have larger incomes but their urban counterparts are much better off indicating that opportunities play a bigger role in this regard. Rural people spend 75 per cent of their income and save the remaining. Savings are larger among those whose annual earrings are in the range of 75 k to 150 k. Rural expenditure on food is 55.4 per cent and the remaining is distributed among various items like housing, transport, etc. In non-routine expenditure, the lion's share goes to ceremonies. Rural credit is institutionalized but non-institutional sources showed an increase in popularity after the economic reforms. In providing credit, co-operatives played a big role. NABARD has a significant role in financing rural projects. Lifestyle analysis shows that a large segment of rural people exhibit the conservative, price conscious, economy-oriented lifestyle of mid- and low-income segments of urban people. Rural sales show potential to the tune of Rs 13,170 billion. Rural retail is now characterized by e-models and PPP approaches.

When technological progress is examined, we find about 81 per cent of villages have electricity. Rural Electrification Corporation (REC), Rajiv Gandhi *Grameen Vidyutikaran Yojana* (RGGVY), *Kutir Jyoti Programme*, Electricity Act 2003 and Rural Electricity Supply Technology (REST) Mission have changed the power scenario in the rural hinterlands. The use of land-based renewable energy and liquid fuels are gaining popularity. The ICT revolution is benefiting rural people as the Government is keen on citizen-services projects. NGOs are also supporting the projects by their involvement and enterprise. There are about 139,081 post offices in rural areas. Project Arrow was launched to modernize post offices and make them capable of handling multiple products and services. The Eleventh Plan target of achieving rural teledensity of 25% by means of 200 million rural connections seems feasible. Rural penetration has gone up from a mere 0.29 in per cent in1995–1996 to 9.43 per cent in 2007–2008. With the rural mobile market growing, there is a huge market for mobile Value Added Services (VAS). A few service providers have already taken the initiative for rural VAS. Rural people are encouraged by government and voluntary organizations to come up with solutions that are cost effective in resolving problems. The Government of India has taken various steps for rural development. Various administrative bodies such as the Department of Drinking Water Supply (DDWS), Department of Land Resources (DLR) and Department of Rural Development (DRD) have been created. NABARD has been set up to ensure credit flows and give support to rural development projects. Multiple schemes are devised and implemented to bring about over all development in rural areas.

Discussion Questions

1. "Rural India is a less developed countryside where the infrastructure is primitive, houses are of mud or brick but rarely painted well, the primary source of livelihood is agriculture, employment opportunities in the organized sector are negligible, eating choices are restricted to home-cooked, simple food, schools are far away, health facilities are rudimentary and—importantly—the youth, while energetic and ambitious, are to be seen playing cards the whole day," says Ajit Gupta of www.ruralnaukri.com. Do you agree?
2. "While mobile phones are widely seen merely as a communications medium, they should really be seen as a new and essential form of infrastructure that will transform a host of other service sectors in rural economies around the world," Discuss.

Short Answer Questions

1. Discuss the impact of environmental variables on the selection of markets by a firm.
2. Briefly describe the changes in the economic scenario of rural areas.
3. Examine the improvements in rural lifestyle and media habits.
4. Elucidate the role of technology in the development of rural areas.
5. Explain how the urban–rural divide is challenged by ICT projects in rural areas.
6. What do you understand by appropriate technology for rural people? Give examples.
7. What is micro-financing? How does it help improve the lot of women in rural areas?
8. Generate a list of rural development schemes and identify their key achievements.

Essay Questions

1. Explain the relationship between environment and marketing decision-making. Identify the major trends in environmental factors.
2. Explain the social factors and examine their implications on promotion decisions of (a) TV companies (b) Postal services and (c) Mobile phones.
3. Discuss the changes in the economic scenario of rural areas. Is the market attractive for food and non-food items?
4. Explain the developments in communication facilities in rural areas with focus on (i) Telephones (ii) Post offices and (iii) Internet services.
5. Explain the rural development initiatives of the Government in brief.
6. Discuss the role of NABARD in promoting rural development with special reference to minorities and women.

Internet Exercise

Surf the Internet and collect data relating to a company of your choice and examine the impact of environmental variables on its rural marketing decisions.

Mini Project

Prepare a marketing environment audit questionnaire to identify environmental forces impinging on firms selling (i) consumer durables (ii) convenience products and (iii) industrial products. Prepare a report and present it in the classroom.

End Notes

1. Eric Bellman, "Rural India Snaps Up Mobile Phones," *Wall Street Journal*, February 2009, available at http://online.wsj.com/article/SB123413407376461353.html.
2. Atul Phadnis, "The Two-in-one Nation!" *The Hindu Business Line*, December 2004, available at www.blonnet.com/catalyst/2004/12/30/stories/2004123000050300.htm.
3. "Urban and Rural Reach of Advertising Media," Lintas Media Guide, Mumbai, January 2008.
4. K. J. S. Satyasai and K. U. Viswanathan, "Persistence of Private Moneylenders in Rural Credit Markets," *National Bank News Review* (April 2008): 15–22.
5. Rupali Mukherjee, "Rural India Promises Growth for Retail," *The Times of India*, April 2009, available at http://timesofindia.indiatimes.com/Business/India-Business/Rural-India-promises-growth-for-retail/articleshow/4371528.cms.
6. P. Raghavan, "Don't Blame Post Offices," *The Financial Express*, 23 October 2009, available at www.financialexpress.com/news/column-dont-blame-post-offices/477877/2.
7. Mehak Chawla, "Pampering the Post," *Data Quest*, 25 April 2009, available at http://dqindia.ciol.com/content/egovernance/2009/109042501.asp.
8. Thomas K. Thomas, "More Mobiles Ring in the Rural Areas than Urban,"October 2009, *The Hindu Business Line*, available at www.blonnet.com/2009/10/24/stories/2009102451950100.htm.
9. Pranav Agarwal, "Over 100 Million Rural Mobile Subscribers in India—Opportunity for VAS," 15 July 2009, available at www. watblog.com.

Case 2.1 *Dakseva, Janaseva*

Winds of change are sweeping the countryside. India Post is an organization that symbolizes the modernization trend in the field of services. It has been given a new name and a new look. In line with the new retailing developments, it is emerging as the one-stop solution for consumer needs. You could soon walk into a rural post office and initiate the process for buying a variety of products and services ranging from a car to ayurvedic products with as much ease as availing information services and insurance policies.

Project Arrow

Project Arrow was launched to modernize post offices. According to the Ministry of Communications and Information Technology, the major features of the project include identity branding (a new logo and a new slogan), designing of exteriors and interiors of offices, upgradation of computer hardware and software, improvements in the delivery of services and spread in connectivity. These new age post offices would serve as a window to the world for the common man—"*Aam Aadmi*"—by focusing on their diverse needs.

New Logo

The new logo, unveiled in September 2008, aims to give the postal service a corporate look and reflects its new approach towards business—an approach that shall aim to leverage technology to connect the nation better. The new logo depicts a bird in flight, done in bold colors like red and yellow. Launching the new logo, the Minister of Communications and Information Technology, A. Raja said, "The bold strokes convey free flight. The choice of colours is red and yellow. Red has been chosen for its traditional association with the postal service. It embodies passion, power and commitment."

New Organization

The (postal) department is committed to transform itself into a viable and sustainable social organization. As part of the process, it is also modernizing its offices. About Rs 2.5 billion has been allotted to modernize 5,000 post offices in the country in the third phase of the process.

The New Age Post Man

The role of the post man has also changed quite a lot. Traditionally, he was considered a part of the rural family. He cannot assume such familiarity now. What he now delivers is very different from what he usually delivered in the past. Communication today is oral, via e-mail or SMS or through telephones. Written communication instruments such as the post card and cover are outdated. The postman delivers official statements and bills of banks, insurance papers and telephone bills or printed promotion materials of products.

Spread

The Department of Post (DoP) has 0.15 million points of presence and about 25,000 direct departmental offices across the country. "While post offices are present in the most backward areas of the country, many other organizations, including banks, have coverage only in urban and semi-urban localities," said M. S. Ramanujan, postmaster general, Chennai city region. Thus, the post office continues to be an organization that has rural presence and the post master is a valued opinion leader.

Tie-ups in Progress

The DoP announced its tie up with telecom player Sistema Shyam Tele Services (the MTS brand) to offer recharge facilities at 50 post offices in Chennai. The partnership will expand to cover the whole of Tamil Nadu. The postal department in Chennai is in talks with companies, including Maruti Suzuki, to help them sell cars in rural areas. Maruti Suzuki has evinced interest to expand its reach to rural areas. Post offices will act as points of sale to sell and collect application forms that will then be submitted to the nearest Maruti dealer. Maruti is planning to sell its low-end as well as mid-size cars through the plan. With this objective of utilizing the rural network, Uttarakhand Post has entered into an agreement with Divya Pharmacy at Haridwar for retailing its health products through a network of 2,716 post offices (about 2,500 of them are rural). The agreement came into effect in July 2007 and by now has done business of Rs 2,259,039 in 2007–2008 and Rs 13,523,293 in 2008–2009, earning a net commission of Rs 462,388 in 2007–2008 and Rs 2,713,158 in 2008–2009 (till December 2008) for the circle.

The department has initiated steps to participate in the Unique ID Project. The DoP will act as a registrar of information dealing with citizens' details. It will be an enrolling body along with other departments, including petroleum, income tax and civil supplies. It will be the only organization in the country to collect and maintain an address database as part of the project.

For discussion

1. Critically evaluate the plans of the Department of Posts (DoP) in modernizing and diversification. Is the DoP trying to gulp down more than what it can chew? Has it subverted its service goal to commercial goals?
2. Suggest suitable business ideas for rural post offices.

Source: Shyamala Seetharamanan, "Rural Post Offices May Sell Cars, Join MTS," 15 October 2009, available at www.mydigitalfc.com; "New Look for Rural Post Offices in India," 18 August 2009, available at www.igovernment.in.

Case 2.2 Rural Outsourcing—The Case of ROPE

ROPE is a social enterprise that provides global customers with access to rural artisans who manufacture diverse products. Mr Sreejith, CEO of Rural Opportunities Production Enterprises (ROPE), says the mission of the organization is "to integrate domestic and international markets with the informal sectors of rural India and generate value for the skills and resources available in these sectors through production outsourcing." He further explains, "We are a part of the TeNeT group of Indian Institute of Technology, Madras, which is the premier engineering institution of India. We focus on combining rural artisans and craftsmen with modern Information and Communication Technology (ICT) applications, to manufacture quality products. It was set up in 2007 with a capital of Rs 7.7 million. Seed funding of Rs 0.5 million was obtained from the Rural Tech and Business Incubator, the Indian Institute of Technology, Madras.

Customers

ROPE has so far supplied its products to more than 30 big and small clients both within and outside India. Some of the prominent names in its client list include IKEA, Chennai, Industree Crafts, Bangalore, CwithCo, New York, TiE, etc.

Production Centres

ROPE Production Centres (RPCs) in villages use local skills and materials to manufacture high quality items ordered by global customers. Currently, there are seven production centre managers who oversee the work of the artisans. They are chosen from areas based on the belief that the talent available in villages can play a critical role in manufacturing quality products. These local managers have access to local skills and readily available raw materials. Also their indigenous knowledge, organizing skills and acceptance within the local communities help in establishing and running the production centre efficiently and effectively.

Products

Currently, RPCs offer production of hand woven and knitted products that include items like natural fibre-based home furnishings such as mats, carpets and window shades, bags, folders, paper bags, prayer mats, wallets and pouches. In the future, ROPE plans to expand into cotton and silk fabrics and apparels.

Competition

Its key competitors are Industree Crafts, and companies that are into corporate gifts and furnishings. Competition in the current products category is from organized factory model manufacturers like big mills, NGO-model producers who are working with artisans from different parts of the country and traditional middlemen or commission agents who buy products from rural producers and sell them to exporters.

The CEO observes, "Factory-model producers cannot compete with us in price as their fixed-cost investments are high in real estate and building and they also cannot offer customization to clients as we do, even at shorter lead times. NGO model producers again, cannot achieve our efficiency in delivery and cost. The middlemen or agents on the other hand cannot actively work with clients to assure quality standards, standard and ethical production processes. Also their scale is limited."

Social Impact

"The money that you spend on buying quality ROPE products is also an investment in a better future for thousands of poor people in rural areas," says the CEO. Currently, ROPE provides work to 200 people (80% of them women). ROPE plans to employ 1,500 people within two years and plans to increase that number to 4,000 people within five years. ROPE artisans have regular work and their average annualized income increased from USD 270 to USD 720. Increased incomes lead to increased savings and investments for the future such as housing, health and education. Apart from financial security, belonging to a larger network of producers and also the sense of catering to global customers increases pride in their work.

Promising Future

Sreejith is aiming for Rs 0.1 billion in revenue by 2012, and 10 times as much by 2020. That customers are appreciative of ROPE's products is evident from the comments of Shilpa Sharma, Head, Product Development and Buying, FabIndia Overseas.

"Given the unique array of natural fibre products that they offer, I feel there is significant potential to develop a whole range of lifestyle accessories with ROPE," she says.

FabIndia placed its first order for floor coverings, table mats and runners with ROPE. The product range and pricing of ROPE reflect its leaning towards fair trade and ethical production. In particular, it is well placed to supply to companies that are committed to the growing global demand for environment-friendly products with eco-compliant packaging. ROPE is ready for IKEA's I-Way audit, which calls for worker-friendly human resource practices, and has applied for the well-recognized Craftmark certification for artisanal products.

Knotty Problems

However, despite these calculations, maintaining supply lines has proved difficult. ROPE's first major order was to provide 100,000 bags priced at the rate of Rs 16 to Tuticorin-based Ramesh Flowers, an IKEA supplier and India's leading player in the natural botanicals sector. "The IKEA sub-supplier order is our first major order," says S. Giridharan, Senior Manager, Production, ROPE. "We needed to scale up by about 10 times in terms of raw material sourcing alone." If the order is successfully executed, Ramesh Flowers has evinced interest in procuring 500,000 bags annually. Scaling up is essential, but order-driven. Earlier, ROPE's lower volumes enabled it to outsource work and procure raw material from rural entrepreneurs. Even as he races to expand overnight, Sreejith nurtures other plans to diversify into textiles and apparel using the same model.

The Model

ROPE's model is unique for several reasons, says Mr Sreejith.

- First of all, the approach is customer driven as it works according to customers' orders.

Customized production is offered as per clients' needs.

- Secondly, the approach competes with modern manufacturers on price and quality. The model is also vastly scalable as there is a large rural need, a vast number of outsourced products, and the production centres require low capital and overheads.
- Furthermore, the use of ICT enables ROPE to carry out efficient operations. In financial terms, the model achieves sustainability through cost coverage and in terms of human resource development, it emphasizes entrepreneurship at every level.

For discussion

1. Critically examine the views of ROPE's CEO on the sustainability of the model.
2. The CEO said, "In the future, we plan to expand into cotton and silk fabrics and apparels." Do you find the idea feasible? What suggestions do you have?

Source: Lalitha Sridhar, "Spinning Rural Profits," *Businessworld*, 20 March 2009, available at www.businessworld.in/index.php/Corporate/Spinning-Rural-Profits.html.

3

Rural Marketing Experiences

LEARNING OBJECTIVES

Upon completion of this chapter, you will be able to:

- Appreciate the marketing approaches of some leading companies based on the public–private–partnership (PPP) model
- Understand how information technology can be gainfully employed in the rural marketing context
- Examine the way marketing initiatives are built around social issues
- State the guidelines for designing rural marketing approaches

Encouraged by the growth in sales from rural India, companies are devising new marketing strategies. For Marico, 25 per cent of its sales come from rural India. Milind Sarwate, head of the company's human resources and strategy division, says, "We have been making products primarily for urban India. But we would focus on increasing our reach in rural areas." Emami, on the other hand, prefers to promote products through channel-level incentives in smaller towns, including wall paintings, door-to-door activities, in-shop promotions, activities in rural markets, fairs and festivals, *kheti mela*, mobile traders or shops on wheels, and video vans. Aditya Agarwal, director, Emami Group, says, "We have introduced new super-stockist networks for rural coverage, with a special focus on West Bengal, Andhra Pradesh, Uttar Pradesh and Maharashtra. The van operations model has also been introduced to make the products reach remote villages."[1]

Dabur India's Vice Chairman Amit Burman says, "Rural and semi-urban India account for almost 50 per cent of our domestic sales. New product introductions have always been the key to Dabur's growth strategy." A Reliance Capital report says, "While the large potential is true, the reality is that rural people are more likely to spend on items that give them status. Spending on a mobile or motorbike that helps one in improving communication and conveyance is more sought after than upgrading to a higher quality soap." This is good news to marketers of durables. LG, Samsung, Sansui, Philips, Maruti, M&M, Tata Motors, Hero Honda, Nestlé and P&G are other major corporations who have ramped up their rural focus. In rural markets, the demand has always been greater for entry-level colour TVs and low-end twin-tub washing machines. However, due to the prolonged summer, most durables-makers have not only exceeded their sales targets but have also found "surprisingly good demand" for top-end models of durables from semi-urban markets.[2]

The emerging rural markets offer exciting opportunities to marketers as well as pose threats of stiff competition from rivals. This chapter discusses the strategies of some leading companies to enable marketing executives and students to come to grips with the diverse elements of an effective rural marketing strategy.

INTRODUCTION

India's untapped rural market holds tremendous growth opportunities for companies that can design the right marketing mix of 4 P's (Product, Price, Place and Promotion) to achieve the 4 A's (Affordability, Accessibility, Acceptance and Availability) for rural consumers. However, when we observe the rural marketing approaches of some companies, we find that they have not narrowly focused on transaction marketing but have gone beyond by employing principles of conversion and development marketing and strengthened their customer base through relationship marketing designs. Hindustan Unilever, CFCL, ITC, Colgate–Palmolive and Hindusthan Latex are examples of such companies. We will now discuss the important initiatives of these companies to gain insights into rural marketing.

CASE OF HUL—PROJECT *SHAKTI*

Hindustan Unilever Limited (HUL), formerly known as Hindustan Lever Limited (HLL), is the largest consumer products company in India. The name HUL came into vogue in late June 2007. The head office of the company is located in Mumbai. There are, in all, 41,000 employees of different categories working in the company.

Mission

Unilever has declared its commitment to people and to "adding vitality to life."

Their focus is on meeting everyday needs of nutrition, hygiene and personal care, and effort is spent on creating brands that help people feel good, look good and get more out of life. Though they operate across different cultures, they respect local cultures and ensure that their products and practices are local culture-specific. They are of the view that customer relationship is the basic foundation of business across the globe. The company sees knowledge management as a potent tool to be used in the service of local consumers—this makes it a truly multi-local multinational.

For achieving productivity, profitability and long-term competitive ability, they emphasize on the highest standards of corporate behaviour towards employees, suppliers, consumers, communities and environments on which they have an impact.

Vision

The vision of HUL is formulated with the inspiration drawn from the service motto given in its mission. This figures the company as an entity that is sensitive to the changing aspirations of its customers. It is responsive in creating competitive and innovative branded products and services that progressively enhance the quality of life.

Products and markets

The products sold to the extent of about four million tonnes nearly accounting for Rs 137.18 billion. HUL's distribution network comprises about 2,500 redistribution stockists, covering 6.3 million retail outlets. About 250 million urbanites and another 250 million rural people are consumers of its 35 major Indian brands. The products marketed by the company range from food items such as flour, biscuits, ice creams, etc. to body products such as soaps, face creams, cigarettes, beverages, etc. used by consumers in their day-to-day life. HUL's brands like Lifebuoy, Lux, Surf Excel, Rin, Wheel, Fair & Lovely, Pond's, Sunsilk, Clinic, Pepsodent, Close-up, Lakmé, Brooke Bond, Kissan, Knorr-Annapurna, Kwality Wall's, etc. are household names across the country and span many categories—soaps, detergents, personal products, tea, coffee, branded staples, ice cream and culinary products.

Corporate social responsibility (CSR) programmes

HUL's corporate social responsibility (CSR) philosophy is embedded in its corporate purpose and "vitality" mission that aims to improve quality of life through their products and their interventions in the communiy.

Adding value to agriculture

HUL has done much to help increase agricultural productivity by introducing the latest technology, sharing and updating best practices, and investing in food processing.

- The average yield of tea at the company's plantations has grown from 900 kg per hectare in the 1960s to about 2,500 kg per hectare now.
- Their tomato extension programme in Punjab has increased the yield per acre from eight tonnes 10 years ago to 20 tonnes today.
- They are the country's largest seller of branded animal feeds; their innovation centre in this business has developed poultry feeds that give a high rate of conversion efficiency.

They understand the need for establishing linkages between agri-business and agricultural development to achieve viability because of their early experience with a dairy plant at Etah (Uttar Pradesh). HUL had an early opportunity to learn this lesson when they first set up the dairy in 1964. The company has increased the availability of milk through a series of focused initiatives in animal husbandry and rural development. As a result, milk production has gone up in the last 20 years from 2,500 tonnes per year to over 30,000 tonnes. There has been an improvement in the incomes of the rural community around the factory.[3]

Water conservation and harvesting

HUL is committed to extending its efforts on water conservation and harversting to the larger community. It has engaged in community water management projects in areas that are adjacent to its manufacturing sites. Box 3.1 describes one such project.

Sanjivani

HUL started *Sanjivani*—a free mobile medical service camp—in 2003 near its Doom Dooma factory in Assam. Villages within a radius of 40 km have been identified for the project. They are centrally located with many bordering villages. The *Sanjivani* project has provided medical assistance to more than 143,364 patients since its inception. In 2007 alone, more than 22,395 patients were treated in 344 camps. In 2008, 31,790 patients were treated through 437 camps. Box 3.2 provides the operational details.

Cause-branding campaigns

Another important aspect of HUL's operations is cause-branding. We briefly describe its cause-branding efforts in this section.

Box 3.1 Water Conservation Projects of HUL

HUL started its pilot project on watershed management around its factory at Khamgaon, an arid region of Maharashtra. As a result, a green belt has come up with about 6,300 trees. Inspired by the success of the project, HUL extended this model to other villages.

Joining hands with the Tata Energy Research Institute (TERI) and Bharatiya Agro Industries Foundation, HUL constructed *bunds*, trenches and check dams in Parkhed village and around 350 families were the beneficiaries. They could cultivate a second crop on a total cultivable area of 470 acres. There was a phenomenal rise in their incomes from around an average of Rs 36,000 to approximately Rs 85,000 per annum per farmer. The experiment was recognized and appreciated at the Johannesburg World Summit on Sustainable Development.

Another project of the kind was taken up in association with an NGO, Vanarai, at HUL's Silvassa manufacturing hub (in the Union Territory of Dadra and Nagar Haveli). First, community awareness was created with Vanarai's help, involving every member of the village. Once the response to water conservation was found to be satisfactory, the villagers were trained to make commitments and contributions to water harvesting. Watershed structures were created to benefit 1,491 hectares and 478 families.

Source: "Water Conservation, HUL," available at ww.hul.co.in.

Box 3.2 Project *Sanjivani*

Project *Sanjivani* aims at creating proper infrastructure and expertise necessary to prevent and cure diseases in the remote villages of Assam. The two-pronged programme envisages (i) awareness creation on issues such as hygiene, child immunization, family planning, etc. and (ii) provision of free mobile medical facilities and basic medical services.

The project covers a radius of 40 km around the factory with two mobile vans equipped with basic medical equipment such as diagnostic kits, blood pressure measuring units, medicines and a mobile stretcher. It is accompanied by a specialized team of one male and one female doctor, two nurses, a medical attendant and drivers.

On an average, 400 Sanjivini medical camps are conducted every year in remote villages surrounding the factory. The project is run in close co-ordination with the local administration and the progress is reviewed every quarter.

The village headman provides support by making arrangements. The unit camps for six hours in a village everyday. Around 100 patients get medical advice and treatment for minor diseases. All patients with critical and chronic diseases are referred to hospitals. About 400 medial camps are conducted in a year.

In association with NGOs and other interested agencies, HUL conducts awareness campaigns on hygiene, child immunization camps, iron supplement therapy, free eye check-ups, family planning awareness camps, anti-tobacco education and anti-alcoholism camps.

Source: "Providing Health Care, HUL," available at www.hul.co.in/sustainability/MakingaDifference/ProvidingHealthcare.aspx.

Lifebuoy Swasthya Chetna (LBSC)

Lifebuoy *Swasthya Chetna* (LBSC) is a rural health and hygiene initiative that was started in 2002. The company worked closely with government bodies such as NRHM and also UNICEF (in 2008) for its initiatives on handwashing. The Indian postal department released a special postal cover on Lifebuoy *Swasthya Chetna* on the occasion of World Health Day (April 7) in 2006. The programme has touched 50,676 villages and 0.12 billion people since 2002. In 2008 alone, LBSC contacted 15,000 villages in Uttar Pradesh, Madhya Pradesh, Maharashtra, Bihar, and Karnataka. Box 3.3 presents the operational details of the programme.[5]

Fair & Lovely (FAL) Foundation

The Fair & Lovely (FAL) Foundation aims at economic empowerment of women across India by providing information, resources and support in the areas of education, career and enterprise. It specifically targets women from low-income groups. The Foundation has renowned Indian women from various walks of life as its advisors. Among them are educationists, NGO activists, and physicians. The Foundation is implementing its activities in association with state governments.[6] A series of projects drawn up to achieve its vision are described in Box 3.4.

Surf Excel—water conservation

Hindustan Unilever's vision is to continuously innovate technologically to reduce water consumption and to conserve water in their manufacturing operations. They developed Surf Excel Quick Wash that needs two buckets of water less than the generally used quantity per wash and is thus, a considerable water-saver.

Rural marketing operations

The company is a pioneer in rural marketing and it has experimented in many ways to increase its rural reach.

Box 3.3 Lifebuoy *Swasthya Chetna*

LBSC was initiated in media-dark villages (in UP, MP, Bihar, West Bengal, Maharashtra, Orissa) with the objective of spreading awareness about the importance of washing hands with soap. It demonstrates that "visible clean is not really clean," thereby proving the importance of washing hands. It targets children as they are the harbingers of change in society and mothers since they are the custodians of health.

LBSC is a multi-phased activity. In the initial phase, a Health Development Officer (HDO) and an assistant initiate contact and interact with students and influencers of the community (Key Opinion Leaders)—village community representatives, medical practitioners, school teachers, etc. A number of tools such as a pictorial story in a flip chart format, a "Glo-germ demonstration" and a quiz with attractive prizes to reinforce the message are used. The "Glo-Germ demonstration" is a unique tool to make unseen germs visible and emphasize the need to use soap to wash hands and kill germs. Each phase of the activity is customized to the needs of the respective group such as interactive games for kids and mothers, etc. The various stages reinforce the message and learnings that are crucial in creating awareness and effecting behaviour change in favour of hand-wash hygiene. The programme involves meeting the local *Panchayat* bodies, especially the *anganwaadi* workers and taking their help in its implementation at the village level.

Source: www.hul.co.in, accessed March 2010.

Box 3.4 Programmes Undertaken by the Fair & Lovely Foundation

The programmes run by the Fair & Lovely Foundation focus on women in cities and villages.

- ***Fair & Lovely Scholarships:*** The Fair & Lovely Foundation has awarded scholarships to over 600 deserving girls since 2003. Fair & Lovely Scholarships of up to Rs 0.1 million are awarded to women for graduate, post-graduate and doctoral courses within India. Recently, HUL extended the scheme to the children of *Shakti Amma* who are part of HUL's social initiatives in rural India.
- ***Fair & Lovely Career Fairs:*** To date, over 600,000 students have benefited from Career Fairs conducted in cities all over India. Fair & Lovely Career Fairs are designed to address the needs of girl students passing out of Class X and XII.
- ***Fair & Lovely Shikhar:*** This aims at inspiring girls by presenting stories of women achievers through TV presentations.
- ***Fair & Lovely Project Suvarna:*** Project *Suvarna* is an identification and training activity aimed at harnessing available talent in selected events of women athletes in the age groups of under 12, 14, 16 and 18. P. T. Usha chose the candidates and trained them at her academy.
- ***Fair & Lovely Project Swayam:*** Project *Swayam* is an initiative in the area of education and enterprise for women by the Fair & Lovely Foundation in association with VRDC (Vanasthali Rural Development Centre). Under this project, women were trained to become pre-school teachers. After completing their training, these women could start their own schools with help from VRDC, through which they got an opportunity to earn their own living. This project was replicated in Bihar in association with a local NGO, *Jan Jagran Sansthan*, in 2005.

Source: www.hul.co.in, accessed March 2010.

Rural divisions

Each business division of HUL dealt with the rural market on an individual basis earlier. Now a rural market division has been set up to deal with rural markets as a single organization.

On-the-job training for rural markets

The company expects executive recruits to spend at least 8 weeks in the villages of India to get a gut-level experience of India's bottom-of-the-pyramid markets. The new executives must become involved in some community projects—building a road, cleaning up a water catchments area, teaching in a school, or improving a health clinic. The goal is to make executives engage with the local population to develop better understanding.

HUL also initiated a massive programme for managers at all levels to reconnect with their poorest customers. They are expected to talk with the poor in both rural and urban areas, visit the shops that customers frequent and ask them about their experience with the company's products and those of its competitors.

Distribution oriented projects

Some of the recognized distribution programmes of HUL are: Operation Harvest, Project *Bharat*, Project Streamline, and Project *Shakti*.

Operation HARVEST

HUL launched Operation HARVEST (Harmonize All Resources in Village to Enhance Sales and Turnover) in 1989 as a seeding exercise with an objective to increase the penetration and the awareness of its brands and to generate demand. The objective was to make the routes viable for coverage by route-schedule vans. This operation was conducted in villages that were not covered by route schedules and where the reach of conventional media was weak.

Around 30,000 villages that had a high growth potential were selected for the operation to encourage trials and identify key distribution and retail points. The villages that were selected had a population of at least 2,000 people and were connected by all-weather roads. The company hired vans and had them fitted with public address systems and in some cases, with audio-visual equipment. These vans covered six villages a day for six days a week. The cycle was repeated a couple of times in the same villages. On reaching the village they would play audio cassettes and video films provided by HUL. These tapes and films had song-and-dance sequences from popular films with advertisements of HUL products coming at intervals. The company representatives distributed free samples and also identified key distribution points. Small shops in these villages were serviced by providing primary products like Lifebuoy and Wheel.

The Market Potential Value (MPV) of the village was determined to estimate whether or not a village had the potential to generate a consistent sale above the minimum threshold of Rs 2,000 per visit per village. If found suitable, the village was included in the standard route schedule of the distributor.

Project Bharat

In 1998, HUL's personal products unit initiated Project *Bharat,* the first and largest rural home-to-home operation to have ever been undertaken by any company. The project covered 13 million rural households by the end of 1999. During the course of operation, HUL had vans visiting villages across the country distributing sample packs comprising a low-unit-price pack each of shampoo, talcum powder, toothpaste and skin cream priced at Rs 15. This was to create awareness of the company's product categories and of the affordability of the products. The personal products unit subsequently rolled out a second phase of the sampling initiative to target villages with a population of over 2,000. Along with Operation *Bharat,* HUL conceptualized Project Streamline to enhance its control on the rural supply chain through a network of rural sub-stockists based in these villages. This gave the company the required competitive edge, and extended its direct reach to 37 per cent of the country's rural population.

The objective was to penetrate 235,000 villages with less than 2,000 population and to increase HUL's reach in rural India from 43 per cent to 75 per cent. About 30 *Bharat* Units were activated to cover 0.6 million households. TV shows (*Ramayana* and *Chitrahaar*) were telecast in the evening at a common place in a village. Coupons were also distributed for a lucky draw. As a result, 0.6 million households were contacted in 10 months. Nearly 20,000 villages were covered. The sales of Fair & Lovely increased by 50 per cent. This activation helped in changing perceptions about using Clinic Plus shampoo for cleaning hair instead of using soap.

Project Streamline (super stockist channel)

In a significant move aiming at long-term benefits, HUL initiated Project Streamline, to further increase its rural reach with the help of rural sub-stockists placed under rural distributors (Figure 3.1). Each rural distributor will have around 20 stockists affiliated to him. The company has appointed 6,000 such sub-stockists who distribute products in remote villages using unconventional means of transport such as tractor, bullock cart, etc. About 6,000 sub-stockists were appointed to cover about 5,000 villages and service 250 million consumers. HUL was able to directly reach 37 per cent of the country's rural population through this initiative.

I-Shakti

I-*Shakti* kiosks have been set up in eight villages in Andhra Pradesh and have been functional since August 2003. During the launch of these kiosks, important village members like the *Sarpanch*, school teacher and doctor are invited to help reinforce relationships with the villagers. The kiosks remain

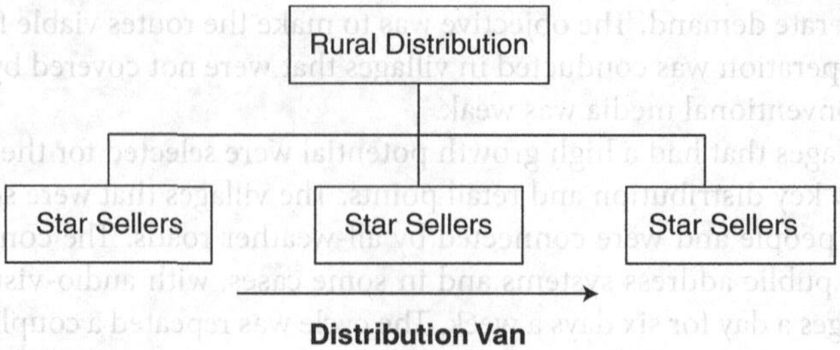

Figure 3.1 Rural Distribution Model—Streamline

open from 9 a.m. to 7 p.m., six days a week. The kiosks offer information chiefly in the form of audio-visuals in the following areas:

- Health and hygiene
- E-Governance
- Education
- Agriculture
- Employment
- Legal services
- Veterinary services

The information provided in the above areas is culled from the best available resources, with additional care being taken to ensure that information, especially in areas like agriculture, is locally relevant and includes inputs form home-grown experts. These experts are also available on request to help provide solutions to problems raised by users through a query mailing system. A farmer from the village can obtain a quick solution to a pest problem plaguing his crops. People can also send queries on health and hygiene to a local doctor for a speedy response. Villagers can avail of discount coupons from the kiosk for medical treatment from doctors operating in local areas.

I-*Shakti* has also tied up with the Azim Premji Foundation to deliver innovative educational modules to students of classes VIII to XII through the kiosk. Local school teachers have also been involved in the process. A similar partnership is in place with Tata Adult Literacy for adult education.

Through I-*Shakti* kiosks, ICICI Bank and HUL provide a new delivery channel for rural India. This offers a multitude of products and services to the rural customer.

In the first phase, Life and General Insurance will be offered through this channel. Other financial services including investment products (equity, mutual funds, bonds), ICICI Bank Pure Gold (gold coins), personal credit, rural savings accounts and remittances will be introduced subsequently. The I-*Shakti* vision is to scale up operations for delivering information services to over 10 million rural people across 7,500 villages.[4]

Project Shakti

Drawing from the Bangladeshi Grameen Bank model, various NGOs, multilateral agencies, government bodies, and public sector banks have set up self-help groups (SHGs) in rural India. These groups function as mutual thrift societies. Ten to 15 women in a particular village form a group that meets regularly. Each member contributes a little money to a common pool. Once the pool attains a threshold, the sponsoring agency steps in and offers micro-credit to one or more members of the group for investment in an economic activity approved by the group (Figure 3.2). HUL stepped into the situa-

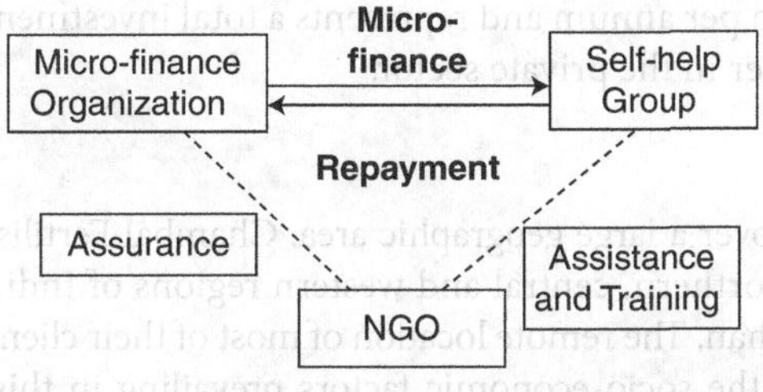

Figure 3.2 Traditional Micro-Credit Models

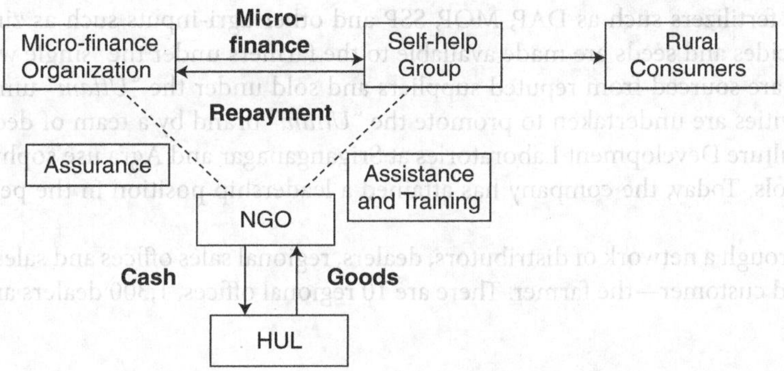

Figure 3.3 Project *Shakti*—The Modified Micro-Credit Model

tion with a simple plan of partnering with micro-credit recipients by offering them opportunities for micro-enterprise (Figure 3.3). Thus, Project *Shakti* was born.

A member of a self-help group (SHG) in each of the 50 chosen villages was appointed as a *Shakti* entrepreneur. As *Shakti* brand endorsers—known as *Shakti Ammas*—they borrowed money from their respective SHGs and with that capital purchased HUL products for sale in their villages. Project *Shakti* is thus, a highly interactive form of selling and engagement that leverages a unique opportunity to communicate, demonstrate and provide experience of HUL brand benefits.

The whole exercise is not an easy task given the low literacy levels, several languages used locally and the sheer scale and diversity of rural India. HUL's partnerships with NGOs and support from state governments facilitate these efforts. Project *Shakti* has played a significant role in aiding economic development in rural India. The *Shakti* brand endorsers earn close to Rs 750 per month on an average and in some cases, their earnings even touch as much as Rs 2,500 per month. This has helped double their household incomes. After initial pilots in 2001, they now have a network of 35,000 entrepreneurs reaching 100 million rural consumers in 100,000 villages.[5]

CASE OF CFCL—*UTTAM BANDHAN*

Chambal Fertilisers and Chemicals Limited (CFCL) was promoted by Zuari Industries Limited in 1985. It is the flagship company of the Rs 50 billion professionally-managed Zuari-Chambal Combine. It has diversified interests in the areas of fertilizers, phosphoric acid, agri-inputs and seeds, agri-biotechnology, textiles, information technology, food processing and shipping. It operates two hi-tech nitrogenous fertilizer plants at Gadepan (Rajasthan), having a total re-assessed capacity of

1.7292 million tonnes of urea per annum and represents a total investment of over Rs 25 billion. CFCL is India's largest urea producer in the private sector.

Marketing operations

CFCL's client base is spread over a large geographic area. Chambal Fertilisers caters to the needs of the farmers in 10 states in the northern, central and western regions of India and is the leading fertilizer supplier in the state of Rajasthan. The remote location of most of their clients, the large number of clients and prospects coupled with the socio-economic factors prevailing in this segment make marketing a challenge.

The company has set up a wide network of 1,100 dealers and 15,000 sales outlets in villages. The company sells its urea under the name "*Uttam Veer*." [6]

Besides urea, fertilizers such as DAP, MOP, SSP and other agri-inputs such as zinc sulphate, bio-fertilizers, pesticides and seeds are made available to the farmers under the "single window" concept. These products are sourced from reputed suppliers and sold under the "*Uttam*" umbrella. Extensive promotion activities are undertaken to promote the "*Uttam*" brand by a team of dedicated field officers. The Agriculture Development Laboratories at Sriganganagar and Agra use sophisticated soil and water testing tools. Today, the company has attained a leadership position in the pesticides business in North India.

It operates through a network of distributors, dealers, regional sales offices and sales representatives, targeting the end customer—the farmer. There are 10 regional offices, 1,300 dealers and 20,000 village level outlets.

Uttam Bandhan

The *Uttam Bandhan* initiative was started in 2000. It is a community welfare initiative that originated under its present name in the state of Rajasthan where the company has its urea plant.

Aim

Chambal's *Uttam Bandhan* is a community welfare initiative that tries to enhance the farmer's income and quality of life. It further seeks to provide employment to educated rural youth.

Employment

Under the auspices of the initiative, the unemployed local youth are trained by the company as extension workers who are otherwise called *Uttam Krishi Sewaks*. About 300 educated, unemployed youth from a rural background are at present acting as *Uttam Krishi Sewaks*. The extension workers earn commission on the sale of specialized products.

Services

These extension workers are obliged to interact with farmers and render the required assistance in their agricultural practices.

Soil and water test

Soil and water samples are collected and tested for micro-nutrients and balanced inputs. Soil test reports are explained and the farmer is educated on the importance of proper soil health and micro-nutrients. Based on thousands of samples tested over the years, soil mapping is being done. The Agriculture Development Laboratories are located at Agra and Sriganganagar and satellite soil testing facilities have been set up elsewhere. The company does not charge any testing fee from *Uttam Bandhan* member farmers.

Farm education

Crop and product demonstrations, field demonstrations and farmer meets are conducted regularly to educate farmers on latest farm practices. Farmers are given training on specialized services that vary from the cultivation of medicinal and horticultural crops, vermi-culture and the use of bio-fertilizers.

Alternate sources of income

Uttam Bandhan looks beyond opportunities provided by land and water to increase a farmer's income. Breed improvement and animal healthcare camps are regularly organized and farmers are educated on proper feed and mineral mixtures for good returns. Goat rearing, turkey farming, bee keeping, backyard poultry, etc. are other sources of income for farmers. *Uttam Bandhan* drives them to enhance income through proper training and by making the facilities available at their doorstep.

Farmers' Web site—www.uttamkrishi.com

Chambal set up www.uttamkrishi.com, a Web site for farmers, in the year 2001. Uttamkrishi.com was one of the first Web sites to be set up for the benefit of the farming community. It has a bottom-up approach to farming solutions as the Web site has been designed region-wise to address the local issues. Broad information on crops and agronomy has been posted. Farmers can access it for free and post queries that are answered by experts.

Farmers' helpline—Hello Uttam

Telephonic helplines called "Hello *Uttam*" have been set up. Farmers can raise issues over the phone by calling one of the local "Hello *Uttam*" helpline numbers. Though the number of centres is limited at the moment, experts are prompt in their response. Information about the helpline is widely circulated and for areas where the helpline is not operational, the farmers are urged to seek clarity from the Government of India's Farmers' Call Centre facility, the Department of Agriculture.

Mailers and AVs

Chambal is particular on proper dissemination of information. For that it has a quarterly mailer "*Chambal ki Chitthi*" that is hand delivered to every *Uttam Bandhan* farmer. It contains valuable farm-related information on activities pertaining to that quarter. Handouts, leaflets, farm calendars, farmer diaries, etc. are distributed extensively. It arranges radio talks, AVs and programmes for farmers on Doordarshan.

The *Uttam Bandhan* programme has been initiated in 10 states with around 80,000 farmers as its members. Services provided are customized taking a farmers' preference into consideration and packaging them according to the agro-climatic zones. Through proper training, demonstrations, expert opinion, quality inputs and non-farm income, the *Uttam Bandhan* farmer has been a gainer in terms of not just increase in income but also quality of life.

Chambal has made use of public–private–partnership (PPP) in an intelligent way. It has involved farmers and experts in the government departments, agriculture universities, agriculture research stations and *krishi vigyan kendras* in various knowledge sharing and promotional activities like crop demonstrations, field days, animal husbandry camps, health check-ups, etc.

Chambal takes several initiatives on its own. They include training farmers, soil testing and encouraging farmers to take advantage of government schemes. It is hailed as a proactive partner in the Government's Agriculture Technology Management Agency (ATMA) initiative.[7]

CASE OF ITC — E-*CHOUPAL*

Indian Tobacco Company (ITC) Limited that started as a traditional tobacco and cigarette producer has grown into a premier and diversified Indian business giant dealing with hotels, agri-business, information technology and fast moving consumer goods (FMCGs). It is one of India's foremost private sector companies with a market capitalization of about USD 4 billion and annual revenues of USD 2 billion. The company, with its philosophy of corporate social responsibility as well as dedication to the cause of nation building, created its International Business Division (IBD) in 1990, as an agri-trading company. To face the challenges of multinational corporations, ITC's IBD decided to use information technology to create a competitive business resulting in USD 150 million business potential trading in varieties of commodities such as feed ingredients, food grains, coffee, black pepper, edible nuts, marine products, processed fruit, etc.

The social consciousness of the company led to the creation of e-*choupals* (meaning gathering places) in 2000, to serve as social gathering places for exchange of information and to also act as e-commerce hubs. Initially the e-*choupals* were engaged to re-engineer the procurement process for soya, tobacco, wheat, shrimp and other cropping systems in rural India. In course of time, it became an e-commerce platform with a low-cost fulfilment system focused on the needs of rural India by creating a highly profitable distribution and product design channel for the company. The system has become a catalyst in transforming rural life by helping to alleviate rural isolation, creating more transparency for farmers and improving their productivity and incomes.

The business model

Unlike pure trading models that do not require much capital investment, the e-*choupal* model required ITC to make high investments to create and maintain its own IT network in rural India and also to identify and train a local farmer to manage each e-*choupal*. A computer is located in the house of a farmer and Internet facility is provided through phone lines using a VSAT connection. It serves 600 farmers on an average within a radius of about 5 km. The cost of each e-*choupal* is between USD 3,000 and USD 6,000 for the set up and about USD 100 per year for its maintenance. It is cost-free to the farmers whereas for the host farmer called *sanchalak*, some operating costs are incurred. The *sanchalak* is obliged to serve the entire community by oath. He is paid commissions for all e-*choupal* transactions.

Benefits to partners

The benefits to the farmers are many.

Information

Through the use of the computer the farmer gets information on various aspects like daily closing prices of commodities at local *mandis*, local price trends and new farming techniques either directly or through the *sanchalak*.

Purchases

Farmers place orders for seeds and fertilizers besides consumer goods from ITC or its partners at prices lower than those available from the village traders, etc. All the products required by the villagers are ordered in bulk by the *sanchalak*.

Selling

Further, ITC directly purchases the crop from any farmer at the closing price of the previous day, enabling him to transport his crop to an ITC processing centre for electronic weighing and for assessing its quality. The payment is made to the farmer directly both for the crop and for its transport. If the quality of the crop is above normal, the farmer is benefited by what are called “bonus points” that are exchanged for ITC products. This is how the e-*choupal* system bypasses the government mandated trading *mandis*. The benefits that the farmer receives such as more accurate weighing, faster processing time, prompt payment for his crop, accessibility to a wide range of information like accurate market price knowledge and market trends enable him to decide when, where, and at what price to sell his products. Generally, the farmers selling directly to ITC through an e-*choupal* receive a higher price for their crops than what they get through the *mandi* system, the benefit being about 2.5 per cent higher (about USD 6 per tonne). The total benefits accrued by the farmers consist of lower prices for inputs and other goods, higher yields, and a sense of empowerment.

The other benefits the farmer receives include the e-*choupal* system acting as a channel for soil testing services and educational efforts to help farmers to improve crop quality. By partnering with banks, ITC offers farmers access to credit insurance and other services.

Benefits to ITC

The system benefits ITC because of lower net procurement costs and by its direct control over the quality of what it buys. It also provides the company direct access to the farmers, allows it to inform them about the conditions of the ground, helps it in improving, planning and building relationships and assists in building a secure supply of raw material.

The other benefits to ITC are the use of the e-*choupal* network and distribution channel for its products, including those of its partners and a source of innovation for new products. There is now demand from farmers to expand ITC services to additional crops such as onions and potatoes. This indicates that the farmers are becoming a source of product innovation for ITC.

When the farmers bring their produce for sale to the ITC processing centre, they can buy seeds, fertilizers and some consumer goods. When some products are aggregated for the whole village and ordered all at once by the *sanchalak*, the logistic costs for ITC are lowered.

The e-*choupal* model enhanced the image of ITC. It demonstrated that corporations such as ITC can play a major role in increasing the efficiency of an agricultural system, which in turn benefits farmers, the rural community and shareholders. Further, a corporation can provide and maintain a key role in the information technology that is used by local farmers for gaining transparency, increasing access to information and rural transformation.

Benefits to society

The e-*choupal* system provides farmers more control over their choices, higher profit margins on their crops and access to information to improve their productivity. The keynotes in the system are more transparent processes and empowerment of local people besides increasing trust and fairness. The increased efficiency and potential for improving crop quality together make Indian agriculture more competent.

However, as the result of introduction of the e-*choupal*, many players in a multi-system have suffered loss of revenue. They are commission agents, *mandi* labourers, *bazaars* near the *mandi*, some *mandi* operators and competing processes. The commission agents have lower incomes after the introduction of e-*choupals* in spite of ITC's best efforts to compensate them for it. The *mandi* labourers engaged in the weighing and bagging produce have been severely impacted by the drop in volume. The revenue of the local *bazaars* that offer products to the farmers has fallen as they have been replaced by shops near ITC hubs. Some regional *mandis* lost taxes for their operations due to diversion of tax payment nearer to the procurement centre.

Spread and operations

Table 3.1 provides details of the coverage of the e-*choupal*. It is spread across 40,000 villages in Madhya Pradesh, Uttar Pradesh, Maharashtra, Karnataka, Andhra Pradesh, Rajasthan, Haryana and Uttarakhand. In these *choupals*, there are 6,000 *sanchalaks* and over 17,000 *upa-sanchalaks*. It has emerged as the gateway of an expanding spectrum of commodities leaving farms—wheat, rice, pulses,

Table 3.1 Spread of e-*choupals*

States covered	10
Villages covered	40,000
No. of e-*choupals*	6,500
Farmers e-empowered	4 million
Sanchalaks	6,000
Upa-sanchalaks	17,000

soya, maize, spices, coffee, aqua-products, etc. The reverse flow carries FMCGs, durables, automotives, banking and insurance. By 2012, ITC has planned to expand the project to 15 states in India reaching 100,000 villages.

Problems and solutions

The problems encountered while setting up and managing these e-*choupals* primarily arise due to infrastructural inadequacies, including power supply, telecom connectivity and bandwidth, apart from the challenge of imparting skills to first time Internet users in remote and inaccessible areas of rural India. Several alternative and innovative solutions—some of them expensive—are being deployed to overcome these challenges, for example, power back-up is being provided through batteries charged by solar panels, BSNL exchanges are being upgraded with RNS kits, VSAT equipment is being installed, mobile *choupals* are being set up, local caching of static content on Web sites is being provided to stream in the dynamic content more efficiently, 24x7 helpdesk is being set up, etc.

Choupal pradarshan khet

This path-breaking initiative brings the benefits of the best agricultural practices to small and marginal farmers. Backed by intensive research and knowledge, this initiative provides agri-extension services that are qualitatively superior and it involves pro-active handholding of farmers to ensure productivity gains. The services are customized to meet local conditions, ensure timely availability of farm inputs including insurance and credit. They also provide a cluster of farmer schools for capturing indigenous knowledge. This initiative that has covered over 70,000 hectares, has a multiplying impact and reaches out to over 1.6 million farmers. In 2006–2007, ITC's unique paid *choupal khet pradarshan* farm extension service conducted over 15,000 field demonstrations in nine states.

Choupal saagar

The brand "*choupal saagar*" of e-*choupal* plans to establish shopping complexes that house a procurement centre, retail store, food court, farmer-facility centre and healthcare clinic. Positioned within tractorable distance from 30 e-*choupal* centres and their user communities, these malls are one-stop destinations for farmers (Box 3.5). ITC has so far launched 24 *choupal saagar* hubs in three states and has plans to open 700 such rural malls by 2012.

New role for traditional middlemen

As the company's e-*choupal* initiative has squeezed out the middlemen or traders who have traditionally bought farmers' produce at *mandis*, there is an attempt at the mall to "integrate the middleman"—by appointing them as *samyojaks* (co-ordinators). The middleman was earlier a principal to transactions. He used to buy from someone and sell to somebody else, and his profit was made out of blocking information and market signals about the price of the farmer's produce. Even though farmers can now get that information at the e-*choupal*, these middlemen still play a very critical role.

S. Sivakumar explains, "The *samyojak* at the *saagar* is in charge of storage, transportation and other logistics and management of bridge financing. He pays first and later collects the money from us in the evening. While we have invested Rs 40 million in setting up the mall, he invests the working capital of about Rs 20 million."[8]

Box 3.5 One-stop Destination for Farmers

S. Sivakumar, ITC's Chief Executive, Agri-business, says *Choupal Saagar* has cost the company Rs 40 million. Every day it may get about 1,100 to 1,200 footfalls and in the week before Diwali, this number may go up to 1,600 to 1,800, with daily sales exceeding Rs 0.2 million.

Coupal saagar is, in real terms, an expansive area with a good variety of outlets and facilities to serve occupational and household needs of farmers. Farm output purchasing counters, a godown, a digital weighing machine, a diesel pump, a soil-testing laboratory and a sale point for fertilizers, pesticides and other agro-inputs are the primary facilities at *choupal saagar*.

An add on to all this is a shopping area with stalls selling daily-purchase convenience products such as soaps, detergents and toothpaste, occasional-purchase products such as watches, clothing and shoes, a range of consumer durables that include entertainment goods such as TVs and DVD players, domestic appliances such as pressure cookers, room heaters, sewing machines and grinders, and automobiles such as motorbikes and tractors. There is an entertainment area too, with video games and swings for kids to while away their time when their parents are on a purchasing spree. To make the place a one-stop centre, a doctor, a bank, an insurance company office and a training centre for farmers have also been made available on the premises. Good quality products, offered at discounted prices with attractive gifts, entice the consumers to become regular customers.

The farmer, accompanied by his family members, brings his produce in order to sell them. While he is busy with weighing and unloading at the godown, his kids enjoy the swings and video games and his wife shops for household items. Together, they enjoy lunch at the cafeteria and drive back home by evening. Before leaving, he buys fertilizers and pesticides and fills his tractor with diesel. The entire shopping experience is so much fun and so purposeful that consumers view it as an "unusual store."

Source: Rasheeda Bhagat, "Ryot choice," *The Hindu Business Line*, 26 November 2004, available at www.thehindubusinessline.com/life/2004/11/26/stories/2004112600290400.htm.

Health and education

The company has initiated projects to promote health and education.

- A pilot project in healthcare services has been launched to provide reliable and quality healthcare services to the remotest villages through leading corporate healthcare service providers.
- Delivery of quality education services to rural areas is another project of interest piloted by the system to provide physical and digital infrastructure for commodity sourcing and consumer retail services.

CASE OF COLGATE—EDUCATION

Colgate–Palmolive India Ltd (CPIL) is a 51 per cent subsidiary of Colgate–Palmolive Company (CPC), USA. CPC's main business is manufacturing and marketing of oral-care products, toilet soap, and shaving products. With an employee strength of 1,130, CPIL has grown to a USD 230 million company with a wide distribution network in India.

Values

Colgate employees worldwide share a commitment to the three core corporate values: caring, global teamwork and continuous improvement. These values are reflected not just in the quality of its products and its reputation, but also in its dedication to serve the communities in which it does business.

Market share

Colgate is a household name in India with one out of two consumers using Colgate toothpaste. Rural areas contribute to 35 per cent of Colgate's sales. Colgate has maintained its leadership and emerged as India's number 1 brand across all categories for eight out of nine years since 1992.

Product range

It is a provider of scientifically proven oral-care products with multiple benefits at various price points. The range includes toothpastes, toothpowder and toothbrushes under the "Colgate" brand, as well as a specialized range of dental therapies under the banner of Colgate Oral Pharmaceuticals. The company also provides a range of personal-care products under the "Palmolive" brand name.

Brand image

Colgate has been ranked as India's number 1 "most trusted brand" across all categories for four consecutive years from 2003–2007 by *Brand Equity's* "most trusted brand" survey. It is the only brand to have been in the top three since the survey commenced in 2001. Prior to this, Colgate was also rated as the number 1 brand by the A&M—MODE Annual Survey for India's top brands for eight out of nine years between 1992 and 2001.

Results of market research

In order to create new demand for oral-care products, CPIL has chosen to increase its reach in rural areas. A Colgate "usage and attitude"[9] survey showed the following:

- More than 20 per cent of India's population still does not use any kind of modern dentifrice.
- About 60 per cent of people surveyed have never visited a dentist.
- While urban consumers appreciate that teeth health depends on one's brushing habits, a high proportion of rural consumers consider "being born with bad teeth" as the most important reason for dental problems.
- Over 90 per cent of the urban consumers use dentifrice products, over a third of rural consumers still use non-dentifrice products.

To increase the sales volume of the toothpaste and toothpowder segment, the following initiatives were crafted:

- New product launches
- Significant hike in marketing expenditure
- Targeting schools to create oral awareness among children
- Sales promotion measures such as small volume low-priced sachets
- Distribution of free toothbrushes
- Rural van distribution and participation in local festivals.

Product innovations

With rapidly evolving consumer preferences, Colgate has been spearheading changes across different product categories through a series of product innovations. The company launched Cibaca Top and Colgate Herbal, two low-priced brands targeted at the semi-urban market. Colgate's low-price offers have also helped to enhance usage levels. The shift in consumer preference from gel-based to white toothpastes has also worked in Colgate's favour, since the company has traditionally been the market leader in this segment.

Pricing for price-sensitive consumers

Colgate resorted to keep its products priced lower than its arch-rival, Hindustan Unilever. As a result, Colgate Gel, Total, etc. are priced marginally lower than similar offerings from HUL. Colgate's dominant position in toothpowder and lower-priced products has helped in increasing the company's sales.

Distribution

From a modest start in 1937 when hand-carts were used to distribute Colgate Dental Cream, Colgate–Palmolive India today has one of the widest distribution networks in India. It spans 2.7 million retail outlets across the country, of which the company services 800,000 outlets directly.

Educational campaigns and programmes: "bright smiles, bright futures"

The company has been delivering oral health education to children in rural and urban India in partnership with the Indian Dental Association (IDA). Colgate's community outreach efforts have touched the lives of millions of children, providing the information, insight and inspiration they need for a healthy life and a healthy smile. Believing that the mouth is the gateway to good oral hygiene, Colgate with its initiatives like "bright smiles bright future" since 1976 and the "oral health month" since 2004, has left no stone unturned to contribute towards the oral health of the nation.

Sports and other events

Joining hands with NGOs, the company has been sponsoring events that encourage children of the less privileged sections of society.

- Colgate has been sponsoring the inter-Mumbai cricket tournament for the physically challenged, organized by Omkar Krida Mandal, an NGO.
- Colgate supported Network in Thane by People Living with HIV/AIDS (NTP+), an NGO. The contribution/pledges supported the education and nourishment of the children infected and affected by HIV/AIDS, thus allowing them to live a life of dignity.
- Colgate has been supporting the Madhu Mehta Foundation, an NGO in Mumbai that hosts a Diwali party for the less privileged children of the city of Mumbai, bringing them joy, cheer and happiness during the festive occasion.

Bright smiles, bright futures (1976)

Colgate–Palmolive, India, undertook a novel oral health educational programme captioned "Colgate Bright Smiles, Bright Futures." It has the twin objectives of teaching children positive oral health habits of basic hygiene, diet and physical activity and encouraging dental professionals, public health officials, civic leaders and, most importantly, parents to play an active role in promoting a child's overall physical and emotional development.

The programme involves dental professionals nominated by the Indian Dental Association who give instructions to children with the aid of audio-visuals and printed literature created by the company. Free samples of toothpaste and healthcare tips are distributed among the participants.

To make teachers active campaigners, teachers' training is made an integral part of the School Dental Health Programme. Besides the on-site programmes, an online school curriculum featuring fun and entertaining activities was also launched. Till date, 235,000 teachers have been trained under the programme.[10]

Oral health month campaigns (2004)

Oral Health Month (OHM) is an oral health awareness campaign that establishes and promotes the importance of good oral-care habits. OHM was first initiated by Colgate in association with the Indian Dental Association (IDA) in 2004 as a six-city programme with 70 participating dentists. The theme for Oral Health Month, 2007 was, "Towards Zero Tooth Decay" and it focused on spreading awareness among the rural population about common oral health problems. It had outreach events like free dental check-ups and oral-care education in schools and villages. It covered 175 cities and towns across 19 states all over the country and included 250 rural and remote corners. The programme staged a unique "Brush Up Challenge" aimed at breaking the existing Guinness World Record for simultaneous brushing by people at multiple locations.

In 2007, in addition to the above, free dental check-ups through 500 ITC e-*choupals* were conducted in Uttar Pradesh, Madhya Pradesh and Maharashtra and toothpaste samples were given to children. The camps taught children the right way to brush, giving free dental health packs with tips and urged them to spread the message of good oral hygiene in their homes and communities. In its sixth year, it was organized for two months through September and October, 2009. It aimed at reaching over 1,000 towns and 40 cities with 15,000 dentists participating through free dental check-ups and awareness generating activities.

Libraries

The importance of libraries in knowledge promotion has been well recognized by HUL. In partnership with "Pratham," it has set up libraries for underprivileged children in economically backward areas in Mumbai. Children are encouraged to imbibe the habit of reading and exploring new avenues of knowledge.

Summer camps

Summer is the time for relaxation and recreation for children. Colgate has brightened the lives of children between 6 and 16 years of age by sponsoring Summer Camps at Dominic Savio since 1981. Not only students of the school but also children from the nearby hutments are also given an opportunity to take part in them. Creative workshops are conducted at the camp. Children who have benefited from this camp often come back as grown-ups to volunteer.

CASE OF HLL—SOCIAL MARKETING

Hindustan Latex Ltd (HLL) is a public-sector unit set up by the Government under the Ministry of Health and Family Welfare in 1966. Today, it has five manufacturing units located across the country with state-of-the-art facilities. In 2009, it was rechristened HLL Lifecare Ltd.[11]

HLL Lifecare Ltd is confident of meeting future challenges to provide products and services to people worldwide, particularly in rural and underserved areas of the nation.

In the global contraceptive market, the company has emerged as a leader with a market share of nearly 10 per cent. In India, it has a market share of over 18 per cent and its target turnover by 2010 is Rs 10 billion. HLL is actively associated with public health programmes of international agencies, the Union Government's National Rural Health Mission, Reproductive and Child Health Project and National Aids Control Programme.

Through diversification from contraceptives to family health care, with a focus on women-driven lifecycle products, and an expansion of manufacturing capacity made recently, a 50 per cent increase in turnover was achieved in the last year. The company's logo was changed to reflect the changes in its operations and focus. The move is from "innovating for generations" to reaching the "bottom of the pyramid in villages."

Product innovation

The company focused on innovation, value addition and development of new products to beat competition. New products such as the spiral condom, the phosphorescent glow condom and the "Moods get closer pack" had all turned out to be hits in the market. It has recently launched the "confidom female condom," a female-controlled HIV/pregnancy prevention device. Two new products—a "vibrating ring condom" and a "three-in-one (dotted, ribbed and foam-fitted) condom" are due to be launched soon. In the healthcare segment, it recently introduced a reuse-prevention syringe under the brand name "Bsure." It had earlier come out with an "auto destructive syringe" called "Autolok" for the National Immunization Programme.

Diversification plans

According to the managing director, the company is now into the diversification mode and would shortly come out with vaccines. It will launch a Hepatitis B vaccine and typhoid vaccine. The company tied up with Acumen Fund, a New York-based philanthropic venture fund to set up a network of "Lifespring Hospitals" with 25–30 bed capacity throughout India to help address the dearth of low-income maternal and child healthcare services. HLL will set up hospitals in 500 villages by 2010. The first such hospital was set up in Maula Ali, Hyderabad.[12]

In Chennai, in a 500-acre facility near NH-7, Hindustan Latex is coming out with the country's first medical park according to the PPP model in the organized sector. About 30–35 medical equipment manufacturing units, including MNCs will be located and Hindustan Latex with its Rs 1 billion vaccine will be the anchor-customer.[13]

Social marketing

The company has focused on social marketing as a thrust area to ensure that quality contraceptives are available to the people at an affordable price. Exports and direct marketing operations have been profitable to the company. However, the company realized the need for family planning and healthcare programmes aimed at the poor and disadvantaged sections of the society and ventured into social sector projects aimed at bringing about planned social change. Hindustan Latex Family Planning Promotion Trust (HLFPPT), a non-profit organization was promoted by HLL to meet this end.

Since its establishment in 1992, HLFPPT has been undertaking the conceptualization and implementation of various social sector projects. The Trust's area of operations extends to the various states of India. Although the Trust was established for promoting the agenda of family planning, its activities have now been broad-based to focus on reproductive and sexual health. Some of the initiatives undertaken by HLL are discussed here.

Mobile health clinic project

A concentrated village-based mobile medical van promotion and distribution programme was proposed to overcome the difficulty in physical distribution of healthcare services and other methods of contraception. This proposal was developed to operationalize a mobile Primary Healthcare Model in the van and to link it to the network of static referral centres at district/town level.

Merrygold health network

HLFPPT has launched Merrygold Health Network in the state of Uttar Pradesh as a social franchising initiative through State Innovations in Family Planning Services Project Agency (SIFPSA) in partnership with USAID, Government of India and the State Government of UP. The trust has committed to establish 70 level 1 franchisees (Merrygold) at district levels as the hubs connected to the next two levels. Level 2 comprises fractional franchisees (Merrysilver) established at subdivision and block level. Level 3 (MerryAYUSH) comprises providers like ANMs, ASHA and AYUSH and acts as the first point of contact with the community and also as the referral support to Merrysilver and Merrygold hospitals. Emphasis is on affordable pricing, quality assurance, customer servicing and efficient service delivery through standardized operating protocols. IT-enabled Hospital Management Information System (HMIS) is also being established. A team of public health and clinical professionals facilitate capacity building and quality assurance. An integrated health insurance policy for the coverage of risk during maternity has been introduced. A branded pharmacy and chain of diagnostic facilities are also being strategized.

Community care centres

Community care centres were conceived to bridge the gap between the community and the hospital in providing health care to HIV patients and to mitigate the impact of HIV on children and women-headed households. HLFPPT is planning to set up 24 such centres in Madhya Pradesh, Uttar Pradesh and Rajasthan drawing support from PACT (Promoting Access to Care and Treatment) and Population Foundation of India (PFI).[14]

Social marketing projects

The highlights of some of the projects are provided here.

Swasthya gram pariyojana

Location: Nearly 2,950 villages of Gwalior, Bhind, Morena, Datia and Shivpuri districts of Madhya Pradesh are covered under this.

Collaboration: The funding from the government for a period of 3 years is Rs 270 million. It was implemented by HLFPPT for the Ministry of Health and Family Welfare (MOHFW), Government of India.

Sales objectives

Promotion of CSM brands of contraceptives, ORS and sanitary napkins.

Development objectives

"Reduction of Total Fertility Rate (TFR)" and "advancement of family health" in rural areas.

Major barriers

Lack of access, affordability and lack of motivation.

Distribution

Through unemployed, educated and mobile rural youth.

Promotion

A comprehensive local media-based Information Education and Communication (IEC) programme.

Achievements: In the project area, the usage of condoms has gone up by 34 per cent and that of oral contraceptive pills by 18 per cent.[15]

Community-based distribution of contraceptives project

Location: Select districts of the socio-economically backward states of Bihar, Orissa and Jharkhand.

Collaboration: Sponsored by MOHFW, Government of India.

Development objectives: To promote the usage of spacing methods, right age of marriage and male responsibility for family welfare among the eligible couples in rural areas.

Sales objectives: To promote and distribute Oral Rehydration Salts (ORS) among children to prevent diarroheal disorders and sanitary napkins to address reproductive hygiene among women.

Distribution: Convergence with existing health service delivery channels. Product distribution through a network of community service providers and *aanganwadi* workers.

Promotion: Promotion elements include the following:

- Information, education and communication
- Brand promotion
- Advocacy with the help of village-based institutions, community representatives, government agencies, etc.

Sukha parivaram

Location: Rural areas of Andhra Pradesh for a duration of 3 years starting from October 2000.

Collaboration: Sponsored by MOHFW and the Government of Andhra Pradesh. Funding of more than Rs 44.8 million from the European commission.

Sales objectives: Selling condoms, oral contraceptive pills, iron and folic acid tablets (for pregnant women) and ORS. Product planning through consumer research.

Development objectives: To reduce the total fertility rate in Andhra Pradesh, child mortality due to diarrhoea by promotion of ORS, reduce the incidence of nutritional anaemia and reduce the incidence of sexually transmitted diseases such as AIDS through the promotion of condom use.

Distribution and promotion:

- Linkages with community-based distribution networks of NGOs, cooperatives, SHGs and women's groups and linkages with government departments such as DRDA, *Panchayats*, etc.
- Enhance capability of graduate medical practitioners to provide family planning services like IUD insertion.
- Enhance the capabilities of non-medical healthcare providers to provide counselling and referral services for IUDs.[16]

Sukhi sansar project

HLFPPT undertook the project in rural Uttar Pradesh to create awareness about the use of condoms and oral contraceptive pills (OCPs). During 1997–1999, it implemented the *Chota Sansar* project in villages that had a population of less than 20,000. During 2000–2003 it took up the *Sukhi Sansar* Project 1 in villages with population up to 1,000 persons and distributed condoms and OCPs through non-traditional rural outlets. During 2003–2006, the second phase of the *Sukhi Sansar* Project was rolled out. At this time the direct distribution system of condoms was strengthened and about 25,000 villages were served on a regular basis.

HLFPPT has initiated social projects in other states too. To make promotion programmes more effective, it has developed a network of RMPs. The networks are named "*Tarang* Network" and the members are called "*Tarang* Partners." RMPs, in the absence of MBBS doctors, make good substitutes for treatment and healthcare counselling purposes.

In Bihar, 6,000 villages in 11 districts of the state are covered through a distribution network of 8,000 outlets, 6,400 retailers and 28 stockists. About two area managers, 25 field sales officers and 12 promotion staff played an active role in supporting the promotion and sales. Around 5.8 million condoms and 0.15 million OCPs were marketed.

Similar results were obtained in Jharkhand. Around 5,000 villages in 11 districts were reached through 6,000 outlets, 8,000 retailers and 22 stockists. They were supported by three area managers, 22 field sales officers and 15 promotion staff. The sale of condoms and OCPs were 5.5 million and 0.12 million, respectively.

In Orissa, the project has started off and so far covered three districts and 1,200 villages. About 1,500 outlets have been activated and 600 retailers have been roped in to sell condoms and OCPs. HLL has appointed two area managers, three field sales officers and six promotion staff to carry the project forward. The resulting sales are commendable. About 5.6 million condoms and 0.08 million OCPs were sold.[17]

LESSONS FROM EXPERIENCE

Companies aiming at selling in rural areas have to go one step beyond normal transactional marketing. The marketing mix should be tested in terms of the 4 A's. Acceptable products, affordable prices, accessible purchase points, and awareness-creating promotions are essential. The development of products within an affordable range requires small packs at low price points. The development of products for acceptance may sometimes require overcoming barriers such as water or power scarcity. A shining example is HUL's detergent that requires less water than other detergents. Promotion should aim not only at creating awareness but also at seeking to develop, transform, and involve rural consumers to secure sustainable sales. Designing wider distribution networks and training channel members to reach the consumer are other vital points in creating accessibility to consumers.

Summary

With the mission of adding vitality to life, HUL has developed a product mix that is represented by 35 key brands. The company has marketed them in urban and rural areas through 2,500 redistribution stockists and 6.3 million retail outlets. To woo both the urban and rural markets, HUL has taken the route of CSR and cause branding. Projects that enhance agricultural productivity, water conservation and health care are significant social responsibility initiatives. Lifebuoy *Swasthya Chetna*, Fair & Lovely Foundation and Surf Excel water conservation are the important cause-branding programmes. Rural marketing is facilitated by the rural division, training of rural salesmen and projects like Operation HARVEST, Project *Bharat*, Project Streamline, I-*Shakti* and Project *Shakti*.

CFCL, an agri-input marketer, has wide geographic markets. For effective reach, it has a wide network of distributors, dealers, regional offices and sales personnel. It has about 20,000 village outlets. To promote sales, it has started the *Uttam Bandhan* programme based on the PPP model. Unemployed youth are trained as extension workers. They interact with workers and provide services like soil and water testing, farm education, and alternate sources of employment. A Web site (uttamkrishi.com), a telephone helpline (Hello *Uttam*), mailers and audio-visuals are employed to promote awareness and interest in products.

ITC, a company with a diversified product portfolio, has decided to use information technology to create a competitive business. The social consciousness of the company led to the creation of e-*choupals* (meaning gathering places) for selling products. In course of time it became an e-commerce platform. A *choupal* serves about 6,000 farmers within a radius of 5 km. *Sanchalaks* (mostly middlemen at *mandis*, who can make investments) and *upa-sanchalaks* provide services required for entire farming operations and sales. It is a place where farmers can sell their produce and buy required goods and services. Now 40,000 villages are covered by e-*choupals*. *Choupal saagars*—large shopping complexes containing a procurement centre, retail store, food court, farmer-facility centre and healthcare clinic have been started. About 24 such malls are presently operating. Besides these, there are projects to promote health and education.

CPIL is committed to three core corporate values: caring, global teamwork and continuous improvement. It is a provider of scientifically proven oral-care products with multiple benefits at various price points. Rural areas contribute to 35 per cent of Colgate's sales. Colgate has been ranked as India's number 1 "Most Trusted Brand" across all categories. Having found that rural people do not use oral-care products, the company developed a strategy that involves initiatives such as new product launches, hike in marketing expenditure and targeting schools to create oral awareness among children. It has taken up sales promotion measures such as selling small-volume, low-priced sachets, distribution of free toothbrushes, rural van distribution and participation in local festivals. Colgate–Palmolive has set up one of the widest distribution networks in India. It spans 2.7 million retail outlets across the country, of which the company services 800,000 outlets directly. The educational programmes include campaigns like "Bright Smiles, Bright Futures" and "Oral Health Month," summer camps and libraries.

Hindustan Latex Limited, now christened as HLL Lifecare, is a global giant in the contraceptives market with a market share of nearly 10 per cent worldwide (18 per cent in India). It is committed to innovation and reaching the bottom-of-the-pyramid population in villages. It has rolled out several new products and diversified into manufacturing vaccines and setting up Lifespring hospitals. Hindustan Latex Family Planning Promotion Trust (HLFPPT), a non-profit organization, was promoted to work for the poor and disadvantaged sections of the society. HLFPPT has implemented several social sector projects that aim at bringing about planned social change in family planning and health care. Some of the initiatives of HLL are: mobile health clinic, Merrygold health network, Health Management Information Systems (HMIS), community care centres, and social marketing projects (*Swasthya Gram Pariyojana*, community-based distribution of contraceptives, *Sukha Parivaram* and *Sukhi Sansar*). These initiatives are based on the PPP model.

Short Answer Questions

1. Name the cause-branding initiatives of HUL.
2. Is Project *Shakti* a viable and capable model for selling in rural areas?
3. Evaluate the effectiveness of *Uttam Bandhan* as a sales promotional mechanism of CFCL.
4. What are the significant benefits of e-*choupals* to the farmers? What will be the reaction of middlemen who lose their business due to this?
5. Is Colgate right in targeting children?
6. The task of HLL is removing stigma and ignorance. Hence, it needs a more person-to-person-based education strategy. Do you agree?

Discussion Questions

1. The Project *Shakti* model is expensive and difficult to manage. Instead, companies do well by relying on the transactional model of distribution. Malhotra (Linterland) supports this view by saying, "While Project *Shakti* might have worked for HUL, it is not an established channel. Reasons like relatively high capital investment, gender roles, and taboos could present an upper limit to those sales numbers. I think a hub-and-spoke model of distribution is the future." Discuss.
2. As Adi Godrej, chairman of the Godrej Group, says, "The challenge [for brands] is to understand the [psyche] of the rural consumer, create better distribution, and [appreciate] the heterogeneity." Discuss the validity of this view by referring to the initiatives of HUL, CFCL and Colgate.

Essay Questions

1. Explain the cause-branding initiatives of HUL.
2. Explain the significance of "*Uttam Bandhan*" in the marketing strategy of Chambal Fertilisers.
3. ITC's e-*choupal* signifies how information technology advantage can benefit rural consumers. Explain this business model and its benefits.
4. Colgate has taken the route of educating children and adults. Evaluate the initiatives taken up by Colgate and suggest innovative initiatives.
5. HLL has balanced its social and economic goals in a judicious way. Do you agree? Support your answer with a discussion on the rationale of its projects.
6. Develop a framework of rural marketing based on the experiences of HUL, ITC, CFCL, Colgate and HLL.

Internet Exercises

1. Develop a paper on Coca-Cola's *Parivartan* programme and present it in the classroom.
2. Compile information on Tata Tea's "*Gaon Chalo*" programme and examine its applicability to other competitive firms.

Mini Project

Form a research team of four members. Develop a questionnaire to collect data from FMCGs and agri-input companies on their initiatives to develop, transform, and involve rural consumers to secure sustainable sales. Conduct a survey and report the findings to the class.

End Notes

1. Pradipta Mukherjee, "FMCG Companies Strategize to Extract More from Rural Segments," *Business Standard*, 28 November 2009.
2. R. Ravikumar and Vinay Kamath, "FMCG, Durables Makers on Rain Watch," *The Hindu Business Line*, 22 July 2009.
3. www.hul.co.in, accessed March 2010.
4. Sweta Chhaochharia, "Project Shakti—A Win–win Situation," available at http://ezinearticles.com/?Project-Shakti—A-Win-Win-Situation&id=1245833.
5. Vinay Kamath , "HLL's Shakti to Help Partners in Rural India," *The Hindu Business Line*, 26 April 2003, available at www.blonnet.com/2003/04/26/stories/2003042601370600.htm.
6. "Zuari-Chambal: A Profile," available at www.naukri.com/gpw/chambal/index.htm.
7. "Public–Private–Partnership—Agriculture Extention Services," available at www.chambal-fertilisers.in/pub-Private-Partnership.asp.
8. Rasheeda Bhagat, "Ryot choice," *The Hindu Business Line*, 26 November 2004, available at www.thehindubusinessline.com/life/2004/11/26/stories/2004112600290400.htm.
9. "October is Oral Health Month with a Unique Rural Thrust," available at www.indiaprwire.com/pressrelease/health-care/200710084954.htm.
10. www.colgate.com, accessed March 2010.
11. "Hindustan Latex Rechristened as HLL Lifecare Ltd," *The Economic Times*, 5 March 2009.
12. "Hindustan Latex Plans Rural Hospitals," available at www.projectmonitor.com.
13. Sarita Varma, "Hindustan Latex to Change Name," *The Financial Express*, 19 March 2008.
14. www.hlfppt.org/whatwedohiv.htm, accessed March 2010.
15. "Hindusthan Latex Limited: CSR Activities," available at www.karmayog.org
16. "*Sukhi Parivaram*: A Social Marketing Programme in Andhra Pradesh," available at www.hindlatex.com.
17. www.hlfppt.org/whatwedo.htm, accessed March 2010.

Case 3.1 Biostadt's Big Leap

Biostadt India Ltd believes that "the growth of India is directly related to the growth of the rural areas." Farmers being the central focus of rural India, it becomes necessary to give them a helping hand by providing them with top-of-the-line agricultural inputs and services. The mission statement provides action guidelines in clear terms.

The belief that India's growth is directly related to the growth of rural areas has been the driving force behind the proactive functioning of Biostadt India Ltd. Recognizing the strategic importance of the farming community to the development of the nation, Biostadt has developed its mission, vision and operational systems to serve the cause of agriculture.

Mission and Logo

Biostadt's focus is on the needs of the farmer and it is committed to offer topline agricultural inputs and services to the farming community with care and responsibility, in India and beyond. It seeks to pursue research to evolve innovative, customized biological tools for sustained productivity and supply to develop high-quality seeds, novel crop protection and aquaculture inputs. It seeks to form alliances with business associates to provide one-stop solutions for crop, animal and health care.

Biostadt's corporate logo depicts three birds signifying the company's main goals—speed, growth and team work.

Growth and Products

Biostadt India has been serving the farming community for over two decades. The growth in the business in a span of just 15 years (from Rs 40 million in 1994 to Rs 2 billion in 2008) is encouraging. It is expecting to touch Rs 5 billion by 2012. Its product range includes insecticides, herbicides, fungicides, hybrid seeds, aqua products and farm services. Biostadt offers an extensive range of high-quality products consisting of insecticides, fungicides, hybrid seeds, aqua products and farm services. Biostadt has ventured into many business areas such as biotechnology inputs, crop protection chemicals, hybrid seeds, Biostadt HI-Q seeds, aquaculture inputs and farmer service centres.

Market Competition

The market for agricultural products in India was highly competitive. Biostadt was competing with rivals such as Dupont and UPL, who were well established in the market.

Aastha Clinics

Biostadt Aastha Clinic (BAC) is a commercially viable rural departmental and service mega store initiated by Biostadt India Ltd. These clinics are opened in partnership with young and dynamic rural entrepreneurs who act as the franchisee for the clinic. A detailed study of the problems faced by the farmers revealed a crying need for initiatives in the fields of health care (human and animal) and farm care. In light of this, BAC was started with the aim of working for the welfare of the farming community by providing professional services for farm care, human health care and animal health care along with all necessary inputs and technology. BAC will provide overall facilities and thereby facilitate better productivity in terms of farm yields, which means prosperity for the farm community.

Loyalty Clubs

Loyalty clubs are formed with the objective of developing a closer relationship with valuable customers. Biostadt endeavours to regularly keep the members informed about the new happenings in the field of agriculture and aquaculture across the globe. Suggestions to improve the company's products and services are also invited. Members are provided a unique membership card to receive special benefits/privileges.

Biostadt Retailer's Club

Biostadt Retailer's Club (BRC) is a unique concept designed for Biostadt's business partners, for a holistic growth. It's a platform to relish the company's objectives of speed, teamwork and growth. It provides a win–win situation to steadfast customers to grow and show their loyalty to Biostadt. As a part of this loyalty programme, each one's endeavour is recognized and rewarded. BRC provides a platform to dealer/retailer friends to interact directly with company personnel.

Tie-ups for Sales

Biostadt has tied-up with petrol pumps such as Hindustan Petroleum (HP), Bharat Petroleum (BP), and Indian Oil Company (IOC) to sell its products in rural areas. The initiative brought multiple advantages to the company for creating awareness, sales and customer feedback.

Meetings

Biostadt organizes farmer meetings and dealer meetings in villages. The meetings educate both parties about latest innovations, technologies and methods of improvement. The farmers are also encouraged to ask questions on the use of products or technologies. The company has appointed a field force of 150 trained people for the same. These people are graduates in agriculture and capable of handling queries.

Video on Wheels

Besides educating farmers, Biostadt brought in the element of entertainment to attract more people. It started playing commercial movies in the villages. The whole idea was called the "video on wheels campaign." Not only the farmers but the whole family was invited to watch the movie. The company also played movies regarding the usage of products and the benefits of using them correctly.

Demonstrations

Biostadt gives live demonstrations of its products by using them on crops to convince farmers as well as to show them the right methods of usage. This is an effective method for advertising and promoting their products.

Aquamalls

Biostadt also took another innovative initiative in the form of the "Biostadt aqua mall." The first aqua mall was opened in Andhra Pradesh. It was a branded concept and acted as an exclusive hub for the farmers to not only buy all the aqua products of the company under one roof but also to access "complete farming solutions."

For discussion

1. In the light of the mission of the company, do you think it has taken right and adequate initiatives to promote its products?
2. Outline your action plan to help the company increase its turnover from Rs 2 billion in 2008 to Rs 5 billion by 2012.

Source: www.biostadt.net, accessed March 2010.

Case 3.2 Godrej Focuses on Rural Markets

Godrej Consumer Products Limited (GCPL) is a major player in the Indian FMCG market with presence in personal, hair, household and fabric care categories. It has reported sales of Rs 4.39 billion and a net profit of Rs 0.7 billion in the quarter that ended on 30 June 2009.

Goals and Targets

The company says that it is focused on growth. It estimates that it will have its best year ever in 2009–2010. The growth in the first half of the year will be in terms of price as well as volume. In the second half of 2009–2010, the growth will be largely led by volumes. Currently, revenues from rural India account for 25 per cent of overall revenues and this will increase in the coming years as rural markets are growing at a higher pace than urban markets. In 2001, the rural–urban sales ratio for GCPL was 23:76. At present, rural business accounts for about 38 per cent of GCPL's revenues. Total sales from the rural market is 50 per cent in case of HUL and 60 per cent in the case of Nirma.The company has set itself a target of raising this to 50 to 55 per cent of revenues over the next three years.

FMCG Cell

The company has renewed its emphasis on rural retailing with the formation of the FMCG cell. Hoshedar K. Press, vice-chairman of Godrej Consumer Products (GCPL), says that historically, the company had primarily been an urban Indian brand. "Post the creation of the FMCG cell, we expect to provide an increased thrust to our rural business. Our objective is to first take the share of rural business to the industry average of around 45 per cent and then, raise it to the predominant share of our revenues," said Press. Widening and deepening penetration in rural areas and small towns and expansion of the portfolio of lower-priced stock keeping units have been identified as the two prongs of its growth strategy.

Product Innovations

As part of its strategy to push up revenues, the company plans to introduce a mix of new products and variants of existing brands in the soap and hair colour category. Its soap brands: Cinthol, Godrej FairGlow and Godrej No. 1 contribute to 65 per cent of GCPL's total sales. GCPL enjoys a market share of 32.6 per cent in the hair colour category. The product category represents 21 per cent of GCPL's total sales. Its hair colour brands include Kesh Kala, Renew, ColourSoft and it also has the *mehendi* brand Nupur. The company's rural share in hair colour is higher than the urban share. The case of soaps is exactly the opposite. Action is necessary to boost the sales of soaps in rural areas.

Distribution

GCPL plans to strengthen its rural foothold by strengthening its rural distribution network. "We are planning to double our presence in 8,000 small towns in the next couple of years. We are also looking at increasing our footprint in 50,000 villages compared to the 15,000 villages we are now present in," Dalip Sehgal, MD, GCPL said.

The company is experimenting with a super stockist distribution system in certain rural markets. Joint rural initiatives among group companies have also been kicked off to leverage each others' strengths. For instance, Godrej Agrovet and GCPL are jointly undertaking certain rural activities to explore the growth potential in rural areas. Godrej Agrovet is into the animal feeds business. In 2008–2009, Godrej increased its reach by 200,000 outlets. The company claims that a Godrej product can now be found in 3 million outlets across the length and breadth of the country.

Low-price Packs

GCPL has launched a variants strategy where it has increased its focus on low-unit packs especially at the Rs 5 and Rs 10 price points. The company has also seen the market and demand for these segments expand rapidly.

Promotion

The Godrej group plans to increase its rural reach using regional media, rural *haats*, ads on walls and participation in rural fairs, among other initiatives. GCPL is also planning to spend 35 per cent more in advertising and promotions compared to last year. This amounts to around 9 to 10 per cent of the company's total sales. A large part of its focus is going to be brand building.

New Initiative

The company is working on tapping salons across the country to promote its brands, especially in smaller towns and rural areas. It has plans to rope in up to 50,000 salons and barber shops in semi-urban and rural areas across the country to promote its hair care brands such as Nupur *mehendi* and Expert hair colour. These barber shops and salons would showcase the entire range of hair colour and other products and serve as a point for promoting them. The company will place combipacks of products such as shaving creams, talcum powders, soaps and hair colours in these salons.

For discussion

1. Analyse the situation and goals of GCPL. Are the marketing goals realistic?
2. Evaluate the steps taken by GCPL to reach the targets and suggest improvements.

Source: Priyanka Dasgupta Brahma and Yassir A. Pitalwalla, "Godrej Plans to Increase Revenue From Rural Market," 3 August 2009, available at www.mydigitalfc.com/companies/godrej-plans-increase-revenue-rural-mkt-835; Kakoly Chatterjee, "Godrej to Beef up Rural Distribution," *The Financial Express*, 1 September 2009, available at www.financialexpress.com/news/Godrej-to-beef-up-rural-distribution/509605/.

Part II Insights

4

Rural Consumer Behaviour

LEARNING OBJECTIVES

Upon completion of this chapter, you will be able to:

- Understand the consumer purchase decision-making process and the factors that influence the consumer and its outcomes
- Know the initiatives that a prudent marketer can take to assist the consumer in his decision-making process and thereby gain from his or her behaviour

The lukewarm response for its new tractor has made Mahindra explore opportunities and limitations in the rural hinterland. Investigations have revealed that farmers depend on opinion leaders for more information as well as confirmation of the truth in the claims made by marketers. A series of deliberations on the design and performance of the tractor led the company to identity the root cause of the problem. The problem was in the wrong perceptions of customers about the tractor's hydraulic system. Based on this understanding the company opted for the experiential marketing route that involved presentation and demonstration of information and individual verification. A meeting of villagers, especially the end users and opinion makers, was organized. Wide publicity about the meeting and the venue was made. As a result of this, there was a good response and both the opinion makers and end users attended the meeting in large numbers. Making use of visuals such as graphs and charts, the efficiency of the tractor was demonstrated and doubts about the flows in design were cleared. Product-engineers from the company answered specific questions posed by the audience members and infused confidence in them. Interested farmers tested the tractor by driving it and examining the benefits of the vehicle.

This kind of experiential approach is not limited to industrial products. For instance, FMCG major Marico utilized the services of hair specialists and local beauticians to endorse its hair oil in the Uttar Pradesh hinterland. Dish TV employed *"Manorajan"* vans to go to villages in Maharashtra and TVS Star City conducted aggressive bike contests in Uttar Pradesh, Punjab and Haryana to focus attention on its motorcycles.

"Connecting with people and understanding their needs is very important. Companies too, need to create brand loyalty," said Priya Monga, business head of Delhi-based experiential marketing firm RC&M that specializes in organizing experiential marketing strategies for companies that want to reach a rural audience.[1]

Every marketer soon becomes connected with what excites the consumers most and tries to find ways to direct their behaviour. As the example of Mahindra indicates, hunches and assumptions do not work in rural markets; systematic exploration is necessary. This chapter begins with the consumer purchase process model and then discusses environmental and individual factors that influence the consumer's decision-making process. The implications of these on marketing are also examined.

INTRODUCTION

The consumer is the basic foundation of every business. What the consumer sees, thinks, prefers and buys is of great importance to marketers in order to finetune their marketing offers and achieve high levels of consumer acceptance and satisfaction. The emergence of the rural market as a viable proposition has sparked a new interest among marketers to explore and understand it. Though some Indian giants like HUL, Godrej, Asian Paints and Philips are in the fray, the profiles of rural consumers are still hazy. Gaining an understanding of the rural market composition and behaviour is considered one of the major current challenges.

RURAL CONSUMERS ON THE GROWTH TRACK

Seventy per cent of India's population, 56 per cent of its income, 64 per cent of its expenditure and 33 per cent of its savings come from rural India.

The rural market now accounts for 54 per cent of all Indian FMCG sales, 59 per cent of durables sales, 100 per cent of agri-input sales including tractors, and 10 per cent to 50 per cent of two-wheeler and four-wheeler sales. Consumerism has altered rural buying behaviour in recent years. Studies indicate a slow but determined shift in the use of different categories of products in rural families.[2] There is a remarkable improvement in the kinds of products used.

The shift is from local unbranded products to national branded ones and low-price products to premium ones. The rural population is upgrading from tooth-cleaning charcoal and *neem* stick to toothpowder, toothpastes and toothbrushes and from traditional mosquito repellents to coils and mats. A study made by the Confederation of Indian Industries (CII) observed that among rural consumers, the knowledge that branded goods offer quality is visible. Established "up market" products of brands like P&G, HUL, Nirma and ITC have found loyal customer bases as compared to the situation 20 years back. The spending of rural consumers on both fast moving consumer goods and consumer durables is on the rise.[3]

About 35 per cent of their income is spent on FMCGs. In August 2008, it was reported that the FMCG industry in India was worth USD 16.03 billion and the share of the rural market was about 57 per cent of that. The growth of rural markets, according to a CII study, was reported to be around 20 per cent. In case of consumer durables, the rural market saw 25 per cent annual growth while the urban growth rate ranged between 7 and 10 per cent.

In view of the growth in consumption and consciousness for high-quality, branded goods in the rural markets, future leadership in markets is linked to attaining the lead position in this segment. As such, marketers have to understand the psyche of rural consumers and finetune their products and strategies to reap benefits and gain a competitive edge.[4]

MODEL OF CONSUMER BEHAVIOUR

The key questions that require answers for understanding consumer behaviour and initiating marketing actions are:

- What stimulates a consumer to look for products or services?
- How does the consumer know about products and services that can fulfil his needs?

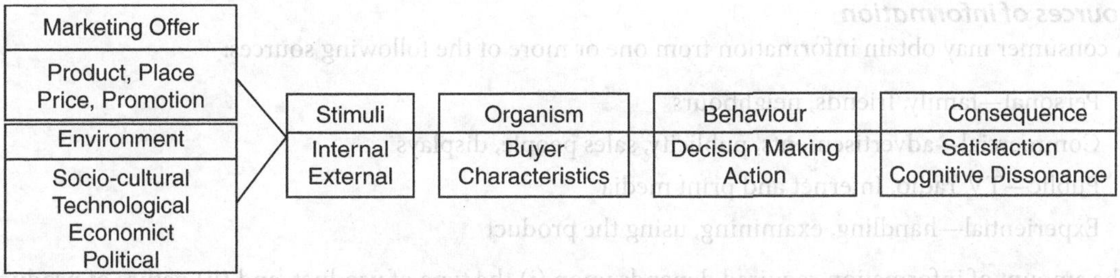

Figure 4.1 Model of Consumer Behaviour

- How do the marketing and environmental factors, along with his personal characteristics, influence the consumer's thinking and his decision-making process?
- How does the buyer take decisions? How does he buy? Where, when and what does he buy?
- How does he consume or use the product or service? What may be his feelings and reactions?

The sequences of all these psychological and physical behaviours in response to marketing and environmental stimuli are portrayed in a model (Figure 4.1). The basic Stimulus–Organism–Behaviour–Consequences (SOBC) model can be adopted to explain consumer behaviour. The model is presented in Figure 4.1.

BUYING DECISION PROCESS

We will try to understand consumer behaviour in the rural context by examining the buying decision process. The buying decision process follows a logical sequence of five steps as shown in Figure 4.2.

Need recognition

The buying process starts when the buyer recognizes a gap between his desired state and the actual state. Such recognition may be caused by stimuli either internal (within oneself) or external (by environment or marketer).

A rural student may feel the need for food (natural phenomenon of hunger) and demand a pizza on observing friends (social comparison) and on being aware of its availability in a nearby place with a discount offer (marketing stimuli). He may enjoy eating it with his friends in style with the feeling that he is one among the trendy, adventurous youth (social environment stimuli) of the day.

Implication for marketers

At this stage, the marketer should help consumers identify their current and future problems and felt or latent needs. To do this, marketers have to research consumer problems and needs and communicate them to the consumer effectively.

Information search

Generally, consumers try to find information pertaining to products that will satisfy their wants in order to make the right choices.

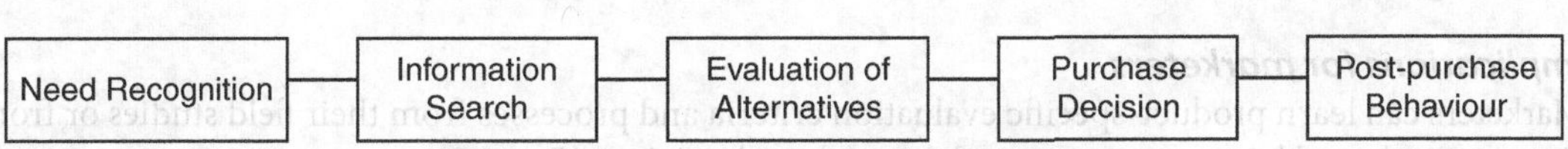

Figure 4.2 Buying Decision Process

Sources of information

A consumer may obtain information from one or more of the following sources:

- Personal—family, friends, neighbours
- Commercial—advertisements, publicity, sales people, displays
- Public—TV, radio, Internet and print media
- Experiential—handling, examining, using the product

The amount of information required depends upon (i) the type of product, and (ii) nature of product.

Type of the product

Products can be classified into two categories as convenience, and shopping or specialty goods. Convenience products are routine purchase FMCGs and require less information relative to shopping goods. The information needs pertain to quality, variety, unique features, longevity, reusability of package, etc. In case of shopping goods, fashion, design, style, durability, performance features like ease, economy, and trouble-free system, will be inquired. Another way of classifying products is based on complexity. High-complex goods like computers, tractors, cameras and refrigerators are high-tech and consumers will look at various sources for information before making a purchase.

Implications for marketers

Search expands with the availability of time. Marketers have to take this aspect into cognizance and design offers to induce immediate buying. Keeping in mind the information needs of consumers, marketers should design communication programmes to reach the consumers and provide adequate and relevant information to them. In view of the low literacy level, audio-visual media become important in rural marketing. TV has been the biggest contributor in bringing consumer awareness in rural India. It is, of course, the traditional marketing methods—demonstrations, displays at fairs and festivals, mobile video vans—that continue to be the marketing man's support system in rural communication strategy. The importance of positive word-of-mouth advertisement need not be overemphasized.

Evaluation of alternatives

How do consumers evaluate the brands that they have come to know and like to consider when making a decision to purchase?

Evaluation process and criteria

The evaluation process varies from product to product depending upon the perceived risk in buying.

- *Convenience goods:* In case of convenience goods (ice creams, soft drinks, toilet soaps, shampoos, edible oils, etc.) that are purchased for one-shot or short-period consumption, the evaluation process will be short and criteria applied are essentially quality and price. Occasionally, the consumer may indulge in impulse buying tempted by the attractiveness of the product or offer. Evaluation will be done carefully, mixing emotional and logical thought processes.
- *Shopping goods:* In case of durables, the evaluation process will be longer, the criteria considered will be functional benefits, operational advantages, maintenance costs and facilities, brand image and social endorsement. In case of clothing and jewellery, views of family members and other social groups, current fashion, price and quality will figure in the list of criteria. Evaluation will be done more carefully and logically. Serious evaluation is found to follow each of the models described in Table 4.1.

Implications for marketers

Marketers can learn product-specific evaluation criteria and processes from their field studies or from surveys conducted by management students and academicians (Box 4.1).

Table 4.1 Evaluation Models

Evaluation model	Criteria application	Application
Expectancy value model	Identifies the attributes necessary. Discusses with others to find the relative importance of each. Arrives at an overall impression of each brand and compares them for choosing the one that scores relatively high among the options.	Motorbike. Considered attributes: style, resale value, fuel economy, pick up, load carrying capacity and fewer maintenance costs and less investment (price). The consumer obtains an overall impression for each brand and then decides.
Lexicographic model	Attributes are arranged in an order of priority. If the first attribute is satisfied, selection is made. If not, the second attribute forms the basis for evaluation.	Let us suppose that the consumer's priority list of attributes is load-bearing capacity, fuel economy, low maintenance costs and price. The consumer chooses one that has high load-bearing capacity. If two options are rated equal on this, the consumer will proceed to the next attribute—fuel economy.
Conjunctive model	A consumer selects a product that satisfies few attributes that he considers important.	For instance, a consumer specifies that price of the product should not be above Rs 55,000 and fuel consumption should not be less than 50 km/litre. The criteria are applied to choose the brand that satisfies them.
Disjunctive model	A brand that has satisfying levels of a chosen attribute will be selected.	For example, if one is interested in buying a motorcycle with high fuel economy, his obvious choice is Hero Honda.

Box 4.1 Studies on the Purchase Process

Saibaba, Ranapratap and Suresh took a sample of 100 consumers aged below 40 years located in Warangal district of Andhra Pradesh and studied their purchase behaviour with reference to two-wheelers. The information sources included advertisements in television (48 per cent), newspapers (28 per cent), magazines (13 per cent) and radio (11 per cent). About 38 per cent of the respondents were influenced by friends, 24 per cent by spouses, 16 per cent by parents and 8 per cent by relatives. The criteria for selection were mileage (44 per cent), price (22 per cent) and driving safety (10 per cent). The consideration set included more than one brand in most cases. About 68.9 per cent considered two brands, 16 per cent considered three brands, and 12 per cent considered four brands. The purchase was made by cash by 50 per cent of the buyers. Only 36 per cent availed of loans from the dealer arranged by a financial company. Reports on performance were positive. The ratings are as follows: excellent (36 per cent), good (21 per cent) and fair (43 per cent).

A similar study with 150 respondents from rural areas in Guntur district, conducted by Seshmohan, Narayana and Ramesh reported the following findings. Need for purchase was

Box 4.1 (Continued)

triggered by oneself in the case of 74 per cent of the respondents. Influence of family was found to be the major factor in case of 21 per cent of the respondents and influence by friends exerted the greatest influence in case of 5 per cent of the respondents. Friends and relatives constituted the major source of information (54 per cent). The major sources of influence in decision making were family members (58 per cent), friends (32 per cent), media (5 per cent) and dealers at showrooms (2 per cent). Approximately 35 per cent of the respondents went alone to make the purchase. About 40 per cent of them were accompanied by friends/relatives. About 57 per cent of them purchased from a showroom in the nearby town. The choice was made based on the following factors: mileage (36 per cent), quality (26 per cent) and design (26 per cent). About 19 per cent of the respondents were dissatisfied and the problems were non-availability of service (12 per cent) and spare parts (5 per cent).

Source: Rudra Saibaba, V. Ranapratap and Vadde Suresh, "Consumer Behaviour Towards Two-Wheelers: A Comparative Study of Rural Urban Consumers of Warangal District (Andhra Pradesh)," *Marketing Master Mind* (April 2008): 63–66; V. V. Seshmohan, M. Narayana, and S. Ramesh, "Understanding Rural Markets: A Competitive Edge in Tapping the Potential in Rural Markets," *Marketing Master Mind* (December 2008): 37–42.

Marketers have to supply information on evaluation criteria and aid in comparison. Advertisements should highlight the unique selling proposition, present role model (farmer for fertilizers or tractors) and a truck driver for engine oil acting wisely in the decision-making situation. Comparative advertisements in newspapers can be helpful to educated consumers and they can act as opinion leaders.

Purchase decision

All the existing brands in the market make a total set. Through information search consumers will become aware of some brands in the total set. Awareness set consists of brands that the consumer is aware of and those that meet the initial buying criteria will be considered for further evaluation. They make up the consideration set. Through application of the final criteria, the consumer evolves his choice set. All the brands in this set are acceptable to the consumer. However, the final choice will be made in favour of one brand. The choice is dependent upon factors influencing the mind of the consumer at this final stage.

For example, a person is interested in buying cement for construction of his house. The marketer should be aware of the place his brand has in the mind of the prospective buyer through the buying process. Table 4.2 illustrates one such typical process with reference to cement brands.

Selection

The factors that influence the final choice are

- Attitude of others (opinion leaders, family members and friends)
- Unanticipated situational factors
- Perceived risk[5]

Table 4.2 Successive Sets Involved in Decision Making

Total set	Awareness set	Consideration set	Choice set	Decision Set
Lanco				
Rasi	Lanco	Lanco		
Nagarjuna	Rasi	Nagarjuna	Lanco	
L&T	Nagarjuna	Rasi	Rasi	Lanco
Zuari	L&T			
Ramco				

The attitudes of others may change the intentions of the decision maker when:

- The other person's views are important to the decision maker and he likes to comply with his advice, and
- The other person has a strong negative attitude towards a chosen brand.

Unanticipated situational factors can be anything like a vendor closing down the shutters of his factory and offering products at heavy discounts, unexpected rains or diseases damaging the crop, introduction of a new brand with tempting offers by a marketer, etc.

Perceived risk is influenced by several factors as shown in Table 4.3. Perceived risk is high when individual products and situational factors influence the thinking process of the consumer.

How does a consumer reduce perceived risk and anxiety? Here are some simple approaches that are followed by intelligent consumers.

- Developing purchase routines
- Decision making by groups

Table 4.3 Perceived Risk Factors

Factors	Description
Personal factors	Lack of self-confidence, information gathered is thought to be inadequate or less accurate
Product factors	Highly complex, high-tech product
Information availability and certainty	Less informed because there is no previous experience of using the product. Also advertisements, demonstrations, and published material (brochures and leaflets) are not very informative. Less certainty because there are many competitive brands with significant differences
Financial factors	High price, investment and operational costs are considerable, it cannot be disposed off without any difficulty and financial loss
Situational factors	Emergency in purchase

- Consulting experts or elderly people
- More information gathering
- Preferring reputed brands or brands with warranties or guarantees

Perceived risk is high among rural consumers because they find it difficult to gather and process information. In view of this, they make collective decisions. As a result, there are single brand villages (Mahindra tractor villages).

Implementation

Finally, purchase decision involves the following questions

- From which dealer to buy the product? In general, agri-inputs are purchased from local dealers, *mandis*, e-*choupals*, and village fairs. FMCGs are purchased from retail outlets, *Shakti Ammas*, door-to-door sales persons, petrol bunks and weekly markets. Durables are bought from nearby towns or *haats*.
- What quantity to buy? The quantity of agri-inputs will be decided based on farm holding and type of crop. The quantity of convenience goods is based on the family budget and the nature of income (daily, weekly or monthly).
- Buy when? The frequency of purchase in case of FMCGs varies from daily to monthly. Durables are purchased when farm income is obtained or at the time of festivals. Agri-inputs are purchased during the farming season.
- Which payment mode to choose? Rural consumers, in most cases, prefer cash purchases. Generally, they take loans for agriculture and prefer to buy land, real estate, gold and durables from their savings.

Implications for marketers

Marketers in this stage encounter a consumer who has made a decision and is about to implement it at the opportune time. The consumer needs moral support to go ahead with his decision. Perceived risk can be reduced by assurance through ads (messages like No. 1 in the market, endorsements of consumers who purchased it, etc.), establishing service centres at nearby locations and personal-selling tactics. Support of social-group members can be won by tie-ups with NGOs and farm advisory agencies, retailer training, and sales persons visiting opinion leaders.

Post-purchase behaviour

Marketers should know the answers to the following:

- What are the feelings of the buyer after buying and using the product?
- What are his reactions when satisfied? When dissatisfied?
- How does he dispose of the product after use?

Post-purchase feelings

A buyer feels satisfied when the perceived product performance is close to his/her expectations. If it exceeds expectation, the customer is delighted. If it falls short of expectations, the customer is disappointed. Then, he develops cognitive dissonance.

Reactions

There are two options for the customer. One is the voice option and the other is the buy option. When messages are transmitted orally from person to person about a product, it is called word-of-mouth advertising (WoMA). This is favourable for the product when the customer is satisfied. The customer spreads good news about the product in the neighbourhood and among his friends and relatives when he is delighted with what he is using. Also, he will repeat the purchase and become loyal to the brand. On the other hand, a dissatisfied customer will create unfavourable WoMA and exercise exit options. He stops buying the product further. Rural consumers are outspoken and like sharing information with others. News of performance failure spreads fast throughout the village.

Disposal

Consumers dispose off the product for several reasons. In case of consumables, disposal may occur as follows.

1. Without using the product fully, it is disposed when they do not like it. They may throw it away or give it away to a neighbour or friend who likes to use it.
2. After using the product fully, the container is disposed. If possible, they may refill it with the same or different product. When it cannot be reused, they throw it away. This may cause environmental pollution problems. For example, sanitary napkins, polybags, disposable glasses, plates, etc.
3. In case of durables, disposal may take place when the decision to replace it is taken. Replacement decision arises when the product has functional value but the consumer prefers to substitute it with a new one of the same brand or a different brand or with an entirely new product. For example, a TVS moped owner may buy a new vehicle of the same brand or change the brand to buy a Kinetic Luna or opt to purchase a new product—maybe Bajaj scooter. The consumer is concerned about resale opportunities and resale price of durables.

Implications for marketers

What can a marketer do to make consumers feel favourably towards the organization? A few guidelines are stated here.

1. Marketers should take proper care in developing expectations of the consumers. Product claims should neither understate nor overstate the performance or characteristics of the product.
2. Marketers may initiate one or more of the following actions to increase the level of satisfaction.
   - Congratulating customers for purchasing the product either by a personal letter or by an advertisement.
   - Informing customers about the size of sales and number of satisfied customers.
   - Educating customers about the proper use of the product to receive better performance and explaining any new usage option.
   - Setting up a customer-grievances cell for speedy redressal of customer grievances.
   - Ensuring timely servicing of products either as per given service schedule or based on customer calls.

ENVIRONMENTAL FACTORS INFLUENCING THE DECISION-MAKING PROCESS

The rural consumer is a member of the society and is influenced by factors in the broad sociocultural–technological–economic–political environment (STEP). The precise questions before us are:

- How do the environmental factors influence consumer behaviour?
- What are the implications for marketing managers?

Socio-cultural factors

Culture

It includes forms of behaviour, norms, beliefs, values and customs that are shared by a society and are transmitted from one generation to the next.

- *Collective processes:* Many rural purchases require collective social sanction. This is unheard of in the urban areas. Wisdom of the elders, suggestions of the leaders and advice of the educated are sought with high regard by rural consumers.
- *Values:* Rural consumers value social conformance in their decisions. As they live in communities, they prefer to have social sanction for their actions. That is why there are brand villages—Escort villages, Nirma villages, etc. Simplicity, honesty, unity and hard work are some the important values cherished in villages.
- *Customs and traditions:* Buying decisions are highly influenced by social customs, traditions and beliefs. Feeding the poor on occasions such as festivals, birthdays or death anniversaries, exchanging gifts between brothers and sisters on the day of Rakhee, celebration of marriage, pregnancy and birth, etc. and celebration of temple festivals are common in rural areas. Belief in religion and worship, belief in the marriage system and spousal responsibilities and belief in the joint family system for the care of children and elderly parents are values practised in the rural areas.
- *Social norms:* Norms influencing individuals are more visible. Norms like "respect elders," "save for the future," "don't lend or borrow," "rendering service to humanity is service to God," "be simple and honest," etc. guide the decisions of rural consumers.
- *Caste:* The influence of casteism is direct and strong. Certain caste groups are forced to locate their houses in the outskirts of villages. Elections and other political activities are mostly caste based. The concept of "caste gods" and *jatras* are prevalent in traditional rural areas.

Implications for marketers

As rural consumers are conservative in their outlook, they take a longer time to be influenced. They do not make quick decisions. They discuss the issue of purchase with other villagers and the headman. Decision making is thus a collective and time-consuming process. However, the rural youth are more open to fresh concepts unlike their elderly family members. They are better educated and have aspirations similar to those of the youth in urban India. The different traditional ceremonies and social norms can be regarded as opportunities to sell products such as garments, food items, gifts, and prayer materials. Festivals offer business for food products, fruits, vegetables, worship material and provide occasions for purchase of consumer durables. Norms of simplicity and honesty require marketers to be open and honest in their product communications and bargains.

Social class

Rural consumers are heterogeneous based on their incomes.

Members of the low-income group mainly buy essential commodities such as food, clothing and shelter.

The middle-income group members venture into buying the following—sewing machines, two-wheelers, TV, mixer–grinders and refrigerators. The rural consumer is more interested in purchasing income-yielding assets like a sewing machine for starting a business, a two-wheeler that is a work companion, or a piece of land that can be tilled. He upgrades his consumption to buy better, premium and expensive goods slowly, after moving to the next income level. The members of the upper middle-income groups are the seekers of a wide spectrum of goods. They look for close substitutes of premium products. The rich indulge in conspicuous consumption and are easy targets for the marketers of premium products.

Implications for marketers

Marketers hope that villagers will use their money to improve their lifestyle rather than to buy assets like gold and jewellery. The challenge is to make them spend on consumables. This is a tough task given that both rural and urban consumers demand value-for-money products. The upper- and middle-class segments of rural markets are positively responding to the stimuli offered by marketers of branded premium products. Thanks to the advent of satellite television and cable network across the country, the rural populace has been exposed to the quality of life (QOL) of urban households. This increased awareness has induced an attraction for premium, quality products that are popular with urban households.

Group

The formation of groups is a natural social phenomenon. Every individual will have membership of more than one group. Interests in education, friendship, sports and games, cultural activities, etc. stimulate individuals to form and join groups. Rural people live in small communities detached from the mainstream of urban life. As a result, they are able to forge close-knit relationships largely within the community. Rural micro-finance organizations identified the strength of these relationships and started using them to build peer pressure to ensure low default rates. The self-help groups operate based on the principle of "collective responsibility." Groups are classified as given below.

Associated groups

They are the groups to which a consumer belongs as a member. Two types of associated groups are briefly explained here.

- *Primary groups:* They are informal groups to which the consumer belongs. The interaction is regular and influential. For example, family, friends and neighbours.
- *Secondary groups:* They are formal groups such as offices, political groups and self-help groups. In Andhra Pradesh the youth are members of self-help groups called *Yuvasakthi* groups and women are members of DWACRA (Development of Women and Children in Rural Areas) groups. Interactions are mostly formal.

Reference groups

These are aspirational groups that serve as guide posts for shaping the attitudes and behaviours of consumers. For instance, sports teams and cultural associations can be reference groups for the rural youth. Reference groups exercise influence in different ways. Reference group influencec can take three forms as given under.

- *Informational influence:* When fellow members use a product, the consumer may simply decide to try the product. For instance, a farmer may decide to buy a fertilizer brand because other farmers are buying it.
- *Normative influence:* Also referred to as utilitarian influence, it occurs when an individual buys in accordance with the norms of social groups with which the consumer has strong ties. A rural youth wears jeans to fit in with the youth group.
- *Identification influence:* It is also called value-expressive influence. It is observed when a consumer buys in accordance with the values of the group to which he belongs. For instance, farmers buy seeds, fertilizers and pesticides to meet occupational requirements in accordance with the farming standards.

Opinion leaders

People, who by virtue of their competence or acceptability wield influence on others, are regarded as opinion leaders. They are well informed and reliable in their opinions. As such, opinion seekers and followers value their opinion. In a village, an opinion leader can be, a *sarpanch*, a teacher, a bank manager, a village development officer, a doctor, a *mandal* youth extension officer or a social worker.

Implications for marketers

Marketers can make use of group dynamics to influence consumers, to spot opinion leaders and encourage word-of-mouth advertising for their products or services. Positive word of mouth (WoM) is sometimes even more powerful than advertising in the mass media. It is, therefore, important for marketers to understand the rural social structure, the hierarchy, the sources of influence, and the flows of information. They should be able to find answers to the following questions:

Who can be the appropriate person to provide evaluative judgements on products and services to consumer groups in rural villages? Who can help the company in the brand diffusion process? Who will buy first and lead others in the product- or service-adoption process? It is found that rural youth are tech savvy and they are the early adopters of products and services that feature new technology. Consider mobile phones and motor bikes. Obviously, it is the youth who can appreciate and talk about them. In case of healthcare products, doctors or social workers can be the right choice. Colgate tapped into school teachers to reach kids through its "Bright Smiles, Bright Futures" programme.

Family

Family is an important organization of consumers in rural markets. Purchase decisions are significantly influenced by family orientation and size and roles played by members.

Family orientation

A person acquires an orientation towards religion, politics, and economics and a sense of personal ambition, self-worth, and love from one's parents. Family orientation is strong in rural areas. Children shape their values and perceptions by observing and socializing with their parents.

Family size

It is a known fact that the quantity of consumables varies with family size. Industry observers are increasingly realizing that at times, purchase of durables has nothing to do with income, but more to do with the size of the family. This is where rural India with its joint family structures becomes an attractive proposition.

Family as a buying unit

Family members play different roles in purchase decisions. The structure of Indian families has been previously characterized as joint families with traditional sex–role orientation (SRO), i.e. the husband predominated in all family affairs. However, owing to influences from the West and socio-economic development, the structure of Indian families has changed to nuclear or extended families (nuclear families plus grandparents). Indian families have become more modern in SRO, such that decision making has become more egalitarian. The power sharing systems in different purchase situations is as given under.

- Husband: Dominant in choosing life insurance, automobiles, television
- Wife: Dominant in choosing washing machines, room furniture, kitchenware
- Equal: Housing, outside entertainment

The voice of children is heard and their preferences are considered with affection and love. Children exercise substantial influence in the purchase of toys, confectionery items, ice creams and story books. They influence the choice of colour, size and shape in case of durables. Older children may educate parents on the utility aspects of consumer durables and influence final brand choices by virtue of their education and exposure.

Implications for marketers

The marketer has to know family sizes and needs to determine the structure of influence in decision making. An understanding of the different roles played by different members in the purchase of products is to be gained to target promotional communication to the right members.

Role and status

Every person is a member of more than one group or organization. In each one of them, the individual has a role and status. Role refers to the behaviour expected of the individual as a member of the group. Status refers to the place given to the individual because of his or her position or achievements. It reflects the general esteem given to him/her by society.

In Indian families, the husband has to play the role of the caretaker for his wife, children and parents. In the process, he is expected to be the chief/sole earner of the family. He is awarded high status within the family group and he will make key decisions such as the purchase of durables and sometimes even consumables.

Status is either ascribed (given by birth) or achieved (earned by virtue of achievements). By birth, one may belong to a high caste or rich family of landlords and hold high status in society. Such people may buy and use premier products to reflect their status. A person may gain high status by means of his education and job (only engineers or doctors in the village). A *sarpanch* and head master enjoy a higher status in a village—people trust them and expect them to be exemplary. Accordingly, they try to make sound purchase decisions and provide rational advice to the people who seek their opinions.

Implications for marketers

The status and roles of consumers is of interest to marketers. Since status and roles are positively correlated in the context of both family and society, marketers address their communication to the key persons after having identified them. In case of demonstrations and personal selling, the key persons are contacted and involved.

Asian Paints understood this concept very well. To promote the *Utsav* range during the pre-Diwali season, company salesmen selected the opinion leaders in villages and painted the village post office or library or the house of the *mukhiya* to demonstrate that the paint does not peel off. Moreover, the salesmen organized meets at the local dealers where the village painters were invited.

The HUL sales person organizes meetings taking the help of *Shakti Ammas* in villages, sets up contests and involves the key persons in the village.

Sociability

In rural areas, individuals are known and identified by their first names. Rural folk like interacting with as many people as possible. The following observations can be made in case of social interactions.

- There are more frequent interactions between the same people.
- The richness of interaction is limited.

The reason is that their exposure to people and information is less. Today, we find politicians, NGOs, social workers, students of rural development programmes, National Social Service (NSS) volunteers, government officials, *anganwadi* workers and other interested persons making a beeline for villages. The new access to information provided by the television, Internet and newspapers have an impact on the sociability of villagers. With villages opening up to information, significant changes in personality and community relationships are observed.

Implications for marketers

The limited sociability of villagers has resulted in poor brand communication and low preferences for branded products. The marketer has to find out the level of sociability of villages.

High-sociability villages (generally the corridor and accessible villages) can be treated as urban-like markets with environmental constraints, if any (like fluoride water, poor fertility of soil, etc).

Low-sociability villages are located at a distance from towns or are remote villages. They must be reached by a company through its sales force or persons who go to those villages.

Companies like HUL and Colgate have educational programmes for villagers to create brand awareness. The *Shakti Vani* Programme educates rural communities about basic health practices. Rural women are appointed as *Vanis* (communicators) and trained to communicate in social fora such as schools and village get-togethers. The *Vani* programme covers topics such as pre- and post-natal care, infant nutrition, sanitation, good hygiene practices, and the prevention of common diseases.

Gender mainstreaming

In India "gender mainstreaming" has become a major programme on the anvil of the Government, NGOs and some corporate enterprises. There has been a spate of legislation, statutes and government policies that are targeted at it. It is also a fact that mere legislation and government schemes do not lead to change. The "solution providers" are democracy, education and economic self-sufficiency. It is education that creates an awareness of women's rights and economic self-sufficiency establishes them. Respect from a male-dominated society comes grudgingly with economic self-sufficiency. HUL's *Shakti* project is an income-generating project for women and contributes to gender mainstreaming. Box 4.2 presents the emerging opportunities for HIV service providers in the context of gender mainstreaming.

Box 4.2 Strategies for Gender-equitable HIV Services

The emergence of HIV in rural India has the potential to heighten gender inequity in a context where women already suffer significant health disparities. Recent Indian health policies provide new opportunities to identify and implement gender-equitable rural HIV services. Potential strategies for gender-equitable HIV services in rural India are responses to the following three questions: (1) What gender-specific patient needs should be addressed for gender-equitable HIV testing and care? (2) What do healthcare providers need to deliver for HIV services with gender equity? (3) How should institutions enforce and sustain gender-equitable HIV services?

Strategies including gender-specific HIV testing and care services would directly address current gender-specific patient needs. Rural care providers urgently need training in gender sensitivity and HIV-related communication and clinical skills. To enforce and sustain gender equity, multi-sectoral institutions must establish gender-equitable medical workplaces, interdisciplinary HIV services partnerships, and oversight methods, including analysis of gender-disaggregated data. A gender-equitable approach to rural India's rapidly evolving HIV services programmes could serve as a foundation for gender equity in the overall healthcare system.

Source: Gita Sinha, David H. Peters and Robert C. Bollinger, "Strategies for Gender-equitable HIV Services in Rural India," available at www.heapol.oxfordjournals.org/cgi/content/full/czp004v.

Implications for marketers

Gender mainstreaming has two implications for marketers:

- Marketing strategies require focusing on this social goal along with other competing goals like environmental protection.
- Marketers should be ready to offer products and services to the market in which women have an egalitarian role in decision making and where they possess purchasing power to buy products of their choices.

Technological factors

Technology has an impact on the occupations and lifestyles of rural people. Occupations such as agriculture, dairy, poultry and animal husbandry have become more productive and profitable. Table 4.4 shows the effects of new technology on products.

New technology has boosted the income of rural folk. It has reduced the drudgery of manual work. It has saved both time and energy and has made farm work acceptable even to the educated youth.

Biotechnology developments

The Indian Government's vision for biotechnology development highlights the need for agricultural biotechnology and the potential it bears for India's growth. Farmers want biotechnologically enhanced crops because they reduce costs and increase productivity. Monsanto, which is committed to serving farmers, sees technology as a driver for future growth in agriculture.

Digital and satellite technologies

Digital and satellite technology has created new sophisticated communication channels and better audio-visual equipments. FM radios, TVs, video cameras and cameras have become part of the rural world, making life more pleasant.

Information and communication technology (ICT) revolution

Today, there are over 15 million villagers in India who are aware of the Internet and over 300,000 villagers have used it! Ten years back, history was created with Public Call Office (PCO) phone booths (essentially, manually operated payphone facilities) opening in every corner of the country. The existing 600,000 PCOs in India will soon be transformed into public "tele-info-centres" offering a variety of multimedia information services. Rural consumers spend time and money to access higher-level information.

Web connectivity through various types of communication hubs is impacting the currency of information exchange. Today's rural environment is characterized by "information access" to education opportunities, exam results, career counselling, job opportunities, government schemes and services, health and legal advice and services, worldwide news and information, land records, *mandi*

Table 4.4 Technology Changes Life

Aspect	Traditional	Modern
Agriculture	Bullock cart, low-yield seeds, conventional manure	Tractors, harvesters, high-yielding seeds, pesticides, fertilizers, pump sets, motors, generators
Lifestyle	*Neem* sticks, bicycles, post cards	Toothpaste, two-wheelers, mobile phones

prices, weather forecasts, bank loans and livelihood options. Communication technology (PCOs, mobiles, and e-mails) has improved exposure to various product and services.

Implications for marketers

The impact of the technological factors can be seen in many ways:

- Competition is based on innovation and value-plus offers. It involves more competition with regard to features other than price. From bare-bone economy models to deluxe, expensive ones, all have to be offered to meet the demand from consumers of different income levels.
- High-tech media available for communications is fast, clear and colourful in imparting information about a product and its usage situations.
- Consumers are better informed and are in a position to make choices.

Economic factors

Economic factors such as inflation/recession, growth in industrial and service economy, competition and increasing supply of goods and services, have considerable influence on individual purchase decisions.

Impact of globalization

The impact of globalization is felt in rural India as much as in urban areas, although it is slow. It has its effect on target groups like farmers, the youth and women. Farmers today, "keep in touch" with the latest information and maximize both productivity and farm incomes. Animal feed producers no longer look only at Andhra Pradesh or Karnataka. They keep their cell phones constantly connected to global markets. In fact, price movements and availability of products in the international market place seem to drive their local business strategies. On the youth, the impact is on knowledge and information while in the case of women it still depends on the socio-economic aspect.

Influence of competition

The market structure consists of MNCs and corporate enterprises in the organized sector and small players in the unorganized sectors. While some of the local products (Nirma washing powder in its beginnings, Ghadi detergent) compete effectively by offering value-for-money products, there are fake brands that vitiate the market. Healthy competition leads to the rise of rural consumerism in the following ways:

- *Increase in choice options:* Wide range of products/brands as well as services are available to consumers with different features at different prices.
- *Availability of information:* Firms are luring consumers with informative and persuasive advertisements and this has reduced the perceived risk in buying products.
- *Availability of retail outlets:* The competitive firms are spreading their distribution networks to reach the rural areas in innovative ways. As a result, the rural consumer has more retail outlets to choose from.
- *Intentional or unintentional purchase of fake products:* Fake products are sometimes purchased intentionally as they are available at lower prices and are also perceived to have a certain degree of reliability. Examples include spare parts, fancy goods and toys. Unintentional purchases occur when rural people fail to distinguish between the genuine product and a fake one because of the limited information provided by the packaging (colour, visuals, size, etc.) of the product. The retailer is a silent observer, if not an active promoter, since he gets a larger profit on selling the counterfeits. This gives scope for counterfeit products to eat into the market share of quality brands. For this reason we find, brands such as "Jifeboy," "Bonds Talcum," "Funny & Lovely," etc. in rural markets.

Influence of recession

Recession has a global impact on urban areas. On the other hand, rural India is set to witness an economic boom with the per capita income having grown by 50 per cent over the last 10 years. This is mainly on account of rising commodity prices and improved productivity. Rural buying of FMCG products, consumer durables, mobiles and two-wheelers has remained buoyant over the past year, even amid the slowdown. This is the effect of easier credit, increased sources of non-farm income in rural areas and stepped-up public spending on infrastructure and employment schemes such as the National Rural Employment Guarantee Scheme (NREGS).

Impact of inflation

Inflation has an impact on consumer spending and choices. During inflationary times, people shift to buying sachets of their preferred brands. One expects the consumer to buy low-priced substitutes when prices increase. But the consumer does not switch to cheaper substitutes. Companies then come out with lower quantity Stock Keeping Units (SKUs) and make consumers switch from higher to lower SKUs. This prevents a shift from premium to popular brands. For example, instead of increasing the price of their Henkel detergent (500 g) from Rs 46 to Rs 50, Henkel has launched a new SKU of 400 g for Rs 40. Others include Wipro, which has offered a 45 g soap at Rs 6, replacing the 100 g pack at Rs 10, and 425 g Pril at Rs 50 (500 g at Rs 55).

Availability of micro-credit

Insurance companies, global software firms and financial services majors are tapping rural areas for micro-finance opportunities. The Indian micro-finance market is now estimated at Rs 600 billion and market demand for micro-credit is over Rs 500 billion.

A recently-released report by Associated Chambers of Commerce and Industry of India (ASSOCHAM) emphasizes the potential of roping in 200 million rural investors by financial institutions (FIs) and insurance companies to provide agriculture, housing, personal and education loans and easy insurance schemes at affordable rates.

Implications on marketers

Consumers now have access to information and product choices. Offering value-for-money brands and services is important. Marketers can utilize mobiles and the Internet to communicate messages to consumers on a one-to-one basis and motivate them to buy their products. Fake products are a threat as the consumers who buy them by mistake may lose confidence in the original brand. A war on counterfeits is necessary to safeguard the interests of consumers and companies. It will be safer for brands to have different pack sizes at different price points to attract consumers from different categories. This will also help to retain the customers during periods of inflation and recession. Financial-services companies have opportunities to tap rural investors to make them buy their services and this will have a positive effect on sales of consumer durables.

Political factors

The philosophy and the decisions of the ruling party and the thinking of rival parties greatly influence the fortunes of rural people. The governments at the centre and state levels are, by and large, helpful to rural people. However, in the development plans so far, the urbanites have benefited more than the rural people. A clear emphasis on the development and protection of rural folk is found in recent plans and development programmes.

Development

The Union Budget 2009 announced a massive Rs 3,250 billion target for agricultural credit, a Rs 391 billion allocation for the NREGS (up by 144 per cent over last year) and liberal increases on rural infrastructure schemes such as Accelerated Irrigation Benefit Programme (a 75 per cent increase) and

Bharat Nirman (a 45 per cent increase) for 2009–2010. This indicates that rural consumption may continue to benefit from the trickle-down effect of all this largesse.

Protection

There are legislations that protect the interests of consumers. Consumers can redress their grievances by taking advantage of the Consumer Protection Act, 1986.

Implications for marketers

Marketers can take advantage of the government schemes. Various central and state government agencies, including those of the governments of Andhra Pradesh, Karnataka, Madhya Pradesh, Chhatisgarh, Uttar Pradesh and Orissa have extended support to Project *Shakti* of HUL. Over 300 NGOs are actively involved in the project. Companies have to educate rural consumers on their rights and the legal protection available to them. They have to organize and promote consumer relationship programmes.

BUYER CHARACTERISTICS

The characteristics of the buyer that affect the buying process include:

- Age and lifecycle stage
- Occupation
- Economic situation
- Lifestyle
- Personality and self-concept
- Psychological factors

Age and lifecycle stage

Buying is influenced by the age and lifecycle stages of people. Table 4.5 indicates consumption patterns by age and lifecycle stages.

Children—favoured consumers

India is being touted as the largest kids-segment market in the world with sectors such as apparel, FMCGs, games, gizmos and toys contributing towards its growth. The Rs 200 billion kids market

Table 4.5 Consumption by Age and Lifecycle Stage

Age	Lifecycle stage	Products
Up to 12	Child	Baby foods, diapers, baby toilet soaps and shampoos, toothpaste, toys, slate, books, pencils, noodles, confectionery items, Vicks Vaporub, Woodwards gripe water, etc.
13 to 19	Teenage	Two-wheelers, cycles, gym and yoga services,
20 to 40	Young	Readymade garments, cell phones, motorbikes, computers, Internet facilities, TVs, sports magazines, services for communication skills and for appearing in competitive examinations
40 to 60	Middle-aged	Credit cards, bank accounts, etc.
Above 60	Old	Books, periodicals, TV, medicines, old-age homes, etc.

is expected to grow at the rate of 25 per cent per annum. Johnson & Johnson is among the leading companies that has products made especially for kids. In recent years, Colgate has introduced a gel toothpaste for kids that comes in two variants with fruity bubble gum flavours—Tweety in bright pink and Bugs Bunny in bright blue. HUL introduced Pepsodent Barbie, Pepsodent Superman and Pepsodent Tom and Jerry. GlaxoSmithkline (GSK) announced the launch of Junior Horlicks Biscuits for toddlers. Dabur has launched Junior Chyawanprash for children.

Children as decision makers

Traditionally, women were seen to be the purchasing agents for the family. Nonetheless, increasing participation of women in the workforce has prompted a shift in this role as children are increasingly the "buyers" for the entire family. Even in families where women do not work, children have been observed sharing this role with their mothers. Children enjoy greater discretion not only in making routine consumption decisions for the family but also in pestering their parents to buy other products desired by them. Contemporary researchers express that children constitute a major consumer market, with direct purchasing power for snacks and sweets, and indirect purchasing influence on big-ticket items. Children have recently attracted considerable attention from marketers because the market for children's products offers tremendous potential (pegged at Rs 50 billion) and because it is rapidly growing. According to available industry data, the chocolate and confectionary market is estimated to be at Rs 13 billion, the apparel market at Rs 4.8 billion and kid's footwear at Rs 10 billion.

Implications for marketers

Marketers traditionally address their campaigns at mothers, who are the primary caregivers of children. Tips are given occasionally on how to take care of babies and growing children who do not eat, who soil their clothes, and who lack in the abilities to excel. So the product communication is mostly educative and illustrative. In most of the cases the model is an expressive child. The same approach may be adopted by marketers in future.

The youth—the liberated consumers

About 40 per cent of all those graduating from colleges fall in the category of the urban youth. They are not very different in education, exposure, attitude and aspirations from their counterparts at least in smaller cities and town. The key characteristics of the youth are[6]:

- They have urban exposure and brand knowledge
- They are users of the Internet
- They are consumption oriented (exposed to western thinking of "earn now and spend now")
- They are ambitious and enterprising
- They like freedom and independence

Implications for marketers

Marketers are increasingly focusing their campaigns on youth-centric messages and throwing up challenges requiring youth involvement. So the product communication is delivered at the ground level in a challenging manner by staying on an "edutainment path."

Occupation

Evidently, the goods and services bought by a person are influenced by the occupation of the individual. A farmer buys a tractor and a carpenter buys a hacksaw. People who work in fields buy shirts and dhoties while those who work in offices wear shirts and trousers.

Implications for marketers

A study of occupational needs provides an understanding of the range of products required. Marketers can make offers tailored to the needs of specific consumers.

Economic situation

The purchasing power of an individual is the prime consideration for marketers. If the disposable income of an individual is high, obviously, he or she can buy a number of popular goods or a few expensive ones. The Max-NCAER India Financial Protection Survey, 2008, has estimated that the average household income per annum in rural areas is Rs 51,922. Of this 77.6 per cent is allotted to expenditure and the reaming for savings. About 55.4 per cent of the routine expenditure is for food and other consumption items. Savings are influenced by reasons like meeting emergencies, education of children, old-age funds, social ceremonies, purchase of house and gifts, pilgrimage, etc.

The rural economy is basically savings oriented due to uncertainty and the long gap in realizing agricultural income. In recent times, due to availability of more financing sources/options, consumers can be influenced to make purchase decisions with little effort. Some of the possible measures influencing consumers in recent times are easy and low down payment, credit card purchase, zero per cent interest loan schemes and the active role of both commercial and foreign banks in coming out with more special programmes due to liberalized economic conditions.

Implications for marketers

Marketers have to find the income sensitivity of the goods and services they offer and make decisions like:

- Offering low-priced pack sizes
- Pricing the goods moderately
- Offering instalment purchase schemes
- Giving heavy discounts or incentive goods with purchases

Today, sachets of shampoos, toothpastes, hair oils, skin creams, cough syrups and several other products tap the vast rural market. The small unit purchasing is convenient to rural people who are mostly daily-wage earners. Sellers of durable products may entice rural consumers by offering easy instalment schemes.

Lifestyle

Lifestyle is a person's pattern of living. The pattern of living is determined by the activities, interests and opinions (AIO) of people.

Activities: Work, hobbies, shopping, social events, etc.
Interests : Food, fashion, family, recreation, etc.
Opinions: About self, society, government, business, etc.

Different researchers have identified different lifestyle patterns. One way of lifestyle classification is by dividing into categories of trendsetters, traditionalists and chameleons. The classification given by NCAER (National Council for Applied Economic Research) lists the categories as destitutes, aspirants, climbers, consuming class and the very rich. A separate classification suggested for women is—a capable homemaker, a career women and a free spirit. Expressions like "quality of life" and "lifestyle" have become popular among the youth and enterprising adults. Responsibility for this goes to: (i) the media, especially the TV channels that publicize lifestyles from all over the world through serials and anchored programmes and (ii) corporations that have roped in celebrities from sports and the film industry. As a result, some of the values communicated among urban and rural people are:

- *Egalitarianism:* Working women deserve support from their husbands in household chores. They should be partners in decision making.
- *Dignity of work:* Household chores can be made pleasant by the use of gadgets. Any family member can do any kind of work.

- *Pleasant looks:* Grooming is important not only for women but also for men. Fairness is not a woman's prerogative alone. Men can also aspire for it.
- *Enthusiasm in life:* We need the sprit of adventure to make our lives more interesting. Food, shopping and work—everything should heighten the spirits of individuals.
- *Physical fitness:* This has become a new wave of interest. Gymming, yoga, naturopathy and ayurveda have become major areas of interest.

Implications for marketers

Obviously, marketers who have understood the present psyche of consumers are busy developing lifestyle products and brand communications to convey one or more of the above-mentioned values. The market for reasonably-priced home appliances, fashion products and grooming centres (hair salons are already adding beauty parlour services for males), quality food items in small packs and natural food supplements is on the rise.

Personality and self-concept

Personality refers to the unique psychological characteristics that lead to relatively consistent and lasting responses to one's own environment. To relate personality to the products people purchase, there are two aspects to be considered—the situation and the person. When in a social gathering, the youth prefer to buy cigarettes, *pan masala*, tea, coffee or cold drinks, etc. While travelling, people prefer to buy mineral water bottles or sachets, food packets, etc. Given the situation, the response patterns vary from individual to individual. A conservative person may offer tea, whereas a jovial, hedonistic type may buy Pepsi for his friends. A person who is not very social will prefer drinking tea standing alone at a corner tea stall.

Implications for marketers

Modern marketers are increasingly concerned about matching products to the perceived self-personality of the individual. For example, take two-wheelers. One can match the personality of a brand and consumer as shown in Table 4.6.

Psychological factors

The three psychological factors that help describe what goes on in the minds of consumers also have influence on his decision making. They are:

- Perception
- Cognition
- Motivation

Table 4.6 Personality of Brand and Consumer

Brand name	Brand personality	Consumer personality
Yamaha	Rugged, dominating, youthful indulgent and vain	Dominating, youthful, highly indulgent and sociable. They are opinion leaders.
TVS-Suzuki	Rational, colourful, youthful, rugged and relaxed	Takes it easy, colourful but not flashy, mature, complex people
Hero Honda	Thrifty, dominating, contemporary and less rugged	Rational, complex, liberal and balanced individual

Source: Subroto Sen Gupta, *Branding Positioning* (New Delhi: Tata McGraw-Hill, 1999), p. 121.

Perception

Perception is the process by which people select, organize and interpret information to form meaningful pictures of the object. Consumers buy products or services that they perceive favourably. The success of brands like Lifebuoy (hard working) and Boost (energetic) is based on positive perceptions. Brand perceptions are also confusing sometimes (see Box 4.3).

It is important to know the three sub-processes in perception—selective attention, selective distortion and selective retention.

- *Selective attention:* People pay attention to things that they consider to be of value.
- *Selective distortion:* People interpret information to support what they already believe.
- *Selective retention:* People remember what, in their view, is supportive to their beliefs and attitudes.

Implications for marketers

Perceptions create impressions that can later be modified by cognitive learning processes. However, the first impression is the best impression. Therefore, marketers should try to create positive impressions by designing products and brand communications properly. Brand images will have a lasting impact on the mind of consumers. As such, decisions like product design, package design, brand name, ad copy and execution, retail choices and display should be consumer-centric.

Cognition and learning

Cognition is the process of information gathering and processing. It results in learning and creation of knowledge and attitudes. It rationalizes emotional thinking and modifies beliefs and faiths.

Box 4.3 It's All in the Perception

Henko failed in Maharashtra because the name sounds like "Hey Nako," which means "No," giving the brand a negative connotation in Marathi. Dabur's health toothpowder containing *tulsi* failed. The use of toothpowder involves spitting. Spitting *tulsi* was considered a sacrilege in the rural areas. Mahindra with its MAXX model passenger car offered metallic colours, an aluminium footstep and an elegant spare wheel cover for the rural market based on an interesting observation. In rural India, cars are generally rented out for functions and ceremonies. The usage pattern necessitates the grandeur that is offered by MAXX with the aluminium footstep, colours and the spare wheel cover. Also the seating can be increased to include 7, 9 or 10 passengers. The success of Cadbury's biscuit, ChocoBix, is based on the popular view of mothers that biscuits are healthy. In some parts of Uttar Pradesh, there is a popular brand of gripe water called "*daei jee ki 112 saal purani ghutti.*" Positioning a product with "daei ji" in focus is a big positive. In rural India "*Daei ji*" or the mid-wife takes the dual role of acting as the gynaecologist and the paediatrician till the child becomes 1 to 2 years old. Moreover, villagers believe in heritage and hence, the 112 years mentioned in the positioning statement adds strength to the perception.

Source: Arun Sri Ram, available at www.markthemarket.blogspot.com.

- *Knowledge helps make decisions*

  If people are educated and intelligent, they learn even complex things quickly. They can develop awareness of product availability, product features, technological advancements, etc. They will be at ease even when making complex purchases.

  The majority of rural people are less educated. There are even illiterate people. What are the consequences of this?

  (i) Learning is slow and step by step.
  (ii) Medium of communication is non-verbal (pictures, diagrams, and human actions).
  (iii) Subject is simple and not abstract.
  (iv) Presentation is in local dialect.
  (v) Learning is by experience—through consumption or hands-on experience.

- *Beliefs and attitudes*

  A belief is a descriptive thought that a person holds about anything. Beliefs may be based on knowledge, opinion, faith or emotion. A rural buyer of a watch holds the belief: "Heavy watches are good in quality, durability and reliability."

  Attitude describes a person's relatively consistent evaluations, feelings and tendencies towards an object or idea. It has thus, three components:

- Cognitive—information evaluation and inference (rational intelligence)
- Cognitive—emotional feelings (emotional intelligence)
- Behaviour—disposition to do or not to do something (action orientation)

Rural consumers have a set of attitudes that influence their purchases. A few of them are:

- Functionality is more important than style and frills.
- Economy can be ensured by making multiple uses of a product
- The difference between local brands and corporate brands is not worthy of consideration. Any product is ok.

Implications for marketers

Marketers should be aware of the learning abilities, beliefs and attitudes of their consumers to make their offers understandable and acceptable.

Brand names should be simple and packaging should be identifiable with a specific colour or mascot. A rural consumer may not be able to read but would say "*Parle ka glucose biscuit dena*" or would recognize the pack by its yellow stripes and the Parle baby. Even in big villages and *kasbas,* consumers refer to Nirma as the *peela* (yellow) powder.

Beliefs, once formed, become emotional and are difficult to change. Brand-image building exercises aim at creating positive beliefs about brands and companies. Marketers design economy products with fewer frills when consumer attitudes lean towards functionality. For example, Cadbury's ChocoBix, a chocolate flavoured biscuit, is based on the consumer insight that rural mothers opt to buy biscuits rather than chocolates for their children.

The attitude towards economic use led to creative application of a product. Godrej black hair dyes were used on buffaloes in Raichur so as to give them a presentable look in the village *haats*. Tractors are used for cultivation, transportation of goods and conveyance of family members.

The prevalence of brand indifference makes fighting copycats difficult. Marketers have to educate the rural consumer on the potential dangers of using fake products and guide them to identify the right products.

Motivation

Motivation is a process of creating motives. A motive is defined as "an inner urge that moves or prompts an action." Motivation to purchase a product becomes positive when the product corresponds to a need or a motive that needs to be satisfied. The motivation becomes stronger and leads to high involvement when such satisfaction is very important to the consumer.

Motives are many

Abraham Maslow propounded a need hierarchy theory of motivation. According to it, individuals have a spectrum of needs placed at five different levels in terms of priority. The need hierarchy and the corresponding product hierarchy of a typical farmer may be as shown in Figure 4.3.

1. Products and services that are basic for living functions: Agricultural implements, pumps, tube wells, bullock cart, fertilizers, seeds, pesticides, houses, marriages.
2. Products that improve productivity and minimize disturbances: Tractors, harvesters, cycles, two-wheelers, insurance, banking.
3. Products and services that give leisure and make leisure a pleasure.
   - Entertainment equipments: Transistors, two-in-ones, televisions.
   - Kitchen appliances: Gas ovens, pressure cookers, mixers, grinders.
4. Products and services that enhance the standard of life and boost self-esteem: Convenience durables like refrigerators, coolers, washing machines, jeeps.
5. Products and services that help realize life's dreams: *Krishi Pandit* Award.

Involvement

It refers to the amount of interest, degree of application of mind and level of engagement in an activity by an individual. It means to obtain end results through a proper engagement process. The degree of buyer involvement (high and low) depends not only on interest in need satisfaction but also on the degree of differences among brands (significant and not). Buying behaviours can be classified as under.

- High involvement behaviours—complex buying behaviour and dissonance reducing behaviour.
- Low involvement behaviours—variety-seeking buying behaviour and habitual buying behaviour

The four types of behaviour are explained in the next section.

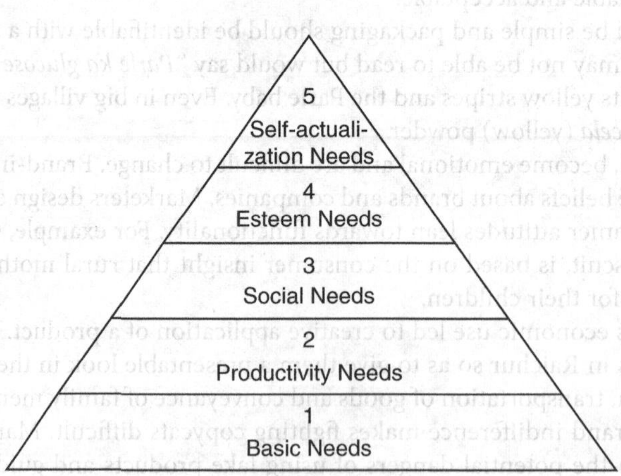

Figure 4.3 Need and Product Hierarchy

Satisfaction

Satisfaction is the result of securing basic benefits attached with a consumers' purchase with reference to "form utility" (design, colour, dimensions, and other features of the product), "place utility" (product availability in desired place), "time utility" (product availability at desired time) and "possession utility" (position of ownership, service guarantees). Besides, according to the acquisition–transaction utility theory, two types of utilities are associated with consumer purchase: acquisition utility and transaction utility. Acquisition utility represents the perceived economic gain or loss associated with a purchase and it is a function of product utility and purchase price. Transaction utility concerns the perceived pleasure or displeasure associated with the financial aspect of the purchase and it is determined by the difference between the internal reference price and the purchase price.

Implications for marketers

Marketers find opportunities to offer products and services that correspond to the needs of consumers. Marketing communication should draw the attention and arouse the interest of consumers. It should also help consumers make purchase decisions by informative and persuasive advertisements, demonstrations and service and product guarantees. An understanding of the satisfaction levels and the causes for dissatisfaction is a must for continuing relationships and generating good WOMA. Marketers have to focus on after-sales service and CRM programmes to create satisfied customers and promote repeat sales.

BUYING BEHAVIOUR PATTERNS

As mentioned above, buying behaviour can be explained based on two factors:

(a) Degree of involvement
(b) Time spent

Degree of involvement

Buyers exhibit different patterns of behaviour in purchasing different types of products and services. They buy cigarettes, *pan masala*, salt, toothpaste, etc. at a nearby shop and do not deliberate much on the characteristics of the product. It is more or less an individual decision taken in a short time. As such, these are referred to as convenience goods. In the case of durables, people visit different shops, take the opinion of many people, evaluate the product characteristics and benefits, check their own financial position and search for schemes of financing or instalment-payment opportunities and then decide their options. These goods are accordingly referred to as shopping goods.

Why do consumers show different patterns of behaviours? The answer is—perceived risk. Buyer involvement is high when the perceived risk is high and vice-versa. Assael[7] distinguished four types of buying behaviour based on the two parameters as shown in Table 4.7.

- Degree of buyer involvement (high and low)
- Degree of differences among brands (significant and not)

Table 4.7 Types of Buying Behaviour

Differences among brands	Involvement levels	
	High	Low
Significant	Complex	Variety seeking
Few	Dissonance reducing	Habitual

Complex buying behaviour

This is seen in case of products such as computers, refrigerators and automobiles. Marketers should initiate the following actions:

- Help consumers learn about the product, its attributes, uses and benefits through detailed ads and exhibitions.
- Make a comparative analysis of features and benefits of products in the print media.
- Train and motivate sales personnel. They can effectively make prospects aware of and interested in products.
- Generate word-of-mouth advertising and influence opinion leaders.

In the rural setting, demonstrations, opinion leadership and trained retail sales persons will be more effective as the literacy levels of consumers are low.

Dissonance reducing behaviour

Products like carpets and furniture are expensive; however, the products of different manufacturers have few differences. However, the consumer is involved because these are products that reflect their social status and their style. The appearance and performance will be talked about and may result in either delight or dissonance. The buyer rationalizes the purchase by identifying certain attributes and uses them as a defence to reduce the dissonance.

Marketers should be smart enough to be aware of the probable arguments in favour of and against a product. On what grounds may the product be appreciated or discounted? Marketers should make their products and offer them with the right amount of logical information using this knowledge. Ads released frequently providing supporting information will reinforce confidence and win the marketer loyal and satisfied customers.

Habitual buying behaviour

Products like salt, wheat, noodles, cigarettes, and *pan masala* are low involvement items with low cost. They are frequently purchased. The consumer is not really bothered about which brand he uses. He will generally ask for the product and not the brand. Some may ask for a specific brand. However, when the preferred brand is not available, they will ask for another brand. They do not postpone the purchase and take the trouble of going to another shop. They buy whatever is available. In such cases, there is a lack of strong brand consciousness.

The question, therefore, is how to convert low involvement products into high involvement ones? How to make consumers brand conscious? Differentiated marketing serves the purpose. The attack can be on two fronts: rational and emotional.

1. *Rational:* Making a rational appeal and raising the consciousness levels of individuals. It may relate to the composition or benefit of the product. Examples: Kissan Annapurna fortified wheat; Horlicks with calcium; Medimix—an ayurvedic beauty soap; Pepsodent 2-in-1 action.
2. *Emotional:* Associating the brand with individual emotions like love, fear, jealousy and wisdom. Examples: Saffola—health of husband; Wills—made for each other.

Variety seeking behaviour

This can be seen in cases where purchasing is less expensive and frequent. Products have significant differences. There exist a good number of brands with different attributes and benefits. For example, confectionery items, ice creams and tourist places. A consumer prefers to buy different items of the same brand or different brands to experience a different sight, smell, sound, touch and taste. Brand switching occurs because of the desire to try out a different variety of the product and not because of the dissatisfaction arising out of the use of a product. Here, the marketer has to take care of three things:

1. *Availability:* Make the products available at different outlets. Avoid stock-outs.
2. *Attraction:* Make products more attractive by offering incentives, advertising as lifestyle products and creating point-of-purchase promotions.
3. *Variety:* Provide a range of variety on a competitive basis. For instance, ice cream marketers such as Quality and Lazza offer a good variety of flavours in different sizes.

Amount of time spent

Purchase behaviour can be classified as given below by the nature of purchase action.

- Planned buying
- Emergency buying
- Impulse buying

Planned

Purchase is budgeted and scheduled in advance. The purchases as such, are well-thought out and predetermined. For example, buying computers, cameras and even provisions for the month are planned.

Emergency

Purchase is made in a hurry to avoid stock-out situations. For example, buying provisions that may be out of stock in a rush; buying an electric bulb in the night when the lamp fails, are examples of this kind of buying.

Impulse

Purchase is made spontaneously, amused or bewitched by a product item, or by taking a decision on the spot without verifying the rationality of the purchase. For example, one may buy a novelty item though its price is high just because it is attractive. Such purchases may include handicrafts, ice creams, sauces, jams, toilet soaps, fairness creams, energy tabs, textiles and garments.

BRAND LOYALTY

Consolidated Coffee Ltd opines, "Brand cynics are growing in urban areas while brands are being looked upon as reliable and trusted in rural markets." Many MNC brands that have long since vanished from shop shelves across the world can still be found in rural India, indicating the longevity of brands once they are adopted. However, the view that the urban consumer is fickle and the rural counterpart is not appears to become weak and unreliable over the years.

Brand loyalty is the consumer's commitment to repurchase the brand and they often help in a lot of positive word-of-mouth advertising for the brand. The brand loyalty found in rural areas is not that kind of commitment; it can be referred to as brand stickiness. Brand stickiness is the repurchase behaviour shown by customers due to the following reasons.

- *First impression:* In rural markets the pioneer creates a lasting impression. The loyalty to such brands is higher.

- *Lack of alternatives:* Many companies have not ventured into rural areas. The entry of a new brand in the rural market is a difficult proposition. The major problem is brand stickiness of rural retailers. The entry strategy should aim at (i) creating shelf space for the product (the retailer may not provide this easily, especially when the existing brand is doing well) and (ii) establishing a symbiotic relationship with him.
- *Perceived risk:* A rural consumer does not easily switch brands due to the fear associated with trying a new brand.
- *Collective decisions:* Belonging to relatively closed societies, rural consumers are slower to adopt new brands and categories than their urban counterparts.

Understanding the difference between loyalty and stickiness, marketers should carefully decode spurious loyalty from actual loyalty and work towards ensuring that customers are not sticking to the brand but are actually loyal to it. In today's highly competitive market; however, the ever increasing range of products available makes establishing brand loyalty easier said than done.

The lesson—it's tough to enter the market, but it's definitely tougher to win over the rural customer for a lifetime.

INNOVATION ADOPTION

As new products are placed in the market, buyers show different degrees of readiness to adopt them. The five adopter groups identified by Rogers[8] along with their probable percentage of consumers are given in Table 4.8.

Innovation adoption, which is typical consumer behaviour, depends on the innovativeness of consumers, the influence of other people and the adoptability of the product. Innovativeness, as Rogers observes is associated with the venturesome; they are willing to try new ideas. Generally speaking, in rural areas the youth exposed to urban life, the students, the white collar employees and a few of the efficient persons in different occupations form the innovative groups exercising personal influence on others. They are the leaders and promoters of innovative products, ideas and services. The adaptability of the product is another important factor influencing innovation adoption. It depends on the characteristics explained in Table 4.9.

Table 4.8 Innovation–adoption Categories

Time lag in adoption	Groups	Percentage	Probable consumer
No	Innovator	2.5	A farmer, better educated and more efficient
Very less	Early adopter	13.5	An educated and efficiency-conscious farmer with adequate resources
Less	Early majority	34	A hesitant but adaptive farmer with moderate resources
Large	Late majority	34	A traditional and less efficient farmer with moderate resources
Very large	Laggards	16	A traditional and less efficient farmer with meagre resources

Table 4.9 Innovator Characteristics

Characteristics	Description
Relative advantage	The degree to which the new product is superior to the existing one
Compatibility	The degree to which the new product matches with values and expectations
Simplicity	The degree to which the new product is relatively easy to use
Divisibility	The degree to which the new product can be tried on a limited basis
Communicability	The degree to which the benefits can be made known to consumers
Affordability	The degree of economy in initial outlay and maintenance costs
Social approval	The degree to which it will gain social or community acceptance

Summary

An understanding of consumer behaviour is essential for formulating marketing strategies. However, information about rural consumers is limited and hazy due to the lack of competence, partial approach, limited knowledge and bias of corporate managers. The model of consumer behaviour comprises stimuli, both internal and external, which include individual characteristics as well as socio-cultural, technological, economic and political factors. In the rural milieu, social customs and sanctions, caste factor, temporary occupations, difficulty in accounting incomes, influence of development groups and opinion leaders such as teachers, *pradhans*, group leaders act as generators of stimuli. A few other factors that provide stimuli include size of the family, status (leader, elected politician, teacher, etc.), sociability, latest technology products and government policies and programmes.

Evidently, buyer characteristics influence purchases. Some of these characteristics are age and lifecycle stage (needs for chocolates or house), occupation (need for a hacksaw or a pen), economic situation (affordability of small packs or large family packs), lifestyle (choosing career-related products or domestic products), personality (buying a dominating Yamaha or a take-it-easy Hero Honda) and psychological factors such as perception (sexuality is a private thing), cognition (linear learning), beliefs and attitudes (function is important, not features) and motivation (hierarchical system of products).

The buying decision process is universal. However, certain differences are found between rural and urban consumers owing to the limitation of information sources (reach of TV is restricted, literacy levels are rising) and limited evaluation capabilities (low learning capabilities). Buyer-evaluation procedures that urbanites usually employ are also employed by rural people but in a less systematic way.

The buying patterns like habitual buying behaviour (*beedi*, soda, salt, etc.), variety-seeking behaviour (ice creams), dissonance reducing behaviour (a mixer or wet grinder that others bought) and complex buying behaviour (a tractor or TV after several discussions with the *pradhan*, teachers, neighbours, field officers, etc.) are visible in rural areas. Further, planned buying (TV), emergency buying (medicines, animal feeds) and impulse buying (clothing, cosmetics) are also observed among rural folk.

Rural buyers are not brand loyalists as they were supposed to be. With improved exposure, increased learning, greater socialization and availability of products they are now becoming comparable to their urban counterparts. Innovation–adoption analysis shows that the politically powerful (*sarpanch*, village development officer) and the educated (teacher, bank officer, school/college educated youth) are among the adopters of innovation.

Short Answer Questions

1. Why do marketers require the knowledge of consumer behaviour?
2. Draw a model of consumer behaviour.
3. Discuss the influence of the marketing offer in creating stimuli among rural people.

Discussion Questions

1. Develop consumer behaviour models for the following products.
(a) Tractors (b) Toothpaste (c) Food products
2. Discuss the purchase processes and suitable marketing actions in case of the following products.
(a) Agricultural implements (b) Pressure cookers
3. Is purchasing always a well thought out, rational process? Can there be impulse buying? Discuss.

Essay Questions

1. Explain the purchase process of consumers. How do marketers shape the decision of consumers at different stages of the process?
2. Discuss the changes in consumer behaviour in response to environmental changes.
3. How do you explain the differences in consumer behaviour based on individual characteristics?
4. "Rural consumers are brand loyal." Evaluate the statement and examine the innovation adoptability of rural consumers.

Internet Exercise

Visit the Web sites of 10 selected companies (five consumables and five durables) and examine their product offerings from the point of view of consumer needs. Are companies guided by the marketing concept or the product concept?

Mini Projects

1. Design a questionnaire and conduct a survey in rural areas to understand consumer behaviour with respect to one consumer durable of your choice.
2. Conduct a focus group study to know the purchase preferences of housewives with respect to detergents.
3. Interview young men and women to know about their lifestyles and aspirations.
4. Visit households in villages, close to the towns and remote ones, and prepare a report on purchases for children (below 6 years) in households of different income groups.

End Notes

1. Bindu D. Menon, "Conducting Field Studies," *The Hindu Business Line*, 29 November 2007, available at http://www.blonnet.com/catalyst/2007/11/29/stories/2007112950020100.htm.
2. "Paradigm Shift in Rural Buying Pattern: CII study," *Business Standard*, 25 November 2009, available at www.business-standard.com/india/news/paradigm-shift-in-rural-buying-pattern-cii-study/20/28/376231/.
3. S. John Manoj Raj and P. Selvaraj, "Social Changes and the Growth of Indian Rural Market: An Invitation to FMCG Sector," available at http://dspace.iimk.ac.in/bitstream/2259/381/1/103-110.pdf.; D. Ashok, "Consumers' Purchasing Pattern in Liberalised Market—A Study on the Household Durable Products," available at dspace.iimk.ac.in/bitstream/2259/322/1/627-639.pdf.
4. "Why the Rural Market is Different," available at www.wpp.com.
5. Richard A. Ashley, "Understanding Your Customer's Perceived Risk," available at www.hort.uconn.edu/agmarketing/distlrnarticles/percrisk.htm.
6. "Rural Youth—A Feature in Event Faqs," June 2009, available at www.anugrahmadison.com/news.html.
7. Henry Assael, *Consumer Behaviour and Marketing Action* (Boston: Kent Publishing Company, 1987), p. 87.
8. Everett M. Rogers, *Diffusion of Innovations* (New York: Free Press, 1962).

Case 4.1 Know Your Consumer and Innovate

CavinKare's success story started with the great idea of launching Chik shampoo in sachets at a low price of 50 paise, and then going on to introduce Meera, Nyle, Spinz, Indica and Fairever, one by one—all based on the understanding of consumer behaviour.

Market Analysis

In 1983, when CavinKare decided to launch its first product—Chik shampoo—the shampoo market had over 200 players with HUL being the market leader with its Clinic Plus brand that was positioned as a health shampoo. Multinational companies sold products in big bottles and not in sachets and they sold only from fancy stores. They did not look at the small *kirana* stores, nor did they look at the rural market.

Consumer Research

CavinKare found that many rural consumers were using bathing soap to wash their hair. The company field force found the reasons—the rural consumer had not heard of soaps damaging hair, and in any case, hair had been washed by soaps for generations. Interestingly, the rural consumer was aware that shampoos cleansed hair better, but the product was expensive at Rs 2 per sachet. Given that India has a tropical climate round the year, women find it hard to maintain the softness and shine of their hair. They often complain about tangled hair. Based on these identified needs and problems, CavinKare conceptualized the 50 paise Chik shampoo.

The research and development team was entrusted with the task of finding a solution to this nagging problem. It came up with a unique formula—Active Double Conditioners.

Targeting and Marketing

Chik Shampoo has targeted both girls and women in rural and semi-urban India.

It used innovative sachet packing and a sachet was priced at Re 1 and 50 paise. When Chik entered the market, Velvette Shampoo was being marketed aggressively by Godrej.

Brand Communication

The new product was launched with extensive communication targeted at the rural and semi-urban masses. It showcased the possibility of soft and manageable hair. The girl in the commercial treated her hair with Chik shampoo and untangled her hair with a single motion of running her fingers through her hair. The advertisement communicated confidence and style along with ease in managing hair. As a result, the communication cut across all social groups.

Sales Promotion

An incentive exchange scheme—"five sachets of any shampoo for a Chik shampoo sachet, free"—was introduced. Later, it was altered. This exchange scheme was introduced to increase the patronage of Chik. With this, consumers started asking only for Chik sachets and sales showed a considerable rise.

Expansion for Growth

Today, among the rural and semi-urban population of India, Chik is the preferred daily shampoo, being the second-largest selling shampoo. The brand has gained the confidence of its consumers and become a household name by catering to their continuously evolving requirements and preferences. The company delighted customers with a range of four refreshing fragrances—Chik Black, Chik Jasmine, Chik Egg and Chik Cool. Further, the company expanded its market share with the introduction of bottles sized at 60 ml, 120 ml, 250 ml and 500 ml. Its new variant, Chik Anti Dandruff Shampoo, contains climbazole and lemon extracts that act on dandruff and itching caused by dandruff.

Meera Herbal Powder

Shaw Wallace had introduced a herbal product; however, it was marketed very poorly. CavinKare introduced Meera Herbal powder and topped the market by gaining 95 per cent market share within six months of launching.

Spinz—The Poor Man's Perfume

Good perfumes came at a huge price and were beyond the means of ordinary people. So the company came out with a Rs 10 Spinz pack.

Fairever

In 1997, the company saw a huge demand for fairness creams. However, Fair & Lovely had a very strong market presence. Research indicates that when a product is good, consumers do not shift to a new brand. However, the company went on to launch Fairever. It contains saffron, which is traditionally used to acquire a fair complexion.

Ruchi Pickles

Food is a huge market. The company decided to make an entry into it and launched Ruchi pickles in sachets. It became number one there too.

The New Initiative

The overall market for shampoos in India is estimated to be at Rs 20 billion a year. The popular segment, where Chik Satin has been positioned, commands an estimated 25 per cent of this market. According to a CavinKare executive, 75 per cent of Chik's sales come from the rural market, while its competitors in the industry sell only 52 per cent of their shampoo brands in the rural markets. In the Indian shampoo market, where sachet (7 ml) format accounts for 75 per cent of the total sales, Chik has been bringing in 90 per cent of its sales in this format.

With new players and new marketing strategies, the shampoo market has become hyper-active and intensely competitive. As a leader in key southern markets, the company has decided to prove its acumen in the bottled shampoo segment. Affluent customers comprise the target market and the competitors are HUL's Clinic Plus and Sunsilk brands. Currently, Chik is being sold in the sachet format, positioned as an economy brand consumed largely in the rural market. Entering the new market segment that Chik is targeting requires changing the image as well. CavinKare's Executive Director, Ramesh Viswanathan, said, "Chik Satin is not a premium or niche segment product. It is slightly higher in the value chain."

For discussion

1. What, in your view, are the key contributing factors to the success of CavinKare?
2. Is the company right in launching Chik Satin—an upward extension? Substantiate your answer by (i) profiling target consumers and their expectations and (ii) probable reactions of its current and potential consumers.

Source: www.cavinkare.com/chikshampoo.html; "Branding Strategies: Chik Shampoo," available at http://strategicbrand.blogspot.com/2007/06/branding-strategies-chik-shampoo.html; S. Kalyana Ramanathan, "CavinKare to take on HUL, ITC in Bottled Shampoo Biz," *Business Standard*, 17 September 2008, available at www.business-standard.com/india/news/cavinkare-to-takehul-itc-in-bottled-shampoo-biz/334627/.

Case 4.2 Caring for One and All

Walk into any small eatery in the southern and eastern parts of the country and you will find it hard to miss the bottle of Horlicks at the cash counter. Horlicks is not a young brand—it has been around for decades. Horlicks' market share of the Rs 2.305 billion milk beverages market is above 50 per cent. The brand that was worth around Rs 8 billion in the early years of the decade, is today 50 per cent bigger at close to Rs 12 billion, bringing in the bulk of the company's annual turnover of Rs 15.8 billion. Rivals know beating Horlicks in the market place is a tough act. Nestlè has stopped making Milo and new entrant Dabur India has decided to stay clear of Horlicks and pitch its Chyawan Junior against GSK Consumer Healthcare's other beverage brand, Boost.

Consumer-centric Products

GSK Consumer Healthcare has decided to use the image of the brand to get into new categories. Zubair Ahmed, managing director maintains, "These categories are relevant and our research shows that consumers need these products. We are not creating needs, we're simply fulfilling them." Recently, it launched biscuits for children, a nutrition drink for women, an energy bar and chilled milk. "We're riding the equity of Horlicks and supplementing it with consumer insights," says Ahmed.

Value-for-Money Positioning

What has worked in the company's favour, says Anand Ramanathan, an analyst with audit and consulting firm KPMG Advisory Services is Horlicks' value-for-money positioning. "Horlicks may not be a cheap product but it's been communicated as a value-for-money product. Parents today are willing to spend more on nutrition for their children and that has helped GSK Consumer Healthcare."

To that extent, Horlicks may have gained over competitors such as Complan that are perceived to be more expensive, a perception that hasn't changed over time. Says Zubair Ahmed, "Compared to competitors, Horlicks is the best value-for-money proposition. Moreover, the consumer gets value for the money spent." For the new launches too, he has in mind a similar value proposition, though final prices will be fixed keeping in mind the target group. "Women's Horlicks is far more expensive than the base Horlicks but that's because the consumer is getting much more and there's no other similar product available. Horlicks Nutribars will be primarily a metro phenomenon to start with, so the pricing has been decided accordingly."

In the late 1990s, market research showed that Horlicks was seen "as a nourishing but boring drink" and it was beginning to lose significance. What's more, consumers were beginning to prefer flavours over nutrients.

So, in 2003, the brand was revamped. It was made tastier and launched in two new flavours—vanilla and honey. The company had earlier launched a chocolate version to try and win over consumers in the North and West who typically prefer chocolate-flavoured drinks. However, the success was limited.

After the 2003 repositioning, the company felt the need for a more direct engagement with the kids and not through their mothers. "We had to acknowledge that today's kids know what they want to drink," observes a company representative. From that day, children became the primary target and mothers became the secondary target for Horlicks. It also led to the genesis of the "*Pran Chanchal*" (livewire children) concept that marked a clear communication divide between Junior Horlicks and general Horlicks.

Meanwhile, the second strategy for staying ahead of the competition was to expand Horlicks' equity in the health food drink (HFD) category in relation to other "solid" nourishment categories such as biscuits, cereal bars and the ready-to-drink milk categories. According to Shubhajit Sen, executive vice-president, marketing, GSKCH, "We realized that there was a clear gap in the market for a biscuit specially designed for toddlers." The outcome was Junior Horlicks biscuits. Fortified with vitamins (B1, B2 and Niacin) and containing no added flavours or artificial preservatives, these are targeted at children between two and five years of age and come in five animal shapes and two variants—chocolate and butter. The product is priced at Rs 10 and Rs 35 for 35 g and 125 g packs, respectively.

The new product launches continued. GlaxoSmithKline Consumer Healthcare (GSKCH) India introduced four new products in three months—Eno Mausambi, Junior Horlicks Biscuits, Horlicks NutriBar and Chilldoodh—the last two marking the company's entry into two new categories, the Rs 0.08 to 0.01 billion cereal bar market and the Rs 0.4 billion ready-to-drink milk category, where Amul and Nestlè control 25 per cent to 30 per cent share, according to various market sources.

The NutriBar, launched in February 2009, has an edge. It reportedly packs in 11 vital nutrients and iron while contributing just 114 calories—an ideal snack for weight-conscious adults. This is currently being hawked in three flavours—Choco Crispy (30 g for Rs 15), Cereal n' Milk (30 g for Rs 15) and Nuts n' Raisins (30 g for Rs 18).

Chilldoodh in 200 ml packs, priced at Rs 17, is also fortified with vitamins and calcium and is set to be sold in modern retail formats, self-service stores and stand-alone fruit juice centres. It is available in four flavours—Choco Dude, Café Stud, Kesar Punk and Yo Mango.

"The idea is to address all age groups. There's Horlicks Lite for the elderly who often have a sugar problem and for the youth we have Horlicks Nutribar positioned on the twin planks of health and convenience," says Ahmed.

Horlicks has, for the first time, tapped the bottom-of-the-pyramid market with a new sub-brand—Horlicks Asha. To lure the price-sensitive, mass consumer, its price is about 40 per cent cheaper than the mainstream brand. While regular Horlicks costs Rs 135 for 500 g, the cheaper variant, Asha, is priced at Rs 85. Rural markets already contribute 30 to 35 per cent to GSKCH's sales. Calling the rural market "absolutely critical" for the company, Shubhajit Sen said that GSKCH has hinged its rural strategy on two aspects—low-unit packs (90 g sachets of Boost, and biscuits at Rs 5) and products tailored for rural consumers, Horlicks Asha being an example.

Reaching the Target Market

Horlicks does not feel the need for a brand ambassador. The ad budget is over Rs 1.94 billion. The radio, through which Horlicks reached out to mothers even 40 years ago, is still an effective channel in states such as Bihar or Orissa where consumers don't have access to television or where power cuts are frequent. In the early years, mothers were the sole target audience since the product catered to the entire family. However, once pester power became big in the 1990s, the advertisements of Horlicks started talking to children too. The change worked because it was also the time when mothers' mindsets were changing—they had become more indulgent and let children drink what they liked, rather than imposing on them a drink of their own choice.

The company believes that the Internet can be a good way to connect with kids. So, there are tips posted on examinations on the Web site "*Exams ka bhoot bhagao*" (Drive the exam-demon away). Besides, the company has also reached out to children with Wizkids, a contact programme that provides a platform for schoolchildren across 25 cities to showcase their talent.

Adding Rural Reach

Under Ahmed, GSK Consumer Healthcare has upped the ante on distribution. In an aggressive "go to market" approach adopted earlier this year, it created a second layer of distributors in smaller towns to supplement the existing chain of around 500 big distributors. Most of these 4,000 sub-distributors were appointed in the eastern and southern parts of the country. The idea, according to Vice President (Sales) Navneet Saluja, is to increase the retail reach by at least 30 per cent. "Right now we reach out to around 25 per cent of the rural market and we hope to extend this reach to about 40 per cent of the hinterland in a couple of years. We're looking to have a presence in towns that have a population of 5,000 people."

For discussion

1. "Something for everyone" is the philosophy of GSK Consumer Healthcare. Has the company succeeded in this regard? Are there any opportunities based on consumer segments and unfulfilled needs?
2. Critically evaluate the promotion programmes from the rural consumer's point of view and make suggestions.

Source: Radhika Sachdev, "Brains and Brawns," *The Financial Express*, 8 July 2009, available at www.financialexpress.com/printer/news/486336/; Ratna Bhushan, "Horlicks Pins its Hopes on Asha," *The Economic Times*, 24 November 2009, available at http: //economictimes.indiatimes.com/news/news-by-industry/cons-products/food/Horlicks-pins-its-hope-on-Asha/articleshow/5262423.cms; Shobhana Subramanian, "Horlicks Stretches Out," *Business Standard*, 14 July 2009, available at www.business-standard.com/india/news/horlicks-stretches-out/363790/.

5

Rural Marketing Research

LEARNING OBJECTIVES

Upon completion of this chapter, you will be able to:

- Recognize the importance of information in marketing decision making
- Appreciate the differences in rural and urban marketing research
- Explain the process of marketing research and the special tools required in the rural context
- Know about the research business and the major research agencies in India

Familiar with the buying habits and preferences of urban consumers, most brand owners falter when it comes to grappling with the distribution of consumer goods and services. However, a bunch of small rural marketing research and consultancy firms have been helping companies, particularly in the FMCG and consumer durables businesses. Pradeep Lokhande, who heads Rural Relations out of Pune, says these are the best of times for him and his team. The firm recently carried out one of its biggest activation events where it identified 1,800 franchises across 10 states to sell Reliance Money's financial products.[1]

Innovations are galore in the rural market. The foremost innovation in rural distribution was Project *Shakti* of HUL that reached out to villages with a population of 2,000 and less. It was designed by MART.[2] Another innovation was brought about in this segment by Mumbai-based Sampark Solutions. The company came on the rural marketing scene in the 1970s. Sampark was the first firm in India to introduce mobile video vans as a medium of promotion in the early 1980s. The high demand for rural marketing services from agri-input as well as consumer product companies encouraged Sampark to introduce mobile vans. Insight Connect teamed up with Tata Motors to sell Tata Magic, a passenger vehicle modelled on the Tata Ace. "We used *burra kathas* or folk art to communicate with the locals and help them understand the product," recalls Khurram Askari, CEO of Insight Connect. Small firms are set to take the next leap forward as new companies in emerging sectors such as telecom, IT, automotive and financial services are gearing up to tap rural consumers in a big way. "We are overbooked, corporations such as Intel, Unilever, Microsoft and others are chasing us," says Pradeep Kashyap of MART, among the earliest entrants in this space.[3]

Two interesting questions emerge from the success stories of research agencies. First, what has made Pradeep Kashyap, Pradeep Lokhande, and Khurram Askari successful in their chosen field? Second, is there scope for new services and new entrants? The market needs more entrepreneurs with sound knowledge and skills. This chapter focuses on rural marketing research and its applications.

INTRODUCTION

Indian rural consumers account for over 70 per cent of the country's population and live in over 600,000 villages across the country. For several product categories, the rural market accounts for well over 60 per cent of the national demand. This is very good news for companies looking to tap rural markets. However, the market is non-homogeneous and individual subsets of the market tend to be rather small and disparate. Demographical, cultural, geographical, and logistical differences are very apparent. The realities regarding the potential of each of these market segments differ. Sound understanding of these differences is essential for formulating marketing strategies for rural markets. As such, an important challenge for marketers is identifying and utilizing sources of information. Among the varied sources, marketing research has a significant place, as it provides specialized and focused information for decision making.

SIGNIFICANCE OF INFORMATION

It is universally accepted that information is a critical factor for decision making. Decision making is often seen as the centre of what managers do—something that engages most of a manager's time.

Types of decisions and information support

Decision making can be divided into three type—strategic, management control and operations control. Table 5.1 presents a brief explanation of marketing information system (MKIS) with examples.

Strategic decision making

This level of decision making is concerned with deciding on the objectives, resource policies and strategies of the organization. This process generally involves a small group of high-level managers who deal with very complex, non-routine problems. The implications of strategic decisions extend over many years. For example, introduction of a new product, starting a new branch and adoption of new technology are strategic decisions taken by an organization.

Management-control decisions

Management-control decisions are more tactical than strategic. Such decisions are concerned with the efficient and effective utilization of resources and performance management. The decision to increase the advertising budget to improve sales and adding new dealers to improve distribution are both examples of management-control decisions.

Operational-control decisions

The focus here is on how enterprises should respond to the day-to-day changes in the business environment. Determining which units or individuals in the organization will carry out the task, establishing criteria of completion and resource utilization, evaluating outputs—all these tasks involve making decisions about operational control. For example, the allocation of territories to sales persons.

Table 5.1 Support of MKIS to Marketing Decisions—Level-wise

Level	Decision/Action	Description
Strategic (Complex, non-routine and unstructured decisions)	▪ Sales trend forecasting ▪ Acquisition of a company ▪ Addition of new product lines ▪ Making decisions regarding entry into a new market ▪ New organization of company ▪ Consideration of new markets and new marketing strategies	▪ Preparation of 5-year sales forecasts ▪ The evaluation of current capabilities summarized in a special way for planning use ▪ Evaluation of capabilities for new ventures based on current or expected developments for alternative strategies ▪ Conducting customer analyses, competitor analyses, consumer survey information, income projection, demographic projections, and technology projections
Management (Tactical decisions)	▪ Making market-trend analysis ▪ Conducting pricing analysis ▪ Selecting credit line ▪ Allocating advertising ▪ Comparing overall performance against a marketing plan	▪ Identifying customers and markets using data on demographics, markets, consumer behaviour and trends ▪ Determining prices for products and services ▪ Analysing performance of sales territories ▪ Analysing distribution and dealer strengths ▪ Preparing reports of advertising budgets ▪ Preparing data on customers, competitor's product and sales-force requirements
Operational (Simple, routine and structured decisions)	▪ Order processing ▪ Evaluating point-of-sale system ▪ Selecting dealers ▪ Hiring new supervisors ▪ Preparing sales orders ▪ Hiring and training the sales force	▪ Entering, processing, and tracking orders ▪ Recording sales data ▪ Provide dealer information ▪ Appointing new supervisors ▪ Presenting promotion ideas ▪ Taking care of the day-to-day scheduling of sales and promotion efforts and periodic analysis of sales volumes by region, product, customer, etc.

SOURCES OF INFORMATION

The major approaches to secure information required for operational and strategic needs of an enterprise are through:

- Gathering intelligence
- Internal reporting
- Marketing research

The kind of support that the three approaches of information gathering can provide to marketing-mix decisions is illustrated in Table 5.2.

Gathering intelligence

A company may initiate the following actions to sensitize organizations and secure information from the sources given below.

1. *Sales Force:* Sales representatives are the eyes and ears of an organization. They can provide information about competitors' products and their moves, attitudes and performance of middlemen and consumer preferences and buying approaches. Being at the grassroots level, they have access to a wealth of information that can be easily accessed. Companies have to train and motivate the sales force to supply the relevant information. The intelligence data can be obtained through periodical letters, meetings and seminars.
2. *Middlemen:* Middlemen may be encouraged to pass on information they consider important to the marketing team. They can act not only as information disseminators but also as idea generators for the company.
3. *Staff:* Managers and other staff members of the organization can be a major source of information when they are motivated to do the following:
   - Scanning the publications—dailies, magazines, journals, research abstracts, government reports, trade journals and reports, etc.
   - Browsing the Internet
   - Attending meetings, conferences, seminars and workshops
4. *Company:* Companies can learn more by participating in industrial exhibitions, development programmes and sponsoring events (music festivals, sports, etc.). Being a sponsor, they can see the world differently and gain access to information, sometimes from unexpected sources.

Internal reporting

Growing enterprises are storehouses of information. The internal records that are of immediate value to marketing decisions are orders received, stockholdings and sales invoices. Given below is a list of the information that can be derived from sales invoices:

- Product type, size and pack type by territory
- Product type, size and pack type by customer
- Average value and/or volume of sales by territory
- Average value and/or volume of sales by sales person

By comparing orders received with invoices, an enterprise can establish the extent to which it is providing an acceptable level of customer service. In the same way, comparing stockholding records with orders received helps an enterprise ascertain whether its stocks are in line with current demand patterns.

Table 5.2 Information Support to Marketing Mix

Mix	Decision	Marketing	Intelligence/Research	Internal records	Decision support
Product	Item (brand) decision		▪ Sales of existing products ▪ Consumer Preferences ▪ Market growth rates and market share trends ▪ Technological advancements ▪ Government polices	▪ Sales of existing products ▪ Profitability data ▪ Production cost analysis ▪ Idle capacity ▪ Request for new products	▪ Sales of existing product design ▪ Concept testing ▪ Screening models ▪ Business analysis
Price	Price determination, price change		▪ Competitive prices ▪ Discount structure in ▪ existence ▪ Channel member preferences ▪ Consumer preferences	▪ Cost data ▪ Company policies ▪ Dealer performance ▪ Discount structure	▪ Mark-up pricing ▪ BE analysis ▪ Supply–demand analysis
Promotion	Personal selling team	▪ Size ▪ Territory ▪ Allocation of target	▪ Competitor's practices ▪ Market growth rate ▪ Potential market size and geographical spread	▪ Current market coverage ▪ Target coverage ▪ Production levels ▪ Budget	▪ Manpower inventory and forecast ▪ Recruitment and selection techniques ▪ Territory-allocation models
	Advertising and sales	▪ Budget ▪ Media ▪ Frequency etc.)	▪ Competitors' practices ▪ Consumer states (awareness, interest)	▪ Previous allocations ▪ Sales and ad expenditure data	▪ AIDA model ▪ Promotion elasticity, Ad budget models
Promotion				▪ Sales force preferences ▪ Previous promotions	▪ Effectiveness measures

(Continued)

Table 5.2 (Continued)

Mix	Decision	Marketing	Intelligence/Research	Internal records	Decision support
Place	Channel decision		■ Competitors' practices ■ Customer characteristics ■ Environmental characteristics	■ Product characteristics ■ Standardization, perishability, bulk service requirements, unit price	■ Channel design ■ Distribution strategies
Dealer appointment			■ Intermediary characteristics ■ Channel members ■ Financial and marketing abilities ■ Competitors' practices ■ Location factors	■ Market coverage need ■ Channel members ■ Number and size ■ Sales turnover	■ Choice of dealers at different locations
Channel management			■ Channel development ■ Customer preference to channels ■ Government policies on channels	■ Channel performance ■ Channel conflicts (complaint data)	■ Channel effectiveness ■ Channel harmony

Marketing research

Marketing research can be viewed as a process and a system. As a process it is a non-routine, specialized activity undertaken with a clear focus and well-defined purpose to obtain relevant data for decision making. From the process point of view, Philip Kotler[4] defined it as "the systematic design, collection, analysis and reporting of data and findings relevant to a specific marketing situation facing the company."

Marketing research can take two forms. It can either be ad hoc and specific-problem oriented or continuous in order to gather information about the trends. In many cases, data is collected to find solutions to a well-defined managerial problem. Research agencies and policy makers attempt to continuously monitor the marketing environment. They undertake monitoring or tracking exercises, often involving panels of farmers, consumers or distributors from whom the same data is collected at regular intervals.

MARKETING RESEARCH—KEY DECISIONS

The key decision areas that require careful consideration of researchers are:

- Defining problems
- Determining the research budget
- Choosing research design (exploratory, descriptive or causal; qualitative or quantitative and based on primary data or secondary data)
- Determining sampling method and size
- Selecting appropriate data analysis tools
- Preparing the research proposal
- Organizing field work
- Analysing and reporting findings

Defining problems

It is often said, "A problem well defined is a problem half solved." Research-problem definition involves an understanding of the information needed by managers and specifying the area of inquiry. Research problems can be formulated using one or more of the following methods:

- Funnelling or narrow-down method
- Problem audit
- Background analysis
- Situation analysis
- Model development

Management problems that warrant decisions exist when there is a gap between the actual situation and the desired situation. When the actual performance falls short of the standard performance, we say that there is a problem. When the current situation is satisfactory but there is scope for improvement, we say that there is an opportunity. In either case, management needs specific and perfect information for sound decision making.

A situation model is a description of outcomes that are desired and the variables that influence the outcomes. The research problem is stated with reference to the

1. Dependent variables, and
2. Independent variables.

The basic questions are:

- What variables determine the outcome and to what extent?
- What are the relationships between them—positive or negative, linear or non-linear?
- How can they be classified—hindering, moderating, promoting or stimulating? Criterion or predictor?
- How can they be structured and shaped to cause the desired outcome?

Based on certain assumptions, the researcher may postulate the relationships of variables for testing their validity, if necessary. The hypotheses not only serve to indicate the researcher's understanding of the phenomena but also help make objective inquiry.
Specification, as such, involves:

(a) Listing the variables to be studied,
(b) Specifying the degree of measurement required,
(c) Formulating testable hypotheses and competing hypotheses,
(d) Defining basic concepts, and
(e) Stating underlying assumptions that govern interpretation of results.

We now illustrate the various components of problem definition.

Management objective: To increase the market share of televisions from the current rate of 20 per cent to 23 per cent.

Management problem: Whether the new model that it is proposing to introduce will be a success?

Research problem: What are the perceptions of consumers requiring a new model?

Decision criteria: The company will introduce the model if 70 per cent of the consumer responses are favourable.

Hypothesis: Consumers favouring the new model are equal to or more than 70 per cent.

Determining the research budget

Research is considered necessary when the available information is inadequate or not very reliable. Managers gather data relevant to the problem on hand from two principal secondary sources:

1. Internal reporting system, and
2. Marketing intelligence system.

When the two sources fail to provide perfect information that can help managers in making decisions without uncertainty, managers will be willing to pay for marketing research. The principle guiding their decision, therefore, is:

> "Conduct marketing research only when the expected value of perfect information (EVPI) is greater than the cost of obtaining it."

As such, the budget decision involves two steps:

1. Specifying the approximate value of information
2. Determining the maximum amount that can be spent

There are two approaches to assess the value of research:

1. Intuitive approach that relies on the individual's ability to judge
2 Expected value approach that utilizes statistical analysis such as the Bayesian approach.

Choosing the research design

Different research approaches are identified based on the purpose, nature of data and sources of data, as given under.

Based on purpose	Exploratory, descriptive and causal
Based on nature of data	Quantitative and qualitative
Based on sources of data	Primary and secondary

Exploratory, descriptive and causal

Available literature classifies research designs into three categories as shown in Table 5.3. When a manager is unaware of the phenomenon, he may initiate exploratory research to gain a basic understanding of it. Next, he may go for descriptive research to have a thorough and analytical view of it. He may opt for experimentation before making huge investments on it.

For instance, a company is interested in marketing its products in the rural market for the first time. The marketing manager is interested in knowing whether rural markets are attractive. He prefers a small-scale survey, a sort of pilot study to assess the attractiveness of the rural market. If the results are positive, he will order for a descriptive research, a large-scale survey to assess the market potential and identify the strategic options. In the final stage, he may undertake experimental research to test market his product in a few select villages to predict the success of the product. If the result is positive, he will implement his marketing plan for the entire rural market.

Table 5.3 Categories of Research

Aspect	Exploratory	Descriptive	Causal
Research purpose	Know the variables	Describe the variables	Verify and validate relationship
Research setting	Natural learning (classroom)	Natural learning (classroom)	Lab experiments, field experiments
Sample scope	Small non-probability samples	Large probability and non-probability samples	Small probability samples
Nature of data	Subjective opinions	Subjective opinions	Objective behaviour
Data collection	Secondary and primary on a small scale	Primary	Primary
Nature of output	Hypothesis	Description	Prediction
	Indicative	Substantive	Confirmative
Application	Growth directions, behavioural trends	Market potential, product usage, sales analyses	New product acceptance, consumer preferences, behavioural patterns

In rural markets, the research is more exploratory in nature as many companies are looking for information to make entry decisions. FMCG companies that have already spread their wings in rural areas such as HUL, Godrej, Colgate, LG, Philips and others are interested in assessing consumer preferences, consumer behaviour and brand loyalty. Hence, they require descriptive and analytical studies. Agri-input companies selling seeds, pesticides, fertilizers and farm equipment will be interested in going from the laboratory to the field and conducting real-life experimental studies to know how well their product works and how it will be received by the farmers.

Quantitative versus qualitative research

Quantitative research is numerically oriented. It requires respondents to give specific answers that are measurable. It often involves statistical analysis. For example, BSNL might ask its customers to rate its overall service as excellent, good, poor or very poor. This will provide quantitative information that can be analysed statistically. Most market research surveys in an urban setting involve using questionnaires with scales for respondents to rate or rank their responses. However, such scaling techniques cannot be used in rural areas as the respondents are less educated.

In qualitative research, there are no fixed set of questions but instead, a topic guide (or discussion guide) is used to explore various issues in-depth. The discussion between the interviewer and the respondent is largely determined by the respondent's own thoughts and feelings. For example, HUL personnel may stop a consumer who has purchased Lux and ask him or her why he or she has chosen the soap. Research of this sort is mostly done face-to-face employing one or more of the following techniques:

- Observation
- Interviews (in-depth interview conducted face-to-face with one respondent, paired-depth interview with two respondents or group interview with 3 to 5 members)
- Group discussion (more than 5 members)
- Focus groups
- Participatory research method

Focus groups are usually made up of 6 to 8 targeted respondents and a research moderator whose role is to ask the required questions, draw out answers, and encourage discussion.

Primary versus secondary market research

Table 5.4 distinguishes between primary and secondary market research. Primary research involves collection of data afresh from the subjects of research through methods such as observation, survey and experiments. It is essential to develop more accurate descriptive and analytical analyses. While it provides accurate data, it has limitations in terms of cost, time and convenience. However, primary research is the only reliable approach when perceptions and behaviours of the target market are to be studied. Secondary research is useful in obtaining an understanding of scenarios, trends and estimates.

Secondary research is based on data collected and published by another researcher or agency. It is, therefore, more economical and easier to undertake when compared to primary research. By investing in secondary market research, target markets can be analysed, competitors can be evaluated and political, social and economic factors can be assessed. Table 5.5 provides secondary data sources in the marketing research process.

One can purchase information directly from agencies or book stores or obtain material from libraries and other public information centres. Information is also available on the Internet (Web sites, blogs, etc.). The information tools developed by research agencies can help managers get the required information with great ease. Some of the tools are given in Table 5.6 to illustrate this point.

Table 5.4 Primary Versus Secondary Research

Base	Primary	Secondary
Nature	Fresh collection needed	To be searched and selected
Sources	Consumers Sales persons Dealers Experts Organizations	Libraries Trade associations Media Internet Research organizations
Methods	Survey Observation Projective techniques Participatory appraisals Experiments	Purchasing from other sources Scanning available databases
Merits	Accurate first hand information	Economical and easier to obtain
Demerits	Expensive, cumbersome and time consuming	Data gaps and non-availability of relevant data
Application	Consumer purchase process, brand loyalty, promotion effectiveness, etc.	Assessing trends in income, savings, and consumption, estimating demand for select goods, understanding the changing rural lifestyles, etc.

Table 5.5 Secondary Data Sources

Sl No.	Data sources	Source specification	Contents
1.	Industry, commerce and trade associations	FICCI, CII, ASSOCHAM	Trade directory and yearbook
2.	Marketing research agencies and associations	Rural relations, MART, Anugrah-Madison, Sampark, Rural Marketing Association of India (RMAI)	Research reports, media statistics and consumer information (semiotic analysis, customer eQ, consumer ID, etc.)
3.	Companies	Colgate, HUL, ITC, Rallis India, and others	Annual reports, brochures, press interviews, and published research studies
4.	NGOs	RASS (AP), Rural Innovations Network (Chennai), CARE (New Delhi)	Project reports and press interviews

(Continued)

Table 5.5 (Continued)

Sl No.	Data sources	Source specification	Contents
5.	Government agencies	NCAER, RBI, Ministry for Rural Development (Central and State government), Mandal Revenue Offices, *Panchayats*, etc.	Population censuses, social surveys, family expenditure surveys, import/export statistics, production statistics, agricultural statistics
6.	Educational institutions	Institutes like NIRD (AP) and NIRMA (Gujarat)	Seminar proceedings, books and research journals
7.	Media organs	*The Economic Times, The Financial Express, Hindu Business Line, Yojana, Kurukshetra,* RMAI journals and other periodicals	Write-ups by freelance journalists, news reporters and experts publicized through audio-visual media (Television, radio, books, newspapers, magazines, journals and the Internet).
8.	Worldwide organizations	International agencies such as World Bank, IMF, IFAD, UNDP, ITC, FAO and ILO	Bank economic reviews, research reports, and articles

Table 5.6 Information Tools of Research Agencies

Tool	Research agency	Information	Decision areas
Semiotic analysis	AC Nielson ORG-MARG	Studies associations of colours, signs and symbols in rural context	Creative advertising and research
Customer eQ	AC Nielson	Brand equity studies (quality, satisfaction and loyalty)	Brand management
Advanced tracking programme	IMRB	Brand health and brand equity studies on a continuous basis	Brand management
Consumer ID	IMRB	Consumer reactions to different variables of a product category	Brand management
Lincompass	Linterland of Lintas	Geographical information system	Market potential, logistics and distribution

Determining sampling method and size

In primary data collection, the researcher has to decide three things:

- Sampling procedure
- Sampling methods
- Sample size

Qualitative research uses non-probability sampling as it does not aim to produce a statistically representative sample or draw statistical inference. Indeed, a phenomenon need only appear once

Table 5.7 Choice of Sampling Procedure

Sl No.	Factor	Probability	Non-probability
1.	Information needed	Totals	Averages or proportions
2.	Expected cost of errors	High	Low
3.	Population	Heterogeneous	Homogeneous
4.	Allowable error	Low	High
5.	Non-sampling error	Small	Large

Table 5.8 Sampling Methods in Rural setting

Sl No.	Method	Description
1.	Random sampling	Population elements are chosen by lottery method or every *n*th unit is selected.
2.	Stratified sampling	Mini-reproduction of the population. Population is first divided into two or more mutually exclusive segments based on some categories of variables and a sample is drawn from each subset.
3.	Cluster sampling	Selecting respondents from certain areas or certain time-periods. In the first stage a sample of areas is chosen; in the second stage a sample of respondents within those areas is selected.
4.	Quota sampling	Sample size is proportional to the population in terms of a chosen characteristic like a demographic variable.
5.	Convenience sampling	Choosing subjects who are available or easy to find.
6.	Judgement sampling	Using judgement to decide who will be included in the sample.
7.	Purposive sampling	Studying the entire population of some limited group (farmers) or a subset of a population (marginal farmers).
8.	Snowball sampling	Researcher identifies one member of some population of interest, speaks to him/her, and then asks that person to identify others in the population that the researcher might speak to.

in the sample. Table 5.7 indicates the factors influencing the choice between the probability and non-probability samples. The need for predictable totals, low allowable errors, high population heterogeneity, small non-sampling errors, and high expected errors favour the use of probability sampling.

The next question relates to the choice of sampling method. Table 5.8 describes some of the useful methods.

The final decision is about the size of the sample that should be used. Should the sample size be large or small? Table 5.9 presents the factors influencing the choice. When time and cost constraints are insignificant, the population is heterogeneous and high level of accuracy is desired, large sample is suggested. Small samples are common in case of experiments and focus groups.

Table 5.9 Choice of Sample Size

Factor	Large	Small
Time available	More	Less
Accuracy	High	Low
Cost	High	Low
Population	Heterogeneous	Homogeneous

Table 5.10 Data-analysis Methods

Analysis	Method
Univariate	*t* test, *z* test, one-way ANOVA, Chi-square test, McNemar test, Cochran *Q* test, Sign test, Mann–Whitney *U* test, Kolmogorov–Smirnov test
Multi-variate	ANOVA, Rank correlation, Multiple regression, Factor analysis, Discriminant analysis, Cluster analysis, Conjoint analysis, Multi-dimensional scaling

In qualitative research, sample size is important only to obtain complete information about the issue taken up for research. As such, a researcher can stop collecting data once information redundancy is achieved. As Sandelowski[5] points out, "determining adequate sample size in qualitative research is ultimately a matter of judgement and experience." In view of this, flexible research designs are desirable to allow researchers to employ iterative sampling and analysis strategies.

Selecting appropriate data-analysis tools

A good number of statistical tools are available for analysing data and drawing inference.

It is imperative that the researcher select the analytic techniques prior to collecting the data and carry out a sample analysis with synthetic data. Such an exercise ensures that the result of the analysis will provide the required information to the researcher.

The type of analysis (parametric versus non-parametric) and the choice of analysis technique (cross-tabulation, hypothesis testing or association) depend on the following factors:

- Purpose of research
- Type of data—quantitative or qualitative
- Number of variables being examined—one or more
- Type of measurement scale used—interval, nominal, ordinal
- Number of samples to be compared—one or more
- Nature of samples—dependent or independent
- Size of the sample—small or large

Table 5.10 provides some of the appropriate techniques for testing hypotheses and measuring association.

Preparing a research proposal

A research proposal needs to be prepared for discussion and approval. A research proposal provides the researcher with a blue-print for conducting and controlling the research project. It facilitates meaningful exchange of thoughts and opinions between the researcher and the decision maker. It helps them to come to an agreement on various terms of the research project.

The elements of a research proposal are:

- Executive summary/abstract
- Background/introduction
- Objectives and hypotheses
- Methodology
- Time schedule
- Research staff and equipment
- Cost estimates—recurring and non-recurring
- Appendices (any relevant information)

Organizing field work

The effectiveness of the design depends on its execution. Regardless of how carefully a researcher has designed his research, the data collected will not be accurate unless the field force does its job properly. Field work can be effective only when it is properly managed.

The key steps in organizing field work

The important steps in field-work management are—the preparation of data collection plan, the organization of research effort and controlling for time, cost and accuracy.

(i) Preparation of data collection plan that specifies:

- Number of supervisors
- Number of field investigators
- Period of data collection and schedule
- Budget

(ii) Organization of research effort:

- Selecting investigators and supervisors
- Training the staff
- Allocating work
- Briefing the investigators
- Compensating the staff for the work turned out

(iii) Controlling:

- Supervising the data collection with respect to time and cost
- Checking the data for validation
- Carrying out corrections, if any, or repeating the data collection wherever necessary

Investigators—selection and training

It is obvious that the entire research effort depends on the efficiency, effectiveness and ethical integrity of the investigators. To be successful, investigators should have the right mindset and appropriate skill.

Table 5.11 Guidelines for Research Investigators

Sl No.	Aspect	Characteristics of respondents	Dos
1.	Appearance	Simple and culture bound.	Dress simply.
2.	Greetings	Greetings and conversations are informal. They try to relate and show affection when interacting with others.	Make a courteous greeting with respect to age (*Namasthe* or *Namaskar*) mentioning a relationship (grandpa or uncle or aunty or mother).
3.	Language and culture	Most of them are not literate and unfamiliar with the English language.	Speak in the local language. If possible, become familiar with the local dialect. A good rule of thumb is that when you can understand the local jokes, poetry and songs, then you may feel you are starting to understand the people's culture.
4.	Rapport	Rural people like to be related. They are open to known people. They have their own apprehensions about urbanites and their intentions.	Engage the respondents in interaction by inquiring on personal and general issues in a casual way showing concern and respect. Be humble, frank and honest in announcing the purpose of research.
5.	Investigation	Rural people are sensitive and naïve. They are slow in understanding and exploring. They are less objective and are relationship-oriented.	Be slow in questioning and getting responses. Be patient. Try to give the respondents a lead role and allow them to speak in their own style at their own pace and in a way they like. Avoid phrases and gestures that may hurt respondents.
6.	Overcoming limitations	Villagers speak in groups. They look for social support and approval.	Encourage group interaction. After gaining trust, obtain individual opinions by asking others to listen to what the respondent says. Let individuals take his or her private time to interact.
		Villagers are less objective. They prefer narrations rather than simple answers and also go off the point establishing unnecessary links to episodes.	Better listen with patience and exercise soft-control options to bring people back on the right track.

Like the rural sales person (as discussed in Chapter 1), the research investigator should have social skills, patience, be respectful and humble, and be courteous and concerned. Table 5.11 presents some useful guidelines in brief. Some important don'ts are:

1. *Don't pretend*: Villagers look at a newcomer with some degree of apprehension. They may avoid you, mistaking you to be a health/insurance employee or micro-finance agent. Sometimes, they gather around you considering you to be a government/NGO employee who has come to discuss some benefits. Avoid promising benefits that you cannot offer.

2. *Avoid direct inquiry:* Do not ask direct questions when conducting an interview in the presence of others. The respondent villager may find it inconvenient to answer and may not like others to talk about it.

3. *Don't touch:* Touching the arm or placing a hand on the shoulder of a villager without first establishing an intimate relationship is not desirable. Male researchers should never touch women.

4. *Avoid suspicious behaviours:* Villagers are traditional in their outlook. In view of this, male researchers should not talk to women without a female assistant. It is always better to interview them in the presence of their relatives.

5. *Don't become controversial:* Avoid speaking about village politics or raising controversial issues that may lead to heated arguments and disputes. Also avoid violating cultural and religious norms. Don't criticize traditions such as the "purdah" among Muslim women.

Locating respondents

The choice of location for conducting interviews is another important consideration in the research process. The following locations are considered appropriate by researchers.

- Women—houses, retail shops, and farms.
- Youth—schools, play grounds, and STD/Internet kiosks
- Men—houses, retail shops, farms, tea stalls, STD/Internet kiosks, *chaupals*, *mandis*, *haats*, banks and post offices.

Studying rural consumers in their natural environments is better than employing CLTs (central location tests) that are non-indicative of their natural surroundings.

Analysing and reporting findings

The heap of data collected makes no sense unless it is properly analysed. Researchers can analyse data manually or with the help of a computer making use of statistical tools. The final step is report writing. The report should be built around the management problem that needs to be solved and for which the research is undertaken. There is no one format that is best for all occasions. The nature of the audience and the topic of the report combine to determine the most describable format. However, the general format is:

- Title page
- Table of contents
- Executive summary
- Introduction
- Methodology
- Findings
- Limitations
- Conclusions and recommendations
- Appendices
- Bibliography

APPROACHES AND TOOLS—CASE FOR INNOVATION

It is a well-known fact that traditional marketing research tools and techniques used in urban areas are not applicable in the rural context. They must fit with the technological and cultural milieu of rural India.

Rural India has traditionally had an oral collectivist culture (forming community relationships and joint families) and information and communication technology is in the nascent stage.

Oral communication: While urbanites can interact with a mix of oral (mobile phones) and written communication (e-mails and fax messages), rural people depend mostly on face-to face oral conversations.

Ascribed status: In urban areas social-class structures are based on jobs and incomes. Social status is achieved and not ascribed. In rural areas, socials structures based on caste, land-holding and wealth are rigid and formalized. Care needs to be taken so as to respect the hierarchical, rigid, social-class structure.

Affiliation oriented: In a less literate collectivistic culture, affiliation needs are stronger. Therefore, a villager's highest priority is to identify himself with his tribe. There is a feeling of collective identity felt by the villager. Individual interviews will be less effective.

Participative: Oral collectivistic cultures are participative in nature. Stage shows, plays, puppet shows have always been popular in rural India owing to their participatory nature. NGOs have been able to appreciate the above fact. This is evident by their increasing usage of role plays and puppet shows. Games can be used as effective marketing research tools that involve collective participation of the tribe.

Emotional thinking: The rural culture is by nature emotional. As such, rural folk are less adept at sequential and rational urban thinking approaches. Articulation of the rural villager's motivations and attitudes is, therefore, difficult when exposed to rational means of testing.

Not spatially equipped: Typical, 5-point, 7-point or 10-point scales used in the urban market are not effective in the rural context because they involve complex understanding on the part of the rural consumer. The rural consumer is not spatially well-equipped. Pictorial scales may be used in their place. Scales can also be simplified to three-pointers that involve less complex processing of information.

Limited information processing: A photograph/painting is highly visual and supplies more information than that can be processed by the rural consumer. In their place, cartoons or caricatures that lack information are cool media sources that provide a participatory role of all the five senses.

PARTICIPATORY APPROACHES

The increasing use of participant observation methods in cultural anthropology provides an important lesson to researchers in marketing. Participatory research methods can be conveniently classified into four main types, each with a distinctive style and ethos.

- Participant Observation (PO)
- Rapid Rural Appraisal (RRA)
- Participatory Rural Appraisal (PRA)
- Participatory Action Research (PAR)

Each approach has its merits and limitations. It is for a research agency to select the best mix of methods to serve their research objectives.

Participant observation (PO)

The researcher actively participates in the rituals and activities along with the tribe so as to understand the shared meanings not as a passive and objective observer but as an active participant. Such socio-participatory roles played by the researcher in the village may lead to important insights that may be overlooked otherwise by objective means of measurements. The researcher can document the lifestyles, customs, values, interrelationships, etc. of the community members.

Rapid rural appraisal (RRA)

In this method, the research team goes to rural areas and collects data using a combination of iterative methods and verification. It may employ the following techniques.

- *Secondary data sources*: Review of books, files, reports, news articles, maps including aerial photos.
- *Observation:* Direct and participant observation, brief aerial observation, do-it-yourself (DIY) exercises.
- *Interviews:* Semi-structured interviews where some of the questions are predetermined and new questions arise during the interview in response to answers from those interviewed. The interviewees may be (i) individual farmers or households (ii) key informants (iii) group interviews (iv) community meetings (v) chains of interviews.
- *Diagrams:* Maps, aerial photos, seasonal calendars, historical profiles, etc.
- *Stories and portraits:* Biographies, local histories, case studies and trend analysis.

Participatory rural appraisal (PRA)

PRA involves local people and outsiders from different sectors and disciplines. Outsiders facilitate local people in analysing information, practicing critical self-awareness, taking responsibility and sharing knowledge of life and conditions to plan and to act.

RRA versus PRA

The differences between RRA and PRA are given in Table 5.12.

Principles of PRA

There are five key principles that form the basis of any PRA activity no matter what the objectives or setting.[6]

Participation and empowerment: PRA relies heavily on participation by the communities, as (i) partners to the research team and (ii) sources of information.

Flexibility: PRA makes use of different techniques for collecting information. The combination of techniques will be determined by such variables as the size and skill mix of the PRA team, the time and resources available, and the topic and location of the work.

Teamwork: PRA is a team method. It is best conducted by a local team (speaking the local language) with a few outsiders present.

Optimal ignorance: It optimizes trade-off between quality, relevance, accuracy and timeliness. This is possible by knowing what is worth doing and what is not worth doing. It avoids unnecessary details, and irrelevant data. It does not measure more precisely than needed.

Systematic: PRA-generated data is seldom conducive to statistical analysis for two reasons (i) it is largely qualitative and (ii) sample size is relatively small. Hence, alternative methods have been developed to ensure the validity and reliability of the findings. These include (i) sampling based on approximate

Table 5.12 Differences between RRA and PRA

Rapid Rural Appraisal (RRA)	Participatory Rural Appraisal (PRA)
Research teams go to rural areas, obtain information and then process and analyse the information.	Research teams go to rural areas, facilitate rural people in collection, presentation and analysis of information by themselves.
The information is owned by the research team. It is not shared with rural people.	The information is owned by rural people but usually shared with the research team.

stratification of the community by geographic location or relative wealth and (ii) triangulation—using more than one, and often three, sources of information to cross check answers.

Inclusiveness: The method allows researchers to involve different people—marginal and vulnerable groups, women, children, the aged and the destitute.

Localization: The extensive and creative use of local materials and representations encourage proper understanding of the research subjects.

Techniques of data collection

PRA is an informal, interactive and innovative approach. It makes use of a similar "basket of techniques" that RRA method employs.[7] They are as follows:

- Secondary data sources
- Observation
- Interviews
- Diagrams
- Stories and portraits

The central part of any PRA is semi-structured interviewing. While sensitive topics are often better addressed in interviews with individuals, other topics of more general concern can be focused on during group discussions and community meetings. The interviewers stimulate debate by encouraging discussion. Diagrams, pictures and symbols are used to facilitate easy understanding and recording.

However, for easy visualization by one and all in the group, the diagrams are drawn on the ground making use of sticks, stones, seeds or other useful materials available at the site of the interview. Later, they are transferred to paper for future reference.

Drawbacks

PRA is not without drawbacks. The following problems are said to be common when the method is applied:

- *Time deadlines*: One common problem is that insufficient time is allowed for the team to relax and mingle with the local people, to listen to them and to learn about the more sensitive issues under consideration. Rushing will also often mean missing the views of the poorest and least articulate members of the communities visited.
- *Credibility:* The reporting of the results of PRA in a standard evaluation report is a challenging process. Individuals unfamiliar with participatory research methods may raise questions about the credibility of the PRA findings.
- *Hijacking:* PRA agenda will be externally driven. This results in legitimacy problems.
- *Formalism:* The "PRA hit team" arrives in a local community to "do a PRA." This abrupt approach is all too common. It will be more exploitative than explorative.
- *Disappointment:* Unnecessary local expectations may be raised. Local communities may view it as a wasteful exercise.
- *Conflict of interests:* The empowerment implications of PRA and the power of its social analysis can create threats to local vested interests, although less so than with PAR. PAR is discussed below.

Participatory action research (PAR)

PAR is a more activist-centric approach in which participants take total responsibility for reflection and preparing the research report. It is a reflective process of progressive problem-solving led by individuals working with others in teams or as a part of a community of practice to improve the way they address issues and solve problems. PAR should not be confused with PRA. PRA is an assessment technique that could be a part of a PAR process. However, it does not encompass the full action-reflection cycle.

INNOVATIVE TOOLS

As the conventional research tools did not prove to be effective in the rural markets, researchers started working out new solutions to problems.

Scaling techniques

Simple, easy-to-understand techniques to indicate varying preferences and feelings have been evolved by rural researchers. Table 5.13 shows some of the popular methods.

Ladder

When used for ranking, the number of rungs correspond to the number of items ranked. For rating purposes, a typical Likert scale on the ascendancy is achieved by the steps on the ladder (Figure. 5.1). The respondent is asked to place a visual card corresponding to the product or preference on a rung according to his ranking or rating.

Table 5.13 Rural Scaling Techniques

Sl No.	Tool	Purpose
1.	Ladder	Rating and ranking
2.	Images of faces	Rating
3.	Colours	Rating
4.	Dice	Rating
5.	Carom coins/Rummy coins/Stacks	Ranking and rating
6.	Playing cards	Ranking
7.	Pigeon holes	Ranking
8.	3-point scale	Rating

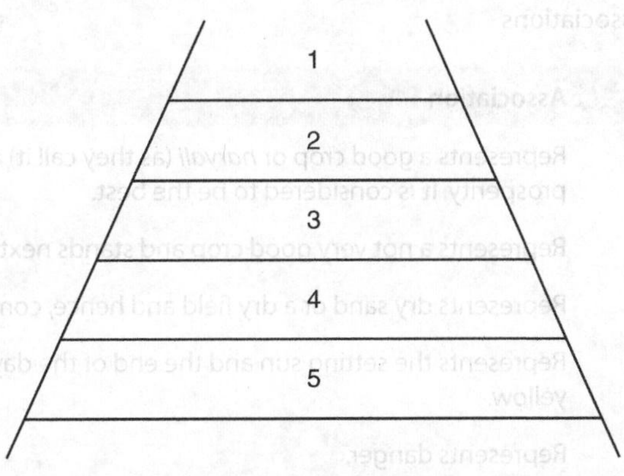

Figure 5.1 Ladder

Images of faces

The images of faces with varying expressions (smiling to wailing) is another useful tool that is used to ascertain preferences and liking (Figure 5.2).

Colour wheels

Colours are very strong indicators and forms of expressing feelings in the rural areas. The selection of colours is done on the basis of the association of rural people with colours as given in Table 5.14.

MART has experimented with success with these colours in its rural research. The colour wheel has a circular base divided into five segments and a rotating pointer (clock hand) attached to its centre. The five segments show different colours or colour shades as given in Table 5.14. The respondent is explained what each of the colours represent and he/she is asked to move the pointer to the colour or shade that represents his or her rating of the item.

Dice

Dice are wooden or plastic piece with 6 faces with varying numbers of holes or dots ranging from 1 to 6. They are commonly used in games like Ludo and Snakes and Ladders. A face value of 1 is the lowest and a face value of 6 is the highest. The respondent is asked to rate the item by assigning the face value of the die to the item.

Rummy coins/Carom coins/Stacks

Fifteen coins are given to the respondents and they are asked to distribute them among the brands under study in order of their preferences—more coins for the most preferred brand. The process usually takes a long time. So stacks of 5, 4, 3, 2 and 1 coins are made. The respondent can easily select the stack by considering different heights of the stacks. Care should be taken to make the stack heights visibly different. If needed, more coins may be used to create stacks with a constant difference.

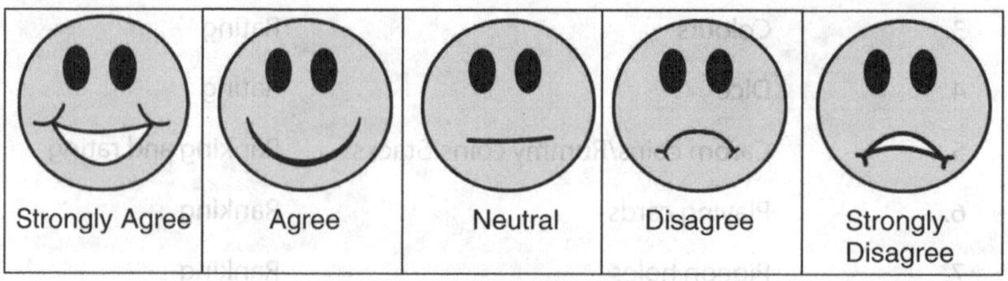

Figure 5.2 Faces with varying expressions

Table 5.14 Colours and Associations

Colour	Rating	Association
Dark green	5	Represents a good crop or *haryali* (as they call it) and hence, represents prosperity. It is considered to be the best.
Light green	4	Represents a not very good crop and stands next to the dark green.
Yellow	3	Represents dry sand or a dry field and hence, comes next.
Orange	2	Represents the setting sun and the end of the day and is placed next to yellow.
Red	1	Represents danger.

Playing cards

Playing cards are well known, especially among rural men. The face cards with K, Q, J, 10 and 9 represent a descending order in terms of values. As such, they are assigned ranks from 1 to 5 in that order.

Pigeon holes

The measurement kit consists of a plastic egg tray, card board cut-outs with visuals of the items to be compared and white tennis balls. The items are placed along the left side of the crate. The scaling is done using the paired comparison method. For example, you are trying to find out the ranking of four brands A, B, C, and D.

The visuals of the brands are placed on the left side of the crate. The respondent is asked to compare pairs of A and B, A and C and so on and to place the ball in the hole against the one that is preferred. Suppose the results are as given under, the conclusion is that Brand A is the most preferred one followed by C and B.

Pair	A and B	A and C	A and D	B and C	B and D	C and D
Preference	A	A	A	C	B	C

3-point rating scales

Researchers interested in conventional scales may use three-point scales, especially when the respondents are school educated.

RURAL VERSUS URBAN MARKETING RESEARCH

Can marketers replicate the urban marketing research approaches, methods and tools in rural areas with the same efficacy? Does the rural–urban divide reassert its presence requiring the invention of different tools and techniques?

The answers to the questions appear to be an affirmative "yes." The time-tested research tools fail to get the desired information from rural subjects, however well you may design and administer them. We now consider the differences between urban and rural research and their implications on marketing researchers.

Respondents

Urban consumers are educated and possess good comprehension and presentation skills. They are marketing savvy and better exposed to marketing offers. They are aware of the wide range of brands. They are independent and assertive. It will not, therefore, be difficult to obtain individual responses, either from men, women or the youth.

Rural consumers, on the other hand, are semi-literate or illiterate. They cannot understand sophisticated terms and tools. Also, they cannot verbalize their responses with the same ease and efficiency as their urban counterparts do. Although they are becoming marketing savvy, with the changing times and rising prosperity, they are less exposed to the brand offers and hence, are less aware of them. Their brand identifications (Nirma is identified as yellow powder; Lifebuoy as red soap) and quality measures might be in a form unfamiliar to urbanites. Rural subjects cannot be interviewed individually. People, nearby, surround the interviewer and the respondent and take part in the interview. The net result will be a mini group response.

Time

Urban life is very time-bound. Urbanities are hard pressed for time, particularly those living in metros and cites. This can be understood from the way they maintain dairies and take part in "time management" training programmes. They are willing to spare very little time for researchers.

The dominance of the time can be understood from the way a multitude of ads define products and lifestyles with a.m. or p.m. A consumer can wake up on Friday morning to "Times FM—a.m. to p.m.", have a 7 o'clock shave, switch on to morning transmission on TV, eat "2-minutes noodles," put on "nine a.m." shirt and pack a "weekender" trouser in a "*kalbhi, aajbhi, kalbhi*" suitcase.

Source: Pawan Bhandari and Rajat Iyer, "Chalk and Cheese," *A & M* (August 1994): 25.

The rural scenario is altogether different. Farm schedules begin well before 7 a.m. and while daily activity is routinized, it is not pervaded with urgency. The attendance demands of rural occupations are a lot more flexible when compared to urban areas. Rural folk may devote time for researchers.

Accessibility

It is easy to access urban people geographically and psychologically. Urban people are more familiar with the different inquiries of market-research agencies. Day in and day out, they are faced with researchers with short questionnaires at places like the home, office, retail outlets, industrial exhibitions, railway stations/bus stations/airports, hotels and hospitals. Some of them might have participated in experiments or acted as panel members. In fact, they suffer from research fatigue. Still, they co-operate as they know the value of marketing research.

Against this, we find rural people are relatively difficult to reach because of physical distances and apprehensions about researchers. Road networking has enhanced the access to about 40 per cent villages. They are connected by all-weather roads and communication lines. The remaining villages are tough to access. When the psychological dimension is considered, both the researcher and the respondent find it difficult to interact. The researchers are used to men and women who know their role and expectations. Villagers cannot understand and appreciate the value of market research. They either consider them as unwanted intruders or mistake them as officers propagating a government scheme.

Secondary data sources

Large volumes of secondary data relating to urban markets is available from multiple sources. Companies that have been in the urban markets over a long period of time have a relative advantage. They have vast accumulated internal data, for example, past and forecasted sales, market environment, product performance, sales force size, potential and performance, product-distribution strength and availability and cost effectiveness of media. There is an established service sector to supplement the readily available internal data. The National Readership Survey IV, Business Men's Readership Survey, National Television Survey III, Television Rating System, Video Watch, ORG Retail audit are some examples of the surveys carried out in the Indian market. Newspapers and magazines occasionally provide coverage of all India trends, urban–rural comparisons and information about metros, state capitals and towns.

Most companies are recent entrants in the rural scene. The result is a paucity of internal historic data. Coupled with this is the fact that the contribution of syndicated research services is meagre. The National Council of Applied Economic Research (NCAER) conducts regular studies and then there are publications, few and far between, such as Villages of India 1991. Very few magazines such as *Kurukshetra*, *Annadatha* and *Khadi Gramodyog* deal with rural issues and present rural data.

Some research agencies have come forward to generate a rural database.

- ORG-MARG set up a rural consumer's panel. The 'R' Panel comprises over 20,000 households whose purchasing and consumption habits are monitored every day. The study covers 16 state clusters, over 1,000 villages and 32 FMCG product categories.
- Initiative Media: The AP Lintas' media-buying arm developed LinQuest—a software package that provides marketers with data on rural India. It is claimed to be the first database to present the census data in an interactive manner. Till now, census data was mostly available as indices. With LinQuest, marketers can simply enter the parameters they seek along with weightages and obtain lists of most suitable districts and all the villages that match the company's requirements. The database can be sorted on five parameters–demographic, literacy, agricultural, civic amenities and income.
- MICA (Mudra Institute of Communications, Ahmedabad) has come out with its exhaustive Rural Market Rating. Additionally, it brings out a quarterly newsletter catering exclusively to the rural sector called "*Ruralscan.*" It has been brought out by Mumbai-based rural communication specialist Sampark Marketing and Advertising Solutions Pvt. Ltd. It covers the rural sector extensively and fills the gap of qualitative information on rural markets on a regular basis. It features case notes, experiences, changing trends, data and information.

Primary data sources

In urban areas, the data sources are many as well as large. The number of experts and middlemen, the size of sales force, the proportion of actual and potential customers and the number of opinion leaders are large in urban markets compared to the rural markets. In urban areas every member of the family can be a source of information. In rural areas, the male head of the family dominates. Women are not allowed to voice their individual opinions. However, the rural market has seen marked transformation with substantial increase in the disposable incomes of rural consumers. The proportion of potential customers of several products is now much higher than in urban markets. The youth are growing independent and women are slowly becoming active through various schemes promoting self-help groups and entrepreneurship.

Sampling

Despite varying linguistic and cultural backgrounds and geo-physical differences, urban markets show a marked convergence in aggregate behavioural patterns. The differences are nullified as a result of high mobility and exposure facilitated by infrastructure facilities, regularity of income receipts, savings patterns moulded by tax problems and time schedules and incomes. Urban consumer sets have a marked similarity. This makes sampling an easy process.

> A profile of the Hush puppies buyer in Delhi on parameters of income, family size, education and occupational status would be reasonably valid for Mumbai or Kolkata. Van Heusen shirts are bought equally by executives working at Brigade Road in Bangalore or Nariman Point in Mumbai.

Differential and limited development of infrastructure, geo-physical differences, variation in literacy levels and differences in proximity to towns have contributed to the heterogeneity in the rural market place. Inter-rural differences are evident between the states and even within a state.

Rajpuria Hundan is a village 24 km from Loonkaransar in Bikaner district in Rajasthan. The village economy is based on rain-fed cultivation of bajra, chana, and maitra (a type of water melon). These crops have a very low monetary yield but the choice is limited by soil conditions and dependence on rain fall. The result is a drop in disposable incomes.

Dabri, a village in Hissar district, Haryana is a picture of rural affluence with *pucca* connecting roads. Most of the cropped area is irrigated. The crops are wheat and cotton.

Most villages in Bikaner district have houses that are semi-*pucca* or made of mud, while in neighbouring Sri Gangangur district, one sees *pucca* or cemented houses.

Source: Pawan Bhandari and Rajat Iyer, "Chalk and Cheese," *A & M* (August 1994): 25–28.

Differences in lifestyles and utility value of products in the rural areas can be better understood with the following examples.

- In Rajpuria Hudan, toothpaste and soap are luxuries whereas in Dabri they are necessities.
- In milk-rich Haryana and Punjab, hair dye has been used on buffaloes and washing machines have been used to make *lassi*.
- In some parts of Rajasthan, utensils are cleaned with sand and ash owing to water scarcity. A washing powder would face competition from these alternatives that need very little water.
- Brackish or hard water in most villages in Bikaner, coastal Andhra Pradesh and Himachal Pradesh is the reason for the low acceptance of soap.

A variable such as income cannot be used to stratify rural samples. The reason is that incomes are uncertain and unaccounted. In the urban context, the income category is the primary criterion for grouping consumers. Often, rural market research utilizes land holding as an indicator of wealth and income. This can be misleading, especially if the study is spread over a large geographic area. The land holding has to be balanced with the productivity and realizations from the crop mix. A farmer growing cotton in 25 acres of irrigated land would be lot more prosperous than a farmer growing food grains or pulses on 200 acres of rain-fed land.

Data collection

Urban and rural research may be designed to get the same data; however, the process of acquiring it differs. Quantitative research is the main strength of many research firms. They take pride in the use of sophisticated instruments. They could be successful with such forms, scales and terms because urban respondents are comfortable with numbers, ratings and time lines.

At NFO-BL for instance, if they want respondents to rank a brand on a five-point scale, researchers prefer to ask repeated questions: first "Is the brand good or bad?" Next, "Is brand x very bad or slightly bad?"

Rural research requires a different approach. The time-tested sophisticated tools fail to evoke the required response.

Likewise, detailed questions need to be asked to simplify the inquiry and to pin down the response. Rural consumers are comfortable with colours, pictures and stories.

In addition, rural researchers make use of participatory research methods.

Table 5.15 Differences in Urban and Rural Market Research

Sl No.	Aspect	Urban	Rural
1.	Respondents	Literate, brand aware, individuals respond individually.	Semi-literate or illiterate, brand unaware. Difficult to obtain individual responses. Generally group responses are available.
2.	Time	Willing to respond. Have time pressures. Spare little time for researchers.	Hesitant, but devotes time.
3.	Accessibility	Easy to access, though many suffer from research fatigue.	Tough to access; geographical distances and psychological apprehensions are barriers. Don't speak easily to outsiders.
4.	Secondary data sources	Internal data, syndicate research, published media. There are many sources and large amount of data.	Very few sources and less data.
5.	Primary data sources	Large number of middle-men, experts, sales force, consumers and opinion leaders.	Fewer number of all categories.
6.	Sampling	Respondents form relatively homogeneous groups. Income can be a criterion.	Heterogeneous groups. Income and land-holding to be carefully applied.
7.	Data collection	Individual focused, use of sophisticated instrument, style and administration. Respondents comfortable with numbers ratings and timelines.	Participatory approaches. Require simplified instruments. Respondents comfortable with participative and naïve approaches of categorization like colours, pictures and stories.

The differences discussed earlier are summarized in Table 5.15. For a better understanding of the differences, the personal experience of two researchers is given here.

RURAL RESEARCH BUSINESS

Rural market research is still at a fledgling stage. While Indian market research is worth Rs 40 billion, it forms barely 10–15 per cent of the total research pie. According to ORG-MARG, the rural market research spend will be around Rs 0.5 billion. However, with the growing importance of the rural markets in corporate marketing strategies, there is an increased recognition of rural specialists in helping companies plan and implement their rural marketing activities. This has resulted in a number of players, both big and small, entering the field in the last couple of years. While the present scenario is very encouraging, there were times when companies planning an entry into rural India faced the problem of knowledge gap. Pradeep Kashyap of MART (Box 5.1) and Pradeep Lokhande of Rural Relations (Box 5.2) are two researchers who had taken initiatives to bridge the gap during those years.

The main players in the rural marketing consultancy and research field are:

1. NCAER, New Delhi
2. AC Nielsen ORG-MARG Research Limited
3. Sampark, Hyderabad

Box 5.1 Pradeep Kashyap—Father of Rural Marketing

Pradeep Kashyap is regarded as the "Father of Rural Marketing in India" for his intellectual contribution to policy making in the context of rural development. An engineer from BITS Pilani, with a post graduate diploma in business management, he followed his passion for rural development and set up MART in 1993. Notable among his contributions are:

- The highly successful pioneering "*Gramshree melas*" to sell rural products in cities. Nearly 300 such *melas* have been held in 60 cities benefiting 100,000 poor women.
- The 3M micro-enterprise model, the most comprehensive approach for large-scale employment generation in rural areas using the micro-finance route. 3M has been approved by NABARD, Governments of Andhra Pradesh, Madhya Pradesh, Rajasthan, Tamil Nadu and Orissa and CARE India.
- He co-created Project *Shakti* with Hindustan Unilever to appoint women micro-entrepreneurs among SHGs as company dealers. 15,000 women in 12 states have benefited and each of them earns Rs 1,000 per month as profit from this business.
- He engineered a novel low-cost, last mile rural distribution model using village volunteers on bicycles for Colgate, Godrej, Eveready, Heinz and others.
- He joined hands with other agencies to form Rural Marketing Agencies Association of India (RMAAI) and became the President of the Association.

Under his leadership, MART was conferred the RMAAI Gold Award for Innovative Long Term Rural Marketing Initiatives for its *Rasoi Ghar* model for HPCL.

Source: www.martrural.com, accessed March 2010.

Box 5.2 Lokhande: Researcher with the Spirit of Service

Pradeep Lokhande, founder of Rural Relations, India's largest rural marketing company based in Pune, is a human encyclopaedia of rural India. He has personally visited over 4,000 villages in India, recorded their populations, markets, education systems, consumer habits, and can rattle off these figures just like that.

Rural Relations commands a network of rural marketers in more than 7,000 villages across India. Lokhande has been recording their populations and capturing facts about markets, education systems and consumer habits in rural India. Giants like P&G and HUL have hired his services. He started the venture of visiting these villages to compile information on them and selling it to companies. He has used his travels to learn about the great digital divide between rural and urban India and is working towards taking computers to 28,000 village schools in Maharashtra, Gujarat, Madhya Pradesh, Rajasthan and Uttar Pradesh. His conviction that computers can do wonders for the confidence and learning style of the children in rural areas prompted him and his team to embark on the project of providing computers to schools, free of cost. They wrote letters to various persons and institutions and the response was overwhelming. With a personal expenditure of about Rs 1,000, he collected computers from the donors and initiated a new movement of computer education in rural areas.

Source: www.indiatogether.org/stories/lokhande.htm, accessed March 2010.

Box 5.3 R. V. Rajan—Crusader of Rural Marketing

R. V. Rajan, Chairman, Anugrah Madison Advertising, was the founder president of RMAAI. Announcing the formation of RMAAI he said, "The association has been formed to improve and develop the cause of rural marketing and protect the interests of rural marketing specialists." One of the important objectives of the Association was to set industry benchmarks in areas of performance evaluation and financial practices. To improve the overall understanding of rural markets by the corporate world, the Association conducts seminars, workshops and conferences, besides offering guidance to the management institutes in running courses in rural marketing. The Association also undertakes syndicated research in rural marketing on selected topics that help to increase the knowledge base of rural marketers, which in turn could help marketers develop better and more effective rural marketing strategies. Further on, the Association also plans to conduct award functions to recognize individuals and organizations who have actively contributed to the growth of the rural marketing industry. To make the Association broad based it has been renamed Rural Marketing Association of India in 2009.

The association has decided to confer the first ever RMAI Lifetime Achievement Award on R. V. Rajan, Chairman, Anugrah Madison Advertising and the immediate past President of RMAI. The Award was given to Rajan for his association with the rural marketing and communication scene for over three decades, during which he has made significant contribution to promoting the cause of rural marketing.

According to Pradeep Kashyap, President, RMAI, "RMAI decided to recognize Rajan's role in spearheading the formation of the Association and also for steering it for four years as the Founder President. He has helped in establishing the Association on a solid foundation by implementing a variety of activities, all of which has helped in creating more knowledge bases on rural marketing."

Source: www.anugrahmadison.com, accessed April 2010.

4. MART
5. ORCN (Ogilvy Rural Communication Network), New Delhi
6. Rural Communication and Marketing (RC&M), New Delhi
7. Initiative Media
8. Anugrah Madison, Chennai

Rural marketing association

A few leading players who have been providing tremendous value-added rural marketing services across the country have decided to come together on a common platform and work towards recognition, credibility and meeting the needs of the rural marketing industry. The founder members of the Association are Anugrah Madison, MART, Rural Relations, Sampark, Ogilvy Activation, Linterland, RC&M, Impact Communications, Kripa Outdoor Publicity, Indian Agribusiness Systems and Rural Eight. Box 5.3 highlights the contribution of R.V. Rajan in the formation and successful functioning of the association.

WHO HAS THE EDGE?

To understand rural markets and design marketing programmes, companies require at least three assets.

- First, they need the resources to undertake a study of the large and diverse rural economy. The kind of explorative study of behaviour that is needed to understand the peculiarities of each segment of the rural market will necessarily be expensive.

- Second, they need to believe that the expenditure is worth their while. This belief must exist with the recognition that the exercise need not always result in a profit-generating project.
- Third, companies must use their technological expertise to create right products and communication for the rural economy.

MNCs versus Indian companies

MNCs have an edge over several major Indian companies for the following reasons:

- They have much deeper pockets than Indian companies.
- They place greater emphasis on research than most Indian companies.
- Being new to this country, they are sensitive to both rural and urban markets. They have no prejudices like urban companies.
- They are technologically more advanced than their Indian counterparts.

These advantages of multinationals are, of course, not impossible for Indian companies to challenge. They can generate resources, develop right attitudes and overcome technological barriers if they make a concerted and determined effort. However, if they are preoccupied with either retaining or expanding their urban market share or reaching out for new global ones, they may find that have handed over the rural backyard to the multinationals.

Large versus small firms

Small research firms are doing good business in this area because the bigger firms are not interested in it. The following reasons may be cited for this.

- The size of rural market research is small. As such, big names in market research are putting a lower priority to it. Rural marketers are generally not looking for nation-wide rural research, just for the data that will bring them profits. Thus, the scale of operations is too small.
- Big agencies do not have the rural touch—their researchers are primarily urban. They find it hard to break the ice with wary rural consumers. They feel more comfortable dealing with men in suits who speak management jargon.
- The core strength of big agencies has always been quantitative research. Since rural marketers are engaged in market development, they are more interested in qualitative data than in numbers. The numbers, they opine, will come later when the market matures.
- Another important reason for the big companies not undertaking research is that their sales forces are out in the field and interacting with retailers on a regular basis while agency personnel visit rural areas for 15 days a year. On the contrary, some of the small rural research agencies have made the following claims.
    a. NFO-MBL has a report called "A day in the life of a farmer." Their researchers wake up at 5 a.m. with farmers, go to their fields, hang around at the *chaupals* noting down what is going on. Clients find it eye-opening.
    b. MART has a permanent field staff of 10 employees with relevant qualifications. They are from a rural background and have lived in villages working with NGOs and thus, gained acceptance. The agency is banking on their comfort levels with rural research. The agency is planning on hiring graduates from IRMA (the Institute of Rural Management) to utilize the thinking, writing and analytical skills that MBAs are famous for.

c. Small agencies are more attractive as they are cheaper. Because they conduct localized research, they do not have to support large overheads. Agencies such as MART quote prices that are 50 per cent lower than large agencies.

However, some large agencies interested in rural research are getting ready for it. MARG and IMRB both have rural knowledge heads who are NGO personnel with acquired wisdom in rural matters.

Summary

In the present competitive business scenario, the support of marketing information in decision making has become indispensable. Marketing information systems consist of four components: (1) internal reporting system, (2) marketing intelligence system, (3) marketing research system and (4) decision support system. Internal reporting system provides transactional data analysis and reports for routine decision making. Marketing intelligence system expands the knowledge horizons of the managers by providing up-to-date information. Marketing research is a problem-specific, non-routine data collection and analysis activity that provides solutions to decision-making problems of strategic importance. The key decision areas that require the careful consideration of researchers are: (i) defining problems, (ii) determining research budget, (iii) choosing research design (exploratory, descriptive or causal; qualitative or quantitative and based on primary data or secondary data), (iv) determining sampling method and size, (v) selecting appropriate data analysis tools, (vi) making research proposals, (vii) organizing field work and (viii) analysing and reporting findings. Choosing the investigators and training them to work in the rural cultural milieu is a difficult task. Urban research techniques cannot be replicated in the rural markets as there are many differences with respect to respondents, time, accessibility, secondary data sources, primary data sources and data collection. New research tools such as ladder, images of faces and colours are being tested by rural marketing research agencies. Rural research is growing in size and value. Many small agencies have already made a mark of their own. However, when MNCs enter the field, they seem to have the competitive advantage by virtue of their resources and professionalism.

Short Answer Questions

1. Explain the role of information in marketing decision making.
2. Define marketing research. When do companies go for marketing research?
3. Briefly explain the steps involved in the marketing research process.
4. Is the qualitative research approach more suitable in the rural context?
5. What is primary research? When is it preferred?
6. What are the sources of secondary data for rural research?
7. Identify the factors that influence the choice of sample in the rural setting.
8. Suggest guidelines for rural research investigators.
9. Explain some of the data collection tools specially developed for rural research.
10. Examine the differences between rural and urban market research.
11. Who are the major players in rural marketing research?
12. Do you think MNCs have more competitive advantage than Indian firms?

Discussion Questions

1. Neither the approaches nor the tools useful in urban research can be replicated in rural research. Discuss.
2. Participatory research tools are qualitative and cannot provide substantial evidence to help make policy decisions. Discuss.
3. Discuss the use of new tools of research in conducting exploratory studies in rural areas.
4. Discuss the role played by any two research agencies in promoting rural marketing research.

Essay Questions

1. Explain the significance and sources of information for decision making with reference to rural markets.
2. Explain the key decisions involved in rural marketing research.
3. Explain the differences between rural and urban marketing research. Suggest guidelines for rural research fieldwork.
4. Discuss the innovative tools and approaches adopted by rural researchers.

Internet Exercise

Visit the Web sites of four research agencies and prepare a consolidated report on the services mix offered by them.

Mini Project

Conduct a study to describe the lifestyle of the rural youth. Include in your sample, rural youth studying in your institute and those residing in their villages. Prepare a research paper that explains your methodology and findings. Draw comparisons between rural youth in your institute and in villages.

End Notes

1. "Reliance Money Goes Rural, Eyes 10,000 Outlets in 5,000 *Talukas*," *Business Standard*, 28 November 2009, available at http://www.business-standard.com/india/storypage.php?autono=29449.
2. www.martrural.com, accessed March 2010.
3. "Helping the Corporate Enter Rural World," 26 March 2009, available at www.adinomics.blogspot.com/.
4. Philip Kotler, *A Framwork for Marketing Management* (Delhi: Pearson Education, 2002), p. 65.
5. M. Sandelowski, "Sample Size in Qualitative Research," *Research in Nursing and Health* (18): 179–183, available at www.ncbi.nlm.nih.gov/pubmed/7899572.
6. Bishnu B. Bhandari, "Participatory Rural Appraisal (PRA)," Institute for Global Environmental Strategies, 2003, available at http://enviroscope.iges.or.jp/contents/eLearning/waterdemo/bhandari_m4.pdf.

Case 5.1 Rural Market Survey

Raj recently attended a seminar on "Rural Marketing: The New Challenge," organized at Time: The Management School. He heard various speakers criticizing corporations for neglecting rural areas. They held forth on the various ways that companies can go rural. Raj, the head of the marketing division of the personal care products division of Sindhu Pvt. Ltd, became curious to know whether the rural markets have changed so much. During his interaction with the management students, he identified a batch of ten students specializing in rural marketing who were quite eager to help him. The ten students went to villages in nearby Vadamalpet in Andhra Pradesh and carried out a survey.

Research Problem: Are villages worthy of consideration for the marketing of personal care products?

Objectives: The objectives of the study are:

1. To find whether villages are accessible to marketers
2. To identify the demographic profile of villages
3. To know more about the products they possess and their brand preferences
4. To examine the existing distribution system

Research Site: Chittoor district is one among the 23 districts of Andhra Pradesh. It is widely known today, because the former Chief Minister of Andhra Pradesh, Sri Chandra Babu Naidu, hailed from it. The district has a population of about 3.26 million, which constitutes 5 per cent of the total population of the state. The district is divided into three revenue division, i.e. Chittoor, Tirupati and Madanapalle. There are 66 *mandals,* 3 municipalities and 1,540 revenue villages in the district.

Data Collection: Data was collected from five villages, i.e. Kadiri mangalam, Obalraj kandriga, Vadamala bazaar, Vadamala gramam and Rama samudram with the help of veterinary medical officers and village assistant officers. Preliminary information indicated that 85 per cent of the population is literate. The mainstay of the villages is agriculture. Keeping this information in mind, a questionnaire was developed to guide the inquiry (see Exhibit 5.1).

Exhibit 5.1: Questionnaire

Village Profile (General inquiry)

- Number of households :
- Population :
  - Male :
  - Female :
  - Children :
- Literates :
  - Male :
  - Female :
- Occupations :
  - Agriculture :
  - Agricultural labourers :
  - Non-agricultural labourers :
  - Salary earners :
  - Business :
  - Unemployed :
  - Others :
- Number of schools :
  - Primary : ( )
  - Secondary : ( )
- Primary health centres : ( )
- Cooperative stores : ( )
- Banks : ( )
- Post offices : ( )
- Distance to nearby town :
- Transport facility :
  - Buses : ( )
  - Trains : ( )
  - Vans/tempos : ( )
- Road facility :

Distribution Profile:

1. Retail outlets

Size	Number

2. Co-operative society
3. *Haats/Melas*
4. Do mobile vans come? Which company sends them? How frequently?
5. Any other way of selling in the village?

Profile of Village Consumers (Individual inquiry):

(a) Product possession

1. (i) Durables related to occupation
   (ii) Consumables related to occupation
2. (i) Durables related to households (TV, 2-in-1, etc.)
   (ii) Consumables related to households
3. Local and national brands in use
4. Spurious brands in use

(b) Exposure to media

1. Is TV watched? What are the preferred channels and programmes?
2. Are newspapers read? Which papers?
3. Are magazines read? Which ones?

(c) Do you take the opinion of someone before you buy? If yes,

Size	Number

Source: TIME: The Management School, Tirupati.

For discussion

1. Evaluate the research design with reference to the problem and objectives.
2. Critically evaluate the questionnaire design.

Case 5.2 Pharma Surveys Rural

Padma Pharma Ltd has decided to go for a special rural marketing drive. When it looked up the available database, it found that there is a lack of proper information about chemists operating in or nearby rural areas and catering to rural markets. It, therefore, decided to conduct a research and contacted Deepti Rural Research and Solutions.

Research Outline

The research agency presented an outline of the proposed research.

(i) Objectives

- To estimate the potential of chemists catering to rural markets
- To analyse the problems that chemists face in receiving supplies and making payments

(ii) Methodology

Rural Market Classification

Rural formulation market has three broad segments.

- Feeder market, which is a small town
- Semi–rural–urban market
- Village market

Therefore, it proposed to cover these three markets. The parameters proposed for selection of the rural market are given below

Sl No.	Parameter	Feeder	Semi-urban/Rural	Village
1.	Absolute population	50,001 to 100,000	15,000 to 50,000	Below 15,000
2.	Communication linkage	Within 15 minutes	30 to 45 minutes	More than 60 minutes
3.	No. of allopaths	35 to 75 (60 per cent are MBBS)	10 to 35 (35 to 60 per cent are MBBS)	Less than 10 (but 10 per cent are MBBS)
4.	Government hospital	Sub-divisional/ District	Primary health centre	Nil
5.	Nursing homes	2 to 8	1 to 2	Nil
6.	No. of chemists	35 to 75	10 to 35	Less than 10
7.	Productivity/ Chemist per day (Rs)	2,500	1,500 to 2,500	Less than 1,500

Information Range

The information focus can be on one or more of the following.

(*a*) *Doctors' Survey*
Qualification, specialty, number of patients seen per day, major ailments normally treated, patients referred to a specialist, major molecules prescribed, source of information of drugs (literature, direct mailers, conference, medical representatives' visits, etc.) and so on.

(*b*) *Hospitals/Polyclinics/Nursing Homes Survey*
Government/private, number of beds, number of patients treated (percentage of patients referred from nearby places), doctors attached to the hospital, whether pharmacy is attached, etc.

(*c*) *Chemists' Survey*
Location, size of the outlet, whether attached to doctor/hospital, turnover, practice of doctors nearby, buyers from nearby villages, place and mode of purchase of stocks, mode of repayment, pharma sales, people's visits, etc.

Inquiry

This study is confined to chemists. A questionnaire designed for data collection is given in Exhibit 5.2.

For discussion

1. Evaluate the questionnaire and suggest improvements.
2. Do you suggest any alternative method of inquiry?

Exhibit 5.2

(Strictly confidential)

QUESTIONNAIRE
DESIGNED FOR RETAIL MEDICAL STORE

IDENTIFICAION NO. | | | | | | | | | |

PART A: IDENTIFICATION OF THE MEDICAL STORES

(Information to be collected by personal observation and also supplemented by interview)

1. Name of the doctor :
   (Note down the name of the store legibly)

2. Address :
   (Note down the address legibly)

Location	
Vill/Town	
District	
State	
Pin No.	
Phone No.	

Distance from nearest town ☐☐☐ km

(b) Whether chemist is a full-time chemist or is keeping medicines with other household amenities?
(Observe and put a tick sign appropriately): Full time Chemist ☐
Chemist keeping other household amenities ☐

(c) Floor area of the shop : ☐☐☐ Sq. feet

(d) No. of employees in the shop : ☐☐

(e) Whether chemist is attached to a hospital/NH : Yes ☐ No ☐

(f) (If yes) Name of hospital/nursing home/primary health centre: ☐

PART B: CHEMIST PROBING

4. When did you establish this store? : ☐
   (Note down the answer using the code numbers mentioned below.
   [(a) Less than 6 months ago (b) 6 months to 1 year ago (c) 1 year to 2 years ago (d) 2 years to 5 years ago (e) 5 years to 10 years ago (f) 10 + years ago]
5. At the time of establishment of the store, what was the total number of stores in this market? (Note down the number of the stores appropriately) ☐ to ☐

6. At the time of establishment, what was the average monthly turnover of the store? (Note down the amount legibly) Rs ☐☐☐☐☐☐☐☐
7. (At present) What is the total number of stores in this market? ☐ to ☐
(Note down the number of the stores appropriately)
8. (At present) What is the average monthly turnover of your store?
(Note down the amount legibly) Rs ☐☐☐☐☐☐☐☐
9. (At present) What is the average monthly turnover of your store in the peak season?
(Note down the amount legibly) Peak season = Rs to Rs ☐☐☐☐☐☐☐☐
10. (At present) What is the average monthly turnover of your store in lean season?
(Note down the amount legibly) Lean season = Rs to Rs ☐☐☐☐☐☐☐☐
11. What is the total number of companies whose drugs are available here?
Could you please mention the name of the top 10 companies according to your sale of products? (Note down the name of the companies below, legibly)
Could you also please mention the share of these companies according to sale of products?

(Note down the shares against the name of the companies below)

Rank	Name of the companies	(Percentage)	Rank	Name of the companies	(Percentage)
1.			6.		
2.			7.		
3.			8.		
4.			9.		
5.			10.		
			11.	All other companies together	

12. (a) Is there any doctor attached to this store? Yes ☐ No ☐
(Circle the appropriate entry)
(b) [If the answer is "Yes" in (a), then] Is the doctor a qualified, registered allopath? (Circle the appropriate entry) Yes ☐ No ☐
(c) [If "Yes" in (a), then] Can you recall the name of the doctor(s)? From where do they come?
[▪ Note down the name of the doctor(s) legibly under Column 1
▪ Write the locality of the doctor(s) under Column 2. Also note down the distance traversed: (a) Less than 1 km (b) 1 to 2 km (c) 2 to 3 km (d) 3 to 5 km (e) 5 to 10 km (f) more than 10 km.
▪ Note down the degree/diploma of the doctor(s) under Column 3]
(d) Also, please tell us when the doctors are available at this store.
(Note down practice time/week, appropriately, under Column 4.
Circle the day code and mention time in the relevant box under Column 4)
Note: Practice time will be written as 7/1000/1300 if the doctor is available from 10 a.m. to 1 p.m. on Sundays.
So, Monday 1, Tuesday 2, Wednesday 3, Thursday 4, Friday 5, Saturday 6, Sunday 7, Everyday 0.
(e) Can you tell us what the average number of patients treated per day by each doctor is?
(Note the number appropriately under Column 4)

Sl No.	Name of the Doctor	Locality with Distance	Degree/Diploma	Practice Time	Average Patients/day
(0)	(1)	(2)	(3)	(4)	(5)
1.				0 1 2 3 4 5 6 7 / 0 1 2 3 4 5 6 7	
2.				0 1 2 3 4 5 6 7 / 0 1 2 3 4 5 6 7	
3.				0 1 2 3 4 5 6 7 / 0 1 2 3 4 5 6 7	
4.				0 1 2 3 4 5 6 7 / 0 1 2 3 4 5 6 7	
5.				0 1 2 3 4 5 6 7 / 0 1 2 3 4 5 6 7	

If needed attach extra sheet.

On an average, how many buyers come to your store to buy drugs, per day? (Note down the response legibly) ______ to ______

Do your customers also come from outside this town/village? Yes ☐ No ☐

(Note down the response appropriately)

Could you please tell us what per cent of your buyers come from each of the following places, i.e. out of 100 per cent buyers of your store of a month how many come:

- From this village/town only
- From outside of this town/village

		per cent
		per cent

(If answer to the above question (*b*) is "Yes" then) Can you recall the name of those villages/ towns?

(▪ Note down the name of the villages/towns legibly under Column 1 below

▪ Also, note down the distance of the villages/towns in complete km under Column 2 below)

Sl No.	Name of the Village/Towns	Distance (in km)
(0)	(1)	(2)
1.		
2.		
3.		
4.		
5.		
6.		
7.		
8.		
9.		
10.		

14. (a) From where do you procure your stock of medicines?
(Put a tick in the appropriate entry under Column 2 below)

Sl No.	Description	Put a tick
(0)	(1)	(2)
1.	Stockist took order and supplied accordingly	A
2.	Wholesaler(s)/distributor(s) took order and supplied accordingly	B
3.	Local agent(s)/youth(s) took order and supplied accordingly	C
4.	Self-procurement for immediate purpose vis-a-vis any of the above methods	D
5.	Self-procure (completely)	E
6.	From the medical representative(s)	F
7.	Others (If any, specify)	G

(b) (If the answer to the above is (a), (b), (c), (d) or (e) then)

(i) Can you recall the name(s) of the stockist(s)/wholesaler(s)/ distributor(s) from whom you normally procure your stocks?

(ii) Also, write the location of such stockist(s)/wholesaler(s)/distributor(s)

Note: Write the proper code of stockist(s): S/wholesaler(s): W/agent(s): A/distributor(s): D in Column 1. Write the name of the wholesaler(s)/agent(s)/stockist(s)/distributor(s) in Column 2. Note down the exact location with the distance code in Column 3 below.

Sl No.	Code	Name of the stockist/wholesaler/agent/ distributor	Location with distance code
(0)	(1)	(2)	(3)
1.			
2.			
3.			
4.			
5.			
6.			
7.			
8.			
9.			
10.			

Distance Code: (a) Less than 2 km (b) 2 km to 5 km (c) 5 km to 10 km (d) More than 10 km (e) Within this market

(C) How do you release payment after procurement?

(a) Do you release cash or pay in kind or both? Release cash: ☐ Pay in kind: ☐ : Both types: ☐

(b) Do you pay cash immediately after supply/collection of products? Yes ☐ No ☐

(c) [If "No" in (b)] Do you procure products on credit and pay after sometime? Yes ☐ No ☐

(d) [If "Yes" in (c)] After how many days you pay? Write in detail.

____

____

____

(e) [If "No" in (c)] Write the payment process in details.

____

____

[Note: For (a), (b), (c), put a tick mark in the appropriate box.
One can use code for (d) and (c): (a) Pay within a week (b) Pay within a fortnight (c) Pay within three weeks (d) Pay within a month (e) Other.]

15. What is the percentage of commission you normally receive by
   (a) Selling drugs of MNCs/Nationalized operators
   (b) Selling drugs of state operators
   (e) Selling drugs of the district operators
   (d) Also, note down whether the shop owner receives more percentage of commission for cash purchases.

16. Can you recall the names of the pharmaceutical companies whose representative(s) have met you in the last fifteen days?
   (Note down the name of the companies in Column 1 below.)

Name of the companies	Name of the companies	Name of the companies
(1)	(2)	(3)

17. Can you tell us what the total size of this market is (in terms of average monthly sales in Rs)? [By your own guess, based on your own experience in this field.] (Note down the value of market in terms of Rs appropriately.)

Rs														

Thank you for your cooperation.

6

Selecting and Attracting Markets

LEARNING OBJECTIVES

Upon completion of this chapter, you will be able to:

- Explain the concept and methods of segmenting markets
- Examine the appropriateness of multivariable segmentation approaches
- Understand the importance of women and youth as the emerging segments
- Discuss the approaches to marketing coverage and positioning

Life insurance companies are resorting to special initiatives to increase business from the rural segment, which they term the emerging market. Insurers see a huge scope in rural areas as penetration is dismally low, especially given the fact that the state-owned insurance giant Life Insurance Corporation of India (LIC) accounts for 30 per cent of the total business premium from rural areas. "We are designing products to suit the emerging markets as we have observed that the premium-paying capacity of people residing in rural areas is lower when compared with those residing in the urban parts of the country. Also, the mode of payment needs to be flexible," said Reliance Life President, P. Nandgopal.

For instance, Bajaj Allianz Life Insurance Company has put a cap on the size of the policies sold in rural areas to increase sales, while Max New York Life is carrying out need-based selling. "Agents are always tempted to sell large-ticket policies due to the high commissions involved. We have capped the ticket size of the policies sold in rural areas to Rs 10,000," said Bajaj Allianz Life Insurance Managing Director and CEO, Kamesh Goyal.

Max New York Life Insurance Company has asked agents to carry out need-based selling. After analysing the client's needs, they customize the products. The private insurer is asking agents to find out how much life insurance one would need in rural areas to cover their needs and provide a policy accordingly. "We are asking agents to sell policies based on the actual assessment of an individual's need in the rural segment," said Max New York Life Executive Vice-President and Head for Emerging Markets, R. P. Singh.

Most players sell similar policies in urban and rural regions. For selling policies in villages, they tie up with district centred co-operative banks and regional rural banks, also taking the help of non-governmental organizations and self-help groups.[1]

The strategies of Reliance Life, Bajaj Allianz and Max New York Life discussed above show how important it is to know and understand the market for achieving success. This chapter deals with the concepts and tools required for studying market segments and designing target marketing strategies.

INTRODUCTION

Marketing strategies require an identification of the markets and an understanding of their differences with respect to affordability, accessibility, acceptance and availability. In fact, in the face of competition, companies thrive on the ability to spot differences and fine-tune a differentiated marketing strategy that matches the diffused preferences of target customers effectively. Accordingly, we find that companies today are developing differentiated offers in terms of products (brands with different names, in different pack sizes and with different formulations), prices (at different price points), promotions (with different communication campaigns) and places (traditional channels, *haats, melas*, e-*choupals*, rural retail outlets, *Shakti* groups, etc.) to win over consumers in different market segments. Both companies and market research agencies are engaged in research to learn more about the characteristics of consumer markets in terms of geographic, demographic, psychographic and behavioural aspects to obtain rich and reliable data and to develop indices to take segmentation decisions. Based on such intelligent decisions, marketers are focusing on attractive segments to reach and serve them effectively and achieve results economically.

CONCEPTS AND PROCESSES

Selecting and attracting markets involves three key decisions—segmenting, targeting and positioning.

- Segmenting is the process of dividing or categorizing the market into different groups based on one or more variables.
- Targeting involves selecting the market segments that can be served efficiently and profitably. It involves making decisions on market coverage strategies.
- Positioning is a market attraction strategy that involves placing the brand in the minds of the customers in the target market.

The various steps involved in the market coverage and attraction processes are given in Table 6.1.

Table 6.1 Steps in the Market Coverage and Attraction Processes

Decision	Actions
Segmentation	1. Identification of various bases for segmenting markets
	2. Developing profiles of the market segments
Targeting	3. Evaluating the market segments for their attractiveness
	4. Deciding the market coverage strategy
Positioning	5. Identifying a set of possible competitive advantages of the brand
	6. Selecting the right competitive advantage
	7. Communicating the chosen competitive advantage to the target customers

CASE FOR SEGMENTATION

Segmentation is the process of dividing a heterogeneous market into homogeneous sub-units. The division is based on the premise that different people have different preferences. India is home to 13 languages, 1,300 dialects, 56 socio-cultural regions and a total of 576,000 villages (Ogilvy-Rural Research). The rural–urban differences and intra-rural differences are apparent in terms of different variables. The following differences substantiate the argument.

Occupational differences

Rural India comprises people practicing all kinds of occupations. The rural consumer could be a bank clerk commuting to the nearest town or an agricultural labourer living in a thatched-roof hut. The small and marginal farmers, agricultural labourers and artisans form the largest segment in the rural market (about two-third) whereas rich farmers constitute about one-third of the rural market. About 69.4 per cent of urban consumers are employed or own businesses as against 22 per cent in rural areas.

Income-level differences

Rural India has an average per capita income that is half of that of urban India. At the bottom of the pyramid, in the income bracket of less than Rs 75,000 per annum, we find 428 million people in rural areas as against 49 million in urban areas.

Different educational levels

About 26 per cent of rural India's chief wage earners (CWEs) are illiterate compared to 7.9 per cent in urban India. Seven per cent of rural CWEs are graduates compared to 29 per cent in urban India. We find differences between villages also.

- The Punjabi farmer has a better standard of living compared to farmers in Bihar and UP. His literacy rate is also at par with those in the urban areas. He likes to spend a lot, especially during the harvesting season. He is quite aware of different brands due to greater penetration of television and due to visits of family members from abroad.
- The villagers in Bihar, UP and MP are characterized by lower literacy rates, caste affiliations and a religious bent of mind. The villages have inadequate infrastructure, especially with respect to the supply of electricity and connectivity. The spending power is also lower.

Thus, we are dealing with extremely fragmented markets where population density is very low. An appropriate segmentation of the highly heterogeneous rural market and identification of the needs of different segments will form the very basis for rural market strategies.

BASES FOR SEGMENTATION

There is no one way of segmenting the market. A marketer may look for one or more variables, i.e. geographic, demographic, psychographic and behavioural to distinguish and describe the market segments. Table 6.2 presents the oft considered variables of segmentation under the classification scheme discussed above.

Geographic segmentation

Geographic segmentation is made based on variables such as zones/regions, states, districts, cities/towns/villages by size, density, climate and culture. The country is divided into states and union

Table 6.2 Segmentation Schemes and Variables

Characteristics	Variable	Categories
Geographic	Zones/region	East, West, North, and South
	Climate	Tropical, Rainy, and Cool
	States	30 States and 6 Union Territories
	Districts	With different market potentials
	Villages	Corridor villages (close to feeder town), Accessible villages and remote villages
	Population density	High and low
	Culture	Traditional versus modern, Socio-cultural regions (56)
Demographic	Age	Under 6, 6 to 12, 13 to 19, 20 to 40, 41 to 60, 60+
	Lifecycle	Infants, children, teens, young adults, elders, seniors
	Gender	Male, female and others
	Marital status	Married, unmarried
	Family size	1 to 2, 3 to 4, 5+
	Income	Rs 25,000 and below, Rs 25,001 to 50,000, Rs 50,001 to Rs 75,000, Rs 75,001 to Rs 100,000, above Rs 100,000
	Occupation	Farmer, agricultural labourer, artisan, non-agricultural labourer, businessman, professional employee, retired person, student, unemployed
	Land holding	Landless, marginal, small and large farmers
	Education	Illiterate, literate, elementary school, high school, college, university
	Religion	Hindu, Muslim, Christian, others
Psychographic	Lifestyle	Trend setters and chameleons
	Personality	Pleasant and assertive
Behavioural	Occasion	Family, religious, national, political and weekends
	Benefits sought	Aesthetic, emotional, rational and moral
	User status	Ex-user, first-time user, regular user and potential user
	Usage rate	Heavy, medium and light
	Loyalty status	Strong ,weak, non-loyal
	Place of purchase	Retail outlets/*Shakti Ammas*, *haats*, feeder towns, mobile vans
	Product possession categories	Product hierarchy

Table 6.3 Villages—Region-wise

Variable	East zone	West zone	North zone	South zone	All India
With less than 5,000 people	181,982	135,936	200,106	73,585	591,609
With *pucca* roads	41,348	44,693	78,217	45,102	209,360
No. of retail outlets	1,089,603	651,285	975,911	980,728	3,697,525
No. of *haats*	18,905	8,380	11,436	3,187	41,888

territories on the basis of language and they can be grouped under four zones/regions as indicated below:

East: West Bengal, Assam, Bihar, Orissa, North-East States

West: Maharashtra, Madhya Pradesh, Gujarat

North: Uttar Pradesh, Rajasthan, Himachal Pradesh, Jammu and Kashmir, Punjab, Haryana

South: Andhra Pradesh, Karnataka, Kerala, Tamil Nadu

Each state is divided into districts for the convenience of political administration. The villages are found under different zones as given in Table 6.3.

It is found that 6,300 villages are in the range of 5,000 or more inhabitants. About 90 per cent of the villages have a population less than 2,000 people. The low density villages are distributed as given under.

- Population of 500 or less inhabitants: 150,000 villages
- Population of 500 to 1,000 inhabitants: 316,800 villages
- Population of 5,000 or less but more than 1,000 people: 102,900 villages

One approach to rural market segmentation is based on the proximity to a nearby town or city. The division may be as shown in Table 6.4.

Culture

Villages with population below 1,000 depend on *shandies*. Promotion by the media will be effective when messages are designed in accordance with the cultural values, traditions, habits, and norms of people in a particular region. As such, the political division is immaterial for the various media. Ogilvy-Rural has divided the country into 56 Socio-Cultural Regions (SCR).

Demographic segmentation

Markets may be divided into segments based on variables such as age, lifecycle, gender, marital status, family size, income, occupation, land holding, education, and religion.

Age and lifecycle

The age and lifecycle classification applicable to urbanites is valid for rural people as well. The specific products for various age segments are given in Table 6.5.

Table 6.4 Geographic Segmentation Based on Proximity to Town

Segment	Characteristics	Implications for marketers
Corridor villages	Close to town (within a 2 km radius). Connected by public and private transport. Free movement to town, wide social networks and exposure to urban lifestyles and markets.	An extension of the urban market. Adopt the same marketing strategy with minor modifications.
Accessible villages	Away from towns. Connected by public transport. Journey to town is time consuming and tiring. Occasional visits to town. Social links with urban people is moderate. Exposure to town life is moderate. Mostly dependent on local markets.	Design channels to reach these places and devise innovative marketing strategy to cater to the unique needs. Supplement with CSR programmes.
Remote villages	Far-flung and widely scattered small villages with a population of 200 to 500 people.	Design innovative distribution strategies with high CSR/development component.

Table 6.5 Products for Different Age Groups

Age segment	Products	Typical brands
Infants	Milk powder, cereals, soaps diapers	Glaxo, Nestlé, Johnson & Johnson, Wipro, HUL
Children	Toothpaste, confectionery, sports cycles, story books, magazines	Pepsodent, Nutrine, Britannia, Parle, BSA, Atlas, Hero, *Amar Chitra Katha* series, *Chandamama*, *Balamitra*
Teens	Toothpaste, face creams, shoes, mopeds, soft drinks	Close-up, Fair & Lovely, North Star, Nike, TVS, Luna, Coke, Pepsi, Thums Up
Young adults	Magazines, shoes, TV, music systems, computers, scooters	*Sportstar*, *Computer Digest*, Reebok, Philips, Sony, Samsung, HCL, Compaq, Bajaj, LML
Elders	Briefcases, spectacles, suiting, cell phones	VIP, Samsonite, Ray-Ban, Bosche and Lamb, Raymond, Park Avenue, Tata Cellular, Magic
Seniors	Rocking chairs, knee pads, self-diagnostic kits, medicines	Modfurn, Conybio, Cipla, Glaxo, Reddy labs

Gender

Gender differences are observed in terms of dress, footwear, cosmetics and other products. Issues specific to women such as gynaecological problems offer marketers an opportunity to supply unique products such as sanitary napkins and estrogen medicines.

Marital status

The influence of marital status is obvious. Some companies can benefit on this ground as illustrated here.

Unmarried:	
Residence	Small size houses/flats, working women's hostels
Eating out	Fast food centres
Occasions	Valentine's day
Married:	
Tourism and hotels	Honeymoon packages
Events	"Best couple" competitions

Family size

Family size and type have significant influences on consumption of goods. Table 6.6 indicates the relationship. It is found that unitary and nuclear families have high per capita expenditure (Rs 7,973 and Rs 5,531, respectively) but low annual total expenditure. Personalized goods can be targeted at such families. Goods that offer values like liberty, status, luxury and comfort can be marketed to them. On the other hand, joint and extended families have more persons in the household and incur large annual total expenditure. However, the per capita expenditure is lower compared to the small families (slightly above Rs 5,000). In rural areas, it is found that large families with low incomes buy consumer durables like TVs. The promotion of consumables as "family products," particularly in economy refill packs, works well with large families. Large families may buy more than one brand of a product to meet specific individual preferences and tastes. As such, multi-brand consumption of a product may be there. While Colgate is perceived as a family toothpaste, Close-up is more personalized with its focus on the youth. Naturally, it makes inroads into families with young members and adequate buying power and co-exists with Colgate.

Income

The importance of income in influencing the purchase decisions relating to quantity and quality need not be over emphasized. Table 6.7 shows that the higher income groups prefer premium products

Table 6.6 Type of Households and Expenditures in Rural Areas

Family type	Percentage of all households	Average family size (no. of persons)	Annual total expenditure (Rs)	Per capita expenditure (Rs)
Unitary (single person or with spouse)	12.2	1.6	12,214	7,973
Nuclear (couple with children)	50.8	4.7	24,617	5,541
Extended (parents with one married child)	28.2	6.1	29,909	5,060
Joint (more than one married sibling)	4.3	10.3	51,551	5,078
Miscellaneous	4.5	8.7	42,003	4,976

Source: Indicus Analytics, available at www.indicus.net.

Table 6.7 Income Distribution and Segments

Annual income size (Rs)	Population (in million)	Convenience goods
>1,000 k	4	Super premium
500 to 1,000 k	10	Premium
300 k to 500 k	22	Premium
150 k to 300 k	111	Value-for-money
75 k to 150 k	239	Value-for-money
> 75 k	428	Cheap (unbranded, fake) products

Source: Indicus Analytics, available at www.indicus.net.

whereas middle-income groups look for economy and discounted products. The low-income groups can afford the unbranded cheaper products or low-unit, low-price branded products.

The rural rich buy premium brands like the urban rich. It is interesting that today even the low-income groups buy some brands that the rich rural people buy. The sale of the premium brands to low-income groups has been made possible through the sachet revolution. Products offered in sachets such as Velvette shampoo, Dairy top and Colgate are highly successful in rural markets. An observation by researchers is that durable products have a hierarchy that corresponds to income levels.

At the low end, demand is for black-and-white TVs, radios, bicycles, stripped models of mobile phones, moulded plastic chairs, simple kitchen appliances, etc. At the higher end, demand exists for home theatres, DVDs, luxury cars, iPods, washing machines, refrigerators, sophisticated mobile phones with multiple features, modular drawing halls and kitchens, etc.

Occupation

Occupational needs vary. Rural India is characterized by different occupational categories as shown in Table 6.8. The identification of specific products provides an opportunity for marketers to develop, design and distribute products to cater to the particular markets.

Land ownership

Land holding is an important indicator of the economic status and expenditure of the household. Table 6.9 provides the profile of rural households by size of land holding. The landless households comprise farm and non-farm employees. Those engaged in farm work will neither have stability of employment nor income. The landlords may have good but not stable incomes. The implications for marketers are: (i) those holding land need farm-related goods, training and information, (ii) they will invest in gold, farms and real estate and (iii) they can be induced to deposit money in banks and purchase insurance. Further segmentation in this category can be based on the size of land holding—small and large. Large land holdings allow the buying of farm machinery and bulk purchase of seeds, fertilizers, etc.

Education

Education provides knowledge and skill. It improves the thinking processes and facilitates the understanding of issues on a higher and wider plane. About 40 per cent of men and 61 per cent of women in India are not literate. However, due to the literacy programmes launched by the government, there has been a considerable rise in literacy levels. Recent reports indicate that illiterates constitute only

Table 6.8 Occupational Categories and Needs

Occupation	Percentage of sample	Needs
Owner and leased farmer	18.6	Seeds, fertilizers, pesticides, tractors, harvesters, pump sets and information about farming practices, market trends and weather
Animal husbandry (owner of live stock, owner of poultry and owner of fisheries)	1.0	Feed, medicines, consultancy
Agriculture and allied workers	24.2	Implements
Artisans/skilled labourers	3.8	Raw materials, equipment, tools, and information on market trends and support agencies
Service and employment (in urban and rural areas)	2.3	Pens, stationery items, conveyance, etc.
Student	14.2	Books and stationery items, conveyance, Internet facility, etc.
Doctors and village health centres	Very few in a village	Stethoscope, BP kit, medicines, syringes, needles, etc.

Table 6.9 Land Holding and Expenditure Patterns

Household type	No. of households (in millions)	Percentage
Landless	58.4	40.5
Marginal (up to 2 acres)	42.9	29.7
Small (2 to 4 acres)	20.4	14.1
Medium and large (above 4 acres)	22.6	15.7
All	144.3	100.0

28 per cent of the total rural population. Table 6.10 provides the literacy levels of men and women in rural areas. Besides education, exposure is also important. It has been observed that the thinking capabilities of rural people, in terms of divergence and association with images, are different from the urbanites. For instance, a horse shown in a condom advertisement (that is an accepted symbol of virility in urban areas) did not make proper sense to the rural consumer.

Religion

The influence of religion on the consumer purchase behaviour is an important consideration for marketers. Religion provides a "code of life" and links the visible real world with the invisible world

Table 6.10 Education Levels of Rural Men and Women

Education level	Males (percentage)	Females (percentage)
Non-literates	40.1	61.2
Primary	32.9	24.0
Secondary	21.4	12.0
Graduates and others	5.6	2.8

Source: Indicus Analytics, available at www.indicus.net.

Table 6.11 Religions of India

Religion	Population	Per cent	Literacy (percentage)	Work participation (percentage)	Sex ratio (rural)
Hindus	827,578,868	80.5	65.1	40.4	944
Muslims	138,188,240	13.4	59.1	31.3	953
Christians	24,080,016	2.3	80.3	39.7	1001
Sikhs	19,215,730	1.9	69.4	37.7	895
Buddhists	7,955,207	0.8	72.7	40.6	958
Jains	4,225,053	0.4	94.1	32.9	937
Others	6,639,626	0.6	47	48.4	995

Source: Census of India, 2001

Table 6.12 Influence of Religion on Product Preferences

Religion	Products/Items	Occasions/Events
Christians	Church, *The Bible*, crosses, candles, rose water, Christmas trees, bells, stars	Good Friday, Easter, Christmas
Hindus	Temples, rivers, icons of god, wicks for lamps, lamps, incense sticks, camphor, coconuts, fruits, betel leaves, nut powder, sandal paste, kumkum	Deepavali, Vinayaka Chaturthi, Krishna Jayanti, Sravana Fridays, Kartika month, Margasira month
Muslims	Mosque, perfumes, white caps, incense sticks, *Holy Quran*, Agar	Id-ul-Fitr, Bakrid, Milad-un-nabi, Muharram

reached after death. It furnishes the dos and don'ts to be followed. Table 6.11 gives some demographic details of major religions in the country. About 80.5 per cent of the population follows Hinduism. Even among Hindus, there are differences in worship and religious codes. The minority religions form niche markets (covering both urban and rural areas) and offer several opportunities to marketers. Table 6.12 shows the product preferences based on religious affiliation.

Psychographic segmentation

While geographic and demographic segmentations provide a physical view of the markets, the true dynamics of purchase can be assessed and marketing offers can be designed only on the basis of psychographics of the people. What people buy is not solely dependent on what they can buy but what they intend to buy. The intentions are shaped by the personality and lifestyle one has chosen to adopt. For example, in some parts of Gujarat, farmers purchased 50 HP (horse power) tractors, though their requirement was only for smaller ones like 25 to 30 HP, to keep up with the neighbours.
As such, marketers are interested in segmenting markets based on the following two variables:

- Lifestyle
- Personality

Lifestyle

Lifestyles are defined by AIO (activities, interests and opinions). With the advent of satellite television and penetration of cable networks across the country, the rural populace has been exposed to the lifestyle of the urbanites. Awareness cannot lead to adoption because of certain limiting factors.

For example, rural students may not have access to well furnished schools, libraries, the Internet, coaching centres, uninterrupted power supply, hair dressers, fashion tailors, cine theatres and other entertainment avenues. This will typically impact their adoption of the lifestyle of the modern urban youth (modelled after a cine/sports star).

Given the same set of facilities and opportunities in both rural and urban areas, we find different lifestyles influenced by cultural trends of the community, opinions and behaviours of reference groups and personality characteristics.

Today, we find that the rural consumer's brand choices are not that different from his urban counterpart's. However, while the brand choices tend to converge, packing preferences don't. By and large, the rural preference is for smaller packs. Wherever an option exists in case of durables, premium models are preferred by the rural rich. The highest selling premium brand of Mirc electronics—KY Thunder Series—found more takers in rural areas. As such, lifestyle segmentation applicable to urbanites can be gainfully employed in rural areas as well when combined with the proper understanding of circumstances.

This is why LG Electronics has graduated from value-plus products to aspirational products for targeting both urban and rural consumers.
One way of lifestyle classification is:

- Trendsetters
- Traditionalists
- Chameleons

A separate classification for women may be helpful. One such classification is:

- A capable home maker,
- A career woman, and
- A free spirit.

The examples provided in Table 6.13 throw light on the influence of lifestyle on product choices.

Personality

Personality refers to the set of psychological and physical characteristics of an individual that determine individual behaviour. These characteristics are unique, making individuals different from one another. Personality can be defined with the help of characteristics such as self-confidence, sociability, adaptability, assertiveness, autonomy, creativity, sensitivity, etc.

Table 6.13 Lifestyles and Product Choices

Lifestyle	Characteristics	People	Products/Brands	Models
Trendsetters	Ambitious for self and family, interested in change, progressive, career minded, achievement oriented, positive thinkers, social, independent, status seeking, have good reading habits, seek entertainment and recreation, prefer love marriages and dual-career families	City-influenced village dwellers with reasonably good income and education, successful farmers and entrepreneurs, teachers, doctors, village-level political administrators, young men and women educated in cities	Latest fashion goods, products with extra features like mobiles with music, camera and the Internet, elegant bikes, fast foods, soft drinks, credit cards, lifestyle magazines, etc. Also, 5C (Car, credit cards, cell phones, clubs, coke) cultural products	Cine artists, sports persons
Chameleons	Active, lack courage and confidence, indecisive, prefer following than leading, favour love marriages and career-oriented women at heart but do not allow full freedom to women, progressive thinkers, have good reading habits, average financial soundness	Farmers, artisans, workers, employees belonging to middle- and lower-income groups, town-educated village dwellers in the middle of their careers	Both aspirational products like those preferred by trendsetters and value-for-money products like the ones used by traditionalists	Cine artists, sports stars, teachers, doctors, *pradhan*
Traditionalists	Passive, hopeful, conservative, emotional, culture bound, contented, under achievers, prefer peace to prosperity and tradition to fashion, home loving, prefer arranged marriages, see women as capable home makers	Elite groups, middle-income category families, retired persons	Durables without unnecessary frills, yoga, homemade diet food, fresh juices, kitchen appliances, newspapers and magazines such as *India Today* and *Reader's Digest*	*Pradhan*, teacher, doctors, elderly people

For example, a person with a pleasant personality will display sociability and creative zeal and show preference to hygiene and skin care products, aesthetic and functional durables, picnics, parties, paintings and photography. Marketers may offer restaurants with good food and ambience, picnic spots, meeting/dining halls, concessional membership cards, cameras, photo films, processing labs, etc. to such persons. Assertive persons try to establish their presence in the group by exhibiting self-confidence, leadership and ambition. Brands like Fair & Lovely, Coke or Pespi, and Scooty Pep convey messages of such kind. Marketers, by experience, found that consumers buy products or brands whose perceived personality matches that of their own.

Behavioural segmentation

The behaviour of consumers is a better guide to segment the market. The following questions may be raised to understand consumer behaviour.

When do people buy?	Occasions
Why do people buy?	Benefits sought
How often do they buy? Once? More?	User status
How much do they buy?	Usage rate
Do they repeat the buy?	Loyalty status
Where do they buy from?	Place-retail outlet
What do they buy?	Products possessed

Occasions

Consumers become enthusiastic to make purchases when there is an occasion to celebrate. Occasions can be classified as under.

- *Family occasions:* Giving a name to a new born child (*barasala*), joining school (*aksharabhyasam*), pregnancy of a woman (*seemantham*), marriages, birthdays, etc.
- *Religious occasions:* Festivals (Sankranti, Deepavali, Dusserah, Christmas, Ramadan, etc.), *melas*, village god festivals, *jaataras*, *Kalyanam* of gods, Brahmostavams, etc.
- *National occasions:* Independence Day, Republic Day, etc.
- *Political occasions:* Elections and meetings
- *Weekends: Shandies* and *haats*

Most of the durables are purchased during the month of January when farmers receive agricultural income. Also, rural people prefer buying required goods when *melas* and *haats* are organized. Generally, purchases are made during the weekends. Purchases are usually made at *shandies* and *haats*.

Benefits sought

The benefits sought from a product depend basically on the needs of customers, though variations may be found from consumer to consumer based on their socio-economic circumstances. Benefits can be classified into economic, aesthetic, emotional, rational and moral benefits. The benefits sought by rural consumers in case of a motorcycle, toilet soap and mobile phone are given in Table 6.14 as an illustration.

Consumers are grouped based on the benefits sought and positioning is effectively done to attract them.

User status

Consumers may be categorized as shown in Table 6.15 based on their user status.

Evidently, each category of users is to be treated as a separate segment and marketing offers should be designed to suit each one of them.

Usage rate

Based upon the size of their consumption, consumers may be categorized as follows.

- Light users
- Medium users
- Heavy users

Table 6.14 Benefits Sought from Products

Product	Motorbike	Toilet soap	Mobile phones
Aesthetic	Sturdy, sleek design, strong, macho like, pleasant colour	Fragrance, skin-glow	Slim, elegant, pleasant colour
Emotional	Sense of fulfilment, status/affiliation	Pleasant experience	Connected to the world
Rational	Easy and quick transport, time saving, family mobility, fuel efficiency and low-cost maintenance (low-cost spares and service)	Value for money, cleanliness, durability	Set at a reasonable price, low-unit cost recharge facility, low-cost call facility, connectivity at all places
Moral	Provides support to family, pollution free	Ensures hygiene at social places	Helps people in need

Table 6.15 User Status and Implications for Marketers

User status	Behaviour	Implication for marketers
Ex-user	Stopped using one brand and using another brand	Target for conversion by highlighting benefits
First-time user	Trial purchase	Reinforce confidence by stating benefits and explain better usages
Regular user	Repeat buy	Educate about better usage or additional usages
Potential user	Users of other brands and non-users	Target for conversion by highlighting benefits

Pack sizes are designed differently to meet the requirements of different users. For instance, Pepsi markets 300 ml bottles priced at Rs 9. It introduced the *Chota* Pepsi (200 ml) at Rs 7 to meet the consumption needs of light users.

Loyalty status

A market can also be segmented on the basis of consumer loyalty to brands, stores and companies. In rural areas, brand loyalty is higher as decisions are collectively made. It is reported that there are Colgate villages, Escorts villages and Nirma villages. However, it is also reported that the brand loyalty is weak in case of toilet soaps. Strong loyalty is reported only in the case of Lifebuoy. Companies may design marketing actions based on loyalty status as given in Table 6.16.

Place

Rural people may buy from the following places and people:

- Retail outlets/*Shakti ammas*
- Weekly *haats* or *shandies*
- Occasional *melas* and *jaataras*

Table 6.16 Loyalty Status and Implications for Marketers

Loyalty status	Goal	Marketing action
Strong	To retain	Improve the features and promotions
Weak	To attract	Identify weaknesses and fortify brand support with good promotion
Non-loyal	To convert	Heavy sales promotion campaign

Table 6.17 Product Possession Categories

Category	Product price	Products
I	Below Rs 1,000	Wrist watches, transistors, fans, bicycles, electric irons, mono cassette recorders, pressure cookers/pans
II	Between Rs 1,000 and Rs 6,000	Two-in-ones, TVs (black and white), sewing machines, mixer-grinders, geysers, vacuum cleaners
III	Above Rs 6,000	Two-wheelers, refrigerators, TV (colour), VCRs/ VCPs, washing machines

- Nearest town, the feeding centre for villages
- Mobile vans

Products may be promoted by developing an understanding of the places where the potential buyers mostly congregate and from where they prefer to buy the products. Marketers are today considering the traditional retail spaces, i.e. *haats* or *shandies* as they realize their potential in promoting sales of several products.

Product-possession categories

It is appropriate to target the buyer on the basis of products he already possesses. The National Council for Applied Economic Research (NCAER) has categorized products to help marketers of durables target the next customer. Table 6.17 shows the product categorization. The categories, as shown in the table, cover most products with prices varying from Rs 100 to over Rs 20,000 following an incremental approach for each category.

The hierarchy is based on the needs and wants of the people.

Category I products are of immediate use to the family or products that tend to be instrumental in supplementing the income in these households.

Category II products consist of a combination of the products that are useful to the households, ease work-strain and act as a source of entertainment.

Category III products show a combination of classy products that fulfil all the above needs.

This categorization can be used as a guideline to target potential customers. Purchases in Category II are made after the purchase of three or four items in Category I. Purchases in Category III are made after purchasing five to six products in Category I and II. Sometimes it can be a straight jump from Category I to Category III.

Table 6.18 Segmentation Tools

Tools	Developers
Thompson Rural Market Index (TRMI)	Hindustan Thompson Associates Ltd
MICA Rural Market Ratings (MRMR)	Mudra Institute of Communications, Ahmedabad (MICA)
LinQuest	Initiative Media of Lintas
Relative Development Index	Centre for Monitoring Indian Economy (CMIE)
Ogilvy Radar	Ogilvy
R-panel	ORG-MARG
Socio-economic classification (SEC)	NCAER
	Media Research Users Council (MRUC) and Indian Readership Survey (IRS)–95
Household Potential Index (HPI)	Hansa Research for Media Research Users Council (MRUC)

Multi-variable segmentation

Very rarely, marketers depend on a single variable for segmentation. To be meaningful, target marketing requires the use of several variables. Attempts to move in this direction were made by companies and researchers and they have come up with different approaches. Some of the popular tools are listed in Table 6.18 and outlined below.

Thompson Rural Market Index (TRMI)

Hindustan Thompson Associates Ltd developed TRMI as a guide to segment markets in rural areas in 1972 and improved it in 1986. They compiled data from 335 districts based on 26 variables. Further, they collected data on the value of agricultural output for each district. It is considered to be the overall indicator of rural market potential as it has strong co-relation with 10 selected agriculture-related variables:

- Agricultural labourers
- Gross cropped area
- Gross irrigated area
- Area under non-food crops
- Pump sets
- Fertilizer consumption
- Tractors
- Rural credit
- Rural deposits
- Villages electrified

Based on the index numbers, the districts have been classified as A, B, C, D and E class of markets as indicated in Table 6.19.

Table 6.19 Classification of Markets

Class of markets	Index range	No. of districts	Percentage of market
A	60.00 to 100.00	22	17.8
B	40.00 to 59.99	39	20.5
C	30.00 to 39.99	54	20.4
D	20.00 to 29.99	86	23.0
E	Below 20.00	154	18.3
	Total	355	100.00

MICA Rural Market Ratings (MRMR)

This has been developed by the Mudra Institute of Communications, Ahmedabad (MICA) in association with ML Infomap Pvt. Ltd, New Delhi to be the perfect table-top multimedia guide to rural India. It is available in a CD-ROM with colourful digital maps and provides the relative market potential of a particular district. The ratings have been arrived at by using six parameters and 42 variables.

- Total value of agricultural output
- Bank advances
- Cropped area
- Irrigated area
- Number of cultivators, and
- Fertilizer consumption

The easy-to-use guide has the following interesting features.

- The results of this research are presented on maps using the Standard Digital Map of India.
- The data is available in electronic media and so can be observed and presented in several different ways with just a click of the mouse.
- Shaded district maps indicate the level of market potential. Since the results are seen on a map, clear patterns of market potential can be "seen."

One can immediately see important facts relating to a district when one clicks on it using the information tool. These relate to bank advances, demographics, infrastructure, and more. Also you can find any district by name, then zoom into it and find the distribution (that is, location) of all the actual rural markets, the "*haats*." Further, you click on a *haat* and you get to know on which day or days of the week the market takes place. Besides, several items of demographic data are also stored for these villages. And finally, the package includes the road and railway map of India, thus enabling one to chart a route to reach the village of one's choice. It was priced at Rs 35,000.

LinQuest

Initiative Media developed LinQuest, a software package that provides marketers with data on rural India. The data can be sorted based on five parameters:

- Demographic
- Agricultural

- Income
- Literacy
- Civic amenities

Depending on the product being launched, marketers will be interested in certain parameters such as literacy levels, male–female ratios, bank deposits, income levels, accessibility (via road, rail and waterways), dispensaries, schools and distance from the nearest town. The LinQuest software allows marketers to assign a weighted average on each of these. The package then lists all the places that satisfy the marketer's criteria. For the rural launch of a regional daily newspaper, the parameters could be villages (population over 10,000), income (over Rs 2,000), distance from the nearest town (not more than 45 km) and literacy levels.

Ogilvy radar

This is a mining tool, which offers a visual depiction of all 579,361 villages and 3,696 feeder towns represented as points on a map. The details obtained are as follows:

Primary census abstract: Population, literacy, occupation and 40 other parameters.

Census village directory: Water resources, education facilities, medical facilities, communication facilities, nearest feeder town and distance and 14 other parameters.

Village retail outlets: Total number and addresses.

Villages are classified into two categories as follows:

- Corridor villages—Within a radius of 2 km on all-metal roads (National Highway, State Highway and District Highway) and a population of over 2,000 (1,451)
- Remote villages—Beyond 2 km from the highway and a population of over 2,000 (132)

Media are prioritized as follows:

- White points (Media Live)
- Green points (Remote villages)
- Red points (Feeder towns)

R-Panel

ORG-MARG, the consumer research agency, launched the first-ever Rural Consumer Panel or R-Panel to provide "a systematically researched information base." The panel monitors purchasing and consumption patterns of the rural consumer in 20,000 households across 1,000 villages randomly selected from 215 districts across India. It provides monthly information on brand preferences, average household expenditure, buying habits like frequency of purchase and brand loyalty, gain–loss analysis, overlap analysis and other important indicators for over 32 FMCG categories.

The panel divided consumers into six groups in the socio-economic classification (SEC), based on the type of house owned and education of the chief wage earner. The panel found that a rural household spends Rs 270 per month on an average on consumer durables, excluding grain. The spending limit varies by SEC, ranging from Rs 441 in SEC1 to Rs 202 in the lowest SEC.

Socio-economic classification

Social class is determined by a combination of factors such as income, education, occupation and others. There are three broad segments in the Indian market: premium, popular and discount. However, there are no formal definitions of these. The rule of thumb is that the top 10 per cent by income

Table 6.20 India's Consuming Classes (2004–2005)

Consumer category	Annual income	Households (percentage)
Very rich	Above Rs 215,000	0.9
Consuming class	Rs 45,000 to 215,000	25
Climbers	Rs 22,001 to 45,000	49
Aspirants	Rs 16,001 to 22,000	14
Destitute	Below Rs 16,000	11.1

Source: "FICCI Rural Marketing Summit 2005," available at www.linterland.com/core/rurallandscape/16.htm.

of any population constitutes the premium market, the next 30 per cent is the popular segment and the last 60 per cent is the discount/mass market. However, a translation of data reveals that the last two segments are roughly equal in terms of total value, though they differ vastly in terms of the number of consumers in each and their respective income levels.

NCAER classification

The construct of consumer classes was first put forward by Dr S. L. Rao and I. Natarajan of the National Council for Applied Economic Research (NCAER) in 1996. They clustered "Consumer India" into five types of groups as indicated in Table 6.20.

MRUC-IRS classification

Media Research Users Council (MRUC) and Indian Readership Survey (IRS)–95 have come out with a new rural Socio-Economic Class (SEC) that maps the rural market based on three variables:

- Education of the chief wage earner
- Ownership of durables
- Type of the house (*pucca*, semi-*pucca* or *kuchha*)

The social classes may be categorized into six groups as indicated in Table 6.21.

The Rural Indian Households are classified into SEC R1, R2, R3, and R4. In the rural classification, the parameters are the education level of the chief wage earner and the type of the house used. Table 6.22 provides the classification.

Household Premiumness Index (HPI)

This was developed by Hansa Research and Media Research Users Council (MRUC) using data from the IRS 2005 survey.

HPI enables a direct comparison of the urban and the rural on the same scale. An interesting inference from this classification is that the analysis "indicates that SEC R1 is close to SEC B2 and SEC R2 is close to SEC D of the urban population." The concept underlying the index is simple—households owning or using a low-penetration item or having a less popular demographic characteristic (like high education levels) get a higher score for that. The scores are then aggregated across all items and a HPI score arrived at for the household. Thus, in place of income, we have a sort of "consumption"/ "ownership"/"characteristics"-based index that is a measure of purchasing power. Table 6.23 shows the HPI scores of different socio-economic classes. Table 6.24 shows the profile of consuming classes in India that may be indicative for rural marketers also.

Table 6.21 Social Classes: Characteristics and Preferences

Sl No.	Class	Characteristics	Preferences
1.	Upper–upper	Social elite, inherited wealth, well-known family background, ascribed status, aristocrats, small in number, reference group for others	Jewellery, antiques, farmhouses, vacations, luxury products at high prices
2.	Lower–upper	Social elite, wealth earned, educated and professional, active in social and civic affairs, aspire and associate with upper–upper stratum	Status symbols—cars, homes, refrigerators, expensive schools, exhibition products, art pieces, sculptures, etc.
3.	Upper–middle	Career oriented, dependent on education and hard work, dual-career families, seek comfort, ambitious	Quality of life products and entertainment, good interior decoration, vacation, etc.
4.	Lower–middle	Average paid employees, small businessmen, college background, fashion-oriented but traditional, dual-career families	Better life products, nice homes, nice furniture, decent school, occasional vacations, travel and tour, regular but economical entertainment
5.	Upper–lower	Above poverty line—depend on loans and advances, hand-to-mouth, dual-career families, traditional, strong family ties, school education	Economy products, instalment and credit buying, low-priced popular brands and local unbranded products
6.	Lower–lower	Below poverty line, daily incomes, low per capita income, poor health and hygiene, dependence on petty loans and charity	Local unbranded products, daily purchases, cheap varieties, buy seconds or collect thrown out clothes, food, etc.

Table 6.22 SEC by Education of Chief Wage Earner and Type of House

Education of chief wage earner	Type of house		
	Pucca	Semi-*pucca*	*Kuchcha*
Professional degree	R1	R2	R3
Graduation/PG	R1	R2	R3
College	R1	R2	R3
SSC/HSC	R2	R3	R3
Class 4 to Class 9	R3	R3	R4
Up to class 4	R3	R3	R4
Self-learning	R3	R4	R4
Illiterate	R4	R4	R4

Table 6.23 Household Premiumness Index (HPI)

SEC class	HPI score	Estimated households (in million)
A1	100.7	2.2
A2	54.9	4.1
B1	28.2	5.3
B2	18.7	5.3
C	11.9	12.8
D	6.8	14.2
E1	5.5	6.7
E2	3.7	10.8
R1	16.1	5.8
R2	7.3	15.9
R3	4.1	56.7
R4	2.5	67.3

Table 6.24 Profile of Consumer Classes of India

Percentage of households	30–50 per cent	51–70 per cent	More than 70 per cent
Samriddha-I	Flat TV, AC, fabric bleaches	PC, deodorant	Four-wheeler, ketchup, camera
Samriddha-II	Four-wheeler, PC	Camera, milk food drinks, ketchup, instant noodles	Washing machine, floor cleaner, ghee
Sampanna	Deodorant, honey, CD player, jam, ketchup, camera	Washing machine, floor cleaner	Mosquito repellent, toilet cleaner, rubs and balms, music system, telephone, motorized transport
Siddha	Instant noodles, motor cycles, milk food, drinks, floor cleaner	Vanaspati, toilet cleaner, telephone, motorized transport	Refrigerator, bank account, fabric whitener
Unmukh	Toilet cleaner, telephone, motorized transport, refrigerator	Mosquito repellent, music system, ghee	Bank account, pressure cooker, utensil cleaner, talcum powder
Saamanya	Mosquito repellent, ghee	Bank account, utensil cleaner, rubs and balms, pressure cooker	Shampoo, toothpaste, TV

(Continued)

Table 6.24 (Continued)

Percentage of households	30–50 per cent	51–70 per cent	More than 70 per cent
Sangarhsi	Music system, pressure cooker, rubs and balms, bank account	Shampoo, talcum powder, toothpaste, TV, fabric whitener	Biscuits, fresh milk
Nirdhan	Vansaspati, shampoo, toothpowder	Fresh milk, biscuits	Detergent bar/cake, washing powder, tea, edible oil, toilet soap, hair oil

Box 6.1 Occupations and Drudgery of Rural Women

Women in the lower-income strata of rural areas are over-burdened with household and occupational work. Women spend a considerable amount of time gathering household requirements from nature. The ecological degradation and depletion of natural resources are responsible for their life becoming harder. Women in water-scarce villages walk long distances and spend long hours in search of firewood.

Women contribute considerably to the household income through their participation in farm and non-farm activities. Landless women work as agricultural labourers for lower wages when compared to men. They take an active role in livestock production, rearing of domestic animals and birds. Some women are engaged in forest-based small-scale enterprises. They make products such as baskets, brooms, and ropes. Women in the coastal areas of Tamil Nadu, Andhra Pradesh and Orissa are involved in fish drying/curing, marketing, hand braiding and net-mending. Information technology has had revolutionary effects on the life of women. Joining hands with IT companies, corporate enterprises and NGOs have set up rural Internet kiosks and trained women to take charge of the information centres.

Source: www.fao.org/sd/WPdirect/WPre0108.htm, accessed March 2010.

EMERGING SEGMENTS—WOMEN AND YOUTH

The changing face of Indian society has brought about new challenges and opportunities. A new India has been envisaged where women and youth will claim more importance, where rural folks will be more demanding and where products and service offerings will be tailored to suit this new set of consumers.

Women's segment

The population of women in rural India is 48.1 per cent and the population of men is 51.9 per cent. Female illiteracy is 62 per cent whereas the male illiteracy rate is 34 per cent. The labour force participation rate of women is 22.7 per cent, less than half of the men's rate of 51.6 per cent. In rural India, agriculture and allied industrial sectors employ as much as 89.5 per cent of the total female labour. Box 6.1 describes the struggle of rural women and Box 6.2 describes the changing lifestyles of educated rural women.

Box 6.2 Changing Lifestyles of Rural Women

The lifestyles of women are changing for the better. Gudia, a 25-year old woman from rural Eastern India is today a different person. She is happy and satisfied with the progress in her life. She had to cross several socio-economic barriers to achieve her goal of pursuing higher education. Even when she joined a nearby school as a teacher, there were comments from relatives and protests from her in-laws.

However, the advancement of civilization spurred by industrialization and government support programmes ushered a new era of hope and challenge. There is inspiration in place of inhibition. Women who are well educated are more liberated and they are aware of life challenges. They are making their niche in the family and society. The much-liberated women seem to be those who are from the upper classes of society and those living in villages that are close to towns and cities. These women are found to be more politically conscious than their counterparts in remote villages. Restrictions on type of work and location of job have now eased off and women are permitted to work outside the villages and accept jobs that were earlier considered suitable only for men. The rural women of Eastern India are today entering into a new society—a society that encourages them to realize their constitutional rights and to enjoy life with a spirit of social and economic freedom.

Source: Satish K.R.T., "The Lifestyle of Rural Indian Women is Changing," 05 February 2008, available at www.groundreport.com

Youth segment

R. V. Rajan, President of RMAAI, defines rural youth as the population aged between 18 and 35 years. He said, "Just as in the rest of the country, this segment forms over 50 per cent of the rural population making it a potent force for the marketers to target."
Why is the rural youth segment important?

- The sheer size of the segment—50 per cent of the rural population—is estimated to be between 25 and 40 years of age.
- They are also earning members who want to live life as per their own choices.
- The rural youth bring brand knowledge to the household and thereby, emerge as key influencers in the purchase process.
- This segment is an early adopter of technology and aspires for more.
- A study by Internet research firm JuxtConsult in 2008 revealed that one out of every seven regular Internet user was from rural areas. The study revealed that rural net users were younger than their urban counterparts.

How are the marketers targeting and addressing the harbingers of change? Box 6.3 presents the approaches of companies.

GUIDES TO EFFECTIVE SEGMENTATION

Marketers are often faced with the dilemma of making a decision whether to segment or not to segment. More often than not, the decision is in favour of segmentation. Hence, the important

Box 6.3 Targeting the New Generation—Youth

Today the face of the rural areas is a new youthful one. A large number of educated, ambitious youths are discarding their traditional outlooks and opting for modern education, careers and even appearances. Even among the families, this change is visible with the youth shedding its traditional dhotis for modern denims and showing preferences for branded watches and cosmetics. Along with this preference for modernity, there is a change in their lifestyle philosophy. The "save-now-and-spend-tomorrow" culture of the earlier generation is losing ground to the "earn-now-and-spend-now" culture.

Describing the business response to changing rural India, Priya Monga, business head, RC&M, said, "Brands are increasingly focusing their campaigns through youth-centric messages and throwing up challenges for youth involvement. So the product communication is delivered at the ground level in a challenging manner in an edutainment path."

Campaigns are designed targeting the youth and employing messages that appeal to them and involve them. Experiential approaches that help engage the youth and make them aware of the merits of the product by themselves are employed. Besides promotion of products, schemes that involve the youth in entrepreneurial marketing of brands are designed to benefit both the firm as well as the participating youth.

Source: "Rural Youth: A Feature in Event Faqs," June 2009, available at www.anugrahmadison.com/news.html.

questions are: How is the market to be segmented and how is the effectiveness of the segmentation to be tested? As discussed above, segmentation can be done using one or more bases. Now, we will identify the criteria used to determine effectiveness of segmentation. Segmentation is effective when it can establish segments that are measurable, accessible, differentiable and substantial.

Measurable

Segments are formed with the help of certain variables. These variables should be distinct, clear and measurable. Only then can segments be described in exact terms and differences between them understood. Companies so far, are not able to reach rural markets due to lack of proper data. In the absence of information related to size, purchasing power and profiles of rural consumers, they were considered to be similar to the urbanites. Today, rural markets are studied by various agencies to obtain useful data for segmentation. Box 6.4 presents a study of Internet users. One can evolve measurable segments with the help of such information.

Accessibility

Reach is important to serve the segments. Till recently, marketers preferred urban markets to rural ones because of the inaccessibility of the latter. They were dependent on mobile vans and nearby town distributors and retail outlets to reach rural consumers. Now, research has established that rural folk can be reached effectively by participating in weekly *haats* or *shandies*. Also, the considerable improvement in the infrastructure has made several villages more accessible.

Box 6.4 Segmentation of Internet Users

According to research conducted by Forrester Research Inc, India would soon emerge as the third-largest country of Internet users in the world. Currently, there are an estimated 50 million to 80 million Internet users and the number is increasing at an average growth rate of 10%–20%. A report by ASSOCHAM supports this estimate. According to it, by 2014, there will be 20 million 3G-based broadband subscribers while WiMax operators cater to 60 million users.

A classification of Internet users is provided by I-Cube 2008 based on a survey conducted jointly by IMRB International and Internet and Mobile Association of India (IAMAI). The details are furnished in Table 6.25. The rural Internet market can be analysed as given under. The potential Internet users are 368 mn literates, of them an easy target can be the 63 mn English-speaking rural persons. These people need training in computer as well as Internet use. The internet non-user segment consists of 9.6 mn computer literates who are to be induced to use the Internet. There are about about 2.2 mn inactive Internet users and they are to be encouraged to use the Internet actively.

Table 6.25 Internet Users in India

Variable	Rural	Urban	Total
Population (mn)	568	250	818
Literates (mn)	368	205	573
English speaking (mn)	63	86	149
Computer literates (mn)	15.1	85	100.1
Claimed Internet users (mn)	5.5	57	62.5
Active Internet users (mn)	3.3	42	45.5

Differentiable

Segments merit consideration of marketers only when they have distinguishing features. Rural consumers are identified as a different segment as their responses are different from the urban consumers' in case of some products and programmes. For instance, in the case of buying wrist watches, rural consumers differ from urbanites. Rural buyers are more worried about the value for money and usually weigh the watch in their hands to gauge how heavy it is. On the contrary, urban consumers prefer light ones equipped with the latest technology.

Substantial

A segment is attractive only when it is profitable. A segment should possess the following characteristics:

(a) Homogeneous—It should consist of people, who are similar in perceptions, learning, preferences, attitudes and action. As such, covering them will be easy.

(b) Large—It should comprise either a large number of light users or a small number of heavy users so that marketing becomes beneficial to the companies. It is observed that rural areas are not homogeneous. Region-wise differences are found in language, thinking and behaviour. However, it is difficult to design separate promotional programmes as the size of the consumer bases is not large enough to make the effort viable.

TARGETING

Segmentation is the process of identifying and establishing alternative market segments. As a next step, targeting involves evaluating the various segments and selecting how many and which ones to target. The three aspects in targeting are evaluation, selection and coverage.

Evaluation of segments

In evaluating market segments, a company has to first identify the criteria for evaluation. The following criteria may be applied to determine the attractiveness of segments.

Profitability

The company has to collect information on required aspects to conduct cost-benefit analysis and ascertain profitability of the segment. Relevant information includes:

- Sales volumes
- Distribution costs
- Promotion costs
- Sales revenues
- Profit margins

Attractiveness

Marketers should know whether they should design effective programmes to attract and serve the market. Smaller companies or new companies may lack the skills, experience and resources needed to serve the larger segments. Some segments may be less attractive when there is already more competition.

Growth rate

A segment's attractiveness depends not only on its current profitability but also, on future prospects. The growth rate of the segment in terms of growth in population, rise in purchasing power and increase in preferences for the use of the products is to be considered.

Company objectives

A company should evaluate the segment opportunity with reference to their short-term and long-term objectives. If a company's objective is to expand the sales, it has to go rural instead of pulling rural consumers to the nearby town in order to buy their products. This is precisely what Onida, Videocon and LG Electronics are doing to promote their TV sales.

Limitations

Finally, a company should examine whether the entry into the segment is acceptable to the society and government. If its entry provokes unnecessary criticisms, the company may have to struggle hard to explain its stand and safeguard its image.

Selection of segments

Selection of the segment(s) can be made by rating the alternative segments on a predetermined scale in respect of the five aspects explained above. An evaluation checklist useful in this context is shown in Table 6.26.

Table 6.26 Segment Evaluation Sheet

Sl No.	Criteria	Rating scale			
		High	Medium	Low	Nil
1.	Profitability	3	2	1	0
2.	Growth	3	2	1	0
3.	Attractiveness				
	Strengths (resources)	3	2	1	0
	Threats (competition)	0	1	2	3
4.	Company objectives (degree of consistency)	3	2	1	0
5.	Limitations	0	1	2	3

Segments may be ranked based on the scores obtained and be considered for selection. Those with high scores will be accepted and others will be kept aside for future consideration.

Coverage of segments

Organizations can choose between four alternative coverage strategies to suit their segmentation approaches.

- Undifferentiated in case of zero segmentation (mass-marketing strategy)
- Differentiated when segmentation is essential (segment or micro-marketing strategy)
- Concentrated when one small segment is selected (niche-marketing strategy)
- Tailored to each customer (customization strategy)

Undifferentiated market coverage

There is no need for segmentation when consumer preferences are homogeneous. A large market is available for targeting. Marketers, hence, design an undifferentiated offer to attract consumers. For some products, the rural market as well as the urban market are considered a homogeneous mass market. Some companies offering such products choose mass marketing strategies. Several products like toilet soaps, shampoos, washing powders, TVs, refrigerators, computers, two-wheelers and services like banking, telecom, medical and education are mass products. For instance, many toilet soap users prefer medicinal value, cosmetic strength, economy and freshness feeling in a toilet soap. Medimix offers all these and claims that it is a beauty care Ayurvedic family soap. This soap appeals to all types of consumers. Fair & Lovely fairness cream, which has spread its tentacles in the urban market, has a high penetration of 75 per cent in the rural market. Other such products are Lifebuoy, Ponds talcum powder, Nirodh deluxe and Sampoorna TV.

Differentiated segment-wise coverage

Differentiated marketing strategy investigates and identifies differences between segments and tries to match the market offer to the desires and expectations of each segment.

The results of such exercise would be

- Strong identification of the company in the product category.
- More costs but higher sales. Hence, more profits.
- More loyal consumers.

Do companies use a differentiated strategy within rural areas? Obviously, there are products that are exclusive to rural areas like fertilizers, tractors, seeds, etc. The following examples explain the use of this strategy.

- *Tractor*: 25 to 30 HP (marginal or small farmer); 50 HP (large farmer)
- *Pepsodent*: 50 g (middle or high income); 15 g (low income)

A segment marketer should be careful in understanding consumer preferences and designing offers. The prerequisites for segment marketing are:

- Understanding of consumer needs and wants
- Awareness of competitors, products and services
- Innovative capabilities of marketers to finetune products and services to the varied customer groups

Selective segment coverage

A niche is a very small group with a distinctive set of traits, where the members seek a special combination of benefits. Niche marketing or concentrated strategy identifies special sub-groups within larger segments and offers different products and services. Concentrated strategy facilitates specialization in serving the segment and achieving higher level of consumer satisfaction, delight and loyalty. However, it is not without risks. In course of time,

- preferences of consumers may change, and
- large companies may become competitors seeing the success of one company.

Generally, large companies may prefer to offer specialized services as a part of their diversification move. O & M has set up "O & M Rural Communication Network" to implement rural communication packages and devise distribution strategies.

Individual coverage

Customized marketing is also termed as one-to-one marketing. Tailoring units, hotels, tourist operators, and doctors provide individualized services. Building contractors build houses or flats to the specific requirements of customers.

Choosing a coverage strategy

Table 6.27 provides a checklist, which guides companies in their making of coverage-strategy choices, with reference to the state of the four variables, for example, company resources, product variability, product lifecycle stage and market variability. For instance, undifferentiated strategy is to be chosen when company resources are moderate, product variability is less, and the product is in the introduction stage in a market that has less variability. The options and determinants are indicated in Table 6.27.

POSITIONING

Positioning is the act of finding a place in the minds of consumers and locating the brand therein. Companies have to plan positions that give their products the necessary advantage in the target markets.

Positioning involves three tasks:

- Identifying the differences of the offer *vis-à-vis* the competitors' offers
- Selecting the differences that have greater competitive advantage
- Communicating such advantages effectively to the target audience.

Table 6.27 Coverage Strategy Options

Variable	Strategy		
	Undifferentiated	Differentiated	Concentrated
Company resources	Moderate	Large	Limited
Product variability	Less	More	Less
Product lifecycle stage	Introduction	Growth	Introduction
Market variability	Less	High	High

Identify differences

The marketing offer may be differentiated along the following lines:

- Product
- Services
- People
- Image

Product differentiation

Products can be differentiated based on attributes such as shape, size, colour, quality, composition and performance. Functional differentiations signify ease in process and benefits of use.

- Mysore Sandal soap comes in three shapes—round, oval and rectangular.
- Close Up has three colour variants—red, blue and green.
- Surf Excel is a high-quality product compared to Wheel—both are from the stable of HUL.
- Coke has 400 calories whereas Diet coke has 1 calorie. Diet Coke is for diabetics.
- Singer sewing machine stitches, "Memory craft" can even scan designs.

Services differentiation

Services may be differentiated with respect to delivery, installation and maintenance. Long warranty periods, free service coupons, service at phone-call distance, 24-hours service, emergency care, etc. are some examples.

People

People who come into contact with users may quite often influence the decision of consumers. In this era of relationship marketing, differentiation by people is worth considering. Service organizations like hospitals, schools, banks, road transport and telecommunication require people who serve with a smile and are efficient. Service organizations mostly emphasize the competencies of their people.

Examples: Saying "Innovative team," "know how to serve," "smile and serve," "professional experts" and "ready to solve your problems," etc.

Image

The image of a brand or company may win over a consumer, even though the product is very similar to a competing product. Image is built by advertisements, symbols, signs, colours, logos, atmosphere of an organization and social activities. The images may be related to attributes such as quality, being high-tech, being a samaritan, achievement, honesty, etc.

Selecting the right differences

When a company identifies several differences, it can evaluate them with the help of the following criteria.

- Attractive — Does it provide value to the customer?
- Distinctive — Is it different from that of its competitors?
- Pre-emptive — Is it very difficult for competitors to copy it?
- Affordable — Can buyers pay for it?
- Communicable — Can the difference be clearly expressed? Is it visible? Understandable?

The evaluation requires the following steps:

1. Identification of attributes, which can give competitive advantage. For example, quality, service, technology and economy.
2. Use of a rating scale. Maybe, a 10-point scale.
3. Rating the attributes on five criteria, i.e. attractive, distinctive, pre-emptive, affordable and communicable as shown in Table 6.28.
4. Then, developing a comparative table of competitive advantages to arrive at an appropriate decision.

Tables 6.28 and 6.29 show the computations.

In Tables 6.28 and 6.29, the economy position has a clear advantage over the service aspect. The other two differences are strengths of competitors. Hence, positioning on economy will benefit the company.

The next question is how many differences to promote?

Roosser Reeves advocated marketers to develop "Unique Selling Proposition" (USPs) for each brand and maintain it. Thus, best quality, best technology, best service, etc. can become USPs. It has to claim that it is the "best" in that respect. However, companies may claim more than one benefit to make its position less vulnerable when it has no one "best."

Table 6.28 Evaluation of Differences

Difference	Attractive	Distinctive	Pre-emptive	Affordable	Communicable	Score
Quality	8	9	4	8	7	36
Service	6	8	5	8	6	33
Technology	6	7	5	8	8	34
Economy	6	7	5	8	9	35

Table 6.29 Competitive Advantages

Difference	Company	Competitor
Quality	32	36
Service	33	32
Technology	34	36
Economy	35	30

Communication strategy

Once the company has chosen the differences, it has to choose an appropriate marketing strategy. A high-tech position may be communicated by futuristic products, classy ads in elite journals and large showrooms with good atmosphere.

CASE 1—ICICI PRUDENTIAL[2]

ICICI's insurance business is organized into two divisions—ICICI Prudential Life Insurance Company and ICICI Lombard General Insurance Company Limited. Set up in 2000 as a joint venture between ICICI Bank India Ltd and Prudential PLC, UK, it has about 750 offices, 22 bancassurance partners and over 0.24 million advisors. It offers a wide array of life insurance products and covers more than 650,000 lives across as many as 17 states in India.

During 2007–08, ICICI Prudential launched its Rural Business Channel by creating a strong infrastructure of nearly 250 branches called micro offices. It entered into the rural market with two plans: *Suraksha* and *Suraksha Kavach*, which are tailor made to the unique needs of rural investors. The plans offer: life cover, low and affordable premiums and hassle free procedure. ICICI Prudential Life Insurance introduced the plans in the rural areas of Punjab, Gujarat, Andhra Pradesh, Kerala and West Bengal during the year 2008.

To increase access and service, it has been working with many Micro Finance Institutions. Innovations include online service delivery system to reduce the costs of serving low-income persons.

Drivers and segmentation

The rural marketing initiative is encouraged by the following factors.

- The penetration ratio of life insurance and health insurance is18 per cent and 1 per cent, respectively.
- The Government of India made it compulsory for all private players to get 18 per cent of the sales from rural markets.
- A recent ORG-MARG study indicated that ICICI Prudential, HDFC Standard Life and Tata AIG have experienced an increase in their market shares by 8.3 and 2 per cent, respectively.

Table 6.30 indicates the segmentation approaches adopted by the company.

Table 6.30 Segmentation and Target Market

Segmentation base	Descriptors
Geographic regions	Andhra Pradesh, Kerala, Punjab, Gujarat and Rajasthan
Demographics	Male, *pucca*/semi-*pucca* house, educated (minimum 10th standard pass)
Social-economic classes	SEC R2—Affluent (income of Rs 0.2 million per annum, 10 acres of land, single source of income) and SEC R1 (very well to do, lots of land, double source of income and politically inclined)
Psychographic	Risk averse, high aspirations for their children, seeks to provide education to children, aspires for better standard of living, dreams of going abroad, always on the lookout for better yield and purchases more land, surplus income, if any, invested in farm equipment, repayment of loan and lends to earn interest
Behavioural segment	Vehicle and consumer durables ownership

Marketing-offer benefits

Schemes relating to pension, education of children or marriage, health support and wealth creation are offered with benefits like security (life insurance, assets and income), bank loan, bulk returns in the future and daughter's marriage (dowry or expensive celebration).

Opinion leaders

The teacher and the *pradhan* are the main opinion leaders.

Positioning and communication strategy

The company slogan "*Jeetey raho* (with you every step in life)" is communicated along with benefits (security—life and occasional needs and income generation) of various schemes for different occasions. The communication adopted the "winds of change" approach.

"Wake up to the new world. Start a new revolution in your lives. Change today for a better tomorrow."

"*Badli zarooratein. Badle Khwaab. Badle duniya. Badle aap.*"

Distribution

Traditional channels (agent and bank assurance) and alternative channels (RRBs, ICICI Rural division, corporate agents, Godrej *Aadhar* and ITC e-*choupals*, NGOs).

CASE 2—MAHINDRA AND MAHINDRA TRACTORS[3]

Mahindra and Mahindra, one among the top ten industrial houses in India, is the only Indian company among the top three tractor manufacturers in the world. Since its inception in 1945, it has retained its core values of introducing rural India to technological advancements and offered a variety of products. It has made its presence in various business sectors: Automotive, Farm Equipment, Financial Services, Systech, After-Market, Information Technology, Specialty Business, Infrastructure Development, Trade, Retail and Logistics.

The Farm Equipment Sector (FES) of Mahindra and Mahindra Ltd (Tractor Division) is a USD 1 billion sector of the Mahindra group of companies.

Segmentation

The tractor industry is segmented on the basis of horse power category. The segments and their market shares are indicated in Table 6.31.

Table 6.31 Segments and Market Shares

Less than 30 HP	Between 30 and 40 HP	Between 40 and 50 HP	More than 50 HP	Industry market share
10 per cent	37.3 per cent	25.3 per cent	31.2 per cent	31 per cent

The "more than 50 HP" category is the fastest growing segment for the industry as well for M&M.

Campaign customization

The company maintains consistency in building the core values of the brand. These are fuel efficiency, technology, style and comfort. *Samriddhi* brand messages are customized to a specific geographical area.

In the south, it did campaigns such as "*Puddling ka Maharaja*" in Tamil Nadu and "*Jashn Josh ka*" in Andhra Pradesh for strengthening the brand–consumer bonding. In the north, it highlighted high-end styling and technology (Arjun Ultra-1 Capsule Van in Punjab, Haryana), Brick Kiln focus (Shaan in Eastern and Central U.P.), and a Potato Special (Western U.P.).

About 40 per cent of FES marketing communications expenditure can be classified as personalized communication (distinct from mass communication). It reaches out through Thematic Vans (product-specific, brand-specific and application-specific).

Target market

The chosen market comprises Shaan Brick Kiln owners and farmers. The key characteristics of the target customers are—sports persons, visitors to *mandis* and ITC e-*choupals*. Some of them are brand loyalists.

CSR activities

The company is active in promoting sports and education. *Shikshak Divas Mahotsav* (supporting the education drive in 1,000 schools, over 0.5 million students) is an example.

Barriers

The economic slowdown has had a spiralling influence across categories. It has affected liquidity and bank financing. 60 per cent of tractor purchases are dependent on finance. This has resulted in a slow-down on consumer off-take.

On-ground innovations

Internet connectivity at FES dealerships (www.mahindrakisanmitra.com providing value-added services) is one move that has been made to strengthen the sales network. Various promotional campaigns undertaken by FES signify innovative abilities of the company (Table 6.32).

Table 6.32 Promotional Campaigns

Campaign	Objective	Activity	Special attraction
Mahindra Tractor *Mahotsav*	Bring the big brand experience at the customer's doorstep	A showcase of all FES products and services under one roof (tractors, spares, services, finance, exchange, agri-counselling)	Participation of rural big brands (ICICI, Castrol)
Arjun Ultra-1 Capsule Van	Establish values of style and technology	Stunning mobile show room	Driving experience through a unique driving simulation game
Jashn Josh ka	Strengthen brand–consumer relationship	Felicitation of loyal customers at their homes as part of a celebration	Invitations extended to prospects and influencers in the village

(Continued)

(Continued)

Campaign	Objective	Activity	Special attraction
Haat riders	Leverage weekly village congregation at a low cost	Trained sales promoters on bikes with inflatable wheels to stand out in weekly *haats*	Personalized communication with prospects and lead generators
HyTEC Hydraulic Van	Establish the precision of Mahindra Hy-TEC hydraulics	Hydraulic operations in a farm relayed on to a centralized computer and projection screen through sensors for demonstration of product efficacy to hundreds of prospects and influencers	

Summary

Selecting and attracting markets involve three key decisions, i.e. segmenting (dividing markets), targeting (selecting a segment to serve) and positioning (placing the brand in the mind of the target audience). The rationale for segmentation is found in the preference patterns in the market that may be homogeneous, diffused or clustered. Four marketing approaches emerge as a result of variations in market focus—mass marketing (homogeneous preferences), segment marketing (diffused preferences), niche marketing (clustered preferences) and customized marketing (individual preferences). Effective segments are those that are (1) measurable, (2) accessible, (3) differentiable and (4) substantial.

Bases for segmentation are broadly classified as geographic, demographic, psychographic and behavioural. Geographic segmentation bases include zones, states, density and climate. Demographic segmentation can be done by employing variables such as age and lifecycle, gender, marital status, family size, income, occupation, education and religion. Psychographic segmentation variables include social class, personality and lifestyle. Behavioural segmentation is considered a better approach since it utilizes the behaviour of consumers that is explicit and real. The variables are occasions, benefits sought, user status, usage rate, loyalty status, place of buying and products possessed. Multi-variable segmentation is a recent development. Thompson Rural Market Index (TRMI), LinQuest and MICA Rating are available to help marketers in this regard.

Targeting involves evaluation of identified market segments, selecting the viable market segments and deciding on appropriate coverage strategies. Evaluation criteria include profitability, attractiveness, growth rate, company objectives, and limitations. Selection may be done objectively by using an appropriate rating method. Finally, one of the three coverage strategies, i.e. undifferentiated, differentiated and concentrated may be chosen. The choice requires consideration of four variables—company resources, product variability, product lifecycle stage and market variability.

Positioning is the act of finding a place in the mind of a consumer and locating the brand therein. Positioning involves three tasks—identifying differences, selecting the differences and communicating them to the target audience. Differentiation can be made in terms of products, services, people and image.

Short Answer Questions

1. What are the three tasks in market coverage and attraction?
2. Explain the rationale for segmentation.
3. What are the prerequisites for effective segmentation?
4. List the bases of segmentation with suitable examples.
5. How do you segment markets based on geographical variables? Illustrate with examples.
6. What is psychographic segmentation? Is it superior to other types of segmentation?
7. Explain how social class can be a base for segmentation. Give the benefits of such segmentation.

8. Identify lifestyles of men and women and show their influence on product preferences with suitable examples.
9. Explain how Indian marketers are differentiating their products based on personality variables.
10. What are the bases of behavioural segmentation? Give examples.
11. Examine the importance and possibilities of multi-variable segmentation.
12. How do you evaluate and select target markets?
13. What is positioning? Give an example.
14. What are the different coverage strategies?

Discussion Questions

1. "Marketing approaches vary with degree of segmentation." Discuss giving Indian examples.
2. Discuss how the following brands can be positioned in the Indian rural market.

(a) Fair & Lovely (b) Reliance money (c) Pepsodent Kids

Essay Questions

1. What is target marketing? How do you segment and decide market coverage strategies?
2. How do you segment and develop a target marketing strategy for the following products.

(a) Bicycles (b) Cosmetics (c) Foot wear

Internet Exercise

Obtain information about the detailed methodology and data employed for constructing Household Premiumness Index (HPI). Contact the IRS team of Hansa Research. The e-mail addresses that can be used are irsinfo@hansaresearch.com and Vineet.Sodhani@hansaresearch.com.

Mini Project

Select one company from each category of the following sectors (i) services, (ii) consumer durables and (iii) FMCGs and analyse the segmentation, target marketing and positioning approaches for a chosen product.

End Notes

1. "Insurers Eye Rural Areas to Revive Business," 14 May 2009, available at http://business.rediff.com.
2. "ICICI Pru Goes Rural with Micro Offices, Biometric Cards," *The Hindu Business Line*, 15 February 2008, available at www.thehindubusinessline.com/2008/02/15/stories/2008021552420600.htm.
3. Sanjeev Goyle, "What Cannot be Measured, Cannot be Bettered," 13 March 2009, available at www.eventfaqs.com.

Case 6.1 Rural Kiosks—Search for Optimization

Rural kiosks are shared-access computer centres run either as community centres or as businesses. Rural PC kiosks face many significant challenges. The following are just a sample of problems that are well-known to practitioners:

- *Economic barriers:* Kiosks often charge per transaction or per service, and these costs are often greater than what many rural villagers are willing to pay.
- *Social barriers:* Discrimination against some customers or avoidance of the kiosk by potential clients due to caste can keep majority of customers away from a kiosk.
- *Confused branding:* Many kiosks try to be all things to everyone, but this is not possible. Farmers may not seek agricultural advice from a place where children play computer games.
- *Educational barriers:* Villagers are either illiterate or lack sufficient education to take advantage of knowledge in document or online form.
- *Mistrust and overabundance of information:* Farmers are bombarded with information, from salesmen, extension workers, neighbours, etc. They can't tell sources of information apart and a kiosk is just another—perhaps more alien—source.
- *Lack of information in a familiar form:* Available information is not in their local dialects, not specific to their geographic region, etc.
- *Poor infrastructure:* Electricity and phone line connectivity is not consistent.
- *Frequent maintenance needs:* Qualified maintenance services can be unavailable or costly.

Kiosk projects try to achieve the dual goals of financial sustainability and social development. However, it is difficult to fulfil both simultaneously. Kiosk operators frequently lack the talent and training required to run these challenging operations. If individual kiosks are difficult, scaling to large numbers is a proportionately greater challenge. ITC, a well-resourced conglomerate and the most aggressive implementer of (e-*choupal*) kiosks, had a large staff of dedicated employees.

Categories of Rural PC Kiosks

Despite the difficulties faced by rural kiosk operators, there are several types of rural PC kiosks that appear to be sustainable with a level of consistency. Of these, entrepreneur success is far more likely if the government actively endorses these centres and additionally closes all other means of providing the particular service offered by the kiosks.

- *Computer-education centres:* Even in remote rural areas, computers signify wealth and upward mobility. As a result, customers are willing to pay significant amounts to learn computer fundamentals.
- *Regular Internet cafés:* Some kiosks evolve to become regular Internet cafes particularly in villages straddling a busy road.
- *Government service centres:* Some kiosks mainly provide government services (e.g., birth and death certificates) and related services (e.g., paying electricity bills).
- *Photo shops:* There are many instances of photo shops that use computers to enhance their services. Digital, still and video cameras are increasingly available and even rural villagers spend lavishly on special events such as weddings where photo and video services are required. In addition, customers pay considerable amounts to have photographs modified by the addition of artificial backgrounds and religious themes.

Classes of Customers

There are at least two classes of customers—the rich and the poor. This results in tricky tradeoffs for kiosk operators. On the one hand, kiosk operators must recover their costs. This requires selling to wealthier clients who are more educated, more experienced in computer use, who expect a state-of-the-art facility with high-end services and who are interested in more advanced offerings. On the other hand, kiosk operators are also often expected to serve the poor. They often require extensive outreach before relevant applications can be found. Serving both is a difficult task. In addition, kiosk operators face a branding decision—whether to market to higher-income consumers or to a lower-income clientele. Marketing to one tends to alienate the other. Local entrepreneurs, left to their own devices, seem to downplay services to the poorest in their communities, in favour of catering to wealthier clients.

Profile of Customers

These kiosks are frequented primarily by students, educated, unemployed youth, and wealthy village residents. Most of the users are male and have completed high school or have a bachelor's degree. They often have prior exposure to computers and are often familiar with basic computer applications such as word processing. There is social pressure for women to remain in their homes or to be accompanied by the male members of their households in public spaces. This pressure prohibits widespread use of kiosks by women, as kiosks tend to be in enclosed spaces and are often operated by men.

Fees

Most rural kiosk enterprises employ a pay-per-use model similar to that used in urban Internet cafés with set rates for each hour of PC use or for each application-specific service (Rs 10 per hour for PC use, Rs 30 for a set of four photographs or Rs 15 per print-out of land record, etc.). While this is an established way to charge for services, it is not the only one. In some kiosk projects, it is observed that an annual kiosk-usage fee encouraged kiosk usage and payment without invoking resistance to paying for computer-based services.

One example is the *e-grama* network, promoted by *Gramin Mahiti Parishat* (GMP), an NGO working to establish computer kiosk enterprises in rural Karnataka. A per-family fee allows any person from the member's family to access the kiosk at any time. Take-up figures have been encouraging. For instance, in a village of around 600 families (about 3,000 people), the e-*grama* centre has 200 families enrolled as members. The E-*grama* encourages its members to pay the kiosk-membership dues on an annual basis. It does so by offering additional "free" benefits with the lump sum payments. For instance, with a one-time 120 Rs annual membership fee, the primary wage earner in the family becomes eligible for up to Rs 25,000 or 50,000 in accidental death insurance for that year. In addition, the e-*grama* membership ID card can be used to get concessions at select hospitals and medical shops in the area.

For discussion

1. Identify the barriers, opportunities and options in decisions relating to the kiosk business.
2. How do you develop a viable business model for a kiosk?
3. How do you fulfil the social goals of serving the poor and women?

Source: Renee Kuriyan and Kentaro Toyama, "Review of Research on Rural PC Kiosks," available at http://research.microsoft.com/research/tem/kiosks; Karishma Kiri and Deepak Menon, "For Profit Rural Kiosks in India: Achievements and Challenges," available at www.i4donline.net.

Case 6.2 LG Reaches Rural Markets

LG—Balancing Urban and Rural Segments

In 2008, LG Electronics India managed to clock revenues of Rs 10.73 billion, a 15 per cent growth over 2007, and is looking at a turnover of Rs 12.5 billion in 2009. The net profit margin was at 4 per cent of sales despite severe pressure on raw material costs. LG decided on a 10 per cent increase in ad and marketing budget to raise it to Rs 4 billion in 2009.

Growth Targets

LG Electronics India, the second-largest LCD television player in the country after Samsung, is looking at becoming the largest player in that segment. Even though the industry is witnessing 4 per cent category growth, LG is looking forward to an optimistic 7 per cent growth by 2009. With this, it aims to increase its market share from the current 27 per cent to a fair 30 per cent by the end of this year.

In 2008, LG held 23 per cent of the market share, far behind Samsung's 37 per cent and was closely followed by Sony with 21 to 22 per cent control over the segment.

Target Markets and Competition

"LG India's vision is to reach every consumer in the country via a route that is most befitting when it comes to practicality. Therefore, we developed a strategy that not only taps every region, state or area but every individual," says Moon B. Shin, Managing Director, LG India.

"For our premium products, we shall continue to focus on the urban markets," he added. The company hopes to alter its portfolio and model mix for the rural market and ensure that all segments are represented at the entry level. "We plan to have a good product mix at the entry level to make use of the rural opportunity," said Mr Ramachandran.

cricket game in TV sets wasn't the only "go local" innovation. LG also offered on-screen displays in five languages and large-capacity, semi-automatic washing machines that would suit Indian families.

Today LG has found that the Indian consumer is evolving slowly in terms of lifestyle preferences and choices and is on the lookout for something new to experiment with. Hence, LG decided to offer the best to the consumer in terms of technology, pricing, looks, features and performance of the product. In 2006, LG India drew up a plan to shed its "value for money" brand image and to become an "aspirational" brand in consumers' perception and to double its turnover by 2010.

Exhibit 6.1 4 A's Framework of Marketing

Acceptability	Product and promotion localization strategy, Hindi and regional language menus on its TVs, tapped local forms of entertainment like annual *haats* and fairs.
Affordability	Reduced cost by replacing four speakers with two speakers, Sampoorna was priced at Rs 3,000 and Cineplus at Rs 4,900
Availability	65 remote area offices under the 40 branch offices are empowered to directly link to the central billing system for orders, 230 service centres and 2,600 mobile authorized service personnel for villages having less than 10,000 residents
Awareness	Mobile vans, exhibitions and road shows.

LG's Strategies

Two years ago the company's top brass was debating how to reach out to rural India. It adopted a two-pronged strategy that has worked brilliantly for LG Electronics, India. At one level, the company figured it needed new cheaper products to lure the rural buyer. At another level, it figured that more offices in smaller towns and cities were the need of the hour. LG moved quickly on both fronts. The 4 A's framework of marketing for LG is in Exhibit 6.1.

The acceptability is enhanced by a consumer-oriented approach, innovations in products guided by value and by adopting principles. The features were carefully chosen and adapted to appeal to Indian audiences. For instance, consumers in South-west India prefer loud sounds and big bass outputs. Accordingly, LG India created Ballad, a flat screen television model that sells only in the subcontinent and comes equipped with 2,000 watt speakers. The

New Product Launches

LG planned to develop 31 models with 100 per cent Star Rating by the end of 2009. These will comprise 19 flat and 12 ultra slim TVs that conform to the BEE (Bureau of Energy Efficiency) guidelines for annual power consumption. The company has already launched eight of these models in the market. The new range sports a complete designer look and XD picture. The TVs are 40 per cent slimmer than the present range obtainable in the market. The Star Rated 21-inch flat TV is expected to carry an MRP of Rs 7,300, while the Star Rated 29-inch flat TV will carry a price tag of Rs 14,900. The maximum MRP of a Star Rated 21-inch ultra slim TV is pegged at Rs 8,300, while a 29-inch ultra slim TV will retail at Rs 17,800. The three major launches of full HDTVs last summer, Scarlet in May, LG 53 in June and Jazz in August were successful.

Value-Plus Proposition

Commenting on the product policy of LG, KSA Technopak Principal Harminder Sahni says, "LG has been careful right from the beginning to offer customers a 'value-plus' proposition. The company does not qualify as a 'budget' models company." Kim—who has been with LG India since 1997—points to a basic characteristic of Indian consumers. "They are very price sensitive. They want the best quality at reasonable prices." Accordingly, LG introduced its economy range in the country that Kim predicted would be "easily accepted." "LG has been a price – warrior while retaining its brand equity," points out Ajay Kapila, vice president, sales and marketing, Electrolux India.

Availability Leads to Profitability

LG's example shows that revenues can rise quickly if you get the mix right. The company says that earlier a single branch office catered to Chandigarh, Jammu and Kashmir and Punjab and generated Rs 180 million per month. Now with more branches, revenue in the same area has gone up to Rs 500 million per month. Similarly other states like Rajasthan now have two branches—at Jodhpur and Jaipur—instead of one.

All these moves are part of LG's efforts to push turnover to a whopping Rs 70 billion by year-end. All this is like great music for rural dealers. A city dealer will today sell a CTV by cutting into his margin, closer to the dealer price rather than the marked retail price. So while he makes 5 per cent to 7 per cent profit, rural dealers make 7 per cent to 10 per cent profit on a sale. "Volume makes up in the city whereas value makes up in the rural area," says an industry observer.

Competition

Mirc Electronics launched its Operation *Vistaar* (meaning expansion) late last year. Mirc is already selling a second-string brand Igo that is slightly cheaper than its Onida range. Mirc says that both Igo and Onida are selling well in the rural areas. Mirc says it had to be careful about diluting the Onida brand. Igo, at Rs 5,000 for a 14-inch TV is priced Rs 500 to Rs 700 lower than the national brands. "We didn't want to dilute Onida's mid-to-premium brand equity by making it mass market," says V. Chandramouli, vice president, marketing, sales and service, Mirc Electronics Limited. Recently the company hired another 100 people for its Igo team.

Videocon, that sells about 40 per cent of its products in rural areas, has just begun a fresh thrust to boost sales outside the metros. It's hoping that by year end about 55 per cent of the total sales will come from the rural areas. But it isn't designing new products for rural customers. So an entry level 14-inch Videocon CTV will sell for Rs 7,000, both in the cities and the villages. The thrust is on CTVs, tape recorders, refrigerators, DVD/VCD players as demanded by rural India today.

Some companies are playing the game slightly differently. Samsung, for instance, insists that it's a high-end technology driven player. That's why the urban areas are still a focus area for it and only 30 per cent of its revenue comes from rural and semi-urban India. Nevertheless, in the last two years, Samsung has looked at increasing awareness and penetration of its products in second-rung cities like Bhuj, Porbandar and Jalandhar. The Samsung Dream Home road shows across the length and breadth of the country have been a step in this direction. "We don't have a rural model or a different pricing strategy. But, the products are focused on semi-urban or urban markets," says Zutshi.

Godrej Appliances has learnt its rural lessons through trial and error. Today, it is present in 900 towns of which 450 have a population above 100,000. Another 250 are towns with less than 100,000 residents. Says Soumitra Ghatak, executive vice president, Godrej Appliances, "To match its new aims, for the first time, Godrej will be advertising on Doordarshan. Till now the company has always advertised on cable television." The company has also redefined its target group from SEC A, B and C to include SEC D as well. Godrej's direct cool refrigerator range starts at Rs 6,500. Godrej admits that it fumbled on the way when it tried to sell cheaper products. Two years ago, it tried to sell a stripped-down fridge called Champion with only half a freezer. However, sales did not pick up so it had to be re-jigged and re-launched with a full freezer. "Product features are important, rural customers are just as aware as the urban customers," says Ghatak.

Perceived Threats of Rural Focus

The increased rural focus doesn't mean the urban market will suffer. Samsung, Onida and even LG are aggressively looking at the urban replacement market for their high-end premium product range. However, industry players warn of dangers in the aggressive rural ramp up. For one, stripping product features in order to lower prices, as some brands are known to do, is a dangerous game to play. Then there are other external problems to surmount like the irregularity of electricity supply and lack of finance options.

"Cracking the rural market is easier said than done," says Godrej's Ghatak. Adds an industry observer, "The rural market will not be about pricing but about how the customer is serviced and treated. If one consumer is not happy, the entire village will know and the company can then kiss that market goodbye."

For discussion

1. Evaluate the marketing strategies of LG and its competitors. Based on the evaluation, develop a suitable model for marketers of TVs.
2. What should be the strategy of LG in future? Is it right in shedding its "value-for-money" brand image and becoming an "aspirational" brand in consumers' perception? Should it retain and strengthen its focus on rural markets?

Source: "LG India to Develop 31 Energy-Efficient CTV Models," available at www.efytimes.com/efytimes/34601/news.htm; Anjana Chandramouly, "LG Group Banks on Rural Markets for Revenue Growth," *The Hindu Business Line*, 20 February 2009, available at www.thehindubusinessline.com/2009/02/20/stories/2009022051750400.htm.

Part III Designing Strategies

7

Product Strategy

LEARNING OBJECTIVES

Upon completion of this chapter, you will be able to:

- Understand product decision situations and approaches to product classification
- Recognize the three levels at which product strategy decisions are required
- Understand the significance of product strategy
- Explain product strategy with reference to acceptability and examine product design considerations
- Recognize different types of product strategies
- Identify the steps taken by companies to counter fake products

The USD 40 billion global white goods major, LG Group, has conceived proactive product strategies based on the understanding that the rural sector is growing faster than the urban sector with high disposable incomes. It has strengthened its focus on rural markets to secure 40 per cent contribution for its turnover from rural sales. V. Ramachandran, director, sales and marketing, LG Electronics, said that rural markets were untouched by the economic slowdown and would "contribute in a major way in durable sales." For the premium products category; however, the company decided to continue its focus on urban markets as the company has an attractive 15 per cent growth there, reporting a turnover of Rs 125 billion in 2009.

The trend in the white-goods industry at present is to introduce feature-rich products, which are not only stylish but technologically advanced. Therefore, LG is looking to launch a mix of energy efficient and innovative products to lure consumers. For instance, LG's new frost-free range of refrigerators is designed to woo Indian customers. LG is keen on new product research and development activities to fuel its expansion efforts and plans are in the anvil to invest about Rs 2 billion. To leverage on its "brand reliability" proposition, it has planned on an investment of Rs 4 billion for marketing and promotional activities. The promotion will be strengthened by after-sales service for gaining a competitive advantage in the market.[1]

The case of LG Electronics reflects the current thinking and approaches of companies aiming at growth and diversification into rural segments. In this chapter, the product related concepts and classifications are explained. The significance of product strategy for a company is outlined and the strategic alternatives are briefly discussed. Finally, the different strategies adopted by Indian companies for rural markets are also highlighted.

INTRODUCTION

On observation, we find that multi-product firms are fighting hard to gain commanding market shares through their product strategies in the dynamic, competitive market environment. As the markets for lifestyle products are emerging, companies are facing intriguing questions such as whether it should introduce low-end models of successful products, create separate brands or continue with the quality image and wait for the evolution of rural markets. In this chapter, we will explore product strategies in the changing context and understand the responses of marketers. The guiding principle is "success requires continuous design and redesign of product mixes."

PRODUCT DECISIONS

Knowledge of product classification is essential not only for marketing but also for entrepreneurial decisions. The important decision situations faced by marketers are:

Entry decision

How to make an entry into a business? The questions that need to be focused on are:

(i) Which product and which market (consumer segment)? Whether to offer FMCGs or durables or services?

(ii) Whether to enter the market with an existing product or an innovative product?

(iii) Whether to offer high-quality, high-price (premium) products or value-for-money (economy) products?

(iv) Whether to go by one product or a combination of different products (product line and mix decisions)?

Growth decision

How to increase sales, revenues and profits? The questions that require attention are:

(i) How to increase penetration levels of the product? Is it by changes in quality, price or promotion (product life cycle strategies)?

(ii) How to sustain growth in sales by creating a competitive edge?

- Is it by innovation (improvement or new product-development strategy)?
- Is it by diversification by opting for either related or unrelated products?
- Is it by integration—backward (supply side input products) or forward integration (consumption side output products)?

PRODUCT CLASSIFICATIONS

Products may be classified in different ways. The distinct product classifications as given in Table 7.1 are important for marketers.

Table 7.1 Product Classifications

Sl No.	Base	Classification	Implications for marketers
1	User	Household goods Occupational requirements	Make an entry/diversification decision based on entrepreneurial competencies
2	Shelf movement	FMCGs Consumer durables	Make distribution decisions that have push effect and support them by promotion and price decisions that have pull effect.
3	Consumer shopping habits	Convenience goods Shopping goods Specialty goods	Design retail outlets to make shopping convenient and pleasant.
4	Customer value (price and quality)	Cheaper products Economy products Premium products	Design product line and make brand extensions
5	Innovation	Original, novel products Imitations	Go in for continuous or breakthrough innovations

Table 7.2 Classification of Products by User Type

Type of user	Consumables	Durables	Services
Households	FMCGs such as toothpaste, shampoo, detergents, biscuits, soft drinks, instant mixes, etc.	Refrigerators, TVs, washing machines, etc.	Product repairs, communication, banking , education, health care, etc.
Occupations	Agri-inputs such as fertilizers, pesticides, seeds etc.	Tractors, two-wheelers, cars, etc.	Counselling services for farming and animal husbandry, investment, banking, insurance, etc.

Based on users and movement of goods

An important classification of products is based on user types and requirements of different types of goods. Who are a company's potential customers and what do they use? Table 7.2 explains the classification with examples.

FMCGs have the inherent characteristic of necessity. They represent inelastic products used for daily consumption. As such, the emphasis of majority of FMCG companies has been on gaining volume growth with mass products.

Based on shopping habits

Products are classified into three categories, i.e. convenience goods, shopping goods and specialty goods based on the shopping habits of consumers as indicated in Table 7.3.

Based on price and quality

Products are categorized into three types based on price and quality considerations.

Table 7.3 Product Classification Based on Shopping Habits

Goods	Product type	Buyer involvement	Buying frequency	Buying decision evaluation	Buying place
Convenience goods (mostly consumables like provisions, toiletries, cosmetics, smoking products, etc.)	Consumables (FMCGs)	Low	Frequent	Simple	Paan shop, *kirana* shop, co-operative stores, fair price shops, fairs and *mandis*. Urbanites buy at *paan* shops, kiosks, provision stores, departmental stores, supermarkets and malls.
Shopping goods (clothing, furniture, home appliances, etc.)	Durables	Moderate	Occasional	Complex	Fairs, *haats, mandis* and shops in feeder towns. Urbanites buy from showrooms, authorized showrooms and chain stores.
Specialty goods (cameras, two-wheelers, tractors, etc.)	Durables	High	Once in life	Complex	Shops in towns or cities

Cheaper goods

Cheaper goods are those that are characterized by low quality and low price. They perform the core function but they lack certain attributes that make their use less comfortable, less pleasant and less desirable.

> **Example:** Nirma washing powder is a cheap product. The packaging is poor. Powder spills over. When the powder is mixed in water, a burning sensation is felt in the skin and palms.

Economy goods

Products with all necessary functional but no fancy features are termed as economy goods. Their price and quality are fairly reasonable. In case of durables, operating and maintenance expenditures are low. As such, they are money savers while being need gratifiers.

> **Examples:** Mopeds, single-door refrigerators, TVs without remote and limited channels.

Premium goods

Premium goods are products that appeal to the ego of the buyer. They are, as economist Thoerstein Veblen described, goods for conspicuous consumption. Being high-quality, high-priced goods, they are known as premium goods and prestige goods.

> **Examples:** Jewellery, silk *sarees*, cars, bungalows, high-priced cosmetics, toiletries and perfumes.

Based on type of product innovation

Products are classified into two categories based on nature of innovation—original, novel products and imitations. Table 7.4 provides examples.

Original, novel products

Innovative products rule the market. An innovative firm will surely succeed. However, it should be careful in making technical innovations in tune with changing market behaviours. There is a long

Table 7.4 Noveltie and Copycats in the Rural Market

Original product	Imitations	
	Novelties	**Copy cat**
Lifebuoy	Nirma buoy,	New Lime Buoy, Nimba buoy
Colgate	Pepsodent	College
Nirma	Wheel	Neerbha, Nima, Nilima, Narima
Fair & Lovely	Fairever	Friends & Lovely

Table 7.5 Industry Classification of Consumer Durables

White goods	Brown goods/Kitchen appliances	Consumer electronics
Refrigerators	Mixers and grinders	Mobile phones
Washing machines	Microwave ovens, cooking ranges	Television
Air conditioners	Iron	MP3 players
Speakers and audio equipments	Electric fans	DVD players/VCD players

list of successful innovative products. For instance, tractors, fertilizers, seeds, pesticides, new farming methods, etc. transformed some parts of poor rural India into prosperous, model villages. Communication devices, colas, cars, cell phones and computers are now changing the face of rural India.

Imitations

Imitations may result in two types of goods depending upon the purpose, commitment and competence of the imitator. A poor imitator will end up in producing deceptive, spurious, fake, copycat products. He dupes gullible customers by offering products that closely resemble the originals. In quality, it is a poor cousin to the original. On the other hand, a competent imitator may even produce an improved version of the original product.

Industry classification of consumer durables

The consumer durables industry can be broadly classified into consumer electronics and consumer appliances. The consumer appliances category can be further segmented as white goods and brown goods as given in Table 7.5.

PRODUCT STRATEGY LEVELS

The product strategy embraces decisions at three levels:

(i) Product mix
(ii) Product line
(iii) Product item

The product mix is a set of all product lines and items offered by the company. A product line is a group of closely related products priced within a range and distributed through some channels to the same customer groups. Table 7.6 shows the product mix of HUL.

Table 7.6 HUL's Product Portfolio and Strategic Objectives

Horizon one	Horizon two	Horizon three
Soaps and detergents	Popular foods	Direct-to-home products
Beverages	Culinary products	Value-added foods
Oil and dairy fats	Personal products	Bread and biscuits
Specialty chemicals	Ice-creams	
Animal feeds	Homecare products	
	New beverages	
Profitable growth	Top line growth	Development and learning

Various strategies adopted at this level are:

- *Width extension:* Adding new product lines (related diversification or unrelated diversification)—diversification strategy.
- *Length extension:* Adding new product items—this extension can be done in three ways: upward (higher-end models), downward (lower-end models) and both ways. When leveraged on a reputed brand it is referred to as brand extension—brand/line extension strategy.
- *Line pruning:* Reducing the number of product items to modernize the product portfolio—line modernization strategy.
- *Depth extension:* Adding new product variants.

SIGNIFICANCE OF PRODUCT STRATEGY

Product strategy refers to the long-range competitive plan involving decisions relating to products, product-line, proper utilization of resources, and achieving marketing goals.

An effective product strategy offers the following benefits.

Achieves product–market fit

A well thought-out product strategy will be able to offer products based on market needs. Thus, it achieves a product–market fit and avoids the pitfalls of marketing myopia. Consequently, it provides insurance for survival.

Encourages innovation

Effective product strategy tends to be proactive in offering products that satisfy not only the current needs but also the future needs of customers. As such, product strategy relies on creativity and innovative techniques. It can be said that innovation is the core of a product strategy.

Provides competitive edge

The success of a firm heavily depends on the uniqueness of the product as there are competitors in almost all sectors. In this competitive era, marketers should set up intelligence systems to understand the product launch moves of the competitive firms. Today, brand wars are considered quite common.

Companies will have to use a well thought-out product strategy to attack and to flank their competition, to defend their positions and to wage guerrilla warfare.

Makes better use of resources

The product additions and deletions, based on rational appraisal of marketing and production strengths and weaknesses allow for better utilization of physical, financial and human resources. It thus helps achieve high productivity levels. Consequently, organizations will not have to worry about idle capacities and a demoralized workforce.

PRODUCT STRATEGIES: ASSESSMENT OF ACCEPTABILITY

In the rural context, marketers have to use two frameworks—the marketing mix of 4 P's (product, price, place and promotion) and the evaluative rural marketing mix of 4 A's (availability, acceptability, affordability and awareness). The product decision is the central decision in the marketing-mix strategy. It should be evaluated on the basis of the acceptability parameter to evolve strategies suitable for the current and emerging rural markets. However, as we discuss acceptability (preferences and penetration), we find it is closely related to another factor—affordability (products within the limits of purchasing power: economy or premium goods)—of the marketing mix.

Acceptability challenge

The first challenge involves identifying the consumer preferences and offering them choices for their consideration and purchase. The acceptance of different products in rural areas can be gauged from the changing preferences of rural consumers, statistics of penetration levels of products and plans of companies to reap benefits form the rural sector.

Preferences for products

Today, we find that the rural market has changed considerably and offers scope for selling modern lifestyle products. Box 7.1 describes the shift in consumer tastes and preferences.

Penetration levels

In recent years, the FMCG sector has continued to grow by 17–18 per cent in terms of volume. The demand from rural India constitutes around 50 per cent of the total FMCG market in India. It accounts for more than 40 per cent of the consumption in major FMCG categories such as personal care, fabric care and hot beverages. However, penetration levels of FMCG players in these areas are still low, especially in personal care and processed foods. Many categories like skin creams (18 per cent), toothpastes (40 per cent), deodorants (1 per cent), hot beverages (3 per cent), and packaged fruit juice (2 per cent) look promising. In well-penetrated categories like shampoos (37 per cent) and hair oils (67 per cent), the per capita consumption is lower than in urban areas. The low penetration levels indicate the potential that such rural markets hold.

The penetration of TVs (36 per cent), refrigerators (5 per cent), washing machines (1 per cent), air conditioners (less than1 per cent) indicates that there is scope for marketing activity.

The acceptance of services is encouraging. For instance, "Today, 60 per cent of all our new consumers are from the rural areas," says Sanjay Kapoor, deputy CEO, Bharti Airtel. This is equivalent to 1.68 million new rural customers a month. Airtel has been adding some 2.8 million subscribers every month for the past one year. Every second new subscriber is from a rural area, observes Pradeep Shrivastava, Chief Marketing Officer, Idea Cellular. In fact, many believe that telecom operators may have reached saturation point in urban areas with penetration at 80 per cent. The rural penetration level is only 10 to12 per cent and the rural rush is understandable.

Box 7.1 Brands for New Consumers

A wave of consumerism is beginning to replace age-old habits. Markets are fast changing from a seller's market into a buyer's market. Dreams and aspirations are materializing into real things and lifestyles. Rural India has slowly begun to adopt the ways of urban living and is emerging into a visible and viable market.

In the morning, the "new" rural consumer brushes his teeth with toothpaste, having done away with the traditional *neem* twig or charcoal powder. After a refreshing bath with a branded soap, he sits down to enjoy a meal cooked by his wife in branded edible oil and sprinkled with little iodized salt to taste. He rides his motorbike to work in the nearest town, dropping off a neighbour or two on the way. During a lull at work, he listens to the radio under a fan. When the heat gets too much, he walks out to a *kirana* shop and cools down with a cold drink, picking up a sachet of *paan masala* before returning to work. On his way home, he looks in at a home appliances shop to buy a pressure cooker his wife had asked for. At home, refreshed after another bath with a branded soap, he sits down for a meal with his family. Simultaneously, he switches on his black and white television to watch the latest serial on Doordarshan.

This change in lifestyle has brought about brand consciousness. The rural consumer is beginning to ask for specific brands and is not just satisfied with product categories. What's in demand are Philips transistors, Khaitan fans, Lifebuoy soaps and Mahindra tractors—not just transistors, fans, soaps and tractors.

Source: "Potential of Rural Markets," available at www.linterland.com/core/rurallandscape/16.htm.

Plans of companies

A large number of companies from different sectors have plans for expansion in the rural markets. The examples discussed in Box 7.2 substantiate the viewpoint.

PRODUCT DESIGN DECISIONS

A product or a service is an offer made by a marketer, which has the ability to satisfy the needs and wants of customers. Products are physical and tangible. Examples are fertilizers, mosquito repellants, analgesics and footwear. Services are intangible and people-based or equipment-based. Examples are soil testing, retailer advice, training and health care.

The key consideration in individual product/service offers is the development of the product at three levels.

1. Core product development
2. Tangible product development
3. Augmented product development

Core product

A core product provides benefits that correspond to the needs specified by consumers. The key questions, therefore, are: What are the needs of consumers? What kind of form and functional utilities are consumers demanding? What are the latent needs and desires of consumers? By obtaining answers from the study of consumers or retailers, the marketer has to work with the manufacturing group

Box 7.2 Plans to Expand Rural Sales

Exide Industries hopes to sell 250,000 batteries for tractors in 2009–2010. It has plans to increase its market share from 14 per cent to 25 per cent in two years. There are 4 million registered tractors in India. Maruti Suzuki, India's leading automobile manufacturer, sells 5 per cent of its vehicles in the rural markets today. The company expects this number to rise to 15 per cent in the next two years. Mahindra and Mahindra, TAFE and other companies are sketching growth plans in a similar vein.

Godrej Consumer Products Ltd (GCPL) has seen rural sales grow by 40 per cent, double of that in urban areas. H. K. Press, vice-chairman, said: "We intend increasing it to 50 per cent within a year. We have project "*Dharti*" for rural India and we cover close to 17,000 villages. We intend covering 50,000 villages soon." Its main competitors HUL, ITC, P&G and Dabur have their own designs.

Bharti Airtel has already announced its intention of becoming a "rural company" in the near future (currently, about 30 per cent of Bharti's wireless subscriber base is in the rural areas).

Reliance Communications is also extending its rural presence. S. P. Shukla, president (wireless) of Reliance Communications opined that the future growth of telephony is in rural areas. According to him, prepaid services will be especially attractive to users in rural areas as it prevents the customer from getting tied down to a fixed-cost service. BSNL, Tata Cellular, Vodafone, and other service providers and Samsung, Motorola and other handset makers are confident about their prospects in rural India.

Elder Pharmaceuticals Limited has set up a dedicated division called "Elvista" to spread its network to villages, towns, sub-urban/periphery markets and hinterland districts. Initial targets are Class II to IV towns and rural markets with a dedicated sales force of 240. "We plan to increase Elvista's marketing strength to about 750 personnel or 'product specialists' by 2012," says Alok Saxena, director, Elder Pharma. The company has earmarked an investment of Rs 0.4 billion for its rural thrust.

Source: Pradipta Mukherjee, "We Intend to Cover 50,000 Villages Soon," *Business Standard*, 4 August 2009, available at www.business-standard.com; "Elder Pharmaceuticals sets up Elvista," available at www.indiaprwire.com/pressrelease/medical/2009071029101.htm; Abhinna Shreshtha and Muntazir Abbas, "Rural Markets Next Frontier for Telecom Operators," 3 June 2009, available at www.cxotoday.com.

to design and develop appropriate products. Sound product strategy should be based on the understanding of the fact that products are transient. However, the basic needs of customer groups remain unchanged. Table 7.7 illustrates this point.

A core product is one that provides important form utility and ensures performance of the basic function. The testing question, therefore, is:

Is the product capable of fulfilling the needs of customers?

Taking the above examples, the relevant questions are:

- Can the toothpowder be used to keep the teeth clean?
- Can the tractor run even when the soil is muddy and roads are rough?

Table 7.7 Need–Product Relationships

Needs	Old products	New products
Brushing teeth	*Neem* sticks, charcoal, ash, rock salt, husk, powder mixtures	Toothpaste, toothpowder and liquids
Washing vessels	Coconut fibre, earthy materials, brick powder, ash	Washing soaps, powders and liquids
Transport	Bullock carts, horses, donkeys chariots, pallanquins	Tractors, LCVs, mopeds, scooters, motor cycles, trains, buses
Irrigation	Wells, canals, water lifters, wind mills	Bore-wells, motors, power generators, pump sets
Hair wash	Shikakai powder, soap nuts	Shampoos and hair care soaps

Tangible product

The product concept becomes visible and operational when psychological needs are specified in physical terms. Any product or service has five characteristics:

(a) Quality
(b) Features
(c) Design/Style
(d) Packaging
(e) Branding

It is in terms of these five characteristics that a consumer expresses the desirable benefits and expects them from a product to satisfy his needs. Accordingly, marketers have to design and communicate "products" with the above five characteristics. The task involves answering two questions:

1. How important is each characteristic to the consumer?
2. How much of each is to be incorporated in product design?

Quality

It is the most important characteristic of a product or service. Quality signifies the ability of a product to meet the following expectations:

- Durability—It should last for a certain period.
- Capacity—It should possess the requisite ability to function.
- Efficiency—It should function better to give desired outcomes with less inputs.
- Economy—Its operational cost, time and energy expenditure are less.
- Reliability—It can be depended upon to provide the desired function and results.

Product designers should necessarily interact with marketers to know how consumers evaluate the quality of a product. Is the consumer dependent on technical specifications? Does he have any other parameters to decide quality levels?

Experience tells us that consumers develop their own norms, notions and beliefs to sense quality. After identifying these norms, notions and beliefs, product designers have to provide physical signs and cues that represent them. These are termed as emotional specifications. For instance, a rural consumer views heavy watches as quality watches; he judges the quality of cement by its bitter taste. Table 7.8 provides the technical specifications and emotional specifications of a few products.

Implications for marketers

Success in marketing is dependent on offering the desired quality products to market segments that are profitable. We can place successful products on a quality spectrum in the market. Figure 7.1 shows examples of products on the quality continuum.

Features

Human beings are progressive in thinking and in their behaviour. They are never happy with what they have. They continually seek improvements for more comfort and convenience. In a lighter vein, someone remarked, "when hunger is satisfied, people demand music." Evidently, bare-bone models of products do not satisfy consumers. They look for features. What are features? Features are extras to a product that are of value to buyers. Features are of two types:

1. Rational, problem-solving
2. Emotional, fancy

The consumer of a product seeks solutions to the problems he has in using the product. Also, he is willing to pay for the solutions. It is the willingness to buy solutions that leads marketers to add features to the "stripped-down" model.

Table 7.8 Product-design Specifications

Product	Technical (Rational) specifications	Sensory (Emotional) specifications
Watches	Mechanical or winding type	Weight
Moped	Fuel efficiency, power	Style and colour
Refrigerator	Capacity in litres	Noiseless, closure of doors
Coffee	Coffee or chicory content	Smell

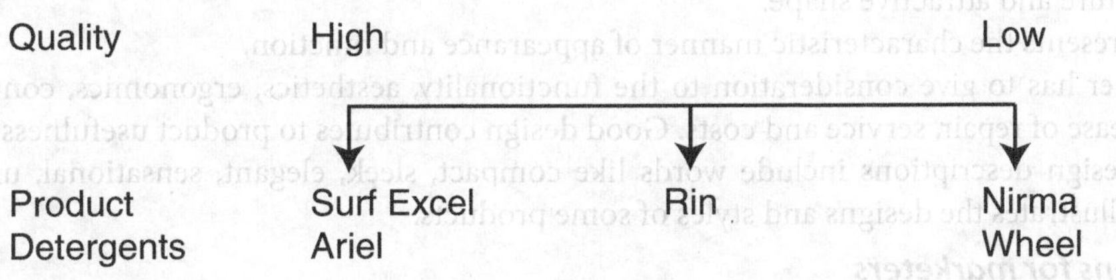

Figure 7.1 Quality Spectrum

Table 7.9 Features of Products

Product	Rational problems	Features	Emotional
35 mm camera	Focusing Lighting Carrying flash Winding Time memory Distance	Auto-focus Flash Built-in-flash Automatic Winding Date and time recorder Zoom lens	Colour Size Finish Few adjustments
Automobile	Discomfort in sitting, heat and dust	Cushion seating, air conditioning	Shape, colour, size, finish

The second type of features are those that capture the attention of the buyers. They are less functional and more fanciful. Table 7.9 presents the features of some products.

Implications for marketers

Rural markets are now becoming prosperous and R-1 and R-2 categories of customers are also looking for features in their products. Instead of thinking about offering bare-bones or stripped models, marketers have to offer features that enhance the utility and convenience in the use of the product.

How many features should be added? Based on market research studies, one can identify numerous feature ideas. They require screening and evaluation on the prime considerations outlined below:

1. *Consumer point of view*—Desirability and affordability of consumer. What is the perceived value of the feature? What price is he willing to pay?
2. *Competition point of view*—Is it necessary, in view of competition? What are the features of the products of competitors? What features do they propose to add? What features do we have to add to become even with competitors? How can we excel them?
3. *Company point of view*—Is the feature profitable? If cost-benefit analysis reveals that feature costs are lower than the price, the feature is viable. Then, it can be added.

Design and style

Design refers to the arrangement of parts, form, colour, etc. so as to produce an artistic unit with functional structure and attractive shape.

Style represents the characteristic manner of appearance and function.

A designer has to give consideration to the functionality, aesthetics, ergonomics, convenience of operation, ease of repair, service and costs. Good design contributes to product usefulness and attractiveness. Design descriptions include words like compact, sleek, elegant, sensational, unusual, etc. Table 7.10 illustrates the designs and styles of some products.

Implications for marketers

It is through design that a product acquires structure, shape and style, which are the three components of personality. Considerations of brand personality occupy central place in the marketer's decision-making process with respect to positioning and target marketing. Rural people are slowly adopting modern lifestyles and the importance given to the design and looks of durables such as two-wheelers, TVs and mobile handsets is increasing.

Table 7.10 Design and Style of Products

Product	Design	Style
Gold Flake Filter Kings	Elegant	Gracious
Annadatha Magazine	Trim and plain	Smart and wise
Garden *sarees*	Geometric	Modern

Packaging

Every product requires a package and a label. Packaging is the process of providing a container or wrapper for a product. Packaging is done at three levels.

1. Primary package—It holds the product, for example, a bottle.
2. Secondary package—It holds the primary package, for example, a cardboard box.
3. Shipping package—It helps carry the packed products from one place to another, for example, a corrugated box.

Implications for marketers

All products need to be packaged for shipping as they are to be transported to different places. Its purpose is mainly protection and handling convenience. Some products need secondary packaging, for example, after-shave lotions, hair dyes, toothpastes, fairness creams, toilet soaps, etc. The secondary package is also found in case of products such as medical syrups and food products such as Kellogs cornflakes. In such cases it should be made attractive and informative. Some products are sold with primary packaging, for example, talcum powder, hair oils, edible oils, beverages, etc. Therefore, the marketer has to make the primary packaging appealing in case of such products.

Branding

Contemporary marketing relies on branding to give products an identity, personality, image, equity, and attractiveness. The brand is a name, term, sign, symbol, design or colour or a combination of them that helps identify the seller's products and differentiates them from those of the competitors'.

Implications for marketers

Branding has gained strategic significance for providing identity and building image for the products. As such, appropriate branding decisions are essential.

Augmented product

Marketers should have the vision to look at the specific needs (core products) of consumers and also their related requirements. They need a broader view to obtain the whole picture of the consumer's consumption to woo him or her with the right offer. It also helps differentiate their offer from those of the competitors'. A holistic approach helps to systematically differentiate the offer. Table 7.11 indicates some of the components.

Augmentation requires fortifying the product strategy with additional force drawn from other P's. As a result, buying and using the product becomes a pleasant and exciting experience. As Karl Van Clausewitz advised, "The greatest possible number of troops should be brought into action at the decisive point. This is the principle of force." When following this strategy to win brand battles, a marketer has to assemble a wide range of benefits to make the offer complete, different and strategically superior.

Table 7.11 Components of an Offer

Product-related	Services-related	Channel
Quality	Ordering	
Design/Style	Delivery and credit	Expertise
Features	Installation	Performance
Packaging	Customer tracking	Courtesy
Brand image	Repair and maintenance	Atmosphere

Table 7.12 Taxonomy of Product Strategy

Sl No.	Strategy	Variants
1.	Product innovation strategies	Urban product in rural segment Rural special (new product development)
2.	Customer-value strategies	Mass product (economy products) strategy Premium product strategy
3.	Product identity strategies	Branding strategy Packaging and labelling strategies
4.	Product lifecycle strategies	Introduction of product augmentation/continuous innovation at various stages of lifecycle (quality, design and features), growth, maturity and decline
5.	Brand-building strategies	Strategic brand management Cause branding
6.	Product-mix re-engineering strategies	Line pruning Line modernization

TYPES OF PRODUCT STRATEGIES

The strategies given in Table 7.12 are used by marketers in the context of rural markets.

PRODUCT INNOVATION STRATEGIES

Product innovations can take two forms: (i) urban products in rural segments and (ii) new products in rural markets. The two strategies are explained here.

Urban products in rural segment (market development strategy)

There are many products that are common to rural and urban markets. They include toiletries, cosmetics, washing powders, communication services, postal services, etc. Box 7.3 discusses some examples.

Box 7.3 Upgraded Product for Rural Markets

Today's rural consumer demands a flat screen television, rather than a cathode ray tube (CRT) television and he prefers foreign brands such as LG and Samsung. There has also been a steep increase in DTH connections in rural areas, states Pradeep Kashyap of MART. His findings are in consonance with Nokia's, which says that the rural consumer doesn't just want an entry-level handset priced below Rs 3,000 but, mid-range models between Rs 3,000 and 6,000. Earlier, a new rural consumer went for a single-colour basic handset; today, he's increasingly choosing a feature-rich colour display phone, says Vineet Taneja, director, marketing, Nokia India.

Apollo Hospitals is serving rural areas in a big way. Aragonda is a village 18 km from Chittoor in Andhra Pradesh. Like in other villages, disease is rampant and healthcare facilities are practically non-existent here. Apollo Hospitals, located at Chennai, has a division at Nellore and Hyderabad. It has set up an Rs 0.1 billion 50–bedded multi-specialty rural hospital at Aragonda for the village and its hinterland that was so far dependant on a poorly-equipped government hospital 10 km away, run by a single doctor. The hospital is a boon to the rural community. Its InfoTech wing, Apollo Health Street, is a joint venture with British Aero Systems and General Electric. It set up the country's first telemedicine centre at a cost of Rs 1.7 million in Aragonda hospital. Soon such centres will be opened at several places in Andhra Pradesh, Assam, Bihar, Rajasthan and Tamil Nadu.

Source: Tejeesh N. S. Behl, "Rural Resurgence to the Rescue of India Inc", *Business Today*, 24 March 2009, available at www.sify.com.

Rural specials (new product development strategy)

A close observation of rural households and situations in which different products are used help understand the importance of redesigning or modifying the products.[2] The manufacturing and marketing men can think in terms of new product designs specially meant for rural areas keeping their lifestyles in view. "There is substantial scope to create products that are oriented towards non-urban sectors," notes Ramesh Kumar of IIM-B.[3]

They can offer either functional or cultural appeal or both. For instance, Chik shampoo developed a jasmine variant to appeal to the cultural tradition of women using jasmine flowers to style their hair in some parts of the country. TVS mopeds created functional value in tune with the "all purpose" vehicle culture and Philips is creating gas stoves and lanterns with functional appeal. Some companies choose to develop products especially to meet the needs of the rural market whereas others have devised schemes that enhance the value of the offer.

Products that meet specific needs

The rural consumer seeks better value for money and is interested in tangible benefits compared with an urban consumer. Take, for instance, the greater market share of Hindustan Unilever Ltd's (HUL) Clinic Plus shampoo over CavinKare Pvt. Ltd's Chik shampoo, though CavinKare made the sachet trend popular in rural India. Similarly, consider the case of the popularity of Britannia Industries Ltd's Tiger brand of biscuits over Parle Products Pvt. Ltd's Parle G biscuits. Box 7.4 describes how companies are tailoring the products to customer needs in the rural space. Box 7.5 describes the battles between mobile-handset makers in terms of products and features.

Box 7.4 Product Customization for Rural People

The farm equipment division of Mahindra and Mahindra Ltd (M&M) has launched a fuel-efficient tractor, *Shaan*. It is an example of utility-driven product development. It helps both in farming and transportation. According to Sanjeev Goyle, senior vice-president, farm equipment sector, M&M, the model works well for brick kilns. As such the company has been aggressively pushing *Shaan* for brick kilns in Uttar Pradesh, Bihar and some parts of Haryana.

The State Bank of India (SBI) has started a zero-balance bank account programme for villagers. Called the SBI Tiny account, there are no physical branches or officials, just a paid volunteer who is equipped with a small box and a cell phone. The box enables biometric measurements (fingerprints) at the time of opening the account to confirm the account holder's identity. The cell phone enables communication with the zonal office to check on available balance. Payments under programmes such as the NREGS and pensions are made directly to these accounts. The advantage for the villagers is that they can withdraw money from their accounts at any time of the day or night. SBI hopes to cover 100,000 villages by 2012. The bank has also tied up with India Post for some services.

Source: Rajeshwari Sharma, "Secrets of Successful Marketers," 25 March 2009, available at www.livemint.com/2009/03/.../Secrets-of-successful-rural-ma.html; "SBI Opens Maiden Gram Panchayat Banking Outpost in Orissa's Sikri," *The Hindu Business Line*, 11 November 2009, available at www.blonnet.com/2009/11/11/stories/2009111151471500.htm

Box 7.5 Unique Phones for India

Nokia is aggressively reaching out to Indian consumers. It unveiled a range of seven new handsets with price tags ranging from Rs 2,000 to Rs 5,000. The phones offer many voice and data features and user interfaces in 75 different languages. The Nokia 1200 and 1208 phones come with a flashlight, localized languages and a teaching mode. Since many people in India's countryside often need to share one phone, Nokia's new models include features that enable multiple users to use each handset. For the first time, the phones have a call-tracking application and a multi-phonebook to make phone sharing simpler for customers at the bottom of the pyramid.

"The sharing of the mobile phone allows many consumers in entry markets to experience the benefits of mobility firsthand, bringing down the cost of ownership," says Soren Petersen, Nokia senior vice-president in charge of emerging markets.

Reliance executives believe that they can match Nokia in appealing to customers from the lower income group. Unveiling the company's new low-cost phones at a press conference in Mumbai, S. P. Shukla, president for the personal business division at Reliance Communications, said, "We are confident of extending the benefits of mobility to an entirely new segment of population in metros, small cities and the rural hinterland."

For Reliance, this push into ultra-low-cost phones is a strategic move. Unlike the GSM handsets sold by its rivals, Reliance's CDMA phones come bundled with air time, making them more accessible to the masses.

Source: Nandini Lakshman, "An Indian Novelty: Cheap Cell Phones," *BusinessWeek*, 4 May 2007, available at www.businessweek.com/globalbiz/content/may2007/gb20070504_055084.htm.

Table 7.13 Product Re-engineering

Sl No	Rural problems	Company	Product design
1.	Water scarcity and impurity	DCM Shriram	Low-cost water purifier especially for rural areas
2.	Power outages	Coca-Cola	Low-cost iceboxes as regular power outages meant families could not depend on refrigerators
3.	Signal problems for TVs	LG Electronics	Customized TV (*Sampoorna*) to pick up low-density signals
4.	Lengthy power cuts and problem of pests	Nokia	Long-life batteries and pest resistant covers
5.	Voltage fluctuations	Samsung	Stabilizer-free operations in its direct-cool refrigerators
6.	Poor quality of water	Samsung	Silver-nano feature in semi-automatic washing machines

Products overcoming problems

Rural people are beset with several problems. Some companies have come out with products that work in spite of such problems. Table 7.13 shows the problems and solutions arrived at through product design.

The problem-solving products not only fulfill needs but also help to improve the productivity of persons engaged in different occupations. We are aware of agri-inputs such as fertilizers, pesticides, tractors, and hybrid seeds that helped increase agriculture productivity. Today, mobile phones are helping shopkeepers, farmers, fishermen and many others. In case of fishermen, it provides them connectivity with their wives and this helps the women feel secure. Box 7.6 presents two interesting cases, one of a grocer and another of a fisherman.

Augmentation by value add-ons

Some companies are providing additional benefits for the purchase of their products. For instance, IFFCO Tokio General Insurance tied up insurance with fertilizers. "For our Sankat Haran Policy (non-crop insurance), we offered farmers a free insurance cover worth Rs 4,000 with every fertilizer bag with the sale receipt also doubling up as a policy document," says N. K. Kedia, director, marketing, IFFCO Tokio General Insurance. Both Bharti Airtel and Idea Cellular offer many value-added services. They provide service messages in the local language of the subscriber, alerts on commodity prices at the nearest wholesale market, English language tutorials and music, especially in the local dialect of the subscribers.

CUSTOMER VALUE STRATEGIES

The purchase proposition of the rural consumer is value for money. The necessity component rather than the comfort and luxury aspects dominate the thought processes of rural people. This is especially true in the case of those whose incomes are farm-based. The uncertainty of farm incomes might have made them more cautious and calculated in their approach.

Mass product strategies

While urban consumers are brand conscious, rural consumers are price sensitive. They are more concerned about functional benefits of the products and the value for the money they pay. Accordingly,

Box 7.6 Products Improve Occupational Benefits

Mobiles are ringing in new ways of working and living for many people. Consider Suresh, a grocer from a small Behra village in West Champaran district of Bihar. To carry out business, he obtains stocks from small distributors in the bigger villages nearby. Earlier, he used to close his shop when stocks ran out and travel to the nearby villages to purchase his wares. Today the little mobile phone has changed his way of replenishing his stock. Now there is neither effort nor time loss because a simple phone call from his mobile helps him replenish the stock. He opted for a mobile connection through Airtel for Rs 1,200 that included a handset. He has power back up to recharge his handset whereas his fellow villagers go every four days to Baisukhva village 8 km away where a makeshift charging station, powered either by diesel generators or truck batteries, allows users to charge their batteries for Rs 5 per shot. With this facility, he carries out his business uninterrupted and with a smile.

Mobiles have brought back smiles to fishermen and their families too. Take the case of Poonathura village in Kerala. More than 150 fishermen have mobile phones. Though the number is small in the 25,000 strong community in the district, the good news is that it is good for business and family happiness. According to Peter, President, Kerala Swathanthra Mathsya Thozhilali Federation, mobile phones are going to be the medium of communication in the future for the fishing community. Although one has to shell out a month's wage to purchase a mobile phone, it is now viewed as a necessity like electricity because of the convenience it offers.

It was a mobile phone that saved the life of Shoban Amaladasan, a fisherman. He was stranded out at sea when the boat engine stalled, stranding him nearly 30 km off the shore. He alerted his friends on the shore and they came to his rescue. Mary, the wife of another fisherman says with a sigh of relief, "Now I am sure about his safety."

Like the grocer, the fisherman is also conducting his business with mobile phones. The fisherman alerts his friends onshore about the availability of a shoal of fish at any particular location. He calls up various agents and distributors while he is at sea to find out who would pay a good price for his catch.

Source: Tejeesh N. S. Behl "Rural to the Rescue," *Business Today*, 19 March 2009, available at http://businesstoday.intoday.in/index.php?option=com_content&task=view&id=10559; Sangeeth Kurian, "When their Catch is a Call Away," *The Hindu*, 2 May 2005, available at www.hindu.com/2005/05/02/stories/2005050208910400.htm.

several consumer durable companies have launched "no frills" economy products to attract rural consumers and low-end urban markets. Box 7.7 discusses the initiatives taken by Godrej and LG to introduce low-end models.

FMCGs and service companies are offering low-unit products and services. In fact, they are swaying the rural market. Every retail shop now displays numerous sachets and small packs to attract the low- and middle-income group consumers. Box 7.8 shows the offers of different types of companies.

Premium product strategy

Rural consumers exhibit preferences similar to those of urban consumers at least in case of some products. Historically, most companies, especially those that hawk consumer durables, have always believed that cheap products do well in the villages. That is not necessarily true. Premium brands are gaining wide acceptance in the rural bastions.

Box 7.7 Affordability Through Low-end Models

According to industry estimates, the total market for refrigerators in India is around 3 million units per annum and is growing at 15 per cent annually. With demand for low-end models picking up, LG, the largest consumer electronics company in India by sales, has designed plans to offer new products to low-end markets. The product range includes direct-cool refrigerators, twin-tub washing machines, solo microwave and CRT TVs. This move is in contrast to its focus on high-end premium products and concern for premium quality image.

Godrej is not very far behind. It has also chalked out plans to woo the low-end customers. It has designed a six-litre refrigerator that is two feet less in dimension compared to standard ones. The new refrigerator is priced at less than one-third the price of the standard model.

The refrigerator will cost Rs 2,500. The entry-level refrigerators that account for nearly 70 per cent of the total market are available at around Rs 7,500–8,000.

Source: "Godrej Plans Ultra-cheap Refrigerators," 6 September 2009, available at www.timesofindia.com.

Box 7.8 Low-unit Products

Idea Cellular introduced a rural calling card that charges only 50 paise per minute for a local call. Bharti Airtel launched a Rs 10 coupon valid for 10 days for the rural markets instead of a Rs 30 recharge coupon valid for a month. LG plans to roll out several new models in low-end segments such as direct-cool refrigerators, twin-tub washing machines, solo microwave and CRT TVs in the first half of 2009.

FMCG giants such as HUL and Colgate have brought out sachets or small units in the price range of Re 1 to Rs 5 for various products like toothpaste, shampoo, detergent, talcum powder, hair oil, cough syrups, biscuits, etc.

Source: Brand Dossier, "LG, Hero Honda, Nicholas Piramal to Focus on Rural Markets," 17 January 2009, available at www.domain-b.com.

Some high profile brands that have been able to gain popularity in rural households are—Ponds talcum powder, Fair & Lovely fairness cream, Surf and Ariel detergents, Pantene shampoo, Denim talcum powder and LG's Golden Eye series models. Qualis, a multi-purpose vehicle of Toyota Kirloskar Motor Limited, has also been received positively by the rural market. The views of two experts confirm this trend (Box. 7.9).

PRODUCT IDENTITY STRATEGIES—BRANDING

Product identification can be made easy in two ways: (i) Branding and (ii) Packaging and labelling. The two tools can be strategically used to gain the acceptance of consumers.

Before we make a case for branding, let us understand what commodity strategy is and how it is not relevant for all products.

Box 7.9 Rural People Seek Better Products

According to Vikram Mehra, chief marketing officer, Tata Sky, most brands still focus on consumers from metros. Brand owners wrongly assume that rural consumers give more importance to the price of a product when compared to parameters such as features, quality, etc. They want value for their money and are ready to pay more for receiving extra benefits. He also felt that rural consumers are wrongly rated as brand unaware though many of them display as much knowledge about brands as their urban counterparts.

Source: **"Rural Consumers Are More Difficult to Reach Out to," Mindshare Brand Equity Compass 2009, 13 February 2009, available at www.afaqs.com/perl/news/story.html?sid=23328.**

Commodity strategy

Products and services that are highly standardized and perceived to be homogeneous are described as commodities. They are unbranded products. Examples are food grains, vegetables, fruits, edible oil, sugar, steel, and edibles. It is reported that as much as 75 per cent of the coconut oil consumed in rural households is unbranded or locally branded.

When sold as commodities, the marketer can differentiate them in the following ways:

(i) *Grading:* Those less familiar with the product cannot recognize quality and the grade specifications help them to choose the quality of their choice.

(ii) *Relationships:* Some consumers trust the retailer and buy the goods recommended by him or her.

The perceived risk in buying the product available in different grades (also, the fear of adulteration) is reduced by the brand promises. This is the reason why urban, and now rural, consumers are shifting to branded goods.

Branding strategy

Branding is a strategy used to gain the acceptance of consumers and secure a competitive edge. There are three levels of decisions involved in the branding policy:

- Whether to brand the product or sell them as commodities?
- If the decision is to brand the products, should it be by the company or the middlemen (distributor or retailer)?
- If the company has decided on a branding strategy, should the name be related to an individual product or the family?

These decisions are to be taken, keeping in mind the psyche of rural consumers and practices of competitors.

First decision: The case for branding

Is the rural market ready for brands? Are the rural consumers able to identify brands and ask for them? The answer is yes. Today, rural consumers are exposed to urban styles and branded products have penetrated into the rural market. Though illiterates constitute about 37 per cent of the population, the transactions are slowly moving in favour of branded products. The case for branding is gaining strength. It is reported that in 18 categories, branded goods account for 80 per cent of sales in rural India. Since, there is a scope for branding, let us examine the arguments for and against it.

Arguments for branding

1. *Provides prestige value to consumers:* Rural consumers are today aspiring for a high quality of life as a consequence of the development schemes of the government and NGOs. Brands symbolize quality. They think the perceived risk in buying will be lower.
2. *Identity helps processing:* A brand name gives identity to a company's product. It helps in recognition and makes processing easy for the company, distributors and consumers. This saves costs and time in manufacturing, warehousing, transporting and order processing for the company when selling the product. Distributors can reap similar benefits in handling the products and selling them. Consumers find it easy to spot and select the product.
3. *Image gives competitive advantage:* Brands earn recognition and reputation by their performance. The image helps the existing products in the line as well as new products. It gives a commanding position to the marketer to charge higher prices than competitors and to convince distributors to carry the products.
4. *Personality convinces consumers:* Brands in course of their association with consumers develop personalities. Advertisers take this opportunity to match the personality of brands with that of prospects. It helps build brand loyalty—a lasting companionship, a strong bondage between a brand and consumer.
5. *Equity enhances value:* By their popularity, brands not only enhance their value-in-use but also value-in-exchange. A company that has built brand image over a period of time by its incessant innovative efforts gets a reward, for example, a premium price offer for its brand from a competitor or interested entrepreneur willing to own it.

Arguments against branding

1. *Category competition:* In rural markets the competition is more between categories rather than brands because rural people are illiterate and gullible. Also, branded products are not easily affordable.
2. *Notion of high prices:* The common notion prevalent among rural consumers is that branded products are high-priced ones. They shun brands for this reason.
3. *Investment-returns doubtful:* Brand building is not an easy task. It requires a great deal of long range investment. It is to be supported by R&D investment, advertising budget and dealer discounts. However, there is no assurance of returns. Many brands have failed. Many are struggling hard despite the good images that they have built over time.
4. *Image and personality are emotional nonsense:* All the talk about brand personality and image are psychological fantasies created by self-seeking marketers. No product sells on brand name. Only when it fulfills a need, does it stay and succeed in the market. The image of a product or brand cannot help other brands. There are many instances of such failures. Brand personality issues are more academic rhetoric. It is an overstretched concept with little practical value. When a person buys the product, the overriding considerations are cost (price and operational economics) and functional benefits. It is true with a vast majority of consumers.
5. *The brand equity concept replaces the old term "good will":* There is nothing new to be argued in favour of a "brand." It is the outcome of business built over a period. Why do marketers glorify branding in this context? It is only an identification factor that helps marketers promote distinctiveness.

Second decision: Brand sponsoring

The marketer has to decide "who has to sponsor the brand." Alternative ways are:

1. Company brand (national brand)
2. Distributor brand (private brand)

Table 7.14 Arguments for and Against Company Branding

	For Branding	Against Branding
1.	Consumers prefer certain national brands	National brands are high priced. Local brands are relatively cheap. Due to price disadvantage, sales will be low. If there is a low priced local product in the same quality range, they prefer it.
2.	Branding reduces marketing costs and improves sale opportunities by its pull power.	Retailers push local brands, as the gains are more by way of heavy discounts. National brand marketers cannot give such discounts.
3.	The power of successful brands helps other products in the line.	Fake brands are rampant in villages. They destroy the image of the brand.

The development of rural marts and retail chains provides the opportunity to leave branding to distributors. The arguments for and against company branding are given in Table 7.14.

Only when the consumer's affordability and quality consciousness are reasonably fair, will national brands be successful. Today, companies are seriously considering supply-chain management to make distribution more active, creative, competitive, productive and profitable. The change in this direction favours branding by companies.

Third decision: Naming a brand

Once the decision is taken to offer a brand name to the product, the following four alternative approaches to naming have to be given attention:

1. Individual names
2. Individual names with company names
3. Product group family name
4. Blanket family name

Individual names

The policy envisages a separate brand name for each individual product. This can be done with or without associating the company trade name.

(i) Individual names without company name: Table 7.15 summarizes the merits and demerits of individual names without company name.

Examples:

Godrej	Cinthol, Marvel, Ganga
HUL	Lifebuoy, Liril, Lux, Pears
P&G	Peposdent, Ariel

(ii) Individual names with company name: Some companies prefer to tag individual brand names with the company trade name.

Examples:

Ponds	Ponds Dream Flower Talc, Ponds Magic
TVS	TVS 50 XL
Wipro	Wipro-Shikakai

Table 7.15 Merits and Demerits of Individual Product Branding

Merits	Demerits
Since decisions are based on individual products, restrictions are less.	Too many names may lead to confusion.
Failure of the product will not have an adverse effect on other products.	Company name will not be known to consumers.
Company can freely resort to upward and downward stretch.	The image of successful brands cannot help other products (brands).
Allows opportunity to give names that have unique associations.	Development costs are high.

The merit of this decision is that the company name becomes popular. It helps to sell other products. However, the negative point is product failures tarnish the image of the company.

Product group family name

Multi-product group companies may choose to name different groups with different family brand names.

Examples:

Raymond: Raymond for textiles; Park Avenue for ready-made shirts, shoes and toiletries.

Group names help to promote a group of products. Hence, development costs are less. The failure of a product will have a limited negative impact only on its group. It permits different groups to develop different psychological associations and evokes appropriate responses.

Blanket family name

This policy advocates naming all the products of a company with one name-family brand name.

Examples:

Usha: Fans, sewing machines, industrial pumps
Nirma: Detergent, toothpaste, soap
Colgate: Dental cream, toothbrushes

When the company name is promoted with all products, a sort of company image is created and it helps new products get instant recognition. It saves time and money during product launches. Also, the benefit of the positive image created by the CSR programmes of the company will add strength to the brands. However, unsuccessful products may dilute the company image.

Brand strategies

Branding should serve the following objectives:

1. Create recognition by less-literate consumers (brand identity) and motivation to buy.
2. Create an image for the brand that helps promote the sales of the product and other product introductions in the family.

Brand identity strategy

The main purpose of a brand is creating easy recognition among the less-literate and innocent consumers in the rural hinterland. The second purpose is to evoke an emotional feeling that surges interest in buying the product. The following guidelines help name brands effectively.

- *Easy to use:* Short and simple words that are easy to pronounce.
- *Easy to understand and associate:* Understand the meaning and its relation to the product.
- *Easy to distinguish:* Not similar to other names (Lifebuoy and Nirmabuoy are very close. Similarly Fairever and Fair & Lovely are confusing).

Table 7.16 gives examples of effective brand names.

Names generate some distinct thoughts in the minds of the people. The name *Sita* is associated with "virtuousness," *Bhima* with "strength" and *Arjuna* with "chivalry." Brand names in a similar way reflect particular characteristics and accomplishments. The associations of brands grow larger, beyond the products with which they are first associated. Brand identity starts slowly with the product to which the name is given. It grows next, to become a symbol, a person and finally an organization. *Vajradanti* means strong teeth. *Chwyavanprash* means ayurvedic solution for youthful energy. Together, they create an image for Dabur as the company that promotes health.

Let us take the example of Philips. Philips brings to our mind electrical products; radios, transistors, lamps, tube lights, televisions, 2-in-one tape recorders, etc. It stands as a symbol for quality and presents an energetic, capable, illustrious person, and an innovative, great company.

Brand extension strategy

Product innovations are a regular feature for a competitive organization. When a product line is stretched, should the new products be launched as separate brands or as extensions of the existing strong brand?

Why line extensions?

The line stretching decision is made for the following reasons:

- *Reaction:* Innovative product items are added as a reaction to competition.
- *Opportunity:* New items are introduced to utilize the existing market gap.
- *Image:* Rolling upward or downward or both ways is done to have a full line company image.
- *Pressure:* New product items are introduced yielding to the pressure of the sales force and dealers.
- *Strength:* Line stretching is done to use the available excess capacity.
- *Desire:* Line stretching is done to fulfill the desire of a top executive or product manager to introduce a new product item.

Why brand extensions?

The decision in favour of brand extensions is made for one or more of the following reasons:

- To make a brand more visible
- To reduce development costs of a brand
- To reduce risk by banking on the image of a reputed brand
- To meet competition or to complete the line of offer

Table 7.16 Effective Brand Names

Guideline	Description	Example
Easy to use (learning and memory)	Short, simple and easy to pronounce, read and remember	Tide, Surf, Rin, Colgate, Dettol
Easy to understand (association)	Meaningful and suggests characteristics and functions of the product.	Medimix, Fairever, Fair & Lovely, Amrutanjan
Easy to distinguish (preference)	Unique, peculiar and distinctive. Not a close imitation of another product.	Clinic Plus, Pepsi, Vicco Vajradanti, Parachute, Tiger

Evaluating brand extensions

Is brand extension beneficial or would it harm a company's prospects? Marketers have to make follow-up studies on the impact of brand extensions. The brand extension decision is considered sound when the following outcomes are observed:

- When the new brand is successful
- When the new brand does not cannibalize the parent brand
- When there is no brand dilution due to the failure of the brand extension
- When there is no brand dilution by brand proliferation

Category brand extensions (variant brands) may wholly or partly cannibalize or eat away the shares of parent brands. However, they may also open up a new segment and boost sales.

Some famous examples of brand extensions are discussed in Box 7.10.

Co-branding

Today, we find offers from two or more brands of the same company or different companies. When a marketer offers one brand with another brand of the same company or another company, it is called co-branding. Such offers may take two different forms:

(i) Ingredient co-branding
(ii) Product co-branding

Ingredient co-branding takes place when

- The maker of the parts, to be visible to the market and to gain image for the brand, insists on publicizing it.
- The part is important and the maker has an image that enhances the consumer acceptance of the ultimate product.
- Competitors are following such practices.

Box 7.10 Brand Extensions

Dettol is a well known brand of antiseptic liquid that is also offered in cream form. Taking the "care" concept as a main feature of the brand, Dettol was launched as "the love and care soap." The launch failed as the care concept did not properly touch the psyche of consumers. After many years, it launched the soap on a protection platform and the soap is doing well.

The case of Maggi is different. First it was 2-minute noodles—a hearty, anytime snack. The brand name was extended to edible products such as sauces, soup cubes, even pickles that are not very closely related.

Vicks—a well known vapour balm—has now extended to cough drops, lozenges and inhalers. Dove's extension is from soaps to shampoos whereas Caterpillar's is from heavy, earthmoving equipment to rugged all terrain cat boots!

Source: Cyril Mani, "Stretching the Rubber Brand," *The Hindu Business Line*, 11 September 2008, available at www.thehindubusinessline.com/catalyst/2008/09/11/stories/2008091150120300.htm.

Examples:

- IBM and Compaq buy computer chips from Intel. They advertise with the phrase "Intel inside."
- Cello and Milton advertise their thermoware saying "We use SAIL steel."
- Kelvinator refrigerator comes with a "Blue Star" thermostat.

PRODUCT IDENTITY STRATEGIES—PACKAGING

When packaging consumer products for rural markets, companies must use prominent logo symbols and colours to ensure that illiterate consumers will be able to recognize the products. Emotional Surplus Identity (ESI) is a concept that that uses the shape, colour and content of a package to differentiate a brand in the eye of a consumer. By creating a bond with the consumer through the package, companies are able to establish a relationship that encourages repeat purchases. Loud, bright colours are typically used on packages to differentiate a product from the others on the shelf and to create a lasting impression in a consumer's mind. Today, we see a variety of packages in use. Let us consider the examples of different packages that offer different benefits.

(i) *Easy to identify and easy to recognize by colours, sizes and shapes:*

- Mysore sandal comes in oval and rectangular shapes.
- Pepsi is recognized by its blue-coloured packaging.

(ii) *Easy to carry, easy to use and easy to dispense:*

- Tetra packs—Soft drinks, milk
- Polythene covers—Sanitary napkins, Dairy milk
- Metal, plastic tubes—Toothpastes, medicines (ointments), fairness creams
- Cardboard/paper packs—Toilet soaps, hair dyes, shaving creams, mosquito coils
- Cardboard/paper packs—Toilet soaps, hair dyes, shaving creams, mosquito coils
- Small bottles—Honey, sauce, jam, tonics and syrups (kids)
- Spray bottles—Air fresheners
- Tear sheets—Medicines (tablets), mosquito mats
- Tins—Threptin biscuits, Protex, Ovaltine
- Lamitubes—Cherry blossom

(iii) *Good to store:* Food grade plastic/glass bottles—Beverages such as Bournvita, Boost and Horlicks, edible oils such as Saffola and Sakola.

(iv) *Attractive to reuse:* Good to store bottles are often reusable.

Packaging as a strategy

Packaging can become a strategic force when developed to solve problems of rural consumers and to outwit competitors. Rural consumers have the following problems:

- *Affordability problem:* There are daily wage earners in large numbers who usually buy small quantities sold in loose packages (soaps and detergent cakes are cut into pieces).
- *Transportation problem:* Protection is required for products when transporting through rough-weather roads.

- *Storage problem:* Storage space is limited for middle- and low-income groups.
- *Less capable of distinguishing brands:* Due to low literacy levels and lack of exposure, rural consumers cannot read brand names and distinguish one brand from another.
- *Inertia in buying new products:* Being traditional, they turn away from new brands. Brands need persuasive power to induce them to make trial purchases.

When the brand name cannot aid consumers in recognizing the product of their preference and choice, packaging can help the consumers to recognize and know about the product. It can be a motivating factor too, when it offers a distinct benefit like reusability or when it allows buying of the preferred product in small quantities at affordable prices.

Communication benefit

Packaging can be an informative and persuasive force to promote the sales of products.

(i) Informative: Purchase decisions are based on the evaluation of the following:

- Product quantity
- Product quality
- Product use information
- Life period of the product.

The evaluation process is made easy through labelling or by presenting information on the package.

(ii) Persuasive: Packages appeal to consumers at three different levels: sensory, emotional and rational. Various benefits are provided to consumers at the three levels as given in Table 7.17.

Small packs

Marketers have realized that it is necessary to offer products at the lowest unit price to enter the rural market. At the same time, innovative packages are necessary to add value to premium products. Innovations that help lower the price are particularly desirable.

Table 7.17 Three Levels of Appeal by Packages

Sl No.	Level	Purpose of package	Package characteristics	Benefits
1.	Sensory	Attention	Attractive	Easy to identify
			Distinctive	
			Visibility	
2.	Emotional	Interest	Adoptability	Easy to carry
		Desire	Compatibility	Easy to use
			Communicability	Easy to store
				Attractive to reuse
				Easy to dispense
3.	Rational	Evaluation	Informative	Easy to know
			Interactive	Easy to store
			Preservative	Good to reuse
			Economical	Fair price

Sachets are plastic pouches that contain approximately 20 ml (0.68 oz) of the product. Since the rural consumer often survives on daily wages, he engages in daily purchases.

Several companies like CavinKare, Godrej and Dabur adopted the "single use" sachet strategy that has worked in their favour. The reasons for high preference for small pack, low-unit prices are:

(i) *Affordability:* The income of rural consumers is unsteady. The sources of income as well as the size of income vary day by day. Hence, they cannot make planned and large purchases. Small pack sizes help the rural consumer pick up the product at a price that he can afford.

(ii) *Usage:* Certain products like detergents and pastes are bought in larger quantities, whereas shampoos, toilet soaps and eatables are bought in small pack sizes. The products that are commonly used by family members are bought in large pack sizes whereas individual-use products are preferred in small packs.

(iii) *Storability:* The storage life of a product also has a bearing on this decision. Edibles, for example, cannot last long unless preserved and kept under ideal conditions. Further, the shelf space of rural consumers is also limited as they live in small huts or semi-*pucca* houses.

(iv) *Benefits for the retailer:* The small pack sizes are convenient for the retailer to do business and promote national brands. The shelf space of rural retailers is less. He cannot afford big premises. Small pack sizes do not demand shelf space.

(v) *Display:* Smaller sizes are easy to display. The colours on the smaller packs are looked at with more interest.

Examples: Many companies have become participants in the package revolution that is sweeping the rural markets and the mid- and low-income strata in urban areas.

- JK Dairy came up with a 50 g sachet of Dairy Whitener at Rs 6.50.
- P&G introduced Vicks VapoRub in a tiny 5 g tin and Tide detergent in 30 g sachets priced at Rs 3.
- Godrej sells its Velvette shampoo in sachets priced at Rs 1.25.
- Marico Industries launched low-priced sachets of hair oil.
- Kothari Products offers *Paan Parag* in sachets.

Implications for Marketers

Manufacturers prefer producing large pack sizes. The economies of scale indicate that small pack sizes are less feasible. However, on the marketing side, the benefits are revealing.

- They strongly induce the rural consumers to buy.
- Trial sales of national brands are on the rise.

Regular sales have gone up for many products. The regional/local players are finding it difficult to face competition from the big players on their home turf.

Combi-packs

Another packaging innovation is "combi-packs." When related products are packed together and sold at economy prices, the consumer finds it a better buying option. For example, combi-packs of toothpaste and tooth brush. An assortment is another innovation. It is a pack of more than two products. The Rs 175 Johnson & Johnson baby care assortment package consisting of a powder, soap, shampoo, hair oil and cream is an example of assortment.

BRAND BUILDING STRATEGIES

When brands are effectively managed, they acquire "value" and become "assets" with "good-will." Effective brand management involves having right concerns and taking appropriate actions as shown in Table 7.18.

Challenges faced by companies operating in the rural market

Companies operating in the rural markets have to recognize that they are threatened by at least two types of competitors operating at the local and national levels. They have to arm themselves against competition from genuine brands as well as competition from fake products.

Competition from genuine brands

Local brands

Companies such as CavinKare (Chik shampoo, Meera herbal powder, Fairever cream, etc), Anchor (100 per cent vegetarian toothpaste), Ghadi detergent powder and Power soap are proof that regional brands can become forces to reckon with. Nirma began as a regional player and became a national player in the course of time. Box 7.11 presents some of the successful ones. They all started in small, concentrated markets, appealing to the local ethos and aspirations of the targeted area. Further, they introduced their brands at the base level, and are all scaling up.[4]

Ghadi, which has a Rs 18 kg detergent also markets "Dog Day," which retails at Rs 50. KAFPL's five kg *atta* pack carries a competitive price tag of Rs 120. They are generous to distributors. While players such as HUL and P&G give 8–10 per cent trade margins, they dole out margins between 15 per cent and 25 per cent to retailers. The proliferation of regional channels has helped local brands to build their strength in a particular area. Some companies are already spending heavily on advertising. Today, KAFPL has an ad outlay of Rs 250 million while Anchor spends around Rs 200 million.

Table 7.18 Brand Management

Concerns	Description	Action
Brand identity	Differentiating the brand from other brands by name, company logo, colour, number, etc.	Protect it from imitation and strengthen it by vivid and distinct packaging and ad campaigns
Brand association	Anything linked to the brand in the consumer's memory	Unique selling proposition in positioning and its communication helps create association
Brand image	This is brand association linked with brand personality	Match brand personality with consumer personality and highlight it subtly in all communication
Brand loyalty	Buying same brand over a period of time without preferring other brands	Continuous monitoring of satisfaction and rewarding loyalty; customer relationship management (CRM) programmes
Brand equity	One measure of brand equity is brand knowledge and it is the sum of brand awareness and brand image	Communication and promotion programmes with distinct messages and promotion measures

Box 7.11 Davids that Toppled the Reigning Goliaths

"Shapers," a sanitary product from Gufic Biosciences has become an irritant for a battery of multinationals such as Johnson & Johnson and Procter & Gamble. It has devised a strategy to increase its market share from 6 per cent to 15 per cent and launch a bouquet of cosmeceuticals (like medicated beauty products). Hasmukhrai & Co's Society Tea is giving a good fight to Hindustan Unilever Ltd and is planning to enter the Andhra Pradesh and Tamil Nadu markets.

Kanpur Trading Company's Ghadi detergent, which has a dominant 40 per cent share in Uttar Pradesh and 10 per cent nationally, is competing with Nirma and Hindustan Unilever. It has plans to go to the neighbouring states. Jyothi Laboratories are the makers of Jiva herbal soap and Ujjala fabric whitener. The herbal soap is slowly dominating the marketplace even as HUL's Ayush herbal offerings are floundering. Ujjala is providing stiff competition to Reckitt Benckiser's Robin Blue.

Surya Foods, the north-based maker of Priya Gold biscuits has became a Rs 1 billion brand. Anchor toothpaste of the Rs 1.50 billion Anchor Health and Beauty Care is wiping the smile off both Colgate–Palmolive and HUL. It is pushing up the numbers of its distributors from the current 2,500 to 4,500 to raise its market share to 28 per cent and launch toiletries and cosmetics.

Dandi salt, positioned as "not an ordinary salt", has an 18 per cent market share and is fighting with Tata salt (40 per cent share) and HUL's Kissan Annapurna (20 per cent market share) in the Rs 5 billion branded salt market. It is from the stable of the Rs 1 billion Surat-based Kunwar Ajay Foods Pvt. Ltd (KAFPL) that is now talking big about the future. It has Friendly Wash detergent retailing at Rs 24 a kg and Sher-e-Punjab *atta* (flour) and hopes to have a bouquet of 25 products on its platter and a turnover of Rs 50 billion.

Ahmedabad-based Paras Pharmaceuticals is the maker of Moov pain relief ointment that has made life painful for Reckitt Benckiser's Iodex, cold reliever D'Cold and anti-fungal creams Itch Guard and Ring Guard.

Source: Nandini Laskhman, "The Big Small Brands Go for Gold," 19 July 2003, available at www.rediff.com/money/2003/jul/19spec.htm.

National brands
There is competition from national players as well. In case of consumer durables in the two-wheeler market, TVS fights against Hero Honda and in case of FMCGs, Godrej, HUL, P&G, ITC and Colgate are competing for a share of the rural market.

Competition from fake products
Haats are popular with the poorest agricultural labourers who consciously buy the duplicate, spurious products that are sold in these *bazaars* since they can't afford the real thing. It is estimated that FMCG companie have lost more than Rs 100 billion to spurious products mostly sold through such local *haats* and *bazaars*.

Protecting brand identity

A marketer has to depend on semiotics and mnemonics to protect brand identity. The dictionary meaning of semiotics is the study of signs, symbols and their interpretation. In the rural context, the interpretation of these signs and symbols becomes the deciding factor to build brand value and image.

Semiotics primarily works best for products that require low-involvement at the time of purchase and have very frequent usage. FMCGs such as soaps, shampoos, tyres and tea are the ones that fit the bill best. Though the signs and symbols help identify products, they may not always succeed in making the consumer remember the product. Mnemonics also becomes crucial to nurture and retain the memory of products in the mind space. Colour, logo and mascot add strength to semiotics (Box 7.12).

Establishing brand personality

Like a person, a brand is a psychosocial being having an appearance, emotional feelings and rational behaviours. Brand personality can, therefore, be described at three levels:

Sensory

How would the brand see, smell, taste, touch, and hear if it is a person? What are its "demographics"? Does it have an attractive and socially acceptable personality?

Emotional

If a brand were to become an emotion, what would it be? What are the underlying subjective, non-functional emotions of the brand? Is it trustworthy? Is it a desirable companion?

Rational

What would the brand, as a person, do? What would it achieve? What are the functional benefits? Is it a person with expertise?

Lux soap, associated with Aishwarya Rai, projects the following attributes—attractiveness, softness and beauty.

Thus, brand personality creates impressions in the minds of people. The impressions left by a brand in the minds of people are summarily explained by the words—brand image. Brand image as perceived by both users as well as non-users is important to marketers because purchase behaviour is influenced by it. Three behavioural patterns are predicted:

1. Consumer buys products consistent with self-image.
2. Avoids buying products inconsistent with self-image.
3. Upgrades to brands that enhance self-image.

Strengthening brand loyalty

Brand loyalty is an emotional product of two psychological attributes—satisfaction and relationship. Marketers have to strive to create these attributes. In a well-knit society of rural consumers, loyalty can be maintained by taking the help of opinion leaders, young members and women. Confidence in

Box 7.12 Reinforcers of Brand Identity

Brand names often depict numbers or animals or symbols such as 555 soap, Monkey brand tooth-powder, Gemini tea (with elephant), Cheetah light matches, Sheru *beedi,* Tiger Mark cigarettes, 3 Roses tea, Tortoise mosquito coil, etc.

ITC sells its Gold Flake brand with yellow colour in the South, where it is associated with prosperity and purity, compared to a golden one in the North, where yellow is often associated with jaundice and ill health. Many companies have changed their logos to make them contemporary. Brooke Bond is one such company. Its new logo enshrines the pioneering attitude, dynamism and heritage of the brand in a better manner.

Box 7.13 *Vishwas* Programme

Mahindra and Mahindra Farm Equipment Sector launched Mahindra *Vishwas* to fulfill the marginal farmer's dream of owning a reliable tractor. It was launched in 2001 with a mission to bring prosperity into the lives of small and marginal farmers by providing them refurbished tractors (of any brand) of benchmark quality along with the support of quality certification, warranty and free services. Mahindra *Vishwas* also helps the customers who wish to exchange their old tractor (any brand) for a new Mahindra tractor by offering them the best price for their old tractor and by helping them in getting a new tractor from Mahindra's dealers. Recently, it announced the opening of its Rs 0.1 billion 3-S (sales, service and spare parts) facility at Hydernagar to enhance the quality of sales and service for Mahindra and Mahindra under one roof. This also includes various financial and insurance support services. The Mahindra Xylo usually comes with a 2-year/50,000 km warranty. The 4-year/100,000 km "shield" extended warranty costs Rs 10,999, if purchased within 30 days of buying a new Xylo.

TVS Motor Company's initiative to expand its network of service centres was followed by the decision to expand its products to new localities. The centres will have highly trained mechanics and an entire range of spares for servicing. They will also house some of the company's models so that prospective customers can take a look at them. "We plan to reach the *taluka* level first and then go deeper into smaller places," S. Kannan, area manager (Maharashtra) said. To support the expansion programme, tie-up arrangements with banks such as ICICI Bank and other nationalized and co-operative are being worked out. This led to the modification of the norms for finance in a manner that allows the rural customer to comply.

Source: "M&M Sales and Service Centre," *The Hindu Business Line*, 3 August 2009; "TVS Motors to Expand Service Centre Network," *Business Standard*, 13 June 2006, available at *www.business-standard.com/.../tvs-motor-to-expand-service-centre-network/246825.*

a product can be created by offering product warranty and service support. Elaborate arrangements for service are to be made to keep up the promises. Box 7.13 presents a typical service and warranty programme of M&M and TVS. Warranty can be a good sales promotion tool when used strategically.

Satisfaction can be created by listening to complaints and solving problems. Relationships can be strengthened by developing emotional bonding through intimate interactions. The three-pronged approach that involves service offers, complaint management and delight creation are given in Table 7.19.

Value addition by communication

The rural market is extremely fragmented and every individual that is being targeted in such a market has extremely limited purchasing power. Large corporate entities need to effectively communicate their brand proposition to rural consumers. They face stiff competion from the unorganized retailers in the rural market who offer their products at cheaper rates. The case of Tata Steel presented in Box 7.14 makes this point clear.

A multi-pronged approach is essential for building a brand in rural India.[5] To make brands memorable and native, sometimes names have to be changed. Take toothpaste, for example. "Dabur *Lal Dant Manjan*" (red toothpowder in Hindi) was rechristened "Dabur *Sivappu Pal Podi*" (red toothpowder in Tamil, the local language) for the South Indian market. Focused brand-building initiatives—like participation at community events such as *melas* (village fairs), *haats* (markets), street theatre,

Table 7.19 Brand Loyalty Management

Sl No.	Focus	Tasks
1.	Service offers	Offer warranty and service at the time of sale Encourage dealers to appoint service personnel /set up company-owned service centres Provide and monitor service performance
2.	Complaint management	Gather customer opinion immediately after sales Set up complaint and suggestion boxes Organize customer meets Conduct satisfaction surveys
3.	Delight creation	Offer greetings Give bonus offers on purchase of other items Offer gifts at chosen occasions

Box 7.14 Tata *Shaktee Haat Hangama* Campaign

Tata *Shaktee* GI corrugated roofing sheets is the category leader in the market. However, the awareness about the brand and its sales in rural markets left much to be desired. The company had been primarily using the electronic and print media to promote the brand and these had limited rural reach. Tata Steel approached MART to increase brand awareness and recall. MART suggested a direct customer-reach *haat* and *mandi* campaign as these marketing platforms are extremely relevant for rural people and are visited by thousands of buyers. A branded modular stall was set up at each location, a public address system was used to attract visitors, games were organized for visitors to increase brand recall and prizes were offered. MART has participated in over 5,000 *haats* from 2004 to 2007 and communicated with over 5 million potential consumers on a one-on-one basis. This targeted consumer approach, touch and feel experience, communication in the local language and enhanced brand recall has resulted in a 40 per cent increase in the sales of Tata *Shaktee* GI sheets.

Source: "Mart: Corporate Sector (Pilot Implementation)," available at www.martrural.com/corporate_pilot_implementation.htm.

van campaigns and puppet shows—generate positive word-of-mouth and influence buying decisions. Word-of-mouth is a huge motivator in such cases.

Cholayil Ltd, the manufacturer of the herbal soap "Medimix," campaigned using mobile vans to promote its brand. "We run a van campaign that visits the interior villages where there are no distributors. We halt the van at specific points [where village folks congregate and watch videos shown on these vans] and give out product samples," says a spokesperson of the company. However, contrary to claims of Medimix's success, Dinesh Malhotra, general manager of Linterland (rural arm of Lintas), believes that "van campaigns can be very expensive." Alternatively, promoting one's brand in large congregation points such as village markets and fairs has a far wider reach and is more cost effective.

Through product trials and free samples, the company was able to generate awareness in this new market. On a similar note, C. K. Ranganathan, managing director of CavinKare, says, "When we entered the rural areas in South India, people used to wash their hair with soap. When we launched the "Chik" brand of shampoo we educated the people on how to use it through live 'touch and feel' demonstrations and also distributed free sachets at fairs. This strategy worked wonders in the rural areas of Tamil Nadu and Andhra Pradesh—two important states in India." Some companies use celebrities to propagate the brand message while others depend on professionals like doctors and elderly persons like grandmothers to offer advice to consumers.

PRODUCT LIFECYCLE STRATEGIES

Product lifecycle presents the four stages of a product's life, known as introduction, growth, maturity and decline. Each stage requires different marketing mixes as shown in Table 7.20.

In the product lifecycle when a brand reaches the decline stage, marketers have two options: (i) dropping or (ii) re-engineering the product. HUL opted for the second choice by re-engineering its brand Lifebuoy, which had strong positive connect with BoP consumers in urban and rural areas. The classic example is explained in Box 7.15.

Table 7.20 Managing the Product Lifecycle

Stage	Marketing mix
Introduction	A basic product, warranties, skimming or penetration price, selective distribution, advertisement to create pull force to generate trial sales
Growth	Product improvements, service offers, price changes for competitive advantage, intensive distribution, ads to generate sales, sales promotions to offset competition and remove inertia among consumers
Maturity	Add features and variants with improvements, competitive pricing, and differentiation by advertising, sales promotion to strengthen pull forces, and CRM to promote brand loyalty
Decline	Phase out the product slowly by making possible gains; Re-engineer the product to give it a new lease of life

Box 7.15 Lifebuoy—Brand Re-engineering

In 2002 Hindustan Unilever Limited (HUL) re-engineered Lifebuoy, its century-old hard, chunky, red carbolic soap. The brand was re-engineered on account of the following reasons: (i) Consumers started opting for softer, good looking soaps that lathered better, (ii) Competition was less and consumers had limited options, (iii) Needs were limited to cleaning, (iv) Whereas earlier, household decisions were taken by men, women slowly emerged as decision makers and (v) No one just wanted a value-for-money cleansing agent with cresylic perfume, they wanted fragrance. A move away from the masculine imagery was needed. The new milled soap was launched as a family soap with a healthy fragrance, in two versions—Lifebuoy Active Red and Lifebuoy Active Orange.

Source: "HLL Re-launches Lifebuoy, Eyes Healthy Sales Numbers," *Business Standard*, 13 February 2002, available at www.business-standard.com/india/news/hll-relaunches-lifebuoy-eyes-healthy-sales-numbers/104410/.

FIGHTING FAKES

The corporate marketer often finds the competition from copycats to be a big menace and debates on the ways of mitigating it. Spurious products, generally marketed by the unorganized, low-end entrepreneurs, somehow make their way into the market and eat away a large chunk of the corporate marketer's profits. The imitations have resemblances that dupe gullible consumers.

Type of fakes

Fake products are of two types—counterfeit products and pass-off products. Counterfeit products are fake products that bear the identical name/packaging/graphics/colour scheme and even the same name and address as the genuine manufacturer. These are manufactured to look exactly like the real product. It is becoming more and more difficult to tell the real "Ponds" talcum powder and "Clinic Plus" shampoo from the fake products.

Pass-off products use similar sounding or are similar in spelling (for example, "Luk" for "Lux," "510" for "501," "Saveena" for "Sabeena," "Sun Max" for "Super Master"). They use similar type of packaging, colours or designs. They are brought out with the motive of misleading and cheating ordinary consumers who are uneducated or in a hurry when purchasing products.

Why do counterfeits thrive?

The primary motive is to capitalize on the trust built by established brands. The marketer of spurious products has less experience and limited resources. As such, he seeks to benefit from the images of the popular brands and low prices of his brands. His profit motive is fulfilled by the following facilitators.

(i) *Willing or gullible consumers:* There is acceptance of substitutes with dubious antecedents. Price consciousness sometimes reigns supreme over quality consciousness. In some cases, the consumer is not aware of the differences between the original and the duplicate. Poor literacy levels make brand recall primarily a mix of phonetics, colour and symbols.

(ii) *Weak brand associations:* Users in villagers are largely first generation users and long-term brand associations are rare.

(iii) *Support from retailer:* Retailers support fakes as the margins offered are higher.

(iv) *Difficulties in taking action:* The costs associated with tracing and punishing multiple sellers and makers of duplicate products are heavy. The lack of clearly defined or effective legal remedies also act as deterrents.

Box 7.16 discusses how the fake-product marketer operates.

Threats to original manufacturers

As a consequence of the operations of the spurious product marketers, corporations loose out in two ways. They lose revenue on account of the loss in sales. The brand image of the product as well as the company is also tarnished. The most affected products are over-the-counter medical products, confectioneries, toiletries, detergents and personal-care products. Some of the examples are:

- Daily milk for Dairy milk
- Kir Kat for Kit Kat
- Coffee Toffee for Coffee Bite
- Mango ripe for Mango bite
- Aasha for Aasai
- Rolo for Polo

Box 7.16 Marketing by Fakes Manufacturers

The ideal time to launch a spurious brand is just after the entry and initial consolidation of the original. By the time the original manufacturer becomes aware of the duplicator or establishes a strong brand image with unique distinctions, the duplicator benefits from his product. The 4 P's of fake product marketing are:

Look-alike product: The copycats resemble the original in many ways.

(i) *Brand—Phonetics:* To woo the largely illiterate customer, the names usually have a close phonetic resemblance to the original—Loveboy for Lifebuoy, Nirbha for Nirma, Teta for Tata.

(ii) *Package—Visuals:* Similar pack designs and pack sizes are adopted. Colours bear close resemblance to the original. Bottled products have the company logo embossed. Generally empties of the original are collected and retailed by these entrepreneurs.

(iii) *Quality—Intangible:* Fake products are generally inferior in quality. However, the consumer cannot gauge that before using it. As such, the consumer largely relies on the retailer's opinion before making the decision to purchase.

Low prices: Lower-end consumer prices are fixed attracting price sensitive, value-for-money rural consumers.

Silent promotion: As higher margins are given to retailers, they advocate consumers to buy these products. Retailer push goes a long way to induce first-time trials.

Limited and anonymous distribution: The copycat seller keeps his identity unknown. He prefers distribution in the local areas where he can establish secret links with retailers. This is necessary to avoid future litigation.

Designing an encounter strategy

Corporate marketers may analyse the situation and embark on an offensive strategy to push out the imitators.

Situation analysis

The following are the negative points:

1. Limited rural reach of media makes educating the consumer cumbersome.
2. Spurious brands have highly localized presences. A successful brand may face a different set of fakes every 200 km, which makes tracing each duplicate source both difficult and costly.
3. Litigation is cumbersome.
4. Costs of surveillance may be more than the benefits secured from additional sales.

The following are the facilitating factors. First, there are a good number of laws to combat fake products.

- Indian Penal Code 1860
- Drugs and Cosmetics Act, 1940
- Prevention of Food Adulteration Act, 1954
- Consumer Protection Act, 1986
- Bureau of Indian Standards Act, 1986 and
- Trademarks Act, 1999

Second, consumers are now better informed and are looking for genuine products.

Components of the encounter strategy

The formulation of encounter strategy requires an intelligent understanding of consumer needs and wants, their perceptions of products and weak points. The strategy components are as follows:

(a) *Complicated packaging:* Packaging could be made more difficult to replicate. Liquid soaps in tetra packs with design patterns are complicated to replicate. Holograms can also be used.

(b) *Products at the low end:* A range of products targeted for the rural consumer could be launched with low price and low quality to counter the spurious products. This can be done by developing franchisee units to manufacture low-end products with a highly localized coverage.

(c) *Rural pull promotion:* Rural sales schemes to reach consumers and enlist support of retailers should be envisaged.

(d) *Promoting quality consciousness:* Local promotion is an effective route to educate villagers. The promotion should aim at highlighting the harm the spurious products can cause to the users and communicating them persuasively to the consumers.

For example, *Bindis* that have an adhesive coating are hawked by many tiny units in the north. On sustained usage, the spurious ones discolour skin, at times triggering allergies.

(e) *Boosting ego needs:* In the highly status conscious village society with rigidly defined community structures, the spurious brands should be depicted as the ideal fit for the down and out.

(f) *Syndicated:* National players could join hands to promote their products in rural areas as well as to counter spurious products.

Summary

The product decision is the primary decision in the marketing mix. A product is anything that satisfies human needs and wants. It can be classified in several ways. Tangibles (physical products such as pen, paper, ice-cream, etc.) or intangibles (services of doctors), consumption goods (cosmetics) or production goods (raw materials), consumables (food and beverages) or durables (furniture), convenience goods (cigarettes), shopping goods (clothing) or specialty goods (cameras), economy goods (without remote and limited channels B&W TVs) or premium products (Lalitha jewellery) and innovations (gel pens), imitations (Nirma buoy for Lifebuoy) and copycats (Lov buoy for Lifebuoy). The final decision is based on brand hierarchy level: global (Pepsi), national (Tata), regional (Siti channel), local (Joy chips) and unbranded (Tamarind).

Product strategy has become essential in view of the growing competition and sophistication in market behaviour. Product decisions include product-mix changes, product-line stretches or modernization and product design considerations such as quality, features, design/style, packaging and branding in developing core and tangible products. Product augmentation requires utilizing the other P's to gain competitive advantage for the product.

Competitive product strategies include identity strategies (commodity versus branding), customer value strategies (mass and premium products), innovation strategies (rural–urban common, special for rural), packaging strategies (small packs and combi-packs), and branding strategies (brand extension, multi-branding, co-branding and brand image management). The monitoring of the product lifecycle is another challenge to marketers as products cannot retain consumer acceptance and competitive advantage over the years.

Short Answer Questions

1. Elucidate the importance of product strategy.
2. Attempt a classification of products.
3. Identify the three levels of product strategy with suitable examples.
4. What are the key elements in product design?
5. How do you classify product strategies?
6. Explain the role of branding in promoting a product.
7. Explain how packaging can make a product appealing to consumers.
8. Identify the key elements in brand building.
9. Analyse the operations of spurious goods strategists.
10. Giving examples, explain brand extension strategy.
11. Do you advocate multi-branding and co-branding policies?
12. Explain the approach you would adopt to enhance brand personality.
13. What is brand image? How do you create and maintain it?
14. Explain the product lifecycle and list the strategies useful at each stage.

Discussion Questions

1. "Needs remain static but products vary." Discuss bringing in the social, cultural and technological influences.
2. R. V. Rajan, managing director of Anugrah Advertising Agency, says, "To communicate effectively, it is important to understand the fears, aspirations, and hopes of the rural consumer." Discuss.
3. "Companies improve quality to attract and retain rural markets." Discuss.

Essay Questions

1. Suppose you are asked to market a fairness cream, how do you augment the product and create brand identity?
2. Explain the innovation strategies being adopted by Indian companies to attract rural consumers.
3. Discuss the customer value strategies used in rural markets with suitable examples.
4. Explain brand image strategies of any two companies operating in rural markets.
5. Describe brand building strategies adopted by any two companies.
6. Explain the product strategies of two brands and evaluate them for their acceptability in rural areas.

Internet Exercise

Collect data on product introductions by FMCGs in a chosen category and prepare a report on the product successes and failures in the rural context.

Mini Project

Visit rural retail shops and obtain information about the range of brands available. Find out the names of the brands popular in the village from retailers. Analyse the reasons. Interact with some of the customers in the village and obtain their opinions on the brands. Prepare a report on "popular rural brands and image builders."

End Notes

1. Anjana Chandramouly, "LG Group Banks on Rural Markets for Revenue Growth," *The Hindu Business Line*, 20 February 2009, available at www.blonnet.com/2009/02/20/stories/2009022051750400.htm
2. "Rural Agricultural Marketing: Strategies for Improving Marketing within Rural Areas," available at www.world-agriculture.com/...marketing/rural_marketing-strategies-improving-marketing-within-rural-areas.php.
3. "Why Companies See Bright Prospects in Rural India," 18 June 2009, available at http://knowledge.wharton.upenn.edu/india/article.cfm?articleid=4386.
4. Nandini Lakshman, "Sizing Up for Battle," *Business Standard*, 19 July 2003, available at www.business-standard.com/india/news/sizingfor-battle/206154/.
5. Preeti Khicha, "Building Brands in Rural India," 8 October 2007, available at www.brandchannel.com/features_effect.asp?pf_id=389.

Case 7.1 Healthy Brand Building—HUL Takes the Lead

Lifebuoy is India's largest selling soap brand from Hindustan Unilever Limited (HUL). It has been synonymous with health and hygiene for the last 100 years and over 70 per cent of India has used Lifebuoy at least once a year. The famous Lifebuoy jingle "*Tandurusti ki raksha karta hai Lifebuoy, Lifebuoy hai jahan tandurusti hai wahan*" is like the health anthem of Indians.

Competitor's Gain

HUL's leading soap brands, Lifebuoy and Lux, have lost market share to Reckitt Benckiser's Dettol, Wipro's Santoor and Godrej's No.1 in the recent past. Together, the two brands still lord over close to a third of the Rs 75 billion market for soaps. Lifebuoy is the market leader with a share of 16.6 per cent. (Lux comes next with 15.5 per cent.)

Fight Back

Hindustan Unilever shaved Re 1 off the price tag of Lifebuoy. Earlier, the country's largest fast-moving consumer goods company had faced the wrath of consumers after it had hiked soap prices on account of higher palm oil costs. They had dumped the brand and gone for value-for-money propositions like Godrej's No. 1.

The company re-launched the soap with a new design and improved consumer value through better formulation. This was followed by higher advertising and trade support. Hindustan Unilever's latest salvo is its new communication centred on swine flu. The "public interest advertisement" opens with the image of a mother washing her child's hand. An informative voiceover follows informing about the importance of washing hands before eating, after sneezing, shaking hands or touching shared surfaces. This can help prevent swine flu. A print campaign too has been launched. The company has conducted rallies in three cities where swine flu was detected in the initial stages. Giving the campaign a further impetus is its digital *avatar*. The company has created a micro-site to educate people on how to protect themselves from swine flu.

Social Interest Tops

Hindustan Unilever maintains that it has always kept the health proposition in mind. "The current advertising campaign is an extension of our effort to use mass media to effectively communicate to people at large to increase hygiene awareness to combat this health threat," says a company spokesperson.

Way back in 1985, Lifebuoy's entry into the Indian market coincided with the outbreak of the plague epidemic. That's when Lifebuoy became a household name in the country. "Lifebuoy *hai jahan, tandroosti hai wahan,*" (where you have Lifebuoy, you have good health) ran the long-playing jingle.

Sometime in 2002, Hindustan Unilever came up with a health and hygiene programme called the Lifebuoy *Swasthya Chetna* (Lifebuoy Health Awareness) in media-dark villages to spread awareness about the importance of washing hands with soap. The insight here was that regular usage of soap helps reduce illnesses like diarrhoea, respiratory infection, eye infection and other such diseases in children.

More recently, Lifebouy came out in aid of the victims of the Kosi floods in Bihar and Aila cyclone in West Bengal.

Can it Be a Winner?

The question is, will all this help Hindustan Unilever? Some brand consultants and experts feel, this will give the brand the much-needed boost. "Surely, the first few who cash in on this will see the best results and I'll wager a bet Lifebuoy's sales are up," says Harish Bijoor of Harish Bijoor Consults. Jagdeep Kapoor of Samsika says that if the brand meets the need, there is no harm in the sales pitch. "Credibility is the key and if Hindustan Unilever can meet the tangible need, it is a win–win situation."

Meanwhile, FMCGs such as Dabur and Reckitt Benckiser have launched similar campaigns. Dabur Chyawanprash boosts the body's immunity and helps protect one's family from swine flu. Reckitt Benckiser has launched an innovative campaign for its Dettol soap to educate consumers about swine flu. The search engine marketing campaign has used about 25 swine-flu related words to promote its campaign. Further, Dettol is also supporting the Global Hygiene Council, which conducts doctors' conferences on the prevention of swine flu.

For discussion

1. Will the first mover's advantage lie with Lifebuoy?
2. "Health campaigns of this kind are short lived," Do you agree? What other social issues can HUL consider for sustaining the health image of the brand in the future?

Source: Byravee Iyer, "Harping on Health," *Business Standard*, 8 September 2009. available at www.business-standard.com/india/news/harpinghealth/369334/.

Case 7.2 Titan Shines in Rural Areas

In a bid to tap the burgeoning jewellery market in rural and semi-urban areas, Titan Industries rolled out the Goldplus stores, mainly concentrated in South India. The rural consumers were looking for purity of jewellery products, a trusted player and an overall good retail shopping experience. Titan Industries catered to these needs through setting up the Goldplus stores, said L. R. Natarjan, vice-president and head of Goldplus and jewellery manufacturing of Titan Industries.

Market Size and Characteristics

The overall jewellery market in India is estimated to be at Rs 800 billion out of which the urban market accounts for Rs 280 billion while the rural and semi-urban market is worth Rs 420 billion. The jewellery market in the rural and semi-urban areas is expected to reach Rs 800 billion by 2015.

In India the consumer psyche is different in the jewellery segment. Gold is valued differently more as wealth of women (*Streedhan*) rather than a fashionable ornament. The unorganized gold and jewellery industry comprised more than 3 million "*karigars*" or workers labouring hard to produce gold artifacts. They focused on weight, karat standards and traditional styles.

Tanishq started off in urban areas in 2000, because urban consumers were willing to dole enough money for a fashionable cause like gold purchase. In 2003, it rebranded to draw the attention of not only English-speaking fashion savvy modern women of India but also women who preferred an eclectic mix of modernity and tradition.

New Segment and New Product

When Tanishq designed jewellery for Oscar nominated fairytale bollywood movie "Paheli" shot in the backdrop of rural Rajasthan, there was a change in the focus on the market segmentation. Tanishq had 80 stores spread over 60 towns across the length and breadth of the country.

Understanding the importance of purity for customers, Tanishq introduced Karatmeter, a machine that, in three minutes, measured the karatage of gold without destroying it.

It helped Tanishq to spread the message that without a trusted brand one can be duped into buying 14 carat gold considering it to be 22 carat gold. The message was loud and clear for any average gold customer in these areas, "The Tata name is like gold in India" and that "There is no company more trusted." Thus, the company ensured a paradigm shift from branding GoldPlus or Tanishq as "jewellery as adornment" to "jewellery as investment."

Titan Industries entered into the rural and semi-urban markets by starting Goldplus stores in Erode

(Tamil Nadu) and Ratlam (Madhya Pradesh) in 2005. The aim was to herald standardization in a largely undifferentiated market by establishing quality benchmarks.

Promotional Measures

Promotional measures such as quizzes, rewards, giveaways like gifting cars on Diwali eve, etc. ensured rural market penetration of GoldPlus, especially in Erode. However, the Ratlam experience was not so encouraging. Enthused by the success at Erode, Titan Industries launched GoldPlus, in 16 places across Tamil Nadu, Madhya Pradesh, Andhra Pradesh and Maharashtra. Speaking at the inauguration of the GoldPlus showroom at Bheemavaram, L. R. Natarajan, vice-president and head of Goldplus and jewellery manufacturing of Titan Industries observed that gold has tremendous historical, religious, cultural, social and economic significance across our country. The absence of standardized practices in markets led to a latent fear among consumers about the purity of gold. He emphasized that GoldPlus aims to establish an emotional connect by participating in every gold purchase need of the consumers with the promise of purity. In line with this assurance, purity certificates are provided for all GoldPlus jewellery products, which guarantees the purity mentioned with the ornaments.

Today, there are 28 GoldPlus stores across the country. They posted a turnover of Rs 2.17 billion during the period of April–September, 2009. To strengthen bonds with rural customers it launched the *Anant* Loyalty programme. Each Goldplus store educates around 1,000 customers per day on jewellery products and facilitates factory visits for its customers to appreciate quality standards in the process of gold manufacturing. A monthly saving scheme called "Golden Future Savings Scheme," which offers buyers multiple benefits like getting more jewellery than what they have paid for, planning future purchases in advance, paying in easy instalments and an attractive free gift at the time of enrolment.

For discussion

1. What are the major considerations in buying jewellery by rural consumers?
2. Is the approach of Titan effective in generating brand preferences and sales?
3. What additional initiatives do you suggest?

Source: "Brand Managers Need to Connect with Rural Consumers," *Business Standard*, 17 November 2008, available at www.business-standard.com/india/storypage.php?autono=340384; "Despite Volatile Price, Tanishq Gold Sales Up," *The Financial Express*, 2 August 2006, available at www.financialexpress.com/old/latest_full_story.php?content_id=136052.

8

Pricing Strategy

LEARNING OBJECTIVES

Upon completion of this chapter, you will be able to:

- Understand the concept, significance and objectives of pricing decisions
- Identify the different pricing policies employed by firms
- Examine the rural pricing strategy from the affordability perspective and distinguish it from the urban strategy
- Explain pricing strategies based on different market segments
- Discuss pricing decisions in relation to distribution, promotion, environmental factors such as government policies, inflation and competition and product lifecycle
- Identify retailer pricing methods

Procter & Gamble (P&G) recently launched two new products, one in the detergent segment called "Tide Naturals" and another one in the skincare segment under the "Olay" brand. P&G Home Products is the wholly-owned Indian subsidiary of P&G, USA. Its portfolio includes brands such as Tide and Ariel in the fabric-care segment and Head & Shoulders, Pantene and Rejoice in the hair-care segment. "Tide Naturals" will be priced at a 20 per cent discount to the core "Tide" brand with a view to halt its decline in market share. P&G lost about 1 per cent of its market share last year.

Tide Naturals is priced at Rs 50 per kg compared with Rs 32 per kg for rival HUL's mass brand, Wheel (a premium of 56 per cent). Small packs of Tide Naturals will be priced at Rs 10 for 200 g and Rs 20 for 400 g compared to the slightly premium Tide that sells at Rs 10 for 135 g and Rs 20 for 270 g. The premium may be too high to increase sales in the highly price-sensitive mass segment. For P&G, there may be cannibalization—Tide Naturals eating into the share of Tide.

The impact that detergents can make on Hindustan Unilever's earnings is not much. The contribution of detergents to Hindustan Unilever's sales is about 12 per cent and analysts say that variations in sales will have a marginal impact of about 2 per cent on the earnings. A down-trade from HUL's Rin to Tide Naturals may take place hurting the sales of HUL. Since Rin accounts for just 3 per cent of

HUL's revenues, the adverse effect is limited. Even then to arrest this, HUL may have to launch a lower priced variant to Rin.

In the fairness cream segment, the encounters of the two companies are in different directions. HUL's Ponds and Fair & Lovely have good image and market standing. P&G has launched "Olay Natural Whiteness" in the fairness cream segment to enhance profitability. It is regarded as lot more premium than the existing premium product "Garnier." As such, its impact on HUL's fairness creams will not be very great.[1]

The battle for market share is an ongoing one. The above case illustrates one of the strategic moves that companies may make either to safeguard or consolidate their positions. P&G's move is an intelligent one in the wake of price cuts taking place. The low-price offer is powered by product innovation and it has the capability of creating a new segment altogether between a value-for-money and cheap-good segments. A series of affordability related innovations such as discounts, low-unit packing, economy packs, freebies, etc. may be triggered by marketers to tactically gain advantage in the overcrowded market place. This chapter discusses the objectives and policy considerations that involve analysis of situations and methods of pricing. It elucidates the strategic approaches necessary to combat competition, satisfy consumers, meet distribution requirements and comply with government policies and legislations.

INTRODUCTION

Among the 4 A's of rural marketing—affordability, availability, awareness and acceptability—the major determinant of consumption is affordability. Affordability is, in turn, determined by two factors—incomes of consumers and prices of the products or services. As such, corporate enterprises are adopting a two-pronged approach of boosting incomes from rural markets through development marketing and by adopting pricing policies and methods that make products affordable. The significance of pricing as an element of the marketing mix has increased with recent trends like market fragmentation and saturation, inter-category competition, de-branding and customization and value-conscious consumption. The future may witness more price wars than brand wars if marketers fail to learn new lessons of value-added marketing.

CONCEPT AND SIGNIFICANCE

The price represents the market value of a product or service. It can be expressed in monetary and non-monetary terms. The price of a product is significant for the following reasons:

- It indicates the market value of a product. It reconciles supply and demand forces and achieves equilibrium.
- Price gives an image to a product. Generally high-priced goods are considered to be high-quality goods.
- Price is a major tool of marketing in designing offers for consumers and a major force in competitive battles.
- Prices of goods possessed and used by consumers help determine their status.

To sum up, price symbolizes quality, value, status and lifestyle for comparison among buyers. It provides signals by which potential buyers and sellers can rationally decide how to allocate their scarce resources. Pricing policy is one of the integral components of the marketing-mix policy of an enterprise. Price decisions are important for the following reasons:

- To determine the level of demand the product can have
- To generate sales, revenues and profits for the firm
- To stay competitive in the market.

PRICING OBJECTIVES

As stated above, pricing decisions are important for estimating demand, promoting sales, creating revenues and profits and outwitting competitors. Since the fundamental goal of any business organization is profit, objectives of pricing should be subservient to it. Whether explicit or implicit, objectives fall into four broad classes as shown in Table 8.1.

Profit objectives

Two major types of profit objectives may be observed:

1. Profit maximization, and
2. Target return.

Profit maximization

Generally, this goal is employed by firms that have made substantial investments and have short payback periods to recoup.

- Innovative product firms that have limited period of protection from imitators will follow this goal. For example, high-tech firms that offer software.
- Traders dealing with perishable goods also have the same strategy. They fix high prices and try to recover the investment along with profits.

Target return

This is common among the firms operating in a competitive world. Profit objectives tend to be set at levels that are viewed as satisfactory from different stakeholders' points of view. The diverse, often conflicting and challenging, concerns are:

- Securing maximum sales without sacrificing profitability.
- Need for liquidity or funds for expansion.
- Desire to recover the investment early.

Table 8.1 Pricing Objectives

Objective	Types
Profit	Profit maximization, target profit
Sales	Gain market share Growth in absolute sales Growth in market share Minimum sales necessary to survive Maintenance of sales volume or market share
Competition	Meet or prevent competition Destroy competition
Development	Gain market share

- Mitigating competition or avoiding public gaze.
- Management attitude of "win–slow" in the place of "make a fast buck", etc.
- Benchmarks such as historical rate of return, industry rate of return, etc.

Most often, this is the goal pursued by manufacturing organizations.

Sales objectives

Many organizations state their pricing objective in sales-related terms. These goals can take a number of forms, such as:

- Growth in absolute sales
- Growth in market share

A firm may be interested in increasing the quantity of sales to increase its customer base and thereby, increase profitability of the firm in the long run. Market share is also a meaningful benchmark of success. However, maintaining or increasing market share depends on two factors.

- Growth in market
- Growth in sales of the firm

If the firm fails to keep pace with the growth in the market and its competitors, its share declines.

Competition objectives

Some firms set pricing objectives in relation to the actions of their competitors. This may be done:

(i) To meet or prevent competition, and
(ii) To destroy competition.

In competitive situations such as oligopoly, firms tend to show price rigidity. When there is a dominating firm, it acts as the price leader and others follow it. The price leader will "police" the prices to maintain similar prices throughout the industry. The smaller firms fear a price reprisal from the larger firm if they deviate from the normal price in the industry. Firms rarely engage in price wars. A lower price is set to block the entry of a new firm or destroy competition. The predatory tactics, when pursued over a long time, will lead to cut-throat competition resulting in losses to the industry and a temporary benefit to consumers.

Development objectives

Firms pursue market development objectives by diversification strategies. Marketers have two options to promote profitability when markets are saturated.

(i) Expanding existing markets by stimulating non-users to use the products or encouraging more use of the product among the users.
(ii) Entering into markets hitherto not considered. The second one is akin to new product introduction. When a firm introduces a new product, it has to decide whether to penetrate or skim the market. The "penetration" objective requires lower pricing whereas the "skim" objective permits higher pricing.

Box 8.1 discusses the profit, sales and competition concerns of firms by using Asian Paints and ITC as examples. Many companies announce their turnover, sales and market share expectations as given in Box 8.1.

Box 8.1 Profit and Sales Concerns

Net sales and operating income for Asian Paints increased to Rs 42.7 billion from Rs 34.19 billion in the previous year—a growth of 24.9 per cent. The operating profit (PBDIT) increased by 0.8 per cent, from Rs 6.17 billion to Rs 6.21 billion. The profit after tax for the current year is Rs 3.62 billion as against Rs 3.75 billion in the previous year. The consolidated sales and net operating income of discounts and excise duty increased to Rs 54.63 billion from Rs 44.07 billion—a growth of 24 per cent. Net profit after minority interest for the group for the current year is Rs 3.98 billion as against Rs 4.09 billion in the previous year.

ITC controls close to 70 per cent of the domestic market for cigarettes. The contribution of cigarettes to the top line is around 65 per cent. ITC has chosen to fix prices, including excise duty hikes. As a result, the company reported much higher operating margins of 25 per cent when compared to its rivals such as Godfrey Philips.

In the tractor battery market, Exide has plans to increase its market share from 14 per cent to 25 per cent. It hopes to sell 250,000 batteries in 2009–2010. The turnover from tractor batteries is Rs 1 billion annually. Maruti Suzuki, India's leading automobile manufacturer, today sells 5 per cent of its vehicles in the rural markets. The company expects this number to rise to 15 per cent in the next two years.

Source: Asian Paints: Director's Report, 31 March 2009; Adarsh Gopalakrishnan, "ITC Books Profits," *The Business Line*, 15 November 2009, available at www.thehindubusinessline.com/iw/2009/.../2009111550621100.htm.

PRICING POLICY

A pricing policy is a standing answer to recurring questions. A systematic approach to pricing requires that decisions on individual pricing situations be identified and codified into a policy covering all the principal pricing problems. A policy approach, well defined and clear cut, is common to all well-managed enterprises. However, for many companies it remains a patch work of ad hoc decisions. The different situations that a company may face in course of its growth are given in Table 8.2. The pricing methods useful in different situations are also indicated.

When marketers face pricing problems, they adopt one or more of the following bases:

(a) Cost,

(b) Competition, and

(c) Demand.

Cost-based approach

The methods under this category are briefly explained in Table 8.3.

Competition-based approach

Competition plays a dominant role in influencing the pricing practices of a firm. The various methods under this approach are briefed in Table 8.4.

Demand-based approach

Methods under this category are based on the assumptions or findings of what the consumer prefers and expects. Table 8.5 describes the methods in brief.

Table 8.2 Pricing Framework

Sl No.	Situation	Method
1.	New product introduction	Cost-plus or mark-up penetration, skimming
2.	Product lifecycle (short)	Payback/capital recovery, rate of return
3.	Growing markets, moderate competition	Cost plus, mark-up experience curve
4.	Mature markets, stiff competition	Leader pricing, competitive pricing (bidding), going-rate pricing
5.	Growing/mature markets, discerning buyers	Discriminatory, differential, perceived value, psychological, value pricing
6.	Product–mix promotion	Product-line, optional feature, captive product, two-part product bundling
7.	Distribution to scattered customers	Geographic pricing
8.	Motivating channel	Discount pricing

Table 8.3 Cost-based Methods

Method	Description
Cost-plus or mark-up	All associated costs of production are computed. Prices are fixed by marking up a fixed percentage over average or marginal costs.
Marginal cost or contribution	Price is determined to recover marginal costs and make a contribution to the firm.
Target return	Prices are set in anticipation of earning a desired target return on investment.
Pay-back method (capital recovery)	Price is determined to enable the firm to cover all costs and capital investments within a specific time period.
Experience curve	An experience curve represents the relationship between costs and cumulative experience. With learning, costs decline and allow fixation of lower prices.

PRICING STRATEGY—THE AFFORDABILITY CHALLENGE

Affordability is the most important concern in rural markets. Rural consumers have low incomes and an orientation for simple living guided by the principles of economy and thrift.

The challenge to rural marketers can be understood by the distribution of rural people by income categories given in Table 8.6. It is evident that the middle-and low-income categories are large and they are either value conscious or price conscious. Table 8.7 furnishes the data on consumer categories provided by NCAER.

Table 8.4 Competition-based Pricing Methods

Method	Description
Leader pricing	Some product items may be priced low to attract customers and to generate more overall demand for other items.
Competitive pricing	It matches the market prices of competitors. It is reactive.
Going-rate pricing (follow the crowd/leader)	The firm prices its products at the same level or below the prices of leading competitors.
Sealed-bid pricing	In industrial marketing, open or closed bids are invited. Firms quote their prices, anticipating what the competitor would quote.

Table 8.5 Demand-based Pricing Methods

Method	Description
Discrimination/Differential/ Variable/ Flexible	Products are sold at two or more prices based on customer segment, product-form, image, location and time.
Perceived-value	The price is estimated and employed based on the perceived value of each component of the product.
Psychological	Based on attitudes of consumers in quality–price relationships (high price indicates high quality) odd prices (convey the notion of a discount or bargain) and reference prices (a price on an average considered right for a product) are determined.
Value	Pricing to generate value satisfaction to consumers. Every Day Low Pricing (EDLP) charges low prices on all days. High–low pricing charges higher prices on an every day basis but lower prices during special promotion periods.

Table 8.6 Income Distribution Across Populations (Population in millions)

Annual income size (in rupees)	Urban	Rural
Above 0.3 million	80	36
0.15 to 0.3 million	119	111
75,000 to 0.15 million	84	239
Less than 75,000	49	428
Total	332	

Source: Indicus Analytics, available at www.indicus.net.

Table 8.7 Consumer Categories

Category	Annual income	Lifestyle
Quality conscious	Over Rs 150,001	Very rich
Value conscious	Rs 45,001 to Rs 150,000	Consuming class
Price Conscious	Rs 22,001 to Rs 45,000	Climbers
	Rs 16,001 to Rs 22,000	Aspirants
	Below Rs 16,000	Destitute

Source: www.naukrihub.com, accessed March 2010.

Box 8.2 Financing Purchases by Rural Consumers

Bajaj Auto is focusing on providing financing schemes to its customers in rural areas both via in-house financing, i.e. Baja Auto Finance Limited and through other financing sources. Hero Honda's strategies include selling during festive seasons, tying up with new dealers, providing finance with local co-operative institutions that are numbered at around 108,779 in India. Hyundai had launched a promotional scheme for rural areas titled *"Ghar Ghar ki Pehchan,"* under which special schemes were offered for government employees in rural areas and members of *gram panchayats* on the purchase of Hyundai Santro cars.

Airtel and Samsung tied up with IFFCO, the world's largest farmer's co-operative, to sell their mobile handsets and services. IFFCO has about 37,000 member units spanning the whole of India. Nokia announced the national roll-out of Nokia Life Tools services that would eventually cover 17 states. Targeted at the rural customer, Nokia Life Tools provides useful information on weather conditions, farm inputs and market prices. Nokia also announced that it plans to offer a micro-financing facility for its phones across 12 states for which it is currently in talks with a few institutions. This facility would be aimed largely at women in rural areas.

Source: Tejeesh N. S. Behl, "Resurgence to the Rescue of India Inc," 24 March 2009, available at www.sify.com; "Nokia Dials Rural Market with New Services," *The Hindu Business Line,* 20 August 2009, available at www.blonnet.com/2009/08/20/stories/2009082051180400.htm.

Hence, the challenge to rural marketers is to provide market offers that consist of products that are reasonably good in quality and low in price. The challenge involves balancing the two important goals of modern corporate enterprises—profit and corporate social responsibility.

Another important finding is that rural consumers are basically against credit purchases. Mayank Pareek, executive officer, marketing and sales, Maruti Suzuki, observed that in contrast to the urban market where 80 per cent of the vehicle's cost is financed, rural consumers pay cash for up to 60 per cent of the price tag. However, the attitude of rural consumers towards credit is changing. Box 8.2 presents the financing routes adopted by companies selling consumer durables and services.

PRICING STRATEGY—RURAL VERSUS URBAN

In urban markets, aspiration is key—it is all about brands, lifestyles and show-off value. This is followed by quality and finally, price. Rural India is driven primarily by price, followed by aspiration and then quality. However, it is important to understand that the Indian consumer, no matter where he or she is or what category he or she belongs to, still looks for a good bargain. That is a unique Indian characteristic. Manufacturers have moved away from the mindset that you can cut quality along with price. One company tried to pass off inferior quality tea leaves in rural markets and superior quality grades for urban markets under the same brand name. This fell flat.

However, re-engineering is necessary in a different sense. According to Harish Bijoor, CEO, Harish Bijoor Consulting Inc., "Companies are realizing that the urban and rural want is largely the same. However, the rural person is savvier and demands real value for money. To offer this, marketers are re-engineering products. Look at the auto segment. The urban man wants a car as does the rural man. Both have the same amount of money. The rural person, however, believes spending USD 12,000 on a car is a sin. He wants it at USD 3,000. The Nano is a solution. Every category needs to operate on the Nano paradigm. The needs are all the same, across rural and urban. The solutions have to be different."

PRICING STRATEGY NEEDS INTEGRATED APPROACH

Pricing strategy requires a holistic approach. Pricing is a part of the marketing strategy. It should be designed as an integral part of the marketing strategy to contribute to the objectives of marketers and the needs and wants of the customer groups. Pricing strategy, therefore, has to pass three tests of effectiveness.

First, is it in tune with the expectations of customers?
Second, is it consistent with the other P's of marketing strategy?
Third, is it competitive enough to achieve the target market share?

The pricing decision is made taking into account product quality, promotion and distribution. The relationships are portrayed in Table 8.8 with reference to the three product strategies in rural areas.

PRICING FOR THE QUALITY-CONSCIOUS SEGMENT

Rural consumers may be more demanding on the price parameter. However, it would be wrong to assume that they are not quality conscious. The volume of high-price products sold in rural markets is small for obvious reasons. Despite lower incidence of premium product purchases, rural consumers across all income segments exhibit a marked propensity to spend on premium high-quality products that are backed by strong brand values, which correspond to their own aspirations and quality needs. According to a recent study on rural marketing by the Confederation of Indian Industry (CII), there

Table 8.8 Price in Marketing Mix

Sl No.	Rural consumers	Product	Price	Promotion	Place
1.	Quality conscious, concerned with functional benefits, value for money	Premium product	High	High	Showrooms, malls, general and fancy stores
2.	Value conscious, price sensitive, concern for functional benefits, no frills, value for money	Mass product	Medium	High	General and fancy stores, super markets, *kirana* stores, *paan* shops and *haats*
3.	Price conscious, no concern for quality	Spurious products	Low	No	*Kirana* stores, *paan* shops and *haats*

has been a paradigm shift in the consumption trend in the rural areas with the focus shifting from price-driven to quality-driven products.

The problem really lies in the market not being able to offer a premium product in the specific context of rural demand. Marketers need to customize and innovate to create products that are relevant and affordable for the rural consumer. If a marketer wants to develop an effective pricing strategy for a quality-conscious market, then, he must know whether the price–quality relationship holds good for the market. Research in this area has established that some people perceive quality based on price, while others do not. Table 8.9 shows the situations in which price–quality relationships are stronger.

Pricing methods

When price–quality relationships are easy to associate, marketers can employ the following methods of pricing.

- Discriminatory pricing
- Perceived-value pricing
- Psychological pricing

Discriminatory pricing

Discriminatory pricing is employed to charge different customer groups differently, projecting differences in the quality of offer. Table 8.10 gives the different forms of discriminatory pricing.

Perceived-value pricing

Companies add features to their products with a view to enhancing their customers' perceived value. For each of the features that enhance convenience, durability, reliability, attractiveness, etc. of the product, the marketer fixes prices to be charged and adds them to the product price to arrive at the final price.

Example: A farmer may assess a tractor by considering several points that are of value to him. He will compare a brand with its competitive brands in terms of price and features such as durability, reliability, cost of maintenance, cost of operation, service quality and warranty. If the brand has higher value, he will decide in favour of it.

Table 8.9 Perceived Quality–Price Relationships

Sl No.	Reason	Strong when	Examples
1.	Quality differences	The perceived differences among brands are large	TVs, home appliances, motorcycles
2.	Quality uncertainty	Consumer does not have the ability to decide quality due to lack of knowledge or absence of clues	Garments, CDs, refrigerators
3.	Price consciousness	Price consciousness is high and price variations exist among products	Toilet soaps, shampoos
4.	Need compulsion	Consumer has peculiar needs that need careful fulfilment	Doctor, teacher
5.	Place of availability	Place where product is sold is stylish	Dealer showrooms
6.	Social consciousness	Consumer buys publicly consumed products	Garments, footwear, jewellery

Table 8.10 Discriminatory Pricing

Methods	Description	Examples
Product-form pricing	Different versions of the product are priced differently but not proportionately to their respective costs	Bound and paperback books at different prices; beverages are offered in different sizes and packs; the unit price differs
Location pricing	Same product is priced differently at different locations	Seats in movie halls
Time pricing	Prices are varied by day or by season	Zoos, parks and museums charge higher prices on Sundays and holidays

Psychological pricing

Individual motivations to buy products can be taken as a basis for charging higher prices. One approach that uses associations for creating motivations is called reference pricing.

Marketers position and sell products at higher prices by having their product endorsed by celebrities, placing the product along with classy products, referring to the purchases made by aspiration or associate group members or by stating that current price is lower than the original one.

For instance, a shampoo is referred to Re 1, match box to 50 paise and a two-wheeler to Rs 10,000. These price levels are acceptable and anything above them is viewed sceptically.

Another form of psychological pricing is image pricing, which is effective in case of ego-sensitive products such as cars, sun glasses, cameras, etc. People prefer to buy expensive brands in such cases as price acts as a signal of quality.

PRICING FOR THE VALUE-CONSCIOUS SEGMENT

The rural consumer is value conscious. The recession may have impacted his budget but not altered his aspiration for quality products. The consumer has became more conscious and has started evaluating the price–value equation while shopping. Instead of downgrading to cheaper substitutes, the consumer is on the lookout for quality products at low price points. This has resulted in a "sachetization" of virtually every category from personal-care (shampoos) to cars (Nano!).

Godrej No.1 offered unmatched quality at 76 per cent total fatty matter (TFM) at an affordable price. While most other brands include talc and other "fillers" to boost manufacturer margins, Godrej No.1 eschewed this path and decided to offer the best quality at the best possible price. This has helped the brand build a loyal base of consumers. This strategy has been strengthened by pioneering "multi-pack" offerings and increasing trials and frequency of usage by introducing stock keeping units (SKUs) at the Rs 5 and Rs 10 price points.[2]

To impress consumers willing to pay for the products of their choice as long as they get "value for money" many other companies are offering innovative products (see Box 8.3).

Two useful pricing methods adopted by marketers to attract value conscious consumers are explained here.

Psychological pricing—odd numbers

Odd endings convey two notions.

1. It belongs to a lower price range.
2. There is a discount or bargain.

Example: Bata has been using such price tactics for many years. TSN Teleshop Centre quotes its prices in the same way.

Box 8.3 Mobiles and Two-Wheelers for the Value Conscious

Nokia launched eight new models in the entry-level segment. Spice, on the other hand, created history by launching the "People's Phone" costing just Rs 800. The handset is a very basic model with no display screen and also lacks SMS facility. Spice has also launched an entry-level affordable colour FM phone, S-525, and an entry-level music phone, S-606, with 1GB internal memory. In the entry-level segment, Samsung launched F250 and J210 that offer strong value propositions to users with their relevant features and affordable pricing. Nokia, along with other players like Motorola and LG, has launched cheaper entry-level handsets to cater to this market. Motorola launched Motofone available at Rs 1,650.

CARE Research observes that the cost-conscious rural populace tends to purchase fuel efficient and lower-priced motorcycles with engine capacity up to 124 cc. "The last few months saw motorcycle sales coming primarily from rural areas while the urban households were reeling under the pressure of the global financial meltdown. Thus, the entry level 75–124-cc motorcycle segment, typically preferred by rural households, witnessed relatively higher growth than the 125–249-cc motorcycles," remarked Ms Revati Kasture, head, CARE Research. "Many rural households, which largely remained insulated from the recent financial crisis, took advantage of the reduction in excise duties as well as lower petrol prices and interest costs and bought motorcycles for themselves," added Ms Kasture. Around 60–65 per cent of the domestic sales in H1-FY10 came from rural areas. "With the cost-conscious rural India foreseen as the growth driver, the entry-level segment would continue to remain significant for the industry in the next four to five years," says Mr D R Dogra, managing director and chief executive officer, CARE Ratings. "Though the 75–125-cc segment is expected to grow at a pace tad lower than the industry growth, this segment is large enough with more than 70 per cent share to be ignored and the action would continue at the bottom of the pyramid," added Mr Dogra.

Source: : Gagandeep Kaur, "Rustic Flavour," 3 June 2008, available at http://. voicendata.ciol.com; "Action Lies at the Bottom of the Pyramid for motorcycle industry, available at www.careratings.com/Current/3/5041.pdf.

Value pricing

Value pricing involves setting prices at a reasonably lower level compared to competitors through careful streamlining of the operations to become a low-cost firm without sacrificing quality. It involves business process re-engineering, supply-chain management, human development and quality management. Many companies in India are adopting this approach as markets are saturated and competition has intensified.

- Whisper, which controls 46 per cent of the Indian market by value has made its Whisper Ultra napkin brand available at a price of Rs 65 for a pack of ten (previously available at Rs 80).
- Reckitt and Colman of India (RCI) has launched Cherry Blossom in lamitubes under Easy Wax. The cost of a 40 g-lamitube is just about 40 per cent the cost of a 40 g-tin can. It is cheaper than plastic bottles as well, with a cost saving of as much as 20 per cent. Also, "squeezability" is the additional benefit. It imports better control on product metering, meaning that the quantity that comes out is what one desires.
- Reusable packing gives additional benefit. Many farmers ask for fertilizers packed in LDPE instead of HDPE sacks.

Skimming versus penetration pricing

At the time of introduction, many companies favour setting high prices to skim the cream off or low prices to sweep the entire ground. A skimming price strategy is preferred when the high price fixed is

Table 8.11 Skimming Versus Penetration Strategies

Factor	Use skimming if	Use penetration if
Price elasticity of primary demand	Inelastic	Elastic
Price elasticity of selective demand	Inelastic	Elastic
Cost of production and marketing relative to potential competitors	Higher	Lower
Economies of scale	No	Yes
Ease with which competitors will enter the market	Difficult for them to enter	Easy entry
Rate at which the consumer will accept the concept	New concept (slow)	Known concept (fast)
Market segments based on price	Segments exist. Can be taken one segment at a time	Mass market exits
The firm's resources to produce and market the product	Small or restricted	Large

aimed at communicating the image of a superior product. Penetration is chosen when the market is highly price sensitive and a low price stimulates market growth. Overtime, the skim price is lowered successively in steps so that the product may slide down the demand curve to pick up other price segments. Table 8.11 compares the two pricing strategies.

P&G introduced Ariel and Tide detergents at high prices. Recently, it cut the prices of most of its laundry and hair-wash brands. The sales of Pantene and Head & Shoulders went up by a whopping 32.8 per cent. Many durables like air coolers, vacuum cleaners and TVs started with high prices and penetrated the market at lower prices. Products like Maggi Noodles, Vicks Vaporub and Rin detergent penetrated markets with introductory lower prices and later went up the price ladder.

PRICING FOR THE PRICE-CONSCIOUS SEGMENT

Price-conscious consumers belong to the destitute (up to Rs 16,000 annual income), aspirant (Rs 16,001 to 22,000) and climber (Rs 22,001 to 45,000) groups. Their affordability is lower. The climbers keep a watch for promotional offers to whet their appetite for quality products. Since branded products are costlier than unbranded, ungraded local ones and are not available in small quantities (the exception is edible oil that is loosely sold), they purchase local brands or fake brands that are relatively cheap. This market can be induced to buy national brands by two methods:

- Small units and low pricing
- Promotional pricing

Many companies have introduced sachets and revolutionized buying in rural areas. Toothpastes, shampoos, detergents, toilet soaps, hair oil, *paan masala*, dairy milk and a host of products are now available in sachets.

Consider the success of Clinic-Plus bubble pack. The 28 ml shampoo pack is priced at Rs 8. The unit price offered is lower compared to a sachet of 8 ml priced at Rs 2.50. Such innovations are expected as rural households change their preferences to buy for a family and a particular period rather than for an individual and for a day's consumption.

Promotional pricing measures include price-offs, discounts or rebates, credit facilities, and low- or no-interest long-term finance schemes.

When it comes to aspirants and the destitute, the same pricing policies will work. Occasionally, they indulge in buying national brands and packed items. They can be encouraged by adopting the ancient system of exchange–barter pricing at the retail level.

This method is being adopted mostly by small *kirana* and general store retailers of remote and tribal areas. The items that are accepted by retailers in exchange include paddy, maize, chillies, ground nut, pluses, etc. depending on the harvest seasons of different crops. The system becomes operative mostly during harvests when labourers get food grains as wages and also when small and marginal farmers harvest their crops.

Another way of inducing these groups to buy can be through the low-priced mini-pack strategy. HUL sells a mini-pack of shampoo, toothpaste, talcum powder and face cream for Rs 15. Sold separately, the products would cost the consumer Rs 27.

PRICING—BASED ON DISTRIBUTION

Companies have to take two distribution aspects into consideration while pricing their products.

(i) Consumers and channel members are widely scattered requiring geographical pricing policy.

(ii) Channel members need motivation to actively participate in sales programmes. It necessitates the employment of discount pricing.

Table 8.12 and 8.13 explain the geographical pricing methods and standard types of price discounts in brief.

Table 8.12 Methods of Geographic Pricing

Method	Characteristics
FOB mill or factory pricing	The buyer selects the form of transportation and pays all freight charges. The seller pays the costs of loading the goods (hence, "from on board") and nets the same amount regardless of the buyer's location. The delivered price to the buyer depends on freight charges.
Uniform delivered pricing	All buyers pay the same delivered price for the same quantity of goods, regardless of their location. The seller pays for shipping and receives varying net prices on each sale based on its distribution costs. This method is used when transit costs are a small part of total manufacturing costs. It aids in maintaining customary prices and allows uniform prices to be advertised.
Zone pricing	All buyers within a geographic zone pay a uniform delivered price. In a single-zone system, any buyer within the seller's entire market area is charged the same price. In a multi-zone system, delivered prices vary by zone. Freight charges are the average costs within a zone area. The manufacturer determines the mode of transportation and pays costs.
Base-point pricing	The firms in an industry establish base points from which the cost of shipping is computed. The base points are usually the areas of greatest production. The delivered price to a buyer reflects the cost of transporting goods from the base point nearest to the buyer, regardless of the actual site of supply.

Table 8.13 Standard Types of Price Discounts

Discount	Description	Objective
Volume	Price reductions for large volume orders	To encourage buying larger and more economical quantities
Trade/Functional	Price reductions for services performed by channel members	To reward channel members for services provided to buyers
Payment Terms	Price reductions for payments made within specific time periods	To encourage buyers to pay sooner and thus, reduce receivables
Seasonal	Price reduction for orders preceding and following peak demand	To stimulate demand in slower periods and to smooth out orders
Promotional	Price reduction for promotional services performed by trade members	To encourage trade members to make special efforts to stimulate product demand

PRICING—BASED ON PROMOTION

Pricing alone cannot generate traffic and purchase. Promotional ingredients are necessary to make the strategy effective. While pricing offers affordability to buy, advertising offers a reason to buy. Sales promotion offers an incentive to buy and also materializes sales. Therefore, marketers develop promotional strategies to support their pricing strategies. By experience, several companies have found that promotional pricing is more effective in generating sales than non-price promo-tools such as contests, exhibitions and demonstration. Table 8.14 describes some of the pricing techniques that companies can use to stimulate immediate purchase.

Promotional pricing strategies are often a zero-sum game. Competitors will copy them quickly and the expected gains may not be realized. Further, the image of the product may be tainted, particularly when price–quality relationship is strong among the consumers. The price reduction offers may lead to the creation of negative perceptions among the consumers with respect to the quality of the product. One has to make a wise choice between promotional pricing and other promo-tools to avoid wastage of resources. In the rural context, promotional pricing will prove effective in promoting sales as consumers here are price sensitive.

Box 8.4 shows what experts in the field have to say about discounts and the benefits of discounts.

PRICING AND ENVIRONMENTAL FACTORS

Among the environmental factors, the major ones are economy and government. They merit attention for tracking on a continuous basis. The technology factor will impact prices, however, such developments require time.

Influence of government policies

Social welfare-oriented governments may decide to intervene in the pricing polices of firms either indirectly through their tax polices or directly by fixation of prices. Sometimes, the government may impose certain duties that may require companies to adopt an innovative strategy. Box 8.5 presents the impact of the government's decision to impose a safeguard duty of 20 per cent on the import of soda ash from China.

Table 8.14 Promotion-pricing Techniques

Sl No.	Technique	Description
1.	Cash rebates or discounts	Textile showrooms and footwear shops offer frequent cash rebates to clear off their inventories.
2.	Price-off	Many consumer durable companies are offering price reductions.
3.	Low-interest financing	TVS-50 and other two-wheeler sellers have been offering schemes of this kind since a long time.
4.	Longer payment terms	LIC polices, housing loan schemes, etc. are spread over a long period.
5.	Warranties and service contracts	There is hardly any consumer durable that comes without this facility. Home appliances carry at least 1 year warranty whereas goods like fans carry warranty for up to seven years. For all these products free service coupons are given for a period.
6.	Loss leader or traffic builder	Retailers put low prices on certain items to serve as traffic builders.
7.	Everyday low pricing	Many retailers like supermarkets are adopting everyday low pricing (EDLP). Their prices are consistently lower than those of others while their quality is the same.
8.	Exchange-price offer	Old products of the same or another brand are exchanged at a lower price for new ones.
9.	Membership cards	Family health cards of hospitals, restaurant cards of hotels, etc. offer a range of reductions based on the number of family members availing it.

Retention pricing

As majority of the farmers are in the small and marginal category, fertilizer pricing is controlled by the government. It is deliberately fixed at a lower level to encourage the farmers to use fertilizers in order to improve the productivity of the agricultural sector. The price is called retention price. An apex body known as Fertilizer Industry Coordination Committee (FICC) undertakes the process of fixing the retention price and its administration.

The retention price consists of three elements and they are:

(a) Variable costs

(b) Fixed costs

(c) Return on investment

The difference between retention price and actual selling price is paid as subsidy by the government. Box 8.6 explains how the government influences pricing in the fertilizer industry.

Influence of changes in the economy

Poor monsoon and crop failures will place pressure on FMCGs to lower the prices or introduce low-priced variants. "Rural consumption remains susceptible to the vagaries of the monsoon," say

Box 8.4 Discounts Lift Performance

According to Aditya Agarwal, director of Emami, the reasons for promotional offers include rewarding loyal customers, passing on cost savings to consumers and inducing trials. Offering a similar view, H. K. Press, executive director and president of GCPL, maintained that companies offer discounts and other incentives to achieve strategic ends such as trial and competitive reaction. Agarwal opined that during trying times, the "save more when you buy more" strategy will be more effective to induce consumers to buy. Sandeep Kaul, chief executive (personal-care products business), ITC Ltd, said that the company's objective is to gain sales for its new brands. To achieve this, its marketing efforts are geared towards enhancing consumer engagement and trial. As a result, the consumer response to its brands, Fiama Di Wills, Vivel and Superia, was excellent.

The power of discounts in promoting sales is strong in case of many FMCGs. An analysis of the aggregate results of 12 leading FMCG companies reveals an 18 per cent year-on-year rise in net profit, while the net sales registered half that growth. The volumes are driven by aggressive advertising and discount offers, with freebies doled out by most players.

A few of Emami's schemes include:

- Emami Pure Skin worth Rs 22 free with Boroplus Advanced Moisturising Lotion worth Rs 98
- Five pieces of Sardija Cough drops worth Rs 5 free with 100 ml of Sardija Cough Syrup worth Rs 50, among others

ITC offers Vivel Di Wills shampoo (200 ml) free with its 75 g bathing soap for Rs 89.

Source: Pradipta Mukherjee, "FMCG Players Bundle Offers to Shore up Sales," *Business Standard*, 15 March 2009, available at www.business-standard.com/india/news/fmcg-players-bundle-offers-to-shoresales/351824/.

the investment bankers of the Noble group and this could affect companies such as Hindustan Unilever (HUL) and Dabur that have the highest rural exposure. In the case of HUL, 50 per cent of its revenues come from rural India, while the percentage is 45 for Dabur, 35 per cent for Colgate–Palmolive, 30 to 35 per cent for Godrej Consumer Products and 25 per cent for Marico. Commenting on the relationship between the monsoon and the FMCG sector, Mr Jaibir Singh Sethi, analyst, consumer and retail, Noble, said, "If the monsoon is not good, it could take the FMCG story off the rails. Half the revenues of some FMCG companies come from rural areas." This assumes more importance, he said, because the urban FMCG is likely to be squeezed narrower in the down trading from premium products to entry level.[3]

Price fluctuations in the economy will influence the fortunes of companies. Box 8.7 describes the reactions of firms to a fall in commodity prices.

Influence of technology on pricing

Technological developments lead to production of new products and services and these lower the cost of operations and production. Initially, high-tech products may be priced high to allow recovery of capital. However, in course of time they will be priced low to increase penetration in the markets. One such case is that of Idea Cellular services described in Box 8.8. Incidentally, the ad campaign of Idea Cellular suggests how technology can impact the life of people (Box 8.8).

Box 8.5 Duties Raise Prices

The government has decided to impose a safeguard duty of 20 per cent on the import of soda ash from China. Soda ash accounts for close to 40 per cent of the cost component of economy-segment detergents. Since the composition of soda ash in high-end detergent brands like Surf (Hindustan Unilever), Procter & Gamble's Ariel and Henkel's Henko is about half compared to the economy segment, premium brands will only be marginally impacted by the safeguard duty. Economy-segment detergents such as Hindustan Unilever's Wheel, Ghadi from Kanpur Trading Company and Fena may become more expensive by 10 to 20 per cent. Marketers of economy-level detergents are in a fix because this segment is very price-sensitive. Increasing prices at a time when companies are pushing volumes at price points of Rs 5 and Rs 10 could hurt consumer purchases.

The total value of the detergent market is estimated to be close to Rs 80 billion. Of this, the economy segment accounts for 30 to 35 per cent. In 2008, detergent companies across the board had increased prices by 10–15 per cent in the economy segment and 20–30 per cent in the premium segment. The hike was on account of increased prices of LAB and soda ash—both key components in detergent manufacturing.

China was the only country from where soda ash imports were affordable. However, with the safeguard duty import, the costs of importing from China will go up. Soda ash is manufactured only by four players—Tata Chemicals, GHCL, Nirma and DCW. These companies are seeking protection and are making huge profits as is evident from their quarterly results.

Source: Ratna Bhushan and Amiti Sen, "Henceforth, Wheel, Fena, Ghadi May Cost You more," *The Economic Times*, 3 November 2009.

PRICING FOR COMPETITION

Finally, the price game is to be played at the market place, facing competitors. What can competitors do? How may a company respond to their moves? Table 8.15 depicts the varied situations.

Selling at a high price

Companies marketing high-tech, high-image and high-quality products keep their prices high and justify them by advertising their superior functional benefits. Surf Excel, Videcon TV, Swaraj Tractor and many other products position their products on the quality platform.
However, companies employ the following price tactics to attract the middle-income segments.

Optional feature pricing

Marketers of durables offer optional product features and services along with the main product. But, an economy buyer can go for a "no frills" model. One example is that of two-wheelers that are offered with additional features such as seat, rear box, sidelights, etc.

Captive product pricing

In pricing its products, a shrewd marketer will consider two types of costs involved in the purchase. These are:

(i) Cost of ownership
(ii) Cost of operation and maintenance

Box 8.6 Price Controls by the Government

The Indian Government controls the retail prices of fertilizers by providing subsidies to safeguard the interests of farmers. The practice of giving subsidy to urea alone has led to the wrong practice of overusing it to increase yields. In course of time, the excess use of urea leads to deterioration in soil fertility and fall in yields. In view of this, the Government of India introduced the new, "nutrient-based" subsidy scheme. According to it, the extent of the subsidy on a particular fertilizer will depend upon the quantity of nutrients it contains. Thus, it aims to give subsidy based on the percentage of four key nutrients—nitrogen, phosphorus, potash and sulphur—in the fertilizer pack.

With the easing of controls, seven fertilizer companies raised prices by 0.10 per cent to 5.96 per cent as follows: Zuari Industries (up by 5.96 per cent), Rashtriya Chemicals and Fertilizers (up by 1.67 per cent), Deepak Fertilizers (1.31 per cent), Nagarjuna Fertilizers & Chemicals (up by 1.39 per cent), Chambal Fertilizers (up by 1.05 per cent), Tata Chemicals (up 0.60 per cent) and National Fertilizer (up 0.10 per cent).

However, the subsidy policy is an intriguing one. By easing controls on the prices of fertilizers other than urea, the Government could reduce the fiscal deficit that rose up to 6.2 per cent of gross domestic product (GDP) last year. But, the rise in fertilizer prices caused an increase in food prices, since the soil nutrients account for 30 per cent of farming costs. Facing protests against soaring food prices, the government has cautioned fertilizer firms that if price hikes are unreasonable, it will re-impose controls.

Source: "Fertilizer Stocks Flare up on Fertilizer Pricing Reforms," available at http://beta.profit.ndtv.com/news/show/fertiliser-stocks-flare-up-on-fertiliser-pricing-reforms-26612?schedules=india.

Box 8.7 Fall in Commodity Prices

While commodity prices had begun falling from the later half of 2008–2009, FMCG companies took time to take advantage of that. They were running high inventories that took time to ease off. To move the goods, some companies reduced prices during the quarter while the soap and detergent category increased the size of their products or offered freebies. This led to an increase in sales especially of low-end products like Godrej No. 1 soap and Ghadi detergent from Godrej Consumer Products. Companies like Emami went the other way and increased prices of some of their products. "We won't go for price reduction. We always have on-going offers and price-related promotions to boost sales," said Aditya Agarwal, director of Emami Group of companies. According to a report of Sharekhan, an equity analyst house, while premium products such as Hindustan Unilever Ltd's soaps and detergents and Marico's Saffola witnessed a fall in volume growth, down-market product like Godrej's Ghadi saw robust growth.

The companies have also got an additional benefit from the government's decision to reduce excise duty in two stages from 14 per cent to 8 per cent across the board. The sharpest advantage has come from the reduction in edible oil prices. Angshu Mallick, vice president (sales and marketing) of Adani Wilmer said, "Consumption increased while prices came down from November 2008."

Source: Rohit Khanna, "FMCG Cos All Set to Reap Benefit from Declining Trend in Commodity Prices," *The Financial Express*, 3 December 2009, available at www.financialexpress.com/news/fmcgcosallsettoreapbenefitfromdecliningtrend-incommodityprices/443503/2.

Box 8.8 Technology for Improved Service and Lower Costs

Cellular service providers are now looking at the efficient use of technology in order to attract new and permanent customers and thus aim at long-term sustainable growth. Several value-added services are available, that are fascinating for the happy-go-lucky types and interesting to frugal minds. An exciting and economy type of service is the popular short messaging service (SMS). It is a major revenue generator with immense market potential. The wide array of its applications testifies to the length and breadth of human imagination. Some of the applications are ad campaigns and promotions, logos, contests, auctions, chatting with celebrities, buying tickets, paying bills and even the latest rage—voting for your favourite performer.

The advent of m-commerce has opened up a new opportunity of making payments for a variety of services through credit cards.

Idea Cellular announced that it has deployed Nokia Siemens Networks Device Management solutions to ensure seamless GPRS services in 20 operating circles, which will now offer improved Internet connectivity to its subscribers. Anil Tandan, chief technology officer, Idea Cellular, said, "Consumers today are using their mobile phones to surf the Web, more than their personal computers. At Idea Cellular, it's important to us that our subscribers enjoy seamless data services so that they can always stay connected. The Nokia Siemens Networks Device Management solution and consulting services will help us achieve that aim, while reducing costs."

Source: Namit Agarwal, "An Idea/Airtel/ Vodafone can Change your life," 23 October 2007, available at http://theviewspaper.net/an_ideaairtel_vodafone_can_change_your_life/.

Table 8.15 Competitive Reactions

Competitor's decision	Company's reactions	Justification
Raise	Raise	Match when costs rise or demand is growing
	Maintain	If additional benefit is not there for the value-conscious markets
	Cut	If there is benefit of technology or large-scale economies or when there is need to kill competition
Maintenance	Raise	Justify price rise by quality improvements
	Maintain	Matching gives competitiveness
	Cut	When costs are low because of technology or large-scale economies or when there is need to kill competition
Cut	Raise	Unusual. May be when quality improvements are made.
	Maintain	Ignore, considering the action of competitor as a desperate step. Appeal to the value-conscious market.
	Cut	Match the price cut to nullify the advantage competitor seeks to get.

Products such as two-wheelers and tractors need spare parts and servicing. Products such as razors, cameras, amusement parks and computers need operating materials such as blades, photo films, entertainment and software. To induce purchase, the marketer may price the products high and keep captive product prices low or vice-versa.

However, there is one danger. Pirates swing into action and flood the markets with dirt-cheap fakes that adversely affect the marketer's position in several ways.

- They reduce the life and performance quality of the product and thereby the image and prospects of the company.
- They lower the sales of the product.

Two-part pricing

Service firms often employ this system of pricing. One part of the price is fixed and the other part is variable depending upon the usage. Charges for electricity and telephone services are examples. The bills carry a fixed charge "rent" and consumption charges proportional to usage at a slab rate or variable tariff.

Product-bundling pricing

There is a move from selling products to systems. An IT kiosk may prefer to buy a system rather than parts such as computers, printers, software, modems, speakers, UPS and services. Buying from one source provides problem-free operations to the buyer as the sellers deliver the entire requirement of products and MRO (maintenance, repair and operations). Fertilizer companies are moving from "single-solution focus" to "farm-management services" focus. The pricing can be done for the entire system, for example, charging for the "turnkey solution."

Promotional pricing

Tactics such as discounts to dealers and consumers, extended warranty or service period, certain free options, strategy of providing extra large packages at the same price, innovative packing, free trial use without any obligation, club membership with the privilege of discounts on other company products, etc. are common features of this type of marketing.

Selling at a low price

Marketers intending to offer products at low prices have two options:

(i) Reduce the price of the premium offer
(ii) Launch a low-priced version

The first option of reducing the price of the premium product is considered to

- Exploit market opportunity (the market at the low end is growing at an attractive pace and costs fall with volumes)
- Counter the threat of losing market share to competitors because the market is price sensitive and rebuilding is a difficult proposition.

This is precisely what is happening in the Indian market. The urban, middle and rural market segments have become attractive and several marketers are either slashing the prices of their high-end products or launching low-end fighter products.

Ind Swift has launched a low-priced version of Atorva Statin by simplifying the production process from 13 stages to nine and indigenizing a vital raw material. A 10 mg tablet in now sold at Rs 5.95 as against the earlier price of Rs 17.90. Its competitors are selling Storvas (Ranbaxy) at Rs 18, Atorlip (Cipla) at Rs 18, Ajitar (Sun Pharma) at Rs 16.90, TC Tar (Unichem) at Rs 14.75 and Atorva (Zydus) at Rs 16.25.

Maintaining the price

Price maintenance is very difficult in the light of competition or increasing costs of operation. If the marketer fails to react to competition, it may result in losing market share and profit margins. However, price maintenance is considered desirable when:

- Market is value-conscious and not merely price-conscious.
- Competition is mild and will not hurt market share gains.
- Rebuilding market share is not a difficult task.

Marketers may adopt the following measures to justify their price maintenance strategy:

- Increase the quantity of product, such as offering "25 per cent extra at the same price" or "buy one, get another free"
- Offer improved product at the same price
- Improve the package design for the same price

The following indicate the possible responses of the price-maintenance marketer to the rising costs:

- Shrinking the amount of the product. It keeps the product within the reach of the consumer. He may learn to use it more frugally.
- Usage of less expensive ingredients.
- Reducing or removing some product features.
- Introducing different pack sizes such as family pack, economy pack and small pack.

In oligopolistic markets, price maintenance is effected by forming cartels. Quite often we hear about cement companies forming cartels. Sometimes, cartels may crack under the pressure of shrinking margins and market down trends.

PRICING BY RETAILERS

Retailers in rural areas can be classified into two types based on the place of their operation.

1. Retailers in feeder towns (semi-urban areas)
2. Retailers in villages

A comparative analysis of the retailer practices in urban, semi-urban and rural areas is made in Table 8.16. It highlights the fact that rural retailers sell small quantities of products, unpacked and loose, at different prices to different customers based on their knowledge, purchasing frequency (daily, weekly or monthly), and purchasing power (wage-goods earners, cash-wage earners, salary earners or farm-income earners) and purchasing mode (barter, credit or cash). They adopt a mark-up pricing policy for all the items that they sell. Their malpractices include adulteration, inaccurate weight and measures and selling fake goods in place of originals. Billing transactions are informal and in some cases, dishonest.

Retailers charge different unit prices from different customers when selling loose quantities. When it comes to branded, packaged goods they sell at the MRP quoted on packages. Promotion of sales by discounts (rebates) and other promotions are quite common. The recession has impacted sales and many companies have introduced several sales promotion measures. Box 8.9 highlights the advantage a consumer can gain during a recessionary period.

Table 8.16 Retailing Comparisons

Retailer	Products	Promotion	Role and influence	Price
Urban* (city or town)	Global and national brands, few local brands	Wide range, intensive	Informative and suggestive, helps identify alternatives	MRP, one price for all, selective discounts to a few, prices displayed, billing formal, no credit, credit cards accepted, selective credit to a few, packed to weights, no adulteration
Semi-urban (small towns) feeder points for villages	National and local brands, few global brands, many unbranded	Limited, mostly POP, discounts and incentive offers	Informative and persuasive, helps evaluate alternatives	MRP in case of branded products, prices of essential commodities are displayed but erratically, different prices offered to different customers based on volume of purchase and knowledge of buyer, loose sales, weights and measures are less accurate, adulteration done, mark-up on items for which prices are not fixed, selective credit policy, billing is less formal
Rural (village selling points)	Few national and global brands, mostly local and unbranded	Marginal, mostly point-of-purchase and road shows	Informative and decisive, helps decide purchase	Mark-up on all items, no display of prices, different prices to different customers based on customer knowledge and type of purchase (barter or cash), improper weights used, adulteration done, loose selling of items, mostly oral billing

* Excludes low-end retailers. Their practices are similar to retailers in semi-urban or village retailers.

Box 8.9 Drivers of Purchase During Recession

During recession, marketers face the herculean challenge of stimulating buying intentions and encouraging consumers to come out of the conservative hood. The marketing tasks, as such, aim at persuading consumers to maintain the current consumption levels, if not increase them, on the one hand and retaining brand loyalty on the other. Winning customers is not easy and it needs a lot of wooing. In addition to the "end-of-season sales" and "discounts up to 20 to 25 per cent," freebies and exchange offers are also employed by companies.

A consumer study conducted between December 2008 and January 2009 by Starcom MediaVest Group reveals that 70 per cent of the respondents from the upper socio-economic classes have started cutting down on big-ticket purchases and travel, while those from the lower income groups are skimping on food and beverages, mobiles, telecom spends and consumer durables. These strategies are not new, but the savings they promise are higher than usual. Says Harish Bijoor, CEO, Harish Bijoor Consulting Inc., "The discount phenomenon is likely to continue for another six months, with more price cuts and innovative offers. However, most promotions will only last till retailers manage to empty out their piled up inventories. Then there are schemes for easy buying."

In case of big-ticket purchases like gold, Tanishq's Golden Harvest scheme could help. If a consumer pays a fixed amount, between Rs 500 and Rs 5,000 for 11 months, the company will match that sum in the twelfth month. If one can persuade 10 members to join the scheme, a Titan watch is given free.

Source: Sushmitha Chowdary, "Money Today," available at www.sify.com.

PRICING AND PRODUCT LIFECYCLE

Pricing decisions are influenced by the stages of the product lifecycle—introduction, growth, maturity and decline.

Introduction

In the introductory stage, a company has two options—skimming pricing or penetration pricing. The choice is influenced by a host of factors as given in Table 8.11 discussed in the context of value-conscious pricing.

Skimming versus penetration pricing

Many companies at the time of introduction favour setting high prices to skim the cream off or set low prices to sweep the entire ground. Skimming price is preferred when high price is aimed to communicate the image of a superior product. Overtime, the skim price is lowered successively in steps so that the product may slide down the demand curve to pick up other price segments. Technology products such as mobile phones and their services started off at higher prices. In course of time, market expansion as well as technological and managerial innovations has led to a fall in the prices. Penetration is chosen when market is highly price sensitive, and a low price stimulates market growth. The product introduced at lower prices may be upgraded to offer premium quality product versions to high-income segments. The upgradation of Lifebuoy by HUL is a classic example of a product that penetrated rural market at a lower price. In course of time, it is upgraded and improved quality versions are offered to match the expectations of rural consumers.

Sometimes, marketers make mistakes in their choices. The classical case of P&G can be cited to drive home the point. Box 8.10 discuses the wrong moves of P&G.

Many durables like mobile handsets and services, air coolers, vacuum cleaners and TVs started with high prices and penetrated the market with lower prices. Products like Maggi Noodles, Vicks Vaporub and Rin detergent penetrated markets with introductory lower prices and later went up the price ladder.

Growth

In this stage, prices are mostly maintained at the same level. Changes may be initiated depending upon the competition and consumer response. Attracted by opportunities, competitors may enter the market. To mitigate competition, low-priced product marketers may consider introducing high-priced models to attract the premium segment while high-priced product marketers may launch low priced varieties.

Maturity

Price (brand) wars commence during the stage. Competitors will launch offensive attacks on the pioneer and the pioneer tries to retaliate and build markets by innovations and price-related promotions. One must be careful in employing sales promo tools that reduce prices. Such measures may hurt the quality image of the product.

Box 8.10 Failure of P&G's Gamble

The global strategy of P&G involves the identification of a large entrenched competitor and introducing a succession of products aimed at different segments with a view to take business away from it. When the major competitor becomes weak, P&G launches a brand against the major brand. When P&G entered the Indian detergent market in 1991, it launched "Ariel," a premium product, pitting it against Surf. The premium strategy was advocated by its CEO Durk Jager. He strongly believed that Indian consumers were on the lookout for a better product than Surf and would pay a high price. However, in this case its global strategy did not work in the Indian market.

True, P&G managed to pre-empt adversary Hindustan Unilever Limited to some extent, but it could not gain the expected market share. It became clear that P&G underestimated HUL's ability to react. HUL reacted with a premium variant of Surf—Surf Excel—to combat the entry of P&G's Ariel. Surf Excel surged ahead with 11 per cent market share relegating Ariel to the second position with a share of 8 per cent. Ariel launched two variants—Green and Blue and Surf Excel countered them with variants like Surf Excel Power and Excel with Power Boosters. Ariel then introduced variants like Super Soaker and Front O' Mat. Between 1998 and 2003, Ariel had nine variants in the Indian market while Surf had five.

The variants did not make much of an impact on the market. Understanding that the Indian consumer market is strong at the middle-income level, P&G took a different route by introducing Tide. Analysts are of the view that P&G floundered by launching Tide as a premium detergent at Rs 120 per kg, just Rs 35 lower than its super-premium sibling, Ariel.

Nikhil Vora, an FMCG analyst with ASK Raymond James, says, "The need of the hour was a value-for-money brand and not another premium brand but P&G did not take that into account."

Source: Shweta Jain and Gouri Shukla, "At Low Tide," *Business Standard*, 19 August 2003, available at www.business-standard.com/india/news/at-low-tide/157714/.

Decline

When sales show continuous decline, marketers have two options: (i) reengineering the brand as HUL did to Lifebuoy or (ii) terminating it by reducing prices and clearing the stocks.

Summary

Price decisions have become very important in the emerging competitive markets. A price represents the value of a product or service in either monetary or non-monetary terms. Price is the revenue generator of a firm, the purchase power index of consumers and allocator of scarce resources in an economy. Pricing objectives include profit maximization, target return, sales growth, market share growth, maintenance of sales volume or market share, survival and off setting and destroying competition. One may pursue one or more of the listed objectives simultaneously.

Pricing decisions are related to different situations such as product and market lifecycle stages, nature of consumers, nature of competition and geography of market. Pricing is influenced by several factors such as cost, demand, competition, product line, channel, marketing strategy of a firm, politico-legal conditions and the management's judgement. Pricing approaches are categorized into cost-based, competition-based and demand-based. Pricing methods under these three different categories make use of different cost concepts and require proper cost identification and measurement. The methods include cost-plus, mark-up, target return, pay-back period and experience curve. Competition-based pricing is done relying on the available nature of competition and response of competitors. Price-leader pricing, competitive pricing, going-rate pricing and sealed-bid pricing are the popular methods. Demand-based methods require estimation of demand. Price discrimination, perceived value, psychological and value pricing are the methods in this category.

Pricing strategy requires employment of methods of pricing to satisfy different market segments, effectively meet distribution needs and government policy considerations as well as challenge the competition successfully. Three market segments, the quality-conscious, the value-conscious and the price-conscious can be identified. The appropriate methods for the different segments are:

- Quality-conscious: Discriminatory, perceived value and psychological pricing,
- Value-conscious: Psychological value, penetration and skimming, and
- Price-conscious: Low prices, premium pricing (small units) and barter pricing.

When products are distributed over geographically dispersed areas, geographic pricing methods such as FOB mill, uniform delivered pricing, zone pricing and base-point pricing merit consideration. Five standard types of discounts are in practice to motivate distributors. They are volume, trade, payment terms, seasonal and promotional discounts. Government policies such as taxation or regulation may affect prices. Administrated prices are found in case of some agri-inputs and essential items.

To face the challenge of competition, companies may react or pro-act, initiating price changes. Competitive pricing policies include price rise, price maintenance or price cuts. Promotional pricing practices include special-event pricing, cash rebates, low-interest financing, longer payment terms, warranties and services, captive product offerings, product unbundling and two-part pricing at the company level and loss-leader and everyday low pricing at the retailer level.

Short Answer Questions

1. Explain the concept and significance of pricing.
2. Elaborate the objectives of pricing.
3. When do firms face pricing problems.
4. Explain the factors that influence the pricing decision process.
5. Do you find differences in the pricing strategy of products for the rural and urban markets?
6. "Pricing should be integrated with other components of marketing mix." Discuss.
7. What considerations are important in pricing high-quality soaps and TVs?
8. Identify the factors that influence pricing toothpastes and shampoos for mid-segment consumers.
9. State the pricing methods based on distribution.

10. How can price and promotion be integrated to promote sales?
11. Give examples of pricing changes influenced by environmental forces.
12. Give examples of price changes made by companies in retaliation to competitors' moves.
13. Enumerate the pricing approaches of retailers.

Discussion Questions

1. "Companies should not change prices frequently. Instead, they can use consumer promotion strategies to increase sales." Discuss.
2. Do you feel that the following firms are right in their choice of approaches to pricing?
   (a) Firm A, making an entry into the market adopts a demand-based approach.
   (b) Firm B, in a saturated market adopts a cost-based approach.
   (c) Firm C, in a growth market adopts a competition-based approach.

Essay Questions

1. Explain the significance of pricing in marketing. Identify the objectives and methods of pricing.
2. How do you price products for different rural market segments (quality-conscious, value-conscious and price conscious)?
3. Discuss the pricing strategies adopted by firms in relation to changes in economic environment and government policies.
4. What kind of competitive pricing strategies did you observe in the consumer market?

Internet Exercises

1. Prepare a report on the pricing strategies of select FMCG companies.
2. Prepare a report on the pricing strategies of select consumer durables companies.
3. Prepare a report on the pricing strategies of select service organizations.

Mini Projects

1. Visit a retail shop and find the price points at which different FMCGs are sold and the response of consumers.
2. Find out the promotional measures introduced by companies of consumer durables and FMCGs that enhance affordability of rural consumers.

End Notes

1. Pallavi Pengonda, "A New Tide," *DNA*, 3 December 2009, available at www.dnaindia.com/money/report_a-new-tide_1319399; Shailaja Sharma, "Heat on HUL: P&G Goes Mass with Detergents," *DNA*, 2 December 2009, available at www.dnaindia.com/money/report_heat-on-hul-p-and-g-goes-mass-with-detergents_1319000.
2. Shailaja Shama, "Godrej Will Focus on Fewer but Bigger Innovations," *DNA*, 7 November 2009, available at www.dnaindia.com/money/interview_godrej-will-focus-on-fewer-but-bigger-innovations_1308213.
3. "Monsoon: FMCG Firms Keep Fingers Crossed," 25 June 2009, available at http://business.rediff.com/report/2009/jun/25/monsoon-fmcg-firms-keep-fingers-crossed.htm.

Case 8.1 Nirma in Dilemma

Nirma Detergents was started by Karsanbhai Patel in 1969. He sensed an opportunity and launched the detergent powder (washing powder) at one-third the price of the competitors. Its mission statement was: "Better products, Better value and Better living." In no time, Nirma Detergent Powder (Nirma Washing Powder) became a household name and people, for whom using detergent powder was a distant dream, wasted no time in purchasing the trial pack. The Nirma Detergent Powder (Nirma Washing Powder) was phosphate-free and was also environment friendly. People liked the product greatly and soon, Nirma became a household name. Today, in terms of market penetration, Nirma is ranked number one in India in the detergent powder category. Nirma broke the myth that better-quality products are always the winners.

Nirma packs are available in 25 g, 400 g, 500 g and 1,000 g packs. The blue-coloured Nirma Detergent Powder (Nirma Washing Powder) that is spray-dried, was launched for the premium segment in 1996 and soon it became a hit. Nirma converted the non-user of detergent powder into a user and provided the customers with better value for money.

Nirma's success in the highly competitive soaps and detergents market was attributed to its brand promotion efforts that was complemented by its distribution, reach and market penetration. Nirma's network consisted of about 400 distributors and over 2 million retail outlets across the country. It offered attractive margins that were higher than the margins offered by competitors.

The 2009 Challenge

Nirma gave Hindustan Unilever Ltd's (HUL) Surf a run for its money in the 1980s. However, it is now battling a shrinking market share in its core business. According to market research agency AC Nielsen, Nirma's market share had dipped to 13.5 per cent in detergents and 6.74 per cent in soaps.

In the Rs 80 billion detergents segment, HUL is in a formidable leading position with a market share of 38 per cent and in the Rs 60 billion soaps category, Godrej Consumer Products Ltd (GCPL) is racing past Nirma with a market share of around 11 per cent.

Analysts attribute the failure of Nirma to its innovation inertia. For long, it has been competing on the platform of affordability while the local and multinational companies in the detergent and soaps market are building their strategies around the three values of viability, affordability and visibility.

According to Jagdeep Kapoor, chairman and managing director of Mumbai-based brand marketing consultancy firm Samsika Marketing Consultants Pvt. Ltd, consumers are shifting from economy brands to aspirational purchases as a consequence of their rising incomes and Nirma has failed to capitalize on this shift.

Analysts say Nirma's brand promotion efforts and pricing strategy have weakened over the past few years. The analysts point out that the firm has not raised its prices for some time despite the increase in prices of LAB (linear alkyl benzene, a key ingredient used in manufacturing detergents) and palm oil (another key ingredient in the manufacture of soap). They add that although Nirma's rivals have products across all price points to mitigate the input-cost effect, Nirma is available in only one plank—value for money.

Nirma needs to resolve this dilemma: Does it want to serve its original customer segment that still wants a cheap product and who may even be ready to compromise on quality; or does it want to move up serving the value-conscious customer, now being served by Hindustan Unilever, Proctor & Gamble or Wipro? If it is to continue to serve the cheap market, Nirma needs to leverage on two things: scale economies and low-cost operations. Nirma has accumulated enough learning to undertake low-cost operations. It has the advantage of backward integration and modern technology. What it needs is to build scale economies with a sharp focus on a limited range of complementary products.

Then Nirma's mission could be stated thus: "A big company dedicated to serving continually the daily needs of the small consumer."

For discussion

1. What, according to you, is Nirma's position in the current market situation?
2. Discuss the strategy to be adopted by Nirma.

Source: "Nirma Losing Froth in Soaps, Detergents Biz," 20 September 2007, available at www.livemint.com/2007/09/20014112/Nirma-losing-froth-in-soaps-d.html; Purushottam Kumar, "Nirma Detergent Powder," *Business & Economy*, 8 May 2008 available at http://ebiz16c.blogspot.com/2008/05/nirma-detergent-powder.html.

Case 8.2 Innovative Pricing Strategy of Idea Cellular

Idea Cellular of the Aditya Birla Group is a leading GSM mobile services operator in India with over 53 million subscribers, under the brand Idea. It is a front runner in introducing revolutionary tariff plans. It is known for its innovative, aggressive, customer friendly and competitive prepaid offerings that it introduced for the first time in India, in an increasingly segmented market. It has been offering affordable and world-class mobile services to varied segments of mobile users. Idea's tariff plans are designed to suit both the high-end users and the low-end, price sensitive consumers.

Spread

The Government of India has divided the telecommunications market for mobile services into 22 "service areas" that are categorized into "metro," Category "A," Category "B" and Category "C" service areas, based principally on a revenue generating potential of the areas. Idea, a pan-India operator, is present in 19 out of 22 telecom circles in the country and has over 47 million GSM mobile subscribers patronizing it.

Major Players

The cellular services market is crowded with three types of players as given under:

- State-owned companies (BSNL and MTNL)
- Private Indian-owned companies (Reliance Infocomm, Tata Teleservices, etc.)
- Foreign invested companies (Hutchison-Essar, Bharti Tele-Ventures, Escotel, Idea Cellular, BPL Mobile, Spice Communications, etc.)

The competition is tough, even though the market potential is unlimited.

Always First

Innovation is central to Idea's offers in terms of value-added services and prices.

- First to launch music messaging with "Cellular Jockey," "Background Tones," "Group Talk," a voice portal with "Say Idea" and a complete suite of mobile e-mail services.
- First in introducing revolutionary tariff plans, with "Super Power," 2 minutes outgoing free and lifelong offer.
- First offer of a loyalty programme, Lifetime Idea, for prepaid customers.
- First in segmented offerings like women's card.

M. D. Prasad, circle head, Bihar and Jharkhand, Idea Cellular, observed that Idea has many firsts in offering world class and affordable telephony services to mobile consumers. Now with the new plans, Idea will redefine the cellular services marketing principles.

New Plan

Two new plans were launched by Idea Cellular to achieve penetration into the saturated Bihar and Jharkhand GSM mobile service subscribers markets. The first one is "pay per second plan", dubbed as "Super Seconds", for all local and STD calls. The existing Idea subscribers have to purchase a special voucher priced at Rs 8, whereas new subscribers have to pay Rs 14. The second one is "Super Saral" which offers customers local call rates of just 40 paise per minute and STD at 60 paise per minute on any other mobile and landline network in the country. For availing this benefit, existing Idea prepaid subscribers can purchase a special voucher priced at Rs 12 and new subscribers can get it for Rs 18.

For discussion

1. Explain the rationale of the innovative price strategy of Idea Cellular.
2. What should be the reaction of competitors, from your point of view?

Source: Sanjay Bafna, "Idea Cellular Launches 1 Paisa per Second in Bihar—Jharkhand," Telecom Talk, 12 October 2009, available at http://telecomtalk.info/idea-cellular-launches-1-paisa-per-second-in-bihar-jharkhand/10983/.

9

Distribution Strategy

LEARNING OBJECTIVES

Upon completion of this chapter, you will be able to:

- Understand distribution from the availability point of view
- Know the distribution practices of leading companies
- Recognize the trends in distribution and rural logistics
- Discuss the coverage decision and the role of geographic information systems (GIS)
- Explain the direct and indirect channels of rural distribution

After decades of hunting for fortunes abroad, India's pharmaceutical companies now plan to strike gold in their own backyards. Large players such as Ranbaxy, Dr Reddy's Laboratories and Piramal Healthcare are all headed to rural India to boost their revenues. The two triggers for this newfound rural thrust are the rising expenditure on public health by the government and the success of smaller rivals such as Mankind Pharma in the hinterland. It is reported that over 60 per cent of the country's total drug sales (Rs 385.72 billion, MAT or moving annual total) take place in metros and big cities.

In order to become the market leader, Ranbaxy wants to reach down to the "last village" in the next five years. Cipla, the current market leader, is increasing its presence with such product categories as pain killers, antibiotics and syrups. Dr Reddy's has set up a rural marketing division, Indura, and a special field force to cater to select rural markets in a few states. Their focus is on scientific education. They want to use innovative marketing tools to address the patients and doctors in rural India. "We began targeting a few states with a contractual field force and now, we are beginning to see good traction in this segment of our business," said Dr Reddy's chief operating officer, Satish Reddy.

Piramal, which has the country's biggest sales force, is increasing its rural presence by adding more field staff.

Pfizer, Merck and Ipca have followed the same route. Most of these marketing personnel only get commission. "The model works well as companies do not incur any additional cost," said Ranjit Kapadia of HDFC Securities.

Analysts said that in the rural market, companies are pushing OTC (over the counter) drugs that can be sold without prescription. "Even in the case of prescription drugs, the rural markets are driven by chemists who act as prescribers in the absence of qualified doctors. The medicines that gain the most are nutraceuticals, vitamins, pain relievers and cough syrups," Kapadia added.[1]

The enthusiastic marketing exercises of pharmaceutical companies in the rural hinterland are an indication of the ongoing revolution in distribution and retailing in rural areas. Executives who are considering a foray into rural distribution have nothing to deter them as there is rich information about the experiences of various companies engaged in the marketing of FMCGs, consumer durables, and agri-inputs. This chapter discusses the perceived problems in the distribution of products to rural consumers, identifies the traditional approaches and presents newer alternatives to reach rural India.

INTRODUCTION

Distribution is central to the success of a rural marketing strategy. Customized and affordable products, effective distribution and focused marketing initiatives are essential factors in building credibility for a brand in rural India. Several changes have taken place making decisions on logistics and channel design much easier to take than before. The availability of information and communication technology driven by communication tools like telephones and the Internet is one reason for the change. The emancipated people who can become retailers or a part of a sales force have made distribution management an enlightened task.

DISTRIBUTION—THE AVAILABILITY CHALLENGE

The major challenge faced by marketers involves supplying products of right quality in enough quantities to meet the needs of customers. India's 650,000 villages are spread over 3.2 million sq. km and 700 million Indians live in rural areas. Finding them is not easy. However, many companies are venturing into rural markets because they have become attractive showing growing demand as discussed in Box 9.1.

Box 9.1 Growing Rural Demand

Here are some estimates of growth in demand. In a paper on "Future of FMCG Products in India," ASSOCHAM projected that by 2012 the demand will touch a level of about Rs 1,233.6391 billion with a Compound Annual Growth Rate (CAGR) of 12 per cent. Approximately, 60 per cent of it will be consumed by folks living in rural and semi-urban areas of the country. This works out to be Rs 740.1835 billion. FMCG products such as toothpastes, skin and hair wash, talcum powders, branded *attas*, dish wash, instant coffees, R&G coffees, ketchups, deodorants, jams, etc. that currently have less than 30 per cent penetration in rural and semi-urban areas, will grow by at least 50 per cent in the next 5–7 years. The report observed that the trend remained almost similar for TV sets and other consumer and electrical appliances. The importance of the rural market for some FMCG and durable marketers is underlined by the fact that the rural market accounts for half the total market for TV sets, fans, pressure cookers, bicycles, washing soaps, blades, teas, salts and toothpowders. The rural market of FMCG products is growing much faster than its urban counterpart.

Source: "Rural and Semi-urban Segments Likely to Capture 60% of FMCG Demand," 24 December 2006, available at www.assocham.org/prels/shownews.php?id=847.

However, the enthusiasm of marketers evaporated when they found that there are several hurdles in reaching the far-flung consumers in the rural hinterland. The impediments in reaching rural customers are as follows:

- Long distances between villages,
- Lack of *pucca* roads connecting villages to nearest townships,
- Lack of adequate transport facilities,
- Lack of proper retail outlets, and
- Lack of mass media infrastructure.

In view these problems, marketers have remained contented by focusing only on corridor villages. However, enterprising companies such as HUL, Colgate, ITC, Coca-Cola, Pepsi and many agri-input companies have forayed into the rural markets and met the availability challenge successfully. Meanwhile, some of the reach problems are solved by government expenditures on roads and Information and Communication Technology (ICT) applications in rural areas. This has prompted many companies to lay more emphasis on rural markets. For instance, the automobile market in rural areas, that till now had been largely restricted to tractors and two-wheelers, is opening up for passenger cars. According to reports, the two-wheeler penetration in villages has been only 10 per cent as compared to 25 per cent in urban areas. The need for high investment, poor conditions of rural roads, lack of finance facilities and lack of service networks have limited the scope of passenger cars in the countryside. However, in recent times we are witnessing a shift in trend as the auto companies are gearing up to explore the huge market potential of the rural areas (see Box 9.2).

Enthused by growing opportunities and improved logistics, many companies such as Exide that have already made a dent in the rural markets are expanding their distribution. Box 9.3 describes the initiatives of Exide.

Box 9.2 Availability of Automobiles

Bajaj Auto is adding value to its existing products and launching new products with a focus on rural markets. Products such as the 100 cc Discover DTS-Si could well attract the attention of prospective buyers in rural areas. Bajaj Auto is setting up 20 outlets in affluent, but severely under penetrated, rural districts. Moreover, it has created specialist dealerships for rural markets called "rural dealerships."

Hero Honda replaced its dealer-driven, decentralized rural marketing with a centralized, company-driven one by setting up a rural vertical. "This includes a 500-strong sales force on the full-time rolls of our dealers to target rural sales specifically," points out Anil Dua, senior vice president, marketing, sales and customer care, Hero Honda.

Maruti Suzuki India generates 10 per cent of its domestic sales from rural sales, numbering 32,000 cars. Maruti has launched its marketing campaign for rural India called "*Ghar Ghar Mein Maruti*" (Maruti in every household).

Source: "Bajaj Auto Targets Growth in Motorcycle Market," *Business Standard*, 18 July 2009, available at www.business-standard.com/india/news/bajaj-auto-targets-growth-in-motorcycle-market/68161/on.

Box 9.3 Exide Initiative—Project *Kisan*

Exide Industries hopes to sell 250,000 batteries for tractors in 2009–2010, up from 170,000 and increase its current market share of 14 per cent to 25 per cent in two years. Under Project *Kisan*, Exide is trying to reach out to farmers through dealers. The company now has 2,800 dealers across 14 states such as Punjab, Haryana, Uttar Pradesh, Tamil Nadu and Andhra Pradesh where the tractor population is very high. This year, around 800–900 dealers will be added to the existing base of 2,800 dealers in the rural areas. The company's turnover from tractor battery sales is Rs 1 billion annually.

Source: "Exide Expects Jump in Battery Sales this Fiscal," 11 November 2009, available at www.thaindian.com/newsportal/business/exide-expects-jump-in-battery-sales-this-fiscal_100273238.html#ixzz0iIIoV2Jl.

DISTRIBUTION PRACTICES

Marketing strategies were recast for the rural areas and rustics were lapping up Pantene, Whisper, Ponds cold cream and Good Knight products that were available virtually at their doorsteps. However, the fact remains that the options available to the rural consumer are nowhere near what they are in the urban supermarkets. For obvious reasons, it is physically impossible for a company to cover all the three million outlets in the country. At best a company can cover about 0.7 million outlets and that is barely around 20 per cent of the rural market. The rest of the market is served by retailers who buy the products from the urban markets. We will now examine how different companies are distributing their products and services in the rural markets.

Distribution practices of FMCG companies

The distribution strengths of three FMCG majors are given in Table 9.1.

Colgate–Palmolive

Colgate's distribution strategy is a three-pillar one:

- Physical distribution reach and the width and depth of it
- Customer marketing approach
- Modernization of sales operations and enhancement of sales efficiencies

Colgate tries to make its presence felt heavily in *haats* and *shandies*, as it finds these to be ideal locations to carry out promotions. Colgate sells products to about 850,000 outlets directly. The approach is

Table 9.1 Distribution Strengths of Three FMCG Majors

Particulars	HUL	Colgate	Britannia
Retail outlets/services	1,000,000	250,000	400,000
Cities/Towns/Villages	50,000	20,000	2,200
Distributors	7,500	2,000	2,500
Rural turnover	50 per cent	35 per cent	30 per cent

one where everyone involved in distribution is treated as a customer who must be kept satisfied. Each stockist, for example, is part of Colgate's incentive plan, such as the "Colgate *Dil Se*" plan for wholesalers. The driving philosophy of Colgate is that a stockist should earn at least twice the return that he gets from a bank deposit since he is investing in Colgate's business. Retail margins vary by product category.

In an effort to modernize its sales operations, Colgate has automated its information system linked to stockists. This helps track market data on a real-time basis and gives a better feel of the market pulse. As it is, it takes about two weeks to move stocks from the factory to the deepest rural retail outlet. Products move from the factory to a central warehouse in each state and then to the stockists, who in turn distribute the stock to retail outlets by vans. Since stockists are Colgate's re-distributors, it's easy to track demand by watching their numbers. The company bases its monthly forecasting on this. Once the entire system is automated, it could be reduced to a week.

Emami

Emami initiated a new level of distribution to increase penetration in rural areas. It has introduced new super-stockist networks for rural coverage, with a special focus on West Bengal, Andhra Pradesh, Uttar Pradesh and Maharashtra. The van operations model has also been introduced to make the products reach remote villages.

Godrej

Godrej Consumer Products (GCPL) Rural initiated a project "*Dharti*" to cover close to 17,000 villages this year and 50,000 villages soon. Consequently, the 4,000 sub-stockists present in rural areas would be more than doubled.

Newspapers are sold using auto-drivers and boat-drivers in Kerala.

BPCL introduced specially designed rural marketing vehicles that move from village to village to fill cylinders on the spot.

Distribution practices of automobile companies

Maruti

Taking forward its successful portfolio of small cars in rural India, Maruti Suzuki is planning to double its outlets in the next two years from 231 to more than 450. This will take the overall figure of outlets in the country to almost 1,000 from the current 680 odd dealerships.

The distribution network in rural India will account for approximately 50 per cent of Maruti Suzuki's network. At present, the company is eyeing its mid-term plan of generating sales of 0.23 million cars in a year from rural India.

Maruti set up an exclusive rural marketing department that has given employment to more than 15,000 people and more than 2,500 rural development sales executives are channelizing the marketing efforts. Maruti is planning to come up with special schemes and initiatives that include tie-ups with *panchayat* members, sponsoring *kabaddi* tournaments and sales fairs.[2]

Bajaj Auto

The company restructured its marketing and distribution network to cater to the different needs of the rural and urban customer in terms of product, infrastructure, working capital, financing, and servicing. According to the new strategy, Bajaj will have four dealer channels. While Probiking will retail the 180 cc plus high-end motorcycles, there will be a series of urban two-wheeler dealers and rural two-wheeler dealers. Three-wheeler dealerships will be the fourth dealership network. The specialist dealerships for rural markets are called "rural dealerships". Currently, Bajaj has over 1,300 service dealers across the country and 1,250 rural outlets. Bajaj set up 20 outlets in affluent, but severely underpenetrated, rural districts. Bajaj wishes to train the sons and daughters of village VIPs, who are also the opinion makers of their respective villages and who can influence the thoughts and decisions of others. Bajaj Auto opted for a self-help group (SHG) model to focus on the rural markets. The move is a bid to double the market share in the value segment of the two-wheeler market from 15 per cent to 30 per cent. As part of its rural focus, Bajaj Auto is also talking to NABARD where the latter will provide names of successful individuals who have performed well under the *Swarnajayanti Gram Swayam Rozgar Yojana*—a scheme for self-employment in rural areas. The company plans to set up over 1,000 service centres through these individuals in the rural belt. The company currently has over 4,000 service centres.[3]

Mahindra and Mahindra

Customization alone meets crop-specific requirements and caters to the diverse farming belts. In a bid to promote customization of tractors, M&M is setting up a string of satellite units that would take up "distributed manufacturing" in line with local demand. The satellite units that would eventually cover the major farming belts are being set up with an investment of Rs 0.04 to 0.06 billion each and would be able to roll out around 500 tractors a month. They would enable farmers to get factory-fresh tractors that would be customized in line with the local requirements. With the satellite units, the company has a target of being present in at least 10 agricultural belts in the near future. Over the years, it proposes to have different types of tractors to suit the cultivation of all types of crops.

Distribution practices of agri-input companies

Rallis

It has one of the most extensive distribution networks in the Indian agro-industry. The network is spread across the country consisting of over 4,000 distributors and a sales force of approximately 0.2 million with over 80 per cent penetration of the country's districts. The eight regional offices, 28 area sales offices and 24 depots are manned by highly experienced sales managers, field officers and field assistants.

It has been leveraging on this strength with initiatives such as the Rallis *Kisan Kendras*—one-stop-shops for agricultural inputs—that provide counsel to farmers on good farming practices. The company provides farm management services to benefit farmers by offering a customized package of practices suited to their land and environment. The company has set up Pesticides Efficacy Advisory Centres (PEACE) in various agro-climatic zones of the country with the objective of spreading farm education among farmers and advising them on current developments in farming practices to increase farm productivity. Trained Farmer's Promotional Assistants (TFPA) are appointed to educate farmers and promote sales of products.

Tata Chemicals

TataChem has set up Tata *Kisan Kendra* (TKK), a centre which offers farmers agri-products as well as agri-solutions. In order to know more about the farmers and their farm characteristics and needs, TKK has profiled farmers and their farms through digitized field maps. It created a Geographic Information System (GIS) that uses satellite images and field maps and helps analyse relevant information such as weather, ground water and soil characteristics on a real-time basis. TataChem organizes soil surveys to obtain complete and clear understanding. It has created a fertility grid of the villages by synthesising the information. The grid indicates the points of deficiencies, allows for better forecasting of pest attacks and provides the exact status of a crop. As a result, a pest attack can be anticipated in advance and arrested.

Distribution practices of consumer electronics companies

- Videocon will launch around 18 models of LCDs, 17 models of refrigerators and nine automatic washing machines. The consumer durables firm is planning to open most of its exclusive retail stores at the regional level to reach out to the rural markets.
- LG has set up 45 area offices and 59 rural/remote area offices.
- Samsung rolled out its "Dream Home" road show that was to visit 48 towns in 100 days in an effort to increase brand awareness of its products.

Distribution practices of mobile services companies

Airtel and Samsung tied up with IFFCO, the world's largest farmer's co-operative, to sell their mobiles and services. IFFCO has about 37,000 member units spanning all over India. Some of the other telecom giants and DTH service providers are looking at using the now almost defunct PCOs as a channel of distribution.

Distribution practices of financial services companies

Almost all banks are using an agent-based model as the typical branch-based model does not work in rural areas due to cost economics. Some of these banks, including ICICI, are looking at tying up with micro-finance institutions and local self-help groups (or creating them if they do not exist already). Many banks have solutions for mobile-based services to reach rural consumers directly. ICICI has gone further in tying up with large corporate majors that have significant presence in rural India and that provide loans/banking services to their distributors/traders. It is also working in tandem with the postal department.

Distribution practices of hospitals

Advances in telemedicine technology has brought improved medical care to villagers. ISRO, Narayana Hrudayalaya, SRMC-Chennai, AIMS-Kochi, Apollo Hospitals, Aravind Eye Hospital, etc. have championed the telemedicine system using VSAT, Wi-Fi, broadband, etc.

Distribution practices of pharma companies

Nicholas Piramal has focused on general practitioners to cater to rural markets to increase its penetration with a field force of 800 people. Most of the pharma companies are looking at post offices as their distribution platform. Some of these companies conduct health-care workshops in the rural areas by tapping the local doctors.

DISTRIBUTION TRENDS

The market trends that have engineered silent but stunning changes in rural distribution are examined below:

Emergence of new customer groups

More and more price-conscious consumers are demanding the best value for the money they spend on the products they buy. They are now brand conscious and looking for exposure, explanation and experience. The addition of the youth and women to the rural market as the active, decisive forces has brought about a sea change in the shopping habits and preferences.

High media exposure

The presence of a highly active media is both a boon and bane for marketers. Brands can be built overnight and can be also demolished in much less time. The penetration of TVs, cable and satellite (C&S) systems, Direct-to-home (DTH) facility, mobiles and corporate media like vans are responsible for the information-rich consumerism in rural areas.

IT revolution

The emergence of the Internet has revolutionized marketing, changing the rules of the game. Portals themselves are becoming brands. Mass customization—one-to-one marketing—is becoming a reality. Why would one need to endure the noise of TV ads when one can go on a virtual commercial tour?

ITC e-*choupals*, I-*shakti* of HUL, *Kisan Kendras*, in addition to Internet kiosks of entrepreneurs, have opened up new windows for information-seeking villagers.

Consumer as seller

A recent trend ushered in by HUL is the engagement of women in rural areas as channel participants. Earlier, Amway had introduced network marketing in which consumers acted as dealers. However, HUL's Project *Shakti* is radically different from that. It is not just a business model like network marketing but a model that aims at the emancipation and empowerment of women.

In response to the market trends, the changes that have taken place in distribution are also baffling but, exciting. They are baffling because they removed time and place barriers for consumers by making products available anywhere and at anytime. At the same time they are exciting because product customization has enhanced the freedom of making choices and purchase activity has become an edutaining and an experiential exercise. Table 9.2 presents the changes in the various elements of distribution.

In view of the changes in distribution patterns, marketers can find many alternative options to make a final decision. Table 9.3 portrays the decision questions that have to be considered such as selling where, when, to who, what and why and the available alternatives. A look at the emergent distribution approaches in practice indicates that the decision maker is also at an advantage. This advantage is intelligently and competitively utilized by some direct marketing companies like Amway to set up network marketing and HUL and ITC in creating public–private–participation (PPP) models that involve consumers in distribution.

Overview of distribution issues and participants

There are four important aspects in distribution networks and several participants as explained in the following section.

Rural logistics

The means of transport include existing ones like animals (bullocks, horses, donkeys, yaks, and zebras and carts driven by them), boats, cycles, motor vehicles, tractors, light commercial vehicles, mini-lorries and vans).

Table 9.2 Changes in Distribution

Element of sales	From	To
Time	Restricted, limited timings	Unrestricted, anytime
Place	Own retail outlets, occasionally public places like exhibitions	Anywhere
Choice	Limited to brands	Any product, in any specification, unlimited
Sales	Products	Products Experiences Relationships Achievements
Result	Customer satisfaction	Customer Participation and satisfaction

Table 9.3 Distribution-decision Perspectives

1.	Selling from where?	
	Home or work place	Door-to-door selling, mobile vans, mail-order selling, tele-marketing
	Commercial places	Industrial exhibitions, *haats*, *shandies*, fairs/*melas*
	Own place	Malls, super markets, showrooms/galleries, provision/fancy/*kirana* shops, medical stores, *paan* shops, co-operative stores, petrol bunks, NGOs
	Anywhere	Internet selling
2.	Selling when?	Limited timings, anytime
3.	Selling to whom?	Company or its agents, syndicates, consumers
4.	Selling what?	Products and services
		Experiences
		Relationships
		Achievements
		Convenience
5.	Selling why?	Profit
		Images
		Business equity

People involved

Sales persons, social workers, rural people (village heads, part-time business people and consumers (HUL's *Shakti Ammas*) are involved in distribution. In rural markets, a new breed of consumers is emerging. A consumer is the insurance agent, the intermediary for a financial product and equally the person who acts as an intermediary distributor of a detergent or a cake of soap. This channel, uniquely, is not restricted to the efforts of the multi-level channel marketers like Amway but, is equally involved in selling products and services as a distributor using a direct mode of distribution. Another channel is self-help groups, which are becoming micro-entrepreneurs assisted by corporations and micro-finance agencies.

Retail outlets

The traditional and innovative models are as given under:

- *Traditional selling points:* Retailers, co-operatives, *mandis*, *haats* and *melas.*
- *Modern outlets:* Fair-prices shops (now becoming malls), NGOs, post offices, *anganwadis*, entrepreneur's outlets and corporate rural malls.

IT-based initiatives

ITC e-*choupal*, i-*shakti*, etc. are examples of IT-based initiatives of companies. Marketers are going on an innovation spree in overcoming the hurdles of distribution. While state governments are expanding fair-price shops to create malls, private entrepreneurs are venturing out to start modernized retail outlets.

RURAL LOGISTICS

Logistics is the organized process of managing the flow of merchandize from the source of supply to the consumers. Thus, it incorporates the following functions:

- Physically moving the goods from one location to another, where location is a distribution centre, warehouse, store or manufacturer.
- Stocking the goods at the location needed in the quantities required.

Good logistics cuts costs, speeds work and improves customer service. A logistics system must be built according to the needs of an enterprise, depending on the nature of products and distances to be moved. Fashion retailers may need to focus on speed while discount retailers on cost.

The Indian logistics industry is characterized by the dominance of a disorganized market. There are numerous transporters with three or four trucks. The freight-forward segment is represented by thousands of small custom brokers and "clearing and forwarding" agents. As a result of the underdeveloped trade and logistics infrastructure, the logistics cost of the Indian economy is over 13 per cent of GDP, compared to less than 10 per cent GDP in almost the entire Western Europe and North America. We need to have a logistics model that reaches out to the potential in rural India, a model that delivers goods and services in a cost-effective manner. This was the theme of the summit on "*Logistics* for Global Competitive Advantage and *Rural* Growth" held at Indian School of Business, Hyderabad (December 5–6, 2006) (see Box 9.4).

A logistics strategy can be either a push or pull strategy. A push strategy has merchandize allocated to stores based on historical demand, the inventory position of the store and the warehouse. The pull strategy has orders for merchandize being generated at the store level, on the basis of demand data captured at point of sales (POS) terminals.

The method of handling logistics largely depends on the nature of product category, the number of outlets and their location. Most FMCG companies employ the "hub-and-spoke system". Whatever may be the system, the distribution centre is a key element that serves several functions, from co-ordinating in-bound transportation, receiving, checking, storing and cross docking to co-ordinating outbound transportation.

Hub-and-spoke distribution model or network

It is a system of connections arranged like a chariot wheel in which all traffic moves along spokes connected to the hub at the centre. A spoke is one of a number of rods radiating from the centre of a wheel (the hub where the axle connects), connecting the hub with the round traction surface.

Tata Motors is using the hub-and-spoke model for the Tata Nano. As per this model, the company's dealers (hubs) in the city will be responsible for maintaining touch points through spokes in

Box 9.4 Rural Logistics on Development Path

Logistics can play a key role in integrating rural and urban India, contributing to employment creation and income generation. Sunil K. Munjal, MD, Hero Corporate Service Ltd, outlined the initiatives launched by Hero Mindmine Institute and the Confederation of Indian Industry (CII) to set up rural business hubs with public–private and *panchayat* (village council) partnership and pointed out that 50 agreements had already been signed in this regard and 100 more were in the pipeline. Logistics players are now seeking ways to address this issue as potential worth about USD 100 million is latent in the rural parts of the country, according to Professor Viswanadham, executive director of the Centre for Global Logistics and Manufacturing Strategies (GLAMS). There is excitement in the Indian logistics and supply chain market, and the effort is also now directed at spotting entrepreneurs who could make a difference to this growing sector.

Source: "V. Rishi Kumar, "Logistics, Supply Chain in Rural Areas Could be Next Big Opportunity," *The Hindu Business Line*, 02 December 2006, available at www.thehindubusinessline.com/bline/2006/12/02/stories/2006120201750500.htm

Box 9.5 Godrej Agrovet Designs Hub-and-Spoke Model

Kick-starting the "Godrej *Aadhaar*" initiative with a 1,000 sq. feet store and a handful of services in December 2004, Godrej Agrovet Ltd is now keen on widening its rural retailing venture in a big way. Within a year of its launch, the "Godrej *Aadhaar*" brand, which is worth Rs 0.02 billion, has grown to become a chain of 18 centres that are operational in Maharashtra, Gujarat, Punjab, Haryana, Tamil Nadu, Andhra Pradesh, besides a few others in Orissa and West Bengal.

Diversified product portfolio: Positioned as a complete solutions provider for the Indian farmers, Godrej *Aadhaar* centres offer professional guidance with an objective to improve productivity, bring higher returns and improve cost–benefit ratio. The services offered range from crop advisory services, soil- and water-testing services, buyback of output, crop finance, supply of agri-inputs and animal feeds, transfer of information (weather, price and demand supply), door delivery of products, etc. In its effort to cater to the complete requirement of the rural household, the last few months have seen the centres diversifying to offer a number of other product categories like durables, FMCG, apparels, footwear, etc. These products are offered through exclusive tie-ups with various companies. According to R. S. Vijan, executive vice-president of Godrej Agrovet Ltd, close to 100 brands are currently associated with the Godrej *Aadhaar* centres and a host of them will be partnering soon.

Hub-and-spoke network: Moving away from the standalone format, the company decided to focus mainly on the hub-and-spoke model to expand further. Explaining the choice of the model, Vijan said, "Now that the brand has made its mark with the target market, the hub-and-spoke model looks to be the obvious option to take this initiative to its next level." In all, the company is targeting 1,000 Godrej *Aadhaar* centres in the next five to eight years and every hub centre will have a minimum of five spoke centres. Targeting a turnover of between Rs 35 and Rs 40 billion in the said period, the company will mainly focus on the northern and western regions to launch these centres.

The company currently has two distribution centres in Maharashtra. Godrej Agrovet will spruce up its distribution centres to effectively service the new centres. The size of a hub store will be around 10,000 sq. feet and the spoke centres will be spread across 3,000 sq. feet. The hub centres are expected to generate Rs 0.04 billion per annum. The spoke centres will generate an annual turnover of between Rs 0.015 billion and Rs 0.02 billion. Around 250 hubs have been planned. Setting up each hub will require an investment of Rs 0.01 billion while it will be between Rs 5 million and Rs 6 million per spoke centre.

Source: Ashish K. Tiwari, "Godrej Aadhaar Is All Set to Take the Hub-and-Spoke Route," December 2005, available at www.dnaindia.com/money/report_godrej-aadhaar-is-all-set-to-take-the-hub-and-spoke-route_1003998.

the hinterland. This model is generally used by two-wheeler companies (like Baja Auto). Since, Nano too is targeting people using two-wheelers; this model will be beneficial for it. This model will ensure a deeper market penetration by Tata Motors. Box 9.5 explains how Godrej Agrovet has designed its hub-and-spoke model.

Box 9.6 throws light on Coco-Cola's distribution model.

Box 9.6 Coca-Cola's Distribution Model

Coca-Cola India has recently modified its distribution chain by shifting from a centralized model to a three-tier hub-and-spoke model. It invested in glass bottles and new vehicles in consonance with the three-tier distribution structure. Large trucks were used to move stocks from the bottling plant to the hubs, medium commercial vehicles were used to move stock from the hub to the spokes and after that auto rickshaws and cycles were used to cater to the requirements of rural markets. "We also modified the use of our returnable glass bottles to meet the demands of the hub-and-spoke model," says a company official. In the centralized model used in urban areas, Coke bottles are moved directly from the plant to retail outlets.

According to industry sources, in the upcountry areas, the responsibility for distribution is shifted to the distributor, based in his territory. These small distributors have their own low-cost means of getting the product to each nook and corner. The stock is transported to the spokes using all types of transport vehicles: cycle, rickshaw, autorickshaw, handcart, camel cart, etc. This is an advantage for Coke because the small distributor has to bear the cost of distribution—earlier the responsibility of the company. While the long-term benefits of penetration accrue to the company, the costs remain less. The companies also use annual *haats* and village fairs to popularize their products. Further, the smaller 200 ml bottles help the company increase sales volumes. "Thanks to larger loads, savings in distribution expenses and a lower price point, the whole [Coke] proposition is very attractive," says an industry source.

Source: Anil G. Jacob, "Picking Rural Pockets," *Business Standard*, 22 April 2003.

The efficacy of the model

The model has its own merits and drawbacks as given under.

Merits

The benefits of the system are economy and efficiency.

- *Transport economies*: The well-defined routes leads to optimal use of transportation resources in terms of loads, costs and time taken to reach the destination.
- *Simplified operations:* Complicated operations like packaging, storing and accounting can be carried out at the hub, rather than at every node.
- *Easy to expand:* Spokes are simple and new ones can be created easily.
- *Customer satisfaction:* For customers, waiting time is reduced and also made predictable. Scheduling is convenient since there are few routes with frequent service.

Demerits

The major drawbacks are inflexibility and unexpected delays.

- *Inflexibility*: Centralization of day-to-day operations may lead to inflexibility. Total cargo capacity of the network is limited by the hub's capacity. Changes at the hub, or even in a single route, could have unexpected consequences throughout the network.
- *Long journeys:* Cargo must pass through the hub before reaching its destination requiring longer journeys than direct point-to-point trips.

- *Unexpected delays:* Delays at the hub (caused, for example, by bad weather conditions) can result in delays throughout the network. Delays at a spoke (for example, because of the mechanical problems of a cargo carrier) can also affect the network.

Of course, the drawbacks can be overcome by efficient management. Route scheduling is challenging for a network operator. Resources must be used carefully to avoid starving the hub. Careful traffic analysis and precise timing are required to keep the hub operating efficiently.

According to Dinesh Malhotra, general manager of Linterland (rural arm of Lintas), the hub-and-spoke model of distribution is the future. As he explains, "We successfully adopted the hub-and-spoke model for Dabur India and it has worked very well. Here, feeder towns, primarily on the highways, serve as hubs where companies can rent a warehouse and stock their products. Spokes comprise 'cyclist salesmen' who then distribute products to small retail outlets in nearby rural pockets."

However, HUL has a different point of view. The challenge for HUL now, is to take its products to towns with a smaller population—under 2,000 people. HUL's conventional hub-and-spoke distribution model, used to great effect in both urban and semi-urban markets, wouldn't be cost-effective in penetrating the smaller villages. Now, with this new distribution model, the smaller markets are now being referred to as "*Shakti* markets."[4]

RURAL COVERAGE DECISION

Differential development of infrastructure, divergent geo-climatic conditions and variations in locational density of village settlements preclude the application of a uniform approach across rural markets. Therefore, the process of coverage decisions involves consideration of the following questions.

- Which villages are similar and are in close proximity?
- What are the distances between villages?
- What kind of terrain it is (plain land, island or hilly area)?
- What are the modes of transport available (road or water)?
- What type of transportation means are available—mechanized vehicles (such as tractors, auto-rickshaws, LCVs and lorries), human driven (like bicycles, three-wheeler rickshaws and handcarts), animal pulled (bullock carts and horse carriages), humans or animals (donkeys, horses and mules)?

Pockets of similarity need to be identified and strategies are to be developed in consonance with individual pockets. Further refinements would be necessitated by local conditions.

An example of a unique solution to a unique condition is the case of Brooke Bond. The company has used itinerant traders who transport their wares to interior hill markets on mules for the distribution of TataChaap packaged tea to rural consumers in Gushwal, Kumaon.

Direct distribution to village settlements with less-than-specific population or number of retail outlets would not be viable. Yet, for future payoffs, systematized distribution efforts are imperative to consolidate brand shares and monitor product movement in a high-growth market segment. Box 9.7 presents a case for analysis.

GEOGRAPHIC INFORMATION SYSTEMS FOR PLANNING RURAL COVERAGE

Geographic Information Systems (GIS) help companies that are trying to identify uncovered markets. Conventional database management software can only answer statistical questions like how many potential customers are out there and which territory has the highest growth. GIS applications, in contrast, can relate all this information geographically. It also allows the user to spatially visualize data thus, revealing hidden relationships, patterns and trends. For example, GIS can answer queries like which locations in the *mandal* are suitable for locating a particular retail outlet? What route should

Box 9.7 Coverage Problem

Rajpuria Hudan is a small village near Lunkaranser in Bikaner district, Rajasthan. Parshu Ram Rathore owns the largest among a total of three retailer outlets in this village. Receiving a 15-day credit line, he purchases stocks on a fortnightly basis from one of the larger shopkeepers of Lunkaranser. He has been doing so for the past three decades. There are no telephones in the proximity of the village. Public transport is limited to a bus rendezvous twice a day at the metalled road head, about 1 km from the village. A marketer aiming to extend distribution to rural Bikaner, or Rajpuria Hudan, might be confronted by the following issues:

- With just three retailers, does Rajpuria Hudan merit direct coverage at all?
- What would the mode of coverage be? Access constraints with low-volume expectations indicate a single visit covering order booking, delivery and collections—a delivery van with sales personnel.
- If the product has an end consumer price of Rs 4 with a net margin to the marketer of 5 per cent and operating costs of over Rs 600 per day for a delivery van with personnel, it would necessitate minimum daily sales of Rs 12,000 (3,000 units) for the operation to at least break-even.
- A well-designed van route would enable coverage of eight village markets in a day at best. Larger inter-village distances would reduce the coverage in the Bikaner area to five.
- A van route could be operated with Rajpuria Hudan and four other markets covered in a day. A repeat coverage could be provided after a fortnight to tally with Rathore's inventory schedule.
- The issue is whether consumption levels would yield off-take of at least 13 units per retailer per day in villages with just three retail outlets? Even if this was possible, what advantage would Rathore and his retailing brethren receive by purchasing stocks from the van?

  With cost considerations occupying centre stage, the marketer offering a price advantage and credit are ruled out. Collections being the perennial month-end bogey, extension of credit to numerous small retailers like Rathore may lead to an accounting mess.

Source: Pawan Bhandari and Rajat Iyer, "Siphoning a Deal," *A & M* (January 1995): 23–26.

distribution trucks take to minimize delivery cost and time? Which are the potential rural areas with greater scope for marketing a particular product? The use of GIS has the following advantages:

- *Easy to use:* Application is fast and it is simple to use. Implementation of GIS made identification of potential markets in the targeted population strata much easier.
- *Fast:* A number of route plans with desired options could be worked out automatically within minutes with the application. Thus, there is a radical cutback in the time between data processing and planning that used to take nine days to produce a single route plan.
- *Flexible design:* Possible route plans could be chalked out on the screen and modifications to the routes from existing markets and stock points has become much easier. Thus, various alternatives can be tried easily through iterations before finalizing on the route plan.[5]

DISTRIBUTION DECISION—DIRECT VERSUS INDIRECT

In direct selling there is a direct trade-off between the buyer and the seller. In this case, no intermediary is involved. The manufacturing firms can sell directly in several ways: (i) company sales staff

(ii) company retail outlets or stalls (iii) mail-order selling (post and telegraph) (iv) telemarketing (v) Internet marketing (vi) company vans, and (vii) consumer-distribution models (network marketing and Project *Shakti*).

Several companies trying to reach out to rural consumers are exploring alternative, cost-effective channels. Use of stockists and company staff for effecting direct sales to rural consumers has also been found to be successful by companies such as Hindustan Unilever, ITC, Colgate, and Godrej. Rural markets or *mandis* are emerging as the target centres for direct sales. Direct selling through company delivery vans, setting up of temporary stalls in rural *melas* or *haats* are few successful examples. BPCL's specially-designed rural marketing vehicles that fill cylinders on the spot by travelling from village to village is an example. ITC e-*choupal* and Project i-*shakti* are examples of Internet-based marketing. The consumer-as-distributor models include network marketing used by companies such as Amway, self-help groups (SHGs) and such networks as Project *Shakti* of HUL.

In indirect distribution, an intermediary is involved between the manufacturer and the buyer. Indirect selling is simple and cheap while direct distribution requires a larger budget. The intermediary can be a channel with one or more members such as sales agents, wholesaler, semi-wholesalers and retailers. Indirect selling is often cheaper than direct selling as the overhead of a company employing its own staff is avoided. However, there are some disadvantages:

- No relationship with the end-user of the product or service
- Loss of control on brand progress and sales

The marketer has to invest resources into managing the relationship with the indirect sales force to ensure that they are working within the bounds of the contract and are promoting products in the most effective manner. In indirect distribution, the hub-and-spoke model is found to be a common arrangement. The syndicated-distribution model is an example of an innovative approach.

DIRECT MARKETING

Companies are embarking on direct marketing campaigns in rural areas. It provides one-to-one communication as well as sales without reliance on retailers. We will discuss the following methods employed by companies.

- Company sales force
- Van marketing
- Stalls at *haats*, *melas* and fairs
- Network marketing
- Internet marketing

Company sales force

Perhaps the ultimate sign that rural India has arrived is in the employment of talent. So far, the talented youth preferred jobs in urban areas. Now, there is a visible change. Educated youth are willing to work in rural areas. There are many training organizations that impart necessary skills to the youth aspiring to make a career in rural India. The routine of a sales person is of course exacting as well as exciting. The journey on rough terrains everyday is arduous but the interactions with the villagers and their hospitality will be pleasing.

Van marketing

Mobile vans have an important role in the distribution and promotion of products in villages. Box 9.8 describes how van marketing takes place.

Box 9.8 Santro Campaign

A convoy comprising two to three video vans and a handful of Santro cars fanned out from a select village to the neighbouring interiors. In the morning, two stalls were set up in the village centre, near a bank or a *choupal*. The video van had promotional videos and was decked with Santro posters on both sides.

"The video van was the 'invitation' for villagers to check out what Hyundai has to offer," says Sandeep Kapoor, managing director, RelioQuick, a company specializing in rural promotions. The van moved into rural hamlets to disseminate information about this "car fair" and elicited information from curious villagers on response cards. In a rural campaign, the company has collected up to 2,000 response cards from villagers. It costs between Rs 70,000 and Rs 0.125 million per month to run a rural van campaign.

By evening, curious villagers surrounded the vans and the stalls. Loud music, promotional videos and interactive games lent a festive air to the fair. People poured into the *shamiana* with their families and surrounded the sales team with questions. All of them recognized the posters of the Santro brand ambassador, Shahrukh Khan. Bankers were on hand to ink a sale while loans were available for rich farmers on collateral. According to company sources, at a campaign executed in February for Hyundai in Mathura, there were 100 enquiries on the first day, of which the company expected to convert 10 into sales within the next month.

Source: Anil G. Jacob, Picking Rural Pockets," *Business Standard*, 22 April 2003, available at www.business-standard.com.

Stalls at weekly *haats, bazaars, shandies*

Haats are weekly markets where people from surrounding villages trade on fixed days. Across the country, there are over 47,000 *haats* that act as distribution points, catering to almost 50 per cent of the rural population. It was found that all states in the country except Haryana, Western Rajasthan and some North Eastern states conducted *haats*. The reasons for the exceptions are—Haryana is almost urban, Western Rajasthan has a very low population density and the North Eastern States are inaccessible. The following observations are meaningful to marketers:

- The number of villages catered by each *haat* is between five and 10 on average.
- Each *haat* draws as many as 5,000 villagers.
- Everything is sold on the ground and there is a large variety on offer. *Haats* do not only sell loose commodities, a significant amount of packaged goods are also sold.
- The sale per *haat* per day is over Rs 0.225 million and the average sale per outlet is approximately Rs 900.
- Sales are usually affected on a 10 per cent margin that gives each stall owner an average daily income of approximately Rs 90.
- The average purchase per visitor is Rs 50.
- More than 90 per cent of the sales in *haats* are made in cash. 5 to 7 per cent is conducted on barter system and the remaining 3 to 5 per cent is on credit.
- Selling overheads are low. Participation fees at *haats* are a flat Re 1 to Rs 5 per stall and this rate is common to a giant like Hindustan Unilever and the smallest local seller.

Why is it preferred by villagers?

The first systematic study of *haats* was conducted only as recently as in 1995. The findings on consumer perceptions are as follows:

- 81 per cent of visitors to *haats* said that they did not make purchases from their respective villages and regularly visited *haats* for their requirements.
- 58 per cent said that they specifically come to buy a particular product and that the purpose of visiting the *haat* is to complete their "shopping list."
- 58 per cent of people who visited *haats* said that the same product was available in their own village but that the shops in the village did not offer them the same variety, price and choice of bargains.

Who are the sellers?

Sellers bring a variety of goods for sale. Sellers at *haats* are typically mobile. They sell in one *haat* on one day and move to another the next day. The reason for this is that villagers in rural India are paid on a weekly basis. *Haats* are usually scheduled on the day that employees get their "*hafta.*"

What types of goods are sold?

Different types of goods are present in a *haat*. The distribution of outlets (per cent of stalls) is as following: agro-related products (39.5 per cent), manufactured goods (24.3 per cent), processed food (13.2 per cent), garments, textiles and handicrafts (8.4 per cent), groceries, stationery and medicines (6 per cent), services (3.3 per cent) and forest products (2.1 per cent).

Advantages to marketers

The following points emphasize the significance of *haats*.

1. *Convenience: Haats* are a readymade distribution network. A lot of re-distribution also occurs through *haats*. The entire market can be compared to large departmental stores in cities where the advantage is a one-stop shopping exercise. These outlets crop up every week, providing consumers immense choice and variety of prices. A large number of retailers and sub-wholesalers also buy from *haats* for their village stores.
2. *Attractive:* The weekend shopping is not only convenient but also entertaining. The markets start early and are over by lunch. Afterwards, there is entertainment. In respect to transactions, it is an attractive place for those who want to buy second-hand durables and those who prefer barter transactions. Further, the freshness of the produce, buying in bulk for a week and the bargaining advantage attract the frugal and hard working rural folk who work the entire week.
3. *Availability:* It is a market for everyone and for everything. Household goods, clothes, durables, jewellery, cattle, machinery, farming equipment, raw materials and a host of products are available.

Implications for marketers

Pradeep Kashyap, director, MART, who has conducted many studies on these markets, observed, "These markets have high potential that corporations are now waking up to." They offer good scope for distribution. For urban marketers with stockist and distributors who don't service remote areas, this form of selling can be a boon. A simple re-distributorship arrangement can be worked out.

Stalls at *melas* and fairs

Melas are gatherings of people for both entertainment as well as the sale and purchase of goods and services. This is another low-cost distribution channel available to marketers. It is comparable with urban events like Wills Trophy, India International Trade Fair (IITF), *Sajavat* or Consumex in which audience participation varies from a few thousand to a few million people.

Why are they held?

Over 25,000 *melas* are held every year all over the country. It is seen that 5,000 of these are commercial *melas*, 2,000 are cultural melas, while the majority (about 18,000) have religious significance. Among the most famous *melas* is the mighty *Kumbh Mela* at Allahabad (*Triveni Sangam*), *Pushkar mela* in Rajasthan, *Kullu Dusshera mela* in Himachala Pradesh, *Sonepur mela* in Bihar and *Makara Vilakku* in Kerala. People from all over the country gather to taste the wonders of India at these places.

When are they held?

Like urban events these *melas* do not require much publicity. The reason is that they are associated with festivals and repeat every year as per the Hindu calendar. The melas are occasions like festivals for people to celebrate and socialize. As such villagers look forward to them with great enthusiasm and in some cases make advance preparations to participate in them.

What about business in melas?

A majority of the *melas* are held during October–November and January–April. These coincide with the *Kharif* and *Rabi* harvests when the farmer's purchasing power is high. With both money and leisure at hand, he is inclined to indulge his family with a day out at the *mela*. He also looks forward to updating himself about the latest farming practices and consumer goods. Visitors to fairs are thus, highly receptive to try out new products and also come with enough money to do so.

- The average duration of a *mela* is anywhere from one to 45 days.
- Rural markets come alive at these *melas* and an average of 0.76 million people visit them. For example, 0.3 million people visited the annual *mela* at Navchadi that lasts for 7 days in Meerut. The largest such *mela* is the *Maha Kumbh Mela* that is visited by an average of 0.12 billion people.
- Women and children participate in *melas* on a large scale.
- On average, 850 outlets are set up in every mela. In fact, it is believed that the *Vali Yatra mela* has been held from the time of the Ramayana and now, has over 3,000 stalls.
- The mood at *melas* is very conducive to making rural folk try out new things. The average spending ranges between Rs 5,000 and Rs 50,000 a day.
- Sales at the Sonepur *mela* of Uttar Pradesh averages Rs 0.4 billion. The average sale per day at a *mela* is Rs 2.5 million.
- The type of outlet by per cent of stalls is as follows: agro-related products (5.8 per cent), manufactured goods (42.0 per cent), processed food (19.5 per cent), garments, textiles and handicrafts (15.6 per cent), groceries, stationery and medicines (9.0 per cent), services (4.2 per cent) and forest products (0.1 per cent).
- At a *mela*, there can be as many as 854 stalls. Some 18.4 per cent of these are local stalls (belonging to a few hundred villages), 40.8 per cent are regional (they belong to a few districts) and 40.8 per cent are national.

Are there differences in purchases made at *melas* and *haats*? The difference between *haats* and *melas* was that only 14 per cent of the products purchased at *melas* were available in the visitor's village. Where almost 40 per cent of stalls in *haats* sold agro-related products, only 5.8 per cent of stalls in *melas* sold such goods. On the other hand, whereas only 24.3 per cent stalls in *haats* sold manufactured goods it was around 42 per cent in *melas*.

Do these *melas* provide an opportunity for sales? Sampling at *melas* is very successful in building awareness of new innovations and initiating trials. Visitors to *melas* are usually cash rich as most *melas* are held immediately post harvest. 73 per cent of visitors to *melas* claimed that they came to buy a specific product. Many brands are advertised and promoted since *melas* are the ideal avenue for attaining product exposure, package familiarity, brand reminder and for word-of-mouth advertising.

How is a *mela* organized? Box 9.9 gives a colourful description.

Box 9.9 Carnival Affair

Imagine an event with assured attendance combining elements of a sports tournament, latest consumer product offerings and a plethora of new concepts, all with an immediate relevance to the visitor's lifestyle—this is a typical rural fair. About three days before it begins, hundreds of temporary stalls spring up on arterial roads leading to the fair ground. A vast range of goods are on offer such as general merchandize, sweetmeats, articles for religious worship, utensils, hosiery, toys, cheap jewellery, cosmetics. There are many eating places too. The fairground itself undergoes a transformation. The layout is decided a month in advance. Areas are marked out for government and private stalls, entertainment and recreational enclosures and food stalls. Ground space is auctioned and contracts for publicity rights are released through bids. Stalls are available on a first-come-first-served basis. The rates spiral upwards as the opening day draws closer. The person bidding for bulk ground space or publicity contracts looks forward to maximizing his returns from one or two fairs a year. "Skim the participants and the visitors," seems to be the operative slogan.

A company sponsoring "lost-and-found announcements" pays Rs 5,000 to the audio-publicity concessionaire who charges Rs 10 per announcement. An average of 20 announcements per day for a 3-day *mela* makes it a win–win situation for the concessionaire who stands to earn a revenue of Rs 11,000 or more from just the regular audio-publicity.

Similarly, rates of Rs 5,000 for a 10 ft by 10 ft stall may peak at Rs 18,000 just before the fair starts. Most fairs have a formal opening and closing ceremony—a single white pigeon and a bunch of balloons suffice to mark the occasions. The first few days witness the setting up of stalls and the like even as the stream of visitors strengthens. By the end of the first week, participants and fairground facilities are firmly in place and the crowds gradually begin to peak.

Many fairs have activities such as cattle trading during the day. The action gathers tempo at sundown with attendance peaking between 8 and 12 in the evening. Stalls usually begin to close past midnight with those stocking food carrying on into the wee hours of the morning.

A large fair could have well over 500 stalls. These include shops selling unbranded items such as flowers, sweetmeats, utensils, agricultural implements, cloth, jewellery, etc. Here, signs inviting customers to pick up any item for Rs 10 are not uncommon. The next lot, company stalls, advertise products ranging from bathing soaps to insurance policies. The presence of all leading marketers of consumer non-durables is mandatory. A well-located Procter & Gamble or Godrej stall with smartly turned out personnel, for instance, is a certainty. The participants are managed either by the company or through the local re-distribution stockist.

At Brooke Bond Lipton's stall for Lipton Tiger tea at Meerut's *Mela Nauchandi*, visitors had to enter through a roaring tiger's mouth. A crowd-puller, the stall was called *Sherdil jawanon ka adda* (a hangout for daring young men). At the Muzaffarnagar *mela*, also in Uttar Pradesh, the stall for Eicher Tractors fascinated visitors—a self-driven demo tractor was in perpetual circular

Box 9.9 (Continued)

motion. A third category of stalls were made up of eating places, photographers, palmists and even quacks. A major part of any fairground is devoted to entertainment and recreation. A circus is a must in a large fair. Sports events such as cart races and wrestling bouts are also conducted. On the cultural side, there are *kavi sammelans*, folk dances, *antakshari* competitions, puppet shows, and of course, the rural floor show—*nautanki*. Over the years, however, the profile of the fair has undergone a change. Audio-visual publicity options have altered from *nautanki* and puppet shows to electronic logo displays and video projections on giant screens that fill the skyline.

Source: Pawan Bhandari and Rajat Iyer, "Carnival Affair," *A & M* (November 1994): 33–35.

Table 9.4 Network Marketing Companies

Product group	Organization
Cosmetics	Aviance, Avon, Biotique, Oriflame
Kitchen ware	Tupperware
Home-care personal	Aviance, Quantum, Modicare products, Nutritives
Books	Time-Life Books, LB Publishers and Distributors, DF Family Learning
Jewellery	Dianet
Insurance	Unique
Health care	Conybio Far-Infra Red products

Network marketing

Network marketing is a form of direct selling. It can take place at two levels.

- *Single level:* Here the distributor appoints sales persons. He earns profits on sales made by him.
- *Multi-level:* The distributor introduces another distributor (a friend or relative, in general), who in turn introduces another distributor. Like this, a network is created. The "network" markets products. Each distributor gets profits on his sales and also a percentage on sales made by his "network" Thus, one earns by "retailing and recruiting."

In India direct selling is still very nascent, with very few players. Table 9.4 shows the players and their product categories.

The major direct selling companies are all members of the Indian Direct Selling Association (IDSA) that is committed to protecting the consumer and laying down the code of conduct for these organizations. Amway is the pioneer in direct selling and the largest selling organization in India and the world. It has a network encompassing 3 million independent business owners, worldwide.

Merits and demerits

In the ongoing multi-level marketing (MLM) practices, one finds both positive and negative features. The positive ones are:

1. *Relationship:* MLM is based on relationships. It relies on successful interactions between two individuals who enjoy what they are doing and who care about one another.

2. *Selling effort:* Very little effort needs to be put for selling. There are a lot of people selling a little each. Small drops make an ocean.
3. *Income:* Distributors earn incomes in three ways (i) retail profit from their own product sales to customers, (ii) discounts on personal monthly purchases, and (iii) commissions based on sales by distributors within their business groups.
4. *Risk:* The company has a 100 per cent product buy-back policy and no inventory requirement that ensures very low risk.
5. *Investment:* To become a distributor, a person has to invest Rs 4,200 to obtain a starter business kit that contains a distributor application form, a selection of products, product and business administration information and business training literature.
6. *Education and training:* No formal education and training is necessary. It provides a firm platform for amateurs to start a set-up of their own with no professional or technical restrictions and no specified or set levels of education or experience. One just needs to be over 18 years of age to become a distributor.
7. *Flexibility:* A distributor can sell the products as per his/her convenience. One can choose his/her timings, fix up appointments and contact persons to promote business.
8. *Satisfaction:* A distributor derives satisfaction by being a proud owner of one's own business. Along with this comes the satisfaction of not having to serve someone else. This is heightened by achieving goals that brings with them a great sense of accomplishment. Further, interaction with friends and relatives is a pleasant experience by itself.

Against this, there are some annoying aspects too. Some of them are listed below:

1. *Strained relationships:* The social relationships with friends and relatives may be polluted by the economic pursuits. Friends and relatives are viewed differently now—as potential customers. The neighbourhood is a market; friends are prospects. Refusal to buy products or to become a distributor have resulted in strained relationships in some cases.
2. *Easier said than done:* Selling is not an easy proposition. Amway distributors in India, for instance, found it difficult to sell the products because they were unfamiliar and far too expensive. Now, many months down the line, the company is adapting to Indian conditions. It is introducing small-sized packs and products like shampoos.
3. *Deceptive schemes:* MLM is often confused with pyramid schemes that are anti-social. It is guided by the principle—many losers pay a few winners. MLM is different. One can join as well as quit the scheme on his own at any time and have his money refunded. It is now, being recognized as a successful and ethical way of doing business.

Network marketing companies have made inroads into corridor villages enrolling the affluent R 1 and R 2 consumers.

Internet marketing

Also referred to as cyber marketing, it is the latest in the series of innovations in retailing—catalogue marketing, special-interest mail order, telemarketing and television shopping. The Internet has become an important new channel much more quickly than anyone would have predicted. Though it started off in the 1960s, it was only in 1993 that its potential as a commerce medium was realized. By 1998, individual Web sites among the hundreds of thousands already in existence were measuring "hits" in hundreds of millions and marketers were eager to tap into the medium because "every body else was there." Today we have success stories of e-retailers like Indiaplaza and Subhiksha that have motivated many companies to set up their own Web sites.

Merits

The popularity of the Internet can be attributed to the following factors:

(i) *Consumer acceptance:* The Internet has attracted people who have an interest in new technology and faith in delivery systems. It has gained wide acceptance. In fact, it has taken only 5 years to achieve a critical mass of 650 million users that the radio took 38 years, television 13 years and cable 10 years to acquire.

(ii) *Low price:* The set-up costs as well as operating costs are much lower for the Internet. Since, the cyber marketer is coming into direct touch with a customer, cyber discounts can be offered (that were earlier given to middle men). Also companies using non-store retailing are selling the products at reduced prices in comparison to store-based selling. Low prices increase sales volume and boost profit levels.

(iii) *Global access:* The Internet's Web browser—a client/server architecture and networks of hyper media database on the world wide web (www)—serve as the technology platform for e-commerce among the Internet-connected communities of customers and business organizations. A study conducted by Forrester Research in February 2000 estimated growth in business from USD 7.8 billion to USD 108 billion in 2004. Global access is a part of this exciting opportunity.

(iv) *Relationships:* The Internet lets companies build interactive relationships with customers because it allows direct links to anyone, anywhere. While some have sites that merely advertise products, others have sites where visitors can obtain information about the company and its product and send e-messages. Some others allow visitors an extra facility of playing games.

Market research findings also showed that Web customers tend to consolidate their purchase with one primary supplier, to the extent that purchasing from the supplier's site becomes a part of their daily routine. Hence, price doesn't rule the Web, trust does. When customers do trust an on-line vendor, they are much more likely to share information with others. Referrals are much more lucrative as "click-of-mouse" is faster than "word-of-mouth."

(v) *Advertising medium:* Ad effectiveness in recent times is determined more by chance than choice. With the rise in the numbers of national and regional channels, marketers are finding it difficult to decide the right channel and right time for their advertisements. However, in the case of the Internet one can be assured of reach and exposure. If a net surfer clicks on to your Web site, he/she is sure to watch your advertisement. What is necessary is to gauge the success by continuous monitoring of the hits and customer trends.

Demerits

Although doing business in the cyber space is novel and exhilarating it can also be frustrating and even unprofitable, both in urban and rural areas. In rural areas it may be even more difficult to successfully employ the Internet due to low literacy levels and poor infrastructure facilities.

(i) *Lack of rules:* At the moment, there are few rules in cyber space. The legal aspects relating to copy right, on-line exchanging and electronic cash transfer are still vague. There is no defined authority to punish those who violate norms. Until these problems are solved, the cyber space will remain a frontier area.

(ii) *Lack of infrastructure:* It is true that communication and electrical power supply facilities are spreading to rural areas. While the development has touched many parts of the rural hinterland, there are several tiny villages that have not yet tasted the fruits of development. Setting up kiosks to cater to the widely scattered, tiny villages will be an expensive preposition. Even in the developed villages, the problem of frequent power interruptions adversely affects the usage of the Internet.

(iii) *Overloaded lines:* In India, net surfer faces problems such as online jams and disconnection after every half an hour. The lines used to carry analog signals of telephones are being used for data transmission on the Internet. These lines are already congested. One has to wait from a few seconds to several minutes for access to the Internet after dialling. These problems are much more common in rural areas.

(iv) *Poor delivery systems:* Indian consumers lack confidence in the delivery systems currently available. TV shopping, for instance, has been around for 7 years now, however, it has never really taken off in India. The reason as one consumer puts it is that "In India what you see is not what you get and hence, I need to touch it, feel it and experience it, before buying it." The failure may be at the supplier or at the transport level. Indian logistics are not yet of international standards in urban areas. In the case of rural India, it is still worse.

(v) *Payment problem:* This is another grey area of Internet marketing. Credit cards have low penetration in India. Only a small section of the country's population possesses credit cards. Also, the credit system is vulnerable to hackers. Alternative methods under consideration are:

- House Accounts—Customers open credit accounts with the company from which they buy.
- Digital Cash—The customer opens account in a bank or a company that acts as an online bank and gets his Personal Index Number (PIN). It is mentioned in all transactions. When the merchant concerned contacts the bank with this PIN, cash is transferred automatically to his account.

In rural India, credit cards have slowly come into vogue. Some banks have already issued "*Kisan* credit cards." However, the number of persons qualifying to have credit cards will be very small, making the Internet a facility for the privileged sections of the rural society.

(vi) *Ability to use:* Computer systems are intimidating to a rural consumer. Lack of exposure, hesitation in using new systems, lack of credibility in the efficacy of buying through the Internet, altogether may keep the rural people away from the Internet. This initial resistance needs to be overcome.

The weak points in the system will disappear slowly with the proliferation of computer services in the rural hinterland. There is a three-pronged approach to minimize the rural–urban divide. Initiatives are being taken by the Government, corporations and NGOs. Box 9.10 and 9.11 discuss the initiatives of an NGO and a corporate enterprise.

Several corporate enterprises have facilitated rural consumer transactions on the Internet. Prominent among them are EID Parry, ITC and Nagarjuna Fertilizers (see Box 9.11).

INDIRECT MARKETING

Go alone versus syndicated

Syndicated distribution is a viable and novel approach to reach rural markets. Under this approach, marketers of household products could group together and consider the formation of a syndicated trading organization that could jointly distribute a collective group of household products in the rural market and enjoy shared economies. The guidelines for formation of the syndicated organization may be as follows:

Box 9.10 Net Entrepreneurship

Punavali kalan in Bundelkhand is a typical village or a fair approximation of one. There is no road, just a dusty trail that leads to this cluster of 500 odd houses; some of them tumble-down structures that look like they'd be washed away by the first downpour. Electricity comes in fits and starts, and the half-a-dozen phones work now and then. Just about a quarter of the 2,748 people who live here are literate. Life centres on farming for the majority, who belong to the backward and scheduled castes. A larger chunk of Punavali is below the poverty line.

Three girls, Rajamani, Madhavi and Priti Parmar run a TARA *Kendra* (kiosk) set up by Development Alternatives (DA), a voluntary agency. TARAhaat.com is a portal that links the user to information services, government agencies and is also a super bazaar that provides access to the kind of services and products that rural India needs.

There has been a steady stream of visitors to the *Kendra* since it opened on an experimental basis in November last year. The sisters charge Rs 40 for surfing the net; assisted surfing costs more. They help download government application forms for a small fee. The farmers drop in to check the different *mandi* rates. Women demand household management tips, *mandi* rates, look at religious sites—the *maha kumbh* was a great hit—visit exotic Web sites, go for a virtual tour or haunt chat rooms. Offline, it is even busier for the girls. There are children queuing up to learn Paint Brush, DOS, Excel and even PowerPoint. Later, there will be special modules for general education. The menu is endless.

Source: Latha Jishnu and M. Anand, "India's Great Digital Hope," *Business World*, 21 May 2001, pp. 28–36.

Box 9.11 IFFCO—ICT Initiatives for Farmers

Indian Farmers Fertiliser Cooperative Limited (IFFCO), which is engaged in the production and distribution of fertilizers, has been in the service of farmers and cooperatives since its inception in 1967. It has set up agri-portals to provide agriculture related information in local languages to farmers and cooperatives. Farmers can access relevant information through its Web site www.iffco.nic.in.

User-friendly features such as intuitive graphic-based navigation, touch screens and audio summaries in important sections are provided. IFFCO has installed about 100 Farmers Information Kiosk in 16 states. Farmers are educated through training programmes and meetings to encourage the use of this facility.

Source: D. K. Bhatt, "IFFCO in the Service of Farmers," Indian Journal of Fertilisers (April 2006): 11–20.

Guidelines

1. Companies willing to work together may contribute to the capital of the organization.
2. It could be privately held and need not be open to the public or government agencies.
3. The distribution by this organization may replace or supplement the existing distribution.
4. A formula for expense sharing is to be worked out in advance by the participating organization.

Table 9.5 Rural Distribution Channels

Level	Channel measure	Place
Level A	Company depot	National/State
Level B	Re-distribution stockists, C&F agents, Semi-wholesalers and retailers	District headquarters
Level C	Semi-wholesalers and retailers	Tehsil headquarters Mofussil towns Industrial townships
Level D	Itinerant traders, vans, petrol bunks, semi-wholesalers, retailers, co-operative societies	*Haats* Large villages
Level E	Retailers, vans, sales people, NGOs, government agencies	Villages

Source: Pawan Bhandari and Rajat Iyer, "Siphoning a Deal," *A & M* (January 1995): 23–26.

Channel levels

A national level marketer who opts for indirect selling will require at least five levels of distribution channels as shown in Table 9.5 and Figure 9.1. They depict product movement routes through interior regions.

Most companies have direct representation in the form of re-distribution stockists at level B and C. Level C in a district would comprise at best 7–10 towns. High outlet density and large customer population permit economies in developing these markets through regular working of sales-cum-distribution vans. On consolidating market penetration, direct representation could be extended to the towns by way of sub-dealers or stockists.

To achieve a winning edge in rural sales, the object is to maximise directed flow and control stocks at levels C to E. Approaching level D requires prior selection of *haat* markets and villages located in contiguous clusters. Sorting of easily accessible census data enables listing of villages with population above a predetermined bracket and also helps in the listing of occurrence schedule of *haat* markets. Various schedules with level C stockists at nodal points could be operated towards self-sustaining distribution rates for level D markets.

The next level is E. The villages are too small to allow economies in van distribution. However, these villages form the bulk of the consumption in rural areas.

Traditional channel members

The traditional channel participants include two categories of people—those who stock and transport goods and those who sell them to other channel members.

Wholesalers

Not withstanding the consumer boom, more than 70 per cent of the rural markets are still beyond the pale of direct distribution. Since, wholesale trade in India has remained largely unchanged over the years there is a need to revitalize it.

The Indian wholesaler is principally a *galla-kirana* (food-grain) merchant who is of the belief that business is speculative rather than distributive in character. He is a trader/commodity merchant rather

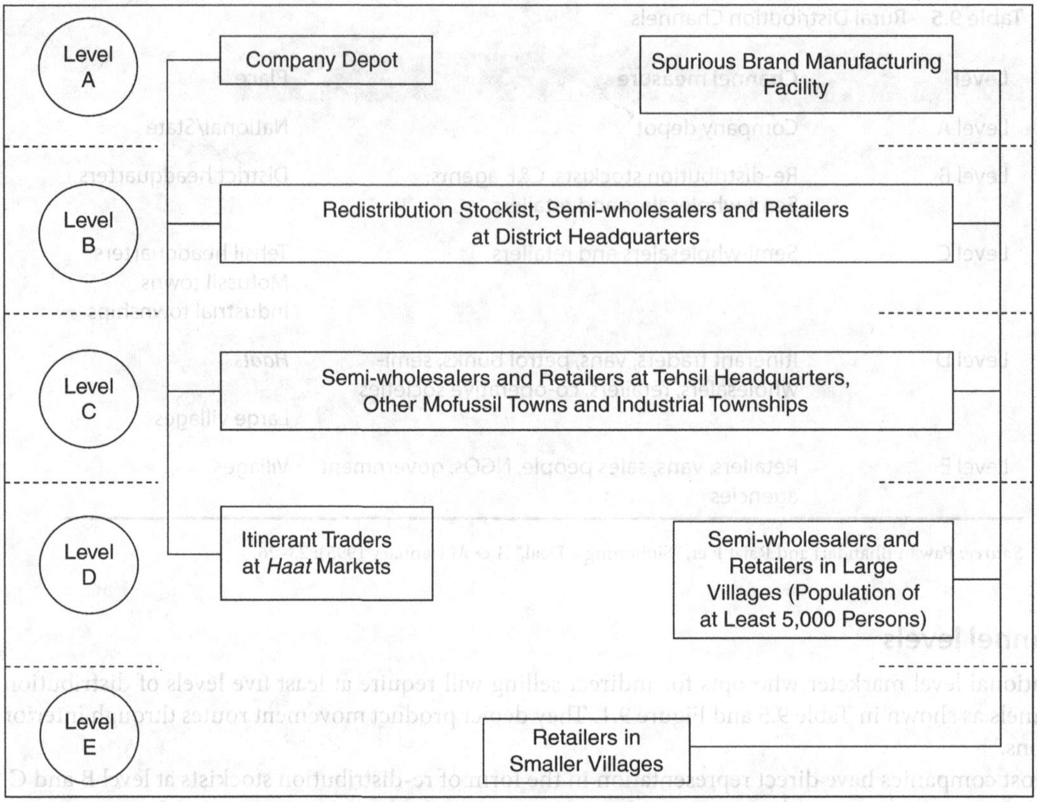

Figure 9.1 Product Movement Routes in Interior Regions

than a distributor and therefore, tends to support a brand during a boom and withdraws support during a slump. The reasons for this speculative character and dormant role of wholesalers are:

- The Indian market was largely a sellers' market. There was no need for an active sales approach.
- Companies laid more emphasis on retailers in urban areas who were present in very large numbers. As a result of retail-based distribution, wholesale-based distribution was weakened.
- Rural markets were neglected by many. The occurrence of retail outlets was low. Therefore, many companies were dependent on wholesalers. Few companies operated mobile vans to distribute products to village shopkeepers.

The current need is to activate and develop wholesalers of the adjoining markets as distributors of products to rural retail outlets and build their loyalties to the company.

It is necessary to adopt a conservative, go-slow approach. Overzealous marketers do not like to depend on the uncertain loyalties of wholesalers. They may aggressively draw up and implement direct-service plans to reach retail outlets and village consumers. This will adversely affect the interests of wholesalers.

Retailers

Village retailers have traditionally been among the most mobile of rural residents. Often doubling up as moneylenders, their occupation facilitates multi-person interaction in the closed village society. As a result, the retailer plays a significant role (refer to Chapter 10 for more details).

The retail outlets are now in for a change with the corporate marketers finding them to be right places for promoting their products.

New channel members

Till recently, selling in rural India followed a pattern. However, with the entry of new players and the surge in rural demand, the structure and dynamics are altering.

Co-operative societies

Co-operatives occupy an important place in India's rural economy in terms of their coverage of population and their share in total supply of agricultural inputs, including credit. India can rightly claim to have the largest network of co-operatives in the world. It is reported that there are 0.5 million co-operatives in the country that span different elements of the economic value chain from production to marketing, procurement to distribution and credit in both agriculture and non-agriculture sectors. Generally, a co-operative exists for 2 or 3 villages. Farmer's Service Co-operatives (FSCs) are mini-supermarkets. Such an arrangement can be tried with others.

Petrol bunks

Petrol bunks have become multi-purpose distribution centres in some places. In view of this, companies are entering into tie-ups with petrol bunks to sell their products. Box 9.12 describes a tie-up between Max New York Life and IOCL.

Box 9.12 Tie-ups to Reach the Last Mile

To reach the diverse and widely spread rural population, Max New York Life Insurance has adopted a multi-channel strategy and is utilizing existing distribution networks. It announced a tie-up with the Indian Oil Corporation. IndianOil will make its approximately 2,000 *Kisan Seva Kendras* across the country available for the sale of Max New York Life Insurance products. This will allow a significantly larger number of people in rural markets to have access to Max New York Life Insurance products.

"We pioneered a unique hub-and-spoke distribution model that is supported by corporate agency relationships, referral tie-ups with state and district co-operative banks and regional rural banks to deepen our penetration in rural and semi-urban markets. We offer need- and aspiration-based products and localized communication for these markets," said Mr R. P. Singh, executive vice president and head, emerging markets.

Speaking on the occasion, Indian Oil Corporation's general manager, retail sales, Mr K. R. Suresh Kumar said, "Through our *Kisan Seva Kendras* we have been successfully reaching vital products, including petroleum products to rural India. From fuel to lubricants, besides insecticides, fertilizers, financial services and FMCG products, our *Kisan Seva Kendras* have proved to be a lifeline for the millions of rural consumers they serve." IOCL has entered into various tie-ups with leading companies like National Seeds Corporation, Indo Gulf Fertilizer, Bank of Baroda, Oriental Bank, Dena Bank, Dabur, etc. to make available their products and services to the rural population. Given the reach of Indian Oil's *Kisan Seva Kendras* in India's hinterland, Max New York Life will have complete access to the rural markets for reaching insurance products to rural customers. This tie-up would also enable the *Kisan Sewa Kendras* to move up the value chain by making life insurance available to the rural consumers.

Max New York Life will start by setting up offices at 100 such Indian Oil *Kisan Seva Kendras* across Punjab, Haryana, Gujarat and Western Uttar Pradesh. Eventually, this model will be extended to other *Kisan Sewa Kendras* across the country.

Source: "Max New York Life Insurance Enters into a Tie-up with Indian Oil Corporation," Max New York Life Press Release, 10 July 2008, available at www.businesswireindia.com/PressRelease.asp?b2mid=16376.

Public distribution system (PDS)

The fair-price shops (FPSs) run by the government can be utilized to sell consumables and low-value durables. The fair-price shops are now becoming malls. As such, there will be greater scope for distribution of FMCGs. Box 9.13 describes how fair-price shops have transformed into rural malls in the state of Gujarat. Other states are also actively engaged in this kind of transformation.

Agricultural-input dealers

Fertilizer companies have retail outlets within a range of 5 km of any village. There is a large network of about 0.282 million agri-input dealers in the country who are the prime source of farm information to the farming community besides the supply of inputs and credit to some extent. Majority of the dealers do not have any formal agricultural education and seldom realize the implication of "laws" related to the handling of agricultural inputs. But as they are basically businessmen, they know about different market forces and if provided with the required knowledge in agriculture, they may become para-professionals and can bring a paradigm shift in Indian agriculture. Given proper training in retailing and financing, they offer an excellent opportunity to marketers of FMCGs and durables.[7]

Box 9.13 Fair-price Shops Become Rural Malls

There are a total of 15,993 fair-price shops in Gujarat. The state government plans to convert them gradually into malls. Earlier, the Civil Supplies Department had imposed certain restrictions on business that could be conducted from FPS premises. Already, 520 fair-price shops across the state have been upgraded into malls and another 1,000 of these shops are being upgraded. The objectives of this scheme are manifold (i) to make FPSs economically more viable, (ii) to make rural malls a bankable scheme and (iii) to provide maximum possible number of consumer goods under one roof. The rural poor need not spend time and incur additional expenses on travelling from villages to towns and back again to meet their day-to-day requirements.

Besides selling items listed as "essential commodities" at a subsidized rate, the plan is to sell what is known in business terms as fast moving consumer goods (FMCG) like grocery items, confectionery and cosmetics, besides postages, cooking gas and SIM cards. The Government will also ensure that rural malls sell nourishing foods like edible oil fortified with Vitamin A, iodized salt and protein-rich pulses. These mini-malls can also sell agro-products like fertilizers and pesticides.

The rural malls have also been planned to be convergence points of information technology and communication (ITC) in villages, providing postal and telecom services. Bharat Sanchar Nigam Ltd (BSNL), Hutch and Tata have shown interest in the scheme. Each FPS, ideally 400 sq. ft in area, will undergo a physical makeover too, with modern interior decoration and swanky display boards. The little additional cost could be borne by branded producers. Each rural mall would maintain computer records.

Dena Bank extended financial assistance to FPS owners to set up rural malls at their existing premises. A closer link between FPS and self-help groups (SHGs) is envisaged. A bulk of the 61,000-odd SHGs in Gujarat comprises women.

Source: "Gujarat to Convert Fair-price Shops to Rural Malls," 31 July 2006, available at http://news.oneindia.in/2006/07/31/guj-to-convert-fair-price-shops-in-villages-as-rural-malls-1154338580.html; Milind Ghatwai, "Mall Gaon," 15 August 2007, available at www.indianexpress.com/news/mall-gaon/210577/.

NGOs

Another alternative is to work with non-governmental organizations (NGOs) that reach the interiors of villages. Ideologies and methods may vary but most NGOs have programmes focussing on sustainable development by providing avenues for income generation. They command substantial influence where the programmes are implemented. Companies may join hands with them for mutual benefit. With NGOs undertaking distribution, companies realize benefits that accrue from infrastructure and grass roots-level networking. As an intervening mediator, an NGO would provide a buffer against delayed retail collections. From the NGO's standpoint, such association with companies could yield employment opportunities for local residents. Box 9.14 narrates Tata Tea's project—*Gaon Chalo*—that utilized NGOs for mutual benefit.

Box 9.14 Tata Tea's "*Gaon Chalo*"

In late 2005, the project "Gaon Chalo" (go to the villages) was launched to counter the growth of local tea companies in Uttar Pradesh and to increase coverage. Earlier sales teams, which investigated sales patterns, reported that Tata Tea was not selling in more than 100,000 villages in UP. The project aimed to increase the sales of its mass brands like Kanan Devan and Chakra and boost the family incomes of all those who are involved in the tea business, right down to the last person in the supply chain.

How did it work? In December 2005, Tata Tea piloted a project in a small village near Varanasi. In the next year, it tied up with 12 NGOs to facilitate its reach across rural UP. To strengthen its distribution network it appointed 500 new rural distributors to cover 20,000 retailers, in about 10,000 villages across UP. Memorandum of Understanding (MoUs) were signed with NGOs (RD-1) to act as main distributors at a district level, collecting various products from Tata Tea on credit before giving them to mobile rural distributors (RD-2), also on credit, who would then visit a fixed number of villages periodically to supply tea to small rural retailers (RD-3). These retailers in turn sold the product to rural consumers. Monthly sales targets were set. The money found its way back to Tata Tea as the RD-3s made payments to the RD-2s on subsequent visits to replenish stock and so on up the chain. Eventually, NGOs made payments and took supplies from the company. As part of initial capital expenses, Tata Tea set aside around Rs 7 million worth of goods to be distributed to 12 NGOs manning 70 districts.

Benefits to all: The unique coalition has borne fruit. According to an AC Nielsen audit, Tata Tea improved its all India share from 18 per cent in January–March 2006 to 21.4 per cent in January–March 2008. The NGOs benefited because their status as facilitators of rural income has improved their image and financial position. The project gave them sustainable funding at a time when international funding was shrinking. An average RD-3 earned an additional monthly income of Rs 300 to 1,000, while an RD-2 earned Rs 5,000 to 7,000.

Product portfolio: It has been proposed that more products (automotives, salt, consumer goods, telecom, insurance, etc.) be added to this permanent, exclusive distribution chain under a programme called Tata Hut.

Source: Sreevalasan Menon, "Uncommon Brew: Tata Tea's Rural Marketing Project Has Changed Lives," Businessworld, 04–10 November 2008, available at www.businessworld.in/index.php/Economy/Uncommon-Brew.html

Freelance traders

In urban and rural areas we find enthusiastic men and women undertaking business activity to boost their incomes during their leisure time. This is a part-time activity and they do it with enthusiasm and self-motivation. Such entrepreneurs are often found selling insurance policies through friends and relatives and churidars and saris mostly from home by spreading messages through word of mouth.

Hero Honda Motors found that village mechanics, local real estate agents, shopkeepers who sell FMCGs or services, were taking motorcycles in twos and threes from the local dealer and selling them by displaying them outside their premises. Of course, the paper work was done by the dealer. Such instances are facilitating, as well as forcing, companies to review their distribution set-ups to ensure that they are present even in the smallest villages.

Mobile traders

There are about 4,00,000 mobile traders and about 19 per cent of them carry original brands of cosmetics and toiletries, according to a study conducted by MART for HUL. Almost half of all mobile traders in northern India are women. On an average, a mobile trader visits five villages per week, covers around 75 households and interacts directly with 5,000 women. An average consumer's one-time purchase from these mobile traders varies between Rs 25 and Rs 75 with as much as 30 per cent of it going to consumer products. They can be trained and utilized by companies to sell their consumer products.[8]

Barefoot salesmen

Companies may train sons of the soil to operate as barefoot salesmen. Fluency in the local dialect and familiarity with persons and the terrain in the area of operation would be among the factors enhancing the efficacy of this approach.

A barefoot salesman, operating on a retailer-cum-commission basis, could book orders from retailers in villages within a limited radius of his village. On aggregating orders that permit distribution economies, he could coordinate with the area stockist to arrange deliveries and make collections. MART has addressed the challenge of creating a low cost and self-sustaining last mile distribution and promotion system and evolved a model. The model is explained in Box 9.15.

Post offices

The Department of Posts in India has launched a series of fully upgraded and completely new-look post offices for the rural population. Called "Project Arrow," the launch aims to transform the existing

Box 9.15 Sales Promoters—MART Model

The MART model involves identifying and selecting unemployed rural youth belonging to village youth clubs in the 18–35 years age group, with a school education, to promote and sell company brands in rural areas. These self-employed entrepreneurs are given rigorous classroom and in-field training in salesmanship. Each promoter is equipped with branded bicycles, umbrellas, storage boxes, T-shirts and caps. The promoter invests small amounts in buying stock from the nearest company-authorized channel partner and sells the same at nearby *haats* and village shops on the way, averaging sales of Rs 700 to 800 per day. His permanent journey plan is carefully prepared keeping in mind the days on which the *haats* are held and including target population strata villages in the coverage. Since, these promoters hail from one of the neighbouring villages and speak the same language they enjoy high credibility among customers. MART has partnered with Colgate, Eveready, Heinz, Goodknight and other brands in rolling out this model in UP, Andhra Pradesh, Maharashtra and West Bengal.

Source: Available at www.martrural.com/corporate_pilot_implementation.htm, accessed March 2010.

India Post infrastructure at an estimated investment of Rs 9 billion across the country. These new-age post offices would serve as a window to the world for the common man—"*aam aadmi*"—by focusing on their needs. Besides providing traditional services in a modern, more efficient and technology-based mode, the post offices will also form an indispensable part of all social and civic initiatives such as the National Rural Employment Guarantee Act (NREGA) and the National Old Age Pension Scheme. With nearly 89 per cent of the network of India Post in rural areas, the project is expected to bring the rural populace in direct communication with the outside world and bring benefits of development to their doorsteps. Corporate enterprises may work out deals with the post offices to sell their wares.[9]

Summary

Distribution is a vital component of marketing strategy. Hitherto, distribution was considered a difficult problem owing to inadequate transport, poor roads and physical linkages, lack of retail outlets and mass media infrastructure. However, the situation has changed, giving ample scope for the entry of corporate marketers into rural markets.

The channel levels include:

(a) Company depot
(b) Re-distribution stockists, C&F agents, semi-wholesalers and retailers
(c) Itinerant traders, vans, co-operative societies, semi-wholesalers, petrol bunks, and retailers
(d) Retailers, vans, sales people, NGOs and government agencies

Newer approaches to distribution include syndicated distribution, relationship marketing through service centres and direct-to-home (DTH) selling. The two methods of DTH selling are network marketing and Internet marketing. Coverage strategy requires consideration of identifying the villages to be covered and mode of coverage.

Short Answer Questions

1. Explain why availability is a challenge in rural markets.
2. Enumerate the distribution practices of consumer durables and pharma companies.
3. State the channel arrangements of FMCG companies.
4. What are the drivers of modern distribution?
5. Identify the problems in rural logistics.
6. What is a hub-and-spoke model? Highlight its merits.
7. What are the methods of distribution in direct and indirect marketing?
8. List the five channel levels of distribution used by Indian companies.

Discussion Questions

1. Discuss the role of retailers in rural markets with respect to distribution, promotion, selling and fostering consumer relationships.
2. Discuss the use of the Internet as a medium of distribution in urban and rural areas. Does it hold promise in the rural areas?

Essay Questions

1. Identify the trends in distribution and present an overview of the distribution choices that a rural marketer has.
2. Explain the direct marketing approaches used in rural areas.
3. Critically evaluate the following options pointing out the merits and demerits.
   (i) Direct versus indirect marketing for FMCGs
   (ii) Syndicated versus individual distribution for consumer durables

4. Describe the significance of *haats* and *melas* in rural distribution.
5. Explain the role of the following in rural marketing.
   (i) Wholesalers
   (ii) Co-operative societies
   (iii) NGOs
   (iv) Barefoot salesmen
6. How do you distribute the following?
   a. *Annadata*—A farmer's magazine
   b. Pesticides
   c. Refrigerators
   d. Fairever

Internet Exercise

1. Collect information on the distribution practices of two select organizations.
2. Analyse the applications of GIS in marketing.

Mini Project

Visit nearby villages and observe the distribution practices that are leading to the availability of products and services to the villagers. Find out the gaps and problems. Prepare a paper on distribution practices.

End Notes

1. Joe C. Mathew, "Pharma World Discovers Bharat," *Business Standard*, 29 November 2009, available at www.business-standard.com.
2. "Maruti Eyes Rural Markets for Car Sales," 15 May 2009, available at www. carazoo.com.
3. "Bajaj Auto Rejigs Distribution Network," *The Times of India*, 26 September 2005, available at http://timesofindia.indiatimes.com/articleshow/1242253.cms; "Bajaj Auto Opts for Self-help Model to Double Rural Revenues," *The Financial Express*, 05 December 2005, available at www.financialexpress.com/printer/news/157454/.
4. Preeti Khicha, "Building Brands in Rural India," 8 October 2007, available at www.brandchannel.com/features_effect.asp?pf_id=389.
5. Suruchi Raina and Vijay Amanna, "GIS for Rural Marketing," available at www.gisdevelopment.net/application/business/pdf/31.pdf.
6. "Max New York Life Enters into a Tie-up with IndianOil Corporation,"10 July 2008, available at www.thaindian.com/newsportal/lifestyle/max-new-york-life-enters-into-a-tie-up-with-indianoil-corporation_10070101.html.
7. Available at http://agricoop.nic.in/PolicyIncentives/diploma_agricultural.htm, accessed March 2010.
8. *Business Today*, 02 January 2000, p.18.
9. "New Look for Post Offices in Rural India," 18 August 2008, available at www.igovernment.in/site/New-look-for-rural-post-offices-in-India/.

Case 9.1 *Har Gaon, Har Aangan*

Market leader Hero Honda launched its "*Har gaon, har aangan*" (for every village, every home) campaign, to make a foray into rural areas. Obviously, it is in place to take advantage of the increase in rural disposable incomes. "They have positioned themselves as a rural India story," says S. Ramnath, vice-president at IDFC-SSKI Securities Ltd, "at just the right time." As two-wheeler sales across the country have slowed, the focus on rural areas has stood Hero Honda in good stead. The company has grown by 12 per cent, while rival Bajaj Auto Ltd has seen sales fall by 23 per cent.

Rural Division

According to the National Sample Survey Organisation (NSSO), while nearly one-fourth of India's urban households own a scooter, motorcycle or moped, only 8 per cent of rural households do so. This is an opportunity for marketers. In 2007, Hero Honda set up a dedicated rural division with the aim of penetrating deeper into small towns and villages across India. These are generally defined as settlements with a population of at least 20,000. For Hero Honda, the share of rural sales has been growing by 2 to 3 percentage points every year; rural areas make up for at least 40 per cent of the company's sales.

Hub-and-Spoke Model

Hero Honda has increased the number of touch points or outlets selling and servicing its products. The company aims to set up 3,500 touch points. Hero Honda's dealerships in districts such as Sawai Madhopur are based on the so-called hub-and-spoke model. Within a district, the company's main liaison is the dealer, typically located in the district headquarters. Under him are "authorized representatives"—smaller dealerships where locals can make purchases and also get their bikes serviced.

The company provides broad guidelines and leaves local activities to these authorized representatives. Vijay Motors in Sawai Madhopur has 10 authorized representatives scattered across the district. Sandeep Aggarwal, its owner, is constantly in touch with them, running promotional activities in villages, holding service camps and helping them tie-up with banks for financing and so on.

A dealer makes an initial investment of Rs 1.5 million to set up his outlet and nets about Rs 0.3 million in profit each year. A dealer may sell between 20 and 25 bikes a month and makes most of his money by servicing them. The dealer showrooms are unassuming to make villagers more comfortable. There is none of the glitz of a city showroom. A visit to Girirad Prasad's Gupta Motors proves this. The entrance is through a cramped room that doubles up as a front office. Inside, the bikes are placed in a small room with whitewashed walls and the heat is almost stifling. However, the workshop looks neat, clean and efficient.

Sell, Not Tell

Rural sales ride more on word-of-mouth publicity rather than advertising. The salesmen of Hero Honda realize this completely. Manoj Gupta, a rural sales executive, maintains, "Making a sale is great, but we aim to form a long-term relationship. It's more important to be seen as a friend of the villagers than as a bike salesman. If they don't buy from me today, that's fine. I need to make sure they think of me next year when they're planning on buying a bike."

The 521 rural sales executives on the rolls of Hero Honda dealers across the country have a gruelling schedule. Take the case of Manoj Gupta. Riding his Hero Honda bike across small towns and villages around Bonli, in Sawai Madhopur district, he meets community leaders, including the local *sarpanch* (village head), school teachers, lawyers, doctors and insurance agents— anyone who plays a role in shaping buying decisions in their vicinity. He makes it a point to visit every village within 10 km of the dealership at least once a month. Armed with pamphlets and brochures on Hero Honda bikes, he is ready to answer any question on the products he sells. However, unlike a regular salesman, he doesn't make an aggressive sales pitch during these visits. He is mostly content sitting and chatting with village folk.

See and Experience

"It's very important to convince village buyers that there's no better deal available," says Sandeep Agarwal. Since, villagers take a long time in making inquiries about prices, price lists are placed across the district at places such as tea shops, the village tailor's shop and the *panchayat* (village council) office. At the sales camp organized by him, a few bikes have been trucked in for the day and are on display at the *panchayat* office. Buyers are free to walk around, touch and feel the bikes, and are rarely pushed into a sale unless they express interest. Villagers take the bikes for test drives and ask Navin Gaur, a rural sales representative, questions on the products. Brijesh Sharma, who oversees Hero Honda's safety initiative for Sawai Madhopur in Rajasthan, explains why bike riders must always wear a helmet. He also lays out a few tips on engine maintenance, the best way to shift gears and signalling while turning.

For discussion

1. Do you appreciate the "sell-but-not-tell" and "see-and-experience" approaches of Hero Honda?
2. Are there any missing links in the distribution plan of Hero Honda?
3. What suggestions would you offer to make it even more effective?

Source: Samar Shrivastava, "Rural Sales Management," *Mint*, 26 March 2009.

Case 9.2 Cattle Feed Distribution—The Anand Pattern

The distribution of cattle feeds under the Anand co-operative system pattern signifies an understanding of the limitations and needs of rural markets. The objective of physical distribution is to supply the right goods to the right place at the right time at the least cost. However, it is a controversial method. There cannot be a simultaneous cost minimization and customer service maximization. Minimum distribution cost means cheap warehousing, transportation, etc. but not at the cost of the quality of distribution service. The buyers of cattle feed are interested in

(a) On-time delivery;
(b) Supplier willingness to meet customer emergency needs;
(c) Careful handling of merchandize;
(d) The willingness to take back defective feeds and re-supply them quickly; and
(e) Supplier's willingness to carry inventory for the customer.

The suppliers have to find out the relative importance of the above service. The efficacy of distribution is also judged in the light of the competitor's efficiency. At the least it has to be as efficient as the competitors.

In most cases, the absence of competitors is more a curse than a boon. When there is no competitor, one has to face the difficulty of non-acceptance of any other outlets except the primary milk co-operative society at the village. The local manufacturer takes full advantage of any lapse on the part of co-operative manufacturers. To keep them away, the society has to offer such services as stated earlier.

Difficult activities involved in physical distribution along with the weightage of the costs are explained in Table 9.6.

Distribution Channel System: Whatever the producer does, he does it to get maximum control over the product till it goes into the hands of the customer. This leads to the adoption of the Vertical Marketing System (VMS), which may be costly and controversial. In a widespread market, an enterprise is not in a position to meet the demands of all customers and satisfy them fully. Here, an agency is required to work as a link between the producer and the consumer. This link does the job of passing on the information and feeding it to the customer and keeping

Table 9.6 Main Elements of Physical Distribution Cost

Element	Weight (per cent)
Transportation	46
Warehousing	26
Inventory carrying	10
Receiving and shipping	06
Packaging	05
Administration	04
Order	03
Total	100

1. Physical Flow:

Supplier — Transporters Warehouses — UNION (CFP) — Transporters Warehouses — PMCS — Customer (Farmers)

2. Title Flow:

Supplier — UNION (CFP) — PMCS — Customer (Farmers)

3. Payment Flow:

Supplier — Banks — UNION (CFP) — PMCS — Customer (Farmers)

4. Information Flow:

Supplier — Transporters Warehouses Banks — UNION (CFP) — Transporters — PMCS — Customer (Farmers)

5. Promotion Flow:

Supplier — UNION (CFP) — PMCS — Customer (Farmers)

CFP = Cattle Feed Plant
PMCS = Primary Milk Cooperative Society

Figure 9.2 Marketing Flows

the producers informed of market behaviour. The marketing flows in the distribution channel of the compounded balanced cattle are given in Figure 9.2.

The flows depend upon (i) the product and (ii) the distribution plan. The channel has been kept as short as possible, involving just the retailer as the outlet for the customer. The warehousing is at the Primary Milk Co-operative Society (PMCS) as the farmers do not have the necessary storing facilities. Moreover, this outlet is available in every village, making the product available almost at the doors of the farmers.

There is an apparent difference in payment and promotion flows. This is because under the co-operative system the payment is hardly in cash. It starts with the farmers. They pour milk at the PMCS and are paid in cash. The farmer pays for the feed from this cash. This milk goes to the union and the bill for it is prepared. The price of the feed supplied to the society is charged to this milk bill itself. So, it does not require banks to handle the money. Though it sounds like the traditional barter system, it is very simplistic and logical.

There is no external agency involved for selling the feed as it calls for personal selling more than advertising. Both the union and the PMCS engage in personal selling.

Therefore, the selection of the distribution channel for any product depends upon how well these flows are handled and facilitated. This calls for an effort-reward evaluation exercise. Figure 9.3 depicts alternative channels.

From a marketer's point of view, the functions that are performed by the channel members are:

- Availability
- Information
- Demand creation

The above model shows the alternatives to meet different market segments. However, in case of selling through the co-operative system, the factory has only one segment to serve—the farmers at the village level. As every district has one cattle-feed factory, it has similar segments though they have to serve different villages. For that it uses the second alternative—taking help of retailers only. This is represented by the primary societies at village levels. This is adopted for getting the maximum control over the distribution, placing and timing of the product. This is also supported by the

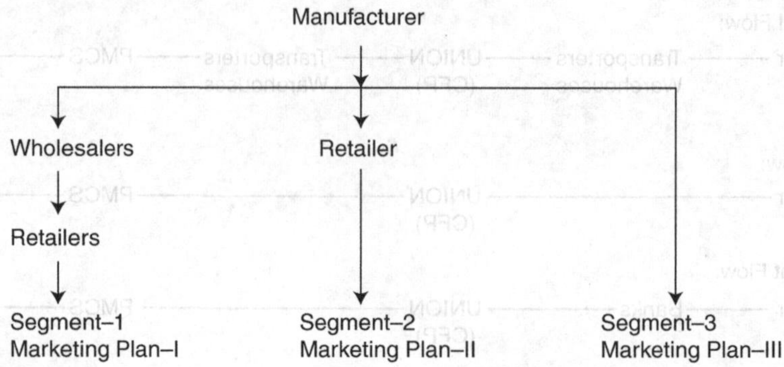

Figure 9.3 Alternative Channel System

fact that the majority of the cattle owners are members of the society and naturally will have more faith in that source than any other outlet. They know that any product coming through the society is a "good"-quality product and is beneficial to them. Therefore, they accept the product almost blindly. In such a situation, distributing the product through other outlets will not only create problems for the consumers but also for the producers and will have a direct effect on the acceptance of the product. May be by doing so, the marketer is creating place utility. Everyday, the farmer goes to the society twice for pouring the milk. Such frequent visits to the society makes it the most appropriate outlet. It satisfies the time utility as the need for the product coincides with the milking of animals and thus, visits to the society. The channel is shown in Figure 9.4.

The channel takes care of the atrocities of wholesalers/middlemen and the farmers get the feeds at the least possible cost. As the objective of the union is to provide feed at the least cost, any addition to the number of middlemen will add to the cost of the feed. These factors force the union to go for as direct a channel as possible.

The non-members cannot buy feed from the union. They can buy it from the society. However, if an agency wishes to buy in bulk, it can buy from the union. They obtain the delivery from the factory and have to make the payment at the union. This usually happens with the government farms. However, this is not a regular feature.

Transportation System: The choice of transportation carriers and modes affect the pricing of the product, on-time delivery performance and the condition of the goods when they arrive. All these affect

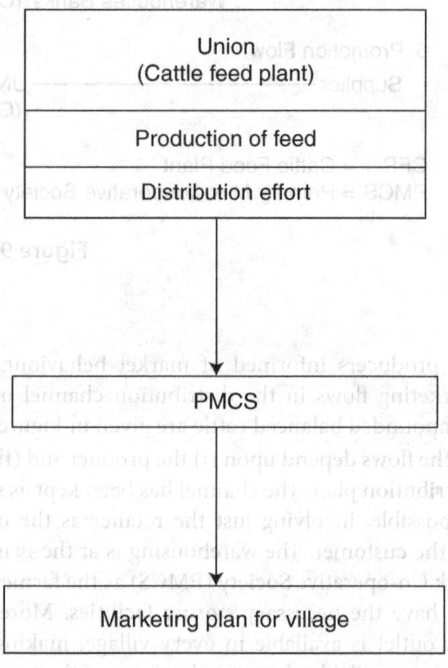

Figure 9.4 The Distribution Channel Adopted for Compounded Balanced Cattle by Co-operative Enterprises

customer satisfaction. It is the main activity in the availability function. It takes care of the time utility by making the product available at the right time and at the right place.

There are mainly two heads of transportation in any marketing set up. One, is the in-house transportation for receiving raw materials and the second, is the outward transportation for getting the finished product to the centre of consumption.

The transportation can be through rail, road or water. However, rail and road are more prevalent modes of transportation and in the case of cattle feed these are the only two modes utilized. In fact, these have so much bearing on the factory that it is desired that the factory is established near the railway tracks or the roads. For the raw materials, both these modes are used, depending on the raw material and the source. However, road transportation is better for the feed. In fact, it is the only way to ship the feed.

This is for two apparent reasons: (a) the villages are connected only through roads; i.e. all the villages do not have railway approach and (b) because of the small quantity bought by a single village, the usage of railway becomes unviable. Since each society does not buy big quantities due to the lack of storage facilities at their end, the frequency of purchase is high and this restricts the use of the railways as the mode of transpiration. However, it does not stop the factory from using the railways for sending the feed to distant places in bulk. One more factor that supports the use of roads is the fleet trucks that are hired by the union for transportation of milk from the society to the dairy. The same fleet is used for transporting the feed to the societies.

One of the most interesting things to be noted in the Anand pattern is the payment made to the transport contractors. They are neither paid on the bulk they transport, nor on the distance covered. They are paid per bag on an average for a particular defined area. For example, the payment at the Dudhasagar Dairy, Mehasana, Gujarat, is *taluka*-wise. It is fixed on the basis of the distance of the *taluka* from the cattle-feed plant. The cost, therefore, differs from *taluka* to *taluka*. But within the *taluka* there is no difference in the cost. Irrespective of the situation of the village, be it the nearest or the farthest, the freight charges per bag are the same.

The case with Amul Anand is different. Here, the district is divided into four regions. The Ahmedabad–Bombay Main Line is taken as the longitudinal basis and the factory as the centre for the latitude, as is depicted in Figure 9.5. The society

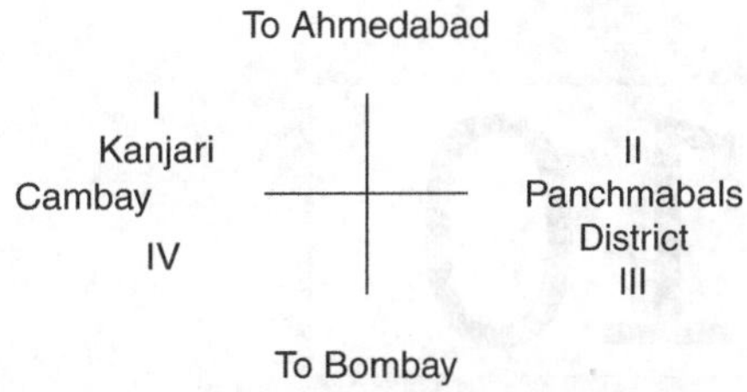

Figure 9.5 Division of Districts

can be located in any quadrant. The cost so arrived at is the average of the overall cost in the *taluka* quadrant.

This system has two major benefits. First, the truck owner will always try to get a truckload instead of making many trips, as the remuneration is on the basis of the number of bags of feed transported. In fact, if the truck owner goes for frequent trips he will lose more than what he gains. Second, this also facilitates out-bound transportation. If one single village does not have a demand for a truckload, it will be uneconomical and hence, the transporter may not like to execute the order. Therefore, the orders from the villages in one route are executed simultaneously to make it a truckload. The transporter goes on dropping the feed in the villages en route. Some orders may have to wait for this. However, the time span between the order and execution is taken into consideration while fixing the inventory at the society level.

Besides these, the union gets a well-maintained fleet as the contractor will not wish to lose orders and keep the trucks idle.

For discussion

1. What are the salient features of the distribution of cattle feed by the Anand pattern?
2. In view of the latest developments do you find any other alternatives of distribution?

Source: P. K. Sinha, "Distribution of Catle Feed, Under Anand Pattern," *Decision*, Vol. 16, No. 3 (July–September 1989): 207–213.

10

Rural Retailing

LEARNING OBJECTIVES

Upon completion of this chapter, you will be able to:

- Know the problems and drivers of retailing
- Understand the different types of retailing and the role of retailers
- Discuss the functioning of different types of malls initiated by the government, entrepreneurs, agri-input companies, petrol companies and urban retailers
- Explain the PPP and e-tail models of retailing
- Recognize the initiatives taken by companies to train rural retailers

A unique training programme "*Parivartan*" was launched by Coca-Cola India for retailers in tier II and III towns across India, to bring about a positive change. The programme seeks to develop skills to survive, compete, sustain and grow in a fast changing retail scenario in the country. As a token of appreciation, the participants are provided an accidental death insurance of Rs 0.1 million, free of cost.

Batches of around 20 retailers, who are typical, small 300 sq. ft *kirana* shop owners, are trained at a time. In a two-hour session, they are trained with the help of audio-visuals, plasma TVs, laptops and LCD projectors. The course content covers the four major issues of retailing—customer, shop, stock and finance. The programme offered various guidelines for effective retailing. The tips provided are varied, ranging from printing a visiting card with a telephone number to treating customers courteously. On the technical side, suggestions relate to building up visibility by focusing on revenue-generating products (20 per cent of products generate 80 per cent revenue), putting up display posters of discounts and organizing a home delivery facility. The programme has covered 20,000 retailers in North India. "Advanced *Parivartan*" was developed based on the feedback from retailers. It covers issues such as shop layout and location, display, basics of finance, knowledge of credit card transactions and people management skills. The response was positive. The feedback collected after each programme from the retailers and impact measures after a gap of three months were impressive. Most of the trained retailers have adopted the best practices they learnt during the programme. The "Coca-Cola University on Wheels" has also covered small towns such as Hoshiarpur, Mukeria, Nakodar, Phagwara, Nawanshahar, Malerkotla, Barnala, Khanna, Moga and Jalandhar among others. Coca-Cola plans to scale up this initiative by taking it across India in the future.[1]

This initiative of Coca-Cola has come at a time when a revolution is taking place in retailing. It is a proactive measure towards building a strong, well-trained retailing network with a sense of corporate social responsibility and long-term business interest. It signals the evolution of professional retailing in India. Already, organized retailing has taken root and is going rural in a big way. This chapter explains the functioning of the traditional retailer. The operations of the emerging organized retail outlets are also outlined in the chapter.

INTRODUCTION

The retail business in India accounts for Rs 7,400 billion with about 12 million retailers. 90 per cent of the retail shops are *kirana* stores. Rural India has 3.7 million shops, spread over 0.63 million villages, with an average of six shops per village with an average sale of Rs 5,000 only. As such, marketers face a huge problem of supplying these shops located in vastly diverse areas. To bridge the gaps in retailing, private sector companies have taken different types of initiatives. Hindustan Unilever has launched Project *Shakti*, under which women's self-help groups act as the last link of the retail chain. India Post is converting itself into a retail chain for a variety of products and fair-price shops that form a part of the government's rationing system are trying to expand beyond supplying just basic food items such as rice and wheat. Some agri-input companies, petro-companies and FMCG players are setting up retail *kendras*. ITC has set up the IT-enabled e-*choupal* network to initiate "e-tailing" in rural hinterlands. The rural retail scenario is changing and the need for developing professional practices is well recognized.

THE RISE OF ORGANIZED RETAILING

Rural retail includes fast moving consumer goods, durables, agricultural inputs and vehicles such as tractors. The rural retail market forms around 40 per cent of the total size of the retail market of India, which according to reports of ASSOCHAM is worth USD 280 billion. Accordingly, the size of the rural retail market will be about USD 112 billion (Rs 5,000 billion). Growing at the rate of around 10 per cent of the size of Indian GDP, it has the potential to double in size in the next 4–5 years.

Present scenario

The present retail scenario is not very encouraging. The penetration of organized retail is very low. Approximately, 10,000 out of the 0.6 million villages in India have access to organized retail services. Owing to the low density of shops per village, uneven concentration of shops and very small size of retail outlets, multiple tiers of distribution have become necessary. As a result, distribution has become inconvenient and costly. In most cases, consumers do not have the opportunity to be exposed to various brands. The reason is that the retailers do not have the resources to stock multiple items and they will stock the brand that sells the most.

Problems of retailers[2]

Many people would be unwilling to start their own stores in smaller villages due to a number of reasons.

Procurement of goods

In the absence of proper connectivity with the feeder town from where the retailer collects goods, there is a constant problem of maintaining adequate stock-keeping units.

Inventory

The retailer has to deal with a large number of stock-keeping units. This results in a large inventory and high inventory holding costs.

Irregular sales

Inability to push sales on a regular basis due to restrictive incomes available with the rural populace is another problem.

Cost of pull strategy

Another problem relates to attracting customers from neighbouring areas. Unless a repeated promotional tool is used, people from neighbouring villages cannot be attracted.

Thin margins

The retailer cannot charge a higher mark-up as the consumers cannot afford to pay higher prices. Retailers have to travel frequently to the feeder town to collect products. As stated above, the retailers pick up their stocks from the nearest company stock point or wholesalers. The cost of travelling cannot be totally passed on to the customers. The margins will be thin in such cases.

Credit sales

Major purchases are made by rural consumers on the basis of credit. As a result, the retailer faces working-capital problems.

Drivers of growth[3]

The drivers are growing population, rising incomes, investment by the Government for development and entrepreneurial initiatives by individuals and corporate enterprises.

Growing population

The number of village households is expected to rise to 153 million in 2009–2010 from 135 million in 2001–2002, probably making rural India the largest potential market in the world.

Rising incomes

The rural per capita income would be Rs 14,000 (USD 350) by 2012 as more families switch to the commercial form of subsistence farming, a big enough jump to spur demand for a wider range of products.

Investment by the government for development

In view of the large investments made by the government in rural infrastructure pushing the income and demand levels, the prospects for organized retail are seen to be bright for rural India. Empowering rural people with education, employment, higher purchasing power, better media exposure and better connectivity with the world outside, provide a massive unexplored pool of consumers.

Entrepreneurial initiatives

Entrepreneurship has been a prime cause of economic development. The same is true in case of the Indian rural economy. Enthusiastic young persons and enlightened corporate enterprises are starting their own outlets. These outlets are revolutionizing retailing because they are comparable to the urban malls.

Today, with many positive changes taking place in the rural economy, rural retailing is on the path of development. Box 10.1 traces the evolution of auto retailing in the rural markets.

TYPES OF RETAIL OUTLETS

The size of the shop and the product mix are dependent on various factors such as the population of the village, income levels and level of economic development and lifestyles of people. Different types of outlets may be found in a village. They may be classified as the following according to the products

Box 10.1 Evolution of Auto Rural Retail

The initial strategy used in the autoretail market was a pull strategy to draw rural consumers to urban showrooms. The automobile companies appointed dealers in the cities and rural customers visited them to make their purchases. In the next phase, the industry eyed the rural market and appointed sales representatives to tour rural areas periodically. Finding good potential in the rural markets, the industry experimented with an "operate-from-the-market" model. Smaller upcountry locations were chosen and representatives were asked to operate "from" that area. With increasing opportunities to promote rural sales, sales force expansion was achieved in the next stage by appointing local representatives to support the extension sales men.

The developments in the market marked a significant change in strategy from pull to push. The large dealers of the district or a particular area set up small showrooms. As the sales did not match the expectations, the industry realized the need for ownership. Sub-dealers were appointed to work under the large dealers. However, the system did not yield good results due to the vested interests of large dealers. To promote business as well as safeguard the interests of dealers in upcountry locations, direct dealers were appointed in upcountry locations.

Source: Dhruv Tanwar, "Rural Marketing Seminar: Go Rural, Don't Wait for Your Customer to Urbanise News," May 2008, available at www.domain-b.com/companies/companies_m/Mahindra/20080510_mahindra_and_mahindra.html.

that they sell: *paan* and provisions (*kirana*), fancy and medical, books and stationery, agri-inputs, cement and hardware, electrical and electronics, Internet and xerox, video and photography, cloth and garments, etc. There may be a couple of outlets selling durables. There will also be in-house sellers especially housewives, who sell select range of *sarees* and other clothes and freelance traders who sell insurance and savings products. In addition, there may be mobile retailers—traders and company sales persons. We do not see this kind of business in small villages. They may have one or two shops selling provisions. In case it is a religious centre, there will be shops selling coconuts and other material for worship. Otherwise, the village wears a quiet, deserted look. The villagers depend on *haats*, vans and mobile traders/salesmen for their periodical purchases. The retail shops in a typical village will be small in size and offer relatively small volumes of stock-keeping units (SKU). Box 10.2 describes how shops vary with the change in altitude over mountainous terrain.

In remote villages retailers will not come forward to start their own retail outlets as they are not economically viable and operationally problematic. Mr Asad Shamsi, who has studied marketing and finance in Germany, conceived a concept that counters all these loopholes of retailing in a rural area. Though the grocers and other shop owners already present in the villages are not happy, they would soon realize how important it is to have an organized plan of action in order to lead the market. Box 10.3 describes the initiative of the 3-A *bazaar* of Shamsi.

In case of consumer durables, especially for automobiles, the service aspect is very important. There is a need to offer regular services to satisfy the customers and promote sales of their vehicles. The automobile companies resolved the problem by employing mobile service vans. Box 10.4 explains the operation of service vans.

ROLE OF RETAILERS

In the rural context, the retailer has a different role when compared to his urban counterpart. The concern for affiliations, open approach in dealing with people, lack of awareness about branded products and willingness to learn found in rural consumers require the retailer to play different roles:

Box 10.2 Retail and Altitude

Retail shops vary from one location to another. Size, specialization and brand mix variations are influenced by the location. Thickly populated metros aid specialization. On the contrary, mountain terrains require different offers. At the foot of the mountain, limited goods find place in shops that can be regarded as local super stores. As one goes up, old tents or stone huts are found. They are multi-purpose outfits offering refreshments, food and lodging. The available products include generic tea, Nescafe, Everyday milk powder, branded noodles, Bonn biscuits, rice, roti and vegetable curry dominated by the tough potato. However, exceptions to the all-in-one shop are found even in these areas. For notebooks, there are exclusive shops till medium altitudes. Some surprising innovations are found as well. The tent restaurant on the way to Stok Kangri in Ladakh has a native refrigerator. The cold stream water is diverted to a pit within to chill the soft drinks. The brand names used also offer surprises. At the shop behind Khati's Jai Nanda restaurant, you will find a small Tata-Bajaj gas cylinder and a Nokia tooth brush.

Source: Shyam G. Menon, "Where the Brands Matter, and Don't," *The Hindu Business Line*, 29 October 2009.

Box 10.3 Retail on Wheels

The 3-A *bazaar* has adopted a novel approach of van marketing. Every morning, five vans stuffed with 1,300 items worth Rs 0.2 to 0.25 million set out for the neighbouring 700 villages. A wide range of products from sugar to shampoo, sanitary napkins to salwar–kurtas are offered to the villagers. Every van is provided with an armed guard to provide security. While the vans touch some of the villages daily, most of the areas are visited on a weekly, fortnightly or monthly basis. The time gap permits daily wage earners to pool up money for making purchases when the van reaches their location. The average sale per day has been approximated to be around 8–10 thousand. Besides a distribution vehicle, the colourful vans act as promotional tools. The orange and blue colours of the van symbolize the fresh shopping experience that the consumers would have from the van.

Source: Vivin Wason, "Retail on Wheels in Rural India," November 2007.

Box 10.4 Service Vans

Faced with the problem of servicing customers in rural areas, Mahindra and Mahindra has utilized the concept of mobile service vans. Arun Malhotra of Mahindra and Mahindra observed that it is far more easy to sell than to service rural customers as the cost of setting up a workshop comprising a paint booth and body shop for a full-service establishment will be over Rs 0.2 million. When service needs are analysed, it is found that 90 per cent of the service needs are of basic, routine maintenance type. Deciding to cover the identified 90 per cent of customer needs, Mahindra and Mahindra introduced mobile service vans. The vans tour rural markets and provide basic servicing and diagnostic services. In case more complex services are required, the customer is referred to the closest service station.

Source: Dhruv Tanwar "Rural Marketing Seminar: Go Rural, Don't Wait for Your Customer to Urbanise News," 10 May 2008, available at www.domain-b.com/companies/companies_m/Mahindra/20080510_mahindra_and_mahindra.html.

Trusted seller

The urban retailer is not trusted. He is seen as a businessman with a profit motive. His viewpoints are evaluated with other sources of information. On the contrary, the rural retailer is seen as a fair person. Villagers trust him in all transactions. Most purchases are on credit basis and this is another major reason for reposing faith in him.

Influencer

The retailer's role as influencer is indisputable. His opinions and recommendations are given due weightage in finalizing decisions. From the tender twig of *neem* to washing powder, retailer testimony has been a vital part of the product adoption process. The role of the urban retailer, on the contrary, is weak. The urban consumers have numerous sources of information. While the retailers opinion is sought, it may not be believed and followed always. A study on buying behaviour of rural consumer indicates that rural retailers influence 35 per cent of purchase decisions.

Brand promoter

Brand promotion has gained ground with the rise in incomes in the rural areas. Further, sachets and small packs are provided by marketers to facilitate easy transactions. Marketers have made brand choices easy by communicating the brand characteristics and benefits through different promotion media and direct one-to-one communication. Despite this, the retailer remains the deciding factor in selling a particular brand. The retail shop is small in size and cannot facilitate shelf displays and browsing experience. Point-of-purchase promotions can arouse interest in the buyers. However, at the time of purchase, it is the retailer who helps in identification and selection of brands.

The presence and sales of spurious brands is ample testimony to this view. The spurious brands enjoy the patronage of the retailer due to the higher retail margins, with lower end-consumer prices, supported by pack formats identical to the original. The retailer does the promotion for fake products.

The urban retailer has a limited role as a brand promoter. He cannot directly recommend the brands. He has to intelligently drive home his recommendation, as urban consumers do not trust him completely. It is through shelf displays and incentive offers that he has to push the brands.

Relationship marketer

The village retailer practices relationship marketing. Most of the consumers are permanent residents of the village. They are dependent on agriculture for their livelihood. The relationship sometimes extends beyond three generations, backed by the historical credibility of the retailer as a product referral. On the contrary, the urban retailer has customers who belong to different locations and different towns. Further, they may not be regular visitors of one retail shop. Also, they do not patronize one shop. They buy from different shops to take advantage of the offers or to have variety in shopping experience. This limits the time span and strength of customer relationship.

Harbinger of change

The village shopkeeper can be a harbinger of change. He is one of the main sources of information and opinion as well as the supplier of products and services. By offering novel products and recommending them with genuine interest, he can bring about a change in the lifestyles of rural consumers.

RURAL MALLS

Rural India needs huge malls that act as one-stop shops that meet all the needs of farmers. They must have the following facilities.

(i) *Mandi:* A purchase centre that buys produce at market-related prices

(ii) *Occupational goods and services:*
- Agri-inputs and implements
- Technical cell that advises farmers on crop-related issues
- Bank that provides credit
- Insurance company that insures produce
- Food-processing unit

(iii) *Home needs:*
- FMCGs
- Consumer durables

(iv) *Medical facilities for people*

(v) *Veterinary services*

(vi) *Entertainment:* A complex that organizes *melas*, bullock cart races and rewards outstanding performance by farmers.

GOVERNMENT-INITIATED RETAIL OUTLETS

The central and state governments have taken steps to transform the congested, restricted and exploitative fair-price shops and Indian post offices in worn out buildings into malls and give the consumers a new shopping experience.

Fair-price shops become malls

Model fair-price shops, described as micro rural malls, are springing up all over Gujarat. Villagers can shop in these malls for all their needs 24x7. The "malls" are in effect model fair-price shops under a programme launched to de-regulate the scope of services of traditional fair-price shops by allowing them to deal with all kinds of goods and services.

Gujarat experiments

There are about 15,000 fair-price shops all over Gujarat. According to official sources, the Gujarat government is planning to have 1,000 multi-purpose malls every year. Already, 512 such "malls" have sprouted and another 508 are on the anvil. Encouraged by the success of the programme, the State has suggested inclusion of the programme in the list of plan schemes to the Central government.[4]

Andhra Pradesh experiments

The Government of Andhra Pradesh has also decided to run fair-price shops as multi-purpose malls. Officials are instructed to make an arrangement with manufacturers so that they (manufacturers) could make available their products at a point to enable fair-price shop dealers to take the commodities on consignment basis. As a result, the consumer will get commodities at cheaper rates. The government has also issued orders asking collectors to provide loans through banks in case dealers approach them. They have also been told to explore the possibility of providing loans from the *Khadi* Village Industries Commission (KVIC) and *Khadi* Village Industrial Board (KVIB) duly treating fair-price shops as rural malls for providing soft loans with differential rate of interest. The State Government, through a Government Order, has also allowed the dealers to provide postal services, life insurance policies, bus-ticket booking facilities, STD booths and ice-cream parlours.

As of now, rice, wheat, sugar, kerosene, palmolein oil and red gram are being sold through the Pubic Distribution System (PDS) network. Following the initiative, companies such as ITC, HUL, major oil companies, Videocon and telephone service providers such as Tata, BSNL and Hutch are supplying their wares. Other products include Life Insurance Corporation (LIC) policies and ice creams. Both state-run and private banks are trying to position themselves in rural areas by making malls the sales link for their financial products. Computers will be introduced gradually to take care of the value added tax (VAT) calculations.

The government would implement this scheme initially, at a village in each of the *mandals* of each district. According to the AP State Civil Supplies Commissioner, Sanjay Jaju, the government has already sent orders in the matter. He further said, the "RFID system will also be implemented within two months at fair-price shops in the five districts of West Godavari, Guntur, Prakasam, Chittoor and Karimnagar on an experimental basis. The civil supplies department will provide smart cards instead of coupons." A ration card holder should take the smart card to the fair-price shop to get essential commodities.

Village malls are believed to increase the incomes of fair-price shop dealers by allowing them to sell more goods and services through such shops. The owners of the shops used to earn between Rs 500 and 2,000 initially, as commission from sales. They can now hope for earnings of Rs 5,000 a month.

However, there are riders. Fair-price shop dealers have to modernize their shops in a phased manner and create more space for mobility, change display systems, computerize and provide water and toilet facilities.

India Post—new age service retailer

The Department of Posts in India has launched a series of fully upgraded and completely new-look post offices for the rural people. According to the Ministry of Communications and Information Technology, these new age post offices would serve as a window to the world for the common man—"*Aam Aadmi*"—by focusing on his needs.[5]

In 2008, two consultants—Ogilvy & Mather and McKinsey—provided a restructuring plan to give India Post a complete new corporate identity. Named Project Arrow, the exercise aims to create technology-driven, new-look post offices, with multi-purpose counters to increase customer footfalls and satisfaction.

New spirit and new look

The new logo, in bright red and yellow is in the shape of a bird about to take flight. The tagline reads "Giving Wings to Your Dreams." The exterior and interior of the post offices have undergone a transformation. They present a contrasting picture to the dark and dingy public image that government offices have in general.

IT support for service upgradation

The project aims at improving the quality of service by being IT-enabled and also, by providing better infrastructure with customer-driven focus. An information kiosk, *Sparsh*, provides information on PIN (postal index number) code, tariff and various services offered by the department.

The multi-purpose counters help manage customer demands faster and better. The range of new services include quick dispatch of passport applications and sale of UPSC and KPSC application forms, e-tickets, gold coins, insurance and financial services. The repositioning of the department aims at increasing responsiveness to market forces, enhancing competitiveness and making it self-sufficient.

New carriers

India Post operates three exclusive aircrafts touching some major cities in the country, including Bangalore, for overnight delivery of mails, speed-post and parcels through dedicated service.

Training to staff

Efforts have been made to improve customer service by training staff in customer relationship management and through the introduction of faster and better services.

New retail centres

All these will now be converted into local retail centres. The idea is to use the existing real estate that's begun to wear a deserted look after the popularity of e-mail services to profitably sell other merchandise, such as off-the-counter medicines, education schemes, auto loans and healthcare services. A select few are also selling text books, *ayurvedic* medicines, gold coins and railway tickets. The plan later, is to look for joint ventures to turn post offices in remote villages into miniature shopping malls.

Services in the rural context

The post office in rural areas will henceforth be a single-window facility for banking, money remittance, transmission and delivery of information. Besides providing traditional services in a modern, more efficient and technology-based mode, the post offices will also form an indispensable part of all social and civic initiatives such as the National Rural Employment Guarantee Act (NREGA) and National Old Age Pension Scheme. With the implementation of Project Arrow, India Post is moving towards the realization of its motto—*Dak Seva, Jan Seva.*

ENTREPRENEUR-FOUNDED MALLS

With the growing opportunities for business in rural areas, some entrepreneurs are exploring new avenues in the rural areas. Nadeem Jafri is one among them. A brief description of his venture is given here.[6]

Hearty Mart

Nadeem Jafri, an MBA from the Institute of Management Studies, Indore, Madhya Pradesh (MP), setup a chain of supermarkets in rural Gujarat, known as "Hearty Mart." Jafri found that the people of Illol village were going to the nearest town of Himmatnagar in Gujarat to buy even a sachet of shampoo. Now people can buy products that they use daily such as shampoo sachets from a shop in their own village rather than travelling to the nearest town.

Jafri ventured into this business with an initial capital of Rs 4 million. After a year, the venture clocked a retail turnover of Rs 6 million, which is expected to cross Rs 7–7.5 million in the current financial year. The first anniversary of Hearty Mart was celebrated by sending a packet of sugar to all its customers along with a signed letter acknowledging their support and at the same time expressing the Mart's desire to continue the "sweet relationship." Indeed, this gesture had tremendous impact on the customers.

Franchisee model

This novel initiative of Jafri percolated into a number of remote villages of Gujarat such as Pipodar, Kakoshi, Vadnagar and Idar, providing a modern retail experience to rural folk aspiring for brands similar to those introduced into their homes by the television.

This model operates on the concept of "two brands under one roof"—Hearty Mart and another chosen by the franchisee. The model also provides a choice to the shopkeeper to disassociate his brand from Hearty Mart and to operate on his own. The first franchise was issued at Illol for a deposit of Rs 25,000. *Sahyog*, Easy Shop and Tiny Shop are the other brand names chosen by the franchisees in Illol, Kakoshi and Pipodar, respectively. The stores are generally 500 to 800 sq. ft in size and those with a size of less than 300 sq. ft, are known as Hearty Mart *Saral* Shops. The latter category of stores have been devised because of the interest shown by the villagers. *Saral* is modelled after the neighbourhood *kirana* stores found in cities. Jafri and his team take care of the initial stocking for the store and claim 1.5 per cent annual royalty from the franchisees. The chain intends setting up about 15 stores in a couple of years.

In a bid to generate more revenue through the stores, the chain is exploring the idea of stocking private labels for products such as *papad*, pickle, *besan*, etc. and so on that are not available locally. Jafri recently introduced *Lutf*, a homemade ketchup that is sold to hotels and other institutions, for sale at the Hearty Mart stores. Good Time is another in-house label for packaged spices that is now being tested.

AGRI-COMPANY RETAIL OUTLETS

Agri-input suppliers have creative and innovative retail formats in rural areas. Here is a brief description of such rural retail outlets.

1. ITC *Choupal Saagar*
2. Tata *Kisan Sansar* (TKS)
3. DSCL *Hariyali Kisan Bazaar*
4. Godrej *Aadhar* and *Manthan*
5. Mahindra *Shubh Labh*
6. Triveni *Khushali Bazaar* (TKB)

ITC *Choupal Saagar*[7]

ITC's zeal in organizing these malls reflects the dominant trend in corporate India of entering every area ranging from contract farming to rural malls, seed research to medicinal plants and food processing to fruit exports.

Choupal Saagar is a warehouse for storing the farm products that ITC buys through its e-*Choupals*. It is one of the first organized retail forays in the hinterland set up by the international business division of tobacco major ITC. This is a hub-cum-supermarket and forms a part of the warehouse.

The first mall was started at a small village called Rafiqganj about 4 km from Bhopal, in the direction of Sehore town. The mall, housed in 5 acres of land, has a warehouse space of 10,000 sq. ft, besides space for storing 10,000 tonnes of grains, with support facilities such as fuel station, food court and training centre. *Choupal Saagar* has a wide range of self-service products ranging from toothpastes to televisions, hair oils to motorcycles, mixer-grinders to water pumps, shirts to fertilizers. Most of the brands sold by it are national in nature such as Marico, LG, Philips, torches from Eveready, shirts from ITC's apparel business, bikes from TVS and tractors from Eicher. This is a pioneering venture in rural retailing with the all-under-one-roof concept.

The idea of the mall is to create a one-stop destination for farmers. The farmer, with his family, drives into *Choupal Saagar* in a tractor trolley, laden with the produce from his field that he proposes to sell. His grain is weighed on the digital weighing machine. The farmer then drives on to the godown to unload the weighed produce. Meanwhile, his kids can enjoy the swings and video games, while his wife may like to move around and select the items she needs for the household. As soon as the farmer gets his cash, the farmer and his family make the required purchases. The family then enjoys its lunch in the cafeteria located in the premises of the mall. Further, the farmer, if he intends to, can even carry fertilizers and pesticides and get a diesel fill for his tractor. The family can drive back home by the evening.

By 2005–2006, the company had opened 30 more rural malls. Recently, the company constructed nine malls, three each in Maharashtra, Madhya Pradesh and Uttar Pradesh. The daily sales of the mall touch between Rs 70,000 and 80,000, which is a reasonably good business proposition.

Business model

- The business model of *Choupal Saagar* is linked closely with the e-*Choupal* initiative of ITC.
- The role of ITC is to create infrastructure such as space, computers and building.
- ITC will charge a fee for the services and items sold at the mall.

These malls will act as a hub for both, branded and locally-produced goods, entertainment options, education, health care and farm advisories. The malls will also generate rural employment.

Tata *Kisan Sansar* (TKS)[8]

Tata Chemicals is India's leading soda ash and fertilizer company. It has had a long association with farmers, supplying high quality urea, a vital input for most crops. In 1998, the company came up with the idea of setting up one-stop shops for the Indian farmer to supply all his requirements from the seed sowing stage to the post-harvest stage. Named Tata *Kisan Kendra* (TKK), it not only offered farmers products but also expert information required by them. Four years later, in 2002, the company decided to expand the offer to provide a range of agri-services and agri-products and re-branded the rural initiative as Tata *Kisan Sansar* (TKS).

Changing mindset

The company is attempting to change the mindset of farmers. It is trying to make the farmer look at farming as a business and not as a subsistence activity. The new outlook implies an openness of mind to seek knowledge, new techniques and ideas. The challenge is customization, designing baskets of products and services according to the needs of each farmer.

One-stop shop

Tata *Kisan Sansar* (TKS) is designed as an information and communication technology-oriented rural project with the aim of helping the farmers to lead healthier lives and carry out sound agricultural activities.

TKS centres offer soil and water testing, contract farming and credit facilitation. Each has a complete range of agri-inputs such as fertilizers, seeds, pesticides, herbicides and micro-nutrients. Agronomists at each TKS share their expertise with farmers and provide the latest information on weather, market pricing and crop production, enabling them to take quick and informed decisions. All the centres are being computerized and a database of farmers is being built up, allowing sharing of techniques and information.

The services offered by the initiative include crop insurance and corporate farming. Apart from offering a range of agri-services, the rural agri-retail outlet also provides many input products such as high yielding seeds and good quality fertilizers and pesticides.

Human-capacity development

Tata Chemicals has tied up with Cornell University's College of Agriculture and Life Sciences, a premier American agricultural college. Professors from the university have interacted with trainers at TKS centres as well as farmers in the field. The focus is on human-capacity building. The company is also trying to set up development centres in association with some agricultural universities.

Tata *Kisan Parivar*

Farmers can avail of TKS services by becoming members of the Tata *Kisan Parivar* (TKP). They can also choose to pay selectively for services. TKP is essentially a relationship-building initiative where Tata Chemicals identifies farmers who are open to new techniques and can also be spokespersons in villages. The 30,000 members of TKP are given training in the latest farming techniques, offered services at a discount and taken for educational trips to agricultural universities. They also get family insurance coverage.

Kisan Sahyog Parivar

The *Kisan Sahyog Parivar* is yet another initiative. Farmers are encouraged to form self-help groups (SHGs) that provide a platform for facilitation of credit as well as learning and sharing among themselves.

Improving lifestyles

Catching up with changes in the lifestyles of farmers, TKS has expanded its basket of products to include lifestyle items. It tied up with Titan for selling Sonata watches, Tata Indicom for telecom services, and Tata BP Solar for solar power products. IndianOil tied up with TKS for setting up fuel stations and selling packaged kerosene. Tata Chemicals is on the lookout for adding credit and crop insurance services to expand further. TKS hopes to strengthen its partnership with farmers with its farmer-oriented initiatives.

Locations

Today, Tata *Kisan Sansar* has 421 franchisee-run centres in the three states of Punjab, Haryana, and Uttar Pradesh and reaches out to over 3.6 million farmers.

DSCL's *Hariyali Kisan Bazaar*[9]

DCM Shriram Consolidated Limited (DSCL), based on its experience in the sugar and seed business, set up *Hariyali Kisan Bazaar*, a rural business initiative in 2002 in the states of Rajasthan, Uttar Pradesh, Haryana, Punjab and Uttarakhand. The retail outlets that numbered five in 2002 increased to 24 by March 2005 and 300 by 2006. In the next five years this number may go up to 500 and spread through all the states of the country.

Goals

The main aim of the initiative is to empower farmers by fulfilling all their occupational requirements and to build farmer-friendly relationships to enhance their productivity.

Range of services

The scope of the project includes the supply of agricultural and daily needs of the farmer such as the availability of inputs, agronomy services, finance and output linkages.

The company wants to develop and customize retail solutions through its initiatives to serve the rural customer better while creating a strong infrastructure for the operations spread over multiple locations. The *Hariyali Kisan Bazaars*, on the whole, are engaged in bridging the last mile providing a complete range of good-quality multi-brand agri-inputs (fertilizers, seeds, pesticides), farm implements and tools, veterinary products, animal feed, irrigation items and other key inputs such as diesel and petrol at fair prices. Financial services (access to modern retail banking and farm credit through simplified and transparent processes and other financial services such as insurance, etc.), farm-output services with opportunities to buyback farm produce, access to new markets and output-related services, other products and services such as fuels, FMCGs, durables, apparels, etc. are also provided.

The company expects the technology platform to be scalable, robust and capable of improving inventory management and controlling stock-outs and overstocking. The operational costs are also expected to be reduced.

The malls occupy an area of about six acres for storing some 400 categories of products such as stock feeds, seeds, fertilizers, veterinary medicines and farm implements all of which cater to the needs of farmers. They function under the management of agronomists who guide the farmers with technical know-how related to agriculture without charging any fees. The malls provide need-based infrastructure to farmers, cater to agricultural land of about 50,000 to 70,000 acres and impact the life of about 15,000 farmers.

The company has linked its *Hariyali* retail outlets with a custom-built IT system to serve rural consumers. The project e-Starr (systems and technology in agriculture and rural retail) offers its solutions to *Hariyali* to extend better services to the farmer. The company has also partnered with software solution providers, SAP and Polaris, to create a unique IT platform.

All the *Hariyali* centres have Internet connection through Reliance Phones and SAT connectivity. As a result, the business processes across all retail stores and in the head office have been simplified, standardized and nationalized. The farmers are provided online information about weather forecasts and market prices with fair and transparent billing. There are now extensive farmer databases with micro-information about farmers' yields to give customized service to them. Farmers are also provided technology services, including training to use the point-of-sales (POS) terminals installed at various outlets.

Alliances

For sales and distribution of its handsets, Motorola has associated with DSCLs *Hariyali Kisan Bazaar* chain of rural/semi-urban utility malls.

Godrej *Aadhar* and *Manthan*[10]

Godrej Agrovet Ltd is a division of Godrej Soaps Ltd and a part of the Rs 34 billion Godrej Group. It was set up as a separate company exclusively meant to be an agri-centre. Right from its inception in 1971, the company has developed and nurtured a close relationship with farmers by providing them with innovative produce and education on world-class farming practices.

Range of services

Adhar and *Manthan* are new concepts initiated by the Godrej Group. Positioned as "*Godrej Aadhaar—Khushiyon Ka, Khushhali Ka*," the new format stores mark the beginning of a chain that shall form the farmer's *Aadhaar* for "*Unnati, Ghar Sansar aur Gaon*," a move from being just a complete agricultural solution provider to being a multi-category retail outlet with wide range of products and services housing a fair mix of brands and private labels. Services such as soil analysis and veterinary care are also offered to farmers. *Manthan*, on the other hand, focuses on the supply of quality animal feed to boost up the dairy and poultry produce both of which are expected to raise the farmers' income.

Godrej Agrovet Ltd entered into a joint venture agreement for rural retailing with Future Ventures India Ltd. It is a Future Group company with 70 per cent stake in *Aadhaar* Retailing Ltd, while Godrej Agrovet Ltd owns the rest. Godrej *Aadhaar*, the agri-services-cum-rural retail initiative with about 66 outlets, is a complete solution provider for the farmer. Based on customer feedback, the venture, of late, has diversified its business to offer a number of other product categories such as consumer durables, food and grocery, apparels, footwear and so on. Thus, this retail initiative meets the total requirements of the rural households.

Aadhar reaches out to 50,000 farmers every month through 300 employees who directly access the produce of farmers from as many as 2,000 villages in the country. This scheme is presently in operation in the states of Punjab, Haryana, Maharashtra and Gujarat. Sourcing from farmers and helping them sell their produce to other retailers is viewed as an extension of the earlier cash-and-carry format of the Future Group.

Aadhar would now serve as a procurement hub for the Future Group's retail formats such as Food Bazaar and KB's Fair Price and even become a supplier to other retailers across the country. All the existing Godrej Aadhar outlets, in a bid to extend their current portfolio, started stocking the Future Group's private labels and financial products. The new brands making their appearance at the *Aadhar* outlets include *Koryo* (for consumer durables) and food brands such as *Tasty Treat and Fresh 'N Pure.*

Alliances

After forging its alliances with such players as GlaxoSmithKline, the Future Group has made it possible for the *Gopika* brand of ghee to be sold at its *Aadhar* outlets. Other brands of products that are catching up in sales at *Aadhar* outlets include financial products like the insurance-based *Future Generalli* and the *Future Card* (the Future Group's loyalty cum credit card).

Mahindra's *Shubh Labh*[11]

Shubh Labh is a rural subsidiary initiative of the USD 2.6 billion Mahindra Group, which is the largest farm equipment company in the country. Mahindra *Shubh Labh* Services have operations in 11 states and leverages the strong Mahindra brand, the 700,000-strong Mahindra tractor-customer base and the 400-plus dealer network, to provide a complete range of products.

The subsidiary also extends services to improve farm productivity and establishes market linkages to the commodity market chain. Its retailing arm, Mahindra *Krishi Vihar*, has been instrumental in increasing the groundnut yield in Rajasthan through a new seed sourced from Maharashtra. It has also introduced a new variety of grapes in Maharashtra. The head of Mahindra *Shubh Labh* Services, Vikram Puri, says that almost 80 per cent of the farmers registered with the company have less than five acres of land and therefore, the company wanted to make farming an attractive proposition through three basic guiding steps:

- Growing what the market requires,
- Improving the crop yield and
- Decreasing the cost of crop production.

The activities of Mahindra *Shubh Labh* Services have attracted the attention of the International Finance Corporation, the financial arm of the World Bank that recently picked up a 27 per cent stake in the company.

With 36 outlets, M&M's *Shubh Labh* network is spread over eight states. Only three centres are run by M&M and the rest are franchisees. The company retails agri-inputs, including M&M brands through *Shubh Labh*. It also undertakes contract farming in over 0.1 million acres. Both oilseeds and cereals have been cultivated in this land besides growing horticultural products, aromatic plants and flowers. It also offers lending support to marginal and small farmers through its agri-input centres under the platform of the Mahindra *Krishi Vihar*. This programme renders assistance through banks to provide loans to farmers with minimum documentation, quick sanctions, and attractive interest rates. Thus, rural lending becomes safer for banks without too many overheads.

Triveni *Khushali Bazaar* (TKB)[12]

Triveni *Khushali Bazaar* (TKB) started its operations at Khatauli and Deoband during February 2005 as a strategic business unit of Triveni Engineering and Industries Ltd.

Triveni Engineering and Industries Ltd is among the 200 largest listed companies in India, engaged in the business of producing sugar, co-generation of power, turbines, high speed gears, water treatment plants and distilleries.

The concept "retail initiative" was introduced with an objective of improving farmer relations with their sugar factories and curbing exploitation and adulteration by middleman in the catchment areas of the sugar plants. The motto of TKB was *"Empowering semi-urban and rural India with a wider choice."*

To give more focus on this activity, its business was transferred to a 100 per cent owned subsidiary, now renamed Triveni Retail Ventures Ltd. The subsidiary operates retail formats in both rural and semi-urban India, with stores mainly concentrated in Uttar Pradesh and Uttarakhand. Headquartered in Noida (Uttar Pradesh), the company operates over 0.125 million sq. ft of retail space, has over 42 stores across 25 towns in India and employs over 300 people.

TKB draws its lineage from the house of Triveni. TKB evolved based on the understanding of rural and semi-urban households; their daily needs and aspirations. The guiding mission is to bring the latest products at the best prices and quality to the customers in semi-urban and rural regions. TKB's value proposition is superior customer service, assured quality, fair prices, speedy transactions and a clean, safe and friendly environment that provides the customer a good buying experience. TKB aims to provide value to its customers through a vast array of strategic tie-ups with institutions across private and public sectors.

The shared values laid down by the company are:

Leadership

The company aims to be a leader in every aspect of its business and in developing its team leadership skills at every level; in its management performance; in the way it designs, builds and supports its products; and in its financial results.

Integrity

The company will always practice the highest ethical standards, and honour its commitments. It will take personal responsibility for its actions, and treat everyone fairly with trust and respect.

Quality

The company will strive for continuous quality improvement in all that it does, so that it will rank among the world's premier retail firms in customer, employee and community satisfaction.

Customer satisfaction

Satisfied customers are essential for the company's success. It aims to achieve total customer satisfaction by understanding what the customer wants and delivering it flawlessly.

Currently, *Khushali Bazaar* has a total of 42 stores. The business has been divided into 3 verticals, namely:

Agri-products and services

This includes seeds, fertilizers, plant protection chemicals, animal feed and nutrients, building materials, farm machinery and equipment, socio-economic activities, soil-and-water testing facilities, farm advisory services and credit to farmers (KCC).

Consumer products and durables

This consists of FMCGs, groceries, consumer durables, imitation jewellery, apparel, colour cosmetics, toys, crockery, kitchen appliances, electrical items, home furnishing, stationery, etc.

Financial services

Triveni Retail Ventures Limited has partnerships with Reliance Money and Max New York Life Insurance Co. to provide life insurance, general insurance, mutual funds, fixed deposits and demat facilities to mention a few.

By 2009, it plans to have a total of 200 stores. The chain currently has 45 outlets that sell agricultural implements, diesel, fertilizers, and consumer goods to the farming and rural community.

TKB has two formats. The larger format has a store area of 4,000 square feet and needs an investment of Rs 3 million to be set up. The smaller format is spread over 800 square feet and requires an investment of Rs 1 million.

"It is difficult to build trust with a rural or a semi-urban consumer. Once the trust is built, it lasts for long, as has been shown by ITC. Triveni will have to leverage on its existing relationships to establish a pan-regional presence," said Shubhranshu Pani, president, retail services, Jones Lang LaSalle Meghraj, a real estate advisory firm.

RETAIL OUTLETS OF PETRO-CHEMICAL COMPANIES

HPCL and IOC are two petro-chemical companies that have taken initiatives to contribute to innovative retailing.

HPCL's *Rasoi Ghar*[13]

The *Rasoi Ghar* (Community Kitchen) Project was initiated as a rural marketing strategy following a study made by MART in 2003 in eight states of India for HPCL. The study found that the poor people, particularly those living in rural areas, cannot afford the LPG initial connection, irrespective of whether it is a 14.2 kg cylinder or a 5 kg cylinder. Further, the poor people in rural areas believed that the cylinder was unsafe and could cause health problems. It then occurred to MART to introduce the concept of "community kitchen" to enable rural women to cook their food items on payment of a meagre amount of Rs 3. The rural households found this acceptable as it was perceived as a clean, efficient, alternate fuel for firewood and was seen as being health and environment friendly.

Today, this scheme has become popular in about six states with thousands of community kitchens operating in areas with a population of above 2,000 owing to its convenience. Its even pollution free. It became successful due to the involvement of the local *panchayat*, which provided the required and easily accessible shelter to socially and economically backward classes. HPCL contributed gas stoves, LPG cylinders and cooking utensils. Ladies from self-help-groups acted as caretakers. The paltry sum of Rs 2 to 3, collected as fees from the kitchen-user families, is used to pay honorarium to the caretaker and to buy refilled cylinders.

The concept was appreciated by women, environmentalists, and voluntary organizations. This economically viable model, as well as the safety and health aspects associated with it, paved the way for the SHGs to facilitate rural women to purchase 5 kg LPG connection through their "kitty" schemes.

The World Health Organization (WHO), through its study, found that the regular use of firewood for cooking can cause the inhalation of the carcinogen benzopyrene equivalent to smoking 20 cigarettes a day. The Maharashtra Forest Department's study sponsored by the HPCL reported that the firewood consumption is around 4 kg a day or worth about ten small trees (shrubs). This rate works out to be 300 small trees a month or 3600 small trees a year. The shift in the women taking the LPG connection would virtually stop deforestation.

In view of this successful endeavour, HPCL started involving Forest Departments, Lions and Rotary clubs for taking the scheme to the rural poor. HPCL collaborated with Maharashtra Pandharkawada Forest Division and set up 32 *Rasoi Ghars* in 800–900 villages each with 70–80 households. As a result, firewood consumption was reduced by an estimated 3.6 million small-sized trees per annum. It is interesting that this scheme has become a national-level programme with the community kitchens becoming hubs for cooking mid-day meals for the school children, as a service centre, as a dealer outlet and serving as tea-cum-*kirana* stores for the caretaker's earnings. This finally led to an enhancement of HPCL's business besides contributing to the overall development of the rural communities, particularly those below the BPL level. The use of LPG gas reduced cooking time in comparison to other fuels.

The concept of *Rasoi Ghars* found new applications in cities also. *Rasoi Ghars* were set up at public places also—AIIMS, King George Hospital, etc. Temporary *Rasoi Ghars* were set up during *Kumbh Melas* at Nasik and Ujjain. About 1500 *Rasoi Ghars* are in operation benefiting 10,000 families all over the country-especially in UP, MP and Orissa. Future *Rasoi Ghars* involving SHGs, Forest Departments and social organizations as also village communities are proposed to be set up.

IOC *Kisan Seva Kendras* (KSKs)[14]

The *Kisan Seva Kendras* (KSKs) are rural malls set up by the Indian Oil Corporation (IOC), the country's largest fuel retailer. These are typically low-cost organized retail outlets being set up by IOC on a dealership basis. The dealer who operates the outlets earns a margin of Rs 1.03/litre of petrol and 60 paise for diesel. These margins are similar to those of regular pump dealers.

The *Kendras* are set up in the dealer's land, the investment being Rs 0.4 to 0.5 million for a *Kendra*. This investment is quite insignificant compared to the Rs 0.01–0.015 billion required for setting up a large petrol pump in an urban area. The *Kendras* are provided infrastructure such as pumps and buildings. To set up a *Kisan Kendra* the minimum fuel sales is 30 kilo-litres (kls) per month. On an average, a *Kendra* is expected to sell fuel amounting to 50 kls per month. The all India average per outlet per month is about 70 kls, which is very impressive according to the IOC. There are some *Kendras* where as much as 200 kls of fuel are sold per month.

These outlets sell non-fuel products besides petrol and diesel. This is being facilitated by its recently appointed consultant Technopak. Dabur India has entered into an agreement with IOC for servicing the growing rural market demands for consumer goods through IOC's chain of *Kisan Seva Kendras*. Accordingly, at all KSKs of IOC (about 1,600), the products of Dabur India are stocked and sold. The products range from health care, oral care, personal wash, skin care and home care.

As of now, the company's non-fuel sales from the segment appear to be worth about Rs 30 billion. The company's overall sales in the financial year 2006–2007 was Rs 2,009 billion. The dealer pockets the entire revenue he earns from non-fuel sales.

The *Kendras* also conduct educational programmes that provide better insights into the field of agriculture. The company has already started 1,180 *Kisan Seva Kendras*.

RETAILING BY URBAN PLAYERS

Some enterprises have started retail outlets taking advantage of their core competencies (like the Raheja group) or connections with villages (like Hatsun Agro Products).

Value retail of the Raheja group[15]

The Raheja group has adopted the internationally popular concept of value retail in its new venture called Inorbit Mall. It introduced a "village" mall in August 2008 as a value-retail showroom at Pocharam village, located about 12 km from Uppal, a suburb of Hyderabad city in Andhra Pradesh. The products sold here are offered at discounts in the range of 20–50 per cent. The company considers the "village mall" a family destination that offers an excellent shopping and entertainment experience. The company has invited local, national and international brand players to set up shops at Pocharam.

The "village" mall at Pocharam occupies an area of 0.4 million sq. ft. The company wants to replicate this initiative in other Indian cities. The rural consumers can go to the village mall in the morning for shopping while their children play in the entertainment area. It will also have cultural shows with popular artists representing various streams performing there through out the year.

Hatsun retail outlets[16]

Hatsun Agro Products is a leading milk and dairy products company having around 5,000 rural logistics centres for milk collection and related activities. The company decided to enter the rural market after having found that it had a cumulative spare capacity of 400,000 sq. ft lying idle. As it can use its existing manpower, the setup cost will be 20 per cent of the business expense for the company and Hatsun Retail will have zero expense.

The company decided to operate the rural retail outlets with minimum overheads and sell household goods at low margins. Hatsun has designed plans to sell readymade garments, textiles and household utensils in addition to the Arokya and Komatha milk brands and Arun brand of ice-cream. This has been hailed by market analysts as a fantastic move by Hatsun though the margins will be low.

PPP MODELS

Many companies have realized the significance of partnering with people and private social organizations in rural areas. Such initiatives have been taken by HUL, ITC and CFCL. HUL's Project *Shakti* and ITC's e-*choupal* have already been discussed in Chapter 3. We will now examine how CFCL's *Uttam Bandhan* operates.

Uttam Bandhan[17]

The *Uttam Bandhan* initiative was started in 2000, by Chambal Fertilisers and Chemicals (CFCL) the flagship company of the K. K. Birla Group. It is a community-welfare initiative that originated in its present name in the state of Rajasthan where the company has its urea plant.

Aim

Chambal's *Uttam Bandhan* is a community welfare initiative that tries to enhance the farmer's income and quality of life. It further seeks to provide employment to the educated rural youth.

Employment

Under the auspices of the initiative, the unemployed local youth are trained by the company as extension workers, who are otherwise called *Uttam Krishi Sewaks*. About 300 educated, unemployed youth from a rural background are at present, acting as *Uttam Krishi Sewaks*. The extension workers earn from commission on the sale of specialized products.

Services

These extension workers are obliged to interact with farmers and render the required assistance in their agricultural practices.

Soil and water test

Soil and water samples are collected and tested for micro-nutrients and balanced inputs. Soil test reports are explained and the farmer is educated on the importance of proper soil health and micronutrients. Based on thousands of samples tested over the years, soil mapping is being done. The Agriculture Development Laboratories are located at Agra and Sriganganagar and satellite soil testing facilities have been set up elsewhere. The company does not charge any testing fee from the member farmers of *Uttam Bandhan*.

Farm education

Crop and product demonstrations, field demonstrations and farmer meets are conducted regularly to educate farmers on the latest farm practices. Farmers are given training on specialized services that vary from cultivation of medicinal to horticulture crops, vermi-culture and the use of bio-fertilizers.

Alternate source of income

Uttam Bandhan is keen on finding alternative ways to improve income-earning opportunities. Besides the land and water avenues, the scope to earn from animal and bird rearing are explored. Some of the income-earning sources identified are: goat rearing, turkey farming, bee keeping, backyard poultry, etc. As a step in this direction, breed improvement and animal healthcare camps are organized to educate farmers on the proper feed and mineral mixtures for good returns.

Farmers' Web site—uttamkrishi.com

Chambal set up uttamkrishi.com, a Web site for farmers, in the year 2001. Uttamkrishi.com was one of the first Web sites to be set up for the benefit of the farming community. It has a bottom-up approach to farming solutions as the Web site has been designed region-wise to address the local issues. Broad information on crops and agronomy has been posted. Farmers can access it free and post queries that are answered by experts.

Farmers' helpline—Hello Uttam

Telephonic helplines, called "Hello *Uttam*", have been set-up. Farmers can raise issues over the phone by calling one of the local numbers of the "Hello *Uttam*" helpline. Though the number of centres is limited at the moment, experts are prompt in their response. Information about the helpline is widely circulated and for areas where the helpline is not operational, the farmers are urged to seek clarity from the Department of Agriculture, Government of India's Farmers' Call Centre facility.

Mailers and AVs

Chambal is particular about the proper dissemination of information. For that it has a quarterly mailer *"Chambal ki Chitthi"* that is hand delivered to every *Uttam Bandhan* farmer. It contains valuable farm-related information on activities pertaining to that quarter. Handouts, leaflets, farm calendars, farmer diaries, etc. are distributed extensively. It arranges radio talks, AVs and programmes for farmers on Doordarshan.

Uttam Bandhan is spread out in 10 states with around 80,000 farmers as its members. Services provided are customized taking a farmers' preference and packaging them according to the agro-climatic zones. Through proper training, demonstrations, expert opinion, quality inputs and non-farm income, the *Uttam Bandhan* farmer has been a gainer in terms of not just increase in income but also quality of life.

Chambal has always believed in public–private–partnership (PPP) in knowledge dissemination. In order to organize crop demonstrations, field days, animal husbandry camps, health checkups, etc. under the PPP mode, it takes the help of experts in government departments, agriculture universities, agriculture research stations and *Krishi Vigyan Kendras*. On its part, Chambal offers its own expertise and training facilities for soil testing to government agencies, shares government schemes with farmers and persuades the farmers to take advantages thereof. It has played a proactive role as a partner in the Government's Agriculture Technology Management Agency (ATMA) initiative.

E-TAILING

Information and communication technology has reached the rural consumers and is transforming the life of rural people. Now they are able to sell and buy with an understanding of the international markets. Many agri-input companies and NGOs have introduced their Web-based initiatives. We will now consider some of the well known e-tailing projects.

ITC's e-*Choupal*[18]

ITC launched three Web-based initiatives (e-*Choupals*) in the year 2000, namely:

- www.aquachoupal.com in Andhra Pradesh for shrimp farmers
- www.soyachoupal.com in Madhya Pradesh for soya farmers
- www.plantersnet.com.in Karnataka for coffee farmers

ITC has placed computers in the houses of *Sanchalaks* (lead-farmer). Each computer is linked to the Internet via telephone or by a VSAT connection. Proper training is provided by ITC to *Sanchalaks* about the use of computer and the Internet. Each *Sanchalak* serves an average of 600 farmers in 10 surrounding villages within a radius of 5 km. Solar-charged batteries are provided by ITC for uninterrupted power supply to the computers.

The following services are provided by the e-*Choupals* to the farmers:

- *Information*: Information on daily closing price of local *mandis*, weather forecasts, etc.
- *Knowledge*: Knowledge about new farming techniques, soil-testing, expert advice, etc.
- *Purchase:* To place order for seeds, fertilizers, pesticides, tractors, bicycles, and other products and services of ITC and its partners
- *Sale:* At harvest time, ITC offers to buy the crops from farmers at the previous day's closing price. The farmers then transport their crops to an ITC processing centre where the crops are weighed electronically, and the farmer is then paid for the crop and transportation fee.

EID Parry's Indiagriline[19]

This is an IT initiative developed by EID Parry in 2001, based on its concept of "Parry Farmers." The initiative mainly concentrated in rural Tamil Nadu by focussing on 271 villages around EID Parry's Nellikuppam sugar factory near Cuddalore. It fashioned a franchise-based business model "Parry Corners" to meet the demand for information and connectivity. These kiosks are owned and operated by franchisees trained to operate the system. They provide advisory services, finance facilities and other occupational information to farmers. The company has been approached by financial services companies for partnering with the channel.

Goals

The strategic goals of the initiative are as under:

- *Distribution infrastructure:* To create bi-directional distribution of products and services into and out of rural India. The infrastructure helps in establishing and managing the distribution channel in an inexpensive and cost-effective manner.
- *Trading infrastructure:* To serve as a platform for trading agricultural commodities and rural industry-manufactured goods as well as provide varied services. It aims at providing the farmers with information on the prevailing prices in local and distant markets for the agricultural products besides guiding and educating them through complex risk-transfer mechanisms.

Range of services

The different services facilitated by the Indiagriline initiative are given here.

- *Procurement:* Relaxation of restrictions on buying, selling and holding of certain commodities including varieties of rice by the Indian Government has opened up a whole new opportunity for EID Parry.
- *Marketing products and services:* The same network that brings produce from the village can be used to transfer goods to the villages. EID intends to leverage this network to sell products in rural India.
- *Desktop and publishing services:* Desktop and publishing services are a key source of revenue for the franchisee. As part of Project e-*Inclusion*, EID Parry, in partnership with Hewlett-Packard, has deployed all-in-one print/scan/fax/copy devices and digital cameras. These devices enable the franchisee to provide a range of services to the villagers.
- *Communication services:* A Parry's Corner kiosk doubles as the local Internet café. Franchisees usually charge customers an access fee for surfing the Web. Information accessed at these kiosks relate to current affairs, education, health, entertainment and the weather. In addition to a data line for Internet access, the kiosks get a telephone line as well.

Education services

EID Parry has used its Parry's Corners to launch adult literacy and computer education programmes. In partnership with NIIT Ltd, a pioneer in the field of IT education, EID Parry organized computer education programmes. In partnership with Tata Consultancy Services, it also conducts an adult literacy programme to educate illiterate women.

Farm extension services

Providing farm extension services is central to EID Parry's business model. The extension services provided in the Cuddalore district focus on paddy, banana, groundnut, tapioca and cashew. For the cane farmers in the region, EID Parry provides the following farm-advisory services:

- Expert visits and crop seminars
- Soil sampling and analysis

The Indiagriline initiative has a good network of partnerships with a wide range of organizations such as Tamil Nadu Agriculture University (TNAU) and its research stations, Tamil Nadu University for Veterinary and Animal Sciences (TANUVAS), National Horticulture Board, AMM Foundation, and Murugappa Chettiar Research Centre. The agriportal (www.indiagriline.com) was developed using in-house expertise (EID Parry's Sugar and Farm Inputs Division and Corporate Research and Development Lab).

TARAhaat[20]

TARAhaat Information and Marketing Services Ltd (*TARAhaat*), promoted by development alternatives group {an alliance between Hughes Escorts Communication, Hewlett Packard, Oracle, KLG Systel, Jaldi.com, Global Development Gateway (sponsored by World Bank and Gates Foundation), Excelsior Ventures Management, LLC and James Martin (one of the world's leading NGOs)}, is an organization that focuses taking the benefits of technology to the rural population.

www.TARAhaat.com is an Internet portal that was launched in 2000, in Bundelkhand near Jhansi in Madhya Pradesh. It aims to connect rural India to the external world. Since then, it has expanded to UP, Punjab and Haryana. The services provided by *TARAhaat* are as follows:

Literacy (TARAakshar)

A literacy programme (in Hindi) to make village people literate.

Education (TARAgyan)

Educational courses are developed and delivered through ICT Centres in UP, MP, Haryana, Punjab, Bihar and Jharkhand.

Information

Information regarding health, nutrition, first-aid, diseases, government schemes, water, agriculture, entertainment, etc. is provided to rural people.

Agri-advisory

Farmers are provided advice on farming and related issues.

Rural entrepreneurship

Rural youth, women and self-help groups are provided information and guidance.

Purchase and sale of products

TARA haat provides opportunity to rural consumers to order a wide range of TARA approved products. TARA vans that are franchised to local people are used to deliver the products ordered by the villagers at their door-step. TARA cards are provided to regular users enabling them to make transactions without paying money in advance.

TRAINING RETAILERS

The recognition of the importance of retailers in rural sales and the emergence of organized retailing are responsible for the recent interest in retailer training. Coca-Cola has already rolled out a large-scale retail programmes to tap the potential in tier II and tier III towns. The programme, called *Parivartan*, focuses on inculcating the knowledge of best practices in the retail business (see opening vignette of this chapter). Dabur is another company that has taken a similar initiative, which has been christened ASTRA.

ASTRA of Dabur[21]

Advanced Sales Training for Retail Ascendance (ASTRA), is a customized training programme for the frontline sales force at Dabur India Ltd. ASTRA is a dedicated audio-visual sales training initiative launched to enhance the quality of field execution. The programme is aimed at managing channel complexities with respect to sales and distribution and is undertaken through "train the trainer" programme using 75 professional actors to train more than 2,000 channel partners across the country. The Astra training consultancy module has been created in five vernacular Indian languages—Bengali, Tamil, Telugu, Malayalam and Kannada.

Through this programme, sales force comprising sales officers, stockists, salesmen, etc. of Dabur and its channel partners were trained. Shopkeepers learnt marketing through role-plays staged by professional actors at their shops. Dabur targeted sales growth of above 15 per cent after implementing Astra. Dabur has a distribution reach of 2.5 million retail outlets across the country. About 75 per cent of the company's sales come form rural areas.

Under Astra, Dabur has categorized its sales and distribution channels into finer segments, such as key grocers, mass grocers, chemists, wholesale, small outlet and modern trade. The programme is designed to address specific needs and expectations of each channel in areas such as trade-activation programmes, trade-promotion programmes, brand/SKU focus, merchandizing and managing channel conflict. It will also run refresher training courses every six months. Every sales officer in Dabur has to work according to a journey cycle that begins on the first of every month.

Summary

The *kirana* format of retailing is most common in India. Retailing sector is growing and making rapid strides even in rural hinterlands. The rural retail opportunities are increasing with the rising incomes and improved infrastructural facilities. However, the farm-dependent consumers form a specific group with peculiar demands. Van marketing is a solution to the problem. Retailing has taken a new turn with the Government taking initiatives to change fair-price shops and India Post into modern retail outlets. Entrepreneurs are also coming forward to make an impact on rural lifestyles. Corporate enterprises are stepping into the retail field and this phenomenon is found in rural areas as well. The companies that have made a mark are agri-input, petroleum and FMCG companies. Rural malls such as ITC *Choupal Saagar*, Tata *Kisan Sansar* (TKS), DSCL *Hariyali Kisan Bazaar*, Godrej *Aadhar* and *Manthan,* Mahindra *Shubh Labh* and Triveni *Khushali Bazaar* (TKB) have been set up by agri-input companies. Two of the petro-chemical companies that have taken initiatives to contribute to the innovating retailing are HPCL and IOC. There are three well-known PPP model retail projects: Project *Shakti* (HUL), ITC *e-choupal* and CFCL's *Uttam Bandhan.* Information technology has made an impact on retailing also. The popular initiatives are: ITC e-*choupal*, EID Parry's India agriline, and *Taarahaat.* Recent developments in retailing required a change in the working of retailers. As such, retailer training has caught the attention of corporate enterprises. Coco-Cola and Dabur have launched retailer training programmes.

Short Answer Questions

1. Explain the major growth drivers of retailing.
2. What are the problems of retailers in rural areas?
3. Identify the growth opportunities for rural retailing.
4. Give examples of mobile retailing.
5. Examine the role of retailers in rural areas.
6. Explain the initiatives of the Government in promoting retailing in rural areas.
7. Briefly explain the functioning of an entrepreneur-promoted retail outlet.
8. What are the range of products and services offered by corporate malls?
9. Explain the PPP model of retailing.
10. Describe how e-tailing spilled into rural areas.

Discussion Questions

1. Discuss the problems and prospects of rural retailing.
2. It is difficult to start a supermarket in rural areas. However, many companies have promoted malls and are trying to succeed. This is a paradox in rural areas. Discuss.

Essay Questions

1. Explain the opportunities and problems in rural retailing. What are the recent developments in organized retailing?
2. Explain the role of the retailer in rural markets. Throw light on the training programmes organized by Coco-Cola and Dabur.
3. Explain the developments in the case of (i) Fair-prices shops and (ii) India Post.
4. Describe the working of any two corporate malls.
5. Can retail entrepreneurs succeed in rural areas? Explain with examples.
6. Explain one of the PPP models of retailing.
7. Describe e-tailing ventures with examples.

Internet Exercises

1. Visit the Web sites of agri-input companies and identify the IT initiatives taken by them to reach farmers.
2. Visit Web sites of any two marketing and research agencies and find out their services for rural retailing.

Mini Projects

1. Conduct a study to prepare a report on rural retail structure in small, medium and large villages.
2. Organize a study on shopping habits of rural consumers.

End Notes

1. "Coca-Cola India Launches Coca-Cola University on Wheels," *The Economic Times*, 3 May 2009, available at http://economictimes.indiatimes.com/features/the-sunday-et/back-page/Coca-Cola-India-launches-Coca-Cola-University-on-Wheels/articleshow/4477620.cms.
2. Soumen Banerjee, "Rural Marketing: Challenges in Distribution and Channel Management," March 2009, available at www.coolavenues.com/know/.../soumen-rural-3.php.
3. CII–Yes Bank Study, "Rural Retail Opportunity Expected to Grow to Rs 2,400 Billion by 2015," 27 September 2007, available at www.moneycontrol.com/news/business/rural-retail-opportunity-expected-to-grow-to-rs-2400bn_305251.html.
4. Virendra Pandit, "Gujarat Government Plans Retail Store Format for Fair-price Shops, *The Hindu Business Line*, October 2006, available at www.thehindubusinessline.com.
5. Radhika Sachdev, "Indian Post Kicks off 3rd Phase of Project Arrow," *The Financial Express*, 5 February 2009, available at www.financialexpress.com/news/indiapostkicksoff3rdphaseofprojectarrow/419403/;

"Modernization of Postal Department," available at http://postalinfo.blogspot.com/2009/09/modernisation-of-postal-department.html.

6. Divya Trivedi, "Mart with a Rural Heart," *The Hindu Business Line*, 3 April 2009 available at www.thehindubusinessline.com/life/2009/04/03/stories/2009040350020100.htm.
7. Munazir Abbas, "ITC's e-*Choupal*: Landmark in Rural Deployment," available at www.cxotoday.com/India/case study; World Resources Institute: Digital Divide: Case Studies: "E-*Choupal*, What Works: ITC's E-*Choupal* and Profitable Rural Transformation," available at www.digitaldividend.org/case-choupal.htm; Abhishek Jain, "e-*Choupal*: e-Empowering Indian Farmers," available at www.itcportal.com/rural-development/echoupal.htm; V. V. R. Babu, "Empowering the Masses: The e-*Choupal* Advantage," available at www.networkmagazeindia.com/2006-05/coverstory-08.shtml.
8. "The Tata *Kisan Sansar*," available at www.tata.com/; "Tata *Kisan* Sansar: The Communication Initiative Network," available at www.comminit.com/en/node/131915/307.
9. "*Hariyali Kisaan Bazaar* Rural Retail Chain in South India," available at www.fibre2fashion.com; Ambarish Mukkherjee, "DCM Shriram May Hive off *Hariyali*," available at www.thehindubusiness.com; "Motorola Ties up With *Hariyali Kisaan Bazaar* to Penetrate Rural Markets," available at www.indiatelecision.com.
10. Prasad Kulkarni, "Rural Marketing: *Godrej Aadhar* Retail Model," 23 January 2008, available at http://prasadkulkarnimarketing.blogspot.com/2008/01/rural-marketing-godrej-aadhar-retail.html; Shalini S. Dagar, "From Farm to Fork," December 2009, available at www.businesstoday.intoday.in/index.php?option=com.
11. "Mahindra Outfit to Set up 50 Agri-centres," *The Hindu Business Line*, 26 April 2002, available at www.thehindubusinessline.com/2002/04/26/stories/2002042600251100.htm.
12. Utpal Bhaskar, "*Triveni Khushali* Plans 200 Outlets by 2009," *Corporate News*, 17 July 2007, available at www.livemint.com/2007/07/17000352/Triveni-Khushali-plans-200-out.html.
13. Preeti Mehra, "HPCL's Rasoi Ghar Project—Weaning Rural Areas Away from Firewood," *The Hindu Business Line*, October 2004, available at www.blonnet.com/2004/10/05/stories/2004100502390200.htm.
14. "Marketing in India," 16 August 2008, available at http://rajeshaithal.blogspot.com/2008/08/kisan-seva-kendra-rural-retail.html; Debjoy Sengupta, "IOC in talks with Peerless to sell Financial Products," 3 January 2008, available at http://economictimes.indiatimes.com/news/news-by-industry/energy/oil-gas/IOC-in-talks-with-Peerless-to-sell-financial-products-/articleshow/2670317.cms.
15. K. V. Kurmanath, "Raheja Group's Inorbit Plans Village Mall," *The Hindu Business Line*, 4 April 2008, available at www.thehindubusinessline.com/2008/04/04/stories/2008040451890500.htm.
16. "The Indian Retail Mantra," May 2008, available at retailmantra.com/2008/.../hatsun-agro-to-convert-rural-dairy.html.
17. "*Uttam Bandhan*–Chambal Fertilisers and Chemicals Limited," available at www.chambalfertilisers.in/ Services.asp.
18. "ITC's e-*Choupal* and Profitable Rural Transformation," Micro Enterprise Development Division of the USAID (2003); V. V. R. Babu, "Empowering the Masses—The e-*Choupal* Advantage," available at www.networkmagazineindia.com/.
19. The Agriportal Case Study, "Parrys Go Beyond, Indiagriline," available at www.worldbank.org.
20. "*TARAhaat*," available at www.dginstitute.com/?q=node/79.
21. Ruchita Saxena, "Dabur Uses Astra to Boost Rural Sales," *Business Standard*, 04 July 2008, available at www.business-standard.com/india/news/dabur-uses-astra-to-boost-rural-sales/327802/; www.dabur.com.

Case 10.1 Expectations on the Higher Side

Ram has undertaken a research study to make a presentation to a rural marketing and promotion company to secure employment. He is impressed by the growth in rural retailing and thought that it can be an interesting field for investigation and discussion. Since organized rural retailing is at its emerging stage, he assumed that there is a need to study the perceptions and expectations of farmers related to organized rural retail outlets to evolve improvement strategies.

Reasons for Entry

An analysis of published literature revealed that the companies entering this arena are lured by two factors, i.e. the vast untapped potential of the rural market and the slowly-increasing purchasing power of the rural population. Lured by the hidden potential, DSCL has started utility shopping centres called "*Haryali Kissan Bazaars,*" Godrej Agrovet has initiated "Godrej *Aadhar*" and Tata Chemicals has started "Tata *Kisan Sansar*"—one-stop shopping malls for farmers that offer a wide range of products, from agri-inputs to lifestyle product items.

Objectives and Methodology of the Study

The study aims at exploring the awareness and preferences of farmers regarding rural retail outlets and analyses farmers' satisfaction with respect to various services provided by them.

Three companies have rural retail outlets in Punjab. DCM Shriram Consolidated Ltd, Godrej Agrovet and Tata Chemicals were chosen by Ram. Two retail outlets of each company were selected at random, i.e. *Haryali Kisan Bazaars* at Ahmedgarh and Kot Kapura, Godrej *Adhaars* at Samrala and Doraha and Tata *Kisan Sansars* at Doraha and Kot Kapura. Two villages were selected in the close vicinity of each selected outlet. These localities were namely Ballowal and Manak in Samrala, Raipur Rajputa and Gudani kallan in Doraha, Jandali Khurd and Begowal in Ahmedgarh and Panjgrain Kalan and Deviwala in Kot Kapura.

A sample of ten farmers per outlet was randomly taken from the list of those farmers who buy from the selected outlets. 60 farmers, who do not buy from these outlets, were chosen on convenience basis from the area in close vicinity of these outlets. By employing a questionnaire, data was obtained from the sample of 60 buyers and 60 non-buyers. Data was analysed to see whether there was significant difference between the responses of buyers and non-buyers using the *t* test.

Findings

The findings of the study are as given under. It is found that there is no significant difference in the views between buyers and non-buyers.

Awareness: All the farmers, even the non-buyers, were aware about the existence of organized rural retail outlets. Advertisements, exhibitions and *kisan melas*, farmer's meetings, field trials /demonstrations and fellow farmers constituted the main source of information. Newspapers and company Web sites are of help to some farmers.

Retail preferences: However, only 39 per cent of them had visited these outlets. The farmers who purchased from organized rural retail outlets gave the following reasons for their purchase: availability of better quality, technical service, veterinary services and home delivery. Others preferred to buy from local shops for the following reasons: credit facility, lower prices and easy availability.

Products/services purchased: Many visit the retail outlets for agri-inputs and technical knowledge. Around 20 to 25 per cent of them purchase FMCGs.

Satisfaction: It was found that the gap between the expectations and perceptions was the highest for credit facility and the minimum for technical knowledge. There is less gap for parameters such as field trials/demonstrations, water testing, soil testing, farmers' meetings, veterinary services, and technical knowledge.

For discussion

1. Based on the findings of the study, what in your view are the areas that need improvement?
2. How do you increase awareness of the retail outlets and customer satisfaction?

Source: Pratibha Goyal, Gagandeep Banga, Babita Pawar and Rajinder Singh, "Rural Retail Outlets in Punjab: A Study of Farmers' Perceptions and Satisfaction," available at www.ignou.ac.in/schools/soss/FINAL_SOSS_CONFERENCE/full_%20papers/C3/P.Goyal%20%20G.%20Banga%20B.%20Pawar%20and%20R.Singh.pdf.

Case 10.2 Retail Format and Strategy

The retail revolution has brought about dramatic changes in the urban areas and has improved the shopping experience and purchase convenience. Since the investors are concentrating more on metros and developed urban centres, rural retailing will remain dormant and traditional. It means that the semi-urban and rural areas that house 70 per cent of the total population of the country will have to depend on spill-overs.

Technopak, a Delhi-based consultancy firm reported that more than USD 35 billion investments are expected in the Indian retail sector by 2013, however, as per current trends, hardly 4 per cent of the total investment will be made in rural areas.

Why Not the Rural Market?

Despite the observed potential to grow in rural areas, why are retailers taking precautions before investing in the rural sector? Explaining the reason, Jigar Pandya, chief operating officer of Real Estate Study and Management Academy (RESMA), observed that the flourishing Indian retail sector is the result of urban consumerism. As the rural area lacks consumerism, retailers may think twice before entering the rural market. Retailers need to devise specialized formats and also change their strategy if they want to achieve success in the rural market.

Which Format?

A wide variety of formats and approaches are available for retailers as given in Exhibit 10.1.

The spending habits of rural customers are not conducive for large retail formats such as supermarkets and hypermarkets. In rural areas, the paying capacity of rural people is less. Moreover, in urban markets the customers buy more than one product at the same time, which helps retailers sustain their profitability. This, however, is not the case in rural and semi-urban markets.

Rural consumers buy mostly on credit. *Kirana* shops sell goods on credit and offer home delivery service. They suffer due to shoddy display, poor hygiene and bad ambience. The rural people are slowly evolving because of their urban exposure. The rural customer, who was used to shopping at the neighbourhood *kirana* store, may now prefer going to a supermarket.

The *kirana* format has its advantages. The management of *kiranas* involves minimal labour costs as the size is small. The focus in *kiranas* is on creating and retaining clients. Retailers are aware of the shopping habits of each customer and deal personally with them. In contrast, a supermarket appeals because of its pleasant surroundings, better product display and the availability of a wide variety of brands. The store has accurate measures and controls and allows economies of scale. A shopper also has the option of shopping for all household necessities under one roof.

It appears that major retailers are favouring medium-sized fair price stores. For instance, the Future Group that operates fair-price stores, a chain of no-frills stores, in cities has plans to grow its rural

Exhibit 10.1 Formats and Approaches for Retailers

Size/Channel Type	Formats
Small to medium	Mobile retailers, hawkers, convenience (*kirana*, provisions and fancy) and speciality stores
Large	Supermarkets, departmental stores and hyper-markets, manufacturer's showroom
Co-operative	Co-operative stores and *sahakari bhandars*
Direct channel	Tele-marketing, Internet marketing, in-home selling, mail-order selling, vending machines

retail venture, *Aadhaar*, in 800 towns and villages in the country.

Question of Logistics

While *kirana* and other brick-and-mortar type stores work well in populated areas, what kind of alternatives can one think of when confronted with small and scattered villages? How about the challenge of geographical distances and the costs associated with overcoming the distances? In most of the cases, rural people are widely scattered and transport facilities are few. The possible solutions are: (i) telemarketing, (ii) van marketing and (iii) Internet marketing. While some of these may not work in remote villages, some others may prove to be prohibitively expensive.

For discussion

1. Which format works best in a rural village with a population of 2,000 and several villages nearby but with limited transport facilities?
2. What kind of retail marketing strategy do you propose?

Source: www.tata.com; Ankur Parikh, "Retail Growth Glory Continues to Escape Rural Markets," 29 May 2008, available at http://sify.com/finance/retail-growth-glory-continues-to-escape-rural-markets-news-default-jegr9qhhbbj.html.

11

Promotion Strategy

LEARNING OBJECTIVES

Upon completion of this chapter, you will be able to:

- Understand the concept and process of integrated marketing communication (IMC) and its role in creating awareness in the rural markets
- Identify the objectives and the promotional tools employed by firms
- Discuss the communication process and media in the context of promotion
- Examine the approaches to designing communication and promotion strategies
- Know how rural advertising is designed

Hyundai Motor India launched a new promotional scheme "Hyundai *Utsav*" in April 2009 to boost sales in rural areas and tier-III cities across the states of Andhra Pradesh and Punjab. The initiative was kicked off in over 50 venues in the two states to reach out to prosperous farmers, money lenders, members of the business community, private companies, government employees, doctors and lawyers across all non-dealership towns to create awareness about the Hyundai brand. The local wholesale marketplace or the "*mandi*" that witnesses a large daily congregation of people was the venue in many places. In order to facilitate rural financing, the company tied up with various public sector banks (PSBs) offering a deeper network in rural villages. Well-trained activation teams were stationed across all the locations to supervise the entire activity, attend to the visitors, offer test drives, educate consumers about loans and schemes and also collate consumer data over a period of about 42 days.

Earlier, Hyundai had launched "*Ghar Ghar Ki Pehchaan*," a first-of-its-kind initiative from an auto maker in the nation. Hyundai Motor offered special schemes on its Santro model to government officials in rural areas and members of the *Gram Panchayats*. Through this special rural scheme, Hyundai Motor India planned to reach at least 58 per cent of Indian villages with a population of 500 or more. The scheme was in operation from 1 May 2008 to 31 July 2008.

Arvind Saxena, senior vice-president (sales and marketing), HMIL observed, "Rising rural incomes, healthy agriculture growth, boost in demand, tremendous growth in rural infrastructure and growing consumerism have opened up new avenues for automobile manufacturers. We feel that 50 per cent of the 220 million rural households are potential car buyers."[1]

The case highlights how a consumer durables company has found marketing opportunities in the rural hinterland and is designing promotional schemes to create awareness, affordability and acceptance. This chapter seeks to explain the concept of integrated marketing communication and discusses the different media used for promotion and communication. It also explains the process of designing communication strategies and promotional mixes. In addition, it discusses real-life examples that provide a deeper insight into real-time practices.

INTRODUCTION

The battle for the rural consumer market has been increasing in intensity over the years. Product promotion has become the biggest challenge for rural marketers today. Only those who can overcome it will emerge successful. A range of promotional tools are being employed by marketers that are referred to as integrated marketing communication (IMC) as a set. The factors that have led to the emergence of IMC include the heterogeneity in target audience, competition, emergence of marketing research agencies with broad services portfolio and the positive results of IMC applications.

IMC—CONCEPT AND MANAGEMENT

During the 1980s, many companies began taking a broader perspective of marketing communications seeing the need for a more strategic integration of their promotional tools. A task force from the American Association of Advertising Agencies developed the definition of IMC as follows.

> A concept of marketing communications planning that recognizes the added value of a comprehensive plan that evaluates the strategic roles of a communication disciplines—for example, general advertising, direct response, sales promotion and public relations—and combines these disciplines to provide clarity, consistency and maximum communication impact.[2]

The integrated management communications (IMC) management process involves the process of planning, executing, evaluating and controlling the use of the various promotional-mix elements to effectively communicate with target audiences. The steps in the management process shown in Figure 11.1 are outlined below.

Establish marketing objectives and plan

The first step in IMC management is to review the marketing plan and objectives. It involves the examination of the marketing plan and objectives in the context of the external environment, especially competition and understanding of the role of advertising and promotion. Marketing objectives refer to what is to be accomplished by the overall marketing programme. They are often stated in terms of sales, market share or profits.

Analyse promotion mix and set objectives

The role of promotion in achieving the marketing objectives is analysed by studying market segments, consumer behaviour and product positioning. The effectiveness of promotional tools and competence of the marketing agency and marketing department are also analysed to determine the promotional objectives. In a broader sense, the promotional objectives will be to inform, to persuade and to remind customers about the company's products/services and to create a sense of satisfaction.

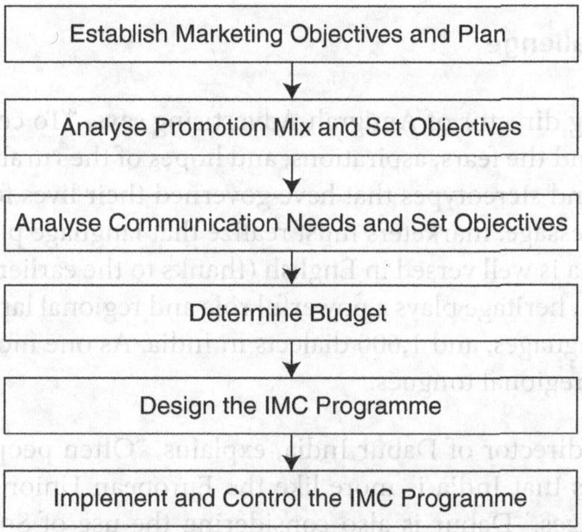

Figure 11.1 Framework of IMC

Analyse communication needs and set objectives

This stage of the promotional planning process examines how the company can effectively communicate with consumers in its target market segments. Communication analysis involves understanding audience characteristics and needs on the one hand and available media and their effectiveness on the other. Communication needs vary with the stages in the purchase process. Communication objectives often include creating awareness, projecting an image, developing favourable attitudes and purchase intentions and enhancing relationships.

Determine the budget

A tentative promotional budget is fixed by using a more simplistic approach such as how much money is available or through a systematic approach such as Return on Investment (ROI). It is finalized after promotional mix strategies are decided.

Design the IMC programme

Based on the promotion objectives and the budget as well as communication objectives, different promotional tools are considered and chosen based on their effectiveness in fulfilling the objectives. Then the objectives, budget, procedures and performance standards for each promotional tool are established.

Implement and control the IMC programme

The IMC programme is implemented as per the established procedures and schedules to achieve the objectives. The implementation is monitored to keep the promotional programme on the successful track. The evaluation criteria include brand recall, brand preferences, brand loyalty, sales, contribution and profit.

AWARENESS AND MOTIVATION CHALLENGE

The major challenge of the IMC programme is creating awareness about products and brands and promoting their sales in rural markets. Let us analyse the target-market characteristics and environment to understand the challenge. Box 11.1 showcases the views of two practitioners.

Box 11.1 Awareness Challenge

As R. V. Rajan, managing director of Anugrah Advertising says, "To communicate effectively, it is important to understand the fears, aspirations, and hopes of the rural consumer." This is not to mention the traditions and stereotypes that have governed their lives for centuries. While communicating the brand message, marketers must realize that language plays a prime role. Though a large part of urban India is well versed in English (thanks to the earlier British rule and modern television), in rural India, heritage plays a powerful role and regional languages are predominant. There are 15 regional languages, and 1,600 dialects in India. As one moves into the countryside, English is replaced with regional tongues.

V. S. Sitaram, executive director of Dabur India, explains, "Often people treat India as one big market but, the reality is that India is more like the European Union—a mix of different cultures, habits and languages." Dabur is also considering the use of South Indian celebrities to propagate the brand message in South India. Marketing companies not only need to customize their communication, but in some cases they must also change their product names to match regional differences. Take toothpaste. "Dabur's *Lal Dant Manjan*" (red toothpowder in Hindi) was rechristened "Dabur *Sivappu Pal Podi*" (red toothpowder in Tamil, the local language) for the South Indian market.

Source: Preeti Khicha, "Building Brands in Rural India," 8 October 2007, available at www.brandchannel.com/features_effect.asp?pf_id=389.

Heterogeneous consumer groups

Rural marketers have to skilfully communicate with a much larger but scattered audience characterized by variations in social classes, language, culture and lifestyles.

Different levels of education and comprehension abilities

Evidently, there are two distinct groups in the rural market. One set of rural people (about 35 per cent) are less educated (even illiterate). They cannot read, write and understand with ease. They do not buy products asking for brands. They identify brands by colours, mascots and graphics. On the contrary, there is a different segment of population, the younger 18–35-years age group. They are educated, more mobile and have urban exposure. They are brand conscious. They ask for brands of their choices. Their brand usage and recall rate is comparable to their counterparts in urban areas. The challenge is to make the less educated understand the message. The less educated comprehend information slowly. They can process linear, logical, simplistic communication with a beginning, ending and a sequence of events. In order to communicate the message, there is a need to use vernacular language, which is dialect-specific. This is a difficult task given that there are 16 official languages and 114 local vernaculars.

Different media habits and reach

Television has the highest reach with penetration of 38 per cent of the rural population in the country. The radio reaches 18 per cent whereas print reaches 15 per cent of the rural population. Cinema has the lowest reach in rural India. It reaches a mere 5 per cent of the rural population.

Gender-wise, TV's penetration in rural areas is 39 per cent for men and 35 per cent for women. Radio reaches 22 per cent of males and 13 per cent of females. Print reaches 20 per cent males and 7 per cent females. Cinema reaches 4 per cent males and 1 per cent of the females. State-wise, the reach of television is highest in Goa, with 83 per cent penetration; it is the lowest in Bihar, with 11 per cent penetration. Radio, like in urban India, has the maximum reach in Tamil Nadu (40 per cent) and the minimum reach in Andhra Pradesh (3 per cent). Print is most effective as a medium in Kerala, with 62 per cent reach and least effective in Madhya Pradesh, with only 4 per cent reach. Cinema has the highest reach in Andhra Pradesh—20 per cent. The medium has the lowest reach in the states of Bihar, Gujarat, Haryana, Chhattisgarh, Orissa, Uttar Pradesh and West Bengal with only 1 per cent penetration in each of these states.

Different lifestyles and cultural adaptations

Culturally, rural people are tradition bound and preserve their frugal habits due to the uncertainty of farm incomes. They uphold religious and social values and take decisions accordingly. They are price conscious and look for value-for-money products. They prefer family associations and like appeals that strengthen the emotional bonds between family members, friends and relatives. While a woman is given the freedom to study and take up jobs, her lifestyle and movements are controlled by social norms. She is not given the same freedom enjoyed by a liberated, independent and decisive urban girl. While advertisements that show her as a growing young girl drinking "Complan," as a job-seeking educated woman using "Fair & Lovely" to improve her chances of getting job, as a hardworking housewife washing clothes with "Rin," as a loving companion to her husband offering "Gemini tea", and a caring mother giving her child a bath with Johnson & Johnson's baby soap are well received, the advertisements that depict women showing off their lustrous hair are not accepted.

Different decision-making groups and approaches

Many rural people live in an open society. Neighbours and acquaintances do not hesitate to encourage things that they consider good and sneer at things that they perceive as bad. Rural consumers are caught in what may be called a social trap and they do not come out of it. Their purchases are influenced by their social relations.

Rural people respect village elders and officials; they bow to peer pressure and share pleasures and pains with family members, friends and relatives. As such marketers have to influence not only individuals but also large sections of people in the village. They have to identify the opinion leaders who may be the village *sarpanch*, doctor, *anganwadi* worker, bank manager or the young children in the family and messages have to be targeted at them also. In this context, interpersonal oral communication becomes all the more important. Interactive media will have more influence than mass media.

However, a section of people, especially the upwardly-mobile, educated youth belonging to the middle class, is emerging as independent decision makers. Even the kids in the middle- and upper-income families make their own brand choices. When they accompany their parents, they wield influence on the choice of brands and when they are sent to do the household shopping they even make the alternative brand choices in case of non-availability of the brand listed for purchase.

One of the results of economic development is social transformation that has liberated women. In developed villages, women enjoy full freedom to make purchase decisions. Dabur India, by research, found that a housewife decides on the usage of the product category and the brand selection and purchase is done by the man. In a village, a young woman was reported to have purchased a refrigerator by making decisions as well as shopping while her husband remained as a passive beneficiary. Advertisers have to take notice of these emergent groups of consumers.

Different social classes and the intentions

Rural consumers are heterogeneous by their incomes. NCAER has divided the market pyramid into five categories—the very rich with annual income of more than Rs 21,500, consuming class (Rs 45,001–215,000), climbers (Rs 22,001–45,000), aspirants (Rs 16,001–22,000) and destitute (up to Rs 16,000). The destitute and aspirants mainly buy essential commodities such as food and clothing. They buy—sewing machines, two-wheelers, TVs, mixer-grinders and refrigerators to supplement their income. The rural consumer is more interested in purchasing income-yielding assets like

Table 11.1 Socio-economic Classes Based on Household Premiumness Index (HPI)

SEC class	HPI score	Estimated households (in million)
R1	16.1	5.8
R2	7.3	15.9
R3	4.1	56.7
R4	2.5	67.3

sewing machines for business, a two-wheeler that is a work companion, or a piece of land to till. Slowly, he upgrades his consumption to buy better, premium and expensive goods, after moving to the next income level. The climbers are the seekers of a wide spectrum of goods. They look for close substitutes to the premium products. The consuming class and the very rich indulge in conspicuous consumption and are easy targets for marketers of premium products.

Hansa Research and Media Research Users Council (MRUC) developed the Household Premium Index (HPI) using a "consumption"/"ownership"/"characteristics"-based index that is a measure of purchasing power. The number of households under different categories according to the HPI is given in Table 11.1. SEC R1 is close to SEC B2 and SEC R2 is close to SEC D of the urban divisions.

Companies desperately hope that villagers will use their money to improve their lifestyles rather than buy assets such as gold and jewellery. The challenge is to make them spend on consumables. This is going to be a tough task given that both rural and urban consumers are demanding value-for-money products.

Different purchases and usage patterns

The influence of purchase patterns in large villages is also visible in the small, remote villages. Companies are recognizing the fact that villagers are becoming more brand savvy than a decade ago, thanks to the introduction of satellite TV in rural homes. Four important and interesting findings in this regard are:

- Penetration of premium products is reported even in the lowest socio-economic classification.
- The one family–one brand view is a myth. Multiple brand usage is noted in many categories.
- The preference for branded products is rooted in the belief that they stand for quality.
- The brand recall for products such as Clinic Plus Shampoo is high.

The reasons for buying a product are varied and multiple. A marketer may offer a product for some use whereas the users may invent some other uses that are unknown to marketers. It is necessary to know and adopt them, to make the message complete and effective.

- A refrigerator is purchased to preserve perishables. However, it is also purchased as an item to be given as part of dowry during marriages by some villagers.
- Televisions are purchased mostly for entertainment. A study by IMRB found that more than one in three televisions was a gift.
- A tractor is purchased by a farmer not just for his own use but also with an intention of renting it out to other farmers.

- A tractor is not only a replacement for the plough, but also a major means of transport to move both men and materials in rural areas.
- In rural Punjab, farmers seek power and vigour from "Revital" health capsules whereas rickshaw pullers expect more energy from it and truck drivers use it for long hours of concentration.

Marketers have to understand the prospective markets to know the usage intentions and expectations. They have to drive home the message of its brand being worthy of all such usages. Thereby, they can initiate first time use. That in itself is half the battle won.

Different purchase propositions

Market analysts found that there are three typical market segments demanding value-for-money products as given in Table 11.2.

While the classification helps simplify the understanding of the market, the movement of one category of people into another category will be quite confusing. The quality conscious are down trading to substitute high-value products with value-for-money goods. Similarly, the value conscious have either reduced their consumption or have down traded to maintain the same living standards. The down trading is particularly noticeable in soaps, detergents, toothpastes, cosmetic products and other segments where cheaper options are available in plenty. A key reason for this shift seems to be an increasing desire on the part of customers to save on small things and go for the big ones. They prefer durables with more features and low prices. Who needs a pricey soap in the bathroom when you can display a gleaming gadget in the living room?

Environmental factors

The communication environment presents some barriers and some facilitators. The barriers include the following:

Media barriers

The key issue in communicating to rural audiences is media access. Unlike urban consumers who are exposed to a proliferation of media channels, rural consumers have limited access to the media.

Distance barriers

The country has 0.6 million villages, spread over 3.2 million sq. metre of area. The road conditions are usually poor. It is difficult to reach the rural consumers in the far-flung villages by van or foot.

Organizational barriers

There are constraints in the organizational aspects too. Budget is a limiting factor. According to estimates by the Rural Marketing Agencies Association of India, the total budget for rural marketing is

Table 11.2 Purchase Propositions of Different Market Segments

Sl No.	Segment	Purchase propositions
1.	Quality conscious	High functional value, style, aesthetics, status, and image
2.	Value conscious	Good functional value, problem-free life, health consciousness, social relationships (love, envy, friendship or national integration), savings and economy
3.	Price conscious	Functional values, social relationships (love, envy, friendship or national integration), low prices, savings and economy

only about Rs 5 billion, compared to the over Rs 130 billion allotted to mass media. This is grossly inadequate to cover the huge potential for different products in rural markets. Of course, clients' reluctance to spend big money for bigger results in the rural markets is because there are no standard performance yardsticks for judging the efficacy of the rural marketing efforts. The TRPs and NRS/IRS data help one to determine the efficacy of TV and press marketing.

Facilitators

Against these barriers, the following facilitators are identified:

Receptive consumers

On the positive side, rural consumers are more receptive to advertising than their urban counterparts. At one time, basic conservatism and diehard thrift would also have been factors; however, exposure to TV has changed all that and created aspirations where once there was resistance to change.

Telecommunications revolution

Of late, the distance barrier is most effectively tackled with communication using STD and ISD booths, cellular phones and such other forms of communication. For instance, an STD booth was placed in a village where no outstation calls could be made. Trade in this village increased by 25 per cent in less than a month.

Innovative tie-ups

Access barriers can also be overcome by piggybacking with large institutions that have a greater reach. For instance, messages and advertising can be spread using the postal department (India Post has already allowed advertising on post cards, envelopes, etc.) and bank representatives. In a few years, commercialization of these services and their sponsorship might even lead to the creation of a "branded postman." If a product is for kids, *anganwadis* and schools are the right places to tap them and their mothers.

Cable and DTH spread

The penetration of television is increasing with the growth of cable operators and introduction of DTH facility. Besides some preferred urban channels, the rural audience has a few exclusive rural channels of substantial significance.

OBJECTIVES AND FRAMEWORK OF IMC

IMC has the basic objective of assisting marketers in the accomplishment of sales and profit objectives. In this direction, IMC may have the following goals:

- To create an understanding of the marketing offer—the risks, benefits, availability and affordability.
- To generate motivation to purchase and use the product/service.
- To establish relationships with the customers by creating brand awareness, brand association and brand loyalty.
- To contribute to the sales and profits of the company.

Tools of IMC

A prospect becomes a customer when IMC provides information for awareness and persuasion to make choices and motivation to buy and use a product. The IMC audience-contact tools can be classified as shown in Table 11.3.

Table 11.3 Tools of IMC

Promotional tool	Communication media and incentives
Direct marketing	Mail-order catalogues, telemarketing, mobile phone short message services (SMS), and direct-response advertisements
Interactive media	Internet (kiosks like e-*choupal*), digital cell phones, van campaigns and folk media
Publicity/public relations	News releases, press conferences, feature articles, films, video tapes, photographs, events, sponsorships, community services and meetings
Personal selling	Company sales force, mobile traders, freelance traders, trained youth and SHG members
Advertising	Product placements in mass media (TV, print and radio), outdoor media like wall paints, hoardings, vans, transportation vehicles (buses, trains and carts), marketplaces such as exhibitions, *haats* and *melas*
Sales promotion	Point-of-purchase displays, consumer incentives (price off, freebies, lotteries, contests, etc.)

Framework of IMC

Based on the above explanation of the objectives and role of IMC, we can say that IMC has two integral parts—promotion and communication. A framework of IMC is presented in Figure 11.2.

PROMOTIONAL MIX

We will now try to understand how the promotional tools are employed by different companies to promote their products and create relationships with customers

Direct communication

Direct media promotions have helped build knowledge of product categories and change long-entrenched living habits. They include direct mailing, personal selling, door-to-door campaigns, telephone calls and e-mails.

Colgate–Palmolive, a leading oral hygiene product manufacturer, entered the rural market at a time when "neem" twigs (the neem tree has herbal properties) and non-dentifrice products like ash, charcoal or salt were the norm for brushing teeth (in fact, in some rural pockets, this tradition still continues). In 2001, Colgate–Palmolive launched "Operation *Jagruti*" to educate villagers about oral hygiene and its benefits vis-à-vis traditional products such as "neem twigs." When gas stoves were marketed initially, rural consumers believed that cooking gas would seep into the food and eventually find its way into their stomachs. Today they are availing of the subsidized offer by the Government.

Videocon is focusing on making its presence felt in the villages. The mechanics of the company make a round of the villages twice a week to assure the villagers of after-sales service as an important component of consumer durables. For this purpose, the company employed 1,800 engineers and mechanics.

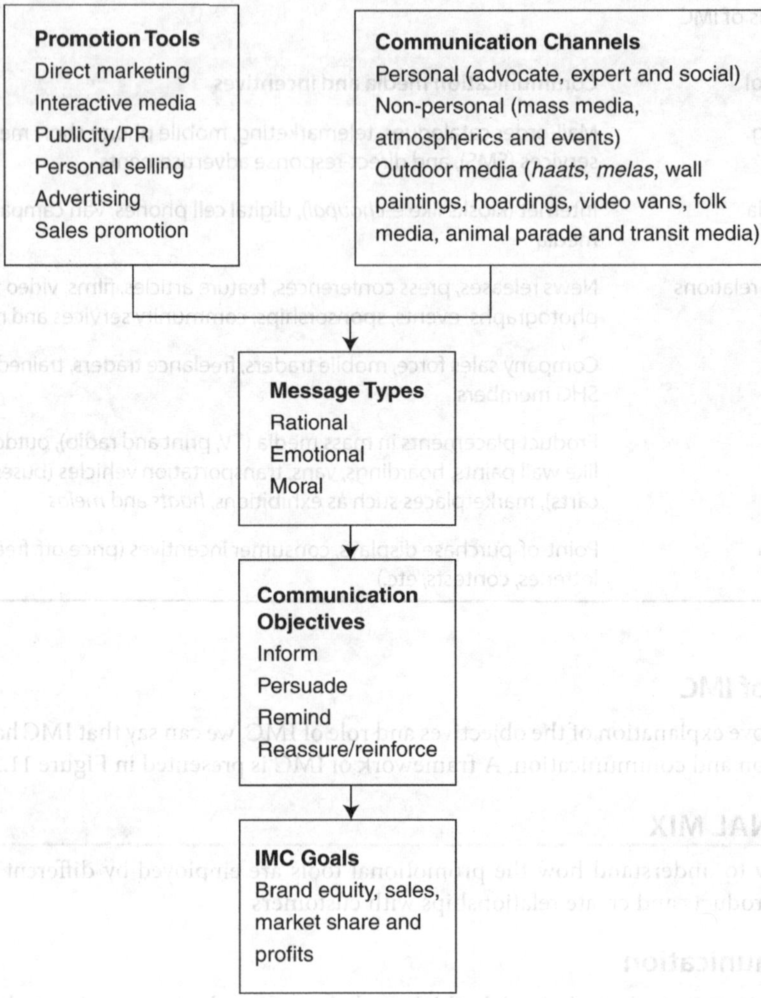

Figure 11.2 IMC Framework

Interactive media

Marico Industries launched a van campaign with the objective of creating awareness for Parachute Coconut Oil pouches in towns with less than 20,000 population in Tamil Nadu. Another objective was to convert loose-oil buyers into Parachute pouch customers. The communication strategy focused on getting women out of their homes to participate in the van campaign that was aimed exclusively at them. The campaign was conducted by women for the first time. A study by Marico showed a 25 per cent conversion from loose coconut oil usage to Parachute Pouch Pack, post the van campaign and a substantial increase in sales from the campaign areas.

Dabur has a participatory programme built around the Dabur Amla Hair Oil brand. It consists of vocational training involving the local community to convert users of loose mustard oil. The company also organized a beauty and talent contest to target rural and semi-urban markets for its beauty products.

Brooke Bond Lipton India Ltd (BBLIL) markets its rural brands through magic shows and skits. Idea Cellular used the folklore art form of *Burra Katha* (a travelling theatre troupe) to build brand awareness.

ACC Suraksha Cement reached out to the opinion leaders, i.e. architects, engineers, contractors, etc. Field meetings with small groups of masons and customers were held. A post-campaign study initiated by ACC revealed tangible improvement in off-take in the state of Karnataka and an extremely positive response from dealers, who believed that the campaign helped in strengthening their hands in influencing decisions.

Publicity/PR

Philips Super Shows were conducted in five district headquarters with the intention of motivating dealers as well as opinion leaders to generate word-of-mouth publicity as a first step. This was followed by extensive van operations in areas with a population of more than 5,000 where audience-participation techniques were used for mouthing the brand, supported by a mass media campaign in the regional press (district-wise edition), rural cinemas, radio, wall painting and intensive merchandizing activities.

Hindustan Unilever's micro-marketing programme in India tapped into women's self-help groups to reach consumers in inaccessible rural markets. Besides selling products, these women help transmit brand communication within rural communities. Building the rural marketing thrust around a social platform helps make it more acceptable to governments, NGOs and other stakeholders. A similar model is being used by Nokia. It works together with micro-finance organizations to sell mobile phones as a means of income enhancement in rural communities. Colgate's rural programmes have a strong community oral-health thrust. They also help build Colgate as an "oral-care expert" and help drive adoption and usage of the category and the brand.

Personal selling

Many LIC agents and ACC representatives make house-to-house visits and provide information about their products. Bankers make a visit to the villages once in a week and address a group of villagers. The villagers gather in the school hall or *Panchayat* office and the banker explains the various financial facilities offered by the bank to the villagers.

Customer contact points

The initiatives that aim at facilitating close interaction between brands and its target customers include "home-to-home" campaigns and the like. Such initiatives provide an opportunity to generate a database of potential customers that can be gainfully used for direct marketing.

Retailer contacts

Some companies reach retailers directly. For instance, as part of a "seeding operation," Wilkinson deputes salesmen in villages whenever it launches a new blade. This not only creates awareness of the new product but also confirms that the product will be available at the nearest retailers. "If you depend entirely on your wholesaler now, you are bound to lose your market to competitors", says Sameer Singh Wilkinson's marketing manager.

Advertising

For its Shaktee brand of corrugated galvanized sheets, Tata Steel Ltd uses the words "*chaddar*," "*teena*" and "*khadag*" to denote corrugated sheets in various rural markets, depending on the local dialect. LG too, uses local languages in advertising.

ICICI Bank introduced a simple innovation such as placing the life-size dummy of a cow mounted on a branded van. It worked well in plugging cattle purchase loans in a programme called *Kamdhenu*. Philips India used to have parades of people dressed as electric bulbs or batteries.

The company also uses wall writing and radio advertising to drive its growth in rural areas. Sellers of cement and asbestos products make use of wall paintings.

HUL used a giant cut-out of Lifebuoy during a boat race in Kerala that is held as a part of the *Onam* festival.

Castrol advertised by painting its logo on both the sides of motorized launches that ferried people across the distributaries of the Ganges. Khaitan fans used the shades of bullock and horse carts to advertise their products.

Colgate, Jyoti Labs and Zandu Balm are some of the companies using radio communication programmes.

Ad films of Vicks, Lifebuoy, Colgate and shampoo brands are shown in rural cinemas halls. The LIC and private insurance companies have been showing short movies in rural theatres to create awareness about life insurance.

Asian Paints promoted its *Utsav* brand of paints by painting the village *Sarpanch*'s house a few months prior to the launch of the brand to demonstrate that the paint does not peel off and is an ideal replacement of *chuna*. The health development assistant of HUL regularly meets school teachers to promote Lifebuoy soap in villages.

Coca-Cola uses a combination of TV, cinema and the radio to reach 53.6 per cent of rural households. It doubled its spend on advertising on Doordarshan. It has also used banners, posters and tapped all the local forms of entertainment.

Sales promotion

There are a host of sales promotion measures that communicate, attract and benefit the consumers. They draw a stronger and quicker response and boost sales.

Offers

While price correction is clearly a focus area, fast moving consumer goods (FMCG) companies such as ITC, Godrej Consumer Products Ltd (GCPL), Emami and Marico are also building on "tactical" promotions, bundled offers and "buy-more-to-save-more" concepts to beat the current recession. GCPL's promotional offers, for instance, include one free cake of soap on purchase of three, and discounts on purchase of linked packs. "Reasons for promotional offers include rewarding loyal customers, passing on cost savings to consumers and inducing trial," said H. K. Press, executive director and president of GCPL.

Sampling

The propensity to try a new product is less among people, particularly in the rural areas. Besides advertising, there should be some promotional measures to induce consumers to buy the products. Sampling as a promo-tool does this job. While advertising creates awareness, distribution of samples achieves both brand awareness and conviction.

The efficacy of sampling in rural areas is, however, debatable. Marketers have varied experiences and different opinions. The arguments against the use of sampling are:

- *Reach problem:* Many a time, people are unsure of whether the samples ever reach the right target, i.e. the decision maker. The final decision makers are away in the fields, working throughout the day. The trial packs never reach them.
- *Conversion lags:* Conversion does not take place easily and immediately. It is a long process. A case in point could be Kelloggs, which took a long time to convert urban dwellers to take to breakfast cereals. So, one can imagine the time it would take to convert rural folk in favour of using brands.

The arguments in favour of sampling are as follows:

- *Brand registration:* The purpose of sampling is not brand sales. It is brand registration. Brand registration is vital in the rural perspective because it may then spread to other products under the same brand umbrella, such as Clinic Plus, hitching a ride on the brand awareness of Clinic shampoo. Sampling goes a long way in the registration of the brands in the minds of rural folk.
- *Brand conversion:* With more number of brands competing for the attention of rural consumers, conversion to a better brand in the same category is a rather difficult proposition. So, sampling is perhaps the only way to achieve this conversion. The expected immediate effect of sampling, therefore, is brand registration. Even this requires the support of sales promotion measures to make the brand the talk of a village.

Instalment schemes

Rural consumers would not have much use for a monthly instalment finance scheme because their income is generated primarily at harvest time. However, growing non-farm income has changed the situation in favour of instalment schemes.

Demonstrations/experiential marketing

Physical demonstrations and word of mouth are very important to rural customers. Since, the usual modes of mass communication such as television and newspapers have very little reach, companies resort to demo-oriented practices. Experiential marketing gives the village folk a touch-and-feel experience.

Demonstration of the products helps customers make an informed choice. Even now, a large portion of the purchases in rural areas is made through cash-down payments rather than on credit. It is for this reason that experiential marketing is important. The *haat* concept provides the opportunity to have a touch-and-feel experience with a wide range of products. This cuts down on advertising costs and the needs of a large section of audience can be met under a single umbrella.

The advertising spend on experiential marketing for rural areas will be about Rs 7–8 billion. According to RC&M, a typical experiential marketing exercise would cost a company anywhere from Rs 1.5 to 5 million.

Mahindra and Mahindra conducted an experiential marketing exercise in Rajasthan for its tractor that was being perceived as having a faulty hydraulic system.

Unilever's Lifebuoy soap used a "germ-glow box" as part of a demo kit to highlight the importance of washing hands with an anti-bacterial soap (the brand's central proposition). The glow within the box helped highlight the germs in the hands and make consumers aware that "visual clean was not safe clean."

COMMUNICATION PROCESS

The function of all elements of the integrated marketing communications programme is to communicate. An organization's IMC strategy is implemented through the various communications it sends to current and prospective customers as well as other relevant people.

Definition

Communication has been defined as a process of exchanging information between two or more people to create a common understanding.

Process

Figure 11.3 shows the communication process model. The process of the communication starts with the sender having an idea to communicate. The idea is encoded to form a message. Messages are

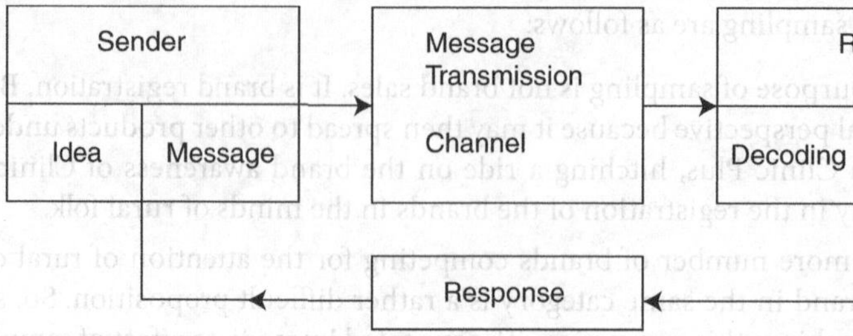

Figure 11.3 Communication Model

Table 11.4 Response Process Models and Effectiveness Measures

Stages	AIDA model	Hierarchy-of-effects model	Innovation–adoption model	Effective promotional tools	Effectiveness measures
Cognitive stage	Attention	Awareness, knowledge	Awareness	Direct communication, interactive media, advertising, publicity, personal selling	Circulation reach, listener/reader recognition, recall, check lists
Affective stage	Interest, desire	Liking, preference, conviction	Interest, evaluation	Interactive media, advertising, personal selling, sales promotion	Brand attitudes, purchase/behavioural intentions, brand recall
Behavioural stage	Action	Purchase	Trial, adoption	Interactive media, sales promotion, personal selling	Inventory, point-of-purchase consumer panel, scanner data
Application	Personal selling	Advertising	Innovation diffusion		

inquisitive, informative or persuasive depending upon the objective of the communicator. In the context of advertising, they carry one or more of the three types of appeals—rational, emotional and moral. These messages are transmitted through a channel to reach the audience. The response from the audience may range from non-observable actions such as storing information in the mind to making a formal inquiry.

Response–hierarchy models

A number of models have been developed based on the stages a consumer may pass through in moving from a state of not being aware of a product to actual purchase behaviour. Table 11.4 shows three of the best known response–hierarchy models.

The different models are developed for different contexts. The AIDA model explains consumer response in the context of personal selling and the hierarchy-of-effects model traces the stages through which the consumer progresses in response to advertising. The innovation–diffusion model describes how a new product is received by consumers and adopted for use. The AIDA model shows that the consumer moves from attention (awareness) to interest and then develops the desire for purchase (propensity to buy or buying intentions) after getting required information about the product and its benefits. The final stage, action, may be reached with or without further prompting by the marketer. The other models are similar but, envisage different stages of movements.

Two-step model of communication

This theory states that the non-personal marketing message is really passed on to an opinion leader who then passes it on to the individual consumer. Marketers as such, attempt to base their marketing strategy on identifying opinion leaders and communicating their marketing message to them.

COMMUNICATION MEDIA

The communication media may be classified broadly into two categories—indoor and outdoor media. Indoor media can further be classified into non-personal media, and personalized media. The various media vehicles are given in Table 11.5.

Non-personalised media utilizes the similarities among the consumers and presents messages that appeal to a large number of people, whereas the personalised media vehicles are designed based on the unique requirements of customers.

Non-personal media

It constitutes three powerful media: mass media, atmospherics and events. We will now examine their efficacy.

Mass media

A medium is called a mass medium when it reaches 50 million people. The prominent mass media vehicles are: radio, TV, the press and cinema.

Radio

Irrespective of the literacy levels of people and the topography and the geographical location of the area of residence, the radio reaches rural people easily. The radio continues to be the principal source of information by habit and choice for many rural people. Earlier, the Indian Radio Industry was limited to the state broadcaster—All India Radio (AIR). Today, with an increase in the number of FM radio stations, the radio has truly matured as a medium of communication and is growing in every possible way.

Table 11.5 Media Vehicles

Indoor media		Outdoor media
Non-personalized media	**Personalized media**	
Mass media (Radio, TV, Print media and cinema)	Advocate	*Haats, mandis, melas*
Atmospherics	Expert	Wall paintings, hoardings, leaflets, video vans, folk media, animal parade, transit media
Events	Social	

The emergence of community radio is a boon for rural folk (see Box 11.2). AIR alone covers around 91 per cent of Indian territory and reaches 99 per cent of the population because of its regional appeal. Private FM players cover the rest. India has around 180 million radio sets, excluding FM mobile phones. The radio programmes too, have a lot of advertising prior to and during the programmes. *Krishi Sandesh* programme (for farmers), for example, has advertisements on pesticides, fertilizers, tractors, etc. Advertising on the radio is popular in India because a number of villages do not have electricity and television-transmission facility. Hence, the radio still remains a popular medium of advertising for rural people.

The radio makes up about three per cent of the advertising pie in India. Radio advertising is moving beyond "spots" or "plain vanilla" advertising. Besides that, radio stations have "activation" divisions that ensure that their clients get on-ground mileage as well. The star advertisers have always been real estate, retail and telecom companies. However, the radio advertising matrix is no longer as simple as that. Today, TV channels (sports, music, reality shows, etc.) are using the radio to drive up viewership.

Television

Television is a very powerful and popular medium in the urban areas. It has expanded in the country at a very fast pace and today, around 50 per cent of the rural population is covered by the TV network. Box 11.3 throws light on TV viewership.

Press/print media

Newspapers, magazines and other publications enjoy high levels of readership in urban areas. According to the National Readership Survey (NRS), 2005, the reach of newspapers and magazines has risen from 17 per cent to 19 per cent and the number of readers in rural India (98 million) became almost equal to that of urban India (101 million).[3]

According to the survey, the growth in the readership of newspapers can be attributed to the growth in literacy, which is measured by the ability to read and understand a language. During 2002 to 2005 the literacy rate had risen from 62.5 per cent to 70.6 per cent in the country. Interestingly, the rise in literacy in rural areas was about 9 per cent from 55.6 per cent to 64.6 per cent, much higher than the 5.2 per cent rise in urban areas (from 79.3 to 84.5 per cent). An important development in the promotion of newspapers is the launch of Internet editions by both English and Indian language dailies. It is found that about 0.3 per cent of the population in the rural areas read English newspapers whereas about 5 per cent read Hindi-language newspapers. The circulation in rural areas is given in Table 11.6.

Box 11.2 Community Radio

Mahila SEWA Trust, Ahmedabad (the Self-Employed Women's Association—SEWA) is an NGO that works for women's empowerment and encourages entrepreneurship. It started its own community radio station 90.4 FM "*Rudi no* Radio" (*rudi* is radio in Gujarati) in Manipur village on the Ahmedabad–Bhopal–Sanand road. The radio station covers an area within a 10 km radius and is run by rural women of the area. These women have had no formal training in mass media. They focus on developmental issues such as agriculture, health and water conservation. The programmes would be produced by rural women and cater to the needs and tastes of the local folk. The community radio station is located at SEWA Academy, in the rural training centre building of SEWA in Manipur village.

Source: "SEWA Starts 90.4 FM 'Rudi no Radio' in Rural Ahmedabad," *DeshGujarat*, 26 December 2009, available at http://deshgujarat.com/2009/11/26/sewa-starts-90-4-fm-rudi-no-radio-in-rural-ahmedabad/.

Box 11.3 Television Viewership

The Audience Research Bureau of Doordarshan discovered that rural agricultural workers, who account for 50 per cent of the rural population, owned only 15 per cent of rural TV sets. There are an estimated 22 million televisions (18 per cent of the 684 million population) sets in rural India. The total TV homes in India stand at 55 million.

The penetration levels vary with the affluence of the states as given under.

- Punjab, Haryana and Himachal Pradesh—over 40 per cent of the rural populace.
- Maharashtra, Gujarat, Andhra Pradesh, Madhya Pradesh and Assam—17–23 per cent.
- Eastern states such as West Bengal, Orissa and Bihar—under 15 per cent.

Due to hindrances, only a tiny 2–3 per cent of the overall rural population watches satellite television at home. It was found that the availability of long hours of film-based programmes had motivated a sizeable number of rural homes in Tamil Nadu, Telugu and Kannada language regions to acquire a cable connection. Doordarshan's strategy of launching DD2 and the regional-language satellite channels is paying off by retaining some audience share for Doordarshan even within satellite homes.

The largest of the satellite channels are Eenadu TV, Sun TV, then DD5 (Tamil) and DD8 (Telugu). In West Bengal the interest in DD7 (DD's Bengali channel) was high, however, the ownership of television sets was low.

As much as 78 per cent of television homes in rural areas still used black-and-white sets. In Kerala, 65 per cent of the sets in rural areas were colour sets.

Source: "A Peek into Rural TV Viewership," available at www.screenindia.com/old/nov28/tele1.htm.

Table 11.6 Circulation of Newspapers in Rural India

Base	(Circulation in million)	Percentage
Any publication	84.3	15.6
Any daily	76.6	14.2
Any Hindi daily	27.3	5.1
Any English daily	1.6	0.3
Any magazine	25.1	4.6

Source: "Indian Print Industry: An Overview," September 2007, available at www.equitymaster.com.

The print media accounts for 48 per cent of the Rs 137.5 billion advertising spend in the country. Anisha Motwani, senior vice-president, marketing, Max New York Life Insurance, said that the literacy wave had just begun and in rural areas, newspapers are a good medium for advertisers "to look beyond wall paintings."[4]

The attractive features of newspapers include the following.

- Both the central and the state Governments undertake development programmes. Newspapers carry such useful information besides the publicity ads of governments.
- Newspapers have regional supplements covering region-specific news that is interesting to the readers.
- Newspapers now-a-days, have a variety of pages catering to the needs of different reader segments—children, youth, women and adults, covering topics on development, sports, cinema, health, personality development, employment, education, religion, etc.
- The youth are emerging as a class of news readers owing to their interest in daily sports columns and weekly special supplements that provide useful information on careers, communication skills, competitive examinations, general knowledge, etc.

Despite the low prices of newspapers (Re 1 to Rs 3), their penetration is less due to the following factors:

- Newspapers do not reach the rural areas in the morning due to poor infrastructural facilities. It is reported that only 16 per cent of the rural population have access to vernacular newspapers.
- The capacity to subscribe to newspapers and magazines is low among rural people. Very few households subscribe.
- Literacy levels are low. Even the average literate person cannot read and understand the technical or classical language of the newspapers, thus inhibiting the process of dissemination.
- The one newspaper for the village subscribed by the *Panchayat* or library cannot be shared by all interested readers.
- Exposure levels are less than 1.5 per cent in case of secondary readership.

Cinema

Cinema is an important medium for rural communication. The films in the theatres attract a good number of people and provide an opportunity to disseminate product information by way of short one- or two-reel advertising films. These films are exhibited just before the start of the movie and during the interval. The effectiveness of in-cinema advertisement is dubious. Sometimes, it may reach and impact more numbers. At times, it may disappoint the advertisers. It can be used for advertising products of mass consumption such as cosmetics, toiletries, medicines, etc. Though people from all strata of society visit cinema halls, the cinema is a comparatively costly medium because of its limited reach.

Atmospherics

Brooke Bond Lipton India Ltd often creates *sherdil jawano ka adda* within its stalls for its Tiger brand. The *adda* offers the local men a chance to test their strength at the grip machine. The decor is changed regularly to increase the traffic to the stalls. The company hires announcers to lure villagers by offering special price-offs. An atmosphere for enthusiastic participation is created.

Events

Events such as *haats*, *jaataras* and *melas* create the right kind of atmosphere for rural consumers to go on a shopping spree. The occasions are marked by socialization and jubilation. For rural consumers, fun, excitement and humour are good ingredients in the product–message design. When advertisement is coined as entertainment it goes down well with the rural audience. Stalls at fairs that combine games with the brand message are preferred routes of brand communication.

Personalized media

While the growing competition has become a big threat, the communication revolution and developments in transport facilities have opened up new opportunities for marketers. Companies can establish contact with their customers in several ways using conventional channels such as dealers, sales persons and researchers and non-conventional channels such as the telephone and the Internet. Here are some examples.

- Fertilizer companies are conducting soil testing for farmers and advising them on the use of the right quantity of fertilizers.
- Companies such as HUL and Godrej are promoting their products through door-to-door selling.
- Social workers, revenue officials and other development personnel who interact with villagers can act as advocacy channels. Marketers of educational institutions, agricultural implements and hygiene products are using this channel of communication effectively.
- Management students and researchers are going rural with a surge of interest in rural marketing. They can be ambassadors for company products when their project work or research is sponsored by the companies.
- Some fertilizer companies have already set up their agri-portals, like *ikisan.com.* The agri-portal of Nagarjuna Fertilizers and Chemicals Ltd, is transforming the rural market like never before. It transforms the local farmer into a global farmer and helps harvest the world.

The personal channel is divided into three sub channels according to the nature of information provided by the communicators (Table 11.7).

Personal influences have a significant role in the rural markets. Here buyers are less exposed to media and are more community bonded. They seek opinions before making final decisions. Companies can activate several sources to influence rural consumers.

i. Distribute products through retail outlets that facilitate interaction.
ii. Create opinion leaders by supplying certain people with products on attractive terms, or work through a community that is influential such as local political leaders, doctors, teachers, etc.
iii. Develop advertising that has high conversational value or interactivity.
iv. Train middlemen to interact with consumers.
v. Establish tele-links for online transactions.

Table 11.7 Personalized Channels

Constituents	Sub-channels	Type of message
Sales people, social workers	Advocate channels	Informative and rational
Professionals (doctors, bank managers)	Expert channels	Suggestive and persuasive
Neighbours, friends, family members and associates	Social channels	Emotional and persuasive

Distribute products for interaction

Companies are realizing that distribution is not an exercise in the mere physical placement of products. It goes beyond. It needs to be animated by people and the atmosphere. Distribution will be effective when the consumers:

(i) Find the outlet a familiar place for a confident entry.

(ii) Find the ambience appealing and compatible with their style of living and reflects their aspirational needs.

(iii) Find the interaction with the retailer and his personnel pleasant and helpful.

Create opinion leaders

Social norms and mores impact the rural consumers in ways different from their urban counterparts. It is found that decisions are mostly opinion-driven. Rural folk value social conformance in their decisions. As they live in communities, they prefer to have social sanction for their actions. That is why there are brand villages—Escort villages, Nirma villages, etc. The wisdom of elders, suggestions of leaders and the advice of the educated are highly regarded by rural consumers. As such, the *Panchayat* head, the school teacher, the doctor and elderly persons play a crucial role in the decision-making process. Accordingly, some companies have started giving more importance to positive word-of-mouth campaigning through opinion leaders.

Advertise with interactivity

Advertisements is newspapers and magazines have limited value in rural areas. More than the radio, TV can impact rural audiences by its audio-visual effects. Compared to these ads, live demonstrations, programmes such as story telling (*Harikatha, Burra katha*, etc.) or skits will be a more powerful media as they provide scope for direct interaction with the audience.

Train middlemen

For a company to stay in the forefront, its representatives should be strong communicators. Their ability to inform and convince consumers is significant as rural consumers are increasingly exposed to as many brand options as the urbanites but, with less education, less media exposure and less experience. Measures are necessary to improve the knowledge of products and skills of persuasion among middlemen.

Tele-links for online transaction

The information revolution is also sweeping the countryside. Remote rural villages scattered far and wide are now being tele-linked with the rest of the world. Villagers are becoming "netizens." Some companies have taken advantage of this revolution (see Box 11.4).

Box 11.4 Tele-medicine

In one respect Aragonda village in Chittoor district of Andhra Pradesh is a village like most others—disease is rampant and healthcare facilities are practically non-existent. In March 2000, the healthcare tycoon, C. Prathap Reddy, chairman of the Apollo Group of Hospitals, set up a Rs 0.1 billion, 50-bed, multi-specialty rural hospital at the village with the country's first tele-medicine centre. This centre cost Rs 1.7 million. Now diagnosis and consultation are available to patients in villages at the same speed and cost at which it is offered to the city dwellers.

Outdoor media

Though indoor mass media is powerful, it does not work effectively in rural marketing for the following reasons:

- Spatial variations in rural markets (differences in locations such as mountains, riversides and deserts)
- Different infrastructural development levels (availability of electricity, the Internet and mobile communication facilities)
- Different receptor exposure levels (literacy levels and interaction with the outside world)
- Different linguistic and socio-cultural norms (differences in language and cultural norms)
- Different affordability levels (variations in purchasing power)

There is a need to explore the local media in view of the limited efficacy of mass media. The outdoor and local media include many useful vehicles such as *haats, mandis,* and *melas* as indicated in Table 11.8.

Haats

There are around 47,000 *haats* held throughout the country mostly on a weekly basis. Out of them, almost 15,000 are big ones catering to a population of more than 2,000. They can be the vehicles for promotion and learning, which can build the brand values. Exposure at these outlets leads to penetration and thereby, a rise in market share. The merits of this medium are:

- They are places where the wares are on display. One can individually see and examine the product. In case of durables such as mixies and grinders, one can watch the demonstration or make a trial use and gain the much-needed product knowledge by experience.
- It is the best way of removing apprehensions and arriving at a decision.
- They are places of social congregation. Hence, they provide an opportunity to exchange views and to collectively discuss and evaluate the product. It may sometimes, conclude in the buying process and result in buying then and there.
- As much as 81 per cent visitors to *haats* are regulars and as much as 85 per cent attribute buying at *haats* to the better pricing offered there. So a *haat* is a better opportunity for promotion than for brand building.

Box 11.5 explains how Tata Steel has utilized the opportunities provided by rural *haats.*

Mandis

There are around 7,600 *mandis,* all over India and they offer a great opportunity to interact with up to 200 farmers a day. In Haryana and Punjab there are no *haats.* As such *mandis* will have a significant role to play.

Table 11.8 Local Media

Selling points	Written media	Mobile media	Folk media
Haats	Hoardings	Video vans	Theatre (street theatre), puppetry, music and dance, stories: *harikatha* and *burra katha,* magic, acrobatics and martial arts
Mandis	Wall paintings	Animal parades	
Melas	Leaflets/posters	Transit media	

Box 11.5 Tata *Shaktee Haat Hangama* Campaign

Launched in February 2000, Tata *Shaktee*, the flagship brand of Tata Steel has earned a reputation of reliability, longevity and strength. It has pioneered the production of 1,220 mm wide GC sheets in India known as "Tata *Shaktee* Wider GC Sheets." It is the market leader in the category of GI corrugated roofing sheets.

However, the company has found that the awareness of the brand and its sales in the rural markets was much lower than expected. As such, it felt that the current promotion through electronic and print media was less effective and approached MART to suggest new promotional measures to increase brand awareness and recall. MART suggested direct promotional campaigns. Since, *haats* and *mandis* are extremely relevant marketing platforms for rural people, they recommended *haat* and *mandi* campaigns. Accordingly, a branded modular stall was set up at each location and visitors were attracted through a public address system. Games were organized for visitors and prizes were offered. About 5,000 *haat* campaigns from 2004 to 2007 were organized and over 5 million potential consumers were contacted on a one-on-one basis. As a result of the three unique benefits—targeted consumer approach, touch-and-feel experience, communication in the local language, there was an increase in brand recall and 40 per cent increase in the sale of Tata *Shaktee* GI sheets.

Source: www.martrural.com/corporate_pilot_implementation.htm, accessed March 2010.

Table 11.9 *Melas* in Different States

State	Mela	Month	Duration (days)	Visitors (in million)
Bihar	Sonepur *mela*	November	30	1
Himachal Pradesh	*Dusserah*	October	10	1
Kerala	*Onam*	August	10	1
Madhya Pradesh	*Kartik mela*	November	30	2
Orissa	*Ratha yatra*	July	10	1
Punjab	*Chappar mela*	September	5	0.5
Rajasthan	Kaila Devi	March	15	2.5
Uttar Pradesh	Nauchandi *mela*	March/April	30	3

Melas

In rural India, annual *melas* organized with a religious or festive significance are quite popular and provide a very good opportunity for product promotion. For example, Fair & Lovely was popularized in the Allahabad *Kumbh Mela*. About 25,000 *melas* are organized annually. Table 11.9 lists some famous *melas* across states:

A mimic of this *mela* concept was conceived by RC&M. Box 11.6 provides a description of the innovative idea.

Box 11.6 Grand Carnival *Mela—Grameenon Ke Beech*

RC&M, the experiential marketing specialist, rolled out a grand rural "carnival" *mela* initiative called *Grameenon Ke Beech* (GKB). It is a unique initiative that provides exposure to rural audiences and takes brand and product interactions to a whole new level. The initiative is based on two reasons: (i) Despite the increasing rural penetration through stand-alone activations, the rural market still remains largely untapped and (ii) Any product or service when marketed to the rural mass with fervour and festive spirit thrown in with good measure, increases brand acceptability and recall.

As a rural *mela* initiative, GKB is a completely syndicated and synchronized *mela* set up in the heart of the rural hinterland. It moves from village to village. According to Priya Monga, business head, RC&M, "It gets expensive for each of the participating brands to get into these villages with specific activities. By creating a common platform at the fairs, we provide brands direct contact with a family that includes multiple target groups."

Kids play a crucial role in bringing families to such places. It provides infotainment, entertainment and greater brand interaction for the audience. Every brand has specific games and tools to attract the maximum audience. RC&M has also conceptualized some syndicated brand games that offer the target group lots of fun and frolic along with lucky draws gifts and prizes. Mimicry artists and magicians have been deployed to increase the entertainment quotient.

GKB is being operationalized in Andhra Pradesh and Maharashtra. Around 960 villages in the 5,000 to 15,000 population strata will be covered. As many as 240 *mela* events have been planned to be conducted over a period of two months. The brand basket of participating clients includes Kodak, Parle, Cadburys, Tata Salt (i-*shakti*), Wipro, Idea, Bajaj, GSK and Airtel DTH to name a few.

It is an all-day entertainment opportunity for the entire family and the reach across the entire campaign is expected to be around 1.2 to 1.5 million people.

Source: "RC&M Rolls Out *Grameenon Ke Beech* in Southern India," September 2009, available at www.indiaprwire.com/pressrelease/advertising/2009091233592.htm.

Hoardings

Hoardings are of two types—stationary and mobile. Large-size hoardings, placed at strategic points will have a good visual impact.

Wall paintings

Though painting on the walls is restricted by some house owners and local administrative authorities, it continues to be a popular, cost-effective option. Many local marketers' as well as corporate marketers use wall paintings. They are less expensive but attractive. They are more effective when they are geographically near the point of purchase such as village shops or *haats*. Where literacy levels are low, it is limited to creating only a visual impact.

Leaflets/posters

This is a cheap and effective means of disseminating product information in detail. However, it has limited applicability in those rural areas where literacy levels are low.

Video vans

The pioneer of the medium in India was Sadhna Bharadwaj, director, Video on Wheels. It started commercial operations in 1989. A van encompasses more than one medium. The audio-visual unit serves as a television and a radio, the banners and posters mimic the print media. A van is manned by three trained personnel. The audio-visual display unit comprises a VCR, a video projector, a PA cassette player, an amplifier, two speakers, a microphone, a 100-inch screen and a UPS. It attracts large audiences because of its entertainment capacity.

How effective is it? Table 11.10 discusses the advantages and disadvantages of the media vehicle. The major players are:

- Video-on-wheels—It is currently running 125 vans and does business to the tune of Rs 0.48 billion.
- Rural Communications and Marketing (RC&M)—It has 50 vans and a turnover of Rs 0.027 billion.
- Rallis India—It started van operations for promotion and distribution.

Animal parade

The attraction that animals have, particularly among children and young people, need not be overemphasized. To cash in on this, companies resort to parading animals with the banners highlighting the product messages.

Mobile displays

Dabur used this novel way of communication. It selected a cluster of 300 villages in Banda district and sent in three bowling alleys. The bowling pens represented the various germs that Chyawanprash protects against.

Table 11.10 Advantages and Disadvantages of Vans

Advantages	Disadvantages
1. Glamour of the medium attracts the audience. As all events, games and competitions are woven around the brand and its image, it is effective.	1. Conventional mass media enjoy higher credibility levels with target audience. Vans lack such credibility due to their localized broadcast and the entertainment nature of the exercise.
2. The influence of direct interaction offered by the medium is powerful, more so in the case of new launches or agricultural products that require intense education.	2. Same vans cater to competing brands within 2 to 3 cycles. A cycle consists of 25 days of van movement in the same areas. As such, the credibility of the message is eroded.
3. The impact and recall levels through this medium is much better than other media.	3. The vans visit villages during the day when most men and women are busy at work.
	4. There is limited choice of software for clients and communication is urban driven. The moment ad spots come in between film songs, people lose interest.
	5. The cost per person reached is higher than TV or radio.

Folk media

To effectively tap the rural market, a brand must associate with the things that the rural folk can relate to. One way of doing this for a brand is to utilize the various folk media. Through this, one can reach the rural folk in their own language and in large numbers.

The importance of folk media has magnified over time as they have continued to evolve with the people, integrating with their experiences and incorporating contemporary themes:

1. *Closely related to people:* Rural communities are by character, closed communities. As such, it is important that the promotion of a brand does not trespass their lives or customs. Folk media have developed over the centuries. They are part of the cultural heritage and true representatives of the essential rural psyche.
2. *Related to hyped events:* Folk media are associated with myriad rituals, celebrations, festivals and other activities where rural folk assemble or come together.
3. *Related to contemporary themes:* Though the art is classical, the themes enacted or vocalized are contemporary. Almost all the folk arts are modernized with the times. Social awareness themes such as gender equality, untouchability, evils of child marriage and the dowry system, drugs or alcohol addiction, etc. are being successfully propagated through this media by NGOs.
4. *Folk media forms:* The performing arts comprise a wide variety of displays. They include:

Theatre (street theatre)	Puppetry	Music and dance
Stories—*Harikatha* and *Burra katha*	Magic	Acrobatics and martial arts

Theatre

Folk theatre is more popular than films in rural India. Folk theatre is found in different forms in different parts of the nation. The art forms in different states are:

Jammu and Kashmir	Gujarat	Kerala	Karnataka and Andhra Pradesh	Maharashtra	Haryana	West Bengal
Kudh	*Bhavi*	*Kuttiyattam*	*Yaksha ganam*	*Tamasha*	*Swang*	*Jatra*

Puppetry

Puppetry acts as a very entertaining and inexpensive medium for communication. Different types of puppets are popular in different areas. For example, there are string puppets in Rajasthan and Orissa, rod puppets in West Bengal, Tamil Nadu and Andhra Pradesh and shadow puppets in Orissa, Kerala, Andhra Pradesh and Karnataka.

Stories

Stories related to kings, patriotic heroes and achievers (*Burra katha*) and of religious gods and spiritual gurus (*Harikatha*) are still popular in rural areas. The storyteller will dramatically insert the brand announcements in the narration at regular intervals.

Music and dance

While music has always been an important part of television and radio commercials, more and more advertisers are now turning to popular folk or cinema songs to attract audiences. Jingles in advertisements are easy to recall and help identify the brands easily. "*Thaduristiki raksha*" of Lifebuoy and "Washing powder Nirma!" resonate with consumers. Music plays an important role in setting an emotional or nostalgic connection with the viewer. When advertisers marry the right song with the right product they can strike a responsive chord with consumers.

Acrobatics and martial arts

Programmes of this kind will mostly attract the youth, sports persons and body builders in the villages. Such programmes can be arranged and brand communication can be transmitted through posters, wall paintings, cut outs and leaflets.

Guidelines for using folk media

Corporate marketers have to keep in mind cultural differences, as well as cost and benefit factors in using the media.

(i) *Choose culture-specific media*: Certain media are popular in certain regions and among certain people. Before choosing the folk art form, culture-specific data must be obtained.

(ii) *Ensure high reach at less cost*: The success of this medium however, is largely dependent on how big the audience is—for that will determine whether the cost-per-contact (CPC) is acceptable.

(iii) *Increase visibility of brand*: While communicating through this medium, it is essential that the brand's message be delivered. There is every chance of it going out of sight and sound in the hype created by the folk media. The important measures needed are:

- Pre-publicity of the brand should be carried out when the event is being promoted.
- Visibility of the brand should be increased by putting up backdrops, banners and sponsorships and in-play brand messages. The brand message should be loud and clear, visible and audible over the entire din.
- Stalls have to be set up for spot selling.

DESIGNING THE COMMUNICATION STRATEGY

For advertising a product or organizing a sales promotion campaign or carrying out personal selling, the key decision that needs to be taken is the decision on communication. Communication is at the heart of promotion. The process of designing a communication strategy involves the following steps.

- Knowing the target audience
- Determining the communication objectives
- Creating the message content or appeals
- Evolving the message structure
- Developing the message format
- Choosing the message source
- Selecting the channel
- Making resource allocation

Knowing the target audience

"Know the consumer" is the first tenet of successful marketing—be it for rural or urban India. The steps in understanding rural consumers are: (i) probing and (ii) profiling. For probing the environment and behaviours, the following questions should be raised:

Who uses the brand?
Who buys the brand, and why?
Who decides which brand is to be bought?

Many companies are undertaking such probing by gathering data on the rural consumer by examining social classes and intentions, receptivity, brand consciousness, lifestyles, buying roles, purchase needs and value propositions relating to community and money. A brief profile of the target audience is prepared based on the data collected.

Determining communication objectives

After analysing the characteristics of the target audience and identifying available media, the next step is setting the communication objectives. The marketer may seek one or more of the following objectives.

1. To achieve awareness among a certain percentage of the target audience.
2. To improve product knowledge among target customers.
3. To strengthen liking or preference to buy the product.
4. To persuade the consumers to buy the product.

In urban markets the emphasis is on brand switching and promoting more usage. However, in the rural markets, many companies are rightly emphasizing on the brand awareness-building objective. This is the route for ensuring more and regular sales according to HUL, Philips, Godrej and Dabur.

Creating message content and appeals

Messages are to be created to induce, inform and persuade the target audience. There should be a theme, an appeal or a unique selling proposition (USP) touching the heart and stimulating the mind. There are three types of appeals: rational, emotional and moral. Table 11.11 shows them with illustrations.

What stimuli may be offered to the rural people to induce them to buy? Emotional appeals like heroism, escape, fantasy, family love, achievement and humour have universal appeal. It is believed that functional elements have stronger appeal for rural consumers than emotional appeals. Quality themes and value-for-money propositions attract many rural consumers.

Evolving message structure

The arrangement of the message in an appropriate order for presentation is as important as message formulation. The message is structured by words, sentences and paragraphs. The message can be tall or short and linear and non-linear.

Tall structures become essential when a marketer desires to explain the product benefits or the company's standing on an issue. Generally, for product promotion short structures with brief messages will be more effective. In the case of rural folks, pictorial presentations make a better impact than verbal

Table 11.11 Types of Appeals

Appeal	Aspects	Examples
Rational	Benefits: quality, value, performance, etc.	Three Roses Tea: colour, taste and flavour
Emotional	Positive: humour, love, pride, and joy	Prestige pressure cooker: those who love their wives cannot say no to prestige pressure cooker
	Negative: fear, guilt, and shame	Hero Honda: pleasure
Moral	Right behaviour, social causes	AIDS campaign, fight-cancer campaign

descriptions, since their ability to read and understand is limited. Linear stories work well with them unlike with urbanites. They cannot process non-linear messages. Simple logic, sequential ordering of thoughts, easy-to-understand arguments and clearly-drawn conclusions are essential to make communication effective.

Developing the message format

The components of the message and their presentation are important aspects in message design. Different media provide different opportunities to format the messages as indicated in Table 11.12.

Pictures, dramatic voices, attractive expressions and colours have more influence on rural consumers.

Choosing the message source

If both the person delivering the message and the message are credible, the message will achieve the objectives set for it. As such, marketers not only make efforts to create appropriate messages but also try to choose attractive, popular or expert sources. The credibility of a message is enhanced by using one of the following sources.

Expertise

Colgate and Pepsodent make use of doctors to recommend their toothpaste brands.

Trustworthiness

The grandma portrayed in Woodward's gripe water is trustworthy because of her experience and the affection she has for children.

Likability

Zandu Balm employed Sachin Tendulkar, who is liked by one and all.

Selecting the channels

The availability of different mass media vehicles offers wide scope to marketers to develop a media-mix that will accomplish the promotional and communication objectives. The selection of promotional tools is determined by the following factors:

Availability

Which media is available? As we have observed, TV is not available in some of the remote villages. Villages without road access cannot be reached by vans.

Frequency

How many insertions are necessary to secure top-of-the-mind position and necessary recall levels? For FMCGs high frequency is necessary to continuously remind and persuade consumers. "Out of sight means out of mind" is a very valid observation in the case of advertising.

Table 11.12 Media Formats

Media	Format aspects
Print ad	Headline, copy, illustration and colour
Radio	Words, voice quality and vocalization
TV/Person to person	Words, voice quality, vocalization and body language (postures, gestures, facial expressions, etc.)

Reach

How many people will read or see the advertisement? A wall painting will be noticed by all who pass through the location. However, how many will pass through the place and care to see it? Similarly an ad in a regional TV channel is likely to be noticed by all the TV viewers of that region. However, in reality, how many watch it? Readership, listenership and viewership surveys may be consulted to gain insights into reach probabilities.

Cost

The cost per contact should be low to give profitable employment of promotional tools.

Impact

Finally, the promotion tools should achieve the twin objectives of communication: (i) awareness of brand and (ii) sales.

Obviously different media vehicles offer different benefits and cost per contact measures. How do different media vehicles fare in terms of reach and impact? We will now discuss the effectiveness of different media in rural areas.

Reach possibilities

Mass media reaches barely 30 per cent of the rural audience. It makes little sense to use this to reach out to rural consumers, unless it is used as a supplementary tool. In fact, the major sources of information gathering and entertainment for the rural consumer continue to be local events and the best way to communicate would be to physically reach out to them by becoming a part of their daily life. Companies that have attempted to use local idioms to convey product message in a meaningful context have had more success.

Impact probabilities

Mass communication is effective in informing and reminding but less capable of changing one's attitudes in the short run. It is to be seen as a two-step flow of the communication process and people exposed to it may become opinion leaders and potential buyers. As opinion leaders they share product information with the less informed people by word of mouth. As potential buyers they share their intentions with family members, friends and relatives. In doing so, they benefit in two ways: (i) they gain social approval and (ii) they obtain the positive and negative views of other people on product benefits.

Atmospherics and events create a sense of excitement and desire to purchase. Though they are not one-to-one interactions, they are capable of generating a new surge of interest in a product and drive one to form purchase intentions.

Outdoor media is effective in persuading one to buy as much as personal media. In both the cases, the consumer is active and his attention levels are high.

Making resource allocation

There should be an objective analysis of the goals and tasks of communication for determining the size and allocations of budget. The rural advertising budget of companies is generally between Rs 0.06 and Rs 0.15 billion. Though it does not seem much, according to an expert, Rs 0.1 billion spent in the villages achieves the same visibility as Rs 0.5 billion spent in towns and cities. MNCs such as Samsung are spending Rs. 0.4 billion on advertising in semi-urban areas.

Promotion should be turned around from the current ratio of 80:20 to that of 30:70. Thirty per cent of the budget should be allocated for urban conventional media with priority sequence to radio, TV and press. Seventy per cent of the budget should be kept aside for rural local media that includes publicity vans, wall paintings, stalls, hoardings and audio-visual publicity at *haats* and *melas*, sampling and other tools.

IMC STRATEGY

When do companies employ an IMC programme and what kind of results do they expect? How does IMC differ for different companies and at different times? Let us take the following situations for discussion to answer the questions.

(i) To sell different types of products
(ii) To help consumer at different stages of purchase decision making
(iii) To assist consumers with different styles of decision making
(iv) To make the product strategy effective
(v) To enhance effectiveness of price strategy
(vi) To serve the distribution strategy
(vii) To face competition

Different products and IMC

IMC strategy differs with the type of product. Consumer durables require a promotion mix that in most cases includes TV ads, hoardings, exhibitions, vans, *haats* and sales promotions. Hoardings are common for tyres, TVs, refrigerators, etc.

Wall paints are seen in the case of cement and fertilizers. FMCGs, on the other hand, require advertisement, wall paintings, point-of-purchase displays, sales promotions and door-to-door selling.

Purchase-decision process and IMC

IMC has the communication objectives of informing, persuading and reminding the customers throughout the purchase process as given in Table 11.13. At the need-recognition stage, marketers can vividly inform or intelligently make suggestions to help consumer identify a need or a need-gratifying product.

In the information-search stage, a larger role is to be played to gain favourable perceptions and help consumers learn more about need satisfying options with specific focus on a company's brand. In the next two stages, messages should be persuasive and should drive the consumer towards decision and purchase. In the last stage, reassuring messages are to be delivered to the consumer to reduce cognitive dissonance and reinforce confidence. In different stages, marketers may employ appeals that are rational, emotional and moral to achieve the objectives (see Table 11.13).

Consumer styles of decision making and IMC

Consumer-decision styles vary with the type of product and level of investment required to own the product. For high-investment products such as consumer durables, involvement will be high. Most of the FMCGs are low-involvement products. High-involvement decisions require more information and IMC has to use tools such as demonstration, personal selling and advertisement. Low-involvement level decisions look for novelty and variety. IMC has to highlight this through advertising, interactive media and sales promotion.

Product strategy and IMC

Product strategy requires appropriate support from IMC. Let us consider the following situations.

Brand promotions

Companies introduce new products based on consumer insights. Consider the following examples. Chik shampoo created the jasmine variant in tune with the culture of women using jasmine flowers to

Table 11.13 Role of IMC in the Purchase-decision Process

Sl No.	Stage	Communication goals	Promotion tools
1.	Need identification	Suggestive. Find solutions to self-identified needs. Induce needs and offer solutions.	Mobile phones, exhibitions, demonstrations, vans, *haats*, *melas* and advertisements
2.	Information search	Informative. Messages may be informative and suggestive (comparative advertising) to help draw conclusions.	Mobile phones, direct mails, ads in print and TV, retail displays, vans, personal selling and public relations.
3.	Evaluation of alternatives	Persuasive. Helps identify criteria for evaluation and present cases of satisfied customers.	Comparative ads on TV and print, sales promotion and demonstrations
4.	Purchase decision	Suggestive. Helps arrive at a purchase decision—what to buy, where to buy, when to buy and how to buy? Information on sales promotion and shop location and telephone numbers.	Door-to-door selling, personal selling, exhibitions, *haats*, *melas*, ads (mobile phones, print, TV and FM radio) and sales promotions
5.	Post-purchase decision	Informative. Information about use of product, service centres, contact numbers and timings. Presentation of customers who are satisfied with the product performance.	Advertisements, customer meets, company letters, gifts and public relations

style their hair in a few parts of the country. Cadburys has launched ChocoBix, a chocolate flavoured biscuit that is based on the consumer insight that rural mothers opt for biscuits rather than chocolates for their children. White refrigerators, for instance, don't sell well in Kolkata and Punjab—while the sea air in Bengal corrodes the paint, the *masalas* used in Punjabi cooking discolour the fridge. So LG offers a range of bright colours in these markets.

Marketers would do well to first understand the consumer preferences and then design messages. Now the role of IMC is to communicate the same message to the target audience and stimulate interest in purchasing the product.

Brand building

The mention of a brand name almost always evokes images that have long been associated with it. For example, Lux is associated with Bollywood-like complexions, Sony with quality, Pepsi with youthful exuberance and so on. To benefit from the image, brand extensions are created. Maggi came into India with 2-minute noodles—a hearty, anytime snack. Since then the Maggi brand has been extended to sauces, soup cubes, even pickles. Vicks, extended itself from the well-known vapour balm to cough drops, lozenges and inhalers. The role of IMC is to strengthen the image and promote consumer patronage.

Price strategy and IMC

Price and promotion are related. High-priced goods require good showroom displays and ads on TV. Good publicity will improve the image of the company as well as the brand. Sponsorships and community service will improve word of mouth. Demonstration in exhibitions or mobile vans will help consumers experience the product. FMCGs that come mostly in economy packs and sachets are generally

Box 11.7 Competitive Promotion

Huntsman Advanced Materials launched Araldite Karpenter, designed for wood bonding in March 2006. The new product is in direct competition with market leader, Fevicol, which has a market share of above 60 per cent. Araldite serves the needs of a gamut of industries with its superior bonding qualities. The product was made available at more than 0.1 million retail outlets across the country, supported by heavy advertising and marketing. The company launched a series of TV and print campaigns and several below-the-line activities such as organizing dealer meets and educating end-users. The brand ambassador, Rajpal Yadav, explained the advantages of the product to carpenters. It aimed at capturing 40 per cent market share in the PVA segment.

Source: Ajita Shashidhar, "Araldite Unveils Wood Adhesive," 24 March 2006, available at www.thehindubusinessline.com/2006/03/24/stories/2006032402001000.htm.

publicized through TV ads, point-of-purchase promotions, sampling and interactive media making loud announcements of price points.

Distribution strategy and IMC

The type of distribution network employed is a major determinant of the promotion network. There are two strategies, namely pull and push strategy. The pull strategy requires heavy promotion to stimulate interest in buying the product. Advertising and sales promotions together create awareness and purchase motivation. In case of push strategy the dependence is more on channel members. The promotion is dominated by personal selling, demonstrations and trade exhibitions.

Competition and IMC

Firms facing competition have three options—to match, to do more or to ignore. There is a need to design the promotion mix intelligently and creatively to obtain maximum benefits at the lowest cost. Box 11.7 explains how Araldite Karpenter deals with competition.

RURAL ADVERTISING

Today, companies can exploit the existing infrastructure in villages to the hilt for brand building. 70 per cent of R1, R2 and R3 markets can be reached through mass media, post offices and postal stationery could also be used, so could the weekly *melas, mandis* and *haats*. Marketers could explore tie-ups with the public distribution system and bank branches, direct mail could be sent to opinion leaders, and word-of-mouth publicity could be built through local service providers such as retailers, barbers, tea-shop and *dhaba* owners.

Unfortunately, we find that majority of the companies are only engaging in short-term, sales-oriented, below-the-line activities. They are ignoring the importance of advertising that can deliver core messages and relate the brand with consumer segments. The following guidelines will be helpful for advertisers to make communication effective.

For FMCGs, use urban ads if they are simple: Some companies prefer to use the same communication package employed to target urban audiences in rural areas. They may design a common television commercial (TVC) for both urban and rural audiences, particularly for FMCG products, provided the communication is not gimmicky and is easy to comprehend.

Box 11.8 Campaign Based on Consumer Insights

The new campaign of GoodKnight featuring Vidya Balan, a popular Bollywood star, focuses on communicating the effectiveness of a moisturiser based mosquito repellent cream with the goodness of natural herbs such as *tulsi* and lavender that help fight mosquitoes naturally while keeping the skin nourished and protected with milk. The ad campaign and concept developed by JWT, communicates the powerful combination of safety from mosquito bites and protection of the skin, while highlighting the product offering through their catchy line "*Machharon ki haar, skin se pyaar!*" Commenting on the launch, Tarun Arora, VP, sales and marketing, Godrej Sara Lee said, "GoodKnight has always offered products that are based on strong consumer insights. The biggest challenge was to overcome the existing mental barriers of people being precarious about using mosquito repellent creams as they are associated with being sticky and harsh on the skin. The new ad positions the product in a way that cues in safety and credibility in a reassuring manner." With such a power-packed campaign and the star power of Vidya Balan, the GoodKnight brand will surely strengthen its supremacy in the market.

Source: Renu Chawla, "Vidya Balan to Spread Goodknight," 1 October 2009, available at www.oneindia.in.

Use urban ads for durables: In case of durables where rational decisions are involved when making purchase decisions, it is advisable to target the opinion leaders first. The urban-oriented TVCs can register well with opinion leaders and help create awareness.

Make ads region specific: Campaigns have to be tailor made for each of the regions where the campaign is to be executed. Therefore, a thorough knowledge of the nuances of languages, dialects and familiarity with prevailing customs in the regions are essential.

Choose right appeals and right brand ambassadors: There are three distinct segments in the rural market—rich (comparable to urban rich in incomes and brand exposure), rural middle (comparable to urban lower middle but with less exposure to brands) and rural poor (whose incomes are meagre and brand exposure is minimal). For real impact down the line, a need-specific communication programme has to be devised. It is essential to gain consumer insights before working on an ad message. The message developed in such a manner is to be endorsed by a person liked or respected by the target audience (see Box 11.8).

Make ads self-explanatory and entertaining: In developing TVCs, the advertiser should remember that rural people do not appreciate complex messages and high profile presentations. A study by MART and Anugrah Madison has corroborated this view.

> MART–Anugrah Madison conducted a study on audience comprehension of the Babool toothpaste commercial by taking a sample of regular TV viewers among men and women in the age group of 18–50 years. The study revealed the differences between urban and rural comprehension. Several rural viewers could not associate with the young couple, child and dog in the story board. One of the oft-asked questions was why a dog was being shown in a toothpaste advertisement.[5]

As such, make presentations rich using simple straight-forward narratives and attractive non-verbal components—pictures, signs and colours.

Maintain consistency in messages: Changing messages and contexts will lead to discontinuity in the identification process of a brand. Strong brand identification requires reinforcement and learning by associations. The ads of Lux, Fevicol, Santoor soap, Fair & Lovely, etc. exemplify this norm.

Summary

Integrated marketing communication is important in rural markets to achieve the twin objectives of (i) creating awareness and (ii) motivating consumers to buy the products and services. IMC integrates promotion and communication to achieve its goals. Promotional tools include direct communication, advertising, interactive media, sales promotion, publicity and personal selling. Communication aims at creating an understanding and it may obtain different responses that range from awareness to action.

The various promotional media vehicles may be classified into mass media (radio, cinema, press and TV), local media (*haats, melas,* wall paintings, hoardings, leaflets, video vans, folk media, animal parade and transit media) and personalized media (direct communication, dealers, sales persons, and researchers). Mass media is a two-level communication process—at one level it reaches opinion leaders and the opinion leaders in turn reach the consumers at the next level. Local media is more effective as it includes several low-cost popular options that have greater impact on the rural psyche. Personalized media continues to have an influence on rural consumers and companies are training their sales persons and dealers to reap maximum benefits from this.

Designing the right promotion strategy is the crux of the problem. Design aspects include message content, structure, format and source. The message can be disseminated with the right choice of media-mix (personal and non-personal) aided by sales promotion and direct marketing efforts.

Short Answer Questions

1. Define IMC and explain its significance.
2. What are the IMC target audience contact tools?
3. Classify response categories of audience and list the evaluative measures at each stage of the response process.
4. Is mass media suitable for rural advertising?
5. What do you understand by interactive media?
6. What are the outdoor media vehicles?
7. How do you classify personalized media?
8. Explain the significance of folk media in rural marketing.
9. List the steps in the message-design process.
10. List the factors that influence the selection of promo-media.
11. Discuss the role of IMC in facing competition.
12. Can marketers use electronic media in rural markets?

Discussion Questions

1. "The rural audience differs from their urban counterparts in many respects. A universal approach will be myopic at present." Discuss.
2. Discuss and develop an appropriate IMC programme for launching a new detergent powder.

Essay Questions

1. Explain the steps involved in message design. Develop messages to promote:
   (a) Readymade garments (b) Insurance
   (c) Pesticides
2. Describe the different forms of local media available to rural marketers. Which ones will be suitable to promote the following?
   (a) Condoms (b) Fairness creams (c) Cement
3. Examine the penetration of mass media in rural areas. Suggest mass media mix for the following and justify your answer.
   (a) Toilet soaps (b) Tyres (c) Airtel services
4. Suggest suitable sales promotion and publicity programmes for:
   (a) Fertilizers (b) Thumps Up
   (c) Rural Internet kiosks

Internet Exercises

1. A study of urban and rural receptivity to advertisements is discussed in www.indianmba.com/Faculty_Column/FC906/fc906.html. Gather similar information and develop a paper on "Developing ad copy for rural consumers."
2. Anugrah Madison is a fully accredited advertising agency catering to the mass media campaign for corporate enterprises. Visit www.anugrahmadison.com/rural_experience.html and prepare a note on van promotion projects undertaken by the agency.

Mini Projects

1. Visit a village and obtain information from local consumers and retailers on the IMC programme of a brand of your choice.
2. Collect information from different sources on the range of promotional services offered by marketing and research agencies.

End Notes

1. Ashish Jha, "Hyundai Launches *Ghar Ghar ki Pehchaan* for Rural India," *CarWale*, 8 May 2008; "Hyundai Drives into Rural India with Hyundai Utsav," *The Financial Express*, 17 April 2009, available at www.financialexpress.com/news/hyundai-drives-into-rural-india-with-hyundai-utsav/448182/.
2. Don E. Schultz, "Integrated Marketing Communications: May be Definition is the Point of View," *Marketing News*, 18 January 1993, p.17.
3. "Survey Finds Significant Increase in Reach of the Press," *The Hindu*, 9 June 2005, available at www.hindu.com/2005/06/09/stories/2005060906801200.htm.
4. Dhaleta Surender Kumar, "Indian Newspaper Congress: Newspapers are Not Yet Dead," 19 May 2008, available at www.afaqs.com/perl/media/story.html?sid=21158_Indian+Newspaper+Congress:+Newspapers+are+not+yet+dead.
5. R. Satish Chandra and B. Sowmya Shankar, "Opening the Rural Eye," 7 October 2008, available at www.indianmba.com/Faculty_Column/FC906/fc906.html.

Case 11.1 Maruti's Game Plan

Maruti Suzuki India Limited (MSIL) has been strategically targeting the rural market since 2008. It has been one of the most effective players in the passenger car industry in tapping the opportunities offered by the rural markets. The company aims to sell 250,000 cars per annum in rural areas. It has launched a pan-India campaign—"*Mera Sapna Meri Maruti*"—to tap the rural market.

Targeting the Opinion Makers

Maruti Suzuki launched a *Panchayat* scheme for opinion makers, covering the village *Sarpanch* (head of local governing body), doctors and teachers in government institutions, rural bank officers, etc. wherein an extra discount is given to make a sale.

Engaging Customers

To communicate to and attract potential customers, various types of *melas* (mass events) are organized wherein local flavour is added by organizing traditional social activities or by leveraging local festivals. While some events such as the *Gramin Mahotsava* are conducted round the year, others are organized near the harvesting season to utilize the cash generated from farm sales. These are in addition to the service camps and used-car *melas* the company organizes on a routine basis.

Innovative Distribution

The company launched non-traditional distribution networks for maximizing coverage with cost-effective approaches.

Extension Counters

These are stripped-down dealerships that operate as satellite outlets for a main dealership in a nearby town. All the enquiries generated from the extension counters are channelized to the parent dealer and deliveries are made at pre-specified dates. Because of its cost-effective sales network, Maruti has been able to cover more than 200 cities. The company has also embarked on various plans to double its sales outlets in rural areas to around 450 in the next two years. The extension counters are connected to the main dealership in a nearby town.

Resident Dealer Sales Executives (RDSE)

A local resident of the village is appointed as a salesman. The resident dealer sales executive (RDSE) tries to generate sales enquiries from local government offices, banks, schools, hospitals, etc. MSIL has announced its plans to appoint 10,000 resident dealer sales executives in rural areas.

Tie-ups

Maruti has tied up with ITC's agri-business division, e-*choupal*, to market its products in rural areas. e-*Choupals* will provide display demonstration and customer engagement services and facilitate meetings with prospective clients.

Credit Financing

Maruti has associated with commercial banks and non-banking finance companies (NBFCs) to extend credit financing facility to rural consumers. It has tied up with public-sector banks that have branches in rural areas such as State Bank of India (SBI) and regional rural banks (RRBs) and local non-banking financial companies (NBFCs) that can provide local "intelligence" to judge the credit worthiness of a rural customer more effectively.

For discussion

1. In the light of the expansion goal, evaluate the promotional mix of Maruti.
2. Is the promotional mix consistent with the marketing mix?
3. What should be the game plan of Maruti in the future?

Source: Shweta Bhanot, "Auto Makers Drive to Rural India," *Indian Express Finance,* 14 September 2009; "Rural Market: A Silent Revolution," December 2008, available at www.ibef.org.

Case 11.2 Fevicol Bonds

In 1959, Pidilite Industries decided to enter into the adhesive or white glue market. Glue is primarily consumed in woodworking. According to sources, approximately 60 per cent of the market share in the overall adhesives market in India is controlled by the company.

Target Audience and Positioning

The company decided to enter the retail market with the product under the brand name Fevicol. It designed collapsible tubes in different sizes in order to cater to different segments of customers. Major sales are driven by carpenters who use Fevicol in woodwork. The USP of the brand is the ease with which it can be applied. The company has become synonymous with adhesives and bonding agents. The punch line of the company, "building bonds," projects and reinforces such an image.

Promotion Mix

Pidilite has launched several initiatives to support carpenters. Fevicol Champion's Club, which helps carpenters to increase their social contact and improve their lifestyle, is one among them. The brand has built strong brand equity over the years and has been able to achieve so much success due to its consistent quality, efficient distribution network and CRM practices.

Creative Ideas

The brand portfolio has been handled by O&M. The creative strategy has been to make bonding a Fevicol attribute. Fevicol advertisements overcome all barriers of region and language as viewers can relate with them easily. O&M won the Campaign of the Century Silver at the 2000 Abby Awards for their Fevicol ad. Fevicol also won them a Lion at Cannes, which is like getting an Oscar in moviemaking. Some of its award-winning TV advertisements include the ones described in the following section.

Ad Campaigns

The origins of the ideas for advertisement campaigns are from day-to-day observations that are presented in an innovative and unique manner. Some of the famous punch lines are "*pakde rehna chodna nahi*", "*aise jod lagae, acche se accha na tod paaye*" and "*lagake haisha jor lagake haisha.*"

"Fevicol *ka mazboot jod*" is the theme of the campaigns. The commercials justify the Fevicol slogan "*fevicol ka jodh hai toote ga nahi.*"

The first ad (1988) is set at a poultry farm where a hen is shown laying eggs. When the caretaker tries to break the egg, it flies off his hand and hits a steel vessel. The steel vessel breaks; not the egg. The caretaker is dumfounded and looks around. He finds that the hen is eating grains from a Fevicol box.

Another ad (2001) shows a bus bursting at the seams with people. Surprisingly no one falls off. The idea was to demonstrate the adhesive as so strong that even the mere mention of the name on the back of the bus (reading "Fevicol: The ultimate adhesive") would ensure a super bond. Yet another ad is set in a carpentry shop where some people are shown watching a movie. The hero of the movie is hanging precariously from the bridge and is asking the heroine not to leave his hand. All of a sudden he falls. The reason—a worker takes away a Fevicol bottle that was placed on top of the TV .

Another interesting ad has a little child asking if anyone has watered the *tulsi* plant. The question flies across the house as each member of the large joint family ask each other if they have watered the plant. The ad pays tribute to the strong bond of a joint family, which stays together no matter what.

Having completed 50 years in India, Fevicol has released a new commercial titled "*moochwali*," positioning it as the "world's shortest feature film." The black-and-white ad film, shot by Prasoon Pandey of Corcoise Films, depicts the life of a little girl who was unable to shake off a moustache pasted on her upper lip during a village play. The film traces her life, through her teenage years, wedding, motherhood, death and finally rebirth, where she is born again with the moustache intact. The ad closes with the tag line "*50 saal se champion*" (winner for 50 years).

"The film is a different cut on the whole bonding angle. We wanted to break away from what we had been doing in the past, and it was nice to come up with something that captured that legacy (of the brand)," said Abhijit Avasthi, national creative director, O&M India, who spent six months labouring over the idea for the new "*moochwali*" campaign. He said, "It has been a magical journey for Fevicol. Today, the brand is a part of every Indian's vocabulary and the brand has endeared itself to the man on the street to such an extent that everyone has an idea for the next Fevicol ad in his pocket. You can't beat that level of engagement."

For discussion

1. "Fevicol is advertised on an emotional and social platform and not on a technical one." Is this justifiable?
2. Abhijit Avasthi, NCD, Ogilvy, said, "The brand has endeared itself to the man on the street to such an extent that everyone has an idea for the next Fevicol ad in his pocket" Do you have an idea for a Fevicol ad? If yes, what is it?
3. Onida has moved away from the "Devil" on finding that it has reached a saturation point. What about the "bond" of Fevicol? Do you suggest any shift from this?

Source: www.pidilite.net; Ankur Jain, "Fevicol," available at http://marketing-and-brands.blogspot.com/2009/03/fevicol.html; "Moochwali: 50 Years of Building Bonds and Award-winning Ads," available at www.livemint.com/2009/11/16220416/Moochwali-50-years-of-buildin.html.

Part IV Applications

12

Marketing of Consumer Products

LEARNING OBJECTIVES

Upon completion of this chapter, you will be able to:

- Identify the products and players in the FMCG industry
- Understand how marketing mix can be developed to promote FMCG products
- Provide an overview of the consumer durables industry
- Describe the marketing mix suitable for the promotion of consumer durables

Tall, snub-nosed and egg-shaped, the Tata mini-car priced at Rs 0.1 million is a contemporary automobile even in the global context. The Nano, as it is called, is put together in such a way that it will appeal to its primary target audience—the buyer upgrading to a car from a two-wheeler. The development team's focus on cost has been two-pronged—keeping production costs low for the company to make the killer pricing possible and also keeping the cost of ownership low. This is a unique combination in the global automobile industry.

There are at least two features in the Nano that the buyer will appreciate. First, the bumpers are large, with the oversized one in front being the most practical. Essentially, this means smaller body panels will take a hit in the event of a collision. With body panels in metal, the cost of repair will be low. Instead of a denting and painting job, just a blow torch repair job of the ABS plastic bumper will do.

The next feature is the elimination of the second windscreen wiper. Besides reducing the car's cost, it also keeps the cost of wiper blade replacement low. As long as the single wiper does the job, the owner will appreciate it that much more just before the monsoon.

The Nano is not only a testimony to the competence of Indian engineers but is also the harbinger of a new revolution in the car market. Renault and Nissan, with their global competence in car manufacturing joined hands with Bajaj Auto, a motorcycle manufacturer that has evolved a competitive cost structure at its plants, to launch a car capable of competing with the Nano in 2011. Other car makers with operations in India such as Toyota, Honda and Volkswagen are developing their own low-cost cars in the price range starting from Rs 0.35 million. Maruti, the leader in the compact car segment, will gauge market reaction to the Nano and watch if the small car is going to eat into some of its products, largely the Maruti 800 and the Alto. Should that happen, it is reported that the company will offer a stripped-down version of either model to retain its position. Little wonder, therefore, that the "low-cost car" *mantra* is now being chanted like never before.[1]

The case of Nano is a pointer to the kind of competition prevailing in the growing consumer markets in India. The markets of the future are the BoP markets and rural markets. The problems posed by these markets such as affordability and accessibility need to be solved by corporate enterprises. Companies have to develop innovative products/services and design marketing strategies that optimize the costs and maximize the margins. Till another marvel arrives, the Nano will be the guiding star for strategists in the consumer-products industry.

INTRODUCTION

India is fast moving towards high-end customized products that are aesthetically designed to complement modern households. The need at this moment is to continuously innovate and come out with product variations across categories to meet the expectations of a varied class of customers. Rural India is fast developing and is catching up with urban lifestyles. It provides opportunities as well as challenges to the companies engaged in the production and marketing of FMCGs and consumer durables. Both the industries are recording double-digit growth and facing intense competition from MNCs and unorganized players. In both the sectors, new products are being introduced with increasing frequency and lifecycles of products are getting shorter, posing threats of obsolescence and loss of market shares. In view of this, managers of consumer-product companies have to be dynamic and aggressive in formulating strategies for survival and success.

FMCG INDUSTRY—AN OVERVIEW

The fast moving consumer goods (FMCG) industry, alternatively named CPG (Consumer Packaged Goods) industry, deals mainly with the production, distribution as well as marketing of packaged goods for all consumers.

Categories of products and players

The different types of products and the major players are listed in Table 12.1.

Some of the leading FMCG companies all over the world are Sara Lee, Nestlé, Unilever, Procter & Gamble, Coca-Cola, Carlsberg, Kleenex, General Mills, Mars, etc. The major players and the value of major FMCG categories are as given under:

- *Personal care:* In this category we find the largest number of brands, i.e. 21, inclusive of Lux, Lifebuoy, Fair & Lovely, Vicks and Ponds. HUL has 11 brands aggregating Rs 37.99 billion or 54 per cent of total market value.
- *Foods:* The foods category in the FMCG market is dominated by Amul, Nestlé, HUL, ITC, Godrej, Britannia and others. This category has 18 major brands, aggregating Rs 46.37 billion. Amul, India's largest packaged food company has a good presence in the foods category with its ice-creams, curd, milk, butter, cheese, etc. Britannia also ranks in the top 100 FMCG brands dominating the biscuits category and has launched a series of products at various prices. Nestlé and Amul slug it out in the powders segment. The food category has also seen innovations like softies in ice-creams, *chapatis* by HUL, ready-to-eat rice by HUL and pizzas by both GCMMF and Godrej Pillsbury.
- *Cigarettes:* Cigarettes account for 17 per cent of the top 100 FMCG sales, and is ranked just below the personal-care category. ITC alone accounts for 60 per cent market share by volume and 70 per cent by value of all filter cigarettes in India.

Table 12.1 FMCG Categories and Players

Segment	Products	Major players
Household care	Fabric (laundry soaps and detergents); household cleaners (dish/utensil cleaners, floor cleaners); air fresheners, insecticides and mosquito repellents, metal polish and furniture polish	HUL, Godrej Consumer Products, ITC, P&G, Dabur and Reckitt & Coleman
Personal care	Oral-care, hair-care, personal wash (soaps), deodorants, cosmetics and toiletries, perfumes, female hygiene products, and paper products	Colgate–Palmolive, Dabur, Lakme, CavinKare, Marico, Fem Care, Emami, P&G, Himalaya, ITC and Godrej consumer products
Food	Staples/cereals, bakery products (biscuits, bread, cakes), snack food, chocolates, ice-creams, branded flour, branded sugar, branded rice, ready-to-eat packaged foods, etc.	Parle Agro, Britannia, ITC, Nestlé, Dabur, Cadbury India, Pepsico
Beverages	Health beverages, soft drinks, tea, coffee, bottled water, juice, liquor, etc.	Dabur, GlaxoSmithKline, Radico, Pepsico, Coca-Cola, United Breweries, United Spirits, Khaitan, etc.

- *Household care:* In this segment Godrej and Reckitt are the two big players. GoodKnight from Godrej is worth more than Rs 2.17 billion, followed by Reckitt's Mortein at Rs 1.49 billion.
- *Hair care:* In the shampoo category, HUL's Clinic and Sunsilk make it to the top 100, although P&G's Head and Shoulders and Pantene are also trying hard to reach the top. Clinic's market share is nearly double the size of Sunsilk's.
- *Herbal products:* Dabur is among the top five FMCG companies in India and is a herbal specialist. Dabur has brands like Dabur Amla, Dabur Chyawanprash, Vatika, Hajmola and Real.
- *Confectioneries:* Cadbury India is the market leader in the chocolate confectionery market with a 70 per cent market share and is ranked number two in the total food and drinks market. Its popular brands include Cadbury's Dairy Milk, 5 Star, Eclairs and Gems.

Size and growth

The Rs 860 billion Indian FMCG industry is expected to register a double-digit value growth and is set to grow by 20–30 per cent in 2009–2010, up from 10–20 per cent in 2008–2009.[2]

The FMCG sector generates 5 per cent of the total factory employment in the country and is creating employment for three million people, especially in small towns and rural India. The SWOT (strengths, weaknesses, opportunities, threats) of the FMCG industry is given in Table 12.2. The major strength of the industry lies in low operational costs and strong distribution networks. The major weakness is the inability to innovate on a continuous basis. There are more modifications than novel products. The growth drivers are expanding markets and innovations. The limiting factors are competition and government restrictions.

Table 12.2 SWOT Analysis of the FMCG Industry

Strengths	**Weaknesses**
Low operational costs	Inflexibility in technology levels
Strong distribution network	Operational costs
Brands with sound image	Less innovative abilities and systems
Opportunities	**Threats**
Growing markets—domestic markets, especially the rural markets	Competition, especially from fake products
Export potential	Entry of MNCs with liberalization
	Excise duties and taxes imposed by the Government

The big firms are growing bigger and small-time companies are catching up as well. According to a study conducted by AC Nielsen, 62 of the top 100 brands are owned by MNCs, and the balance by Indian companies. Fifteen companies own these 62 brands, and 27 of these are owned by Hindustan Unilever. Pepsi is at number three followed by Thums Up. Britannia takes the fifth place, followed by Colgate (6), Nirma (7), Coca-Cola (8) and Parle (9). Personal care, cigarettes, and soft drinks are the three biggest categories in FMCG. Between them, they account for 35 of the top 100 brands.

Recession and reactive strategies

FMCG is a recession-proof industry. "By definition, FMCG addresses a very core need in the consumer's life and so it is less prone to economic swings than high-ticket items such as televisions or even apparel," said Mr Hemant Kalbag, principal, AT Kearney.[3]

The economic recession has not impacted the performance of the companies that have manipulated their marketing strategies intelligently. Adi Godrej, chairman of the Godrej Group and Harsh Mariwala, chairman of Marico Ltd, opined that there will be strong growth both by value and by volume because of value-for-money products.

The beverage industry in India is estimated to grow at 17 per cent despite the slowdown in the economy. On the personal-care front, deodorants, shampoos and talcum powders could see double-digit growth. For instance, CavinKare registered 23 per cent sales growth in 2008–2009 and anticipates 30 per cent growth this year, according to Mr Vineet Trakroo, vice-president (marketing), CavinKare.

Different companies have reacted in different ways to sustain and increase sales.

Price increases

Some companies like HUL resorted to price increases. They have also been well-absorbed by the market. Akhil Kejriwal, an analyst with Enam Securities, observed, "There has not been any drop in demand for consumer products at popular price points. However, there may have been some narrowing in demand at the top end of the market; in the mass market, demand continues to be strong, both from rural and urban markets."

Price cuts

Companies like P&G and Godrej resorted to price cuts. "While volume growth is likely to be strong for most categories, it is expected to decelerate for discretionary categories. Lower input costs will result in margin expansion, leading to growth in operating profit for the FMCG industry," said an industry analyst.

Innovations

Some companies resorted to new product launches and brand extensions. The extensions of brands such as Navratna cool oil and Boroplus are examples for this.

Focus on rural markets

With the urban market reaching near saturation, companies developed strategies for penetrating deeper into rural and semi-urban markets.

Rural market—a new opportunity

According to a research study commissioned by the Associated Chambers of Commerce and Industry in India, rural areas are propelling the demand for FMCGs, passenger cars, two-wheelers and organized retail goods at a comparatively faster pace than the urban areas and thus, leading to a healthy increase in the revenue of companies despite the global recession. "The FMCG sector in rural areas is expected to grow by 40 per cent against 25 per cent in urban areas," stated ASSOCHAM. However, no time frame for these predictions has been given by the Association. With current estimated value of over Rs 5,600 billion, or nearly 40 per cent of the total retail market valued at Rs 14,000 billion, the rural retail market will remain the potential area for growth.

Several FMCG firms, including ITC and DCM, have been registering faster and higher growth in the sales of their goods in the rural markets as compared to the urban markets. This has significantly added to their bottom lines.

Significance of the FMCG sector

According to a research analyst at RNCOS, a leading market research and information analysis company, "Increasing penetration of the FMCG sector in rural areas is leading to the development of rural India over the last few years." However, to grow strongly and rapidly, rural areas should effectively address widespread and fundamental problems such as developing infrastructural facilities and improving education levels.[4]

Prospects of FMCGs

The future outlook for FMCGs is very promising. The following factors are responsible for the optimism in industry circles.

- The middle class and the rural segments of the Indian population are the most promising market for FMCGs, and there is an opportunity to convert them as buyers of branded products.
- The per capita consumption of almost all products in the country is among the lowest in the world.
- Technology is advancing to facilitate innovations that are affordable to the middle and BoP segments of the Indian market.

Growth is possible if companies focus on innovation of quality products at affordable prices and design effective marketing strategies.

MARKETING MIX

The marketing mix of FMCGs is a combination of the various elements given in Table 12.3.

The choice of the elements to design a marketing strategy requires a customer-centric long-term view, aggressiveness and innovative spirit. Consider the approach of Arvind Mills and Nicholas Piramal (see Box 12.1).

Table 12.3 Rural Marketing Mix for FMCGs

Components	Choices
Product	Innovative products, small pack units, functional products with desirable trendy features.
Price	Popular price points, economy (minimal total cost of operation).
Place	Feeder towns, village retailers, *haats*, vans, co-operative stores, agri-input dealers, NGOs, petrol bunks, post offices, mobile traders, *melas*, SHGs, *anganwadis*, company sales force and agents (trained local youth). Transport by local buses, bicycles, auto-rickshaws, animal carts or animals, humans, trains and boats.
Promotion (communication)	Directly mailing opinion leaders and select customers, exhibitions, van campaigns, animal parade , FM radio, local newspapers, local TV channels, hoardings, wall paints, tin plates tied to trees, transit media (bus, horse/bullock-cart sides), posters, leaflets, point-of-purchase promotions, interactive media (demonstrations), stories—*burra katha* and *harikatha*; magic shows, meetings/workshops, contests, sports, etc.
Promotion (motivation that indirectly leads to economy and excitement)	Price-offs, extra quantity at same price, gifts, two for the price of one, etc.

Box 12.1 Aggressive Innovation

Arvind Mills has charted out an aggressive growth strategy targeted at the rural markets. The idea is to revolutionize the rural distribution of shirts and *sarees* by involving pan shops. The challenging question "Why can't we sell a shirt at a pan shop in a village?" was posed by Kulin Lalbhai, the youngest son of the group's chairman, who is the chief manager of Arvind Retail. Driven by the innovative idea, there has been a new focus on product and package innovation. It has been decided to bring out products with special finishes and blends for ethnic wear for both men and women. While a *saree* made of non-silk material will have the look and feel of silk, a shirt will retain its texture even after 30–40 washes. Small easy-to-retail packs of 12 shirt pieces will be distributed in the place of the 16-metre rolls.

Nicholas Piramal has decided to intensify its promotion by directing its field force of 800 people to be in constant touch with general practitioners, and utilizing post offices as the new distribution platform. It will also conduct health-care workshops in the rural areas by involving local doctors.

Source: Bhargav Trivedi, "Arvind Mills Weighs Direct Selling Plans," *The Economic Times*, 5 December 2009, available at http://economictimes.indiatimes.com/news/news-by-industry/cons-products/garments-/-textiles/Arvind-Mills-weighs-direct-selling-plans/articleshow/5302173.cms; Malapati Rajasekhar, "Some Attempts to Penetrate into Rural Markets: A Look at Rural Distribution Systems," 31 May 2008, available at http://ruralindia.blogspot.com/2008/05/some-attempts-to-penetrate-into-rural.html.

DETTOL CAMPAIGNS FOR HYGIENE

Dettol, the 76-year old iconic brand from Reckitt Benckiser, is well on its way to achieving a turnover of Rs 10 billion. This is because the brand has been clocking a double-digit growth even at a time when most others, including market leader Hindustan Unilever, have been losing market share. The brand's revenues were pegged at Rs 9 billion in July 2009, according to data from AC Nielsen.[5]

Consumer preferences

According to Arvind Singhal, chairman, Technopak Advisors, Dettol has been able to command a premium because of the consumers' preference for a brand that has never deviated from its health platform. The peculiar odour of Dettol is one of the most omnipresent smells in dispensaries, clinics and hospitals. As an antiseptic germ-killer and a potent disinfectant, Dettol must be unparalleled in medical history.

Brand-building initiatives

There are multiple reasons for Dettol's growth:

- Consistent positioning
- Smaller packs
- Careful brand extensions
- Stable pricing

"It is amazing to see how brand Dettol has been built over the last so many years with a message that is relevant even today. They have almost become a generic category in health," says Singhal.

Positioning

The Dettol brand is positioned as a bodyguard that protects people from the unhygienic world outside by fighting germs and infections. This positioning is strengthened and reinforced by all decisions on packaging and band extensions. "It has been able to guard the brand message and not let the brand occupy any other position in the consumer's mind," points out Singhal. Other brands, he feels, have tried to jump on to the bandwagon of health, but have had shorter lives because of the lack of such a focus.

Package identity

The packaging of all its products is distinct in their own way. The green and white colours and the sword have become symbols for fighting germs and infections, reinforcing the brand's positioning as a bodyguard.

Brand extensions

Dettol has successfully extended germ protection—the USP of its flagship product, the antiseptic liquid, to soaps, hand washes and shaving creams.

Performance of brands

Soaps, launched in 1981, have been the biggest growth driver for the company accounting for around 75 per cent of the total revenue. According to AC Nielsen's April–May 2009 report, the market share of soaps has risen to 7.7 per cent from 6.5 per cent in a Rs 75 billion market that is growing by 8–9 per cent in value and by 2–3 per cent in volumes.

The remaining products are also doing well.

- Dettol Liquid handwash, despite retailing at a higher price than competitors such as Fem and Lifebuoy, has maintained a lead in this segment with a 60 per cent market share in the Rs 1 billion market.

- Dettol shaving cream has 30 per cent share in the Rs 2 billion market. Meanwhile, it is planning to launch herbal soaps and is testing them in Tamil Nadu.
- Dettol liquid antiseptics, is logging 20 per cent growth in the Rs 1.5 billion market. The brand is the leader (85 per cent share) with its nearest competitor, Johnson & Johnson's Savlon not being able to make much headway.

Small pack size

Dettol liquid handwash and soaps have been introduced in smaller pack sizes. As a result, distribution shot up by 25 per cent and volume sales by 35 per cent in markets such as Bihar, Orissa and Madhya Pradesh.

Communications and promotion

The biggest challenge has been low consumer awareness on hygiene and inertia in taking purchase decisions.

Message-source credibility

The brand is also endorsed by the Indian Medical Association. This has resulted in increased credibility and acceptance.

Tailor-made communications

According to TAM data, Dettol's brand communication had 60 per cent share of voice (percentage of Gross Rating Points generated by the category) over the last seven months, 100 per cent in liquid antiseptics and 13–14 per cent in soaps. Its communication has been carefully different for urban, semi-urban and rural markets. The company is planning to increase advertising spends by 30 per cent.

Education for awareness

Dettol has taken the education route to spread awareness. One-fifth of the ad spends of the company go into non-mass media in smaller towns. The promotion includes the following:

- Visits to schools, hospitals, and housing societies
- Doctors tell audiences about the basics of hygiene (workshops and meetings)
- Wall-paintings
- Dealer boards
- Vans with products
- Awareness literature
- *Surakshit parivar* campaign—the programme educated people about hygiene issues and handed them kits with Dettol products.

Swine flu—an opportunity for Dettol

"The flu vaccine isn't ready; instead, keep the virus at bay by keeping your hands clean," this is what a doctor says in advertisements made to make people aware of the steps to be taken to prevent swine flu. The Hygiene Council's country representative, Dr Narendra Saini, urged people to think beyond flu vaccines and anti-virals. "Good hand hygiene is the first line of defence against the spread of many illnesses," he maintains. A recent council survey across eight countries found that only 42 per cent Indians believe hand hygiene can prevent the spread of flu.

CONSUMER DURABLES INDUSTRY—AN OVERVIEW

The Indian consumer durables industry has witnessed considerable changes in the past couple of years. Changing lifestyles, higher disposable incomes coupled with greater affordability and a surge in advertising has been instrumental in bringing about a sea change in consumer behaviour patterns.

Categories of products and players

This industry consists of durable goods used for domestic purposes such as televisions, washing machines, refrigerators, microwave ovens, mobile phones, etc. Consumer durables are the products whose life expectancy is at least three years. These products are hard goods that cannot be used up at once.

The consumer durables industry can be broadly classified into consumer electronics and consumer appliances. The consumer appliances category can be further segmented as white goods and brown goods as shown in Table 12.4.

Most of the segments in this sector are characterized by intense competition, emergence of new companies (especially MNCs), introduction of state-of-the-art models, price discounts and exchange schemes. MNCs continue to dominate the Indian consumer durables segment and this is apparent from the fact that these companies command more than 65 per cent market share in the colour television (CTV) segment.

The major players are LG, Samsung, Sony, Whirlpool, Videocon, Godrej, Philips, Nokia Bajaj Electricals and Maharaja Appliances. Their product mix includes the major categories of white goods.

Penetration levels

The penetration level of consumer durables is very low in India when compared with other countries. Table 12.5 shows the penetration levels. This translates into a vast unrealized potential.

Table 12.4 Classification of Consumer Durables

White goods	Brown goods	Consumer electronics
Refrigerators	Mixers and grinders	Mobile phones
Washing machines	Microwave ovens	Televisions
Air-conditioners	Cooking range	MP3 players
Speakers and audio equipments	Iron	DVD/VCD players
	Electric fans	

Table 12.5 Penetration Levels of Consumer Products

Product	Urban (in %)	Rural (in %)
TVs	76	34
Refrigerators	32	5
Washing machines	NA	<1
Computers	5.4	<1
Air-conditioners	3	<1
Mopeds/Scooters/Motorcycles	28	10

Demand drivers

The demand for consumer durables is driven by changes in the environment and industry.[6]

Environmental factors

There are many environmental factors favourable to the emergence of a competitive and prosperous consumer durables industry.

- Double-income families and the resulting increase in incomes have spurred the demand for better lifestyle products. The Rural Employment Guarantee Scheme and good agricultural production over the last four years has created disposable incomes in rural areas.
- Technology advancements set into motion the digital revolution that enabled production of a host of products spanning the entire technology spectrum. MP3 music files, personal video recorders, game machines, digital cameras, appliances with embedded devices and other media and services have set off a battle for dominance among corporate enterprises and they are in turn wooing urban and rural consumers.
- Availability of credit for purchase of durables has made a big impact. Apart from steady income gains, consumer financing has become a major driver in the consumer-durables industry. In the case of more expensive consumer goods such as refrigerators, washing machines, colour televisions and personal computers, retailers are joining forces with banks and finance companies to market their goods more aggressively.
- Rural electrification programme has provided electricity to many villages and very soon the electricity factor will not be an impediment for the use of durables.

Industry factors

- *Competitive strategies:* As per a survey conducted by FICCI on the Indian consumer durables industry, a shift in consumer preferences towards higher-end, technologically advanced branded products has been quite discernable.

  This shift can be explained by the narrowing differentials between the prices of branded and unbranded products added with the high quality of after-sales service provided by the branded players. The shift has also been triggered by the availability of foreign branded products in India owing to lower import duties coupled with other liberal measures as introduced by the Government.
- *Promotional strategies of companies:* With increasing competition, companies are working hard to promote their products through heavy advertising and sales promotion measures. They are offering hefty discounts and long-term warranties to win over customers.
- *Increasing share of organized retail:* Organized retail is growing and it is estimated that it would garner a 10 per cent share by 2010 from a mere 3 per cent share at present.[7]

Growth rates and size

The urban consumer durables market is growing at an annual rate of 7–10 per cent and the rural durables market is growing at 25 per cent annually. Some high-growth categories within this segment include mobile phones, TVs and music systems. The growth rates of other important durables are given in Table 12.5. The consumer electronics segment registered an overall growth rate of 9 per cent in 2005–2006 and now, it is over 10 per cent.

The consumer durables industry is set to grow by more than 15 per cent in the financial year 2009–2010 (Table 12.6). The market for consumer durables (including entertainment electronics, communitarian and IT products) is estimated to be at Rs 32 billion (USD 7.1 billion).

Table 12.6 Growth Rates of Durables

Product	Growth rates
Colour TVs	25–30 per cent
Refrigerators	18–22 per cent
Washing machines	15–20 per cent
Air-conditioners	32–35 per cent
Others (including VCDs and DVDs)	35–40 per cent

Recession and reactive strategies

In spite of a deficient monsoon in 2009, which led to 316 districts in 13 states being declared drought-hit, rural markets have proven to be resilient because of two reasons. One, the agricultural prices and agricultural output have been growing very well over the last 5 years. Though there was a drought, agricultural prices have risen. As a result, rural discretionary income has grown. The second reason is prevailing positive sentiment. Together these reasons have ensured that these markets remain lucrative and attractive destinations for those selling goods and services in the countryside. A survey carried out by RMAAI has revealed that 59 per cent of durables sales come from rural markets.[8]

Different companies have taken different measures eyeing the rural markets. The following examples are illustrative of such initiatives.

- LG has set up 45 area offices and 59 rural and remote-area offices. Moreover, it has outlined plans to invest around USD 40 million towards the development of entry-level products targeted at rural markets.[9]
- Samsung has also rolled out its "Dream Home" road show that was to visit 48 small towns in 100 days in an effort to increase brand awareness of its products. Samsung expects that its rural revenues would increase to USD 287.7 million in 2009 from USD 164.4 million last year. The company also plans to expand its sales channel by 25–30 per cent in rural India.[10]
- Whirlpool has plans to reach villages with a population between 100,000 and 500,000 in the first phase. In the long run, it proposes to provide access to potential customers in villages with a population of 50,000.[11]
- Videocon is planning to offer a wide basket of 18 models of LCDs, 17 models of refrigerators and nine automatic washing machines. It proposes to increase the number of its "Digi World" outlets to around 100 this year from the existing nine by penetrating into Class B and C cities.[12]

Prospects for consumer durables

The consumer durables industry has good prospects as many companies are overcoming weaknesses by adopting new technologies, investing in R&D and streamlining operations to reduce costs. The opportunities are very attractive and the threats can be overcome by strengthening distribution networks and service operations. Table 12.7 provides the SWOT analysis of the industry.

Table 12.7 SWOT Analysis of the Consumer Durables Industry

Strengths	**Weaknesses**
Strong distribution network Brands with sound image	Inflexibility in technology levels Operational costs Less innovative abilities and systems
Opportunities	**Threats**
Growing markets—domestic markets, especially the rural markets Export potential	Competition, especially from unorganized players; in the organized sector, competition among players is on the basis of differences in prices and well-acknowledged brands Demand is seasonal and cyclical Bargaining power of customers Entry of MNCs with liberalization Excise duties and taxes imposed by the government on the import of most raw materials

MARKETING MIX FOR DURABLES

The marketing mix of consumer durables is a combination of the various elements given in Table 12.8.

Table 12.8 Rural Marketing Mix for Consumer Durables

Components	Choices
Product	Innovative products, functional products with desirable trendy features, aesthetics such as style and colour, brand image for reliability (functional efficiency) and durability (fewer repairs)
Price	Products in premium (high quality–high price) and economy segments, economy (minimal total cost of operation), bundling or combo offers and festival discounts
Place	Feeder towns, village retailers, *haats*, vans, co-operative stores, agri-input dealers, NGOs, petrol bunks, post offices, *melas*, SHGs, company sales force and agents (trained local youth)
Promotion (communication)	Directly mailing opinion leaders and select customers, exhibitions, van campaigns, vehicle parade, FM radio, local newspapers, local TV channels, hoardings, wall paints, interactive media (demonstrations), stories—*burra katha* and *harikatha*; magic shows, meetings/workshops, contests, sports, etc.
Promotion (motivation that indirectly leads to economy and excitement)	Warranties, service coupons, discounts, gifts and financing schemes, service vans and centres
Promotion for relationships	Customer relationship programmes such as special exchange schemes (buy-back schemes) and club memberships with discounts on services and spares

Box 12.2 Beating the Heat with Innovations

Consumer durables giants have come up with innovations to beat the heat. Samsung has introduced a "Fresh tech" series in its range of refrigerators where a freshness lamp is placed inside the refrigerator that emits red LED rays on the stored fruits and vegetables. The effect, the company claims, is akin to what sunlight has on plants. Besides keeping food fresh, the new range also keeps bad odour at bay. Videocon Industries is bracing up for the summer with at least nine new models in the refrigerator category in addition to their present range of 32. The new crisp cooling technology has been introduced after intense consumer feedback, which indicates a trend towards larger capacities. Electrolux launched a new range in refrigerators—the Deo Fresh Direct Cool series and Frost Free Deo Fresh refrigerators that addressed the issue of cross odour of food.

Voltas has introduced triangular air-conditioners to fit discreetly into room corners. Chinese durables company TCL India has air-conditioners that blend technology and style. It is available in colours such as fresh vibrant blue, silver, green, yellow and even pink to go with the home or office décor. Their air-conditioners are available with a new air vitamin energizer technology that emits recharging vitamin radicals. This new line-up has been introduced to bring "consumer-relevant innovation" to Indian homes.

Source: Bindu D. Menon, "Consumer Durable Majors Find New Ways to Woo Buyers," *The Hindu Business Line*, 7 April 2008, available at www.thehindubusinessline.com/2008/04/08/stories/2008040851280500.htm.

A customer-centric long-term view, aggressiveness and innovative spirit are required when making the choice of the elements to design a marketing strategy. We find that innovations have now come to occupy the centre stage of marketing strategy. Box 12.2 highlights recent innovations.

Marketers also use combo offers as another competitive marketing tool. This has to be considered as prices of consumer durables have already reached a threshold limit and there is no scope to pull it down further. So, there has been a shift in trend from normal discounts to solution marketing. This is more prevalent in case of high-end products. Offers like discounts, gift vouchers and other schemes could not provide desirable margins. As such the companies have begun offering combo products. Such offers help manufacturers boost sales and also, ensure a saving of anything ranging between Rs 5,000 and Rs 25,000 for the customers with most of it coming from high-end products.

NOKIA SETS CONNECTIONS

The great Indian mobile revolution is all set to move to the rural part of the country with handset manufacturers gearing up to come out with market-specific products to acquire maximum share. The next big opportunity for telecom companies will be in the hinterland where two-thirds of the country's 1.17 billion population live.

Nokia—the world's largest manufacturer of mobile telephones—is aiming to tap business potential in the rural market. According to the Association of Unified Telecom Service Providers of India (AUSPI), as of 31 March 2008, rural tele-density in the country stood at just 9.2 per cent vis-à-vis the urban tele-density of 65.9 per cent. Figuratively, the all India rural wireless subscriber base stood at 0.622 billion, while the all India urban wireless subscriber base stood at 1.98 billion.[13]

Growth facilitators

There are many factors driving handset manufacturers and operators to the rural market.

Low price of handsets

The fall in the handset prices along with the availability of services at extremely competitive prices has made mobile connectivity accessible to the lower strata of society, which has mostly remained untapped. Handsets are available for as less as Rs 1,000 and affordable prepaid packages have made mobile telephony very tempting for the mass market.

Expansion of infrastructure

The Department of Telecom is planning to launch the second phase of mobile phone expansions covering around 0.2 million villages. This is a key driver for this market. A new beginning to develop infrastructure services was made in June 2007 with subsidy support from the Universal Service Obligation Fund (USOF) of DoT. Under the scheme, about 11,000 additional towers will be set up in areas with a population of 500.[14]

Hurdles to be crossed

Apart from the growing competition, companies entering rural markets have to take into cognizance the following limiting factors.

Geographical dispersion

According to an Ernst & Young-FICCI study, low income and geographical variance pose difficulties for network layout, as well as for setting up of distribution channels in remote areas.

Low returns

Further, the low ARPU (Average Revenue Per Unit) generated by rural customers does not immediately offset return on investment and revenue for rural outlay for private operators.

Marketing strategy design

The key elements that form the marketing strategy have been worked out as follows by Nokia.

Pricing versus features

As one goes down the income pyramid for expansion, pricing becomes the most crucial element. "Affordability is one of the key factors, and our effort will be in the direction of making our products more accessible to rural consumers, be it easier finance or pricing itself," says Sunil Dutt, country head, Samsung Mobile Business. However, Anil Arora of LG and Lloyd Mathias, senior director, sales and distribution, India and Southwest Asia, have taken a different view. They see the rural market as an evolving one and emphasize that features, style and design are also important. Accordingly, the strategy of LG focuses on prosperous consumers who are looking for high-end phones that offer both quality and utility at affordable prices. The entry-level market strategy of Motorola Mobile Devices addresses the needs of an aspiring Indian consumer who considers features, style and design along with affordability while choosing a handset.

Though many players say that pricing is just one of the factors, the prices of the handsets are continuously falling, making mobility more appealing. Moreover, the customers are looking at the total cost of ownership. "Handset manufacturers have to come out with features that are specific to the needs of the rural consumer. Basically, affordability, access and availability are going to play a key role," says Naresh Priyadarshi, head of Synovate Business Consulting India. Motorola has appointed Bharti TeleTech as its national distributor, to supply products through 20,000 retailers throughout the country.

Spice recently introduced a handset priced at just Rs 800. LG has the Bullet series phones targeted at this segment. LG has also recently launched the KP106B catering to the rural segment. This basic phone is targeted at high-capacity users with high talk-time requirements and also supports the best-in-class battery.

Motorola, on the other hand, has its Motoyuva series, Motoflip W220, Motoflip W375 and Motorola W218. The company has come out with features targeted at the rural segment such as Hinglish predictive text input, Hindu calendar, Indian wallpaper, Hindi texting, phonebook storage, and vernacular languages. It believes that these features are likely to appeal to the rustic part of the country.

"Rural consumers seek a value-for-money proposition. In most cases the demand emerging from the rural market is for sturdy handsets that have strong battery life. Also, voice and easy text messaging are other essential and important features in an entry-level phone. Nokia 1100, one of the best selling Nokia models was specifically targeted at the rural segment with long battery life and came with a torch," says Devinder Kishore, director marketing, Nokia India.

Price versus cost of ownership

It is recognized that the rural consumer is not just looking at price (initial outlay) but, also at the cost of ownership (initial outlay + talk-time charges). In view of this, bundled schemes have become the order of the day. "Handset manufacturers would have to work in tandem with operators to reach out to new subscribers in the rural market. This is mainly because the consumer is looking at total cost of owning a mobile and bundled schemes become very important in this scenario," says Priyadarshi of Synovate.

Bundling is rationalized on the following grounds:

- The rural population sees it as a key value proposition.
- Due to decreased ARPU realizations, companies would like to reduce their spending. This way, handset manufacturers as well as telecom companies could pass on the benefits to the customers in rural areas.
- Both handset manufacturers as well as telecom companies will be able to take advantage of each others distribution network to ensure a higher market penetration. Lesser-known handset manufacturers will also get an opportunity to garner higher sales on account of brand image of renowned service providers.

"Nokia has always been at the forefront as far as extending affordability to consumers is concerned. As part of our strategy, we essentially look at maximizing customer value by reducing the total cost of ownership for consumers. We will continue working with operators and the government to drive down the cost of mobility thereby, making it affordable and bring the benefits of mobile communication to the Indian consumers," says Devinder Kishore, director, marketing, at Nokia India.

Distribution and promotion

The main challenge in marketing is creating availability and awareness for rural consumers.

Nokia India has entered into a partnership with SKS Microfinance, which has 653 branches across 15 states and it is looking for more such tie-ups. Recently, it entered into a partnership with HCL for the distribution of its phones.

Nokia started the Rural Van project about two years back. The van forms a travelling retail and distribution centre designed to improve awareness of the benefits of mobility.

Last year the company also decided to start its own distribution efforts and has set up a number of concept stores in metros and tier-1 cities. "Making our products, as well as services available in rural India is our key focus this year. As of now, there are 130,000 mobile outlets in the country, out of which 75,000 are Nokia brand outlets," says D. Shivakumar, VP and MD of Nokia India.

"LG has a distribution network in place to leverage on as a competitive advantage," says Priyadarshi of Synovate.

Samsung has recently strengthened its distribution network in the country by appointing SSK and Link as its distributors for mobile sales in the western and eastern parts of the country, respectively. The company already has Telemart and United Telelinks as its distributor in the northern and southern parts of the country. "We are targeting alternate distribution networks to reach the rural market, which is the next growth area for the mobile industry. We are also looking at tying up with local co-operatives to push handset sales in the rural segment. Samsung recently tied up with the Indian Farmers Fertilizer Co-operative (IFFCO) for rural telephony, which will take our handsets to the countryside. We will use

IFFCO's co-operative network for marketing our handsets. The handsets will be especially beneficial for accessing commodity prices to agricultural inputs, among other benefits," says Dutt of Samsung.

Smaller players such as Meridian Mobiles are also planning to tweak their distribution channel to cater to the rural segment of the market. "We are expanding our distribution network in a large manner to reach out to rural customers and facilitate them both in terms of products and services. For this, we are also in the process of recruiting 100 strong channel partners in different areas," says Rajiv Khanna, CEO, Meridian Mobiles, India.

Nokia is also looking at micro-finance as a major initiative to increase mobile penetration in the country. The company is currently running pilots and trials to gauge consumer response in select markets and will soon come out with specific offerings to make buying a mobile phone more affordable.

Value-added services

Vernacular content will become a key differentiating factor in the Indian rural market in all likelihood. As companies enter the innermost areas of the hinterland, where the proportion of population that understands English is negligible, the true value of vernacular languages will emerge. Since, the rural market is extremely price sensitive, it is likely that volume economics will come into play and VAS providers will offer applications in small denominations. Language and ease of use are going to be major concerns. Handset manufacturers have already started working on specific content for the masses. "Nokia is working with a host of content providers and we have kick-started a programme for farmers, including solutions ranging from providing information on market prices for agricultural products to weather updates and financing options," says Devinder Kishore, director, marketing at Nokia India.

Summary

India is fast moving towards high-end customized products that are aesthetically designed to complement modern households. The two important types of goods that dominate consumer markets are FMCGs that are consumed periodically by households and consumer durables that have a lifespan of more than a year. The Rs 860 billion Indian FMCG industry is expected to register a double-digit value growth and is set to grow by 20 to 30 per cent in 2009–2010. Major categories in FMCGs are personal care, foods and beverages and household care. Some of the major players in the organized sector are HUL, Godrej, P&G, ITC, Dabur, Cadbury, Reckitt, Britannia, Amul and Nestlé. According to the study conducted by AC Nielsen, 62 of the top 100 brands are owned by MNCs, and the balance is owned by Indian companies. FMCG is a recession-proof industry. Different companies have reacted in different ways to sustain and increase sales. Price cuts, innovations and focus on rural markets are the reactions of FMCG players.

The Indian consumer durables industry has witnessed a considerable change in the past couple of years. The consumer-durables industry can be broadly classified as consumer electronics and consumer appliances. The consumer-appliances category can be further segmented as white goods and brown goods. Penetration levels of TVs in rural areas are the highest, being 34 per cent. For other products, penetration levels are below 5 per cent. The growth rates are very attractive. Quality improvements and combo-products are the major aspects of the marketing strategy.

Short Answer Questions

1. Provide a classification of FMCGs.
2. What is the size of the FMCG market? What are the growth drivers?
3. Prepare a SWOT analysis of the FMCG industry.
4. How have FMCG companies reacted to the recession?
5. State the marketing mix of FMCG companies.
6. Provide a classification of consumer durables.

7. What is the size of the consumer-durables market? What are the growth drivers?
8. Prepare a SWOT analysis of the consumer-durables industry.
9. How have consumer durables companies reacted to recession?
10. State the marketing mix of consumer durables companies.

Discussion Questions

1. Ability to innovate economy products with good quality is the key to success in FMCG markets. Discuss.
2. Product design and strong distribution networks with service capability is at the core of the consumer durables marketing strategy. Discuss.

Essay Questions

1. Explain the concept and growth opportunities of the FMCG industry.
2. Suggest a suitable marketing mix for FMCG companies. Take a product of your choice and explain how it is marketed.
3. Identify the categories and growth opportunities of consumer durables.
4. Suggest a suitable marketing mix for consumer-durables companies. Take a product of your choice and explain how it is marketed.

Internet Exercises

1. Visit the Web sites of any two FMCG companies and collect information on their rural marketing strategies.
2. Visit Web sites of any two consumer-durables companies and collect information on their rural marketing strategies.

Mini Projects

1. Take an FMCG product and identify the major brands. Gather information on the competitive marketing (product, price, promotion and distribution) strategies of the leader and the followers in the rural markets.
2. Conduct a SWOT analysis for a consumer durable product marketed by a company of your choice. Also, document the strategies adopted by the company to penetrate into the rural markets.

End Notes

1. S. Muralidhar, "The Great Indian Engineering Feat," *The Hindu Business Line*, 23 March 2009, available at www.thehindubusinessline.com/2009/03/23/stories/2009032350900700.htm; Murali Gopalan, "A Turning Point for the Car Industry," *The Hindu Business Line*, 23 March 2009, available at www.thehindubusinessline.com/2009/03/23/stories/2009032350850600.htm.

2. Shobha Kannan and Divya Trivedi, "FMCG Industry Set for 20–30% Growth On Increased Rural Demand," *The Hindu Business Line*, 20 June 2009, available at www.thehindubusinessline.com/2009/06/20/stories/2009062050780500.htm.
3. Lalitha Srinivasan, "FMCG Set to Record Double-digit Growth Despite Recession," *The Financial Express*, 20 April 2009, available at http://www.financialexpress.com/news/fmcg-set-to-record-doubledigit-growth-despite-recession/448813/; ASSOCHAM, "FMCG Sector to Grow by 25 Per cent Despite Slowdown" December 2008, available at www.thaindian.com/.../fmcg-sector-to-grow-by-25-percent-despite-slowdown-assocham_100129432.html.
4. "FMCG Demand Surging in Rural India," 21 April 2009, available at www.rncos.com/Blog/2009/04/FMCG-Demand-Surging-in-Rural-India.html
5. Sayantani Kar, "Dettol Finds Wealth in Health," *The Business Standard*, 7 September 2009, available at www.business-standard.com/india/news/dettol-finds-wealth-in-health/369236/; "Dettol Rolls Out Campaign to Promote Hand Hygiene Concept," *The Hindu Business Line*, 11 September 2009, available at www.thehindubusinessline.com/2009/09/11/stories/2009091151831900.htm.
6. Yogima Seth, "Consumer Durables Industry Brings a Shift in Marketing Strategy," *The Financial Express*, February 2008.
7. "Strong Consumer Demand Spells Cheer for Industry: FICCI Survey, www.thehindubusinessline.com/2009/10/20/stories/2009102050901500.htm
8. "Indian Consumer Markets," available at www.investingintamilnadu.com.
9. "LG, Hero Honda, Nicholas Piramal to Focus on Rural Markets," 17 January 2009, available at www.domain-b.com/brand_dossier/marketing/20090117_rural_markets.html.
10. "Rural India Unleashing the Hidden Potential," *The Economic Times*, 1 October 2009, available at http://economictimes.indiatimes.com/news/economy/indicators/Rural-India-unleashing-the-hidden-potential/articleshow/5074060.cms.
11. "Whirlpool Eyes Rural Markets in India," *The Economic Times*, 04 June 2009.
12. Press Trust of India, "Videocon to Invest up to Rs 200 cr on Marketing," *Business Standard*, May 2009, available at www.business-standard.com.
13. Gagan Deep Kaur, "Handset Strategy," *Voice & Data*, November 2009.
14. "DOT to Start off Mobile Service Phase II In Rural Areas," PIB Press Release, 27 August 2008, available at www.pib.nic.in/release/rel_print_page1.asp?relid=41946.

Case 12.1 Aventis Arrives

Pharma major, Aventis has essentially been a tier I (big city) player in India and its current revenue from the rural market is negligible. They expect to grab a 1.5–2 per cent share of the rural market in the next 5 years. At present, the Rs 360 billion Indian drug retail market is growing at 14 per cent annually. Aventis Pharma hopes that increasing awareness about health care and rise in income will drive the growth in rural regions. The Indian drug market is highly fragmented. Cipla is the market leader with just 5 per cent market share. The rural market accounts for about 20 per cent of the country's total drug retail market. Aventis Pharma, which was earlier known as Hoechst Fedco Pharma Pvt. Ltd was incorporated in the mid-1950s.

Attractiveness of Market

About two-thirds of India's 1 billion-plus population live in rural areas. Considering the prevalence of disease patterns in these areas such as respiratory, gastrointestinal and nutritional diseases, Aventis Pharma has identified some broad therapeutic areas to be targeted in the rural marketplace.

Competition

Besides Aventis Pharma, several other multinationals are charting out strategies to exploit the potential opportunities in India's growing villages.

GlaxoSmithKline and Abbott Laboratories have reportedly ramped up plans to enter the largely untapped rural markets of India in a big way.

MNCs including Eli Lilly, Novo Nordisk, and Novartis are also chalking out programmes to tap the rural customer.

At present, seven states are being targeted by Novartis. More than 16,000 pharmacies now have access to the company's low-priced products that are being marketed in various pack sizes. By using audio-visual interface through health advisors in villages, Novartis is spreading awareness on health issues. Similarly, Novo Nordisk is using mobile clinics to spread awareness. Eli Lilly has opted for taking the assistance of Self-Employed Women's Association in Ahmedabad to educate patients about such diseases as tuberculosis.

Strategy to Win

"The India rural push is in line with the company's global strategy of becoming a fully integrated health-care company involving partnerships with other service providers such as clinicians, diagnostics services and even non-profit organizations for value-added services to improve quality of health care by bridging the gap between treatment and diagnosis along with better access to medicine," said Shailesh Iyyangar, managing director, Aventis.

The new initiative that will also see a rebirth of its erstwhile Hoechst identity in the country will be a three-pronged strategy involving education and training for rural doctors, facilitating diagnostics and other value-added services by partnering with clinicians, diagnostics and other infrastructure companies and non-profit organizations, besides improving access to medicines by launching low-cost generic drugs.

The over Rs 10 billion Sanofi-Aventis India's current share of the Indian drug market is around 2 per cent. "We expect that the rural initiative would provide an additional Rs 5 billion in sales for the company in India over the next five years," said Iyyangar.

Product Portfolio

Aventis has launched a rural market division with 10 products and a sales team of 300 people in an attempt to garner a bigger share of the fast growing Indian rural market. It plans to gradually expand the drug portfolio and launch another five drugs soon. These drugs that are made by 3–4 Indian companies on contract will target those diseases, which are widely prevalent in rural regions such as respiratory, gastrointestinal and nutritional diseases.

Pricing

Aventis Pharma plans to manufacture the product meant for the rural markets through Indian manufacturers on a contract basis to make them cost-effective and on par with the offering prices of companies operating in rural markets. Accordingly, the company has set up a new business unit, in which drugs will be branded under the brand name Hoechst and sold in rural markets. The idea is to remain competitive compared with unbranded as well as branded generics.

Place and Promotion

According to Mr Ayyangar, increased awareness about health care and rise in income will drive the growth in rural regions. In India, doctors are key players in the pharmaceutical market as they prescribe specific brands of medicines to their patients. Conventionally, firms employ a field force to market their brands to doctors. In rural areas, that would be prohibitively expensive in relation to the potential returns. So, firms have devised new methods of reaching out to them. Holding workshops is one. Another is to outsource the field operations. Novartis India Ltd hires "health advisers" who go to villages and also bring doctors for health camps who prescribe medicines. Dr Reddy's Laboratories Ltd has a contracted field force for the rural market.

Aventis envisages the enrolment of at least 100,000 doctors in rural India in its training and continued medical education programme under a non-profit banner in the next five years. The initiative, known as "*Prayas*" (which means endeavour), will operate under a new division—the Hoechst Business Unit—within the Indian company, Aventis Pharma Ltd. Hoechst, a well established name in the drugs and pharmaceuticals market in the past, was transformed into Aventis Pharma after the worldwide merger of two top drug makers, Hoechst AG and Rhone-Poulenc SA in 1999. Hoechst had a strong presence in the Indian pharmaceuticals and veterinary market at the time.

Sanofi-aventis India conducted 554 workshops during the pilot phase initiated since May 2009 for over 3,200 doctors across Bihar, Uttar Pradesh and West Bengal. Soon, the company will extend the programme to Maharashtra, Madhya Pradesh and Andhra Pradesh covering about 30,000 doctors.

The move is to indirectly help the company's medical representatives gain better access and intimacy with doctors in rural areas and small towns. Later, the company will rope in non-governmental organizations (NGOs) and local governments through a public–private–partnership (PPP) model to help the poor in rural India access quality medicines.

Future Outlook

At a later stage, Sanofi-aventis India may look at exporting to neighbouring markets and manufacturing branded generics itself. According to company officials, it will also launch affordable branded generics for chronic diseases as well as combination drugs.

The emphasis at present is on infectious diseases that are more prevalent and are also cheaper to treat. However, companies will be eyeing the spread of lifestyle diseases such as diabetes and cardiovascular-related ailments that are reported to be on the rise in rural areas too. Firms cite figures of 65 per cent of the population not having access to medicine. 70 per cent of the population lives in rural areas. The rural market is estimated to contribute around 20 per cent of the total pharmaceutical sales. For large firms, the contribution is unlikely to be significant, yet. However, that will change. They just need to emulate the success of consumer goods firms that get at least 50 per cent of their sales in some products from the rural market. "We will make significant investments to create infrastructure in rural markets," said Shailesh Ayyangar.

For discussion

1. Critically evaluate the rural marketing strategies of Aventis.
2. Suggest new initiatives keeping in mind the growing competition, changing market demands and the company's long-term goal for having a rural market share of 5 per cent by 2015.

Source: "Aventis Launches Rural Market Division, Eyes 2 per Cent Share in 5 yrs," *The Economic Times*, 11 December 2009; "MNC Pharma Firms Line up to Tap India's Rural Market," December 2009, available at www.dancewithshadows.com.

Case 12.2 Marketing Water Purifiers: The Godrej Way

"We are currently working on several product categories, including water purifiers and solar lanterns," says George Menezes, chief operating officer, Godrej Appliances, the consumer electronics and appliances division of Godrej and Boyce Manufacturing Co. Ltd. "The company is aiming for a unique position in all products, including premium, mid-end and really affordable, in terms of pricing and features," said Kamal Nandi, vice-president, sales and marketing. The appliances division of Godrej is growing at more than 20 per cent with an estimated turnover of Rs 14 billion for the current fiscal.

Market Potential

The total water purifier market size is currently estimated to be at Rs 15 billion, according to PricewaterhouseCoopers (PwC). "The size of the rural market is still unknown but, definitely the potential is huge, which is why big companies such as HUL and Tata Chemicals Ltd have entered the segment," said P. Rashmi Upadhya, managing consultant, strategy and practice, PwC.

Competition

Tata Chemicals, the latest entrant, has launched a water purifier, Tata *Swach*, joining HUL's Pureit. The two companies use chemical purification technology that is cheap, unlike reverse osmosis (RO) or the UV technology being used by players such as Eureka Forbes, Kent RO System Pvt. Ltd and Whirlpool India Ltd.

Product

The company is developing a water purifier for the rural markets. It "may not require after-sales service for the entire lifetime," said Kamal Nandi, without elaborating on the technology to be used. Godrej has earlier launched UV (ultra violet) water purifiers for the urban market priced at Rs 6,500. However, for the rural product, the company has used a different technology.

Price

As for the price, Kamal Nandi said, "If we are selling a refrigerator for about Rs 3,000, that's the kind of value-for-money approach we would take for other products as well." Tata *Swach* has a starting price of Rs 749.

Place

Marketing experts are of the view that to be successful in rural areas, a company needs to have the pricing strategy, network and after-sales service in place. The company has decided that the new utility refrigerator will be sold through the rural channel that involves NGOs, micro-finance companies and community workers. The same channel will be employed to sell other durables developed for rural consumers.

Promotion

Another critical issue that the companies would need to deal with is acceptability and product preference. "It is difficult for consumers living in remote villages to understand the need for and accept such products," said Rajesh Shukla, senior fellow, at the National Council of Applied Economic Research or NCAER. Also, the television set takes first preference when it comes to choice of appliance, he said. Still, this also allows companies to make people aware of other products, given that the penetration level of the TV is about 30 per cent in Indian villages, reaching about 200 million people, who "could be prospective buyers for other consumer durables items," Shukla said.

According to Pradeep Lokhande, founder of Pune-based rural marketing agency Rural Relations, one of the hurdles is the expectation of subsidies on water purifiers in rural areas. As such, firms have to overcome this expectation. They should have the right distribution model and a strong after-sales service network.

For discussion

1. Given the competition from two high-profile companies, do you think Godrej can succeed in the rural market?
2. What are your suggestions for Godrej to promote water purifiers?

Source: Vijaya Rathore, "Godrej Plans Rural Push with Purifier, Refrigerator, Lantern," 10 December 2009, available at www.livemint.com/2009/12/10210226/Godrej-plans-rural-push-with-p.html.

13

Marketing of Agri-inputs

LEARNING OBJECTIVES

Upon completion of this chapter, you will be able to:

- Explain the concept and classification of agri-input products
- Discuss the marketing of seeds, fertilizers and pesticides
- Describe the marketing of durables such as tractors
- Analyse the marketing of farm services

The emerging market regimes offer several opportunities as well as pose many challenges for agricultural growth and development. More than 80 per cent of agricultural holdings in India are less than 2 hectares in size. How would these small and marginal farmers be integrated with the process of agricultural growth and development as a result of the integration of markets due to globalization and liberalization? How would they adapt to the changing technological development and cope with the new institutional environments, the majority of which are market-driven?

Improving competitiveness of small farmers by improving access to new technology, inputs, credit and insurance, calls for institutional and product innovations. Several models are now being experimented with throughout the country. The Farmers' Club Programme initiated by NABARD envisages efficient use of agricultural credit in scientific ways. Currently, a strong network of 17,976 farmers' clubs covering 524 districts in 29 states and the Union Territories are in operation. About 40,885 villages have benefited through 12,234 SHGs linkages that involved nearly 1,590 voluntary agencies and *Krishi Vigyan Kendras* (KVKs). The club undertakes the responsibility to coordinate and ensure credit support among the members, and foster better bank–borrower relationship.

Enlightened corporate enterprises are not very far behind. Mahindra and Field Marshall have come up with mini-tractors. Tata Chemicals designed the Tata *Kisan Sansar*. It provides value addition by fulfilling credit needs and providing information and advice on better agronomic practices apart from the supply of quality agri-inputs at a single source point. Tata *Kisan Sansar* (TKS) evolved a "hub-and-spoke" model. Competent scientific and technical staff along with *Krishi Preraks* serve 101,040 farmers covering 25,260 villages.[1]

The challenges taken up by NABARD and Tata Chemicals are illustrative of the innovative behaviour expected of corporate enterprises and government agencies concerned with the promotion and development of agriculture. In this chapter, we will explore the marketing initiatives suitable for agri-input companies and examine the practices of a few select companies.

INTRODUCTION

Agriculture is a major occupation in the Indian rural economy. About 41.3 per cent and 34.6 per cent of the population fall under the occupational categories of self-employed in agriculture and labour, respectively. In view of this, the importance of agricultural inputs and farm services need not be overemphasized. The agri-input sector is dependent on advances in research and development and farmers' adoption of modern farming techniques. The market is crowded with different types of companies—multinational to local—offering a good variety of products ranging from consumables to capital goods. Companies provide products for different types of customers—marginal to large farmers.

CONCEPT AND CLASSIFICATION

Marketing of agricultural inputs is a process of delivering manufactured or processed inputs or services to rural producers.

Classification

Agricultural inputs can be classified into two categories—consumable inputs and capital inputs—as shown in Table 13.1.

MARKETING OF SEEDS

Seeds form the fundamental and crucial input for sustained growth in farm production, often stimulating the use of new methods, machinery and yield-enhancing agro-inputs.

Although the Indian seed market is one of the largest, it is almost exclusively supplied by locally-produced seeds. Farmers retain the seeds of major food crops (wheat, rice, sorghum, millet, corn, and pulses) and commercial crops for many years and the largest volume of seed trade involves local

Table 13.1 Classification of Agricultural Inputs

Consumable inputs	Capital inputs
Seeds	Tractors
Fertilizers	Tillers
Pesticides/insecticides	Pump sets
Diesel, oil	Sprinklers, harvesters
Electricity	Threshers, dusters and sprayers

exchanges of established self-pollinating varieties. The seed replacement rate in most crops is very low, with the exception of cotton and some vegetables.

Hybrid seeds

The use of hybrid seeds is mostly confined to cotton and to some extent to corn, millet, sunflower and a few vegetables. However, awareness about the high yield and quality of produce from hybrid seeds is growing and this is attracting farmers to switch over to hybrids.

Major players

The Rs 40 billion Indian seed industry is dominated by private players. It is estimated that the private seed sector consists of more than 150 players, who account for nearly 60 per cent of industry turnover in terms of volume while the 13 state seed corporations, state Farms Corporation of India (SFCI) and the National Seed Corporation account for the rest. The composition of the seed industry, by volume of turnover, has reportedly reached a ratio of 60:40 between the private and public sectors.

The private seed sector now comprises some 20 or so large players (with sales turnover exceeding Rs 200 million), several medium companies (with sales turnover between Rs 200 million and 20 million) and a large number of small, unorganized players (with sales turnover less than Rs 20 million) with local presence. Mahyco, Navbharat, Nuziveedu, Rasi, Ankur, Brahma/Paras, Tulasi and JK Seeds are the prominent players in the private sector. Mahyco is the first private enterprise in India to produce and market hybrids of cotton, sorghum, pearl millet and sunflower. Also, it is the first Indian company to commercially grow and market transgenic Bollgard cotton—India's first transgenic crop in 2002.

Most large multinational seed companies now have presence in India (either as a joint venture or with 100 per cent equity) with their main focus on biotechnology. These include Monsanto, Bayer Crop Science, Syngenta, Advanta, Hicks-Muse-Tate, Emergent Genetics, Dow Agro, Bioseed Genetics International Inc., Tokita Seed Co., and Nunhems Zaden BV.

Seed development

The present arrangement in India for variety development, testing, evaluation and release are as follows[2]:

- New varieties are developed by the Indian Council of Agricultural Research (ICAR), State Agricultural Universities (SAUs) and private seed companies.
- Varieties that show some promise are entered into the All India Co-ordinated Trials (AICT).
- AICT is operated by SAUs, ICAR institutes, and State Agricultural Departments under the auspices of ICAR.
- Results of the AICT are presented at the respective annual workshops of participating scientists working on the particular crop, where recommendations are formulated for submission to the Variety Release Sub-committee of the Central Seed Committee.
- The Variety Release Sub-committee of the Central Seed Committee makes final recommendations to the Agriculture Ministry on which varieties should be released and notified.

Private seed companies get breeder seeds free of charge from public-sector companies and obtain information on the availability of seeds with public research institutes. Under the "consortium" model, the private companies can develop parental lines working with ICRSAT. They often cross parental lines with in-house genetics to produce proprietary hybrids. It is observed that private seed companies are marketing about 500 hybrids of field crops and vegetables.

The Indian seed programme follows the "limited generation system" of seed multiplication in a phased manner. The system recognizes three generations of seeds, i.e. breeder, foundation and certified seeds and provides safeguards for quality assurance in the seed multiplication chain to maintain purity of variety as it flows from the breeder to the farmers. Seed availability and consequently, the production gap against requirement have improved substantially as indicated in Table 13.2.

Marketing

Seed marketing includes activities such as production, processing, storage, quality control and distribution of seeds. From the point of the intermediary, seed marketing refers to the actual acquisition and selling of packed seeds, intermediate storage, delivery and sales promotional activities.

Product

Three types of seeds are available in the market: (i) seeds from produce, (ii) hybrid seeds developed by research agencies and (ii) fake seeds. High-quality, hybrid seeds are desirable as they enhance agricultural productivity. Fake ones are harmful and they should be detected and destroyed.

Pricing

Seeds are critical inputs in farming. As such the supply–demand forces play a great role in price fixation.

Price fixation by the government

In the public sector, the National Seed Corporation is usually the retail price setter. The government determines the prices of seeds marketed by the National Seed Corporation on a cost-plus basis. Apart from the procurement price of the seed, cost of processing, certification cost, interest on capital, profit margin, transportation cost and dealers' commission are also considered in arriving at the prices of seeds. The National Seed Corporation revises the prices of seeds after taking market forces into account in addition to covering their costs to prevent diversion of seeds into consumption.

Price fixation by private traders

Private traders set their prices in relation to prices fixed by the National Seed Corporation. Under normal conditions, the seeds are priced a little higher than the prevailing grain prices and improved varieties are priced much higher. Exploitation of farmers by charging exorbitant prices is found under two situations: (i) when supply is less than demand and (ii) a new hybrid variety is introduced.

Supportive role of the government

The government plays an active role in ensuring that even marginal farmers can afford seeds. Box 13.1 presents the role played by the Andhra Pradesh government to counter the strategies of Monsanto, the leading manufacturer of genetically engineered seeds in the world.

Table 13.2 Seed Availability

Year	Availability in quintals	Percentage change
2005–2006	140.50	6.22
2006–2007	148.18	5.47
2007–2008	194.31	31.13
2008–2009	250.35	28.84

Box 13.1 Government Restricts Exploitation

Exorbitant prices: The Andhra Pradesh government took Monsanto to the Monopolies and Restrictive Trade Practices Commission (MRTPC) challenging its exorbitant price for Bt seeds. In 2005, the company was charging Rs 3,785 per kilo of seed. The MRTPC ordered a rate reduction that the company challenged before the Supreme Court but was unable to get a stay order. In 2006, three state governments fixed the price of a Rs 450 gram packet at Rs 750. In April 2008, seed companies asked for an increase to Rs 800 per packet. However, this was refused. The Gujarat government decided to sell Bt seeds through its seed corporation to keep prices in check.

Complaints and bans: The Tamil Nadu government has banned the sale of seeds from Mahyco over complaints of crop failure in Dharmapuri district. Bt cotton varieties made by the Indian seed major had earlier been blacklisted by Andhra Pradesh after crop failures in the 2004 *kharif* season. In Dharmapuri, thousands of farmers are in distress. They told the district collector that their Bt cotton crop failed due to sub-standard seeds. Cotton crop on at least 2,500 acres (1,012 hectares) has failed and about 2,000 farmers have been affected. The state government has taken serious note of the problem and ordered an enquiry.

Source: Sujata Madhok, "The Hi-tech Seeds of Child Labour," May 2008, available at http://infochangeindia.org/200805267154/Children/Features/The-hi-tech-seeds-of-child-labour.html; Shailesh Kumar, "Tamil Nadu Blacklists Mahyco's BT Cotton Seeds after Crop Failures," 14 February 2007, available at www.indiaenvironmentportal.org.in/node/16012.

Subsidies are declared by the central government whenever it is found to be necessary to support farmers. In August 2009, the Indian government announced the decision to increase the subsidy on seeds of different crops up to Rs 2.88 billion to mitigate the impact of drought and hoped *kharif* losses would be made up to some extent, especially now that rainfall had improved. "We have decided to distribute good-quality seeds in time to farmers and have stepped up subsidy to the extent of Rs 2.88 billion so that farmers get subsidy directly, which will get reflected in the pricing of seeds," Finance Minister Pranab Mukherjee told reporters after the first meeting of the Empowered Group of Ministers (EGoM) on drought.[3]

Seeds are distributed through government agencies and private intermediaries. The government and public-sector agencies include the Agriculture Department, the Agro-industrial Corporation, research institutes and agricultural universities. On the private side, the co-operatives and individual traders (dealers, distributors and retailers) facilitate the movement of seeds to farmers. The four-channel distribution network is shown in Figure 13.1.

The National Seed Corporation and the State Seeds Corporations have their own sales points for seed marketing. In some states, the Department of Agriculture also sells seeds through their field staff. The Agro-industries Corporations of the states encourage private entrepreneurs to establish agro-service centres in rural areas by providing them with training and arranging supplies of farm inputs for subsequent sales to farmers.

In case of traders, we find distributors and dealers handling seeds along with food grains, oilseeds, spices and vegetables and agricultural inputs such as fertilizers, pesticides, agro-chemicals, etc. A distributor or stockist is appointed for a region that may consist of one or more states. The distributors appoint dealers at the district level. Normally 15 to 25 per cent commission is given to distributors who pass 12–22 per cent to the dealers while the retailers get 9–19 per cent discount on sales.

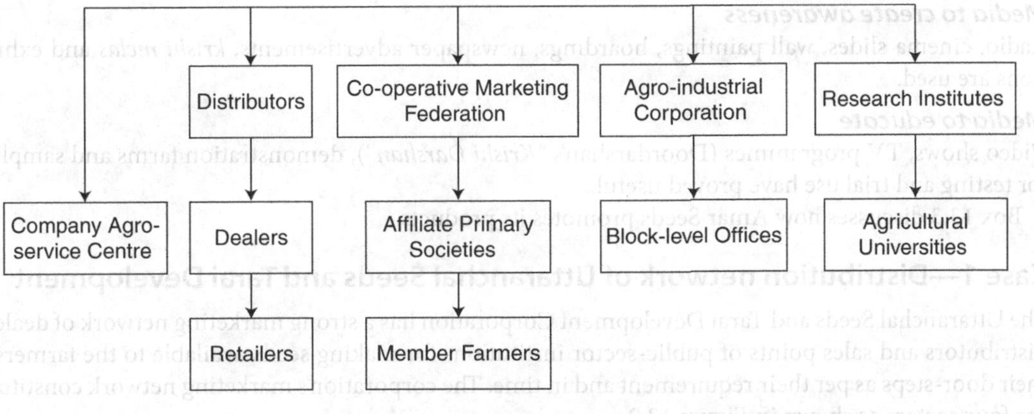

Figure 13.1 Distribution Channels of Seeds

Box 13.2 Role of Post Offices in Facilitating Sales of Seeds

Farmers in some villages in Jalgoan use their local post offices not only to buy stamps and send letters, but also to order seeds, fertilizers and pesticides. The initiative of MCX, the country's leading commodity exchange has managed to link farmers with seed companies through five post offices covering 15–20 villages in Jalgaon. Typically, a farmer places an order with the post office for the quantity of seeds required and pays 10 per cent upfront. The post office in turn arranges for the requested seeds through MCX from the seed company. The farmer pays the remaining cost after receiving the seed packets that are dispatched through the postal department.

In June, MCX arranged for seeds worth Rs 0.129 million and fertilizers and pesticides worth Rs 0.108 million through its tie-up with Shriram Fertilizers and Chemicals Ltd.

Source: Suresh P. Iyengar, "MCX to Tie up with Mayhco for Seed Distribution in Jalgaon," *The Hindu Business Line*, 9 December 2007, available at www.blonnet.com/2007/12/09/stories/2007120950940500.htm.

Innovative approaches such as enrolling post offices and employing the Internet have been used in recent times. Box 13.2 explains how post offices are assisting in the sales of seeds.

Promotion

Trust is the key factor in the sales transaction of seeds. Farmers are apprehensive about the quality of seeds (fake seeds rule the market) and prices charged by the seller. Poor quality of seeds will lower productivity and sometimes, may result in losses. As such, the promotion programme should have the following objectives:

1. Creating trust in the company—in the quality of its seeds and prices.
2. Creating trust in the trader who can sell the genuine seeds with assurance.
3. Educating on how to gain from the seeds—right from sowing to harvesting.

The following media can be employed to achieve these goals.

Media to create awareness

Radio, cinema slides, wall paintings, hoardings, newspaper advertisements, *krishi melas* and exhibitions are used.

Media to educate

Video shows, TV programmes (Doordarshan's "*Krishi Darshan*"), demonstration farms and sampling for testing and trial use have proved useful.

Box 13.3 discusses how Amar Seeds promotes its products.

Case 1—Distribution network of Uttaranchal Seeds and Tarai Development

The Uttaranchal Seeds and Tarai Development Corporation has a strong marketing network of dealers, distributors and sales points of public-sector institutions for making seeds available to the farmers at their door-steps as per their requirement and in time. The corporation's marketing network constitutes the four sectors as shown in Figure 13.2.

Agricultural seed stores

Various sales points under the Agriculture Department of the state are engaged in the distribution of seeds produced by the corporation.

Co-operative seed stores

Co-operative seed stores/Primary agriculture co-operative societies are in operation under the Co-operative Department of the state for distribution of agricultural inputs including seeds. These sales

Box 13.3 Promotion by Amar Seeds

Established in 2001, Amar Seeds is in the business of providing genetically pure quality seeds to farmers. The company's operations are carried out in the states of Maharashtra, Karnataka, Tamil Nadu, Madhya Pradesh and Gujarat. It has a well-qualified, experienced and trained sales work force. They carry on extensive as well as intensive sales campaigns of the company's seeds in the areas allotted to them. The distributors and dealers regularly provide guidance to the farmers about agricultural practices and the marketing of produce.

Source: www.amarseeds.com, accessed March 2010.

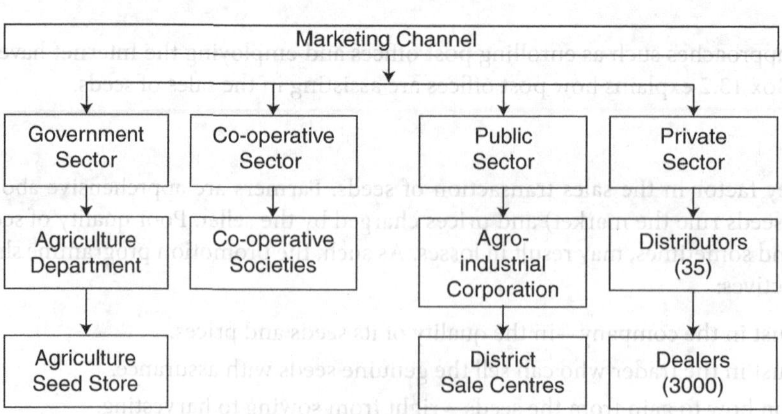

Figure 13.2 Distribution Model

points sell seeds and other inputs to the member-cultivators of the Co-operative bank under the Crop Loan Scheme. Non-members can also buy on a "cash-and-carry" basis.

Agro-industries sale outlets

District-wise sales outlets run by the Agro-industrial Corporation throughout the state are also engaged in distribution of seeds to the farmers. These sales outlets also provide other agricultural inputs along with seeds.

Horticulture department sales counters

Horticulture Department sales counters are also engaged in the distribution of vegetable and potato seeds specifically produced by the corporation to the farmers of the state. These sales counters also provide technical knowledge to the cultivators regarding horticulture through their extension services.

Private-sector distributors and dealers

About 35 distributors and 3,000 dealers in the private sector are also distributing seeds of the corporation throughout India.

Apart from the above, sales points of national level organizations such as Chambal Fertilisers and Chemicals Ltd (CFCL), National Agricultural Cooperative Marketing Federation of India Ltd (NAFED), Indian Farmers Fertiliser Cooperative Ltd (IFFCO), and Krishak Bharati Cooperative Limited (KRIBHCO) are also distributing Pantnagar seeds through their sales points.

All the above sales points provide seeds to the cultivators, along with other agricultural inputs like fertilizers, pesticides, insecticides, implements, etc. under the "one-window delivery system." The network, over all, is in a position to provide seeds of the corporation to the farmers within a radius of 5 kms.

The corporation has a strong network of dealers and distributors in other states also. In the case of Bihar, distribution is made mainly through large numbers of private-sector distributors and dealers. In West Bengal, apart from a strong network of private-sector distributors and dealers, the seeds are also distributed through the sales points of West Bengal State Seeds Corporation. In Assam, the distribution is made mainly through the State Seeds Corporations on specific orders like in the other states of the country.

Order-delivery system

As per the terms and conditions set out by the corporation, the distribution agency has to reserve its accepted indent almost four months before the actual sale time covered with 10 per cent advance. Crop seeds are made available according to variety at the regional godowns based on the reservation made by different distribution agencies. The seeds are delivered from the godowns of the corporation to distribution agencies on payment of its balance cost or under definite payment arrangements at the dealer's price and margin for local transport. These distribution agencies sell the stock to the farmers at the retail rates fixed by the government. The dealers get a commission of 9 per cent and the distributor between 2.5 and 4.25 per cent on slab basis that is quite remunerative to them.

In case of states other than Uttaranchal and Uttar Pradesh, the stock is supplied by wagons/trucks directly to the dealers on payment of 25 per cent advance. The remaining cost is covered through a bank/regional office before delivery of the railway receipts. The dealers and distributors also get stocks from buffer godowns.[4]

Case 2— Marketing strategies of Nuziveedu Seeds Ltd

Nuziveedu Seeds Ltd is a leading hybrid seed company in India.

Product and research

The company's hybrid seeds are produced in collaboration with about 42,000 seed producing farmers and are used by 5 million farmers across the country. The cotton seeds supplied by the company are planted in 35–40 per cent of the areas where cotton is cultivated. This contributes to producing 40–45 per cent of the best-quality cotton in India. Besides cotton, the company is also strong in crops such as rice, maize, bajra, jowar, etc. The company's R&D has evolved excellent hybrids in cotton by the name of "Bunny" and "Mallika" that produce very high-quality cotton fibre besides giving high yield to the farmers. The R&D department of the company also evolved several excellent hybrids and improved plant types in rice, maize, bajra, jowar, etc. At present, NSL is using the GM traits for imparting "insect resistance in cotton" and selling the largest quantity of Bt cotton seeds in India. NSL is also developing GM traits on its own and through contract research for cotton and other crops.

Processing and storage

NSL established all the required research farms, seed conditioning (processing) facilities as well as conditioned storage godowns for seeds around Hyderabad and several other strategic locations across the country.

Place

The company is present in about 15 major agricultural states with offices at Hyderabad, Delhi, Guntur, Ahmedabad, Akola, Indore, Davangere, Bangalore, Chennai, Lucknow, Jaipur, Patna, etc. The company has also developed excellent systems of production, quality assurance and distribution. The marketing network consists of eight regional offices, 639 distributors, 1,395 dealers and over 20,000 sub-dealers.

Promotion

Through its qualified and trained personnel, NSL helps farmers in increasing their productivity so as to make the farmers reap the benefits from the superior genetics supplied to them through the company's seeds.

Future plans

After having established itself as the top player in cotton, NSL is now working on increasing its market share in rice, maize, jowar, bajra, sunflower, chillies, soybean, wheat and various vegetable crops.

Fighting fakes

Keeping in mind the large-scale spread of unapproved Bt cotton cultivation across cotton growing states, the All India Crop Biotechnology Association (AICBA) felt that it had become necessary to educate and create awareness among the agricultural inspectors, traders, dealers and the industry on the prevailing laws by holding workshops. This would go a long way in helping the industry grow by offering quality seeds to the farming community at an affordable price.

The initiative of AICBA emphasizes the need to understand how the fake seeds are distributed.

Illegal Bt and the seed market

In the 2004 season, illegal Bt was priced anywhere between Rs 800 and Rs 1,200 per packet. With its seemingly effective performance and its lower price, illegal Bt is a threat to legal seeds, whether Bt or otherwise. In Gujarat, for instance, the market leader, Vikram Seeds lost its non-Bt market rapidly because of illegal Bt.

There are several factors that facilitate the spread of illegal Bt seed.

- Firstly, it can be priced lower than legal Bt because the seed value does not have to be shared with the gene supplier. Even if legal Bt hybrids improve their performance or lowers their prices, illegal Bt could compete by further lowering its price.

- Secondly, the illegal Bt coming out of Gujarat is regarded as being of good quality within Gujarat. It is served by a large network of seed producers and distributors. Anecdotal accounts of grower experience speak of farmers receiving quality assurance from this network.
- Next, illegal Bt generates large gains for seed dealers and seed producers and, therefore, can be shared with local authorities that have the power to enforce seed laws.

However, there are factors that also constrain the spread of illegal Bt.

- Seed dealers and producers cannot use normal banking facilities nor can they use regular commercial channels for dealing with first-time buyers (i.e., seed dealers from outside their area of operations). As such, transactions have to be based on trust and carried out in cash. Illegal trade becomes difficult to carry out without kinship networks that are geographically restricted.
- Illegal Bt is marketed without a company name and a bill of purchase. Illegal Bt producers do not possess the formal means to communicate quality especially to growers located outside their traditional areas of operation. In Gujarat, some illegal seeds are known by brand names such as *Kavach* and *Rakshak*. However, it would be difficult to build these brands over geographically dispersed areas.
- In areas outside Gujarat, growers confronted with the issue of spurious Bt have become cautious. One estimate is that 30 per cent of all seeds marketed as legal Bt in Maharashtra is spurious. Kurnool in Andhra Pradesh is another centre for illegal Bt production and proliferation. In these places, distribution systems developed by the Gujarat seed producers may not carry over easily.
- In course of time, legal Bt could outperform illegal Bt seeds.

Measures to be taken

Obviously, the operations of fake marketers are harmful to the farmers and also to the economy. Measures are necessary to curb them. The Government has to set up law enforcing agencies and strengthen them. Agricultural extension personnel should help farmers become aware of fake seeds and support them in the purchase of genuine seeds. Through their sales force and extension/agriculture promotion assistants, private companies should render assistance to farmers in the purchase of seeds as well as cultivation practices.[5]

MARKETING OF FERTILIZERS

Fertilizers can be described as any substance, organic or inorganic, natural or artificial, that supplies one or more of the chemical elements required for plant growth.

It is the most important among all the inputs purchased by the farmer. For boosting agricultural output, the use of chemical fertilizers has an important role. India's soil, though varied and rich, is deficient in nitrogen and phosphorus—two plant nutrients that together with organic manure influence crop return. The use of fertilizers increases land productivity and eases the nutrient constraints on multiple cropping and land development programmes.

Market structure

In the present scenario, there are more than 57 large and 64 medium and small fertilizer production units under the Indian fertilizer industry. The 57 large-sized fertilizer plants in the country are manufacturing a wide range of nitrogenous, phosphatic and complex fertilizers. Out of these, 29 units produce urea, 20 units produce di-ammonium phosphate (DAP) and complex fertilizers, 13 plants manufacture ammonium sulphate (AS), calcium ammonium nitrate (CAN) and other low-analysis nitrogenous fertilizers. Besides this, there are about 64 medium and small-scale units in operation producing single-super phosphate (SSP).

Production of fertilizers

The fertilizer industry made rapid progress during the past decade. Fertilizers can be classified into two categories—chemical and bio-fertilizers. There has been considerable increase in the domestic production of fertilizers over the years but, not enough to keep pace with the growth in consumption. Hence, to meet the growing demand, the Government imports from other countries.

Bio-fertilizers are bacterial cultures mixed with an appropriate inert material, referred to as carrier. Bio-fertilizers offer several advantages. First, they are based on low-cost technology. Second, they supplement the availability of nitrogen and increase the availability of native and applied phosphates. Third, they are eco-friendly being a renewable source of energy.

Bio-fertilizer usage is popular to a reasonable extent in the states of Madhya Pradesh, Maharashtra and Tamil Nadu. At present, there are about 110 units producing bio-fertilizers. Installed capacity of the bio-fertilizer production is about 17,000 tonnes with an annual production of 10,000 tonnes. The annual potential demand has been estimated to be around 40,000 tonnes.

Demand determinants

Fertilizer demand is influenced by the following factors.

- *Rainfall and irrigation facilities:* Adequate and well-diversified rainfall gives the farmers confidence to invest in fertilizers along with well-equipped irrigation facilities.
- *Relative prices of fertilizers:* Indian agriculture is characterized by small holdings and demand for fertilizers tends to be price-sensitive. If there is significant price differentiation between fertilizers, demand will move in favour of the cheaper fertilizers, even if it is not the most appropriate one.
- *Cropping pattern:* This determines the need and timing of fertilizer purchases.
- *Government policy:* Government policies and frameworks (subsidy and price controls) influence pricing, production and distribution of fertilizers.

Product

Fertilizers are classified into three groups based on the mix of nutrients—nitrogenous (N), phosphates (P) and potassic (K).

- *Straight fertilizers:* The fertilizers that have a single nutrient like N or P or K are called straight fertilizers. Examples of such fertilizers are ammonium sulphate, urea, calcium ammonium nitrate (that supply only nitrogen) and single super phosphate and triple super phosphate (that supply phosphate).
- *Compound fertilizers:* The fertilizers that contain more than one nutrient are called compound and complex fertilizers. For example, di-ammonium phosphate (DAP) is a complex fertilizer that supplies both nitrogen and phosphate.
- *Specific-mix fertilizers:* The fertilizer mixtures that supply all the three nutrients in proportions required by different crops and for different regions are referred to by this name.

Brand names

According to the Fertilizer Control Order (FCO), fertilizers have to be marketed only by their generic name and not by any trade or brand name. Usually, companies add their company name to the generic name, for example Mangalore Chemicals and Fertilizers Ltd sells urea under the name Mangala Urea. Southern Petrochemical Industries Corporation Ltd calls their product SPIC Urea.

Labeling

The bags should clearly indicate product mixture details. The proportions of the three nutrients say, NPK 20:20:20, should be given.

Price

Price is an important factor in the purchase of fertilizers. The costs of the agricultural output is influenced by fertilizer prices and the quantity of fertilizer used. For this reason, Government intervention is considered necessary to control prices.

Price controls

Presently, fertilizers except urea have been de-controlled in view of the improved supply situation and with the aim of reducing the burden of subsidy. However, de-control resulted in price hikes.

Subsidy

Subsidy aims at providing fertilizers to the farmers at a price lower than its economic price. Differential rate of subsidy on nitrogenous, phosphatic and potassic fertilizers was used to correct the imbalance in the use of nutrients by the farmers. However, after the de-control of P and K fertilizers their prices rose sharply and it resulted in distorted use ratio of N, P and K.

Distribution system

Fertilizers are produced only at select locations and imported fertilizers arrive at seaports. The distribution system has to carry out the functions of storage, transportation and sales to the farmers spread throughout the country. The marketing costs are as follows: freight accounts for 50–55 per cent, the distribution margin accounts for 18 per cent and handling and storage for 10 per cent.

Storage

While fertilizer production is continuous throughout the year, its use is seasonal. In India, there are two main cropping seasons: (i) *kharif* (April–September) and (ii) *rabi* (October–March). Fertilizers are stored before the onset of each season. Consumption is characterized by a peak period followed by lean spells. Therefore, storage is an important factor in fertilizer marketing and distribution. There are about 2,060 central and state warehouses with an aggregate capacity of 30.1 million tonnes. In addition, the Food Corporation of India has a storage capacity of 23.95 million tonnes. The co-operatives have about 65,970 godowns with a capacity of about 14.12 million tonnes. These godowns are used for storage of food grains, fertilizers and other commodities.

Sales

There are 0.26 million fertilizer sales points in the country, out of which 70 per cent are in the private sector and the remaining 30 per cent are operated by either co-operative societies or other public-sector institutions like State Agro-industries Corporations.

The different channel types are:

(i) *Traditional channel:* These include consignees, dealers, distributors, wholesalers and retailers.

(ii) *Direct channel:* Some companies sell directly to farmers through their company sales depots or service centres.

(iii) *Co-operatives:* The pattern of fertilizer distribution in the co-operative sector varies from state to state. Generally co-operative networks operate through a three-tier system. However, in some states the system works on a two-tier basis. In a number of states, the apex co-operative marketing federation functions as a wholesaler. The village-level primary agricultural co-operative societies (PACS) are the ultimate units in the co-operative structure. These societies act as the retail sales points for fertilizers. Nearly 50 per cent of the total PACS are involved in the fertilizer business. The village level societies generally receive fertilizer supplies either directly from the co-operative wholesaler, i.e. apex marketing federation or from primary district marketing societies.

Credit facility

Generally, two types of credit facilities are available in the fertilizer sector for fertilizer distribution and use. One type is distribution credit that a dealer uses for buying fertilizers from the manufacturer or wholesaler. The second type is production credit that a farmer uses for purchasing inputs, of which fertilizers are the major one. Various agencies provide credit to the agriculture sector in different forms. These include co-operative banks, regional rural banks, commercial banks and other agencies.

Promotion

Farmers require advice in the choice and application of scientific fertilizers. In view of this, promotion should be a two-pronged one:

(i) Creating awareness of the different brands and mixes of fertilizers
(ii) Instructions on how to use fertilizers—timing, quantity and method of application.

Promotion for awareness can use mass media (radio, cinema slides, wall paintings, hoardings, newspaper advertisements, *krishi melas* and exhibitions) but, promotion aiming at education requires interactive media. It is for this purpose that many private companies and government agencies have their farm extension services.

Case 3—Marketing strategies of Zuari Industries Limited

Over three decades ago, Zuari Industries Limited (ZIL), promoted by Dr K. K. Birla, entered the Indian corporate scene by investing in fertilizers in Goa. ZIL markets its products like urea and complex fertilizers—Sampurna (19:19:19), Samrat (18:46:0), Samarth (10:26:26) and NPK 12:32:16—under the *Jaikisaan* brand.

Distribution

With their marketing head office based at Zuarinagar, Goa, the company has a network of regional marketing offices in the states of Goa, Maharashtra, Karnataka, Andhra Pradesh and Tamil Nadu. Zuari Industries Ltd has over 2,000 dealers and 5,000 sub-dealers who market its various brands of fertilizers and other agri-inputs. Zuari-Chambal has an enviable strength in its ability to leverage its deep understanding of the rural market. It has built a huge rural infrastructure that stretches across most of India and touches remote villages through a combined network of approximately 50,000 village-level outlets.

Promotion

Faced with the major challenge of educating farmers to enhance their yields through increased use of fertilizers and adoption of scientific methods in farming, Zuari devised its service-oriented marketing strategy and organized innovative education programmes for farmers. The frontline task of extension education was undertaken through agricultural graduates. Attaching great importance to selection of the right type of dealers, Zuari familiarized dealers with their role as "change agents."

Krishi sudhar programmes

Field visits and one-to-one farmer contact programmes of the company are categorized under the *krishi sudhar* programmes. These programmes of regular nature are common to the entire marketing area. The various activities being organized under this programme are promotional squads, intensive farmer-contact programmes, soil testing days, soil test results recommendation days, etc. The promotional squad is a fortnight-long programme of contacting the farmers at their doorsteps, providing spot solutions to their field problems and acquainting them with modern agronomic practices.

Each squad, consisting of agricultural graduates and field assistants, is equipped with a well-decorated van. They visit farmers at their doorsteps and organize farmer meetings, group discussions, method demonstrations, literature distribution, etc. Wherever possible, the help of subject matter specialists from various departments is taken to guide the farmers.

Similar programmes undertaken on a smaller scale spanning 4–5 days are called intensive farmer-contact programmes.

Crop seminars and farmer-training programmes

To update farmers' knowledge on crop production, Zuari organizes crop seminars and farmer-training programmes for farmers on regular a basis in the entire marketing area. Faculties are drawn from agricultural research stations, agri-universities, the Department of Agriculture, etc. These programmes facilitate one-to-one interaction with subject matter experts.

Educational tours

Zuari uses the "seeing is believing" principle of extension education. Farmers are taken on educational tours to agricultural research stations, sugar factories, agricultural universities, progressive farmers' fields, *krishi melas*, etc.

Krishi Samrat Award

To honour excellence in agriculture and recognize the valuable contribution to the community at large, Zuari instituted *Krishi Samrat* award in 1985. This award is given to outstanding farmers with proven leadership in the marketing territory.[6]

MARKETING OF PESTICIDES

At about 2 per cent, India accounts for only a small part of the global agro-chemicals market; however, the year-on-year growth is about 10 per cent in terms of value. The market size is estimated to be at Rs 30 billion. The use of pesticides is considered necessary to protect the plants from various types of diseases and to control pest attacks. In agriculture, the use of pesticides starts from the pre-sowing stage. The soil is treated against nematodes before sowing. Then, the seeds are treated against seed-borne diseases, rodents, etc.

Categories

Agro-chemicals can be classified into five groups as given in Table 13.3.

Usage pattern

The usage pattern is found to be varied on account of several factors.

Global differences

The world market for agro-chemicals is primarily dominated by herbicides, which has a 46 per cent share followed by insecticides at 29 per cent and fungicides at 17 per cent. In sharp contrast, in the Indian market, insecticides have the lion's share of 76 per cent followed by fungicides with 13 per cent. Herbicides have a share of only 10 per cent. The low consumption of herbicides in India is on account of cheap labour available for weeding operations.

Regional differences

The consumption pattern is skewed in favour of certain states like Andhra Pradesh, Karnataka and Punjab where scientific farming practices are given greater attention.

Table 13.3 Classification of Agro-chemicals

Group	Brand name/Formulations
Insecticides	BHC, DDT, Malathion, Monocrotophos, Endosulphan, Methyl parathion, Phosphamidon, Phorate, Dimethoate
Fungicides	Dithane, Copper Oxychloride, Organo-Mercurials
Herbicides	2-4-D, Butachlor
Fumigants	Ammonium phosphide, Methyl bromide, Ethylene di-bromide
Rodenticides	Zinc phosphide, Ratafin

Seasonal differences

Largely, pesticides are consumed by two major *kharif* crops in India—cotton and paddy. Since, the two crops are sown and reaped between the months of July and November, this is the peak demand period for agro-chemicals.

Crop differences

Cotton accounts for 40–50 per cent of the pesticides consumption while other crops like rice, vegetables and wheat consume less.

Extension services

Corporate farm service centres such as ITC e-*choupal*, Tata *Kisan Sansars*, EID-Parry Argroline, Rallis *Kisan Kendra* and Mahindra *Krishi Vihars* have been assisting farmers in rationalizing the use of pesticides.

Exposure and literacy

The exposure to global practices through TV and the Internet as well as workshops and farmer meets organized by corporate firms have had a positive influence on the pesticide-use practice of farmers.

Market structure

The domestic agro-industry has about 80 players in the organized sector and more than 6,000 in the small-scale sector. More than 60 technical grade pesticides are manufactured indigenously by 125 producers. Others are engaged in making pesticide formulations. There are large numbers of subsidiaries of MNCs such as Monsanto Chemicals, Bayer (India), Novartis (India) and Cyanmide Agro. R&D is a key factor in this business. However, many Indian firms invest less in R&D. The top 10 companies account for 80 per cent of the production.

The formulators buy technical-grade material and prepare various formulations for the ultimate users in different concentrations for different crops and also for different types of pests and diseases. The formulators are free to manufacture and market any combination or concentration of pesticides or insecticides from the basic chemicals. They are also free to use any trade or brand name for their products.

Nature of business

Production in the agro-chemical industry is essentially a conversion job. Raw materials and labour are the major cost elements. Environmental considerations have resulted in high regulation for the industry. The industry is basically generic in nature with nearly 70 per cent of the molecules being off patent. In the off patent market, wide distribution network, strong brand image and superior product quality are major factors that help retain competitive advantage.

Product

The products differ in form and use for different crops. However, there are also products that are insect specific and can be used for many crops. The products are mainly available in two forms, i.e. powdered form and liquid form. The pesticides/insecticides in powdered form need dusters for application, while those in liquid form need sprayers for application. Most of the farmers do not possess the applicators. They either borrow from their neighbours or hire it from agro-input vendors.

Pricing

As there are no government controls, prices of pesticides are determined by normal demand and supply forces. Competition and excessive capacity build up together led to a steady decline in the prices of generic products. In addition, discounts and credit facilities are offered to win customers. Nearly 80 per cent business is conducted against unsecured credit, the period for which varies from 30 to 120 days. As they are generally purchased at the middle or the end of the crop cycle when a farmer's cash flows are lean, the incidence of bad debts can be quite high. In this respect, products that target crops that have a shorter cash-to-cash cycle such as paddy, or commercial crops, would be better placed than others.

Distribution

The distribution of pesticides is similar to that of fertilizers. It is carried out through state departments, co-operatives and private dealers. There are about 79,000 outlets for pesticide distribution in the country. The margins for the distributors range between 5 and 10 per cent and for the dealers it is between 10 and 18 per cent. To promote cash sales, dealers sacrifice a part of their margins and sell at lower prices.

Promotion

The promotional measures used to promote agro-chemical products are usually the same as those used by fertilizer manufacturers/marketers. As the product is a problem-solver, farmers may try to become aware of them on their own. However, inappropriate use of pesticides will result in further problems. As such, it is important to activate opinion leaders (peers, educated persons and *sarpanch*), local dealers, company farm-services agents and agricultural scientists from agricultural departments and universities to educate farmers on how and when to apply pesticides.

The media generally used for awareness creation are: television, newspapers, radio, wall paintings, hoardings and cinema slides. The media for education include the following: field demonstrations, farmers' meets, agriculture fairs (*kisan melas*), credit facilities and gifting applicators.

Case 4— Marketing by Rallis India Ltd

Rallis India Limited is a leading manufacturer of pesticides in India. There are around 20–25 technicals manufactured by it. Other than pesticides, it deals in seeds and fertlizers.

Takeover by Tata Chemicals

Tata Chemicals, which generates over 40 per cent of its revenue from fertilizers such as urea, DAP and NPK has annual sales of about Rs 122 billion. It has taken over Rallis India, which has sales of over Rs 8.5 billion from crop protection products that include pesticides, insecticides, seeds, micro-nutrients, etc. and contract manufacturing of agro-chemicals for multinationals. Rallis is the sole distributor for Tata Chemicals fertilizers in its main markets in the north and north-east regions. Tata Chem manufactures about 12 per cent of the urea produced in the country by the private sector. It also manufactures inorganic chemicals such as sodium bicarbonate, soda ash, salt, bio-fuels and fresh farm produce as part of a joint venture.

Agro-chemicals division

The agro-chemicals division with its well-established distribution network, manufacturing infrastructure and state-of-the-art research and development facilities help Rallis partner world players to provide best-of-the-breed agri-business solutions.

Product

The product range includes insecticides, fungicides, herbicides and intermediaries. The company has eight factories.

Distribution

Tata Chemicals has a strong marketing presence in the north and east, while Rallis is strong in the west and south. It has eight regional offices, 28 area sales offices and 24 depots that are manned by sales managers, field officers and field assistants. In the last 12 months, Rallis has rationalized its dealership network by reducing the number of dealers, especially in common areas, from 8,000 to 1,500 with increased focus on pesticides. According to analysts, rationalizing the dealership network has helped Rallis reduce its finished goods inventory with dealers and efficiently manage working capital.

Rallis Farm Management Services (FMS)

It is ideally placed to bring the farmer closer to the consumer. Under FMS, Rallis helps identify the consumer's requirements of produce and works backwards to help the farmer grow the specified crop, such that he is able to harvest and sell market-driven produce.

Rallis undertakes contract farming, providing all inputs to the farmer including seeds, fertilizers, pesticides and also farm equipment. It helps the farmer arrange for finance, get recommendations on the application of quality pesticides and fertilizers and ultimately ensures purchase of his produce at appropriate prices.

Rallis Kisan Kendras (RKKs)

Rallis has established four Rallis *Kisan Kendras* in order to provide the farmer/grower with a whole continuum of services designed to enhance his own profitability as well as to bring in efficiencies into the whole gamut of agri-practices. Each *kendra* has the infrastructure and trained personnel to organize agronomic advice and to impart training to the farmers, genuine agri-inputs, soil-and water-testing facilities, assistance in the availability of credit to the farmers, post-harvest management including sorting, grading, packaging transporting and then delivering to the identified market.[7]

MARKETING OF TRACTORS

The Rs 90 billion Indian tractor industry has shown a steady growth since the liberalization period. Good monsoons for the past 10 years, leading to good harvest and good prices of agricultural crops have created more demand for tractors.

Market dynamics

In the past few years, the tractor market has moved from a seller's market to a buyer's market as competition from both the existing and new manufacturers' intensified and fresh capacity was created. This has created a scenario where dealers have been maintaining higher inventories so as to provide a wider choice and immediate delivery to the farmer. Tractor prices in India are about a quarter of the similar powered tractors in international markets.

Major players

Till the late 1990s, domestic players dominated the tractor industry. Once the sector was thrown open to foreign players, the new entrants brought in high-end, higher horse power (HP) tractors. The three MNC tractor manufacturers, New Holland (US), John Deere (Italy) and Renault (France), have entered the Indian market through collaboration-cum-joint ventures with L&T, Greaves and International Tractors Ltd, respectively. Among the major players, Mahindra and Mahindra, Escorts, Punjab Tractors, Tafe and Eicher have a presence across the major segments.

Demand determinants

The various factors that affect the demand for tractors are as follows.

Government policies

All agriculture-related industries in India have been highly controlled by the government and tractors are not an exception to this. The important government policies that affect the tractor industry are excise duty and licensing.

Usage of tractors

In India, tractors are mainly used for three basic purposes, i.e. for farming operations, for transportation and as a source of power.

- *Source of power:* Tractors are used for seedbed preparation, irrigation and harvesting. Tractors help in reducing the time required for these operations. It is also used as a power source in farms for harvesting, pumping of water, etc.
- *Transportation:* Tractors are also used in the transportation of people, fodder, food grains, etc. from rural areas to the nearest market place and in earth-moving and forest-clearing operations.
- *Industrial applications:* Tractors are used like loaders, forklifts, road rollers and baggage haulers at airports.

The use of tractors in operations other than farming is sizable and as per industry estimates, it ranges from 40 to 50 per cent of total tractor utility in the country.

Land-holding pattern

The optimal land holding required for different HP tractors is approximately 8–10 hectares for 1,800 cc or 25 HP tractors, 25–30 hectares for 35 HP and for land holdings beyond that, higher HP tractors are required. However, the actual relationship between different land holdings and the power of tractors is dependent on earning stability, type of soil, type of operation and affordability by farmers.

Irrigation potential

As of now, about 65 per cent of the total irrigation potential has been achieved in India. Thus, there is still some way to go before making Indian agriculture free from the vagaries of the monsoon.

Monsoons

The monsoon has a dual impact on demand. While on the one hand, poor monsoons cause hardening of soil and weakening of farm animals and call for a greater need of tractors. On the other hand, a poor monsoon also leaves the farmer with low purchasing power. As such, the demand during monsoon failure would depend on state support in terms of subsidies, concessions, etc.

Availability of credit

Nearly 95 per cent of the purchases of tractors are through loans taken from banks and agricultural institutions. The loans given for tractors by banks are re-financed by NABARD under the head "farm mechanization," which includes power tillers, harvesters, engines, pumps, etc. besides tractors.

Income of farmers

The improvement in procurement prices of controlled agricultural products leads to increase in disposable income of farmers and in turn, their purchasing power. The farmer would then be in a position to increase his share of the initial investment in the tractor.

Implementation of scientific farming practices

Farm mechanization would not be feasible without a complete package of scientific farming that would include irrigation, use of high-yielding variety seeds, fertilizers and modern farming practices such as intensive cultivation and multi-cropping.

Purchase criteria

It is found that while only 10 per cent of rural households own tractors, almost 35 per cent use them, relying on rentals. Although the domestic tractor market is now facing stagnation, companies see good long-term prospects in the country, where tractor ownership is just 19 for every 1,000 farmers. The important things that a farmer looks for when purchasing a tractor are:

1. Horse power of the engine
2. Low cost of operation (low maintenance cost)
3. Reliability of product
4. Ease of operations
5. Price
6. After-sales service
7. Easy availability of spare parts
8. Resale value
9. Availability of finances

Product uses and categories

Tractors are mainly used to prepare land for sowing seeds and to transport the agricultural produce after harvest. They are also used as sources of power in operating other machines such as winnowers, threshers, chaff cutters, and power sprayers/dusters. The nature of the demand for tractors originates from the need to perform the operations of land preparation and transportation. The tractor sector is segmented into three types—small, in the range of 21–30 (HP), medium, in the range of 31–40 HP and large, in the 41–50 HP range.

Price

The present cost of tractors is anywhere between Rs 0.3 million and Rs 0.6 million. Despite the availability of high-technology products equipped with four-wheel drives, synchromesh gears and even air-conditioning, it is the good old price equation that still rules the roost in the Indian tractor markets. Offerings with a high price line "make a mockery of the requirements of Indian farmers whose purchasing power is less. The manufacturers should concentrate more on providing a greater value for money in their lower-end models, which are within the reach of Indian buyers," says a senior official of a tractor company. With tractors below 25 HP constituting 10 to 15 per cent of the total sales of 2,60,000 units (it was just 5 per cent two years back), experts feel there is huge scope in the small-tractors segment. M&M launched a tractor priced at only Rs 0.15 million.

Distribution

The channel of distribution is simple for tractors as shown in Figure 13.3. Three players in the channel are—company sales force, company agro-centres and dealers. The major concerns to be addressed in distribution are: (i) making tractors available, (ii) making credit facility available, (iii) assisting farmers in making choices and (iv) providing service and spare parts.

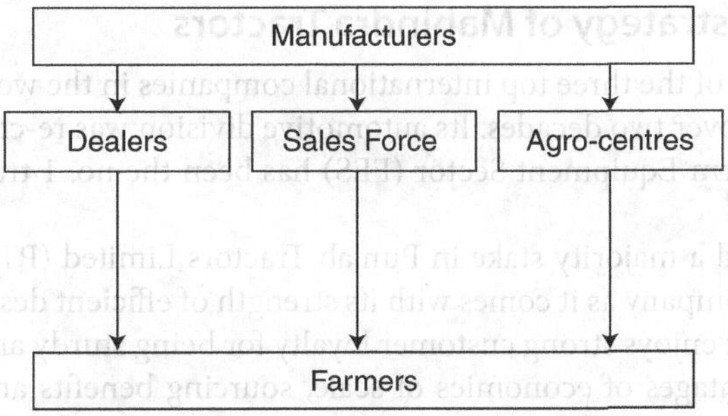

Figure 13.3 Channel of Distribution of Tractors

Product availability

There are more than 2,000 dealers in the country. The companies have dealer support programmes for (i) providing finances, (ii) training them to educate farmers and maintain relationships and (iii) managing their outlet efficiently. It has been observed from the market that single-brand dealership is the norm and more than two models are sold by dealers on an average to cater to the different requirements of farmers.

Credit availability

It has been observed that 90 per cent of tractor sales are through credit. Co-operative banks and banks for agricultural development play an important role in tractor sales by providing credit to farmers. Most of the time, banks will play the role of a sub-dealer (mediator), as the banks will buy the tractors from the dealers on behalf of farmers (loan applicant) so that the required documents can be kept in custody by the banks for their recovery of loans. The loan repayment periods vary from 5–10 years.

Information availability

A tractor is a heavy-investment, long-life product. As such, it falls under a complex buying category that requires high involvement and long time for decisions by the buyer. Hence, farmers will need more information and more time to make a decision for purchasing a tractor. They need assistance from the company sales personnel and dealers. Company sales personnel have a key role to play. They have to visit the farmers and carry out discussions using a problem-solving approach and suggest the purchase of a tractor when a genuine need can be established.

Promotion

Educating farmers about the use of tractors and a good service offering will build a good brand image in the minds of the farmers, which in turn will be spread through word of mouth to other farmers. As mentioned earlier, a tractor is a capital-intensive product. Hence, targeting opinion leaders is also a good strategy for tractor promotion.

Educative media that can be used for this include *kisan melas*, personal selling, exhibitions and *haats*. Mass media (radio, advertising in local newspapers and TV channels), wall paintings, hoardings posters and pamphlets are some of the informative media that can be used too.

Customer relationship management (CRM)

Since, tractor is a capital good that requires support from service centres of the dealer, it is necessary for tractor manufacturers and dealers to provide information and service support to farmers on a continuous basis.

Case 5—Marketing strategy of Mahindra Tractors

Mahindra Tractors is one of the three top international companies in the world. It has been the undisputed leader in India for over two decades. Its automotive division was re-christened the Farm Equipment Sector Division. Farm Equipment Sector (FES) has been the no. 1 tractor brand in India since 1983.

Mahindra had acquired a majority stake in Punjab Tractors Limited (PTL) in early 2007. PTL is a good strategic fit to the company as it comes with its strength of efficient design (strong R&D abilities) and the brand *Swaraj* that enjoys strong customer loyalty for being sturdy and reliable. Benefits of this acquisition include advantages of economies of scale, sourcing benefits and vendor rationalization. Post the Mahindra-PTL merger in February 2009, PTL is now a part of Mahindra FES. It is known as the *Swaraj* Division. The company has achieved a growth rate of 20 per cent.

Competitive strategy

M&M is also considering plans to further sharpen its competitive edge. The plans are based on the following assumptions.

- Demand for tractors is heterogeneous. Success in the tractor business would, to a large extent, be determined by the promptness with which manufacturers respond to the heterogeneous demand.
- In the longer run, fresh demand will be driven by states in the west and south and high-powered segments of the country, while Punjab and Haryana will witness more replacement demand. Demand is also expected to arise out of the increase in irrigated crop area that has stagnated of late.
- Customization alone meets crop-specific requirements and caters to the diverse farming belts.

Distributed manufacturing for customization

In a bid to promote customization of tractors, M&M is setting up a string of satellite units that would take up "distributed manufacturing" in line with local demand. Having built its first satellite factory at Rudrapur in Uttar Pradesh, the company is now setting up its second assembling unit near Jaipur.

The satellite units that would eventually cover the major farming belts are being set up with an investment of Rs 0.04–0.06 billion each. They would be able to roll out around 500 tractors a month. They would enable farmers to get factory-fresh tractors that would be customized in line with the local requirements.

With the satellite units, the target is to be present in at least 10 agricultural belts in the near future.

Product innovations

Its main tractor facility at Kandivli has been converted into a product development centre, while the product assembly is shared between the Nagpur factory and the satellite units. M&M is the biggest investor in product development in tractors. Over the years, it proposes to have different types of tractors to suit cultivation of all major crops. It launched "pudding special" for catering to paddy belts. The company is also planning to roll out tractors with specific application for other crops such as ground nut, potatoes and sugar cane. Mahindra hopes to revive its domestic sales, which declined by five per cent to 90,037 tractors in the last fiscal year (2007–2008), by attracting more farmers with a low-cost model.

Product

Brand Mahindra sells a range of tractors that include *Bhoomiputra*, *Shaan*, *Sarpanch* and *Arjun* Ultra-1, with each (except *Shaan*) having a range of variants based on the horse power (HP) and other attributes. Over the years, Mahindra brand of vehicles has come to represent high quality, ruggedness, durability, reliability, easy maintenance and operational economy. FES sells its 15 HP to 75 HP category tractors in the domestic market as explained in Table 13.4.

Table 13.4 Tractor Sizes of Mahindra

Category of tractor	Brands
Less than 30 HP	*Yuvraj*, 265 DI 1 *Sarpanch*, 265 DI *Bhoomiputra*
30 to 40 HP	*Arjun* 445 DI, 275 DI TU *Sarpanch*, 275 DI TU, *Bhoomiputra*, 475, DI *Sarpanch*, 475 DI *Bhoomiputra*
More than 40 HP	*Arjun* 555 DI, *Arjun* 605 DI, 575 DI *Sarpanch* , 575 DI *Bhoomiputra* , 585 DI *Sarpanch*
Farm Implements	Rigid tine cultivator, mounted offset disk harrow, spring loaded tiller, mounted disc plough, leveller

Price

The present cost of tractors can be anywhere between Rs 0.3 million and Rs 0.6 million. The cheapest variant that is likely to be launched in a year, targets small holding farmers who still use bullock carts to till the land. "Our idea is to provide low-cost farming solutions to farmers. The proposed model will be small but will do the primary function of tilling land," said Mr Ashok Sharma, senior vice-president, Farm Equipment Sector, Mahindra and Mahindra.

Distribution—reach and credit

FES also has the deepest distribution reach with more than 680 dealers along with the widest service network across India. The increased participation by Mahindra and Mahindra Financial Services Limited in retail financing of *Swaraj* tractors has also helped to mitigate the uncertainty of bank credit during this quarter.

Customer relationships management

FES has a large customer base of more than 2,100,000 customers (including *Swaraj*). The sector has time and again topped the customer satisfaction chart because it has not spared any occasion to celebrate with its customers.

Swatantra mahotsav: Celebrating the spirit of freedom, on the 60th anniversary of the country's independence, Mahindra and Mahindra Limited flagged off Mahindra *Swatantrata Mahotsav*—a week-long programme that presents the farmer with a host of benefits, such as zero per cent interest scheme on loans, exchange of old tractors, labour-free service and health check-up camps for farmers. The benefits were offered between 13th and 19th August, 2007 at Mahindra Tractor dealerships across the country. Mahindra and Mahindra Limited extended its unique "*Jai jawaan se jai kisaan*" rehabilitation scheme for the brave soldiers of the country. Under this scheme, Mahindra tractors were made available at attractive prices across Mahindra Tractor dealerships to soldiers of the Indian Armed Forces.

Samriddhi centre: Samriddhi centres were conceptualized to educate farmers about various technological inputs that would keep them abreast with world-class solutions for farming issues.

Mr Gautam Nagwekar, chief operating officer, Farm Equipment Sector, M&M, said, "Mahindra Tractors has always been looked upon as a customer-centric organization and always seeks to bring technological innovation for its customers. The *Samriddhi* centre is a milestone in our journey towards farm tech prosperity."

The *Samriddhi* centres will provide:

- Soil-and-water testing facilities to farmers
- Productivity demo farms

- Agri-counselling facilities
- One-stop finance shop
- Tractors and implement's sales and service

The soil testing facility will help farmers to analyse their land for its PH, EC (Electrical Conductivity—Ion Exchange), TDS (Total Dissolved Salt), OC (Organic Carbon), primary nutrient's (nitrogen, phosphorous and potassium) and secondary nutrient's status. Water is analysed for its PH, EC, TDS, carbonate, bicarbonate, chloride content. Based on the test results, crops suitable for the available soil and water, the quantum of nutrients to be applied for the prescribed crops with time and number of application are conveyed to the farmers.

The demo farms guide farmers at different stages of the crop (land preparation to post harvest) through method and result demonstrations to bridge the gap between the "actual" and "attainable" yield. Agri-counselling is be provided by experts/scientists from the best agricultural universities and research institutes across the globe. The finance counter provides vehicular as well as personal finance. At the same time it facilitates the sales of tractors and other agri-implements.[8]

EXTENSION SERVICES

Farmers are willing to invest more to receive higher incomes. One of their critical investment needs is getting agriculture services. So far, agri-services like helping farmers improve crop techniques and advice on ways to improve farm productivity has mostly been provided by the Government for free. However, the quality of service has been poor, rendering them less useful. In view of this, agri-input companies have set up their own farm service centres with Internet facility.

Initiatives by the government

The Agriculture Ministry decided to recruit the village youth to enhance the research extension-farmer-market model, suggested by the National Commission on Farmers (NCF). The weakening of the extension services in the public sector and negligible progress of private extension support, despite government efforts, has created a vacuum in the farm extension system. The Ministry is of the opinion that there is a need to increase investments in local research and make research institutions accountable. The increasing complexity of production and marketing requires information dissemination and training in the use of modern technologies for which qualified graduates would be recruited to tutor the rural unemployed.

ITC extension services

ITC Ltd has now taken up the concept of agricultural extension services called "*choupal pradarshan khet*." The new initiative will have agricultural scientists advising 7,500 farmers about good farm practices across Uttar Pradesh, Madhya Pradesh, Rajasthan and Maharashtra during the *kharif* season. Senior scientists from the National Research Centre for Soyabean (Indore) and University of Pantnagar, as well as post-graduates from agriculture universities will supervise farmers from pre-sowing until the harvest.

Mr S. Sivakumar, CEO, ITC-International Business Division, said that a participative-cluster model was being implemented where the registered farmer takes up the demonstration on one acre of his land holding and also bears the cost of all recommended nutrients and protective inputs. An average field that is representative of the village is chosen for showing the value of adequate agri-inputs and risk mitigation technique and 8–10 farmers are invited to participate in the training. Farmers would be charged Rs 150 for classroom training, product literature as well as around five visits from these agriculture experts during the crop cycle.

For an extra price, farmers can also buy foundation seed and weather insurance. Of the 7,500 registered farmers, around 4,000 have opted for weather insurance. This insurance would cover the crops against excess rainfall during the sowing, vegetative and reproductive phase of the crop at a premium of Rs 250.

Expertise is also being drawn in from various agri-input companies such as Khaitan Fertilisers and Chemicals Ltd, Bayer Crop Science, Pro Agro, CLASS India, Tata Agrico and Sygenta India. "The idea is that these progressive farmers could become agri-consultants in their village to create a ripple effect in the adoption of modern farming techniques to augment production," said Mr Sivakumar.[9]

Hariyali Kisan Bazaar (HKB) centre

The 302 outlet-strong *Hariyali* network of DCM Shriram Consolidated Ltd (DSCL) is currently catering to a million rural customers—80 per cent being farmers—across UP, Punjab, Haryana, Rajasthan, Madhya Pradesh, Maharashtra and Andhra Pradesh. They include 83 "centres" owned by the company and 219 leased-in "stores." Rebalancing the farmers' nutrient portfolio, use of new generation pesticides and new techniques like inter-cropping *matar* (pea) with sugarcane, are some of the learning points at a *Hariyali* centre.[10]

Summary

The marketing of agri-inputs has an important role to play on account of the dependence of the rural economy on agriculture. Agri-inputs can be classified as consumables (seeds, fertilizers, and pesticides) and capital goods (tractors and others). Hybrid seeds are in demand in the seeds market. There are different players with seed development capabilities. Seed development is encouraged by research organizations and regulated by the Government. Fake seeds are being sold causing losses to farmers.

Bio-fertilizers are gaining ground in the market. The determinants of fertilizer demand are rainfall and irrigation facilities, relative prices of fertilizers, cropping pattern and government policy. Fertilizers are categorized into straight fertilizers, compound fertilizers and specific fertilizers. Fertilizers are sold under company names. Credit and information are important for distribution reach.

Pesticides (agro-chemicals) can be classified into insecticides, fungicides, herbicides, rodenticides and fumigants. The usage pattern of pesticides employed for plant protection varies from region to region due to soil and climactic conditions. It also varies with season, type of crop and farming practices. The pesticides market is dominated by large players who make technical grades and formulations. In the marketing of pesticides, promotion plays a key role with the twin purposes of creating awareness and educating farmers on the use of pesticides.

A tractor is a capital goods item and as such, is a high-involvement product in terms of purchase. A quality product with service guarantees, the right price and good promotion form the key elements in the marketing mix of tractors. The tractor sector is segmented into three types—small, in the range of 21–30 HP, medium, in the range of 31–40 HP and large, in the 41–50 HP range. Now the trend is towards manufacturing and marketing of mini-tractors.

Extension services are promoted by the Government and corporate enterprises to educate farmers and assist them in purchases and farming applications. Examples of corporate centres are ITC e-*Choupal* and Mahindra *Krishi Vihar*.

Short Answer Questions

1. Prepare a classification of agri-inputs.
2. Explain seed development procedure.
3. Diagrammatically present the distribution model of seeds.
4. Describe, in brief, the structure of the fertilizer market.
5. How do you classify fertilizers?
6. Identify the demand determinants of fertilizers.

7. What are the three availability needs in the distribution of fertilizers?
8. Prepare a classification of pesticides.
9. Explain the factors that influence usage pattern of pesticides.
10. Identify the segments in the tractor market.
11. What are the demand determinants of tractors?
12. Explain the role of extension services offered by corporate enterprises.

Discussion Questions

1. Marketing of agri-inputs is solution oriented rather than product oriented. Discuss.
2. Farmers are exposed to a wide network of interaction–influence systems while purchasing agri-inputs. Discuss.
3. Can a firm sell all agri-inputs through the same channel?

Essay Questions

1. Describe the marketing strategies adopted by a seeds marketer.
2. Explain how fertilizers can be marketed citing examples from the Indian industry.
3. Discuss the marketing strategies of pesticide companies.
4. Examine the marketing strategies of any two tractor companies and develop a marketing model for tractors.

Internet Exercise

Visit Web sites of any four companies dealing with agri-inputs and prepare a report consolidating their approaches to the marketing of agri-inputs.

Mini Project

Visit farmers in a village and obtain information on the farming practices and the role of different agri-inputs. Identify the brands of agri-inputs that they are aware of and their preferences for various brands.

End Notes

1. National Academy of Agricultural Sciences, "Innovations in Rural Institutions: Driver for Agricultural Prosperity," December 2007, available at www.ncap.res.in/upload_files/others/oth_11.pdf.
2. "Indian Seed Industry under Transition," Global Agriculture Information Network Report, December 2003, available at www.fas.usda.gov/gainfiles/200312/146085513.pdf.

3. "Subsidy on Seeds Hiked to Rs 288 cr; Rainfall Deficit Down," 25 August 2009, available at www.zeenews.com/news558295.html.
4. www.pantnagarseeds.com/marketing.htm, accessed March 2010.
5. "A Good Year Again for BioAgri," July 2006, available at http://biospectrumindia.ciol.com/content/CoverStory/10607144.asp.
6. www.zuari.in; "ZIL in the Service of Farmers," available at http://www.faidelhi.org/IJF-April-06/ijf1_6.pdf.
7. "Rallis India," available at www.indiacatalog.com/profiles/chemicals/rallis_india_ltd.html.
8. www.mahindra.com; Manu P. Toms, "Mahindra Plans Ultra Low-cost Rural Tractor," *The Hindu Business Line*, 30 April 2008, available at www.blonnet.com/2008/04/30/stories/2008043051660200.htm.
9. Lalitha Srinivasan, "FMCG Majors' Battle on Rural Turf Intensifies," 12 June 2009, available at www.financialexpress.com/news/fmcg-majors.../475069/; Radhika Menon, "ITC Starts Farm Extension Services," *The Hindu Business Line*, August 2006, available at www.thehindubusinessline.com/bline/.../2006081502160300.htm.
10. Harish Damodaran, "DCM Shriram Hariyali Market Adopts Extension Route to Drive Sales," *The Hindu Business Line*, 3 July 2009, available at www.the-hindubusinessline.com/2009/07/03/stories/2009070351951800.htm.

Case 13.1 Small Is Beautiful

India's leading diesel engine manufacturing firm, Fieldmarshal, has forayed into the mini-tractor segment. Fieldmarshal launched three mini tractors of 9.5 HP, 12 HP and 15 HP with multi-utility applications for the farmers.

Need Analysis

"The mini tractor was the result of the feedback received from the end-users of our various products, mainly farmers," claimed Deepak Patel, marketing director of the company. The Central Mechanical Engineering Research Institute (CMERI) located at Durgapur in West Bengal had recommended in a survey that there was a need of tractors with lesser capacity.

Agriculture requires multiple applications like tilling land, pumping out water using the engine of a tractor, ploughing land, post-harvest transportation, explained S. S. Jogelaker, president of the company. The applications by themselves required only 12 HP to 15 HP each. Large tractors in India have a capacity of 25 HP to 75 HP, with most tractors being in the 25 HP to 35 HP range. It was then that the company decided to roll out three mini tractors of 9.5 HP, 12 HP and 15 HP, Jogelakar said.

Acceptability

As far as the quality of the product was concerned, Jogelekar said the mini tractor had cleared all testing conditions of the Central Farm Machinery Training and Testing Institute (CFMT&TI) under the Ministry of Agriculture of India located at Budhni near Bhopal in Madhya Pradesh. In terms of fuel efficiency, the mini tractor offered many advantages, he added.

Affordability

Big tractors generally cost Rs 0.3 to 0.4 million while a mini tractor costs Rs 0.15 million. A big tractor used 3.5 litres of fuel to accomplish a particular task for which a mini tractor consumes only 1 litre of fuel.

Distribution

The company has a very extensive marketing network comprising 2,200 distribution outlets along with 21 distributors in the country. Its core focus after that would be on establishing local assembly plants in the other states of the country to reach out to customers quickly in case of sales and after sales-service and spare replacements.

Promotion

Talking about the initial market response received for the mini tractor, Dipak Patel said, "Currently, we are hardly able to cater to the domestic requirement as far as the demand in Gujarat and the Saurashtra belt is concerned." Fieldmarshal's distributor in Jharkhand recently made a detailed presentation on its mini tractors to the state government, highlighting their multi-utility capability despite the marginally higher cost. The minister was satisfied with the product and the company was looking at a major order of at least 1,000 tractors from the state of Jharkhand itself, added Patel.

Recent Innovation

Bhanjibhai Mathukiya, a small innovator from Junagadh, has created a mini tractor of 10 HP, after being moved by the plight of the small groundnut and orchard farmers in Saurashtra. Mahesh Patel, chief innovator at the Grassroots Innovation Augmentation Network that has been incubating the small tractor, says that non-exclusive rights of the invention have already been taken up by an Anand-based company, with many others showing interest.

"Working with the students of the S. P. Jain Institute of Management and Research, Mumbai, we have priced the product at just above Rs 0.16 million, which is sure to be a hit with farmers who are otherwise helpless in a market flooded with high-power tractors suitable for use in a large land holding only," said Patel.

A Rider

Meanwhile, local companies have begun to price their low-powered tractors aggressively since they import components and engines from China and Taiwan. This has also led to bigger tractor companies rethinking their plans for the lower-end markets.

For discussion

1. What should Fieldmarshall do in the light of competition?
2. How should the Anand-based company market the new 10 HP motor?

Source: Archana Mohan, "Gujarat Innovator Creates Rs 1.6 lakh Tractor," *Business Standard*, 18 December 2007, available at www.business-standard.com/india/news/%3Ci%3Egujarat-innovator-creates-rs-16-lakh-tractor%3Ci%3E/307895/; Himanshu Bhayani, "Fieldmarshal Eyes Market for Mini Tractors," *Business Standard*, 24 August 2005, available at www.business-standard.com/india/news/fieldmarshal-eyes-market-for-mini-tractors/220714/.

Case 13.2 *Uttam Bandhan*

Zuari–Chambal was promoted by Zuari Industries Limited in 1985. It is the largest fertilizer complex in the Indian private sector.

People and Operations

Chambal relies on the strength it derives from its human resource. It has a pool of more than 1,000 professionals who have years of experience in their respective fields. The thread that binds Zuari–Chambal in harmony is its unique culture steeped in the tradition of integrity and ethical business practices. The two mega fertilizer plants have a total re-assessed capacity of 1.7292 million tonnes of urea per annum. Both Gadepan I and II represent a total investment of over Rs 25 billion (USD 500 million).

Marketing

Chambal Fertilizers caters to the northern, central and western regions of India and supplies its produce to 10 states. The company markets urea under the brand name "*Uttam Veer*." With ten regional offices, Chambal has a 1,300 strong dealer network and 20,000 village-level outlets to assist distribution.

Besides urea, fertilizers such as DAP, MOP, SSP and other agri-inputs as zinc sulphate, bio-fertilizers, pesticides and seeds are made available to the farmers under the "single-window" concept. These products are sourced from reputed suppliers and sold under the "*Uttam*" brand umbrella. Extensive promotion activities are undertaken to promote the "*Uttam*" brand by a team of dedicated field officers. The Agriculture Development Laboratories at Sriganganagar and Agra use sophisticated soil-and-water testing tools.

Uttam Bandhan

To establish a closer brand and to provide personalized services to farmers, Chambal has started the "Uttam Bandhan" programme, a community welfare initiative. Crop and product demonstrations, field demonstrations and farmer meets are conducted. Farmers are given ongoing training on specialized services that vary from crop diversification, animal health care, need for balanced inputs and use of bio-fertilizers. Soil-and-water sampling and testing are also conducted for free. To excite the new-age farmer, a Web site, www.uttamkrishi.com, provides information on the weather, suitable cropping techniques and markets. It is an endeavour to help improve farm productivity by providing online information on various agriculture practices. Farmers can access the Web site at the "*Uttam Krishi* Clinics" set up by the company and at agriculture universities, agriculture research stations and Krishi Vigyan Kendras. Chambal has set up "Hello *Uttam*" call centres where agriculture experts respond to farmer queries on the phone.

Chambal has engaged bright, unemployed youth from villages as "*Uttam Krishi Sewaks.*" They are trained in the latest agricultural techniques and provide specialized services to farmers. They are self-employed and earn from the commission on the sale of specialized products.

Environmental Protection and Safety

Chambal is deeply committed to environmental protection, pollution control and maintenance of ecological balance. Over 0.2 million trees and shrubs, a hundred species of birds, non-predatory animals and exotic fish are all found at Chambal's Gadepan complex covering an area of 1,060 acres. In fact, Chambal has been accredited with the prestigious ISO 14001 certification by M/s DNV (Netherlands) for its environmental policies and management. In recognition of its environmental practices, Chambal has received awards from the Fertilizer Association of India and World Environment Forum.

Social Contribution

Chambal's commitment to fulfil social responsibilities has been there even before production commenced. It has ongoing schemes for water harvesting, health care, rural infrastru cture, education and women's empowerment. Chambal has built a check dam across River Kalisindh, close to the Chambal plant. The dam stores six million cubic metres of water. Under the "rural healthcare programme," Chambal provides basic health care facilities in the villages neighbouring the facility. A mobile medical unit with a doctor and a trained nurse visits the villages daily providing free checkups and medication.

Chambal has helped to provide infrastructure required for drinking water to neighbouring villages. Chambal has also provided education aids for rural schools. It constantly tries to improve the quality of life and to provide opportunities for self-employment in rural areas.

For discussion

1. Examine the marketing strategy of Chambal Fertilisers. Is the strategy well designed in your view?
2. What are the missing links or desirable improvements in the strategy?

Source: "Zuari–Chambal—A profile," available at www.naukri.com/gpw/chambal/index.htm, accessed March 2010.

14

Marketing of Services

LEARNING OBJECTIVES

Upon completion of this chapter, you will be able to:

- Explore the marketing of savings and investment services
- Examine how financial institutions undertake the marketing of credit services
- Discuss the approaches to the marketing of insurance services
- Describe the marketing mix employed for the marketing of cellular services

In an interview with the *Business Line*, Ajai Puri, director and CEO, DTH, Bharti Airtel, narrated one of his experiences in a rural area: "I saw three boys in a small village just before Nadiad in Gujarat carrying a DTH box in a bag. I asked them if they had a TV. They said no, not yet, but had Rs 5,600 for a 21-inch television that they would get next week."

According to Puri, for five years the DTH industry has targeted cable as competition and, therefore, stayed focused on the top 300–500 towns and the 70 million-plus cable and satellite (C&S) homes. "We decided to be game-changers and target 230 million households and all those 150–160 million households that are not part of C&S because they don't have access to it. Because, I believe as mobile telephony made people buy handsets, DTH, when made available, will make people buy colour TVs."

Movie channels make a difference. Unless there is a Sony Max in rural Haryana, they don't want it. In Chandigarh, service providers will not be accepted unless they provide access to ETC, PTC and *Chardi Kalaa*—the three channels that showcase different *gurudwaras*. ETC showcases the Golden Temple, PTC the Bangla Sahib and *Chardi Kalaa* shows the Sis Ganj Sahib. "Rural sales in Maharashtra went up because we had IBN *Lokmat* that became the most popular channel during the recent elections," Puri maintained. He further says, "So, depending on your pin code, we can offer Kannada, Telugu or Tamil channels. It looks like simple business; however, it's a deep-rooted consumer insight, segmented business."

The farmer family with two mobiles and an additional income of Rs 3,000–4,000 is the target. Most farmers cultivate two big crops, each of which gives them some extra money with which they buy something for the family. Television is the only means of entertainment in rural areas. The mobile and TV are life enhancers, every other gadget is a convenience. Now, a locally-made,

14-inch television is available for Rs 3,500, which is equivalent to the price of two mobile phones. All rural mobile households have two mobiles, one for the farm and one for the home and, if they can afford two mobiles they can afford a TV next.[1]

Every other rural marketer is trying to emulate what Ajay Puri did for Airtel to improve their opportunities in rural areas. The case highlights three observations: (i) rural people grab opportunities to improve their quality of life; (ii) they save with a clear purpose and (iii) make purchases in a planned manner. Based on this preliminary understanding of the rural transformation in progress, this chapter examines the approaches of different companies offering different services to rural consumers.

INTRODUCTION

One of the key challenges to marketers is the delivery of an improved standard of living to the people. Improvement in the quality of life of rural people depends on the quality of products as well as services offered to them. On the one hand, services marketers are turning their attention to meet development obligations imposed on them by the Government and; on the other hand, they are trying to tap the emerging market potential in rural hinterlands. Among the services, financial services rank first as it is the engine for the growth of the rural economy. Closely associated with financial services are insurance services that provide financial security to rural people. The other important services are life enhancers—cellular services, TV channels and DTH.

MARKETING OF SAVINGS AND INVESTMENT SERVICES

The financial market in rural areas is expanding and offering a variety of financial products to meet the needs of savings and investment of rural people. Their credit needs are also being met. First, we will identify the major players in the market. Then, we will examine how savings and investment opportunities are provided and credit financing is offered.

Major players

The sources of finance can be categorized into two—unorganized and organized. The unorganized, informal sources comprise relatives, friends and money lenders. The organized, formal sources constitute commercial banks, non-banking financial institutions, co-operative credit societies and microfinance institutions.

NABARD

The National Bank for Agriculture and Rural Development (NABARD) was established as a development bank for providing and regulating credit and other facilities for the promotion and development of agriculture, small industries, cottage and village industries, handicrafts and other rural crafts and other allied economic activities in rural areas. Its aim is to promote integrated rural development and secure prosperity of rural areas.

Regional Rural Banks (RRBs)

RRBs were originally conceived as low-cost institutions with a rural flavour and their primary role was akin to that of commercial banks, as in raising deposits and lending onwards for a profit. Except that, these banks targeted rural and semi-urban areas for deposit mobilization and primarily, lent small loans to marginal farmers. Presently, 86 RRBs are operating in the country with 15,107 branches in 615 districts. A RBI report stated that 86 RRBs extended new loans to the extent of Rs 412.73 billion to 9.4 million borrowers as against Rs 384.64 billion during 2007–2008 to 9.3 million borrowers. Of this,

Table 14.1 Types of Refinancing Facilities Offered by NABARD

Agency	Credit facilities
Commercial banks	Long-term credit for investment purposes, financing the working capital requirements of Weavers' Co-operative Societies (WCS) and State Handloom/Handicraft Development Corporations
Short-term co-operative structure (state co-operative banks, district central co-operative banks, primary agricultural credit societies)	Short-term loans (crop and other loans), medium-term (conversion) loans, term loans for investment purposes, financing weavers' co-operatives, State Handloom Development Corporations for working capital by state co-operative banks
Long-term co-operative structure (state co-operative agriculture and rural development banks, primary co-operative agriculture and rural development banks)	Term loans for investment purposes
Regional rural banks (RRBs)	Short-term (crop and other loans) and term loans for investment purposes
Non-governmental organizations (NGOs)—Informal credit delivery system	Revolving fund assistance for micro-credit delivery innovations and promotional projects

Source: www.nabard.org, accessed March 2010.

the share of priority-sector loans issued was 82.6 per cent. In terms of the number of borrowers' covered, the share of the priority sector was about 84 per cent of the total loans issued during 2008–2009.[2]

Co-operative banks

The co-operative credit structure (CCS) of India was set up to serve the needs of both short-term and long-term rural credit in the country. Short-term credit is supplied in rural India by three institutions:

- State co-operative banks (SCB)
- District central co-operative banks (DCCB)
- Primary agricultural credit societies (PACS)

Long-term credit is supplied by the primary co-operative agriculture and rural development banks (PCARDB). The state co-operative banks, now 29 in number, finance, co-ordinate and control the workings of the central co-operative banks in each state. There are now 367 central co-operative banks and over 92,000 primary agricultural credit societies in the country with a membership of over 100 million.

Commercial banks

While there are around 600,000 villages in the country, there are only about 45,000 rural branches of public-sector banks and regional rural banks. The result is a huge demand–supply gap. Around 60 per cent of India's rural population does not have access to banking services.[3]

Under the Government's policy, all domestic banks (including private banks) and foreign banks are, required to provide 40 per cent and 32 per cent of their net banking credit to the priority sector, respectively.

Two innovations, namely micro-finance and *Kisan* Credit Card (KCC) Scheme, have emerged as the major policy tools to address the problems associated with the distributional aspects of rural credit.

SAVINGS AND INVESTMENT

An important activity in the finance sector is the mobilization of savings in the form of deposits and channelling the funds for investment.

Savings and investment behaviour

A survey conducted by Max-NCAER revealed that around 81.4 per cent of households at the all India level save some part of their earnings—the figure is 88 per cent for urban India and 78.5 per cent for rural India.[4]

Reason

The predominant reasons for savings in a majority of households are emergencies (81.2 per cent) and education for children (79 per cent). Other reasons for savings are ensuring security for old age (66.7 per cent), saving for social ceremonies (63.9 per cent), saving for buying or building a house (44.8 per cent), for improving or expanding business (43.5 per cent), for buying large consumer goods (19.8 per cent) and gifts(17.5 per cent).

Preferred mode of saving

Almost 42 per cent of households keep their savings at home and about 45 per cent of the households opt for bank deposits. The other modes of savings are deposits in co-operative societies (3 per cent), in post offices (5.4 per cent), in insurance (1.8 per cent) and in others like chit funds (2.7 per cent).

Owning an account in a financial institution

About 59.2 per cent of households in rural India hold accounts in a financial institution.

Indebtedness

A fourth of rural households (25.2 per cent) have outstanding loans. Incidence of indebtedness is low in case of regular earning households. It is high (27.5 per cent of households) in case of those who are self-employed in agriculture.

Stability of household income

About 50 per cent of rural households expressed confidence in the stability of their incomes. This shows that half of rural Indian households live in uncertainty about their incomes.

Investments

The investment patterns are as given in Table 14.2. It is observed that the propensity to invest is higher among the regular income-earning households.

Table 14.2 Investment by Households—Occupation-wise (Percentage of Households)

Investment type	Salary/ Wages	Self-employed in non-agriculture	Labour	Self-employed in agriculture	Others
Stock market	43.6	34.6	8.9	10.7	2.3
Small savings	48.7	18.7	7.6	21.4	3.6
Life insurance	39.9	25.8	9.1	21.5	3.7

Savings and investment opportunities

Financial institutions and India Post have opened up opportunities for rural people to save and invest their surplus amounts.

Bank deposits

All the commercial banks offer savings accounts and fixed deposit schemes. They are promoted through advertisements in the print media and leaflets. By a notification issued in January 2006 the Reserve Bank of India (RBI) allowed banks to appoint "business correspondents" to offer savings accounts on behalf of banks in remote rural locations. The business-correspondent model offers an alternative structure to branch-based banking to ensure outreach of formal-sector financial services to every citizen in the country.[5]

Postal saving schemes

India has a very organized and well-maintained postal network with post offices even in small villages. The Postal Department offers many financial services termed as postal saving schemes. The saving schemes include National Saving Certificates, Post Office Savings Account, Public Provident Fund, *Kisan Vikas Patra*, Postal Life Insurance and Senior Citizen Savings Scheme. These saving schemes tend to compete with the bank deposits as they offer tax benefits under Section 80 C of the Income Tax Act.

Mutual funds

In India, mutual funds are financial instruments. These funds are collective investments that gather money from different investors to invest in stocks, short-term money markets, financial instruments, bonds and other securities and distribute the proceeds as dividends. The mutual funds in India are handled by fund managers, also referred as portfolio managers. The RBI has permitted commercial banks and RRBs to offer mutual funds.

Marketing strategies of banks

Commercial banks and post offices have to recognize the need for an innovative marketing mix and design new products and take advantage of IT solutions.

Offer innovative and affordable products

Bank of India (BoI) has started mobile banking service in rural areas.[6] The service will be useful in villages that do not have banks. Villagers would be given a special type of SIM card. The customers can conduct their banking transactions through the mobile phone and would also get to know the balance in their account.

The State Bank of India (SBI) has started a zero-balance bank account programme for villagers. Called the SBI Tiny account, there are no physical branches or officials, just a paid volunteer who is equipped with a small box and a cell phone. The box enables biometric measurements (fingerprints), at the time of opening the account to confirm the account holder's identity. The cell phone enables communication with the zonal office to check on available balance. Payments under programmes such as the NREGS and pensions are made directly to these accounts. The advantage for the villagers is that they can withdraw money from their accounts at any time of the day or night (withdrawals are never for more than a few dollars). SBI hopes to cover 100,000 villages by 2012. The bank has also tied up with India Post for some services.[7]

ICICI Prudential Liquid Plan, a money market mutual fund (MMMF) product offers easy liquidity and low entry requirements. It invests solely in money market instruments that are forms of debt that mature in less than one year and are very liquid. Treasury bills make up the bulk of the money market instruments. An advantage, compared to bank savings accounts, is that MMMFs earn compound interest; the interest earned is reinvested in the principal, thus earning more interest. In fact, MMMFs

Box 14.1 Efficient Banking Services are Elusive

According to a study conducted by the National Council of Applied Economic Research (NCAER), only over 15 per cent depositors and 21 per cent borrowers found quality brochures/pamphlets in local languages in Orissa as against 54.1 per cent customers at the national level. In this regard, private-sector banks fared the worst with a low percentage 10 and 30, respectively. The time interval for disbursing loans stood at only 13 days nationally; it is 23 days in Orissa. Nationally, private banks take only 13 days to sanction and disburse a loan but in Orissa they take 25 days. Similarly, when 71 per cent received banker's assistance on investment decisions nationally, in Orissa only 49 per cent availed of the service. In Orissa, of the borrowers surveyed, 33 per cent took loans for agro purposes followed by 25 per cent for commercial activities and 1 per cent for housing/construction activities, respectively.

Source: RBI sponsored study conducted by NCAER in Orissa, available at www.ncaer.org/downloads/MediaClips/Press/effservelude.pdf.

have been offering returns that are not only higher than returns on bank savings accounts, but even bank fixed deposits.[8]

Improve service quality

In rural areas, service is more important as the customers are less educated. The need to bridge the service gap is highlighted by the NCAER study given in Box 14.1.

Organize promotion

Investor education in mutual funds is the key to take the message of this investment avenue forward in these markets.

"Business correspondents" have to be appointed to offer savings accounts on behalf of banks in remote rural locations.

Advertisements in TVs, FM radios, print media, transit media and hoardings are used to promote savings and investment products.

Engage in CSR activities

Community service programmes have to be undertaken for the benefit of the rural people. For instance, Canara Bank has schemes such as rural clinic services, rural service volunteers, *jala yoga* (provide safe drinking water to SC/ST/Backward communities), *Hari Kalayana Yojana* (literacy classes, health care, cleanliness campaign, tree planting, sanitation, drainage and other extension programmes) and a retail mobile marketing van for sale of household products, articles made by women entrepreneurs and artisans.[9]

Marketing mix of banking services

The marketing mix of banking services is given in Table 14.3.

MARKETING OF CREDIT SERVICES

Though debt is not part of the culture of rural India, the need for taking loans for farming purposes such as the purchase of agri-inputs or tractors is quite common.

Credit needs

The credit needs of rural people are two-fold:

Table 14.3 Marketing Mix of Financial (Savings and Investment) Services

Mix components	Decisions
Product	Combo products linking deposits with loans and insurance, emphasis on service quality
Price	Small savings with periodical (also weekly) payment facility
Place	Branches, business correspondents, agents in case of postal savings, tie-ups with *Kisan kendras*, companies and NGOs
Promotion	TVs, FM radios, the print media, transit media, hoardings, van campaigns, word of mouth, leaflets, CRM
Community service	Social responsibility programmes

Occupational needs

Those engaged in agriculture, animal husbandry, poultry and cottage industry require funds to carry out their production activities. They also require finances for purchase of automobiles (tractors, LCVs and two-wheelers). The requirements can be categorized into two: capital for long term investment and working capital for day-to-day operations of their enterprise.

Household needs

Credit is necessary when incomes and savings are not adequate to meet routine and non-routine household expenditure of the family. Borrowing for education of children, marriage of daughter or for performing social ceremonies is quite common in rural areas.

Credit repayment behaviour

Rural folk are more community oriented and spend a lot of time interacting with one another. This makes for a better collections environment, as the chances of default are lower when your reputation in the society are tied in, as opposed to the anonymous facelessness of the urban borrower who skips on payments by moving house and changing his phone numbers. Dhruv Talwar of Mahindra Financial says, "The company gets 75 per cent of its payments in cash and has a less than one per cent rate of bad debts." Box 14.2 gives the ingredients of a successful recipe.

Credit instruments and intermediaries

To meet the credit needs of the rural people, especially the poor, in addition to the short-term and long-term loans of banks, micro-finance and *Kisan* credit cards have been evolved.

Micro-finance

Micro-credit/finance is defined as provision of thrift, credit and other financial services and products of very small amounts to the poor in rural, semi-urban and urban areas to enable them to raise their income levels and improve living standards. The loans and credit extended are typically small ("micro"). They are provided in varying contexts, either to individuals or groups, ranging from personal micro-credit to small enterprise support and rural finance. The institutions that provide micro-finance and credit services are diverse, including non-governmental organizations (NGOs), credit unions, non-bank financial intermediaries and commercial banks.

There are more than 200 MFIs in the country, of which the top 20 account for 80 per cent of the total MFI portfolio. The Indian micro-finance sector is expected to grow nearly 10 times by 2011 to a size

Box 14.2 Credit-collection Formula

The factors responsible for lower loan delinquency levels at Mahindra Financial are as follows:

- **Responsibility of one person:** The person evaluating and approving the financing of an asset is the same person who collects payments on that loan.
- **Customized credit:** Mahindra Financial allows the equated monthly instalments (EMIs) to be varied based on the customer's cash flow, making it possible for a farmer to make three lump sum payments in a year as opposed to monthly payments that are suited more to an urban salary earner.
- **Convenience in collection:** Collection of repayments was offered at the doorstep, in cash and even in coins.
- **Continuous monitoring:** The chance of spotting a possible delinquency at daily intervals as opposed to monthly ones ensured that the system works.
- **Opinion makers help:** In rural markets, there are a few key people who act as the opinion makers, such as teachers, doctors and medical practitioners, *Sarpanch/Panchayat* members, the *Patwari*, and the local bank manager. Their help is sought by appealing to their prestige and esteem and seeking their opinions. Financial incentives only work sometimes in these cases.

Source: Dhruv Talwar, "Go Rural, Don't Wait for Your Customer to Urbanise," 10 May 2008, available at www.domainb.com.

of about Rs 250 billion from the current market size of Rs 27 billion, at a compounded annual growth rate of 76 per cent.[10]

The small credit needs of borrowers in India have not been met successfully. The fact that 60 per cent of the population in India do not have a bank account provides ample evidence for it. Micro-finance institutions play a key role here by meeting the credit needs of this section of the population. At the end of March 2009, micro-finance constituted 1.29 per cent of the gross credit of scheduled commercial banks, an increase of only 0.27 per cent over the previous year. Micro-finance institutions added 8.5 million customers and Rs 57.80 billion to outstanding loans in 2008–2009.[11]

Non-governmental organizations (NGOs) have a crucial role as intermediaries between banks/MFIs and rural customers. Consider the case of Society for Resource Integration and Development Action (SRIDA) that illustrates the development role of an NGO (see Box 14.3).

NGOs can also help people obtain purchase loans. For instance, ACCESS Micro-finance Alliance (AmFA), the largest network of fledgling MFIs in India, provided finance to buy water purifiers. ACCESS took up the task of supplying clean drinking water to poor households once it had identified the seriousness of the drinking-water problem. It has joined hands with Hindustan Unilever Ltd (HUL) to encourage the purchase of water purifiers. It has organized programmes on safe drinking water to build awareness in order to stimulate demand. Financial support has also been provided through micro-finance institutions. Improvements were noticed in the health of clients with the increased use of water purifiers. This led to a reduction in absenteeism from work and school.[12]

Kisan credit card

The *Kisan* credit card scheme (KCC) aims at providing adequate and timely support from the banking system to the farmers for their short-term credit needs for crop cultivation. This mainly helps farmers purchases inputs, etc. during the cropping season.

Box 14.3 SRIDA—In Service of People

SRIDA is involved in micro finance activities through SHG formation and its bank linkages with financial support from NABARD, as well as the *Zila Panchayat*, Jabalpur. Besides SHGs formation and linkages programme, SRIDA also has its micro-finance promotional initiatives "*SAMPARK*"—a community-level savings and credit programme that has reached out to more than 1,500 members among the marginalized and needy community in Jabalpur, Mandla, Dindori and Seoni districts.

The organization has more than 250 functional SHGs of which more than 150 SHGs have bank linkages with SBI, Bank of Maharashtra, UCO Bank, Central Bank of India, Allahabad Bank and district co-operative banks. Through its team efforts, the organization has made more than 200 women SHGs from disadvantaged communities in Mandla and Jabalpur district. Besides these, SRIDA has got the opportunity to initiate and play the lead role for the promotions of micro-finance activities in the Mahakaushal region through the Mahakaushal micro-finance forum supported by SIDBI.

Source: www.ngosinfo.com, accessed April 2010.

Co-operative, regional, rural and commercial banks have issued about 0.085 billion *kisan* credit cards across India and sanctioned credit of about Rs 3,700 billion to them as on 31 March 2009 according to the Reserve Bank of India's "Report on Trend and Progress of Banking in India 2008–2009." Banks have issued about 0.015 billion KCC and sanctioned about Rs 501.50 billion to farmers. Uttar Pradesh, Maharashtra, Gujarat, Andhra Pradesh, Madhya Pradesh and Karnataka are some of the leading states in terms of amount sanctioned to farmers.[13]

Credit needs and bank strategies

Traditionally, short-term loans ranging from Rs 50,000 to Rs 0.1 million have worked in rural areas. However, with renewed interest in agriculture, banks foresee tremendous opportunities for rural credit. Agriculture, today, covers not only food crops but also commercial crops (cash crops), horticulture, spices, medicinal plants and floriculture. Allied industries such as poultry, fisheries and animal breeding come under agriculture. While small farmers make borrowings in the range of Rs 10,000 to about Rs 0.3 million, farmer groups can avail credit up to Rs 2.5 million. The size of the loan amount determines the rate of interest and it varies between 7 and 13.5 per cent.

Most farmers avail of small loans to set up small-scale industries targeting exports or inter-state trade. Poultry and allied areas constitute about 25 per cent of agricultural lending and have grown in scale. People who used to own a backyard pen, today invest in 0.1 million chickens. Bankers say these businesses are growing due to genuine demand and are confident of loan repayment.

Term loans for crops are also popular. These take into account a crop's entire lifecycle and provide for working capital, harvest capital and some cash even during off-season periods to help the farmer continue with his livelihood.

The Indian Overseas Bank has designed area-specific loans. For example, the West and East Godavari regions have been classified as inland fisheries, Guntur as poultry, Mercara and regions near Coorg as coffee plantations. Their loans are customized to help such businesses thrive. The bank has a tie-up with CAMPCO to fund areca nut production in the South Canara region.

Many banks have tie-ups with companies such as TAFE, Eicher and EID Parry to finance loans for farm implements and sugarcane production. Besides self-help groups, banks are also looking at tie-ups with organized financiers (non-banking financial institutions) to market their loan products.[14]

Indian Bank is utilizing several approaches to provide credit facilities to rural customers:

Account-linked credit

Indian Bank has brought 81 villages across the country within its fold by providing 100 per cent banking services through the implementation of the financial inclusion (FI) project. The bank has offered a no-frills account (that does not require the maintenance of a minimum balance) and as a product under the FI project, offered customers credit without security.[15] Box 14.4 presents the successful exercise of financial inclusion in a village.

Credit through SHGs

Indian Bank has so far credit linked more than 0.23 million SHGs to the tune of Rs 15.4548 billion as per reports in 2008.[16]

Tie-ups with NGOs and companies

Commercial banks have tied up with NGOs and companies to provide credit to rural people and SHGs. Box 14.5 describes a project initiated by ICICI Bank.

Box 14.4 Financial Inclusion Project

Vagarayampalayam hamlet in Palladam *taluk* of Coimbatore district is connected by an all-weather road. It has a primary health centre, veterinary centre, primary and high schools and an *anganwadi*. The missing link probably was a bank's presence to create the habit of thrift among the economically weaker sections. Indian Bank decided to tap the potential. The villagers said they were disinclined and nervous to approach a commercial bank. Getting a loan from a bank was, according to the villagers, "not easy and a time-consuming process." Instead, they preferred the moneylender, who came to their immediate rescue—"no questions asked," they added. The existence of a co-operative society in its vicinity, villagers say, was not of much help.

Creating awareness: The bank officials have, over the last two years, persistently attempted at creating awareness about the bank's services by organizing sensitization camps and finally managed to bring the entire village within its fold.

Credit offer: Out of a populace of 3,178, comprising mostly of agricultural labourers, the bank identified 2,416 persons eligible under the FI project.

"We not only helped them open accounts with us but, have extended savings bank overdraft facility to five (identified) needy customers such as a barber, a newspaper agent, a photo frame shopkeeper, a petty shop owner and a lady engaged in power loom operations. We have sanctioned 17 general credit cards and 12 *Kisan* credit cards. We have enabled one of the SHGs to tie up with HUL for marketing HUL products," Mr Ramakrishnan, the Vagarayampalayam Branch Manager, said.

Outcome: Indian Bank has managed to rescue 1,000-odd households from the clutches of pawnbrokers and private money lenders. The villagers appear a relieved lot as they are now able to access funds at cheaper rates.

Source: L. N. Revathy, "IOB Initiative Frees Villagers from Money Lenders," *The Hindu Business Line*, 23 May 2006, available at www.thehindubusinessline.com/2006/05/23/stories/2006052302222100.htm.

Box 14.5 No White Space

The ICICI Bank rolled out a new initiative "no white space" to increase rural credit offtake. Rural credit would be approximately 20–25 per cent of its total portfolio within the next three years. The rural project envisages having a kiosk or a franchisee every 10 km in the rural heartland. "We would have our presence spread all over India but, it would not be through opening of rural branches. Instead, we can reach the farmers with the support of corporate houses and self-help groups. Information technology would play a key role too," said Mr Kamath, then managing director and CEO of ICICI Bank.

ICICI Bank proposed to create partnerships with 200 micro-credit institutions by 2008–2009. Regarding the partnership with the corporate houses, Kamath said that the bank was looking at companies (dealing with fertilizers, seeds or providing other inputs to the farm sector) that have a relationship with farmers.

Source: "ICICI Bank Sees Big Scope in Rural Credit," *The Hindu Business Line*, 12 August 2005, available at www.thehindubusinessline.com/2005/08/12/stories/2005081202720600.htm; Gargi Banerjee, "Rural Banking with ICICI Bank," *Economic Strategy, Businessworld*, September 2006.

Table 14.4 Marketing Mix of Credit Services by Banks

Mix components	Decisions
Product	Loans—short-term and long-term loans, small to large amounts, combo products—savings account tied loan
Price	Priority lending rates determined by RBI and reasonable interest rates in other cases
Place	Branches, tie-ups with micro-finance institutions, companies and NGOs
Promotion	Sensitization programmes—meetings with opinion leaders, NGO channels, SHG channels
Community service	Social responsibility programmes

Marketing mix of credit services by banks

The marketing mix of banking services is given in Table 14.4.

MARKETING OF INSURANCE SERVICES

The insurance sector in India is one of the booming sectors of the economy and is growing at the rate of 15–20 per cent per annum. Together with banking services, it contributes about 7 per cent to the country's GDP. The insurance sector in India was liberalized in March 2000 with the passage of the Insurance Regulatory and Development Authority (IRDA) Bill, lifting all entry restrictions for private players and allowing foreign players to enter the market with some limits on direct foreign ownership. Presently, there are 16 life insurance companies and 15 non-life insurance companies in the market.

Size and growth

According to a May 2008 ASSOCHAM report titled, "Insurance in Next Two Years," the size of the insurance sector was estimated at USD 12.8 billion and it is likely to see a never-before growth of 200 per cent, reaching USD 51.2 billion by 2009–2010. Rural India is an opportunity worth USD 23 billion for the insurance companies if they provide the right product mix. According to the international consultancy firm, Celent, the rural life insurance market will grow to a potential of USD 1.9 billion by 2015 from the current USD 487 million. Out of the 78 per cent households with awareness about life insurance in rural India, only 24 per cent were policy owners. India's untapped rural market holds tremendous growth opportunities for life insurance companies with business worth USD 231.67 million for insurance firms. Only 8–10 per cent of the rural households are covered by life insurance. Therefore, the insurance sector has tremendous potential in the coming years.

Types of insurance

The various fields covered by insurance companies in India include:

- *Life Insurance:* For students, children, family, individual, etc.
- *Health insurance:* For self, for family, accidental insurance premium, medical claim policies, etc.
- *Non-life insurance:* Home or house insurance and other property insurance, auto insurance (for cars, motorcycle and other two-wheelers, commercial vehicles), infrastructure-projects insurance, travel insurance, real estate insurance, mobile insurance, etc.

Apart from the insurances mentioned above, there is a growing trend for reassurance—insurance for the insurer. Reassurance helps primary insurers take risks that are beyond their capacity but, without jeopardizing their financial stability when mass settlement cases arise. Such cases occur at the time of natural calamities. The major player, the General Insurance Company (GIC), has taken up the role of national insurer. GIC is paid 20 per cent of the re-insurance business of all insurance companies.[17]

Insurance companies employ insurance agents and brokers to sell their insurance policies and products. A work license from the insurance regulation department is a must to sell any insurance plan. The insurance premiums offered vary from company to company and also from policy to policy. The premium asked for depends on the risk factors involved as in the case of the lives of Indians under the British rule that were riskier and demanded higher premiums.

Major players

The major players in the insurance sector are:

- LIC (Life Insurance Corporation of India) still remains the largest life insurance company accounting for 64 per cent market share.
- ICICI Prudential Life Insurance Co. Ltd is the biggest private life insurance company in India. It experienced a growth of 58 per cent in new business premium.
- Bajaj Allianz Life Insurance Co. Ltd ranked second (after LIC) in the number of policies sold in 2007–2008.
- SBI Life Insurance Co. Ltd ranked 6th in 2007–2008 in terms of the number of new policies sold.
- Reliance Life Insurance Co. Ltd ranks 5th in new business premium and 4th in the number of new policies sold in 2007–2008.
- HDFC Standard Life Insurance Co. Ltd ranks 6th among insurance companies and 5th among private players.

- Birla Sun Life Insurance Co. Ltd moved to the 7th position in 2007–2008.
- Max New York Life Insurance Co. Ltd was pushed down to the 8th position from the 7th in 2007–2008.
- Kotak Mahindra Old Mutual Life Insurance Ltd reported a growth of 80 per cent, moving from the 11th to the 9th position in 2007–2008.

Marketing strategies

The Government is keen on promoting insurance in rural areas. As a result, RBI has imposed certain restrictions and announced liberal measures.

Focus on rural sector

IRDA issued certain obligations to insurers that they need to fulfil to safeguard the interests of the rural and social sector. Accordingly, 5 per cent, 7 per cent, 10 per cent, 12 per cent and 15 per cent of insurers in that order, during the first five financial years, should be from the two sectors. An analysis of data from seven life insurers for 2007–2008, accounting for at least 80 per cent of the market, reveals that all of them topped their individual targets laid down by IRDA.

ICICI Prudential Life, for instance, covered 117,000 customers in rural areas in 2007–2008, as against its target of 25,000. "All our regular product offerings are made available to the customers in the rural segment. The company also offers a small ticket-size policy called "*Suraksha*," a micro-insurance policy, to suit the needs of the rural customers," said Rishi Srivastava, senior vice-president and head, rural business, ICICI Prudential Life. In the case of SBI Life, the firm was expected to sell 18 per cent of all its policies in the rural areas. It ended up selling 22 per cent.

According to the India Invest Incomes and Savings Survey 2007 by IIMS Dataworks, a Noida-based retail finance research firm, 58 per cent of India's 105.4 million insured population (out of a total of 321 million people who constitute the country's paid workforce) are from the rural areas. However, in terms of penetration, or the number of policyholders compared with the total population, urban India is ahead. Thus, penetration in urban India is 47 per cent (which means that almost one out of every two paid workers in urban India is insured), while it is only 27 per cent in rural areas.

Combo products

Instead of offering single protection for life or non-life aspects, insurance companies are now coming up with combo products. However, the problem being faced by the companies is the existing norm by IRDA that allows a life insurer to have tie-ups with only one non-life insurance company as far as sales of products is concerned. Soon the rule may be changed to allow insurance companies to have more riders. In fact, combo products offer many advantages. First, cost to the customer will come down, income of the channel will go up, the commission value as charged by the agent as a percentage of the premium will also go up and above all, the cost of the channel will come down. If the product is designed with similar tenure, multiple risks can be covered and cost of office can also be shared between the life and the non-life insurance companies.

Grassroots level distribution

Rural and social sector policies are sold through a multi-channel approach, including hiring agents from villagers and tie-ups with banks, non-governmental organizations and micro-finance institutions. RBI has allowed entities such as individual *kirana*/medical/fair-price shop owners, PCO operators, agents of government-sponsored small savings schemes, insurance agents, petrol pump owners and retired teachers to act as "business correspondents" (BCs) of banks. A notification by the RBI said that allowing banks to appoint BCs (agents in common parlance) was part of its financial inclusion initiative.

Touching promotions

Promotion of life insurance requires creative approaches. The need to protect against a possible loss cannot be put across in straight-forward communication. Advertisements in TVs, FM radios, print media, transit media and hoardings are used to promote the insurance concept and products. However, concept selling is a difficult exercise. ICICI bank's innovative "*Kamdhenu* Cattle Loan Campaign" won an award at the WOW Event and Experiential Marketing Awards, 2009 as it could touch rural hearts. Box 14.6 provides more details about the campaign.

Life Insurance Corporation (LIC)

The Life Insurance Corporation (LIC) of India, founded in 1956, is the largest life insurance company in India owned solely by the Government of India. LIC presently has seven zonal offices and 100 divisional offices situated across the country. In addition to an even distribution of 2,048 branches located in different towns and cities of India, LIC also has a network of around one million agents who solicit life insurance policies to the public.

Innovative, affordable combo product

LIC pioneered the introduction of combo products. "*Jeevan Madhur*" is an endowment assurance plan, available to both males and females without any medical examination covering individuals in the age group of 18–60 years. The sizes of the premium and payment periods are designed to suit the rural people. The minimum premium is Rs 25 per week, Rs 50 per fortnight and Rs 100 per month, which is expected to be well within the reach of the targeted group.

Tie-up for distribution

LIC has associated with COMAT Technologies (P) Ltd (COMAT), by appointing them as its "corporate partner" to offer a wide array of insurance services in the rural market through its 1,250 rural business centres. Traditionally, individual agents were appointed to create awareness about LIC's services

Box 14.6 *Kamdhenu* Cattle Campaign

The *Kamdhenu* cattle loan campaign is a joint campaign by ICICI Bank's Rural and Microbanking and Agri-Business Group (RMAG) and ICICI Lombard General Insurance.

This campaign was launched with the aim of generating awareness about loans for cattle purchase and cattle insurance in rural areas. The campaign won the award for best rural marketing programme of the year at the WOW Event and Experiential Marketing Award 2009. Mr Roopesh Kajrolkar, head, marketing, RMAG, who received the award on behalf of ICICI Bank said, "These WOW awards given to us are a recognition of our innovative efforts to reach out to rural markets. Our campaigns have touched the hearts and minds of thousands of customers, which is also evident from our business results. The campaigns have also helped us in positioning ICICI Bank as a 'potential fulfiller' for the rural customers."

According to Mr Pranav Prasad, head, rural and agriculture business group, ICICI Lombard General Insurance, "The *Kamdhenu* initiative was aimed at creating awareness among rural consumers about protecting their assets and hedging their economic loss in the event of injury to the cattle due to illness or other perils." The *Kamdhenu* campaign also received the prestigious Rural Marketing Association of India (RMAI) Award in December 2008.

Source: "Kamdhenu—An Integrated Campaign for Cattle Loan," ICICI Bank Press Release, 12 March 2009, available at www.icicibank.com/aboutus/pdf/wow_awards.pdf.

in the rural market. In an effort to provide more services in the rural market, LIC choose COMAT's rural business centres that are equipped with professionals and trained employees to reach out to rural citizens in a more efficient and effective manner. The objective of the collaboration is to make information about products and services easily available, improve accessibility for trouble-free premium payments and enable smooth settlement of claims in the rural sector.

SBI Life Insurance

It is a joint venture between the State Bank of India and Cardif, a BNP Paribas company. The State Bank of India enjoys the largest banking franchise in India. Along with its 7 associate banks, the State Bank Group has the unrivalled strength of over 14,500 branches across the country.

Innovative product

"*Grameen Shakti Shakti*" is a dual-benefit life insurance product to safeguard the group member who provides protection with maturity benefits at affordable rates. It offers "protection" to the "family" of the group member and it offers survival benefit to the "group member." The premium can be paid yearly throughout the entire term of the policy.

Distribution

SBI Life extensively leverages the SBI Group as a platform for cross-selling insurance products along with its numerous banking product packages such as housing loans and personal loans. SBI's access to over 100 million accounts across the country provides a vibrant base for insurance penetration across every region and economic strata in the country ensuring true financial inclusion. Agency channel, comprising the most productive force of more than 25,000 insurance advisors, offers door-to-door insurance solutions to customers.

Tie-up for distribution

SBI Life Insurance has tied up with Coromandel International Ltd to offer insurance in rural areas in Andhra Pradesh. According to the tie-up, Coromandel would sell SBI Life Insurance products to its rural customers through its "*Mana Gromor*" brand of rural retail outlets. The small ticket Unit Linked Products (ULIPs) and traditional plans of SBI Life would be sold by 427 outlets. Each centre would cover 30–40 villages having 5,000 farm families in the radius of 20 km. A dedicated senior insurance professional would be positioned in *Mana Gromor* to provide need-based insurance solutions to the rural farmer community. In addition, in the second phase, another six dedicated insurance managers will be counselling farmers, one each for each of the six zones.

Marketing mix of insurance services

The marketing mix of insurance services is provided in Table 14.5.

Table 14.5 Marketing Mix of Insurance Services

Mix components	Decisions
Product	Combo products tied to life, non-life and deposits
Price	Small premiums with periodical (also weekly) payment facility
Place	Agents, all retail outlets, part-time agents (retired teachers, housewives and youths), tie-ups with *kisan kendras* and companies
Promotion	Advertisements, word of mouth, hoardings and leaflets

MARKETING OF CELLULAR SERVICES

The telecom sector is one of the booming sectors of the Indian economy. There are a large number of mobile subscribers in India and with the next 100 million to come from non-urban areas; many Indian mobile service providers are targeting the rural market with aggressive tariffs and low-cost handsets. Almost all operators listed below have huge plans for rural India.

- Bharti Airtel
- Idea Cellular
- Tata Teleservices
- Spice Telecom
- Reliance Communications
- Vodafone

Target market

Cellular services constitute one of the most popular telecom offerings of current times, along with the Internet. It has attracted a consumer segment which wants to be in touch with colleagues, friends and relatives 24/7. Earlier the services were introduced with high prices and catered only to the high-income groups who could afford the hefty outgoing and incoming charges. With the advancement of technology and growth in volumes, the cell phone has become a mass product. It is being considered as a necessity item and today, we can see a cell phone in every pocket. Box 14.7 explains how the cell phone has become part of the poor man's life.

Penetration

According to the Telecom Regulatory Authority of India (TRAI), the country currently has more than 400 million wireless subscribers. Tele-density (phones per hundred) has also reached the 37.94 mark; of which rural density is still low at 12.62 per cent. A Confederation of Indian Industries (CII) and Ernst & Young study report said that around 100 million (40 per cent) of the next 250 million Indian wireless users are likely to be from rural areas and by 2012, rural users will account for over 60 per cent of the total telecom subscriber base.

Box 14.7 Poor Man's Budget Item

Cellular phones are a clear status symbol. Many poor households in the developing world have been able to successfully redirect a part of their household budget towards the purchase of cellular handsets and payment of operating costs. This demonstrates that rural consumers with limited incomes can and will pay for a new product or service if it is sufficiently desired. The drive for modern appliances/communications and ingenuity of users is evident from how rural users purchase cellular handsets despite having no access to electricity for charging. Users have to take or send the units to towns for charging purposes. Interestingly, it was noted that in South Africa and Nigeria, the liquor industry has actually experienced a reduction in sales as people redirected disposable income to cell phone costs.

Source: World LP Gas Association, "Developing Rural Markets for LP Gas, Key Barriers and Success Factors," 2005, available at www.worldlpgas.com.

Lowest prices

The prices offered by cellular companies in India are some of the lowest in the world. The penetrating price policy has given the opportunity to expand the market without limits. Time and again, charges of predatory pricing have been levelled against the cellular companies for offers such as lifetime free prepaid services. These type of offers are introduced in order to capture the market and attract more customers as every operator is trying to control maximum market-share.

Intense competition

The market is characterized by intense competition. Box 14.8 highlights the entry plans of major companies.

In the cellular services industry, the reaction from competitors is instantaneous and hence, there is hardly any first-mover advantage. It is a completely different scenario in the case of fast moving consumer goods (FMCG), as any FMCG needs days and sometimes weeks to be introduced into the market. While in comparison, the products or services introduced by cellular providers have to catch the fancy of the customers right away. Oherwise, they would be ineffective. In some cases, competitors have responded to such offers by announcing their own plans within a span of a few hours.

Value-added services for revenue generation

A serious problem faced by the cellular industry is the low average revenue per user (ARPU). One has to invent and discover new ways of generating revenue all the time. Cellular service providers are now looking at the efficient use of technology in order to attract new and permanent customers and thus aim at long-term sustainable growth. The best example is the short messaging service (SMS) facility, which is now a major revenue earner for all cellular operators. The market potential of SMS has proved to be great. It facilitates various forms of communication such as chatting, voting, advertising, campaigning and participating in contests and auctions. Even e-commerce can be conducted through SMS. The following are some of the major value-added products that are found in the rural market.

- *Reuters Market Light (RML):* Reuters has dispensed comprehensive agriculture-related information on a pilot basis in Maharashtra since April 2007.
- *IFFCO Kisan Sanchar Limited:* It is a joint venture between Bharti Airtel and IFFCO to provide rural-specific telecom services to rural households; it was set up to expand rural coverage from 0.32 million to 0.5 million villages by 2010.

Box 14.8 Go Rural Plans of Mobile Companies

Bharti Airtel has announced its intention of becoming a "rural company" in the near future. Currently, about 30 per cent of Bharti's wireless subscriber base is from rural areas. Reliance Communications is also extending its rural presence. Prepaid services are especially attractive to users in rural areas as it prevents the customer from getting tied down to a fixed cost. Reliance Communication has targeted the rural segment by its "*Grameen* programme" for rural subscribers. Spice Telecom is in the process of launching local market rates for commodities across Karnataka to connect with rural customers. BSNL has budgeted an investment of USD 125.38 million on rural infrastructure.

Source: Namit Agarwal, "An Idea/Airtel/ Vodafone Can Change Your Life," 23 October 2007, available at http://theviewspaper.net/an_ideaairtel_vodafone_can_change_your_life/.

- *Soochna Se Samadhan:* This was started by One World Network in collaboration with Reliance Mobile from 2006.
- *Mandi-on-mobile service:* It is run by the state-run BSNL in Uttar Pradesh.
- *Fisher Friend project:* This was a pilot project launched in Tamil Nadu and Pondicherry aimed at the fishing community.
- *LifeTools:* A project by Nokia, a package providing agricultural information and educational services, slated to be commercially launched in 2009.

Major players and initiatives

Telecom operators and OEMs have realised the importance of rural India. OEMs are also looking at getting a piece of the rural mobile-market pie. Take the example of Nokia. The mobile giant has tied up with service providers such as Airtel and Idea for launching an educational initiative in order to give rural users a live experience on mobility services that include hands-on training on making the first phone call and sending SMS with localized content.

According to Vipul Sabharwal, director of sales at Nokia India, Nokia's retail strategy is focused on making Nokia handsets available in every town or village that has a mobile retail outlet and mobile network. The company also has deployed Nokia vans across the country to further reach out to tier 3 and 4 towns and villages and to educate rural consumers on the benefits of mobility.

BSNL

BSNL is attracting consumers through its low-cost schemes. Being a state-owned player, BSNL could cover rural areas and this helped it increase its subscriber base. On the other hand, private players are leaving no stone unturned as is evident from the presentations by two executives at the Rural Marketing Association of India (RMAI) Seminar on rural telecom in Delhi, held on 3 July 2009. Box 14.9 gives the highlights of the rural marketing initiatives discussed at the seminar.

Vodafone

Vodafone took over Hutch's Indian business in 2007. The country was painted red with the "Hutch is now Vodafone" campaign to publicize its arrival. Vodafone introduced a new service offer "*Gappa Goshti*." It was a unique offering to the rural population keeping in mind affordability, accessibility and customization to their requirements. It is an innovative product designed to suit the needs of the market and to create a long-term association with the rural markets of India (Box 14.10).

Idea Cellular

In 2008, Idea Cellular of the Aditya Birla Group company launched an "education for all" ad campaign (Box 14.11) featuring its brand ambassador, Bollywood actor Abhishek Bachchan. To promote this thought, they have also tied up with an NGO Nanhi Kali, and NDTV. For Idea, the rural segment accounts for 40 per cent of total sales and 50 per cent of net subscribers.

For penetration into rural areas, most of the operators follow a varied distribution system. "Operators are now looking to roll out services in every nook and corner of the country. There is a huge untapped market and operators now have a rural-focused rollout plan," says T. V. Ramachandran, director-general, Cellular Operators' Association of India. The operators are now taking into consideration villages with as few as 1,000 people to provide services. "A few years ago, operators would not consider rolling out telecom services to areas with a less than 10,000 population. This has now come down to 5,000, and in a few years would get into clusters of villages that have just 1,000 people," says Pradip Srivastava, chief marketing officer, Idea Cellular. In the current scenario, it seems that private operators have found monetary potential in villages and to tap that, they are on a hunting spree.[18]

Apart from the traditional three-tier distribution system, service providers, distributors, retailers and operators are now roping in rural distribution channels such as the postal department or public distribution system.

Box 14.9 Rural Promotion: You May Do Like This!

Rajendra Chourasia, COO-MP of Chattisgarh Idea Cellular explained: "At Idea, we wanted to understand our consumers as much as possible before we marketed our products and services to them. Hence, before the launch of our campaigns, around 150 people from our marketing department spent a couple of days in villages interacting with the villagers to understand their needs. Following this, we came up with the marketing campaigns for the brand. Establishing the rural connect was a multi-pronged approach for Idea." On television, Idea has a programme called "TV Jalsa" that is aired on Doordarshan. The company also has two programmes running on AIR FM called "Idea *Madhur*" and "*Masti Ki Pathshala*" for the rural areas. Word-of-mouth marketing spreads the brand's message more effectively in the rural markets. Hence, Idea tries and engages the villagers during all its activities in these markets. Moreover, every village has a set of influencers like the *Sarpanch* or headmaster in the local school. They are invited to inaugurate the local network tower or are engaged in some other activity that ensures that there is enough buzz created in the area. The brand also uses vans and canter activities on a regular basis to drive home the brand message. Local *mandis* and *haats* are also used regularly as activation spots for the brand.

Raj Kumar Jha, national creative director, Ogilvy Action, maintained that brands have to go beyond van and canter activities to strike a chord with rural audiences. He highlighted the need for brands to be recognized and endorsed by villagers and presented clippings from regional-language music videos that incorporated brand names in their lyrics. "For rural markets, it is a successful communication plan only if your brand gets into the common lingo of the region," Jha says. Citing examples of brands that have managed to create a connect with the rural audience; Jha also noted that the rural population gave a lot of preference to the "colour" factor. He underlined the need for brands to differentiate their communication plans in accordance with this.

Source: Manish Ranjan, "Rural Telephony: Connecting India's Heartland," 04 July 2009, available at www.exchange4media.com/e4m/izone1/izone_fullstory.asp?section_id=4&news_id=35198&tag=30791; "In Rural Marketing, the Need Is to Go Beyond Van and Canter Activities," 07 July 2009, available at www.eventfaqs.com/index.php?rlink=topstory/top_stories.

Box 14.10 Vodafone's *Gappa Goshti*

Vodafone Essar launched Vodafone "*Gappa Goshti*" for prepaid customers in the rural markets of Maharashtra and Goa. Vodafone *Gappa Goshti* is a pack that allows Vodafone prepaid customers in villages to form the *Gappa Goshti* community and discuss business, market trends, stay connected with family, near and dear ones at just 30 paise/minute. Existing customers can recharge with the Rs 101 paper voucher, while new customers can enjoy this offer with the Rs 101 Vodafone prepaid card. Once purchased, any regular talk time recharge option can be used with Vodafone *Gappa Goshti*. This pack comes with lifetime validity and will be available at retail outlets across villages in Maharashtra and Goa.

Source: Sanjay Bafna, "Vodafone Launches Gappa Goshti," 15 May 2009, available at http://telecomtalk.info/vodafone-gappagosthi-plan/3851/.

Box 14.11 Idea—Education for All

In 2008, telecom service provider Idea Cellular launched its "education for all" campaign featuring its brand ambassador, actor Abhishek Bachchan. The new campaign was launched in two phases. R. Balakrishnan, chairman and national creative director, Lowe India, says, "The Idea campaigns have been specifically tailored to bring mobile telephony closer to the Indian consumers. By integrating a social message into the new campaign, we are not only reinforcing the difference that can be made through the use of modern technology but also the power of a new idea." Sanjeev Aga, managing director, Idea Cellular, says, "We believe that new ideas can change our lives, a thought that has been central to our brand promise from the beginning." "The new campaign addresses a very relevant social theme—education for all, especially the girl-child. I am pleased to be playing a part in this campaign and contributing towards making a difference through the power of the idea," Abhishek Bachchan said.

Source: "Idea Cellular Launches 'education for all' Campaign," 01 July 2008, available at http://indiaeducationdiary.in/showebn.asp?newsid=106.

Tata Teleservices has adopted a multi-pronged strategy to reach rural subscribers. It has joined hands with Impetus Technologies to launch the value-added service (VAS) *Mandi Bhav* for the rural market. This service offered to Tata Indicom subscribers will help farmers and commodity traders get spot prices from all markets for any commodity of their interest. It will be in real time, enabling them to make informed and prudent buy and sell decisions. Farmers can look forward to information on 500 commodities in about nine languages—Hindi, Marathi and English to begin with. TTSL plans to reach out to rural subscribers through *panchayats* by holding local level plays, by calling them or by sending personalized messages, by participating in rural *melas* and through the Tata *Krishi Sansar* centres.[19]

Spice mobiles

In 2008, Spice Telecom, Punjab's premier telecom service, launched a first-of-its-kind handset combo offer that included a unique handset and a Spice connection. Aptly called "Sabka Spice," the handset combo offer was made available at only Rs 599. The Sabka Spice offer is economically a very attractive offer as the prepaid connection comes with one-year validity and zero rental for one year along with a call rate of 50 paise. Similarly, the postpaid connection comes with very attractive local, STD and roaming call rates. The low-priced handset has unique features: long battery life, talk time of 3.5 to 4 hours and stand-by time of 250–300 hours, an intelligent audio interface system—a substitute for LCD. With this mechanism, alerts on the mobile were called out, which meant that even those who couldn't read could use the phone just by following the audio alerts. The handset also offered a choice of languages including English, Hindi, and Punjabi, a speaker-phone, a universal charger, which meant the phone could be charged using any mobile phone charger, speed dial and intelligent LEDs comprising red LED and blue LED.[20]

Bharti Airtel

Bharti Airtel is adopting various routes in varied market segments. They have tie-ups with low-cost handset manufacturers to reach out to the lower-end market segment. They have also tied up with Canteen Stores Department (CSD) to launch Airtel *Jai Jawaan* prepaid cards for defense personnel. These cards are available across 1,900 CSD outlets in the country, starting from Leh to Kanyakumari, Misamari to Kuchh.

Some operators are also inking deals with rural initiatives such as ITC's e-*Choupal*, *Haryali Bazaar* stores of DCM Sriram, and Godrej's *Aadhar* stores. Industry sources say that the state-owned BSNL is planning to tie-up with rural co-operative banks to push its service more aggressively.

In one of the innovative methods, Bharti Airtel has tied up with Mumbai's famous "*Dabbawalas*." These lunchbox carriers distribute homemade food packed in lunch boxes to Mumbai office goers. Everyday, this strong community of around 5,000 people take lunch boxes to thousands of Mumbaikers with nearly 100 per cent accuracy. And now, after this tie-up, they would distribute Airtel mobile prepaid cards, recharge coupons, and bundled handsets. The company is all set to leverage the large distribution network of the "*Dabbawalas*" to reach out to a larger consumer base.[21]

Reliance

Reliance Communications Infrastructure Limited has announced the signing of a joint venture with KRIBHCO, a premier co-operative society. This joint venture is a significant step forward that would result in an unmatched platform that would go a long way in providing mobile services in rural India. Box 14.12 explains how the joint venture is mutually beneficial.

Marketing mix for mobile services

The marketing mix for mobile services is given in Table 14.6.

Box 14.12 Joint Venture for Mobile Services

In September 2009, KRIBCO, a premier co-operative society with an unmatched marketing presence in rural India and Reliance Communications Infrastructure Limited, India's largest telecom service provider announced a joint venture to form KRIBHCO Reliance *Kisan* Limited (KRKL). This joint venture created a first-of-its-kind distribution model covering 72 per cent of the Indian population through a network of over 25,000 co-operatives, 6,300 member co-operatives and 60 "*Krishi Seva Kendras*" spread across the length and breadth of the country. The unique distribution model created by the joint venture company would distribute a range of telecom and non-telecom services to bridge the urban–rural divide. Over and above the state-of-the-art and most-affordable range of GSM and CDMA services, Reliance Communications would also soon unveil a wide range of products and value-added services customized for the rural markets. In future, KRKL would also distribute products and services of other business enterprises of Reliance ADA Group including Reliance Capital, Reliance Entertainment and BIG TV DTH. The joint venture would provide an additional source of business to the agricultural co-operative societies and help in strengthening the rural economy and the co-operative movement of the country.

Source: "KRIBHCO and Reliance Infrastructure Forge Rural Marketing Joint Venture," available at www.brandstoday.in/2009/06/15/kribhco-and-reliance-infrastructure-forge-rural-marketing-joint-venture/.

Table 14.6 Marketing Mix for Mobile Services

Mix components	Decisions
Product	Simple handsets with lifetime free prepaid service and a range of value-added services (music, farm services, etc.) and combo offers
Price	Affordable prepaid charges, recharge coupons, group subscriptions without SIM card
Place	Co-operatives, *dabbawalas*, corporate malls, Canteen Stores Department (CSD), retail shops, *haats* and *mandis*
Promotion	Vans, advertisements with celebrities in TV channels, sponsoring programmes (movies and TV serials), FM radio and opinion leaders

Summary

Financial services need to be provided to encourage savings, investment and credit facility to all those people who require it for meeting their household and occupational needs. Micro-finance and *Kisan* credit cards are innovative tools in addition to short-term and long-term credit offered by banks and co-operatives. Similarly, thrift in SHGs and investment in mutual funds are new phenomena. Insurance provides protection against uncertain incomes and life and it can be promoted by designing combo products combining life with non-life and bank deposits. The Internet has emerged as a gateway for information and entertainment in rural areas. Its promotion is carried out by the Government and NGOs. Many agri-input companies have set up Internet kiosks. Mobile Internet is a new product and it is promoted with easy-to-use features and low tariffs. Mobile services have become a necessity and the challenge is to make handsets and talk time available at affordable prices. The total cost of ownership is important and it is promoted by a wide distribution network.

Short Answer Questions

1. Describe the credit needs and savings habits of rural people.
2. What are the sources of credit?
3. Explain the role of micro-finance in the rural context.
4. What is the size of the insurance market? How is it growing?
5. Explain the market potential of Internet services.
6. Give an estimate of the market size of cellular services.

Discussion Questions

1. In the rural context service–quality considerations are unnecessary. Discuss.
2. It is difficult to develop a universal marketing model applicable to all services. Discuss.

Essay Questions

1. Describe the marketing strategies of commercial banks in rural areas.
2. What are the sources of credit? How can bad debts be reduced?
3. Discuss the marketing strategies of any two insurance firms.
4. How do you market Internet services to (i) the youth (ii) women and (iii) farmers?
5. Explain the cellular marketing strategies of any three service providers.

Internet Exercise

Prepare a report on cellular marketing in rural India based on data available on the Internet.

Mini Projects

1. Conduct a study of rural people to ascertain their preferences for investment in the stock market.
2. Interview the youth in rural areas and find out their needs for Internet services.

End Notes

1. Meera Mohanty, "Mobile, TV are Life Enhancers," *The Hindu Business Line*, 29 October 2009, available at www.thehindubusinessline.com/catalyst/2009/10/29/stories/2009102950010100.htm.
2. "RRBs Perform Better After Amalgamation," *The Hindu Business Line*, 24 October 2009, available at www.thehindubusinessline.com/2009/10/24/stories/2009102450810600.htm.
3. "Promoting Rural Savings Through MMMFs," available at www.ifmrtrust.co.in.
4. MAX-NCAER Survey, *The Marketing Whitebook*, (New Delhi: *Businessworld* Publication, 2009–2010), pp. 397–401.
5. "RBI Gives Nod for Appointment of 'Business Correspondents'—Banks Can Now Offer Loans, Accept Deposits through Agents," *The Hindu Business Line*, 26 January 2006, available at www.thehindubusinessline.com/2006/01/27/stories/2006012702580100.htm.
6. "Bank of India Starts Mobile Banking Service in Rural Areas," 28 November 2009, available at www.dnaindia.com.
7. Lison Joseph, "How SBI Tracks the Rural Fingerprint," 30 March 2009, available at www.livemint.com.
8. S. G. Anil Kumar and Nitin Chaudhary, "Access to Micro-savings for Remote Rural India," 27 August 2009, available at www.ifmrtrust.co.in.
9. www.canarabank.com, accessed March 2010.
10. Ashish Sinha, "Dhanax—Online Lending Platform For Micro-loans," 27 February 2008, available at www.pluggd.in/indian-startups/dhanax-online-lending-platform-for-micro-loans-agri-loans-social-investment-1200/.
11. "Banks Fare Poorly in Micro-finance: Kidwai," *Business Standard*, 27 October 2009, available at www.business-standard.com/india/news/banks-fare-poorly-in-micro-finance-kidwai/374364/.
12. www.accessdev.org/microfinance-amfa.php, accessed March 2010.
13. "More Farmers Get Kisan Credit Cards," *The Hindu Business Line*, 24 October 2009, available at www.thehindubusinessline.com/2009/10/24/stories/2009102450740600.htm.
14. Archana Venkat, "Banks Aggressive on Rural Portfolio," *The Hindu Business Line*, 05 June 2006, available at www.thehindu-businessline.com/2006/06/05/stories/2006060501941400.htm.
15. "Indian Bank Ropes in 81 Villages Under Financial Inclusion Project," *The Hindu Business Line*, 22 May 2006, available at www.blonnet.com/2006/05/22/stories/2006052201571400.
16. "Indian Bank's Credit to SHGs," *The Hindu Business Line*, 06 March 2008, available at www.blonnet.com/2008/03/06/stories/2008030652231100.htm.
17. "Insurance Companies in India," available at www.indiahousing.com.
18. Thomas K. Thomas, "Call of the Village," *The Hindu Business Line*, 02 April 2007, available at www.thehindubusinessline.com/ew/2007/04/02/stories/2007040200030100.htm.
19. Preeti Parashar, "Tata Teleservices, Impetus Join Hands to Launch Mandi Bhav for Farmers," *The Financial Express*, 23 January 2009, available at www.financialexpress.com/news/tata-teleservices-impetus-join-hands-to-launch-mandi-bhav-for-farmers/414058/.
20. www.spiceindia.com, accessed March 2010.
21. Gyana Ranjan Swain, "Mission Rural India," 02 December 2007, available at http://voicedata.ciol.com.

Case 14.1 Giving Wings to Savings

Post office savings banks (POSBs) in India were established in 1882 by the British Government to mobilize savings. Today, there are 154,000 POSBs. POSB offer various schemes to suit the needs of a diverse population. Some of them are listed below.

- Post office monthly income scheme
- *Kisan Vikas Patra*
- National savings certificate VIII issue
- Public provident fund (15 years)
- Post office recurring deposit
- Post office time deposit (1 to 4 years)
- Deposit scheme for retiring and retired employees
- Sector post office savings account (DSRGE/DSRPSU)

Hari Sundar and Prashob Jacob collected data from a sample of 171 persons to understand the perceptions of customers on the schemes and service offered by POSBs. The sample comprised respondents from different categories such as salaried employees, housewives, business people and students.

Findings

The following findings were obtained after the analysis of data:

Reasons for saving: About 25.4 per cent of the respondents saved for children's education, 10 per cent of the respondents for retirement safety, 17.2 per cent to buy household articles and 12.4 per cent to construct a house.

Reasons for not choosing the offered schemes: About 38.7 per cent of the respondents reported that they were not aware of the schemes. The other reasons were that the schemes were less attractive (24.3 per cent), insurance scheme was better (13.5 per cent), lack of adequate income to save (12.6 per cent) and delays in service (1.8 per cent).

Preferred instruments: The two most preferred instruments were *Kisan Vikas Patra* and Monthly Income Scheme (MIS). About 28.3 per cent and 23.3 per cent of respondents have accorded their preferences to the schemes in that order.

Conclusions

After the analysis a conclusion was reached that many of the respondents were interested in investing in post offices. At the same time, a considerable chunk of the sample was unaware of the schemes.

Suggestions

The possible actions that can be taken by India Post are summarized below:

- The Government must create more awareness among rural people about the saving schemes and the benefits availed through it as it has not reached the people properly.
- Good, reliable Government-authorized agents should be appointed so that people find it easy to hand over the money in order to increase mobilization of savings.
- More attractive schemes have to be designed and offered.
- The post offices should be computerized and more staff members have to be appointed to reduce delays in processing.
- There must be a change in the infrastructure facilities of post offices to create the right ambience.
- The staff should be more hospitable. Training the staff for efficient working and maintaining courteous relationships with customers is important.

For discussion

1. Critically evaluate the findings and suggestions.
2. How can post offices be modernized so as to increase their share in the rural savings pie?
3. Can you suggest an innovative savings scheme for post offices to attract people of low-income categories?

Source: G. Hari Sundar and Prashob Jacob, "Post Office Savings and Its Relevance in Rural Areas—A Study on the Impetus for Rural Investment with Reference to Kumbalangi in Cochin," *Vidwat*, Vol. 2 (January–June 2009): 26–34.

Case 14.2 Mobile Internet Services

Incorporated in 1996, as a part of the Tata Group conglomerate, Tata Teleservices already enjoyed strong brand recognition and played a leading role in the Indian telecom sector, actively developing and offering technologies and services in both fixed and mobile telephony. To bring the mobile Internet to a pan-India population, Tata needed a tool that could deliver a full, fast Internet experience, as well as offer unique market-specific features. Tata evaluated its options and found that Opera Mini met these needs. A significant technical advantage offered by the Opera Mini solution is lower battery usage. In a market like India, where mobile telephony has reached places where electricity is intermittent or rare, heavy demands on a mobile handset's battery life are prohibitive. The "heavy lifting" of Internet browsing is done on the Opera Mini servers and battery life is conserved.

Tailored Product

Tata's target population comprised people who had in all likelihood never seen or used the Internet before on any device. Users would need more fundamental guidance about what the Internet is and how it could be useful for them. Additionally, to make a real mark in the target market, the Internet browser had to be capable of rendering local language fonts to transcode local languages on servers For example, the English language is dwarfed in use by Hindi throughout India. Reaching these populations would require exceptional localization efforts, made much easier with localization options in Opera Mini.

Pricing

Pricing is simple, flat-rate and understandable. Tata provides a flat-rate pricing plan to its users that is simple to understand and mirrors the pricing structure consumers are used to seeing in Internet cafes. The flat-fee packages are available to pre-paid and post-paid customers at a price of Rs 10 for one day, Rs 30 for seven days and Rs 49 for 15 days (a kind of per-day, per-week, per-month pricing scheme). This allows the consumer the flexibility to predict and/or decide what amount s/he intends to use. There are no data limits imposed, so the customer is clear about what s/he will be paying for in his/her monthly bill.

Promotion

Tata pushes promotional SMS messages that advertise the availability of Opera Mini. Also, point-of-sale representatives are well-trained advocates of Tata's mobile Internet offer, informing potential subscribers about Opera Mini and the services available, as well as describing its use and educating consumers. Tata has employed other methods, such as enclosing advertising material with customer bills, top-of-deck positioning on the mobile portal and free seven-day trial use of the mobile Internet service on Opera Mini to encourage download and use.

Through the marketing channels that Tata employed, Tata emphasized its unique value proposition, condensing the message to four key points—access affordability (inexpensive handsets), simplicity (user friendly), pricing flexibility (straightforward, simple pricing structure offering a choice of subscription), and multilingual support (crucial in multilingual, multicultural India).

For discussion

1. What is the target market for mobile Internet services?
2. Is the marketing mix of Tata Tele Services appropriate to reach the target market?

Source: "Operamini Case Study: Tata Teleservices" available at www.opera.com/business/file/Business_case_TATA.pdf.

15

Social Marketing

LEARNING OBJECTIVES

Upon completion of this chapter, you will be able to:

- Understand the concept and elements of social marketing
- Know the social campaigns of government agencies, pharma companies and others

Lifebuoy's *Swasthya Chetna*—meaning "health awakening"—campaign, launched on 9 May 2002 by HUL was as unique a rural health and hygiene education programme as ever undertaken in India by a corporate enterprise. As recognition of its social contribution, a special Lifebuoy *Swasthya Chetna* postal cover was released on the occasion of World Health Day by the Chief Post Master General of Maharashtra Circle, K. Noorjehan. It was the first time that an Indian brand received such recognition. The programme reached about 200 million people over five years.

The laxity in health care, leading to diseases such as diarrhoea, was the theme of the campaign. It is reported that a child succumbs to diarrhoea every 30 seconds. According to a report by WHO, simple hand washing with soap and water would reduce 48 per cent of diarrhoeal diseases. Based on this report, Hindustan Unilever developed the *Swasthya Chetna* campaign. The objective of the programme was changing the basic health habits of villagers and their attitudes towards hygiene. The multi-level campaign involved opinion leaders such as village elders, school teachers, and health development officers. Children were educated using presentation aids such as flip charts, glow-germ demonstrations and quizzes to develop them into influencers in the community. In the next stage, the health officers interacted with the parents while involving the children. Follow-ups through subsequent contacts were made to reinforce the message and cultivate new habits.

The message was spread through mass media such as wall paintings, *haats*, fairs and festivals. Cinema vans were employed based on the well-known fact that rural consumers like films. They showed popular movies, interspersed with product advertisements. HUL introduced an affordable 18 gram bar of Lifebuoy soap for low-income people that would be enough for one person to wash hands once a day for 10 weeks. The campaign was replicated successfully in other countries like Bangladesh and benefited close to 3,100 villages.[1]

The exemplary initiative of HUL is worth emulating for its right mixture of immediate social concern with long-term profit objectives.

The evolution of public–private–participation (PPP) models involving the Government, NGOs and corporate enterprises is a happy augury to the socio-economic revolution sweeping the countryside. The model can be successful only when it understands and applies the concept and techniques of social marketing. This chapter deals with the nuances of social marketing and discusses the initiatives of some change agents.

INTRODUCTION

Rural markets call for a unique marketing strategy and distribution model. FMCG companies commonly seek emotion-laden social touch points such as fairs and exhibitions on religious and social festivals, road shows, etc. to market their products. They undertake social marketing, in general, as a part of their corporate social responsibility. Some companies, however, resort to promotion of product-related social causes; examples are Lifebuoy *Swasthya Chetna* and Reckitt Benckiser's Dettol Swine flu campaign. The case of pharma companies is different. Social marketing is a key ingredient of product marketing for them.

CONCEPTUAL FRAMEWORK OF SOCIAL MARKETING

What is social marketing? The following definition explains the concept.

Social marketing is the systematic application of marketing, along with other concepts and techniques, to achieve specific behavioural goals for a social good. In social marketing, the distinguishing feature is its primary focus on social good.

Though social marketing and commercial marketing make use of the same concepts, they differ in context and purpose. A commercial marketer aims at creating a customer by influencing him or her to like and purchase a product or service whereas a social marketer seeks to influence clients to create a change in behaviour by reducing negative behaviours such as cigarette smoking or encouraging positive behaviours such as condom use.

Focal points in social marketing

Social marketing is a complex, intellectual and social process that requires understanding people, designing change, inducing initiatives and modifying the environment of behaviours.

Target audience

Identify the target groups and put them at the centre of every decision. Social marketing begins and ends with the target audience. In order to influence the target audience, understand their behaviours and the reasons.

Action

Action is the process of heightening awareness, shifting attitudes and strengthening knowledge relevant to desired behaviour.

Exchange

Change in behaviour implies giving up certain behaviours or modifying an old behaviour or accepting a new one. This happens only when there is a positive gain that adequately compensates the loss of the old behaviour. Change agents must offer incentives to motivate the target groups to make changes in their lives.

Competition

The social world is full of good and bad options. The target audience can always choose to do something apart from what is being advocated. For example, junk food (pizzas, burgers, potato chips and soft drinks) competes with native food; formula feeding competes with breastfeeding because of convenience and participation by other family members. Competition is intensified and rationalized by the participating organizations and peer pressures. Pepsi promotes lifestyle soft drinks and fast foods. Friends may encourage a college student to drink alcoholic beverages.

Marketing mix[2]

The "4 P's of the marketing mix" are to be understood as given in Table 15.1.

Additional social marketing "P's" are as indicated in Table 15.2.

Strategic questions

The 10 strategic steps in developing an initial social marketing plan are as given under.

1. Identification of social (or health) problem.
2. Designing actions that best address the problem.

Table 15.1 The 4 P's of the Marketing Mix

Product	The desired behaviour communicated to the audience, the associated benefits, tangible objects and/or services that support behaviour change. For example, giving up drinking will offer benefits such as savings, family happiness, social approval and good health.
Price	Cost (financial, emotional, psychological or time-related) or barriers the audience faces in making the desired behaviour change. For example, giving up drinking involves costs in the form of loss of company of friends and perceived social status and relaxation.
Place	Location—where they will access the programme products and services and where the audience will perform the desired behaviour. For example, interventions may include offering immunizations in a neighbourhood or mobile clinic, offering nutritional information on a restaurant menu or grocery-store food shelf, or placing condom vending machines in club or bar bathrooms.
Promotion	Communication through media channels, promotion materials and activities.

Table 15.2 Additional Social Marketing P's

Publics	"Publics" refer to both the external and internal groups involved in the programme. External publics include the target audience, secondary audiences, policymakers and gatekeepers, while the internal publics are those who are involved in some way with either approval or implementation of the programme.
Partnership	Teaming up with other organizations in the community that have similar goals for creating synergy.
Policy	Decisions that help remove barriers and change the behaviour of the target audience. Social marketing is particularly useful in removing barriers that prevent behavioural change. A legislation prohibiting child labour is important to curb child-employment practices. Sometimes, community norms are also to be changed to ensure effective implementation of legislations.

3. Identification of people to be influenced (target audience).
4. Knowing the benefits expected by the target audience for adopting the new behaviour.
5. Recognizing how much the audience trusts your offer—is it real and true?
6. Comparing your offer with that of the competitors to know whether your offer is superior to that of the competitors' and beyond the expectations of the audience.
7. Identifying the best time and place to reach members of your audience (the idea is to reach them when they are most disposed to receiving the intervention).
8. Determining the frequency and source of intervention, so that it works.
9. Integrating a variety of interventions to make them work in a coordinated manner to influence behaviour.
10. Finding out the availability of resources and deciding whether to carry out the strategy alone or in partnership.

NATIONAL RURAL HEATH MISSION CAMPAIGNS

The National Rural Health Mission aims at providing accessible, affordable, effective, accountable and reliable health care to all citizens and in particular to the poorer and vulnerable sections of the population. This is consistent with the outcomes envisioned in the Millennium Development Goals and general principles laid down in the National and State policies, including the National Health Policy, 2002 and National Population Policy, 2000.

A wide range of campaigns are being implemented by states to address identified needs/specific gaps in health services. Some of the campaigns are described here.

Safe motherhood

Chiranjeevi Yojana in Gujarat, *Ayushmati* Scheme in West Bengal, *Mamta* Friendly Hospital Initiative in Delhi and *Saubhagyawati* Scheme in Uttar Pradesh are health financing schemes that are designed under the public–private–partnership model to benefit women belonging to the below-poverty-line (BPL) category. They aim at providing emergency obstetric care and transport services.

Family planning

United States Agency for International Development (USAID) funds and ICICI Bank implements the *Bindaas Bol* campaign in nine states. The campaign has been designed to promote condom use by men. An integrated communication and marketing approach has been used for the campaign. Celebrities have been involved in mass media campaigns. Innovative distribution approaches have been used to reach retailers. Partnerships have been formed with condom manufacturers, marketers and health providers.

The *Aadarsh Dampati Samman* has been instituted in Uttar Pradesh to encourage family planning behaviour among men. Men who follow the two-child norm and who have opted for male sterilization are considered as role models under the scheme. Under the scheme, Rs 500 is awarded to two men every year per sub-centre.

Child care

A community-based approach, *Kano parbo na*, has been started in West Bengal. It is aimed at reducing low birth weight and malnutrition. By transmitting the good practices of mothers with healthy children across the community, the scheme tries to improve feeding practices of mothers.

A week-long intervention programme called *Panchamrit* campaign has been initiated in Rajasthan. Immunization is one of the five services covered under it. The *Ankur* Project in Maharashtra provides care for new born babies at home by community health workers.

Adolescent reproductive and sexual health

The *Saathiya* Youth Friendly Project in Uttar Pradesh is a programme that aims to educate out-of-school girls on contraception and sexual health. Training is imparted to the girls at youth information centres.

Health care

The healthcare programme called *Saathi Bachpan Keos* promotes the use of oral rehydration salts for treating diarrhoea. The programme has been implemented in 33 towns across eight states in North India. A campaign called *Bodhana Nauka* (Information boat) was initiated to create awareness about water- and vector-borne diseases among people living in the water-logged Kuttanad region in Alappuzha district of Kerala.

Service delivery

Different transportation modes are used in order to access various places. These include mobile health clinics (operating in seven states), mobile boat clinics (Assam), mobile helicopter services (Tripura hilly zones) and floating dispensaries (Narmada basin of Maharashtra).[3]

PHARMA HEALTHCARE CAMPAIGNS

MNCs such as Novartis, Roche Diagnostics, Novo Nordisk and Eli Lilly have drawn up blueprints to tap the rural healthcare market in India that suddenly appears to be attractive like never before. The rural market makes up 17–18 per cent of the country's USD 8.1 billion pharma market. It can be observed that pharma companies eyeing the rural markets are incorporating social marketing in their overall marketing strategy. The following examples illustrate this point of view.

Novartis—*Arogya Parivar*

Novartis introduced the *Arogya Parivar* model that aims at ensuring availability of products at the same prices but, different pack sizes, in pharmacies in villages across seven states, including Maharashtra, Gujarat, Chhattisgarh and Haryana.

The model supplies medicines to over 16,000 pharmacies. Initially, 24 products from the Sandoz generics and consumer healthcare business unit that addresses tuberculosis, mother and childhood malnutrition, respiratory and gastro-intestinal problems will be sold to the rural masses. "Our stockists in district towns supply to village pharmacies. There would be no difference in pricing of medicines in rural and urban areas. Price points will remain the same. The idea is to give it in smaller packets. This is a social business. We have an emerging social category that needs health care," said Mr Ranjit Shahani, vice-chairman and managing director, Novartis India Ltd. "We also create awareness on health issues using audio-visual interface through health advisors in villages," he said.[4]

Ipca laboratories—*Jeevan Rekha*

The aim of the *Jeevan Rekha* programme of Ipca laboratories was to create cardiac awareness by means of free blood pressure check up camps using BP machines. Those who were detected with high BP were explained its long-term effects and advised that it can be prevented by using Tenolol. The one-month long pilot run of the campaign added new prescriptions of about 1,000 patients to their list. The second run of the campaign was carried out in the Vidharbha region of Maharashtra in July 2009.

Touch points for these campaigns have always been the PHCs, hospitals and nursing homes, retail chemist shops, dispensaries of doctors, consumers, residential areas and markets. RW Promotions, a company that hosts medical camps has helped companies such as GlaxoSmithKline, Nicholas Piramal create brand awareness, a new database of doctors and medical shops beyond medical representatives' limits. The use of mobile dispensaries and pre-publicity vans in all the campaigns resulted in the opening of new markets, and created new opportunities and avenues in untapped markets.[5]

Novo Nordisk—diabetes project

Novo Nordisk, the diabetes major, has set up the Novo Nordisk Education Foundation. It launched a project in Goa called the "Changing Diabetes Barometer project."

Partnerships

It was launched under the banner of "Global Changing Diabetes Leadership" forum in association with the Goa Government in Goa.

Aim of the project

Through this project, the company aims to undertake a massive diabetes-control programme towards making Goa free from diabetes-related amputation, blindness, nephropathy and other complications.

Place

It is operated through mobile clinics and primary health centres. Mobile clinics go to villages and screen people for diabetes.

Product

The campaign involves creating mass awareness about diabetes, conducting diabetes screening programmes, enabling practical training camps for medical professionals, and improving treatment of diabetes with a focus on reducing complications related to diabetes.

Promotion

Anganwadi workers are health workers trained in various aspects of preventive health, nutrition and child development covering rural areas. Through this programme, 74 *anganwadi* workers responsible for maintaining health records of 1,000 to 1,500 people in their area were trained.[6]

MARKETING OF FAMILY PLANNING

In case of family planning, companies, in general, undertake initiatives to educate their own employees as well as local community residents. Box 15.1 presents how Indo Gulf carried out a campaign in collaboration with a government agency.

Box 15.1 Family Planning Campaign by Indo Gulf

Indo Gulf has taken up social projects that cover about 1,000 villages and touch the lives of more than 0.3 million people surrounding the fertilizer plant at Jagdishpur and the Birla copper plant at Dahej. For the projects, Indo Gulf has collaborated with the SIFPSA and the State Health and Family Welfare Department. The central theme of the projects is family planning and reproductive health in a broader context. With the key focus on the well-being of women and childcare, Indo Gulf adopted a holistic approach to provide easy access to quality family planning services in villages. The range of services includes distribution of contraceptives, antenatal and postnatal counselling and medical check-ups and immunization of children. Rural weekly clinics are held in the village interiors for the benefit of the local populace of Jagdishpur. More than 14,200 couples and more than 11,000 children, aged one month to five years, immunized since the programme began in 1998–1999 have been the beneficiaries to date.

Source: "Corporate Concerns—Indo Gulf Family Planning," available at www.change.godrej.com/septoct/corp_con.htm

HLL—*Swasthya Gram Pariyojana*

Hindustan Latex Limited (HLL) is the leader in the manufacturing of contraceptives and an organization with a keen sense of social responsibility. HLL formed the Hindustan Latex Family Planning Promotion Trust (HLFPPT) when it realized the need for organizing family planning and healthcare programmes for the poor and disadvantaged sections of the society. The Trust conceptualizes, designs and implements different types of social projects and through this provides a wide range of services.

HLFPPT implemented a community-based contraceptive social marketing programme approved by the Ministry of Health and Family Welfare (MOHFW), Government of India (GOI), in select districts of Bihar, Jharkhand and Orissa. The GOI provided funds for a period of three years to the tune of Rs. 0.027 billion.

The project was aimed at family planning promotion by removing the three major barriers in promotion of spacing methods in rural areas, i.e. lack of access, affordability and lack of motivation. The promotional approach involves the following tasks and goals.

- Reduction of Total Fertility Rate (TFR) through distribution of contraceptives through unemployed, educated and mobile rural youth and encouraging their use through a comprehensive local media-based IEC programme.
- Advancement of family health through the promotion of sanitary napkins and oral re-hydration salts (ORS).

The implementation of the project called for an integration of local resources such as *anganwadi* workers as service providers at the last village level. They form an important link in the programme.

The results of the programme were encouraging. The use of condoms went up by 34 per cent and that of oral contraceptive pills increased by 18 per cent.[7]

MARKETING OF HEALTH CARE

Players in the healthcare sector are designing innovative models to reach rural people. The PPP model of CARE Hospitals is an example of an innovative approach in the marketing of health care.

CARE campaign

As per budget estimates, the Government spends roughly Rs 300 per person/year to provide primary health care. However, it is important to have PPP models to provide quality health care to rural people. In the 2008 budget, the Central Government announced SOPs for setting up hospitals in tier II and III cities. The SOPs, such as a five-year tax holiday and insurance schemes, have provided impetus to CARE hospitals to experiment with the integrated health care model.

Strategy

The strategy is to emerge as an integrated healthcare provider with presence in primary, secondary and tertiary spaces.

Project and collaborations

The Rs 0.02 billion experiment is carried out in collaboration with ITC. The pilot project was launched in Nagpur and the plan was to replicate the project in other states based on the results.

Health information

About 40 e-*Choupals* will be located at a *Choupal Saagar* and each e-*choupal* will cater to three to four villages. The operational details are as follows. In the first phase, village health workers will be trained. There will be three to four village health workers in each e-*Choupal*. Meanwhile data will be collected to map the health profile of the million-strong population. "Smart devices" will be developed together with a reputed corporate hospital like CARE Hospitals to capture basic health information in electronic format.

Product

A 100-bed, multi-speciality hospital set up at Nagpur is electronically linked to three smaller medical centres located in Yavatmal, Wardha and Amaravati.

Price

The idea is to provide health care at affordable price levels. Emphasizing this point, Dr Reddy of CARE Hospitals group observed that the efforts are to test the public–private–partnership (PPP) model, to deliver high-quality and cost-effective primary health care and also to establish a sustainable network in rural areas.

Place

The telemedicine facility covers nearly 400 villages with a million-strong population. The electronic and video link between Yavatmal, Wardha and Amaravati villages and the Nagpur hub will facilitate efficient service delivery.[8]

MARKETING OF AIDS PREVENTION

AIDS-awareness campaigns are organized in a big way in our country. We find government agencies, NGOs and corporate enterprises working together to create synergistic effects. Box 15.2 discusses NACO's partnership with soft drink majors.

Campaigns of Reliance Industries

Reliance Industries Limited is a well diversified private enterprise with a workforce of 25,000 employees. It has taken up social health projects covering its large workforce and social community.

Early initiative

As an industrial site, Hazira has a large migrant workforce employed in several local industries. The presence of these industries has also contributed to a large, floating population of truckers in Hazira. Concerned about the risk of infectious diseases in such a population, the local government sought corporate support to set up HIV and tuberculosis programmes at the workplace and in medical camps in local villages and on local highways.

The programme began by establishing a well-equipped health centre at Hazira, in Gujarat, to provide tuberculosis treatment based on the strategy recommended by the World Health Organization

Box 15.2 NACO Campaign

The National AIDS Control Organization is a division of the Ministry of Health and Family Welfare that provides leadership to HIV/AIDS control programmes in India through 35 HIV/AIDS Prevention and Control Societies. The National AIDS Control Organization (NACO) has chosen a piggyback strategy and appealed to both Coca-Cola India and Pepsico India to put AIDS awareness slogans on Coke and Pepsi bottles and caps and use their individual 1 million-strong retail network for selling low-cost condoms.

The main idea behind tying up with Coke and Pepsi was that they have tremendous rural reach and are mostly consumed by the youth, which also happens to be the segment that needs AIDS education the most. However, since, the profit margins on condoms supplied by NACO are low; most kiosks in rural and urban areas do not want to partner with NACO.

Source: "AIDS! What's Your Company Doing?" 24 September 2005, available at www.rediff.com/money/2005/sep/24spec.htm.

(WHO), known as DOTS (Directly Observed Treatment, Short-course). The centre, that also offered information on HIV prevention, later expanded to treatment and other services for AIDS patients. It also provides counselling, education and training and disseminates information on nutrition. In 2004, the district tuberculosis programme approached Reliance to collaborate in efforts to address tuberculosis in Hazira. Together, these two events gave the management the impetus to initiate a full-time HIV and tuberculosis programme at the company's Hazira location.

Full-time HIV and tuberculosis programme

The company's management began by discussing possible intervention strategies with *Lok Vikas Sanstha* (LVS), a local NGO specializing in public health.

Target audience

In 2004, LVS had conducted a baseline survey on the prevalence of sexually-transmitted infections in Hazira and found that among the local population of migrant workers and truckers, the prevalence rate was close to 12 per cent. The target group included truckers (drivers and crew members), contract and migrant workers, employees of local enterprises and members of the local villages.

Products

The Reliance HIV and AIDS programme has two components: awareness and education and treatment. It aimed at removing the strong social stigma associated with HIV and psychological fear and depression among the patients. Also, it offers treatment to patients. Patients seeking treatment for sexually-transmitted infections receive counselling on topics such as modes of HIV transmission, the relationship between HIV and sexually-transmitted infections and the use of condoms. The centre also provides antiretroviral therapy. It offers emergency care including intravenous drugs, fluids and ambulance services. Also, among the other services offered at the centre are yoga training, *pranayama* coaching (breathing exercises to boost physical and mental spirits) and nutritional support.

Price

The centre provides a number of free medical tests for HIV-positive patients and at a heavily subsidized cost for others, including pregnancy tests, blood screening for syphilis, urine microscopy and biochemical examinations such as liver-function tests, blood sugar test and lipid profile. Patients suffering from malnutrition, weighing less than 40 kg receive food and nutrition supplements.

Place

The discussions with LVS led Reliance to set up a DOTS tuberculosis and HIV centre at Mora village on 15 May 2004 to provide medical services (both general and tuberculosis related). The centre is housed in a community hall provided by Mora's *gram panchayat*. Involving the *panchayat* helped create a sense of ownership among the local villagers.

Promotion

Reliance held a series of discussions with the Gujarat State AIDS Control Society in order to obtain a better understanding of the nature of HIV prevalence in Hazira. These discussions made it clear that generating awareness among high-risk groups was a priority in stemming the spread of the epidemic. Reliance thus, ensured that its awareness programme extended beyond its employees and local villagers to high-risk groups in local industries. Reliance has developed a multi-pronged approach to HIV and AIDS awareness and education in the local community:

- *Community mobilization team*: A community mobilization team with representatives from both Reliance and LVS frequently visits neighbouring villages (Damki, Suvali, Batlai, Junagaon, Vasva, and Rajgiri) to disseminate information.

- *Health camps:* In nearby villages, it conducts mass awareness programmes through health camps. Sessions held at these camps discuss other health issues along with HIV to diffuse the focus and thus, lessen the discomfort of addressing HIV-related topics. Diagnostic and referral services are also provided in the health camps. Reliance bears the cost of both the health camps and any subsequent treatment.
- *Different media:* Reliance has also posted several educational banners in Surat and used street plays, poster exhibits and video shows.

Barriers

The limiting factors to the programme are identified for removing barriers in future.

- *Poor public health services:* The government's public health system often lacks the basic medical services and expertise required to administer quality care to AIDS patients. While this may not directly hinder the operation of the centre, an effective government system would help both support the services offered by the Reliance centre and extend coverage to more patients.
- *Retention of village outreach workers:* Retaining village outreach workers has been a challenge for the programme staff with workers often dropping out after receiving training. Continually training new outreach workers has been costly and time consuming.
- *Social stigma:* Reliance faced initial challenges in its awareness and education programmes because of the social stigma associated with HIV and AIDS and sexually-transmitted infections. Workers hesitated to ask questions during training sessions though they often returned to clear up misconceptions. Villagers were concerned about the proximity of the medical centre to their homes, fearing that it could expose them to infections from visiting patients.
- *Monitoring and evaluation:* Reliance's employees believe that monitoring and evaluation of the programme need to be strengthened with clearly defined targets established for evaluating all partners.
- *Financial sustainability:* The Gujarat State AIDS Control Society provides funds to LVS for its counselling, training and dissemination services and for the cost of medicines. Thus, the continued support of LVS as a programme partner depends largely on the continued financial support of the Gujarat State AIDS Control Society.

Future plans

The programme has already reached nearly 300,000 people—truckers (drivers and crew members), contract and migrant workers, employees of local enterprises and members of the local community. Reliance is now initiating a process of replicating the programme at other company sites. In addition, the company is considering implementing similar HIV and AIDS initiatives at Reliance gas stations on the highways, targeted at the trucking population.[9]

Summary

Rural markets require development approaches that integrate social development with marketing tasks. Social marketing is the systematic application of marketing along with other concepts and techniques to achieve specific behavioural goals for a social good. Social marketing is a complex, intellectual and social process that requires understanding of people, designing change-inducing initiatives and modifying the environment of behaviours. Social marketing is done by government agencies, NGOs and corporations. Prominent among social campaigns of FMCGs are Lifebuoy's *Swasthya Chetna* and Dettol's swine flu prevention campaigns. Pharma companies have made social marketing an integral part of product marketing. Illustrative of this kind of initiatives are the campaigns of Novartis (*Arogya Parivar*), Ipca Laboratories (*Jeevan Rekha*), and Novo Nordisk (Diabetes project). HLL's *Swasthya Gram Pariyojana* campaign is an example of how a company can promote a product considered to have social stigma. Reliance has teamed up with other organizations to campaign against HIV/AIDS in a big way.

Short Answer Questions

1. Define social marketing.
2. What are the focal points of social marketing?
3. Explain marketing mix of social issues.
4. Identify the strategic questions relating to social marketing.

Discussion Questions

1. Social marketing aims at social change that requires psycho-social changes in individual and groups. Discuss.
2. For social marketers, the HIV/AIDS issue is one of the most challenging issues among all social marketing issues. Discuss.

Essay Questions

1. Define social marketing. Explain the major elements in social marketing.
2. Explain the role of the National Rural Health Mission in promoting health in rural areas.
3. "Social issue advertising is an integral part of pharma marketing." Do you agree? Give examples of social marketing by pharma companies that support the view.
4. Explain how marketing of family planning is done by corporate enterprises.
5. Examine how health care is marketed by government agencies and corporations.
6. Describe how AIDS prevention has been taken up as a serious issue and campaigned for in India.

Internet Exercise

Gather information from the Internet and prepare a report on "marketing of social issues by corporate enterprises."

Mini Projects

1. Meet the executives of local industrial enterprises and prepare a report on the activities undertaken by them in respect of (a) family planning, (b) health care and (c) AIDS prevention.
2. Design social campaigns linked to (a) Fair & Lovely (b) Savings account.

End Notes

1. www.hul.co.in, accessed March 2010.
2. "The Basics of Social Marketing," available at www.turningpointprogram.org/Pages/pdfs/social_market/smc_basics.pdf.
3. Arun Kumar Sharma, "National Rural Health Mission: Time to Take Stock," *Indian Journal of Community Medicine*, Vol. 34, Issue 3, July 2009.
4. "Novartis India Launches '*Arogya Parivar*' to Tap Rural Market," available at www.aarogya.com.
5. "An Initiative Towards Rural Health Care," *Express Pharma*, 16–31 July 2009, available at www.expresspharmaonline.com/20090731/management09.shtml.
6. Arshiya Khan, "Greenfield for Pharma Companies," *Express Pharma*, 16–31 August 2009, available at www.expresspharmaonline.com/20090831/market01.shtml.
7. "Hindustan Latex Limited," www.karmayog.org/csrothercompanies/csrothercompanies_7932.htm.
8. M. Somasekhar, "Rural Healthcare: CARE to Leverage ITC's e-*Choupals*," *The Hindu Business Line*, 06 March 2008.
9. "RIL: A Unique Initiative for AIDS and HIV Infected," 08 December 2009, available at www.casestudy.co.in/ril-a-unique-initiative-for-aids-hiv-infected/.../08/.

Case 15.1 Campaign for Health

Elder Pharmaceuticals Limited was set up in 1983 in the state of Maharashtra as a private limited company. The values of the company include behaviours characterized by honesty, integrity, ethics, and performance based on individual dignity, team work and mutual respect and customer satisfaction through high-quality standards of products and services.

Strategy

Alok Saxena, international director, Elder Pharmaceuticals feels, "Rural markets offer potential volume growth, which has not been tapped by most of the pharma companies." Elder has decided to go rural through its Elvista division and developed plans aimed at moving towards tier II to IV towns, villages, and *talukas*. To start with, the plans have been envisaged for penetrating the interior markets of Uttar Pradesh, Maharashtra, Andhra Pradesh, Bihar and Rajasthan. An investment of USD 8.21 million is proposed.

Product Mix

The product mix offered by the division has 16 brands including the Eldervit Injection. The aim is to offer a full range of products that top the therapy preferences of rural people. The basket includes antibiotics, multi-vitamins, digestives, pain killers, cough syrups, antipeptic ulcerants, etc. Niche brands such as Venex, Protocream, Mucodyne, Mucobron have been focussed on. Small packs have been designed to suit the purse of the rural people. For example, the topical pain reliever "Ontac Gel" has been launched in a small blister sachet pack.

Outreach Techniques

Elder has adopted a multi-pronged approach to promote products by creating a dedicated sales team comprising 250 personnel to cover a targeted number of about 70,000 doctors supported by taxi tours, mobile health clinics and public awareness programmes.

The healthcare professionals would be exposed to continuous medical education programmes. Medical camps would be held periodically to create awareness about health problems and company products among rural folk.

Medical Camp: Will it Work?

Elder has decided to organize medical camps periodically in villages with the twin objectives of (i) creating health awareness among rural people and (ii) gaining brand acceptance from both doctors and rural people.

Though Venkatesh Srinivasan, director, RW Promotions maintained that the rural public had been very receptive of these medical camps and the hindrances faced by the pharma clients had been few and far between, there are still some problems as given under:

First, there is a lack of awareness about the ailments among the rural people. A poorly educated rural population is a major challenge in this case.

Second, patronage of drugs depends purely upon the family doctor's opinion and the follow-up by local sales team with the doctors and patients. The lack of qualified doctors makes it challenging for companies to get patronage for chronic ailment products.

Third, there is the need to follow-up to obtain the necessary stocks and infrastructure in these markets.

Here are the economics of the medical camp campaign. The van has a 30-day route cycle and about 70–80 medical camps will be held during the campaign period. The overall cost of a medical camp campaign would be between Rs. 0.45 and 0.5 million, depending upon the drug being promoted. On an average, a medical camp touches around 100 to 200 people.

For discussion

1. Would you consider the marketing procedures of pharma companies to be part of social marketing?
2. Is organizing a medical camp a worthwhile proposal? What are your suggestions to make medical camps effective campaign tools??

Source: Arshiya Khan, "Greenfield for Pharma Companies," *Express Pharma*, 16–31 August 2009, available at www.expresspharmaonline.com/20090831/market01.shtml.

Case 15.2 Multi-pronged Attack

In India, the fight against HIV/AIDS began when the first case of HIV was detected in Chennai in 1986. The Government of India launched the National AIDS Control Programme (NACO) and the response to it has been constructive and yielded positive results. The Kerala State AIDS Control Society (KSACS) was a state-level autonomous society registered under the Charitable Societies Act with members drawn from all key government departments. It works under the aegis of the National AIDS Control Organization (NACO), which is a part of the Ministry of Health and Family Welfare of the Government of India.

The National AIDS Control Programme (NACP) has completed two phases and is currently in the third phase (NACP III). The first phase (1992–1999) focused on creating awareness about HIV/AIDS, modernizing blood banks and building the capacity of health personnel at different levels. The second phase (2000–2007) gave a thrust on interventions in high-risk behaviour groups and expansion of the counselling and HIV-testing facilities. The current phase (2007–2012) seeks integration of prevention, care and treatment programmes to halt and reverse the HIV epidemic.

Why a Mainstream HIV/AIDS Prevention Programme?

The proposed integrated approach to eradicate HIV/AIDS requires a multi-sectoral response to HIV prevention. This is the main objective of the National AIDS Control Programme (NACP). The elevation of the concern requires mainstreaming the programme to facilitate involvement of the authorities beyond the health sector. Now, it is campaigned for not only as a health issue but also as an issue with strong socio-economic ramifications making it everyone's business.

Multiple Dimensions of the Issue

The mainstreaming effort brought the following issues into the forefront:

- Stigma and discrimination against victims of HIV/AIDS,
- Social isolation or discrimination issues faced by HIV-positive persons at workplaces,
- Access to medical care, availability, affordability and awareness,
- Sexuality-related problems and
- Legal problems such as denial of property rights to HIV-positive persons.

Organizational Set-up

A broad-based campaign of the kind envisaged requires wide organizational set-up, resources and commitment of authorities. The National AIDS Council at the Centre, working under the Prime Minister, is assisted by the State AIDS Council, under the chairmanship of the Chief Minister. It draws people from different sectors to make the campaigns broad-based and effective.

Identified Partners and Responses

In case of KSACS, involvement of 11 government departments, including Social Welfare, Education, Labour, Police, Prisons, Tourism and Local Self Government was envisaged through alliances to spread the message against HIV.

The Social Welfare Department provides education on nutrition for women and children living with HIV. *Panchayats* implement several targeted intervention programmes.

The Prisons Department and the Railways have set up counselling and testing centres inside six major prisons and at select railway stations, respectively.

Organizations are advised to mainstream the issue by adopting policies and practices that sensitize staff about HIV and reduce the risks.

Business Enterprises Invited

As a part of the mainstreaming initiative, the KSACS has given a call to the business community to become campaign partners. It approached the Technopark group of companies and has initiated efforts to identify and involve major industries and institutions. Explaining the aim of involving the business community, a senior KSACS official said, "We would like every enterprise to respond to the challenge of HIV/AIDS by identifying how best they can integrate HIV-prevention activities into their core business."

For discussion

1. Do you agree with the view that HIV/AIDS programmes are multi-dimensional ones that require different organizations to respond?
2. Prepare a presentation highlighting your response to the call of KACS as an executive of an enterprise in the following sectors (a) Service, (b) FMCG and (c) Agri-inputs.

Source: C. Maya, "KSACS Draws up Pro-active Campaign," *The Hindu*, 14 December 2008, available at www.hindu.com/2008/12/14/stories/2008121453220400.htm.

16

Agricultural Marketing

LEARNING OBJECTIVES

Upon completion of this chapter, you will be able to:

- ▶ Understand the existing system of marketing of agricultural products
- ▶ Appreciate the need for improving the commercialization of agri-outputs
- ▶ Recognize the participation of corporate enterprises in agricultural activity

The government of Uttar Pradesh has decided in favour of the public–private–partnership (PPP) model for procurement and marketing of agricultural produce. The decision was taken in order to reduce the on-field losses and to provide alternative channels to farmers for selling their produce at the best prices, A number of marketing resource centres would be opened across the state in partnership with private players to provide information and assistance regarding handling, grading, sorting, packaging and transportation of agricultural harvest to local farmers.

Usually, the farmer's lack of reliable and easily accessible information results in low realization of market price for the produce and gross wastage of harvest on various accounts such as rodents, pests, rotting and transit losses. It is expected that these losses will be reduced and the best market prices will be provided to farmers by various mechanisms such as grading and sorting. The lack of proper and adequate storage in the state has time and again resulted in heavy losses to farmers and traders.

Specialized cells have been proposed to cater to region-specific produce storage needs. Accordingly, there will be potato marketing centres in central UP and mango centres in Malihabad and Mentha centres in Barabanki. Initially, the land will be leased out to private players for a period of 30 years and in future the lease period will be reduced to 20 years. The marketing centres will attract private players to set up latest technological facilities such as radiation plants for enhancing the shelf life of produce, ripening chambers for fruits and auto-grading facilities. With all the farmer-friendly arrangements, the centres will provide farmers a chance to make choices—they can take their produce to the open market or sell directly to the companies at the centres.

The centres will be opened on the basis of the findings of ongoing studies for identifying various "agro-climatic" zones in the state to enable the availability of best equipment and technologists for the local farmers.[1]

The latest initiative of the Government of Uttar Pradesh is a step in the direction of strengthening the democratic structures and policies of our nation. It will also go a long way in improving marketing practices and providing benefits to the farmers. In this chapter, we will examine the marketing practices in vogue along with certain important developments.

INTRODUCTION

Agriculture is the life-line of the Indian economy. As such, a good agricultural marketing system that stimulates scientific farming and enhances the standard of living of farmers is important. Developing a sound marketing system and making it effective is a major concern of all the participants and stakeholders. Several steps have been initiated by the Government to facilitate effective marketing practices. The entry of corporate enterprises into the field of agriculture and privatization of markets are the two significant developments that may have a positive impact on agricultural marketing in future.

MARKETABLE SURPLUS

The concept of marketable surplus is very important for the development of markets. Marketable surplus is different for different commodities. Marketable surplus is a surplus that is available for sale after meeting (i) family needs, (ii) seed requirement, (iii) kind wages, (iv) gifts to relatives and friends, etc. In case of food grains, surpluses are generally low.[2] They vary from zero (with small and marginal farmers) to 70 to 80 per cent with large farmers and those in surplus areas. In general, marketable surpluses in food grains are in the range of 45–50 per cent. In the case of cash crops and in those commodities that are used as raw materials in industries, surpluses are to the tune of 80–100 per cent. In fruits and vegetables that are grown on a commercial scale, surpluses are above 90 per cent. Thus, markets have to be well-organized and efficient for the commodities that have large surpluses.

CONCEPT AND FUNCTIONS

Agricultural marketing consists of all the functions and services used in moving the commodities from the producer to the final consumer. It includes all activities that create different utilities—time, place and form—for the ultimate consumer.

Concept

The National Commission on Agriculture defines agricultural marketing as a process that starts with a decision to produce a saleable farm commodity. It involves all aspects of the market structure of system, both functional and institutional, based on technical and economic considerations and includes pre- and post-harvest operations, assembling, grading, storage, transportation and distribution.[3]

The Indian Council of Agricultural Research defined it in the following manner:

> It is the involvement of three important functions, namely (a) assembling (concentration), (b) preparation for consumption (processing) and (c) distribution.[4]

Agricultural versus manufactured-goods marketing

The differences between agricultural and manufactured-goods marketing and their implications for the agricultural marketer are given in Table 16.1.

Table 16.1 Agricultural Versus Manufactured Goods

Base	Agricultural commodities	Manufactured goods	Implications
Perishable	Yes	No	Immediate sale or special storage facility
Seasonal	Yes	No	Storage facility for distribution for items like food grains
Variations in quality	Natural	By design	Grading
Processing	Needed	Finished	Miller/processing agent is an intermediary
Size	Bulk	Varying quantities	Transport is essential

Functions of agricultural marketing

The essential functions of agricultural marketing may be described as follows:

- *Assembling:* This involves collection of produce for sale in *mandis* or larger markets.
- *Grading and standardization:* Grading is the sorting of the commodities into different groups on the basis of size, variety, taste, quality, colour, etc. Standardization fixes the grades and does not allow them to vary from season to season and year to year. Grading and standardization are used interchangeably.
- *Processing:* Processing is the conversion of farm produce into more consumable forms. For example, conversion of wheat into flour, hulling of paddy into rice, etc. Processing imparts form utility.
- *Transporting:* Transportation takes place through different means such as road, rail, air and water and aims at creating place utility.
- *Storing:* Storage is the holding of produce from the time of production until it is needed by the consumers. Storing creates time utility. Some products such as fruits and vegetables are stored for short periods. Also, they require facilities like cold storage.
- *Distributing:* It relates to channels that take produce to a large number of consumers.

TYPES OF AGRICULTURAL MARKETS

Agricultural markets can be classified into primary markets, secondary markets and terminal markets.[5]

Primary markets

Primary markets are periodical markets locally called *shandies* or *haats*. They are generally held in an open place once a week on a particular day. Commodities produced in the surrounding villages are sold in these markets. Besides agricultural produce, a number of other articles required by rural folks, for example, locally made agricultural inputs such as threshers, hannovers, winnovers, etc. and consumables such as pulses, salt, jaggery, oil, fruits and vegetables, spices, clothes, hosiery products and ornaments of cheap metal, are sold. The salient features of this market are:

- *Convenient place:* As the producers and buyers are from nearby places, the market is a convenient place for them to transact in. Problems of transportation and costs are minimized.
- *Cash payment:* Village producers receive immediate payment after the sale of their produce.

Secondary markets

They are regular wholesale markets and are known as "*mandis*" or "*gunjs*." They are situated at district headquarters and towns. The quantum of commodities transacted is in bulk. Large quantities of commodities arrive from other markets into these markets. Middlemen, market agents, weighing men and commission agents are involved in the marketing system. Facilities like grading, packing, warehousing, loading, transportation, telephone and banking facilities are available. There are about 2,500 secondary markets in India.

Terminal markets

In terminal markets, the produce is either finally disposed of to the consumer or to the processor or assembled for export. The terminal markets are located in highly populated cities such as Mumbai, Chennai, Delhi, Kolkata, Bangalore, etc. The following functions are performed by the market committee:

- *Assembling of goods:* Products from different local and primary markets are assembled here so that they can be transported, economically, from one market to another.
- *Grading:* The produce is graded based on the quality and specifications of different types of consumer groups.
- *Warehousing:* Agricultural produce can be stored in state warehousing, central warehousing and FCI godowns. In case the capacity of the godowns is insufficient, private godowns are rented by the market committee to store the available marketable surplus.
- *Distribution for processing:* The marketable surplus is distributed to mill owners and processors who further process it and sell it to retailers or consumers.
- *Financing and risk bearing:* The marketing committee undertakes the functions of financing and risk bearing. It buys the produce that is not covered under the minimum support price on auction basis and may sell it in future when the prices are fair in the market.
- *Price maintenance:* The terminal-market committee, being agents of the Government, play an important role in stabilizing prices in varying demand–supply conditions.
- *Commodity exchange:* Commodity exchange is at the heart of terminal markets. It is an independent organization of dealers in certain commodities. It does not make purchases and sales on its own but, provides a place where the goods can be bought and sold economically and without any discrepancies. The activities are carried out under certain set rules and regulations and under the supervision of the authorities of the exchange.

Besides the classification of agricultural markets into primary, secondary and terminal ones based on location, there are five more important classifications based on (i) frequency of holding, (ii) commodity handled, (iii) volume of transactions at a time, (iv) nature of transaction and (vi) number of commodities.

On the basis of frequency with which they are held

Markets can be classified into daily markets, weekly markets, bi-weekly markets and monthly markets.

Based on the types of products traded

We may classify markets as grain markets, cotton markets, fish markets, fruit and vegetable markets, etc.

Based on the volume of transactions at a time

Wholesale markets: A wholesale market is one where commodities are bought and sold in large lots or in bulk. These markets are generally located in either towns or cities.

Significance: A wholesale market becomes a place of congregation for different businesses and over time the population tends to get concentrated. It acts as an extremely important link in the marketing chain of all commodities including farm products. The market balances supply and demand and determines the prices of commodities.
Types: Wholesale markets can be classified as primary, secondary and terminal wholesale markets.

- Primary wholesale markets are essentially assembling centres located in and around producing regions. The transactions in primary wholesale markets take place mainly between farmers and traders.
- Secondary wholesale markets are generally located between primary and terminal wholesale markets. The transactions in these markets take place between primary wholesalers and traders of terminal markets.
- The terminal markets are generally located at the large urban metropolitan cities or export centres and cater to the large consuming population around them or in the overseas markets.

Retail markets: A retail market is one in which commodities are bought by and sold to the consumers as per their requirements. Transactions in these markets take place between retailers and consumers. The retailers purchase the goods from wholesale markets and sell them in small lots to the consumers in retail markets. These markets are very near to the consumers.

Based on nature of transactions

Agriculture markets are classified based on the types of transactions in which people are engaged. The classification includes spot and forward markets.
Spot or cash markets: Markets in which goods are exchanged for money immediately after the sale is called the spot or cash market.
Forward markets: These are markets in which the purchase and sale of a commodity takes place at a time (t) but, the exchange of the commodity takes place on some specified date in future, i.e. time (t)+1. Sometimes, even on the specified date in the future (t+1), there may not be any exchange of the commodity. Instead, the differences in the purchase and sale prices are paid or taken.

Based on the number of commodities

A market may be general or specialized on the basis of the number of commodities in which transactions are completed. These would include:
General markets: Markets in which all types of commodities, such as food grains, oilseeds, fibre crops, *gur*, etc. are bought and sold are known as general markets. These markets deal in a large number of commodities.
Specialized markets: Markets in which transactions take place only in one or two commodities are known as specialized markets. The examples are food grain markets, vegetable markets, wool markets and cotton markets.

MARKETING SYSTEM

The need for having a marketing system for agricultural products need not be over emphasized. The agricultural marketing system in India is characterized by different markets, agencies and channels.[6]

The objectives of an efficient marketing system are to address the concerns of farmers and consumers, such as:

- To enable farmers to sell products at reasonable prices.
- To make available all products of farm origin to consumers at reasonable price without compromising on the quality of the produce.

Obviously, the fulfilment of the first objective requires good infrastructure for transport, storage, distribution and a well-functioning market mechanism.

Table 16.2 Agricultural Markets and Agents

Classification of markets	Agents
Primary market	Producer, the village or itinerary merchant, pre-harvest contractors, commission agents, transport agents, etc.
Secondary market	Processing and manufacturing agents are the additional functionaries. Financing agents, such as shroffs, banks and co-operatives.
Terminal or export market	Commercial analyst and shipping agent.

Marketing agencies

The transfer of produce or goods takes place through a chain of middlemen or agencies as shown in Table 16.2.

A number of middlemen are involved in the marketing of agricultural produce as per the details given below:

Landlords

They are big cultivators and buy surplus produce from farmers and sell the same in *mandis.*

Village beoparis

They set up a shop in the village and sell consumption goods. They purchase produce from farmers and may act as financiers to other poor farmers. They visit neighbouring markets to know the prevailing prices and they sell the produce in nearby markets or in the village.

Mobile beoparis

They do not have shops in the village. They move from village to village and purchase the produce from farmers. They transport the produce to the nearby markets.

Commission agent

This is a person who buys agricultural produce and makes the payment on behalf of his principal trader. He keeps the goods in his custody and delivers it to the principal trader in due course. He charges commission as per the agreement between him and the trader.

Mandi level

Three types of commission agents operate at the *mandi* level and they are:

i) *Kachcha arthatias:* They are commission agents and they act for the sellers including farmers. Sometimes, they provide money to farmers on the condition that the produce will be sold to them. The *kachcha arhatia* has limited financial resources and his sphere of activity is purely local. His commission is known as the *arhat* and is about 2 per cent of the value of the produce.

ii) *Pucca arthatias:* They are wholesalers and big commission agents. They act on behalf of traders as well as farmers. They are processors of rice, oilseeds and dealers in cotton/jute, etc. They advance money to the farmers and earn commission on sales of produce as well on the advance given to farmers.

iii) *Dalals:* They link buyers and sellers and earn commission.

The following observations are pertinent with reference to functionaries.

- The functionaries have their own set up. They may be individuals, partners or co-operatives.
- They may buy and sell on ready and future basis at a price determined by the forces of supply and demand.

- Each functionary renders some service in the process of marketing and also earns a varying margin of profit for himself.

Marketing channels

The channels of marketing of agricultural produce are as given under.

- Government channel
  Producer > Government department > Consumer
- Co-operative channel
  Producer > Co-operatives > Consumer
- Private channel
  Producer > Village merchant > Wholesaler > Commission agent (*dalal*) > Retailer > Consumer

The government channel is used mainly to protect farmers as well as domestic consumers. In case of food grains such as rice, wheat and sugar, the government purchases the produce from farmers and supplies it to consumers through the public distribution system. When farmers cannot get proper prices for their produce, the government announces support price and buys from them. The government channel operates with the co-operative or private channels. In Maharashtra, the government channel operates in the marketing of milk along with co-operative and private channels.

The co-operative channel is used partially along with the private channel in the case of important fruit crops such as grapes, pomegranates, bananas and oranges.

In the private channel, too many intermediaries result in high costs. The commodities become expensive for the final consumer and this reduces the producer's share in consumer's prices. Nearly 60–70 per cent agricultural produce is sold through this channel. In some fruit crops, in addition to the above, the pre-harvest contractor takes ownership of fruit gardens while fruits are still on the trees.[6]

TERMINAL METHODS OF SALE

In the terminal markets, sales take place in a variety of ways as explained here.[7]

Hatta system (undercover)

Though dealing undercover is not a healthy marketing practice, it is still prevalent in copra trade. Copra makers take their produce to the market and contact the broker with copra samples, commonly called *"oneeda,"* in one basket, which moves from one broker to another. The settlement of the price for the produce is determined in a secret manner without uttering the price in open. The buyer and the broker engaged by the seller determine the price through pre-determined secret codes of prices for every one of the five fingers of their left hand, which is held hidden under the cover of a towel. They touch each finger alternatively by offering the price that has been fixed for the difference fingers. The rates are known to the buyer and the broker; however, not to the sellers. The deal is finalized at the price arrived at secretly. After the consultation of the broker with the seller, both firmly hold their particular finger under the cover of a towel. This practice was in vogue among the copra/coconut-oil merchants in Travancore and Kochi. The copra merchant might not get the payment for copra immediately. When the next lot is brought to the market, the merchant gets the amount that is due for the previous consignment.

Auction system

This is one of the common methods of selling farm produce. It has two variants.

Open bid system

The method involves the following steps.

- The produce brought for sale by a farmer is inspected for quality by those who would like to purchase it. This allows elimination of disputes regarding quality.
- In the presence of the farmer, the commission agents or brokers or some other trader will take part in the auction and announce their bids.
- The offer of the highest bidder will be accepted. The farmer has the discretion to refuse the offer if he considers it low.

The merit of this system is the openness that gives a sense of satisfaction to the farmer that he is not cheated. The demerit is that it is a time consuming process.

Closed bid system

In this method, the produce that is brought to the market is arranged in lot sizes. The intending buyers inspect the lots, record the bid in their tender slips supplied by the market committee and deposit it in a sealed box. They sign in the priority register. In the case of a tie (when bids of two bidders are the same), the one who deposited first will be declared the winner. The tender box is opened and the market secretary or superintendent announces the highest quotation on the public address system. If the price is not acceptable, the farmer has to inform the same to the officials of the marker within the stipulated time. Thus, the process takes less time than the open bid system and ensures a fair price to the farmer.

Private agreement

In this method the farmer enters into a sales transaction without the influence of intermediaries. Tobacco and cotton are generally sold through this method. The merit of this system is that the farmer gets the final price without deduction of commission for middlemen. The demerit is that the buyer may exploit the innocent farmer by over weighing, manipulation of accounts, deductions of unauthorized allowances and through delays in payments.

Sale by sample

The sale transaction is made by showing samples to the buyer. The buyer and seller negotiate the price based on the grade of the sample.

Dara sales

A flat price is offered to the heap of agricultural produce without grading the contents.

Jalap sale

The buyer purchases the standing crop of the farmer well in advance of the harvest at a price fixed on the date of the bargain. The buyer may pay an advance amount of 50 per cent of the value of the sales transaction to the farmer.

Moghum sale

This is entered into when a farmer requires credit to carry out farming. The cultivator borrows from traders and agrees to sell the produce to them on a set date. The agreement is oral and is based on mutual trust. The price paid will be the one prevailing in the market on the date of delivery.

REGULATED MARKETS

Most State Governments and Union Territories have enacted legislations such as the Agricultural Produce Marketing Committee Act to ensure efficient regulation of agricultural-produce markets.[8] These regulated physical markets have been established to ensure a reasonable amount of profits to agriculturalists for their crops and other agricultural products.

Currently, there are more than 7,500 such markets in the country. Most of these regulated markets are wholesale markets. Other than these markets there are also around 30,000 rural periodical markets of which 15 per cent function under the ambit of regulation. Presently, the average reach of a single regulated market is 459 sq. km. This means that farmers have to travel a long distance with their produce to avail this facility. The Central and State Governments are in the process of creating more regulated markets so that the command area of each market does not extend beyond 80 sq. km.

Basic facilities such as internal roads, boundary walls, electric lights, loading and unloading facilities and weighing equipment are available at more than 80 per cent of the markets. Farmers' rest houses exist in more than half of the regulated markets. Infrastructural facilities that the Government plans to extend to all regulated markets are auction platforms, drying yards and cold storage units.

Objectives of regulated markets

The objectives of regulated markets are as follows:

- To ensure reasonable gain to the farmers by creating an environment in markets conducive to the fair play of supply and demand forces.
- To regulate market practices and attain transparency in transactions.
- To aim at providing proper method of sale, correct weighing, prompt payment and various marketing-related services
- To provide a democratic set up to control and manage markets.

Functions of the market committee

A "market committee" is set up to control marketing activities. The committee consists of representatives of farmers, commission agents and government nominees. The committee issues licenses to the commission agents, weighing men and other functionaries. The rate of commission to be charged is fixed by the committee. Weighing is done properly by the weighing men appointed by the committee.

ICT CHANNEL

In the current era of information technology, farmers can use information and communication technology (ICT) for building sustainable marketing linkages.

The ITC e-*choupal* is the best example in this context. Through the creative use of information technology, ITC e-*choupals* have been creating sustainable stakeholder value by reorganizing the agri-commodity supply chains while simultaneously improving the competitiveness of small farmers and enhancing rural prosperity. The e-*Choupals* also sidestep the value-sapping problems caused by fragmentation, dispersion, heterogeneity and weak infrastructure. ITC takes on the role of a network orchestrator in this meta-market by stitching together an end-to-end solution. This system eliminates the traditional *mandi* system that involved a lot of middlemen as a result of which farmers failed to get the right value for their produce. The solution simultaneously addresses the viability concerns of the participating companies by virtually aggregating the demand from thousands of small farmers, and the value-for-money concerns of the farmers by creating competition among the companies in each leg of the value chain.[9]

CASE 1—MARKETING OF COCONUTS

The marketing of coconuts differs from that of other fresh fruits due to the natural durability of coconuts. Coconuts are sold as fresh tender nuts, as water nuts as well as matured and dry nuts. Coconut is mainly cultivated in the southern states, i.e. Kerala, Karnataka, Tamil Nadu and Andhra Pradesh and nominally in the coastal areas of Maharashtra, Goa, Gujarat, Orissa and West Bengal.

Sales channels

Coconut farmers have two channels for disposal of their coconuts—the direct channel (leasing) and the indirect channel. Nearly half of the coconut farmers in general and two-thirds of the marginal and small farmers in particular have been observed adopting leasing as the mode of disposal of their coconuts. The indirect channel is the most prominent channel adopted among coconut farmers.

Processing—husking

Matured coconuts are generally disposed of by farmers in un-husked forms for want of nearby market places. However, farmers located near market places, de-husk the coconuts and sell them as husked nuts. Farmers from the areas where the husks are not utilized for retting and coir purpose store the coconuts for two to three months, particularly the nuts harvested in the monsoon season. In Kerala, Karnataka and Andhra Pradesh, farmers keep nuts for several months and sell them as dry nuts for making edible copra.

Storage practices

The storage practice for matured coconut differs from place to place and in accordance with marketing practices. Producers, merchants or exporters store coconuts in different ways. The farmers and local village merchants store coconuts in their houses. In markets, coconuts are stored in godowns owned by the wholesalers or commission agents. Since matured coconuts are meant for immediate consumption or crushing for oil, they are not warehoused for longer periods. The matured nuts meant for copra making are stored as un-husked nuts immediately after harvesting and undergo further ripening to improve the quality of copra obtained. The husk obtained from such nuts loses the quality required for coir-making purpose. The matured nuts are not stored but husked immediately after harvesting in places where husks are used for retting and nuts are sold for milling purpose. The matured nuts meant for consumption of water and kernel are stored for a period of a few weeks to three months by the farmers in their garden itself, as they fetch premium price when the colour of the nuts become brownish. This type of storage has been observed in some districts of Maharashtra, Karnataka and Kanyakumari district of Tamil Nadu.

Channel members—transporting, grading and pricing

The personnel and agencies involved in the marketing of coconuts and the marketing practices followed are discussed below:

Village merchant (copra maker)

In Kerala, the village merchants are the first purchasers of the nuts from the producers. Traditionally, the price of coconut is determined by the price of coconut oil prevalent in the market. The accepted norm followed in Kerala is that the price of one quintal of coconut oil is equivalent to the price of 1000 nuts, i.e. the cost of a single nut is equivalent to 100 g of coconut oil.

Middlemen (copra merchants)

The middlemen, who are also merchants, convert the coconut into copra by sun drying or kiln drying or by following both the methods. It takes around seven days for producing standard-quality copra. In most of the cases, copra is sold at the stage when moisture level is 10 to 12 per cent. This is commonly known as "*ghatti*," for which the corresponding amount is deducted by the traders. The best quality copra has 6–7 per cent moisture. The price of the copra is calculated on the following basis (a) the price of oil per candy, (b) the price of cake per candy and (c) less sales tax and crushing charges. Since, the marketing prices of coconut oil always fluctuates, the copra makers have to rush to the manufacturer of copra by reducing the drying period. In some villages, drying of copra is carried out in a crude form of copra-kiln. It results in the manufacture of inferior-quality copra. The small copra makers in villages sell their lots to big processors and thus, there is more than one intermediary involved before it reaches the millers.

Traders (millers)

The copra thus procured is brought by the traders for further sale to millers. The transportation involved is either by country boats or bullock carts. Generally, traders are associated with particular millers but, they can go to other agencies if they have not taken any advance payment from the miller.

In Kerala, most of the units are situated near the back waters facilitating water transport. The trader take about 10 per cent of the copra procured as sample to the miller for approval and then bargaining starts.

Wholesale traders adopt the practice of grading copra based on the quality factors prevailing in the trade. The coconuts are categorized into two forms, fresh and dry, while copra is classified into edible and milling. The edible copra is classified as ball copra and cup copra, depending on the quality. Edible copra is further graded as copra from dry nuts, copra from semi-dry nuts and copra from fresh nuts. Each grade is again classified into different trade names such as Office Pass, Rassi, Rajpur, Moong, etc. The Office Pass grade is generally used for milling purpose and sold to millers.[10]

CASE 2—MARKETING OF COTTON

The marketing of cotton commences from the harvesting of *kappas* and ends after the lint is procured by the millers. The farmers normally bring their produce to the nearest market by cart, truck or by other means after packing it in bales. It is sold by the grower to the village merchant without the intervention of any intermediaries.

A majority of the cultivators are now disposing off *kappas* in the secondary wholesale markets. In the secondary wholesale markets, business is conducted in accordance with local customs and practices. In case of centres with regulated markets, the transactions are governed by bylaws framed by the market committee and approved by the State Governments. The marketing committee is responsible for providing storage space, arrangement of auction, inviting tenders, announcement of market rates and providing market information. The market committee collects market cess and commission agents charge commission for the services rendered.

The open auction system is generally followed in most of the secondary markets for each individual seller's produce. Based on the grades decided, cotton lots are put to public auction where commission agents or wholesalers participate. The commission agents do all the work in handling the *kappas* on behalf of the farmer and arrange to sell it either in the presence or absence of the farmers. The farmer gets the value of his produce after all these deductions.

The wholesaler normally transports the cotton to Mumbai or arranges to gin it locally and sells the cotton lint to the textile mills, exporters and traders dealing with consuming mills or engaged in inter-state trade. Mumbai, Coimbatore, Ahmedabad and Kanpur are some of the important terminal markets, of which Mumbai is the largest.

With the establishment of a number of ginning/spinning mills in the private and co-operative sectors in many *taluks* and districts, the bulk movement of *kappas* and lint to weaving mills located in Mumbai and Surat has been reduced in recent years. Mostly, the lint/*kappas* is consumed locally. When there is surplus lint, it is moved to distant places for selling.[11]

MARKETING FINANCE

Farmers require credit for production and domestic purposes. The loans taken by farmers can be classified in different ways as shown in Table 16.3.

The sources of finance can be classified into non-institutional and institutional sources.

Table 16.3 Loans—Types and Purposes

Base	Categories	Description
Time	Short-term loan	For agricultural operations. Period will be less than 15 months.
	Medium-term loan	For purchase of agricultural machinery, digging of well, etc. Period ranges from 15 months to 5 years.
	Long-term loan	For making permanent improvements on land, purchase of tractors, etc. The period of loans extends beyond 5 years.
Purpose	Production	For seeds, fertilizers, pesticides, payment of wages, digging of wells, making permanent improvements on land, etc.
	Consumption	For family expenditure on food, clothing, etc.
	Occasions/Problems	For litigation, performance of marriage, birth/death of family member and festivals.

Table 16.4 Non-institutional Sources of Finance

Sl No	Lender	Description
1	Friends/Relatives	Money is lent based on emotional relationships.
2	Landlords	Money is lent on the understanding that the produce will be sold to them.
3	Mobile traders	Money is advanced for short periods and also for procuring agricultural produce from cultivators.
4	Small commission agents (*kachcha arhatias* in Northern India)	They procure produce from villagers and arrange to sell it in the nearby *mandis*. As soon as the money is received from the *mandis*, they make payment to the cultivators.
5	Wholesale commission agents (*pucca arhatiyas*)	Deal is made on bulk quantities of commodities and with finance traders as well as farmers.
6	Professional moneylenders	Money lending is the main business and they charge exorbitant interest rates, as high as 40 per cent per annum.
7	Non-professional moneylenders	Money-lending activity is a side business for village merchants or traders in agricultural produce.
8	Indigenous bankers or shroffs	They finance traders, local industries and villagers.

Non-institutional sources

The participants in this segment of financing are given in Table16.4.

Institutional sources

The major sources of financing for agriculture are the government, co-operatives, regional rural banks, commercial banks, farmers service societies (FSS), large-sized *adivasi* multi-purpose co-operative societies (LAMPS) and micro-financial institutions.

The government

Low-interest loans for both short as well as long-term are provided by the government. They are known as "*taccavi* loans." These are generally provided in times of natural calamities. However, this cannot be a major source of agricultural finance.

Co-operatives

Different co-operative institutions provide different types of loans. State co-operative banks (SCBs), district central co-operative banks (at district level) and primary agricultural co-operative credit societies (at village level) provide short-term and medium-term loans, whereas long-term loans are provided by the central land development banks (at state level) and primary land development banks (at *taluk* level).

Regional Rural Banks (RRBs)

RRBs were set up to provide loans to small and marginal farmers, landless labourers and village artisans. They are set up at places that have potential for agricultural development but marginal institutional credit facility. These loans are given for purposes related to crop production.

Commercial banks

Nationalization in 1969 had changed the character of commercial banks. Priority-sector lending guidelines were formulated giving major thrust to agriculture credit. Today, they form the largest source of institutional credit to agriculture.

Farmers Service Societies (FSS)

These are registered co-operative bodies and they advance different types of loans to weaker sections for different purposes and different periods.

Large-sized Adivasi Multi-purpose co-operative Societies (LAMPS)

LAMPS came into existence in December 1971. They were reformed on the lines of FSS to supply credit to tribals.

Micro-financing

Micro-financing has emerged as a prominent source of financing in recent years. Financing is done in three ways. In the first method, banks take initiatives to form and finance SHGs, directly. In the second approach, NGOs take initiatives to form SHGs and facilitate direct financing by the banks. In the last mode, NGOs and other agencies form SHGs and act as financial intermediaries.[12]

CORPORATE AGRICULTURE

Many corporate enterprises such as PepsiCo, Bharti, Reliance and GGCL are engaged in agriculture by contract farming methods and participate in the distribution of agricultural products such as food grains, vegetables and fruits.[13]

PepsiCo

PepsiCo is a pioneer in the concept of contract farming. Under this, the company performs two tasks. One, it educates and supports farmers in farming by transferring the best agricultural practices and technology. Second, it procures the produce at a guaranteed price. For this venture, PepsiCo set up a 27-acre research and demonstration farm in Punjab where it conducts farm trials of new varieties of tomato, potato and other crops.

The company aimed at cultivating farm supplies required for its production activities. The objective was to ensure the supply of the right produce at the right time in required quantities to the company's processing plant. Accordingly, it focused on developing region- and desired produce-specific research, as well as extensive extension services.

The initiative worked and a change in attitudes and behaviours of farmers was achieved. Encouraged by the success of contract farming in tomato in several districts of Punjab, the company replicated the model in food grains (Basmati rice), spices (chillies), oilseeds (groundnut) and other vegetable crops like potato.

The company undertook contract farming of potatoes involving about 10,000 farmers in over 10,000 acres across Punjab, UP, Karnataka, Jharkhand, West Bengal, Kashmir and Maharashtra. It tied up with the United Breweries Group to cultivate barley partnering with 1,200 farmers in Rajasthan.

Bharti

Indian telecom giant Bharti has moved into the global fruit and vegetable market through a joint venture with a unit of UK-based finance group Rothschild. Field Fresh Foods incorporated in September 2004, is an equal-partnership joint venture between Bharati enterprises and ELRO Holdings India Ltd, an investment company of the Rothschild family.

The business model proposes to link Indian fields to the world market by providing fresh, quality produce to the markets worldwide through contract farming. It is leasing large tracts of land in Punjab and Rajasthan and has developed an arrangement with a group of farmers in Uttaranchal as well. Field Fresh has 78 farms with 4,200 acres on lease in Punjab producing beans, snow peas, carrots, okra, baby corn and other vegetables for export to Europe and the Middle East. The leased arrangement is increasing the income of farmers significantly. The lease rate in Punjab is anywhere between Rs 12,000 and Rs 15,000 a year, which the farmer earns over and above his annual income.

Reliance

Reliance Industries formed a bio-tech venture—Reliance Life Sciences—in 2001, to engage in cropping and sale of medicinal and herbal plants. A herbal garden in Navasari, Gujarat, was developed for growing plants like ashwagandha, patchouli, geranium and lemon grass. From them, Reliance Life is extracting aromatic oils under the brand names ReliCare Pa, ReliCare Ge and ReliCare Le, respectively. These are anti-bacterial and anti-fungal in nature. Using contract farming, Reliance is planning to enter the business of food processing and export of fruits and vegetables. It is establishing a chain of cold stores in Punjab to support the venture.

GGCL

Thapar Group's Global Green Company (GGCL) has a contract farming arrangement with 12,000 farmers in Andhra Pradesh and Karnataka to grow gherkins. The company markets about 30,000 tonnes of gherkins and over 95 per cent of the company's products are exported to 23 countries. The end result of the business model is substantial earnings of hard currency from international markets.

COMMERCIALIZATION

Commercialization is a multi-faceted phenomenon with its orientation depending on the technology, policies and the location-specific objective conditions. In a nutshell, it refers to production with a market orientation. The transformation in agriculture during the last six decades suggests that our agriculture has acquired commercial characteristics on a significant scale. The commercialization process faced several constraints in the past and many of these constraints are relevant even today, when new constraints are also being experienced.[14]

Marketing constraints

An inefficient agricultural marketing system has been a major impediment in the growth of marketed surplus and in the realization of remunerative prices by farmers. In spite of the best efforts by the state, weaknesses still persist. Some of the maladies that affect agricultural marketing are the presence of unduly large number of middlemen, long marketing channels, malpractices by the intermediaries, information gap due to the lack of free and effective flow of information.

Input–supply constraints

The supply of inputs in adequate quantities and within time is essential for the success of commercial projects. For example, to establish plantations successfully, supply of quality seedlings is a prerequisite. In the vast rain-fed tracts of our country, water is a major constraint for undertaking land-based commercial ventures.

Technology constraints

The lack of suitable technology and non-adoption of the available technology pose severe constraints. Technology is capable of easing some of the constraints. For example, tissue culture can solve the problem of non-availability of quality seedlings in adequate number. Water saving technologies such as drip/sprinkler irrigation can ease the water shortage in rain-fed areas to a large extent. Recent advances in information technology can bridge the information gaps in the agricultural marketing system.

Infrastructure constraints

Constraints on account of adequate infrastructure are galore in the agricultural marketing system in our country. Lack of roads, cold storage facilities, transport (including refrigerated transport) facilities, air cargo, pre-cooling, etc. are some of the problems plaguing the system. Inadequate post-harvest facilities relating to processing, grading, packing and erratic supply of electricity, etc. is also a major impediment. Delays in electrification are yet another important constraint.

Institutional constraints

The present level of the exploitation of agro-based hi-tech potential in the country has been observed to be very low. The supply of credit is inadequate to meet the demand notwithstanding the significant role played by NABARD and credit institutions. The lack of awareness among entrepreneurs, bank personnel and other implementing authorities about the relevance of hi-tech facilities and the absence of effective coordination among different agencies involved are the major constraints.

The existing provisions of the Land Ceiling Act in the country impede large scale cultivation. Most hi-tech and commercial ventures require large extent of area under cultivation to achieve the break-even point.

Socio-economic constraints

The socio-economic profile of our agriculturalists is not always conducive for adoption of new technology. As the green-revolution technology was scale neutral, it could enlist the participation of most of the farmers sooner or later, irrespective of farm size. However, the new commercial agricultural ventures are capital intensive, require in-depth knowledge and involve high degree of risk and hence, are not amenable for less educated individual farmers.

Summary

Agricultural marketing is vital for the development of rural India. The concept of marketable surplus is important to ascertain the quantity to be marketed. Agricultural marketing involves assembling, grading and standardization, processing, transporting, storage and distribution. Markets are variously classified. An important classification is one that identifies primary, secondary and terminal markets. An efficient marketing system enables farmers to realize fair prices and makes products available to final consumers at fair prices.

Several agencies are involved in the marketing of agricultural produce in the primary (village merchant, mobile traders and commission agents), secondary (processing and manufacturing units and wholesalers) and terminal markets (commercial analysts and shipping agents). The three channels of marketing of agricultural produce are the Government Channel (Producer > Government > Department > Consumer), the co-operative channel (Producer > Co-operatives > Consumer) and the private channel (Producer > Village merchant > Wholesaler > Commission agent (*dalal*) > Retailer > Consumer). To ensure fair play, state governments have passed the Agricultural Produce Marketing Committee Act and established regulated markets. The latest channel is the one influenced by ICT (for example, ITC e-*choupal*).

Sales take place in the terminal markets in a variety of ways. Some ways are *hatta* system, auction system (open or closed), private agreement, sale by sample, *dara* sale, *jalap* sale and *moghum* sale.

Agricultural financial requirements can be long term and short term. The sources of finance are institutional (commercial banks, co-operatives, regional rural banks and societies) and non-institutional (friends and relatives, mobile traders, small commission agents, wholesale commission agents and money lenders). Today, corporations are making an entry into farming through contract farming methods. Pepsi, Cadbury, Reliance, etc. have made a mark and contributed to rural prosperity. Commercialization of trade is important for wealth creation for farmers. However, it is limited not only by marketing constraints, but also by input–supply, technology, infrastructural, institutional barriers and socio-economic barriers.

Short Answer Questions

1. What is marketable surplus?
2. Define agricultural marketing.
3. List the functions of agricultural marketing.
4. Briefly explain one classification of agricultural markets.
5. Identify the agencies in the agricultural marketing system.
6. Explain any three methods of selling in terminal markets.
7. Explain the purpose of regulated markets.
8. How can ICT improve marketing of agricultural produce?
9. Identify the uses and sources of agricultural finance.
10. What is contract farming?
11. Explain in brief the agricultural operations of a corporate enterprise.
12. List the constraints to commercialization of agriculture.

Discussion Questions

1. The entry of corporate enterprises into agriculture will harm small and marginal farmers. Discuss.
2. Privatization of markets will lead to irregularities and fraudulent practices. Discuss.

Essay Questions

1. Explain the nature of the agricultural marketing system in India.
2. Describe the role of middlemen in different markets. How are sales made in terminal markets?
3. Explain the working of: (a) Regulated markets (b) ICT in agricultural marketing
4. Discuss the role of corporations in agricultural marketing.
5. What are the barriers to the commercialization of agriculture? How can they be removed?

Internet Exercise

Search for information on federations set up by the Government for promoting agricultural marketing and prepare a report.

Mini Project

Visit (a) village markets (b) *mandis* and prepare a report on their functioning.

End Notes

1. Vishnu Pandey, "Uttar Pradesh to Adopt PPP Model for Agricultural Marketing," *Business Standard*, 25 November 2009, available at www.business-standard.com/india/news/uttar-pradesh-to-adopt-ppp-model-for-agricultural-marketing/377537/.
2. "Agricultural Marketing," available at www.indiaagronet.com.
3. "Agricultural Marketing in India," available at www.world-agriculture.com/agricultural_marketing/agricultural-marketing.php.
4. M. S. Rao, "Problems and Prospects in Agricultural Marketing," 25 October 2008, available at http://profmsr.blogspot.com/2008/10/problems-and-prospects-in-agricultural.html.
5. Satyaveer Singh and Subah Singh Yadav, "A Road Map to Wholesale Market Infrastructure – PPP Model," available at www.afcindia.org.in/february_2010/chapter4.pdf.
6. "Marketing Systems: Functions, Agents, Enterprises and *Channels*," available at www.ilri.org/html/trainingMat/policy.../x5547e18.htm.
7. "Regulated Markets," available at www.agribusiness-atoz.com/html/RegulatedMarket.html; "Marketing Policies," available at www.agronet.com.
8. "Regulated Markets," available at www.cosamb.org/markets.html; "Agricultural *Marketing* and Storage." available at www.krishiworld.com/html/agri_storage1.html
9. "Let's Put India First," available at www.itcportal.com/rural-development/echoupal.htm.
10. Government of India, Ministry of Agriculture and Co-operation, Directorate of Marketing and Inspection, "Production and Marketing of Coconut in India, 2008," available at www.agmarknet.nic.in/ProductionCoconut.pdf.
11. "Cotton Marketing," available at www.ikisan.com/links/knt_cottonMarketing.shtml.
12. G. S. Chahal, "Agricultural Cooperation, Finance and Business Management," available at http://nsdl.niscair.res.in/bitstream/123456789/497/1/pdf+revised+cooperation+final.pdf.
13. Nihar Mohapatra, Tapas Ranjan Moharana and Subidita Pattanaik, "Corporate Sectors in Agribusiness: A Win–Win Business Model," 27 April 2009, available at www.indianmba.com/Faculty_Column/FC1005/fc1005.html.
14. K. J. S. Satyasai and K. U. Viswanathan, "Commercialization and Diversification of Indian Agriculture," 1997, available at www.nabard.org/fileupload/DataBank/.../OC%205.pdf.

Case 16.1 Corporatization of Agriculture

Time and again, experts have suggested measures to improve the competitiveness of Indian agriculture. At a workshop on "Agri-marketing in India: Opportunities and Challenges" organized by the Justice K. S. Hegde Institute of Management at Nitte in Udupi, experts emphasized the need for liberalization and private partnership in agricultural marketing.

The country should take advantage of its primary sector by going in for corporatization of agriculture production and marketing. Dr N. K. Thingalaya, chairman of the Academic Council of the institute, said, "In the WTO era, India can take advantage of its primary sector by corporatization of agricultural production and marketing and through public–private partnerships."

The structural inadequacies of Indian agriculture such as the small size of operational holdings and the insufficient infrastructure facilities are the hindrances in increasing the sector's contribution to a rapid growth. Corporate farming could be one of the processes that can be considered for improving the sector's efficiency. The workshop suggested that the feasibility of the corporate farming efforts made by some major corporations should be examined on a larger scale. However, the political sensitivity of its operational dynamics should be taken into consideration. The country has a competitive advantage for the marketing of agricultural produce in the global market. This advantage must be harnessed for the prosperity of rural India. Integrating farm business with production, processing and marketing may be necessary to ensure better value addition to the agricultural sector.

For discussion

1. Identify the proposed ways and purpose of liberalization and private partnerships in agriculture.
2. Do you think corporate farming is a sound approach in the WTO era? What other approaches can be examined and Why?

Source: "Corporatization of Agriculture Output, Marketing Emphasized," *The Hindu Business Line*, 26 April 2007, available at www.thehindubusinessline.com/2007/04/26/stories/2007042600942300.htm.

Case 16.2 Welcoming Private Markets

The agriculture ministry is considering providing liberal incentives to private entities to encourage them to set up wholly privately owned and operated markets for perishable farm produce, ending the state monopoly over agricultural marketing. At least 10 states, besides the Union Territory of Chandigarh, have already identified more than 30 sites for setting up private markets to be called terminal markets, for trading in fruit, vegetables and other perishable farm goods. Many States have gone a step ahead and invited "expressions of interest" from private companies, financial institutions and co-operatives for this purpose.

However, the response from the private sector has not been encouraging chiefly due to the paucity of incentives offered to them. The main sop at present is the option for equity participation (up to 49 per cent) by the state or central governments. The ministry is, therefore, considering additional incentives, which could be offered to make the scheme more attractive for the private entities. Under this novel initiative, aimed at reforming agricultural marketing, the proposed terminal markets with state-of-the-art facilities will be constructed by private enterprises with the support of selected financial institutions and the state governments. The market operators would be free to levy user charges for their services. The proposal for setting up the terminal markets under the National Horticulture Mission was approved by the Cabinet Committee on Economic Affairs (CCEA) in November 2006 paving the way for the state government to undertake the spadework for this purpose. The state governments have to identify land for such markets and create legal and regulatory framework by amending their Agricultural Produce Marketing Committee (APMC) Act for enabling private entrepreneurs to operate in the markets on a level playing field with existing markets.

About 13 states have responded and taken action. Eleven states have identified sites and many of them have held conferences with the potential participants and financial institutions to pave way for inviting formal expression-of-interest letters. The Agriculture Ministry has already circulated the operational guidelines of the scheme to the states that have amended their APMC Act to facilitate direct marketing and setting up of markets in the private sector. These private markets will have a "hub-and-spokes" format. Under this, the terminal market will constitute the hub that will be linked to a number of collection centres constituting the spokes, located in key production centres to facilitate easy access to markets by the farmers. The facilities to be provided at the markets will include electronic auctions, cold chain and logistics support from the primary collection centres located at convenient places. The markets will be set up by corporate or other private enterprises or by co-operatives themselves or through the outsourcing route. The concerned private entity could even be a consortium of entrepreneurs from agri-business sectors, cold stores, transporters, warehouses or other agri-infrastructure providers.

For discussion

1. Do you consider privatization of markets to be a good idea?
2. What kind of measures do you think are necessary to make them beneficial to farmers?

Source: Surinder Sud, "States Plan Incentives for Agri Marketing," *Business Standard*, 15 January 2008, available at www.business-tandard.com/india/storypage.php?autono=310737.

17

Marketing of Rural Industry Products

LEARNING OBJECTIVES

Upon completion of this chapter, you will be able to:

- Know the different artisan products and problems faced by artisans in marketing them
- Identify ways to improve the marketing of rural artisan products
- Understand the steps taken by the Government to promote rural tourism

The Government of India has come up with the idea of rural business hubs (RBHs) to connect rural producers and rural markets to national and international markets with the help of business houses. Being developed as an answer to China's successful "town and village enterprises" scheme, the hubs would aim at promoting agriculture and allied activities as growth engines for rural development and rural non-farming enterprises so that rural employment is generated.

Tie-ups: The central government has facilitated the signing of 50 MoUs between India Inc. and district-level institutions—mainly *gram panchayats*, and farm producers' associations—for the establishment of these hubs across select districts in Uttaranchal, UP, Tamil Nadu, Karnataka and Haryana in the first round.

Structure and roles: In terms of overall structure, the promoting partners of the hubs have the option of getting incorporated as a formal company under the Companies Act or getting registered as a partnership firm. *Panchayati*-level institutions are essentially being roped in to play the governance role, while technology and resources are to be mobilized by the respective business houses partnering them. The financing of these hubs is being envisaged as a self-sustaining business proposition on the public–private–*panchayat*–partnership principle and support is also envisaged from specialized institutions such as NABARD and KVIC.

Focus areas: The initial focus will be on the plantation of jatropha, fruit processing, seed production, organic food preparation, dairying, handicrafts and handlooms, brick-making and electricity generation through bio-mass. While ITC entered into an agreement for partnering 11 fruit processing hubs in Uttaranchal, DI Oils came forward to set up three jatropha plantations and bio-diesel hubs in Haryana. Another thrust area is handlooms and handicrafts.

SEWA has launched a handicrafts and handloom products hub in Uttar Pradesh and NIFT has proposed a RBH dealing in artwork and design of garments.[1]

The setting up of rural business hubs to promote rural products is one of the many initiatives taken by the government. A broad institutional network comprising corporations and government departments and boards has been created to support rural artisans and entrepreneurs. In this chapter, we discuss the various measures aimed at improving the lot of rural artisans and take a cursory glance at the promotion of rural tourism.

INTRODUCTION

The rural products of India are unique, innovative and attractive. A wide variety of products such as agriculture and household implements, handicraft items, food products, embroidery and clothes are manufactured in rural areas and offered for sale in urban markets. Among the products, the handicraft items that represent the unique skill and art form of rural artisans have significant attraction not only for metro buyers but, also for foreign nationals. They are appreciated for their "ethnic origin" and "indigenous design and appearance." They attract a premium in the market for these two features. Developing an appropriate marketing network and promoting rural products by highlighting their significant features has been a challenge for the Government, NGOs and rural entrepreneurs. Today, corporations are joining them to promote products of rural entrepreneurs and artisans.

ARTISANS AND PRODUCTS

The village small-industry sector consists broadly of two different segments.

i) Traditional industries (for example, handlooms, *khadi* and village industries and handicrafts, etc.)

ii) Modern small-scale industries (mills, factories, power looms, etc.)

The artisans comprise blacksmiths, carpenters, weavers (carpets, durries, *khesh*, *sarees*, etc.), potters, *mudha* makers, hand-tool makers, farm implement makers, metal-ware (silver, brass, copper) makers, sculptors (wood, metal clay, stone), handicraft makers, etc. The Task Force on Handicrafts for the eighth five-year plan in 1989 defined the term handicrafts as follows.

"Handicrafts are items made by hand, often with the use of simple tools, and are generally artistic and/or traditional in nature. They include objects of utility and objects of decoration."

The artisans are the heirs to tradition. Most craft people have learned their skills from their parents and grandparents as a continuity of tradition that is being passed on from one generation to another. They have made their regions proud of their work. Box 17.1 provides examples of craft category items that are unique to a specific region. Thus, the artisans, on the one hand, are regarded as custodians of the heritage of India, and on the other, they play an important role in village life through their repair and maintenance services.

ARTISANS LEFT BEHIND

As a socio-economic group, artisans are among the poorest. Research shows that households headed by artisans, in general, have much lower net wealth and almost all (90 per cent) are landless. While some of them have migrated to other occupations or become casual labourers, others are stuck with their traditional work technique due to the lack of required ability and mindset.

It has been revealed that the main cause behind the fruits of scientific and technological developments not reaching these artisans is their non-involvement in the rural development programmes.

Box 17.1 Crafts and their Ethnic Origins

***Kalamkari* paintings:** *Kalamkari* art is distinct in its form and usage of colours. *Kalamkari* paintings from Andhra Pradesh illustrate stories from Puranic legends and the famous epics—*Ramayan* and *Mahabharata*. The craft has been in existence in Kalahasti for several generations. All colours are fast and derived from plants, barks, flower seeds, leaves and roots of various plants. The Vaghri community of Gujarat also specializes in *Kalamkari* paintings. The outline is made on the cloth by a fine bamboo stick and different colours are filled with a date-palm stick brush.

Leather carving: The hand-carving tool on leather is popular in Auroville and Pondicherry. The terracotta leather enables the artist to execute carving and braiding work by hand. The item is coloured after carving and braiding. Gold embossed painting on leather has a unique charm of its own. The leather is pasted on iron and wood, geometrical drawings are made and flowers, leaves, and figures are drawn with a thin pen brush. A specially prepared paste made from *guggal*, *sakkar*, gum, and fenugreek solution is applied on the drawings. Thin and fine pieces of gold are pasted on leather with sugar solution and enamel paint.

Metal: Jaipur is the hub for chased, engraved, enamelled, lacquered and encrusted metalware. A wide range of items, including vases, perforated lamps, table tops, fruit bowls, planters, jewellery boxes and picture frames can be found. Ink wells, pen cases, styluses, compasses and holders are the other outstanding brass, iron or silver items found in Rajasthan.

Source: www.craftandartisans.com, accessed March 2010.

The scattered and diverse nature of this industry has prevented politicians and policy makers in India from understanding or formulating effective policies or strategies by which this segment of the population can be made part of a general advancement.

Recognizing the significance of the role of rural artisans in shaping the growth and development of the country, the National Institute of Science, Technology and Development Studies (NISTADS) undertakes science and technology (S&T) studies for the weaker sections with a focus on rural artisans and research and development (R&D) personnel, on the one hand, and development functionaries on the other. Several such studies have been carried out. The insights obtained from rural artisans are listed below.[2]

- *Government negligence:* Non-coverage under agricultural relief programmes and non-involvement in rural development programmes.
- *Lack of opportunities:* Lack of skill improvement and technology upgradation opportunities, lack of specialized markets, non-availability of quality raw materials, lack of proper infrastructural facilities and lack of linkages with development institutions and banks.
- *Individual weaknesses:* Weak financial power and poor communication skills.

MARKETING PROBLEMS OF ARTISANS

The artisans continuing in their occupations could not market their products successfully due to various reasons discussed here.

Product-side problems

The products of artisans have becomes less competitive. Skills of rural artisans continue to be old and the technology used is traditional. Mass-produced factory goods are preferred because of their standardization, modernity and low prices.

Modern technology has enabled machines to imitate even the most intricate designs that were once the exclusive domain of the artisans, developed and perfected over centuries and passed down from generation to generation. Though artisans are creative, they do not risk innovations. Any form of innovation implies an element of risk and investment of capital. Given that most Indian artisans live on the margin of subsistence, they have virtually no reserves to invest in technological innovations (physical capital). Further, rural artisans lack guidance in product design and development based on an understanding of the demand of the market. Due to lack of market research facilities and urban exposure they tend to be product oriented and not customer oriented.

Price-side problems

Artisans face price disadvantages. For instance, cheap plastic products have wiped out the market for earthenware. Artisans cannot charge lower prices than mill-made products because of the following problems.

High raw material costs

The infrastructure with which rural artisans produce their handicrafts is quite inadequate in comparison to what is required to satisfy consumer demand. For example, in the carpet industry, small producers who make handmade carpets compete for the same supplies with large factories. The large-scale economies of buying put the large producers in an advantageous position.

High interest rate

As more than 90 per cent of rural artisan households are landless, they have minimal resources to mortgage or use land as collateral for a loan. In such situations, informal credit plays a critical role in the production and expansion of artisan's enterprise. They are forced to take loans from local middlemen and moneylenders at exorbitant rates of interest.

Place-side problems

Craftspeople who reside in small distant villages find it difficult to access urban areas and metro cities that are now the main markets for craft products. The middlemen exploit them as they are only interested in maximizing their margins.

Exhibitions, fairs and handicraft stores are now prevalent in much larger numbers than they were earlier. Still more needs to be done.

Promotion-side problems

Artisans do not have strong communication and promotion skills. The economic status of artisans is far from satisfactory and this makes their advertising power weak. Their education level is low and they lack exposure to information and communication technology. Their shyness, weak communication skills and tendency to remain “small” and “satisfied” are major barriers to personal selling. Heavy competition from modern and large industries (high-tech products with heavy advertising and promotion) obviously negate their chances of promotion.

INSTITUTIONAL FRAMEWORK FOR DEVELOPMENT

Central and state government entities, voluntary non-government organizations and co-operatives are working together to help artisans to improve their lives. The reasons for promoting crafts are:

- The crafts sector contributes to foreign exchange earnings through exports.
- It provides additional earning opportunities for the rural population, especially during the weak agricultural seasons. It adds to the overall disposable income of the rural economy.
- It is labour intensive and investment in this sector can provide more employment than large industries. For every rupee of value added in this sector, the capital required is roughly one-third of what is needed in larger industries.
- Rural art, based on the tradition of centuries is the manifestation of the culture of a region.

There are widespread institutional networks of different organizations that exist to support rural artisans. These organizations have been established at all levels and for almost all product categories. The nature of these organizations varies from being a commission set up by an act of Parliament, to a board, corporation or a registered society, etc. The list of the organizations set up with an objective for promoting the cause of artisans is given below.

R&D institutions

- Indian Agricultural Research Institute (IARI)
- National Institute of Science, Technology and Development Studies (NISTADS)
- Advanced Materials and Process Research Institute (AMPRI)
- Central Institute of Agricultural Engineering (CIAE)
- Central Leather Research Institute (CLRI)
- Central Food Technological Research Institute (CFTRI)
- Central Glass and Ceramic Research Institute (CGCRI)

Financial and marketing institutions

- National Bank for Agricultural and Rural Development (NABARD)
- *Khadi* Village and Industries Commission (KVIC)
- Central Co-operative Bank (CCB)
- District Industries Centre (DIC)

Technical training institutions

- Indian Agricultural Research Institute (IARI)
- Central Institute of Agricultural Engineering (CIAE)
- Central Leather Research Institute (CLRI)
- Central Food Technological Research Institute (CFTRI)
- National Bank for Agricultural and Rural Development (NABARD)
- Haryana Institute of Rural Development (HIRD)

Advisory boards

Different boards have been set up to advice governments in policy making.

- The All India Handicrafts Board
- All India Handloom Board

- Central Silk Board
- Jute Advisory Board

Corporations

Various corporations have been established to promote quality production and to lend marketing support to artisans.

- The Handicrafts and Handlooms Export Corporation of India (HHEC)
- The North-Eastern Handicrafts and Handloom Development Corporation Ltd [NEHHDC]
- The Central Cottage Industries Corporation Pvt. Ltd (CCIC)
- The All India Handloom Fabrics Marketing Co-operative Society Ltd

Government offices

- Office of the Development Commissioner for Handlooms
- Office of the Development Commissioner for Handicrafts

All India associations

There are all-India organizations for India's three most popular handicrafts items—hand-printed textiles, carpets and *zari*. These associations serve as platforms for consultations among manufacturers and exporters on the one hand and the Handicrafts Board on the other. The board uses the following associations to disseminate information useful to craftsmen:

- All India Carpet Manufacturers Association, Varanasi district, UP
- All India Federation of *Zari* Industry, Surat, Gujarat
- All India Textile Hand-printing Industries Federation, Mumbai

State and Union Territories corporations/departments

The Central Government provides grants and loans to encourage the states to boost the production and sale of their handicrafts. The states in turn assist particular sets of handicraft producers and products depending upon the number of people engaged in them and the market potential the products have. Each state and union territory has a department looking after development and promotion of handicrafts. Many states including Arunachal Pradesh, Daman and Diu, Delhi and Goa have public-sector corporations for marketing handicraft products. A few state corporations dealing with small-scale industries and other products have taken up marketing and export promotion of handicrafts.

Voluntary organizations

Certain voluntary organizations are running regional handicrafts training institutes for women under the all India Handicrafts Board.

- Handicrafts Teacher's Training College (the Arts and Crafts Society), Mumbai
- Regional Training Institute of Handicrafts (*Bharat Sevak Samaj*), Dharwar, Maharashtra
- Regional Handicrafts Training Institute for Women (Andhra *Mahila Sabha*), Hyderabad
- Regional Handicrafts Training Institute for Women (*Karma Kutir*), Kolkata

DEVELOPMENT MEASURES

Development of rural artisans requires a two-pronged approach—(i) improving the socio-economic conditions of artisans and (ii) strengthening the production and marketing of their units.

Inclusive development programmes

The government rural development programmes should include rural artisans for improving their living conditions.

Participatory approach in all rural development programmes

The government policies need to consider livelihood approaches that put the people at the centre of development projects and take a wider and better informed view of the opportunities and constraints that characterize the lives of the artisans. This will increase the effectiveness of the different developmental measures taken up by the government for the rural artisans.

Social security support

Just as farmers and other weaker sections are provided relief and support in the form of subsidies, loan waivers and pension schemes, artisans should also be considered for such preferential treatment.

Organizing artisan groups

Organized artisans would be in a better position if a good business plan is evolved to approach financial institutions for obtaining financial support and marketing agencies to market their goods.

The alternative approaches to organizing are:

Organizing into self-help groups (SHGs)

Village artisans can be organized into self-help groups. The organized effort will help them to develop better produce and enjoy the benefits of economies of scale. So far, 1.5 million self-help groups have been formed for 3.7 million artisans.

Formation of co-operative societies of craftsmen

Craftsmen can come together in the form of registered co-operative societies to protect and promote their interests.

Formation of a trust

A trust can be formed by a local NGO or a corporate enterprise interested in marketing the products of artisans and improving their living conditions. It can help artisans in marketing and production for some time. The trust can facilitate the formation of an organized group with a distinct organizational structure when the group members become capable and resourceful.

Technical education and training

Training and education aims at enhancing the craft skills as well as the entrepreneurial skills of rural artisans. Provisions for entrepreneurial training for rural artisans can help them manage their micro-enterprises in a better manner. The training programmes can be conducted by different government agencies and co-operative organizations. Supply of Improved Toolkits to Rural Artisans (SITRA) was launched in July 1992, as a sub-scheme of Integrated Rural Development Programme (IRDP) and a number of crafts persons were supplied improved hand tools within a financial ceiling. The rural artisans are trained under the Training of Rural Youth for Self-Employment (TRYSEM) scheme.[3] Box 17.2 explains the efforts of the *Khadi* and Village Industries Commission (KVIC) to organize artisans.

Box 17.2 KVIC Organizes Artisans

The *Khadi* and Village Industries Commission (KVIC) took two villages in Orissa in its fold under the cluster-village programme. Through the programmes, it was decided to encourage the leather industry in Jayapur and bamboo craft in Erkana village. The Commission is supporting the artisans of these two villages by providing training to further sharpen their professional competencies. They are being trained in the use of new technology. High-end technical support is provided to these artisans. About 534 rural entrepreneurs have been selected by the Commission to set up small-scale industries. KVIC has a good track record of having set up 4,853 small-scale units in Orissa under the National Rural Employment Generation Programme. In the direction of social welfare, its initiatives include insuring rural entrepreneurs. It has insured 1,220 rural entrepreneurs under the *Janashree Bima Yojana.*

Source: www.orissalinks.com, accessed April 2010.

Credit facilities

A capital fund for purchasing raw material and assisting with wages when stock is being prepared can be of great help to rural craftsmen. Credit facility can be of vital help for innovative artisans to overcome technological obsolescence and undertake quality production. Two types of instruments are to be considered by commercial banks:

- Collateral-free loan facilities based on marketing opportunities and viability of project.
- Artisans' credit cards—just like the *Kisan* credit cards, artisans may be considered for extending credit facility.

MARKETING INITIATIVES

Various initiatives are being considered and introduced by the Government and NGOs. We discuss some of the important ones here.

Awareness meets and market research

Rural artisans need to be aware about consumer lifestyles and the traditional product fit for manufacturing their product range. At least, informal market research has to be conducted to understand the changes in the preferences of customers with respect to colour, shape and design. This can be done by participating in fairs and exhibitions where artisans can interact with the customers directly with respect to their needs and preferences. Box 17.3 presents the initiative taken by the Development Commissioner Handicrafts, Ministry of Textiles in Kashmir.

Agencies

Entrepreneurs and artisans can market their products on their own or through co-operatives. The state can do it for them through its procurement agencies. Today, developmental thinking on market linkages has reached stage three—linkages through companies or industries.

- *Co-operatives:* While this is conceptually a sound approach, the success achieved by co-operatives is limited. The institutions slowly got corrupted.

Box 17.3 Workshop for Creating Awareness

A state-level workshop on handicrafts was organized by the Development Commissioner Handicrafts, Ministry of Textiles, Kashmir with the aim of creating awareness about different schemes. Hundreds of artisans, stakeholders including NGOs and entrepreneurs participated in the workshop. Bindoo Ranjan, design consultant, National Institute of Design (NID), Ahmedabad, deliberated on the importance of design development in handicrafts marketing and diversification in designing. "There is need to adopt improved technology and brand building in handicrafts," Ranjan said. Afrooza, of ICICI Lombard spoke on various aspects of the Rajiv Gandhi *Shilpi Swasthya Bima Yojana* (RGSSBY). ICICI Lombard had also arranged a health camp on the occasion. The workshop was followed by a question–answer session. It was resolved that all grievances would be redressed for effective implementation of the schemes.

Source: www.greaterkashmir.com, accessed April 2010.

Box 17.4 Urban *Haat*

The State-owned Handicrafts Development Corporation (Poompuhar) set up a one-stop outlet at Mahabalipuram to promote the interests of the state's artisans and their handicrafts. Touted as an "urban *haat*" (market) along the lines of the famed "*Dilli haat*" in New Delhi, the outlet was set up on a four-acre piece of land owned by the Tourism Department. It will allow the nearly 0.65 million artisans in Tamil Nadu to display and sell their wares directly to foreign and domestic tourists. "There will be 140 to 150 stalls. We will keep changing the theme to accommodate all artisans," said D. Rajendran, the chairman and managing director of the Tamil Nadu Handicrafts Development Corporation. It provides space for shelf display, dormitories for artisans, an exhibition hall, food courts and public convenience facilities.

Source: Sandhya Soman, "'Urban *Haat*' Planned at Mahabalipuram," *The Hindu*, 13 September 2006, available at www.hindu.com/2006/09/13/stories/2006091302710600.htm.

- *Government agencies:* As for the linkages provided by the state, these offer uncertain sustainability. Bureaucrats are in a hurry to promote the artisans when the concerned minister or politician is interested. Their interest wanes when ministers and politicians lose interest. Further, they lack the marketing and technical skills needed to support the artisans.
- *Industries:* Given this context, one can conclude that profit-oriented industry linkages are a more sustainable and a more scalable alternative. To make an effective market linkage, industries can play a significant role. Companies can use the social infrastructure (self-help groups, etc.) as an alternative procurement and distribution chain and vice versa. This initiative of industries will also strengthen the backward and forward linkages of the rural market, besides accelerating the innovation of rural products.

Retail centres

The state governments can help organized co-operatives of craftsmen to establish retail outlets in the cities where there is good demand for rural craftwork. Specific markets for artisans such as *Anaaj Mandies* may be encouraged. Box 17.4 describes the initiatives of the Tamil Nadu government to eliminate middlemen.

Exhibitions and fairs

Exhibitions and fairs create a direct interface between customers and producers. They improve the opportunities for craftsmen to (i) sell their products, (ii) book orders and (iii) obtain formal and informal feedback from actual and potential customers.

Exhibitions by government bodies

The Ministry of Rural Development has decided to hold exhibitions of products made by SHGs at regional and national levels.

Regional craft-based fairs

Since 2003, the Government has been conducting regional fairs that have so far covered Delhi in the north, Hyderabad in the south, Mumbai in the west and Bhubaneshwar and Guwahati in the east. Box 17.5 discusses how fairs are held and how they have benefited artisans.

International fairs and exhibitions

The Indian diaspora and international citizens can become aware of the rich cultural heritage and unique crafts of India by visiting international festivals such as India Day Celebration in Washington, etc. where products by Indian artisans are put on display. In addition to immediate sales on the site, the other benefit is the promotion of rural tourism.

Museums

Museums arouse curiosity and the desire to possess products that we like the most. The National Handlooms and Handicrafts Museum (NHHM) was established at *Pragati Maidan*, New Delhi. NHHM is spread over a sprawling area of 5 acres. It comprises about 20,000 rare and distinctive pieces reflecting the excellence of Indian craftsmen. It is an important showcase and promotional platform for the artwork of artisans from across the country.

Box 17.5 International Fairs—An Opportunity

Organized jointly by the Ministry of Rural Development and the Council for Advancement of People's Action and Rural Technology (CAPART), the annual SARAS–2007 at India International Trade Fair (IITF) displayed a variety of products prepared by rural artisans, self-help groups and NGOs. The SARAS movement began in 2003–2004. So far, 67 fairs have been organized exhibiting a variety of rural products under one roof, providing an opportunity for sales.

Ram Kishor Raiger, a rural leather artisan, observes, "We were surviving in the bounded areas of our village through small local sales. The Endogenous Tourism Project (ETP) has given us the chance to display our art and craft skills across the country. Due to these opportunities, our art and economic level has improved." From 16–27 February 2008, crafts persons from 18 different ETP sites of the country got the opportunity to sell and demonstrate their arts and crafts at the Toshali National Crafts Mela organized in Bhubaneswar by Orissa Tourism, supported by the Ministry of Tourism, the government of India and the United Nation's Development Programme (UNDP).

Source: Raghuvansh Prasad Singh, "Rural Artisans Need Support in the Era of Global Marketing," November 2007, available at http://rural.nic.in/publication/Nov2007/gb_nov_eng07.pdf; "Toshali National Crafts Mela," available at www.orissatourism.gov.in/new/Toshali_ekram.htm.

Telemarketing

Different tele-shopping companies operate all over the world offering various types of giftware and handicrafts, jewellery, fashion, health and beauty products, household and consumer goods, collectibles and home accessories.

Web marketing

e-Marketing has caught the imagination of consumers the world over and it is worth Rs 370 billion annually. It is a very effective tool to establish an organization without the help of intermediaries. This media can be of great use for obtaining orders from new customers and repeat orders from regular customers. Organizations (SHGs, co-operatives) can create their Web sites or Web pages to display information about their products to the entire world. The development and promotion agencies of the government can use this to market the products and educate artisans.[4] Box 17.6 showcases the efforts of development agencies.

EXPORT MARKETING

Craftsmen can explore the export markets if they organize themselves by forming SHGs or co-operative societies. The export councils set up by the government will also assist the artisan groups.[5] Box 17.7 discusses the initiatives of the Export Council for Handicrafts (EPCH).

We will now outline the steps involved in organizing the export marketing effort.

Market identification

National level commissions, boards, corporations and export promotion councils can conduct research with respect to the different markets where particular handicraft products have potential for exports. They can also enable the select handicraft organizations or artisans to display their products in the exhibitions that are organized in different countries from time to time.

Awareness of export regulations

Artisan groups, planning entry into export markets, need to know the export procedures and agencies that help them.

Box 17.6 e-Marketing Portal

The Central Cottage Industries Corporation of India Ltd (CCIC) and the Handicraft and Handlooms Export Corporation of India Ltd (HHEC) have jointly developed an e-marketing platform. The portal presents high-quality graphic displays of a wide variety of handicrafts and handlooms products along with their description, origin and place of production. Procurement is made easy, with a single-window gateway, easy navigation in a customized interface, e-payment facility through major debit/credit cards, online tracking of the shipment and a transparent redressal mechanism. The Web sites of the Office of the Development Commissioner (Handlooms) and National Institute of Fashion Technology (NIFT) with regional language interface facility, display about 1,500 free, downloadable contemporary designs. They help weavers and artisans in developing latest products and enable them to capture both domestic and export markets.

Source: "Mr Maran Unveils e-Marketing Portal for Handicraft and Handloom Goods," 20 August 2009, available at www.fibre2fashion.com/news/association-news/ministry-of-textiles-india/newsdetails.aspx?news_id=76291.

Box 17.7 Exports of Handicrafts

Inspite of being a low-value portfolio in the country's exports basket of USD 170 billion, handicrafts exports employ seven million people. Millions of artisans have been facing tough times due to a demand slump in major international markets. Exports declined by 48.35 per cent to about USD 1.8 billion in 2008–2009 and have contracted by 24.58 per cent to USD 789.30 million till August 2009.

The Foreign Trade Policy of 2009–2014 has also encouraged handicraft exporters in the direction of new markets. In the policy, provisions have been made to allow all handicraft exports to be considered as special focus products that attract an incentive of 5 per cent duty credit scrip. Additionally, 52 items have been added in the special focus products, while the market-linked focus product scheme has been expanded to incentivize exports to Algeria, Egypt, South Africa and Brazil.

The Export Council for Handicrafts (EPCH) has adopted a three-pronged strategy, including capacity development, design enhancement and aggressive marketing to boost exports. It is diversifying its export basket by tapping emerging markets such as Latin America and Africa, among others. EPCH is organizing a number of awareness programmes on quality improvement for handicrafts, including technology upgrade for workshops, packaging, ISO bar-coding, statutory compliance and quality control measures. It is also setting up 25 common facility centres at important handicraft clusters. Besides, several new clusters are being provided the status of "town of excellence."

Source: www.infodriveindia.com, accessed April 2010.

Development product literature

They have to develop brochures displaying and describing the range of products. The information should be in English as well as in the native language of the target market.

Choosing the right channel

The alternative channels that can be employed by the handicraft organization for exports are as follows:

- *Wholesalers:* Tie-up with specialized wholesalers having a narrower but in-depth range of handicraft products.
- *Importers/distributors:* Most Indian handicrafts companies use importers/distributors to market and sell their handicrafts lines.
- *Commission agents:* Independent commission agents working on around 15 per cent commission provide Indian companies with direct access to the market and direct control.
- *Department stores:* Department stores prefer to deal directly with manufacturers. Their buyers are very specialized and only handle a limited range of products. Artisan groups may establish business contacts with the buyers.
- *Mail order:* The mail-order houses in foreign countries may be contacted to secure orders for the products.
- *Web marketing:* By placing product information on a Web site, artisan groups can create awareness and promote sales.

Box 17.8 Success Story of Lepakshi

Lepakshi is the name of a temple town in Andhra Pradesh that is reputed for its beautiful sculptures created during the Vizianagaram dynasty. With such a well known name, Lepakshi retail outlets set up by the Andhra Pradesh Handicrafts Development Corporation Ltd (APHDCL) for marketing handicrafts gained not only a brand image but also a high ranking in the hierarchy of other handicraft brands such as Cauvery or Kairali or PoomPuhar. In the export markets, "Made in India" is a prestigious label to market handicraft products and the good news is that Lepakshi of Andhra Pradesh Handicrafts Development Corporation Ltd (APHDCL) got a geographical indicator (GI) status. In all, there are nine products with GI status under Lepakshi's umbrella and another 10 are in the pipeline.

Enthused by the success, the corporation has evolved plans to open franchisees in overseas markets. To start with, it has initiated steps to open franchisees in the US market. Though the markets are dull due to recessionary trends, surprisingly, there is a lot of demand for items from the Lepakshi brand and the corporation is making efforts to improve sales by conducting exhibitions. In Chile and Hong Kong, there is a huge demand for red sanders products for its auspiciousness in these countries. In the domestic market, the corporation is planning to set up stores in the premises of important temples.

The support given by APHDCL to about 0.2 million artisans of the state is manifold. Lepakshi, with its brand status and favourable markets, is helping to market the artisans' products overseas. To ensure quality production and right supplies, the corporation is providing unique and exquisite designs taking the help of Indian Institute of Crafts and Designs, Jaipur. Artisans are provided with newer and more modern designs that would help to revive the rich heritage of the state.

The soaring prices of raw materials is a problem area. To resolve this, the government of India has allocated about Rs 0.01 billion as a grant for setting up a "raw material bank" that has the capacity to store about 50 tonnes of teak wood and red sanders wood. Taking this opportunity, APHDCL has set up a "raw material bank" and the State Forest Department is making the necessary procurements. With this arrangement, raw materials are made available to the artisans at concessional rates. Other measures include training programmes to develop latest designs and toolkits, cash awards every year to encourage the artisans, insurance worth Rs 0.2 million and medical reimbursement up to Rs 15,000 a year.

So far, APHDCL has set up 18 Lepakshi showrooms, including two outside the state in Kolkata and Delhi. Every year, the corporation holds about 100 exhibitions at different places in the country to promote sales. Established in 1982, the corporation has made good progress and has set an ambitious target of achieving business worth Rs 0.65 million in 2009–2010.

Source: B. V. Mahalakshmi, "Andhra Pradesh's Handicraft Brand Lepakshi Gets GI Status," *The Financial Express*, 26 April 2009, available at www.financialexpress.com/news/andhrapradeshshandicraftbrandlepakshigetsgistatus/451209/; "More Lepakshi Showrooms to be Opened in State," *The Hindu*, 20 June 2009, available at www.thehindu.com/2009/06/20/stories/2009062058970200.htm.

Promoting selectively

Different markets will have different preferences. An understanding of "what sells where" is important to direct marketing efforts. Artisan groups have to adopt niche marketing approaches based on market research data and feedback from international exhibitions.

Building a brand name

The importance of building a brand name need not be overemphasized. Brand building is possible only when a concerted effort is made to promote a group of products. Box 17.8 presents the successful case of brand building by Lepakshi.

ROLE OF NGOS

The economic reforms and liberalization saw the Government vacating several areas to let private-sector entrepreneurship flourish and contribute to the growth of the economy. A similar paradigm shift is needed to transform NGOs from their dependence on aid and grants from within and outside for transforming the rural scenario in the country. This is sought to be achieved by engaging them in micro-finance and micro-entrepreneurship activities for the overall development of the rural areas and to promote the welfare of the people of rural India. The role of NGOs in training and financing rural entrepreneurs and artisans as well as promoting the sales of the products is significant. Box 17.9 illustrates their contribution.

Box 17.9 Retail Outlets Managed by NGOs

Samruddhi is a different kind of shop managed by Rural Innovations Network, an NGO. *Samruddhi* means prosperity in Sanskrit. Tamil Nadu has only two *Samruddhis*—one in Kasipalayam and another in T. N. Palayam, both near Erode. *Samruddhi* showcases 18 products developed by people in rural areas. The products were innovatively developed by the people to meet their needs and not with a commercial motive. The products on display include a cost-effective stove that burns on pellets made from waste, a paddy seeding machine, a battery-operated power sprayer, a low-cost milking machine, small devices to increase fuel efficiency in LPG stoves, etc. Both the stores depend on *Samruddhi Ammas* and *Aiyas* for selling their products. The shops have four *Aiyas* and eight *Ammas* who bring them business. There are field-level executives who oversee the operations. The shops need a monthly sale of Rs 0.15 million each to break even.

Women in Banaskantha have a rich heritage of crafts; the Aahirs are known for their fine embroidery, the Rabari women for beautiful mirror work, the Mochis make attractive leather items and the Harijans do patchwork and beadwork. A craft development centre set up at Radhanpur provides skill training, design documentation, product development, supply of raw materials and marketing. A Delhi-based organization, *Dastakar*, has played a committed role in developing the Craft Development Centre with support received from the Development Commissioner (Handicrafts) of the Government of India.

SEWA has set up a direct marketing outlet, Banas Craft, in one of the main commercial areas of Ahmedabad to build up a good market for their products.

Source: Karthik Madhavan, "Marketing Innovative Products and Providing Employment—Samruddhi Does it All," *The Hindu*, 04 November 2007, available at www.hindu.com/2007/11/04/stories/2007110454960500.htm.

Box 17.10 Rural Tourism

The government of Rajasthan has sanctioned Rs 0.015 billion for promoting rural tourism sensing the opportunities in the segment. The Department of Tourism of Rajasthan has picked up three villages—Khejdli and Khichan in Jodhpur and Sorsen at Baran—for the same. The three places offer three different attractions. Demoiselle Cranes flock at Kichan during winters and are a major attraction for tourists. Sorsen, in addition to flocking birds, offers blackbuck sights. Khejdli is famous for the stories of human sacrifice to save trees. A fair that is organized during winters is drawing a lot of foreign tourists to the small town.

Changes in sightseeing interests are being recognized by analysts. It is found that people are no longer interested in sites showcasing monuments, handicrafts, architecture, heritage, etc. They are interested in going beyond regular tourism and love seeing places that offer a rustic aura.

The government is drafting plans to promote eco-tourism in suitable areas and building the required infrastructure such as roads and amenities to ensure access, comfort and affordability. The Rajasthan Tourism Development Corporation (RTDC) has been entrusted with the responsibility of creating the required infrastructure such as connecting roads to these villages, sanitation facilities and toilets and resting spots for visitors. It is believed that the development of these places would not only promote tourism but, will also provide employment to the locals and improve the economy of the rural areas.

Source: "Government Bets Big on Rural Tourism," *The Times of India*, 19 December 2009.

MARKETING OF RURAL TOURISM

India has a culturally rich heritage. In its tourism policy of 2002, the government initiated steps for promoting rural tourism so that the economic benefits from tourism can reach the rural regions. Developing rural tourism usually means showcasing the ethnic arts, crafts, culture and lifestyle in its traditional setting and providing a platform for tourists to experience this. It also means promoting the concept of home-stays in the host community. However, more importantly, success lies in how well the rural youth is trained in dealing with international and domestic tourists and maintaining tourism sites.

The government of India in the Tenth Plan identified tourism as one of the major sources for generating employment and promoting sustainable livelihoods. The Union Ministry of Tourism, in collaboration with UNDP, has launched the Endogenous Tourism Project linked to the existing rural tourism schemes of the government. Box 17.10 explains how the Department of Tourism of Rajasthan has developed rural tourist places.

Summary

Rural products are unique because of their ethnic origin and indigenous design. Marketing them is a big challenge for the government, NGOs and artisans. Products crafted by artisans have a wide range and represent a specific region. Artisans are economically backward and less equipped with marketing skills. Both the Central and the State Governments have taken initiatives such as setting up of institutions, corporations and offices and allocating funds for various development and marketing schemes. The important marketing initiatives are organizing urban *haats*, setting up specialized showrooms, holding exhibitions and training of artisans. Export marketing is promoted by setting up export agencies and encouraging participation of artisans in international fairs. NGOs are not only encouraging appropriate technological innovations but, also showcasing them through retail stores set up by them in urban areas. Another important aspect of rural promotion is rural tourism. Tourism is promoted by eco-tourism projects being operated on a PPP model.

Short Answer Questions

1. What are artisan products?
2. What is the economic status of artisans?
3. Why could artisans not sell their unique products?
4. Outline the measures initiated by the Government to improve socio-economic conditions of artisans.
5. List the marketing tools used to promote artisan products.
6. How do you promote export marketing of artisan products?
7. How is rural tourism promoted by the government?
8. Explain the role of NGOs in the marketing of artisan products.

Discussion Questions

1. Marketing of rural artisan products begins with the development of artisans and ends with brand building. Discuss.
2. Rural tourism sells experiences and not only material artefacts. Discuss.

Essay Questions

1. Explain the opportunities for marketing of artisan products. Examine the problems faced by artisans in selling their products.
2. Explain the role of the Government and NGOs in promoting rural products.
3. How is rural tourism promoted in our country? Suggest measures to improve it.

Internet Exercises

1. Visit the Web site of one of the handicraft promotion boards and prepare a note on its activities related to the promotion of artisan products.
2. Visit the Web site of the Directorate of Tourism (DOT) of State and prepare a paper on "rural tourism—role of DOT."

Mini Project

Visit two nearby villages and find out the products sold to urban markets. Prepare a report on the existing system of marketing and methods to improve it.

End Notes

1. Anil Sasi, "Rural Biz Hubs: 50 MoUs Inked with District Level Bodies," *The Hindu Business Line*, 26 December 2006, available at www.thehindubusinessline.com/2006/12/26/stories/2006122603480100.htm.
2. S. S. Solanki, "Unorganized Sector of Workers: Rural Artisans," available at www.nistads.res.in/indiasnt2008/t6rural/t6rur5.htm.
3. "Poverty Alleviation in Rural India: Programmes and Strategy," available at http://planningcommission.nic.in/plans/planrel/fiveyr/9th/vol2/v2c2-3.htm.
4. Rajveer Singh, "Direct Marketing of Artisanal Products Through the Internet," available at www.idrc.ca/en/ev-83705-201-1-DO_TOPIC.html.
5. Raghuvansh Prasad Singh,"Rural Artisans Need Support in the Era of Global Marketing," available at http://rural.nic.in/publication/Nov2007/gb_nov_eng07.pdf.

Case 17.1 Promoting Rural Products

The need for generating employment for rural artisans and promoting profitable and sustained development of traditional industries is well recognized by the government, NGOs and other development agencies in the country. However, a look at the current marketing scenario indicates that many of the marketing issues have not yet been resolved to the desired level. Issues such as demand assessment, brand identification, product promotions, etc. are still in the evolutionary stage, calling for sophistication and professionalism. It is important to take stock of the attempts made so far in the direction of supporting artisans before thinking about future directions.

Stock Taking

The initiatives can be examined as those related to the advancement of artisans and promotion of traditional handicrafts.

Artisan-focused Initiatives

Government bodies as well as NGOs have taken steps to provide training to the artisans to improve their skills in making their products and using simple machines, setting up work sheds and providing residential space. Some states have availed of foreign aid, for example, the Indo-Dutch Karnataka Industrial Sheds Project. Like many welfare programmes, the efforts in this direction were subjected to scathing criticisms on aspects such as the quality of the sheds, the agencies responsible for construction, the procedural delays and injustice in case of the selection of beneficiaries, the indifference of officials and development agents and on social aspects (medical care, social infrastructure and the subordinate role of women).

Many welfare programmes are designed and implemented for the welfare of the people in rural areas. As there is no special recognition of the category of artisans, in many a case, they are grouped along with agricultural labourers and non-farm workers. As a result, it is complained that the cultural carriers are often subject to negligence.

Analysis of institutional credit given to artisans reveals that a base is created by the participating institutions like co-operatives, RRBs and commercial banks. However, the contribution is still marginal.

Handicrafts-marketing Focused Initiatives

The measures taken to market the products appear to be in the right direction, however, the results are not impressive.

Availability—local to global: Most rural artisans are used to selling their products in local rural *haats*. The selling opportunities have now increased with the involvement of NGOs and the governments at various levels. They have helped in promoting the sale of these products outside the confines of the local environs at *melas*, exhibitions and fairs. The products have moved from villages to major urban centres and even to foreign countries.

Awareness and preferences: The diversity of Indian culture led to the creation of diversified products that represent the regional cultures and locally-available raw materials. Each state has a rich heritage of art and craft to market to the domestic as well as foreign tourists. Therefore, in many states, government bodies were created to devote time to market "culture" and the "artisan products," working in close association with tourism and archaeological departments. They are expected to create awareness and preference for the products and tourist locations. This would encourage rural tourism on one side and sale of artisan products on the other. In some states, the government bodies were asked to set the example by extending preferential treatment to the artisan products at the time of procurement. Different avenues for employment are being explored for rural artisans. For instance, the government of Andhra Pradesh set up an animation academy to train rural artisans as animators.

Challenges

A general assessment of the situation of artisans and the marketing of handicrafts reveals that as an entrepreneur, the individual or the group of rural artisans need attention and support. The development challenge is based on the following observations:

- Most of the products are still sold at the local rural *haats*. This means that the products have limited demand in terms of quantity and quality and do not fetch a good price. As a result, the skills of artisans are not put to right use, incomes are low and the quality of life is poor.
- Awareness building is not fully effective or far reaching, not only in global markets but also in domestic markets. Barring occasional advertisements by the promotion agencies, publicity by the Government on special occasions and periodic exhibitions and *melas*, there is no devoted and concerted exercise in creating awareness of "culture" and "artisan products."
- To facilitate availability at different locations, exhibitions and *melas* are utilized. In addition, urban *haats* are also set up. Cultural programmes are organized to create an atmosphere of enthusiasm to make purchases as well as to support traditional arts. Despite this, urban *haats* are not able to draw potential buyers.
- An intelligent market analysis is imperative for attracting and sustaining customers for any product. In the present context, the rural poor with their limited knowledge and finances cannot carry out this exercise. The government bodies are less capable because of their bureaucratic culture.
- Information Technology support to the marketing of artisan products is appreciated and Web sites are created by the government bodies as well as artisan associations. The Web sites though, are formal and dull when compared to the advertising of other commercial products.

A View

What is perhaps necessary is a break from the top-down approaches that dominate the management of issues related to rural artisans and the products, replacing the planning that starts from where the artisans are. It is more important to develope a USP for the craft by redefining *swadeshi* spirit with a new social and cultural meaning and protecting intellectual property rights.

For discussion

1. Develop a model that presents the approaches to develop the work of artisans indicating the facilitating and restraining factors and the agents involved.
2. Do you agree with the view that "to sell products made by artisans, you have to sell your culture first"?
3. Recommend a viable and self-sustaining solution that addresses the issues outlined in the case.

Source: D. C. Misra, Avijit Dutta, Omkar Rai, Rama Hariharan, Rajiv Goel and Manie Khaneja, "Rural Bazar—Ideas of Today for a Better Tomorrow," available at http://crisp.nic.in/ruralbazar/Concept.htm.

Case 17.2 Selling With Enthusiasm

Shaffi Pehalwaan runs an exquisite handcrafted products' stall on Brigade Road in Bengaluru. The 75-year old artisan charms customers with his zeal, wit and painstakingly crafted products.

Fun in Selling

Work becomes fun-filled when one works with passion. For every item displayed in the stall, Shaffi uses an interesting tale to make his sales pitch. For instance, he takes the giant wheel and rotates it clockwise and says that in fancy fairs, one can see the giant wheel that keeps rotating in the same direction and cheerfully rotates the giant wheel in the opposite direction with a broad smile and adds, "My giant wheel rotates in the other direction too!"

Down Memory Lane

Sayed Shaffiullah aka Shaffi Pehalwaan hails from Chenapatna, a small town situated at a distance of 45 km from Bengaluru. The town is now famous for its wooden toys and lacquerware. Everyday, Shaffi travels from his native place to Bengaluru to sell his products.

The business was founded by his father, Shah Sayed Miyan, who received training from Nizam Hazrat, a master artisan from Chenapatna. He received opportunities to visit countries like Japan on assignments and improve his outlook. After honing his skills, he gathered a workforce of 50-odd men and developed them as seasoned craftsmen.

When Pehalwaan took over, he brought about changes in the style of functioning by introducing machines and increasing the sourcing of products. He established ties with hundreds of artisans living in Chenapatna and surrounding areas. An artisan working under him earns between Rs 200 and Rs 500 per day, depending on his or her skills.

Trade Avenues

The small stall of Pehalwaan measures 5 by 5 yards and he pays a monthly rent of Rs 10,000 for it. He displays a wide array of products that shine in different colours and spark of different ideas. In addition to the income from sales in his stores, he also earns at least Rs 6,000 from the supply of goods to Cauvery Emporium. Pehalwaan is also capable of dealing with gems and jewellery and works for many traders.

Creative Inspiration

Artists need creative inspiration and smart learning capabilities. For inspiration, Pehalwaan looks beyond the local culture and arts. Pehalwaan has visited many countries—Indonesia, Malaysia, Hong Kong, Singapore, etc. and learnt from their diverse artistic designs and cultural traditions. He became interested in visiting foreign locations to improve his business when he observed that a vendor from Alipur who bought goods from him used to sell them in Bangkok. Inspired by his business abilities, Pehalwaan has travelled extensively. With a smile he observes, "My products don't have a religion."

Success Recipe

What is the secret of his success? His honest answer to this question in his own words is,

"Before employing people to work for you, you should master the work yourself. I enjoy my trade and I always try to pull off a good bargain—sometimes I win, sometimes the customer wins."

Consumers often leave the shop wondering whether it was the products or the sales pitch that compelled them to buy.

For discussion

1. Identify the characteristics of a successful artisan.
2. How can artisans be trained to acquire such characteristics?

Source: Binesh Kutty, "Selling Handicrafts with Enthusiasm," *Dare,* 01 March 2009, available at www.dare.co.in.

Part V Looking into the Future

18

Future of Rural Marketing

LEARNING OBJECTIVES

Upon completion of this chapter, you will be able to:

- Identify the change patterns in the environment that have an impact on future rural marketing practices
- Highlight the key aspects that require attention of rural marketers
- Appreciate the innovation potential of rural people and recognize the role played by NGOs in developing appropriate technologies

Is the economic revolution taking place positively impacting the life of people in rural India and transforming it into a busy market place for the nation's top selling companies? The responses to this question seem to represent diametrically opposite views. For instance, K. V. Kamath, the non-executive chairman of ICICI is of the opinion that corporations have a great future in rural areas. Contradicting this view, analysts ask, "If this is true, why should India rank a dismal 66th out of 88 countries on the 2008 Global Hunger Index?" It is reported that as many as 12 of the 18 states measured, including "vibrant" Gujarat, technology-savvy Karnataka and the rice bowl of India—Tamil Nadu, are in the category of "alarming" states. The report of the National Commission on Enterprise in the unorganized sector also supports this argument. The report clearly states that the per capita expenditure of 77 per cent of India's population, the bulk of which lives in the rural areas and is equivalent to 836 million people, is not more than Rs 20 a day.

Foreign companies and collaborations are invited to aid the socio-economic transformation in India. The American agri-business giants Monsanto, Cargill, Walmart and ADM entered the rural retail segment through the Indo-US Knowledge Initiative on Agriculture Research, Development and Marketing (KIA) agreement. However, to the dismay of everyone, they are not interested in collaborating on agricultural research. There is an element of unfairness in their stand. According to some studies, a rural landscape of the size of 1,000 acres provides earnings to the tune of Rs 0.3 to 0.7 billion every year to agricultural-input companies. If at least a part of this money is used for the development of villages, they would look bright and vibrant. However, the villages of India have been victimized for long. This is what is referred to as reverse terms of trade.

The people at the bottom of the pyramid in India usually do not get a fair deal. A poor woman in a self-help group who wants to buy a goat to earn her livelihood has to pay an average interest of 24 per cent. Whereas, a person intending to buy a TV, refrigerator or a two-wheeler has access to interest-free loans. Marketers present dreams of a pleasant life to the people at the bottom of the pyramid because economists opined that GDP will grow when more people buy consumer durables. Those witnessing the drama in the rural markets cannot resist the temptation of asking the question "Who said selling dreams is only Bollywood's prerogative?"[1]

The views expressed above represent a despondent outlook and suggest that all is not well in rural India. They are cautionary statements and encourage unbiased thinking to crystallize the challenges that lie before the three developing organs of our country—the Government, NGOs and corporate enterprises. Transforming rural India, including the less accessible villages, requires powerful grassroots level socio-technical innovations that would enable their empowerment. This final chapter takes a cursory glance at the changing patterns and focuses on the progressive use of such socio-technological innovations.

INTRODUCTION

Cultivating markets in rural India will continue to be an attractive proposition to domestic and global companies. Together, globalization and the information revolution will impact rural India, and the rural–urban divide will gradually be narrowed. The prosperity created by development programmes on one side and connectivity (both road and information) on the other will gradually revolutionize the life of farmers, the youth and women. While the youth will lead the consumption groups, women will make their unique contribution to the development of rural markets. The marketers who understand the rural market and fine-tune their strategy are sure to reap benefits in the coming years. It is inevitable that in the future, the leadership in any product or service is linked to leadership in rural India.

CHANGE IN PATTERNS

There is a tectonic shift in market demographics. There is a steady rise in disposable incomes and visible change in consumer lifestyles. The following views of business executives elaborate this point of view. Girish Rao, vice-president, marketing, LG, observed, "Today, rural India is not 100 per cent dependent on an agrarian economy. Unlike in the past, where the ratio between those who were involved in agriculture and in other vocations was in the ratio of 75:25, that proportion is today estimated to be 50:50. Further, a lot of educated folk are getting white-collar jobs in nearby towns but, still have close ties to their rural homes."

With the increasing penetration of cable TV, the Internet and improvements in transport infrastructure, the line between urban and rural areas in terms of exposure is vanishing. Debashish Das, president, Linterland (Rural Initiatives), maintains, "The rural consumer is as exposed to films like the recent multi-starrer *Dhoom II* and is as conscious about acquiring a swanky mobile handset as his urban counterpart."

Anurag Gupta, country head, Ogilvy Activation opines, "The rural consumer is far savvier now and demands nothing but the best." Marketers have taken into cognizance the shifts in demand patterns from a low-key, largely utilitarian consumer base that has changed to a high-profile hedonistic consumer base. In fact, it is observed that the gap between the expectations and lifestyle aspirations of rural and urban consumers has gradually narrowed over the years. In line with the changes, it is reported that from a mere 2 per cent in the late nineties, most companies today, are dedicating 25 to 30 per cent of their total advertisement spend towards priming the rural market.[2]

WINNING STAKES—SOCIAL ASPECTS

Many things may change, however, family sentiments and socio-cultural relationships remain the same. Corporate enterprises have to win over rural consumers on these counts.

Regional differences

Rural marketing is highly influenced by regional differences. According to Das of Linterland, out of the 597 districts in India, only 100 are comparable in any way to urban markets and these are the markets that most big players are cultivating to get their future volumes. Despite the developments, a rural communication exercise has to be region specific. There are not only distinct cultural differences but, also climatic differences. Communication campaigns in the villages of Madhya Pradesh should be different from those in the villages of Orissa or West Bengal. For instance, the beauty needs of a woman in Rajasthan will differ from those of a woman in Kerala.

Scalability, as such, continues to remain a huge issue. Sandip Bansal, country head of Xpanse Asia, advises that marketers of national brands have to constantly keep the consumers across the country engaged. For this, they have to evolve brand-specific and market-specific solutions that are cost-effective. Anurag Gupta, country head, Ogilvy Activation opines that rural marketing cannot be considered a simple, one-time exercise. He says, "Rural marketing is not just about pitching a tent in a *haat* or a *mela* or sending a van to the villages. It is about a company going to the villages and engaging the consumers there, seducing them, and making them loyal to its brands."[2]

Emotional connect

Striking an emotional chord with rural India has now become the mantra of success for most companies. Here is an example.

VVF Ltd, the Rs 2.5 billion FMCG company, launched a helpline called the "*Jo Saundarya Sakhi*" in rural India to promote its soap brand, JO. The soap was positioned as a brand with quality ingredients, offered at an affordable price. The company felt there was a need to go beyond this positioning to gain top-of-the-mind position in the target market. To achieve this, "*Jo Saundarya Sakhi*" offered women household beauty tips. The message the brand communicates is that it understands and provides for the needs of its consumers.[3]

The experiences of Tata Teleservices and Rallis India discussed below highlight the importance of forging an emotional connect with rural consumers.[4]

"In rural communities, communication takes place mainly among defined family groups. So, they want a service that allows them to call families in and around their village at reasonable rates," says Darryl Green, CEO of Tata Teleservices. The company's family-and-friends (*Parivaar*) programme at special calling rates has been well accepted.

The *Kisan Sahyog Parivar* is yet another initiative. Farmers are encouraged to form self-help groups (SHGs) that provide a platform for facilitation of credit as well as learning and sharing among themselves. The focus is not on selling Rallis products but, on making the company a trusted friend of the farmer. "Very often, solving a problem may not require the use of our products. The farmer sees our technical field assistant (TFA) as a knowledgeable friend and increasingly relies on his advice to improve yields," says Dr Venkatrao Sohoni, managing director, Rallis India.

EMERGING SEGMENTS—WOMEN AND YOUTH

A woman's place in Indian culture doesn't often leave her with the freedom to make her own choices. Many cannot go out shopping or visit friends without permission from their husbands. 62 per cent of women believe that domestic violence is acceptable and the majority of husbands agree. In villages where cable was introduced, women's attitudes towards themselves and their role changed quite dramatically. For these villages, women's autonomy rose to indicate as if they had been educated for 5.5 years; their acceptance of spousal abuse fell by 10 per cent; their hope for a male child instead of a girl dropped by 12 per cent. It was noted that after the arrival of cable, girls between 6 and 10 years old were 10 per cent more likely to go to school. Also, for women who were under 35 years old, birth rates fell by half in a given year.[5] The socio-economic development measures taken by the Government have resulted in the empowerment of women. Women now represent a new consumer group with significant choice-making power. Two significant roles of women are discussed below.

Promoter of rural products

Women are actively promoting rural products with the help of NGOs as can be understood from SEWA's contribution presented in Box 18.1.

Women as consumers

Way back in 2002, a study conducted by Lavanya Panchapakesan and Namita Bharadwaj of Management Development Institute (MDI), Gurgaon showed that women are exercising considerable influence in purchase decisions. Understandably, several development programmes thereafter, have led to the increased empowerment of women. The findings of the study are given in Box 18.2.

Youth—leaders of change

With fresh minds and open outlooks the youth are receptive to changes and they can easily become the promoters of change. Many IT and other companies are focusing on this segment. For instance, Maitrya Doshi from Pune, the Indian representative of Canada-based organization "Taking IT Global" has embarked on a mission to encourage tech-savvy youth to involve themselves in bridging the digital divide by taking up ICT projects in various parts of rural India.[6]

The educated youth in rural India are exposed to urban influences through TV and satellite channels. They have images, either real or of a celluloid kind, of how their counterparts in cities live. Most of it is of the elite, and many of them aspire to similar lifestyles.

Already 40 per cent of all those graduating from colleges are rural youth. If they could, many of them would go to the cities. However, employment opportunities are limited. Therefore, many are staying put in villages, setting up businesses there or in the nearby towns and cities. The implications of the above in marketing terms are: (i) Villages of relevance to marketers of branded goods are urbanizing rapidly and (ii) The hierarchical structure is gradually breaking down and the hegemony that elders had in decision making at the family and community levels is concomitantly lessening. Therefore, young people are either given a say in the decision-making process or they have simply taken over the process.[7]

Box 18.1 SEWA Empowers Women

In 2004, Self-Employed Women's Organization (SEWA) set up a rural marketing network called *Rudi Bazaar*. The bazaar is managed by SEWA'S rural women members. Twenty five commonly used products were launched to begin with. All products made, packed and sold by women members of SEWA are sold under the brand name "Rudi." Small and marginal farmers gain as they sell their produce to these women instead of *shroffs* or middlemen. The produce (mainly agri-based products) of over 4,000 self-help groups comprising over 0.35 million women of 14 districts of Gujarat are procured, graded, sorted, cleaned and packed and sold though the network. Hindustan Lever Ltd (HUL) and Grassroots Trading Network have assisted SEWA Gram Mahila *Haat* (SGMH), the agricultural marketing arm of SEWA in providing the necessary technical expertise and capability in setting up the network.

Source: "Sewa Unveils Rural Marketing Network of Women," *Business Standard*, 10 December 2004, available at www.business-standard.com.

Box 18.2 Empowered Rural Women

A study conducted by Lavanya Panchapakesan and Namita Bharadwaj of MDI, Gurgaon classified "women" into the following five categories:

- Unaware—non-influencer and non-buyer
- Aware—non-influencer and non-buyer
- Aware—non-influencer and buyer
- Aware—influencer and non-buyer
- Aware—influencer and buyer

A majority of rural women are aware of many brands and are influential in decision making. They form the target market for selling. The other categories are targets for creating awareness and interest. Regarding brand preferences, it is found that less than 50 per cent of the women showed brand preference. In case of household FMCGs, clothes, jewellery and cosmetics, influence exercised by women is high. Ghadi, Nirma, Surf, Lifebuoy, Lux, Fair & Lovely, Dabur Amla and Dabur Laal Dantmanjan are among the frequently mentioned brands. The study suggested that mobile door-to-door traders—*pheriwaalas* can be the right choice for distribution. Data for the study was collected from different categories of women—rural rich, rural poor or landless, patriarchal families, women-headed households, among Hindus, Muslims and tribals in four districts of Uttar Pradesh.

Source: Preeti Mehra, "How to Woo the Rural Woman," *The Hindu Business Line*, 23 July 2002, available at www.thehindubusinessline.com/2002/07/23/stories/2002072301340600.htm.

ICT—TRANSFORMATION AGENT

Information and communication technology is in the process of creating a global village. Rural people are utilizing the Internet to improve their lives.

Mitra Technologies, for example, has been working on developing a handicrafts e-trade centre that would connect producers directly to wholesale and retail buyers resulting in increased efficiencies in marketing and production. This extra-net based computerized network would connect producers to buyers in a B2B environment. Mitra has transformed the lives of artisans in Orissa. D. Behra, member of Mitra Technologies said, "We wish to network more than 10,000 artisans all over the country and showcase their craft to the global market for higher gains."[8]

The eSwasthya project launched by the Bihar Institute of Economic Studies (BIES), on the other hand, would allow the poor in the Madhubani district to gain access to better health at lower cost by providing them with smart health cards. These cards would contain their entire health history, which can be accessed at local community health centres.[9]

TECHNOLOGY AND INNOVATION—A DRIVER

"Over 70 per cent of India's population lives in the rural areas, but 70 per cent of electricity generated is used in urban areas," says A. K. Vora, managing director of Tata BP Solar. "Even in the future, rural areas will continue to get an unequal share of power, because urban needs will keep on increasing," he adds. However, the trend will change as increasing numbers of corporate enterprises are finding appropriate low-cost technologies to help solve rural problems. Two illustrative cases are discussed in the next section.

Tata BP Solar[10]

Tata BP Solar has a slew of products such as solar home lighting systems, solar lanterns, solar cookers and solar hot-water systems. They have also designed the following innovative packaged solutions for specific segments in rural India:

- Sunbank, a customized package for rural banks that are being computerized. The package consists of a power pack along with solar modules, batteries and controllers and provides power for three to six hours a day. The company is also looking at providing power to ATMs.
- Suraksha, a solar-powered communication system, helps police stations function effectively.
- India has thousands of primary health centres; however, most of them have very little or no power and vaccines need to be refrigerated at temperatures lower than 6°C. The health centre package, Arogya, includes a solar-powered vaccine refrigerator manufactured indigenously by the company and approved by the World Health Organization (WHO).
- In Madhya Pradesh, the *Rajya Siksha Abhiyan* supplied computers to over 3,000 rural schools. However, this proved to be ineffective because schools did not have the power to operate them. Tata BP Solar is proposing to put together a school package called Tejas that will power computers, TVs, lights and fans. Specific packages for e-governance and *panchayats* are now being developed.

Godrej *chotukool*[11]

Godrej has gone in for several engineering innovations to keep the prices of their products low. *Chotukool* is one such innovation. The number of parts in *Chotukool* has been reduced to just 20 instead of the 200 that go into regular refrigerators and the size is also small. "It's a reverse engineering of sorts," says G. Sunderraman, vice president, corporate development, Godrej & Boyce. *Chotukool* does not have a compressor. It looks like a 43-litre cool box that is loaded from the top and can run on battery. The refrigerator weighs only 7.8 kg, runs on a cooling chip and a fan similar to those used to cool computers. Given the power shortage in the countryside, it also uses high-end insulation to stay cool for hours without power. The operational cost is low—the refrigerator consumes half the power consumed by regular refrigerators. It costs around Rs 3,250, which is 35 per cent less than the prevailing brand "Champion." Champion is targeted at the rural audience and is priced at Rs 6,790.

RURAL INNOVATIONS

Rural India needs ideas that can deliver inclusive, eco-friendly and sustainable prosperity. A handful of individuals—better known as social entrepreneurs—are making a difference by blurring the boundaries between business and social good. These rural and indigenous innovations come from two sources—first, farmers, semi-literates, illiterates and slum-dwellers who have managed to change things by marrying their own innate genius to their inherent understanding of ground conditions; and second, innovations taken from more traditional sources such as universities and independent engineers that are then adapted to suit Indian traditions and conditions.

According to the Chennai-based Rural Innovations Network (RIN), there are over a thousand innovations in the villages and a majority of these go unnoticed as the innovator rarely has the wherewithal to commercialize it. Box 18.3 presents examples of grassroots innovations.

A grassroots innovator from Madurai has created a machine to peel garlic without damaging its quality. An entrepreneur from Singapore read about an areca nut peeler on the National Innovation Foundation Web site and placed an order. For each innovation or instance of traditional knowledge documented, there are thousands waiting to be tapped. The poor are not just the "bottom of the pyramid" or simply consumers of products. They provide knowledge and drive innovation. More

Box 18.3 Rural Innovations

A stove that uses both kerosene and electricity was invented by Balubhai Vasoya, a resident of Ahmedabad in Gujarat. Mansukhbhai of Gujarat modified an Enfield diesel motorcycle into a tractor-like vehicle as he could not afford to buy a tractor. He simply removed the back wheel and replaced it with a spiked cylinder. To milk cows effortlessly, Rural Innovations Network (RIN) designed a manual milking device—J S Milker. It is a simple vacuum driven portable machine and has become successful in South India. Now, it is marketed in Gujarat, where milk co-operatives are present in large numbers.

A 70-year old farmer, Anna Saheb Udgave of Sadalga village in Karnataka's Belgaum district, developed a low-cost drip irrigation system in view of the water crisis in his village. He later evolved it into a mega sprinkler and called it Chandraprabhu Rain Gun.

Deepasakhti Pooja Oil, an innovative product is commercially manufactured by KP Castor Oil Works in Coimbatore. It is a blend of five different oils prepared as per the Indian *shastras*. The blended oil does not produce any soot but, gives a bright flame. It lasts longer and the fumes produced repel disease-causing bacteria. A banana stem injector was developed by Manoharan, a lathe owner of Batlagundu in Tamil Nadu. It is similar to a syringe and can be used to inject pesticides into the psuedo-stem of the disease-infected banana plant.

Source: Shobha Warrier, "Innovators in Rural India? You bet!," 24 March 2004, available at www.rediff.com/money/2004/mar/24spec1.htm.

than 50,000 innovations and instances of traditional knowledge were scouted across 300 districts of India by the National Innovation Foundation (NIF) with the help of the Honey Bee Network.[12]

From the above exposition, we can say rural India is changing in several respects—socially, economically, and intellectually. It is no exaggeration if we say that rural India creates more than just poverty. A wealth of ideas awaits. If the creativity is harnessed and entrepreneurial spirit and skills are fostered, rural markets can come up in a big way.

Globalization will impact target groups such as rural households at the bottom of the pyramid, farmers, fishermen, artisans, youth and women. The advancements in technology and collaborative development programmes of the government and NGOs are expanding opportunities for improvements in the quality of work and life for different categories of people. Rural markets are responding enthusiastically to the stimulus provided by the communication and promotional campaigns and reasonably priced innovative product and service offers of corporations.

In conclusion, one can say that the rural markets are enticing and marketing to rural consumers is exciting. However, the winners in the rural marketing game are those who can fine-tune their strategies based on a clear understanding of the different types of rural consumers and their current and future expectations.

Summary

Development for marketing is the mantra for many companies. Rural India is changing for sure, but, cultivating it requires cultural learning and technological tools. The emerging women and youth segments offer good business opportunities by their lifestyle and consumption patterns and also by their contribution to the household purchase decision-making process. Affordable and acceptable products, when made available with emotional connectivity, will sell in rural markets. Information and communication technology and grassroots-level rural innovations assisted and promoted by NGOs, corporate enterprises, young entrepreneurs, etc. are spearheading the process of rural transformation and women (the *shakti* of India) are very much involved in the change process.

Short Answer Questions

1. Highlight the changes taking place in rural India.
2. Explain the significance of social connectivity in ad campaigns.
3. How is the community concept useful in designing products?
4. Can women be a new segment for FMCGs?
5. Explain how the youth can become opinion leaders in the household.
6. Citing an example of one ICT application, show how development can take place in rural areas.
7. Explain two rural innovations.

Discussion Questions

1. Is the rural woman ready for lifestyle products? Discuss.
2. "The youth will take the lead in rural consumption patterns in the future." Discuss.
3. Grassroots-level innovations can only transform rural India. Urban innovations can help only urbanized rural villages. Discuss.

Essay Questions

1. Discuss the changes taking place in rural markets. What are the opportunities and challenges faced by rural marketers?
2. How can corporate enterprises promote rural transformation as well promote collaborations with the government and other corporate enterprises in the future?
3. Examine the role played by NGOs in developing appropriate technology and increasing the purchasing power of rural people.

Internet Exercise

Visit the Web sites of innovation-assisting NGOs and prepare an essay on "rural innovations and the role of NGOs."

Mini Project

Visit two nearby villages and explore the changes that have taken place during the last two years and identify the changing preferences and lifestyles of households having children above 15 years of age.

End Notes

1. Devinder Sharma, "India Together: Corporates Look for Gold," 31 January 2009, available at www.indiatogether.org/2009/jan/dsh-ruralgold.htm.
2. Ajitha Sasidhar, "Getting the Other Half," available at www.business.outlookindia.com.
3. *ibid.*
4. www.tata.com, accessed March 2010.
5. Robert Jensen and Emily Oster, "The Power of TV: Cable Television and Women's Status in India," 23 September 2008, available at http://home.uchicago.edu/~eoster/tvwomen.pdf.
6. www.ciol.com, accessed March 2010.
7. Francis Xavier, "Marketing to Rural India," 11 October 2001, *Catalyst*, available at www.hinduonnet.com/businessline/catalyst/2001/10/11/stories/1911o05b.htm.
8. www.ciol.com, accessed March 2010.
9. www.bies.in, accessed March 2010.
10. "Tata BP Solar India Limited: The Largest Solar Company in India," available at www.india-buildinginfo.com/virtual-clean/tatabp/index.htm.
11. www.thinkchangeindia.org, accessed March 2010.
12. "Potter's Wheel: Rural India Creates More Than Just Poverty," 15 July 2005, available at www.nif.org.in/bd/outlook_potterwheel.

Case 18.1 Advertising on Two Wheels

Innovations in the field of out-of-home (OOH) advertising are being witnessed year after year. The Indian consumer is bombarded with 100,000 advertisements a day displayed on more than 250 channels plus innumerable advertisements on billboards. A novel concept in outdoor advertising, the "adrickshaw" was reported in 2009.

New Idea

Suyash Trivedi, a management graduate from Narsee Monjee Institute of Management Studies in Mumbai launched AdScoot, an OOH venture in Mumbai. As a result of interactions with entrepreneurs and marketing professionals, he came up with the idea of offering advertising space on two-wheeler scooters. So far, rickshaws were being used to carry backlit ad displays. The backlit flex displays of the size 24" x 48" x 30" will be mounted on the scooters re-modelled to meet the specific requirements of the clients with the help of a bike-designing company. Riders wearing uniforms will not only distribute promotional material but, also interact with prospective buyers.

Target Advertisers

The ad scooter is targeted at the small-and-medium enterprise (SME) segment that has few cost-effective advertising options available. The scooters can move easily from one locality to another, advertising products and distributing samples, even in rural areas. The scooters are monitored with the help of global positioning systems (GPS), fitted to the scooter. A beginning has been made by mainly targeting the rural markets in Gujarat and Maharashtra.

Merits and Problems

Evidently AdScoot is economical, innovative and traceable. The clients are charged on an hourly basis for each scooter hired. As such, the SMEs get value-for-money promotional services. However, analysts and advertisers are anticipating some problems.

According to Mangesh Borse, director, Symbiosis Advertising, maintenance can be a big problem. The ad display will be exposed to heat and dust and keeping it clean will be a tough challenge in rural areas connected by dusty roads. Another problem is related to creativity in advertisements. Ads should be simple and easy to understand.

Raghu Khanna, chief executive officer, CashUrDrive, expressed similar concerns about maintenance. According to him, there are two serious problems. One is that the medium will work more in favour of local advertisers and would not be able to effectively contribute towards brand-building exercises. Second, monitoring the campaign is a major problem as it is dependent on the integrity of the rider.

Looking Ahead

Raj Mohanty, senior business director, Poster Publicity, remembers seeing ad scooters at an exhibition in China. He observed, "In terms of display, ad scooters look promising; though there is a need to rework the pricing of the media." His advice is based on the optimistic view that rural India is growing at a great speed and different media owners have greater opportunities. Pricing is critical to success because a mobile van is available for Rs 0.1 million for a month and an advertiser will obviously go for a cheaper option.

For discussion

1. Evaluate the new media vehicle for its effectiveness.
2. Suggest guidelines for marketing this vehicle.
3. Suggest guidelines for the usage of this media vehicle by SMEs.

Source: Rohit Nautiyal, "AdScoot to Brand Scooters in Rural Areas," 23 October 2009, available at www.afaqs.com/perl/ooh/news/story.html?sid=25293.

Case 18.2 Insurance Takes a New Path

Excellent companies do not do different things; they do the same things differently. Tata AIG Life Insurance has embraced the opportunities provided by rural business and has taken many initiatives to build a rural base. The rural mandate for life insurance companies in India has established two obligations. One, a part of the company's annual business (in terms of number of policies) should come from rural areas, gradually rising every year from 7 per cent in the company's first year to 18 per cent in the sixth year. Second, the business should cover a certain number of people in the informal or unorganized sector, in both urban and rural areas. Vijay Athreye, assistant VP and head (rural and social) at Tata AIG Life Insurance said, "We decided to treat it as a business opportunity rather than an obligation."

Hurdles to be Crossed

Insurance selling requires not only interest in selling but also in servicing, especially in rural areas. However, in rural areas, there are two bottlenecks. One is the lack of motivation among agents to service policies. The agents are concerned with earning their livelihood and look for opportunities that give them large commissions. The agents receive a 40 per cent commission on the first year's premium. In subsequent years, the commission varies between 6 and 10 per cent. Another problem is the lack of infrastructure that makes servicing difficult. Selling in rural areas requires understanding and dealing with realities such as illiteracy, superstitions and lack of birth certificates or proof of age.

Segmentation

Athreye segmented the rural market into three tiers. The top one comprises the "almost urban" people and rich farmers and the middle one consists of the rural "middle class." The third is the "bottom of the pyramid." It is this segment that requires attention and Athreye says, "We had to find a way of addressing the last segment, as it would help us fulfil our obligation as well as generate incremental new business."

Empowerment of Women

A development-oriented solution to the problem of neglected service was found by involving women. It positions insurance as a supplementary livelihood activity and creates a channel to handle micro-insurance. Instead of the usual agents, Tata AIG decided to engage service-oriented organizations and people who will be satisfied with small earnings. The decision to involve women in selling is based on the idea of contributing to the cause of capacity building of women. Explaining the idea, Athreye says, "In rural areas it's very difficult for women to find a source of income. We encourage women to become our micro-insurance agents."

Collaborations

Tata AIG collaborated with the Department for International Development (DFID), an arm of the British Ministry of Finance that funds activities in rural areas, on a matching funds basis. Together, they created a corpus fund to develop the grassroots-level community workers' infrastructure and collaterals. Women are trained to promote and service micro-insurance to landless adults in the state who work as daily-wage labourers.

The Experiment

Training the women at designated training centres for 100 hours as required by the Insurance Act was a big challenge. Rural women could not stay for so many days in a city. Tata AIG shared this learning, both in India and abroad. As a result, a new micro-insurance regulation has come up. According to the new regulation, micro-insurance agents in villages need only 25 hours of training. In a strategic move, AIG formed Rural Community Insurance Groups and trained them. Each group consists of five members. Tata AIG takes them around in their own branded vans that are also used for collection and policy servicing. In about four three-day capacity-building modules, women are trained in soft skills, insurance skills and data management. The results are impressive. About 150 women could make earnings of around Rs 700 (USD 15) a month and some women who developed competencies of selling regular products to the rural middle class and thereby, earn as much as Rs 2,000 (USD 43).

With necessary modifications to suit local conditions, the model has been replicated in other parts of the country. For instance, in states like UP and Rajasthan, men don't allow womenfolk to go out of the house for work. Tata AIG approached NGO field workers and volunteers to overcome this problem. With efforts of this kind, the company could involve large numbers of women and empower them. Women agents are typically cluster leaders or office bearers of rural self-help groups (SHGs) and constitute 60 per cent of the 460 rural agents selling micro-insurance.

New Products and Approaches

To make the insurance products affordable, the company has designed no-frills, low-priced personal products that focus on savings. A small premium of Rs 150 (USD 3) to Rs 300 (USD 9) provides insurance coverage of between Rs 15,000 (USD 320) and Rs 20,000 (USD 430).

The company has involved many NGOs, co-operatives/women federations and MFIs in mentoring and monitoring the programme. Under new micro-insurance regulations companies can now pay 20 per cent commission throughout the product's tenure. Thus, a steady income is assured to micro-agents. The company has settled many claims involving local NGOs to make sure that the money is given to the right beneficiary and the proceeds are used well.

Impressive Results

The company has operations in about 10 states (Andhra Pradesh, Kerala, Tamil Nadu, Karnataka, Maharashtra, Gujarat, Jharkhand, West Bengal, UP and Rajasthan) and has 50,000 policy holders, many of them belonging to the bottom-of-the-pyramid (BoP) category. The achievements have made the company proud and provided it confidence to look ahead for bigger things. Vijay Athreye, assistant VP and head (rural and social) proudly announces, "Our policy-holder survey shows that it is the very first time that they (BoP category) have bought an insurance policy and it is our women agents who have reached out to them."

The Guiding Philosophy

The business philosophy of Tata AIG has tenets such as targeting the "bottom of the pyramid," creating choices by offering value-for-money products, gaining footholds and moving up by making investments, generating long-term profits and working on making it a sustainable business. Emphasizing the importance of choices and services, Athreye maintains, "The biggest thing about development is having choices. We are educating people about insurance and about the product choices they have by offering them the relevant services at their doorstep, including frequent collection of premiums."

For discussion

1. Examine the innovative strategy used by Tata AIG. What are the salient features of the strategy?
2. Offer suggestions to improve the strategy.

Source: www.tata.com, accessed March 2010.

Part VI Cases

Cases

CASE 1 BAJAJ DISCOVERS NEW OPPORTUNITIES

Even though the domestic motorcycle industry grew by 3 per cent in 2009, Bajaj automobiles registered a negative growth. India's second-largest two-wheeler manufacturer plans to reverse the trend this year. In order to achieve this, the company will focus on redesigning its existing range of bikes and will also target the rural market, since the urban market has been registering flat growth.

Bajaj Decides to Change Gear

Bajaj Auto's decision to exit the scooter business has triggered a wave of nostalgia evoked by Bajaj's famous "*Hamara* Bajaj" campaign. Bajaj is keener on the motorcycle segment rather than scooters.

"We will exit the scooter market because we don't see much sense in it. If we are to be a motorcycle specialist, we cannot make scooters," announced Rajiv Bajaj, managing director, Bajaj Auto. The logic does not make much sense. According to the Society of Indian Automobile Manufacturers (SIAM), the scooter segment is booming. The market leader, Honda Motorcycle and Scooter India Pvt. Ltd (HMSI), the Indian unit of Japanese Honda Motor Co. Ltd, sold about 1.1 million units this year and is targeting a sale of 1.5 million units next year. Mahindra Two Wheelers Ltd (MTWL), the new entrant, has tasted success by selling 7,020 scooters in November 2009. However, the performance of Bajaj Auto was disappointing. During November 2009, Bajaj Auto sold only 154 units of its "Kristal" scooter.

Innovation Neglected

Bajaj has to blame its dormant attitude for its failure. While the competitors have taken the innovation route and launched upgraded, novel products based on fresh R&D and improved features (such as auto gears), performance and mileage, Bajaj continued with its iconic (but now defunct) geared scooters. A meek attempt at innovation was seen in case of the 100 cc gearless "Kristal," the features of which are hardly on par with what the competitors are offering. The indifferent and insensitive attitude of Bajaj Auto led to the unnatural and untimely death of its scooter segment.

Re-entry into the 100 cc Segment

Bajaj did exit from the 100 cc motorcycle segment after failing to catch up with market leader Hero Honda. Though the market share of 100 cc bikes has declined from 80 per cent to 65 per cent, the decline has not occurred as fast as Bajaj expected. Bajaj has a meagre 9 per cent market share in this segment while it was a market leader in 125 cc+ segment. The fact that Hero Honda is doing well amidst recession can be attributed to the booming sales of its 100 cc bikes in the rural market.

Indian Market—Preferences

India's market is divided roughly into two categories, urban and rural, depending on the needs and resources of consumers in these areas. For example, pricing and fuel efficiency matters most for rural consumers whereas the urban consumer would prefer more power and style in a motorcycle. In an effort to capture the younger, tech-savvy urban consumer market, Bajaj ignored the rural market and did not launch any new variant in the 100 cc segment in the past two years.

Rediscovered Opportunity

In light of this, Bajaj is revamping its portfolio and has already launched nearly half a dozen bikes in 2009. Bajaj's Pulsar brand found strong association with sports lovers. Focusing on the domestic sports segment, Bajaj launched Pulsar 220 and another variant, the Pulsar 135 LS. The latter is powered by a 4-valve DTS-i engine and is priced at Rs 51,000 (ex-showroom Delhi). At the lower end, Bajaj has Platina, a 100 cc motorcycle. In addition to this, the new 100 cc Discover DTS-Si motorcycle has been launched.

Discover—New Driver

According to ARAI–IDC (Indian Driving Cycle), Discover returns a fuel efficiency figure of 89 km/l. Under standard conditions, fuel efficiency is expected to be around 125 km/l, higher than the XCD 109 km/l. Bajaj is yet to get the ARAI figures under standard conditions. The new 100 cc Discover has "Digital Twin Spark Swirl Induction," a 2.0 version engine and other features including electric start, nitrox suspension, longest wheelbase in the 100 cc segment, 5-speed gear—a first in the 100 cc segment—and maintenance-free battery.

It is expected that with rising fuel prices the bike would hold relevance for cost-conscious customers. It is available in three colours—black with green stripes, black with red stripes and black with blue stripes. Bajaj Discover 100 cc comes in only one variant and is priced Rs 40,000 (ex-showroom Chennai).

Discover will be available in showrooms across India. Bajaj is aiming to increase its domestic monthly sales of motorcycles to 0.15 million from the existing 0.11 million per month through the launch of new products. Products such as 100 cc Discover DTS-Si could well attract the attention of prospective buyers in rural areas. The company could put the thrust on providing financing schemes to their customers in rural areas both via in-house financing, i.e. Baja Auto Finance Limited, as well as making finance available through other financing sources as well.

Bajaj will promote its new bike as a long-distance bike and is going to do a series of outdoor promotional activities. "Rediscover India with Discover 100 cc" would be the message of the campaign. As part of the campaign, Bajaj will take its customers from cities to suburbs to highlight the mileage of the bike.

DISCUSSION QUESTIONS

1. Did Bajaj pay a huge price for ignoring the rural market?
2. Is Bajaj's decision to exit the scooter segment a wise one?
3. Do you think it can tame the 100 cc segment this time?
4. What are the strategies that Bajaj can use to compete with Hero Honda?

Source: Sucheta Dalal, "Bajaj Auto: Will History Repeat Itself Time and Again?" 14 December 2009, available at www.suchetadalal.com/?id=ae206ca0-d75f-2e0f-4b2601282de1&base=sections&f; "Bajaj Auto Targets Growth in Motorcycle Market," *Business Standard*, 18 July 2009, available at www.business-standard.com/india/news/bajaj-auto-targets-growth-in-motorcycle-market/68161/on.

CASE 2 MARKETING OF DTH SERVICES

Most people living in rural areas can't afford to pay Rs 200 to 400 towards the monthly cable fees even if it is made available. Currently, with the advances in technology, private companies (Dish TV, etc.) are trying to introduce the concept of DTH—Direct to Home. This can be made available everywhere in the country. The credit for making it widely known goes to India's first free DTH Service—DD Direct Plus launched by Doordarshan on 16 December 2004. DD Direct Plus opened up a new world to the rural masses. It also provided new opportunities to the private players. However, it could not sustain interest for long due to the poor service quality of the channel.

Players

DTH allows the beaming of satellite programmes directly into your home through a personal dish. DD Direct offers 33 free-to-air channels whereas Dish TV and Tata Sky offer about 100 channels each. The players in this market are:

- Dish TV
- DD-Direct Plus (government-owned)
- Tata Sky
- Reliance Big TV and
- Airtel Digital TV

Market Potential

Of the 220 million homes in the country, around 116 million have television. This number is growing by 4–5 per cent per annum. It is reported that there are about 68 million cable homes and about 45 million plus do not have cable connections. About 104 million homes are yet to purchase TVs. Exhibit 2.1 presents the market potential and tasks for DTH service providers. As much as 70 per cent of the DTH subscribers are accounted for by the rural areas and tier II cities.

According to experts, DTH is estimated to reach around 20 million homes by the end of 2009–2010. Analysts say the DTH industry is adding five to seven million customers every year. In terms of geographical location, North India and Western India together account for over 8 million DTH subscribers while the southern market accounts for 3 million. The states of Maharashtra, Goa, Punjab, Uttar Pradesh and Rajasthan are the leaders in DTH subscription, contributing over 6.5 million DTH connections to the overall base.

The industry is estimated to touch Rs 30 billion in the current financial year compared to Rs 15 billion in 2008–09. The sector is presently taxed highly by the government. DTH companies pay service tax, licence fee, excise duty, VAT and

Aspect	Households (In million)	Task
Total homes	220	The maximum potential
TV homes	116	Currently target market
Homes without TVs	104	Market for TV and DTH to tie-up and gain
TV+DTH	13	Retain penetrated market
TV + cable homes	68	Market for conversion
TV+DD1 (No cable or DTH)	45	Market ready for attraction

Exhibit 2.1 Market Potential for DTH

entertainment tax, which amounts to a total tax component of almost 50 per cent per user. If the government reduces the tax and fixes a proper content-buying price, the DTH industry will grow by 15 million every year.

Awareness and Preferences

According to independent surveys, about 35 per cent of the population is now aware of the DTH platform and may consider this option. Rural people are finding DTH services more worthy than the cable operator's offerings as service quality is good and there are no technical glitches. Movies of one's choice, entertainment on demand and interactivity have helped direct-to-home (DTH) players make gradual but certain inroads into the cable-driven Indian market. As most consumers do not have adequate knowledge of the benefits of DTH, service providers have to educate consumers to gain market share.

Dish TV and DD Direct Plus have the most penetration within the rural markets. In the top 100 metros too, Dish TV and Tata Sky are the preferred brands. The southern market is dominated by Sun Direct while Tata Sky is the dominant DTH brand in high-income households.

Strategies

In rural areas, Dish TV runs fleets of vans for demos, installation as well as selling hardware and pre-paid vouchers. Experts say providing regional language channels is one of the easiest ways to reach out to customers in rural areas. Besides these, launching channels at regular intervals also motivates customers to invest in the product.

DD Direct Plus

Prasar Bharti (Doordarshan) has joined hands with Igo TV from Mirc Electronics Ltd to co-promote DD Direct Plus channels. The recently launched Igo DTH TV has an in-built DTH receiver that enables the viewer to receive 33 free-to-air television channels as well as 12 AIR FM radio channels without a cable connection. This cutting-edge digital technology not only provides better reception quality but also saves the consumer from buying a separate set-top box and recurring cable connection charges. Prasar Bharti and Igo TV will promote the DTH concept through a series of joint marketing campaigns for a period of two months:

- *Emphasis on quality:* The Igo brand has been working towards the betterment of the rural/low-income group consumer by offering value-added products with latest technology and high quality at most affordable price points.
- *Focus on areas without cable:* In the first phase, 92 districts of Madhya Pradesh, Gujarat, Bihar, Uttar Pradesh, Chhattisgarh, Jharkhand, Rajasthan and Maharashtra will be covered. These states currently have low cable and satellite connections.
- *Van and melas:* Mobile van promotions and rural *mela* participation will be undertaken extensively where the consumers can experience DD Direct Plus channels. On-ground support staff will interact and educate the audience, demonstrate the features of the television and the broadcast range of DD Direct Plus.
- *Outdoor activities:* Various outdoor activities such as wall paintings, hoardings and bus shelters will also be undertaken during the promotional month.

Dish TV

Market leader Dish TV, run by Zee Entertainment Enterprises Ltd (ZEEL), has the first-mover advantage and was the first private company to start DTH operations in India in 2005. Dish has an overall subscriber base of over 17 million and has seen a 57 per cent growth since December 2008. The company's rural penetration strategy consists of the following measures:

- *Rural vans:* In rural areas, Dish TV runs fleets of vans for demos, installation as well as selling hardware and pre-paid vouchers.
- *TV commercials*: Bollywood actor Shahrukh Khan is featured in its marketing campaigns to sell connections. Khan still features heavily in the Dish TV ads.

Tata Sky

Tata Sky is the second-largest DTH operator with 4.2 million subscribers. The strategy of Tata Sky comprises the following initiatives:

- *Call centres:* It has set up three call centres at Hyderabad, Pune and Chandigarh and supports 11 languages.
- *Tie-ups:* It has tied up with ITC e-*choupals* and godrej *aadhars* to tap rural customers. When a farmer sells his produce at an ITC e-*choupal*, he has cash in hand and can use it to subscribe to DTH services. Similarly, when a gas cylinder from IndianOil is delivered at a house, the delivery boy carries Tata Sky pre-paid vouchers that can be purchased by the user.
- *TV commercials:* The commercials featured Bollywood star Aamir Khan for increasing subscriptions outside the main urban areas.

Bharti Airtel

Airtel Digital TV, which began offering services in October 2008, has about 1.1 million of the total 15 million net installed DTH subscribers as of August 2009. The company is likely to add 1.6 million new DTH subscribers by March 2010. The strategy of Airtel is characterized by focus on non-cable areas, village-contact activities and improvements in the quality of channel attraction.

Focus on non-cable geographies: The company has initiated an aggressive strategy to acquire customers outside the cable space. It will now target rural areas in Maharashtra, Andhra Pradesh, Gujarat, Rajasthan and UP and as many retailers as possible.

Village-contact activities: Ajai Puri, CEO, DTH Bharti Airtel said, "Through village-contact activities, we ensure deeper penetration into the hinterland. After crops seasons, we give demos at *mandis* because farmers are cash rich and are able to commit."

Quality improvements: Besides offering the product at competitive prices, DTH operators say using advanced mpeg4 technology with DVBS 2 and HD services in the product also helps to increase the number of subscribers. There has been an increase in demand for products with these technological qualities due to their clarity in picture.

Reliance Big TV

Direct-to-home service provider Reliance Big TV, part of Reliance Communications, has earmarked Rs 0.5 billion for a new media campaign that it has just rolled out to enhance its subscriber base. The six-week campaign across media including print, TV commercials, out-of-home and online space, is built around the concept—"joy of owning Reliance Big TV." To increase brand awareness and visibility, Reliance Big TV DTH has embarked on an "entertaining and educating rural Andhra" promotion that covers remote educational institutions and the IT sector across Andhra Pradesh. As part of its on-ground activation, Big TV has rolled out float vans with Big TV branding, loaded with a dummy dish for doing the rural rounds in the state.

The on-ground team has captured small towns such as Kakinada by installing more than 3,000 connections during the promotion. More than 90 per cent of the town was connected with Big TV DTH. Vijayawada, Visakhapatnam, Tirupati, Kurnool, Srikakulam, Warangal and surrounding rural towns are being targeted in the first phase.

DISCUSSION QUESTIONS

1. Analyse the marketing approaches and initiatives of DTH service providers.
2. Develop a comprehensive marketing strategy to be a model for DTH service providers (use subheads such as consumer behaviour, target market, positioning, marketing mix, etc.).

Source: Rashmi Pratap, "DTH Operators to Bridge the Urban–Rural Divide," *The Economic Times*, 22 September 2006, available at http://economictimes.indiatimes.com/news/news-by-industry/media/entertainment-/entertainment/DTH-operators-bridge-the-urban-rural-divide/articleshow/2015662.cms; Priyanka Akhouri, "DTH Players Eye Tier-II Cities, Rural Markets for Bigger Subscriber Pie," *The Financial Express*, 05 October 2009, available at www.financialexpress.com /news/dth-players-eye-tierii-cities-rural-markets-for-bigger-subscriber-pie/524986/0; "DD-MIRC Electronics Tie-up to Promote Direct Plus Channels," *The Hindu Business Line*, 07 February 2006, available at www.thehindubusinessline.com/2006/02/07/19hdline.htm; R. Ravikumar, "Reliance Big TV Targets 'Quality' Subscribers," *The Hindu Business Line*, 14 October 2009, available at www.thehindubusinessline.com/2009/10/.../2009101450130500.htm.

CASE 3 STRATEGY OF ACE

Tata Motors, India's largest company in the automobile and commercial vehicle sector, has consciously decided to focus on being a customer-centric company rather than a product-centric one, developing products that fit customer requirements rather than making customers adjust their requirements to suit existing vehicles.

Need Identification

Tata commercial vehicles are known for their reliability and durability. Seven out of every 10 trucks on Indian roads proudly carry the Tata logo. However, the smallest vehicle it manufactured was a four-tonner that was too big to be economically deployed in large numbers in small towns. The requirement was for an optimal vehicle that could economically carry smaller loads and reach out into small towns and villages. Issues such as purchase price, cost of operation and reliability were critical.

Requirements Analysis

The company classified its customers into a four-level pyramid with the help of McKinsey (Exhibit 3.1).

The company targeted customers largely from semi-urban and rural areas, who fell into the two bottom layers of the pyramid that cover 85 per cent of the market. The rural customer is not too aware of features and benefits and is found more at the lowest end of the pyramid. The educated, urban customer lies at the second level. The challenge, as competition increases, is to bring out products that provide the benefits of one segment at the price point of the lower segment.

Through its interaction with customers, the company learnt that the five essential attributes that they look for in a small commercial vehicle are lower operating costs (as compared to a three-wheeler), reliability, durability, safety and comfort and most important of all, a viable business proposition.

Commercial vehicles are business investments. If a customer is not able to earn the money to be able to pay back the acquisition price and earn some profit, s/he is not going to buy the vehicle.

Design and Development

The company realized that the entry level vehicle for the semi-urban and rural market was a product between a three-wheeler and a pick-up truck. The team put together to develop the new model came out with the Tata Ace in 2005.

A sturdy vehicle that can carry loads up to 1.5 tonnes over distances up to 300 km, the Ace is a four-wheeler at a price slightly higher than a three-wheeler. However, it offers greater stability, safety and comfort. More importantly, the operating cost was extended to a product lifecycle cost that covered purchase cost, operating cost and resale price. The Ace's USP is its low product lifecycle cost. It is essentially a last-mile load carrying vehicle, also useful in congested cities.

Customer type	Evaluation criteria
Only-performance customer	Who is willing to pay a higher price
Looking-for-a-balance customer	Who weighs both price and performance
Return-on-investment customer	Who is willing to pay a price for better value
Acquisition-price-sensitive customer	Who considers price, not performance

Exhibit 3.1 Classification of Customers

Launch

Ace, the mini-truck, was exhibited by organizing road shows through villages where the features and benefits were demonstrated. Customers were encouraged to test drive the vehicle. Using the metaphor of an elephant (a mother elephant representing the Tata truck), the Ace was simply called the baby elephant!

Changing Lives

Research had indicated that owning a four-wheeler increases the family's status in rural areas. However, the market is extremely price sensitive. "The Tata Ace, therefore, is an emotional brand at a functional price. In addition to a business, it enabled the customer to climb the social ladder," says U. T. Ramprasad, head—marketing communications. He adds, "Semi-urban and rural customers use Tata products for their day-to-day livelihood. Their belief and trust in the Tata brand is huge."

Sales and Service

As markets continue to move towards semi-urban and rural areas, the company is extending its reach through a unique concept called 1S outlets that handle only sales. At over 300 such outlets across India, customers can see and buy the product within 50–100 km of their village. Apart from its dealers, Tata Motors has tied up with local garages for servicing and has also organized training programmes to enhance their service skills. A mobile service van supplements their reach.

DISCUSSION QUESTIONS

1. Evaluate the marketing strategy of Tata Motors. Are there any gaps in their launch strategy?
2. Do you have any suggestions to offer?

Source: Sujata Agrawal, "Reaching Out to Rural India," July 2006, available at www.tata.com/company/Articles/inside.aspx?artid=m73PWlDIJmU=.

CASE 4 ASHA—NOURISHING NEW HOPE

"We continuously identify and cater to the needs of various consumer segments. With Asha from Horlicks, we are looking at offering a health drink for the emerging consumer class," says Shubhajit Sen, Executive Vice-President (Marketing), GlaxoSmithKline Consumer Healthcare.

GlaxoSmithKline has rolled out another health drink, Asha, under the Horlicks umbrella targeting the low-income groups in the urban markets and rural consumers. Asha evolved from Horlicks as a result of research conducted by the company, which reflected a need to extend a low-cost product for the hitherto neglected segments.

Previous Moves

Research conducted by the company in the 1990s indicated that though considered nourishing, Horlicks was perceived as a boring drink. While consumers were moving towards flavours, Horlicks had not changed its old look and feel. Thus, the company re-launched the brand and positioned it as a pleasurable nourishment drink aimed at children in the age group of 8–14. Three new flavours were introduced—vanilla, honey and chocolate—and a new look and design was given to the packs.

Things began to move fast when Zubair Ahmed took over as the managing director of the company. The company has plugged most markets with new products—Horlicks Lite for the elderly, Junior Horlicks for young kids, Women's Horlicks for women, Mother's Horlicks for lactating mothers and Horlciks Nutribar for young adults. "Over the years, what essentially was a malt-based drink has evolved into a wholesome brand catering to various age groups and geographies," adds Sen.

Affordable Product

GlaxoSmithKline Consumer Healthcare discovered that people in rural areas were not regular users of Horlicks because they were short of cash. They could afford to buy it rarely and would make it last for months. The company needed a product that could be used on a regular basis. Consequently, Asha, the new drink from Horlicks was priced at Rs 85 for a 500 g pouch pack—way below the price tag of Rs 135 on a Horlicks pack of a similar size.

Acceptability

In-house research carried out by GlaxoSmithKline and published health data showed that a significant proportion of Indian consumers in rural areas have different nutritional needs because of their dietary habits and work patterns. Typically, these consumers meet these nutritional needs through unbranded products such as finger millet and broken wheat. However, the quality of these products varies and they are often nutritionally inadequate. Direct interaction with consumers also revealed that many people from rural areas had moved to urban centres in large numbers. With both members of the family working and no support system, people were worried about falling sick. They needed a health drink that could safeguard them against illnesses.

After taking all these factors into account, GlaxoSmithKline Consumer Healthcare's team of researchers decided to make a product that was nutritionally superior but, easy on the pocket. Thus, was born Asha from Horlicks. "The name Asha stands for hope, and the brand believes in supporting the hopes of the emerging consumer class to access a better life," adds Sen. Of course, the company has added its flagship brand, Horlicks, to the name.

Competition and Strategy

Horlicks is the largest brand in the Rs 23 billion health food drinks market (it is growing at a rate of 20 per cent per annum) in the country with a share of over 50 per cent. Cadbury's Bournvita and Heinz's Complan have 15 per cent share each. Such is the brand equity of Horlicks that Nestlé has withdrawn its brand called Milo from the market. Dabur has entered the market with Chyawan Junior as a rival to GlaxoSmithKline other brand, Boost, and has stayed clear of Horlicks.

The introduction of Asha is a strategic move. This is the first time the company is trying to split the market into income groups. Sector experts say there's more to Asha's launch than meets the eye. Complan has gained market share of late, which has caused sufficient concern to GlaxoSmithKline Consumer Healthcare. Both the brands have been fighting tooth and nail in the advertising space. In 2008, Horlicks came out with a campaign that made a dig at Complan's theme of 23 vital nutrients. This resulted in Heinz filing a case in the Bombay High Court. It then came out with its own advertisement that compared its virtues against those of Horlicks. The television ad campaign claimed that Complan provides nutrients to children and enables them to grow twice as much as others. Obviously, GlaxoSmithKline Consumer Healthcare filed a counter in the Delhi High Court. Meanwhile, the competitors moved fast and launched products to arrest the growth of Junior Horlicks. While Heinz India has launched muesli as a breakfast meal, Cadbury has introduced Bournvita Li'l Champs.

In addition to the intense rivalry in the urban markets, another significant factor influenced the introduction of Asha. The rural markets make up about 30 per cent of the revenues of GlaxoSmithKline Consumer Healthcare. This figure is well below other fast-moving consumer goods companies like Hindustan Unilever and Marico. These companies and others active in the rural markets obtain 40–50 per cent of their sales revenues from rural markets. Glaxo decided on new initiatives such as the launch of Asha after it recognized the untapped opportunities and the power of innovation in making rural markets an engine for growth. It strengthened its distribution infrastructure to make sure that its products are available across markets. It added 4,000 sub-distributors to its existing 500 distributors in smaller towns. With these initiatives, the company hopes that the share of rural regions in its sales will go up by about 10 per cent over the next two years.

Cannibalization Problem

However, will Asha not eat into Horlicks's market? "Horlicks has been expanding and we want to make sure that we don't hurt the baseline equity of Horlicks," says Sen. Hence, the new product will be sold as Asha from Horlicks. It will be a separate brand. The company is also working on a brand-building exercise. The marketing team has developed a series of street plays to introduce the product. It has also tied up with a micro-finance group to promote the product. The ultimate objective is to gain an entry into schools and spread the brand's message.

DISCUSSION QUESTIONS

1. Analyse the strategy of GlaxoSmithkline and consider its appropriateness in the emergent context.
2. Will Asha get the expected results? If no, what suggestions do you make to build the brand and make it achieve expected results?

Source: Byravee Iyer, "Horlicks' New Hope," *Business Standard*, 8 December 2009, available at www.business-standard.com/india/news/horlicks-new-hope/00/33/378808/.

CASE 5 AN ALL-WEATHER FRIENDSHIP

The Nagarjuna group was founded by the late K. V. K. Raju, a professional technocrat, in 1973. It is one of the rapidly growing business houses in India. The group's asset base will cross USD 5 billion in the next five years. The group has significant presence in the steel, fertilizers, chemicals and financial services sectors of the country.

Nagarjuna Fertilizers and Chemicals Limited (NFCL), the flagship company, is the first gas-based fertilizer factory in South India. Construction began in 1988 in Kakinada in Andhra Pradesh and commercial production commenced from 1 August 1992. In 1998, it doubled the capacity of urea to 1.4 million tonnes. The other companies of the group offering agricultural solutions are Vijayalakshmi Insecticides and Pesticides, Nagarjuna Agri-chem Ltd, Nagarjuna Agricultural Research and Development Institute and Nagarjuna Haifa India Ltd (Vietnam).

The new logo of the group symbolizes a dynamic and value-based organization actuating the concept of trusteeship. The logo exemplifies the group's inner strength through the core values of organizational concern, commitment, quality and integrity towards its stockholders and customers. The central circle symbolizes the sun, the source of prime energy of the solar system. The five circles also symbolize the five elements of the universe and spirit of continuity. The triangle represents the planet Mars, which from time immemorial has symbolized prosperity, success and an abundance of energy. Therefore, it represents the upward flow of perennial energy towards the mission of the group.

The Company's Mission

The company visualizes itself as a highly trusted business partner of Indian farmers and seeks to serve society through its business. It aims at becoming the leading agri–input supplier in the country meeting the farmers' need of quality inputs for improving their productivity through latest technologies and services of committed and knowledgeable team of people.

Marketing Organization

The marketing head office of the company is located at Hyderabad. The organizational structure is depicted in Exhibit 5.1. With more than 3,000 dealers over 11 states across the country, the department handles a turnover above Rs 8 billion for its product range comprising 25–30 products.

It has six marketing zones across the country—two in Andhra Pradesh (one at Vishakhapatnam and the other at Hyderabad) and one each in West Bengal, Orissa, Maharashtra and Karnataka.

Market Share

NFCL is the leader with a share of 50 per cent in the 4 million tonne urea market, which is growing at a rate of 10 per cent. The primary competitors in the urea market are indicated in Exhibit 5.2.

Product Portfolio

The company has a range of products that include:

- Fertilizers
    - Manufactured urea (1.4 million MTs p.a.)
    - Traded fertilizers (0.2 million MTs p.a.) (MOP, DAP, Urea, AS, ZSSP).
- Pesticides
- Seeds
- Speciality fertilizers
- Other plant nutrients

Pricing

The government controls the prices. There is an excise levy of about 8 per cent on urea. The MRP of a 50 kg urea bag is Rs 238.50. However, competition has induced price wars and most of the companies are selling 50 kg bags at Rs 220.

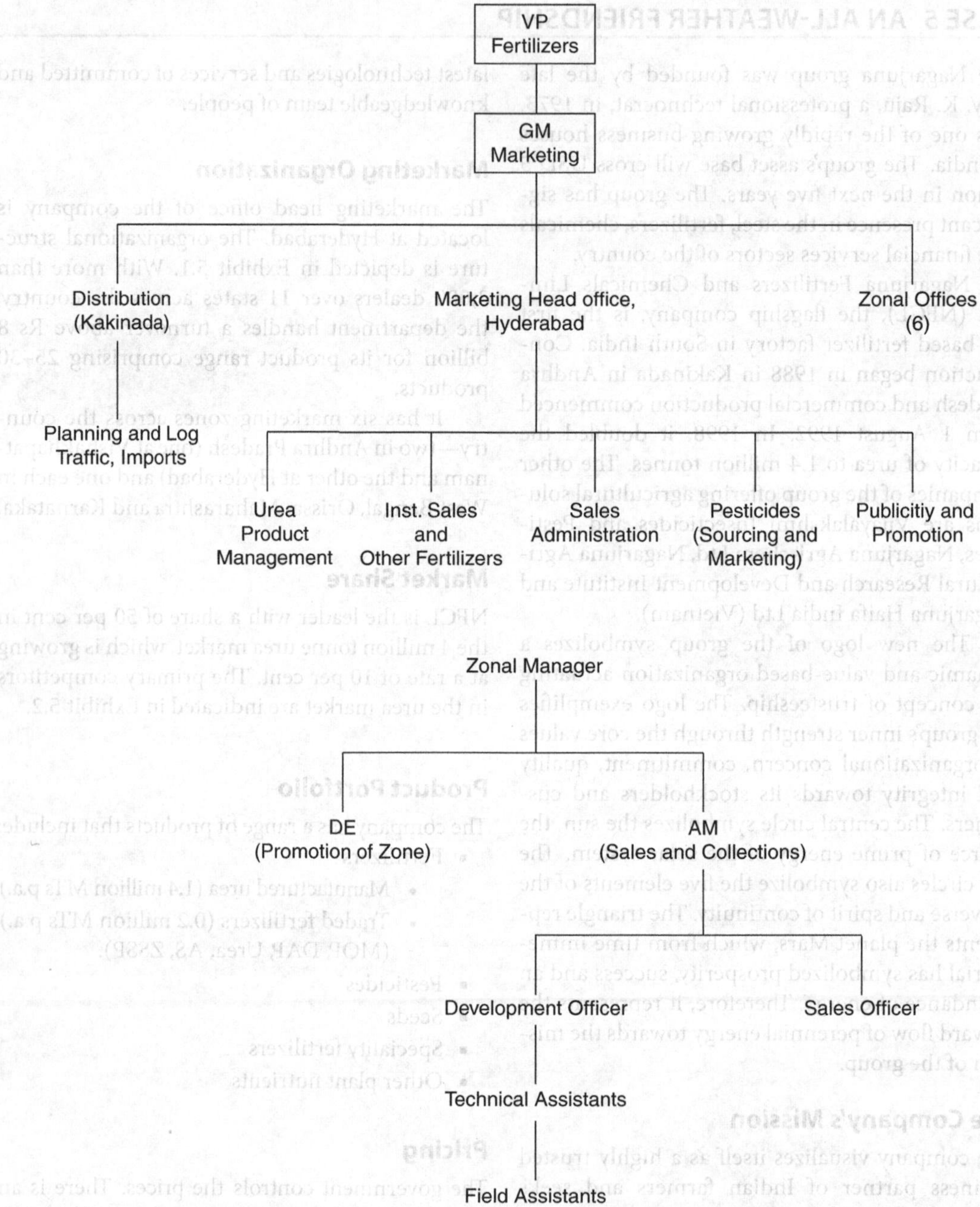

Exhibit 5.1 Marketing Organization of NFCL

State	Competitors
Andhra Pradesh	KRIBHCO, RCF, SPIC, MFL, NFL and ZACL
Orissa	IFFCO, NFL, Oswal and DIL
West Bengal	IFFCO, TCL, IG, NFL, Oswal and DIL
Maharashtra	RCF, KRIBHCO, IFFCO, GIWFC and GSFC
Karnataka	MFL, RCF, ZACL, KRIBHCO and SPIL

Exhibit 5.2 NFCL's Competitors

The Government of India fixes the *kharif* season and provides 100 per cent transport subsidy. The monthly movement is monitored by the Ministry of Fertilizers, Government of India, under the Essential Commodities Act, and the quantity is supplied based on that.

Distribution

The company's distribution network of dealers and consignees is spread over three states as shown in Exhibit 5.3. About 80 per cent of its distribution is concentrated in AP.

State	Dealers	Consignee	Total	Sales Locations
Andhra Pradesh	2609	6695	9304	6025
Orissa	284		284	387
West Bengal	158		158	287

Exhibit 5.3 Distribution Network

The company made its decision regarding location based on a survey finding that AP is among the first three states of the country in terms of consumption of fertilizers and East Godavari is among the top five districts in terms of fertilizer consumption in AP. Its other strengths are:

- Well planned internal siding and loading facilities
- Incoming wagon availability and proximity of traction line
- Operations streamlined by ISO 9002 systems and procedures

Promotion

The design of promotional activities depends primarily on two factors—(1) understanding of consumers and (2) choice of push or pull strategy. The company has also undertaken a study of its market and consumers.

Consumer Profile

The main characteristics of farmers are:

- Agriculture is more a way of life than a profession for the Indian farmer.
- Farmers generally feel insecure because of the overdependence of Indian agriculture on the monsoons.
- Though uneducated, many of the farmers exhibit good crop knowledge and common sense. They are shrewd decision makers.
- They show eagerness to acquaint themselves with new technology. However, they may not adopt readily due to financial reasons.
- Farmers are influenced more by the success of other farmers than by extension activities or advertisements and the sales-promotional efforts of the Government or commercial organizations.
- Farmers are dependent on revolving credit with high interest and often pay in kind to their financiers. They show high degree of loyalty to such financiers who are mostly traders and commission agents.
- Farmers are highly price sensitive due to the low margins involved in agriculture. Also, the returns are doubtful because of the dependence on the monsoons and other factors beyond their control.

Promotional Activities

The promotional activities in the rural markets require a strong focus on developmental activities and fostering of relationships with dealers.

(i) Dealer Front

1. **Rebates:** Quantity rebates of 1–2 bags are given to dealers when they cross the target.
2. **Credit:** Credit facility is extended to dealers with an interest of 1.5 per cent. However, collection of credit payments poses a problem for the company.
3. **Dealer's meets:** Whenever a product is introduced, a meeting of dealers and sub-dealers is organized.

(ii) Customer Front

The promotion is development oriented and takes the educational route. The company spends about Rs 0.45 billion towards development and Rs 0.01 billion on advertising.

Farm Management Services (FMS)

NFCL has set up the Nagarjuna Agricultural Research and Development Institute (NARDI) to provide R&D support and initiated a uniquely beneficial programme—FMS. FMS provides a gamut of services, which include:

- Situation-specific technology transfer
- Providing feedback for site-specific consultancy
- Total involvement from the soil testing and land preparation stage to the post harvest stage
- Involvement of eminent scientists from NARDI in the exercise
- Ensuring recording of farm practices
- Helping in risk mitigation

Advertising

Advertising is done in farmer's magazines like "*Annadata*" and prime time shows on TV. Outdoor advertising include wall paintings, hoardings and *shandy* centres. An audio-visual van makes rounds covering 3–4 villages in a day. During the night, the van provides entertainment—film songs or cinema shows.

Field Promotion

The field promotion becomes intense just before the *kharif* and *rabi* seasons, i.e. between August and October and December and February. The activity is multi-pronged and inclusive of:

- *Growers meetings:* For landlords of 10 acres and above, orchard growers, etc.
- *Crop seminars:* This involves about 50–60 farmers based on the pests and diseases prevalent in the local area. Research scientists of the local government Agricultural Department are invited.
- *Scientists' visit to the field:* Technical assistants of the company, retired or in-service research scientists of the Agricultural Departments visit the farm and advise the farmers.
- *KVK training: Krishi Vignan Kendra* at Kakinada organizes training classes for three days for about 900 farmers in a year. The annual expenditure may be any where between Rs 2.5–3 million.
- *Big farmer meetings:* Every year 10–15 meetings of the big farmers are conducted in which 30–40 members take part.
- *Spot demonstrations:* Farmers are educated by showing them photos of different farming practices. 15–20 farmers take part in each batch.

The field activity at villages hinges on field assistants. The company ensures that qualified persons who can fluently speak the local languages and mix with farmers are selected. Young farmers are roped into service and trained. They organize meetings. The field assistants are given a fixed coverage plan—a cluster of 12–15 villages. They have to cover 2 or 3 villages in a day. Field assistants are advised not to sell products directly. The marketing mantra is—"Friendship with farmers finds you customers."

Forging New Friendships

Globalization has opened up new cultural windows and unforeseen business doors. NFCL has ushered in the new revolution with a vision. "Rural prosperity through enhanced knowledge and technology" and a mission "to enable continual enhancement of agricultural production and rural prosperity to make Indian farmers globally competitive" are the goals.

The new revolution at NFCL has been ushered in by its new agri-portal called ikisan.com. The new agri-portal will speak to every farmer in his language, no matter which part of the country he may be in. It tells him about the best farming practices, the latest technology, soil conditions, anything and everything that he might want to know. In fact, to begin with, it will bring all the benefits of FMS. It brings the world to the farmer because everything the farmer needs to know is just a click away.

Staying Together

The winds of change are here. It is an opportune time to forge friendships. Also, it is a testing time for farmer relationships. A strategy for retaining friends and winning their favours need be developed.

R. L. N. Murthy, senior manager (marketing development) suggests the following tips:

- A rupee in hand is better than two on paper. Motivate farmers to buy in cash by offering attractive incentives at the beginning of the season.
- Aim for high-volume and high-value margins. Market concentration should be on commercial crops. These farmers can offer to pay more for quality products.
- Buy the distributor's loyalty. Consumer loyalty often flows through the distributor. Make special favours to him.
- Sell usage more than a product.
- Educate about the usefulness of the product and its usage. Do not persuade people to buy your brand.
- It is often said that seeing is believing. Instead of focusing on company sponsored demonstrations, it is preferable to showcase the fields of farmers who have voluntarily used the company's brand.
- Develop trust.
- Many agents and traders resort to cheating the farmers in connivance with government officials. Win the farmer. Be a reliable friend.
- Help in the marketing of produce. By helping farmers in disposing off their produce, you not only win their goodwill but also ensure clearance of their debts to the company.
- Offer technical services to meet competition. Provide services to improve farming practices, such as technology transfer and co-operative farming with an understanding of the farmers' competitive needs.
- Focus on integrated farm development. The agri-input marketing programme should envisage an integrated development approach for the benefit of the farmer community than a narrow area/crop or season-based plan.

The following development programme can be considered for this purpose:

- Formation of farmers' clubs to discuss their problems and possible solutions.
- Interaction with scientists, experts and successful farmers to learn and solve problems.
- Training on the proper use of inputs and farm equipment, particularly that of spraying.

- Participation in exchange programmes like field days, farmers' meets and TV/Video programmes.

DISCUSSION QUESTIONS

1. Outline the characteristics and needs of farmers and identify the future opportunities and threats.
2. Appraise the current marketing strategy of NFCL.
3. Suggest modifications in strategy that NFCL needs to make to face future markets.

Source: Field interviews; R. L. N. Murthy, "Management Strategy for Farm Inputs," *Indian Management* (November 2000): 57–59.

CASE 6 HEROES FOR A CAUSE

The Heroes Project, initiated by Hollywood actor, Richard Gere and socialite, Parmeshwar Godrej, is a beacon of hope for those who have been living a life of stigma and ostracism. The project aims to advocate and educate the masses on issues related to HIV/AIDS through the Indian media, the entertainment industry and business houses. It was launched nationwide in 2004 after a tie-up with the Avahan India AIDS Initiative, an offshoot of the US-based Bill and Melinda Gates Foundation. The project received funding of USD 2.4 million from the Bill and Melinda Gates Foundation for a period of three years. The Henry J. Kaiser Family Foundation also collaborated with the project by providing technology for the production of campaign advertisements and creating awareness about the project in the Indian media.

Star Partner

The project announced its first public education partnership with STAR Television Network in July 2004. STAR TV volunteered to air messages by allocating airtime and providing content writers. Thus, the partnership provided the project with a reach of an estimated 70 million viewers and huge amounts of free airtime across their various channels over a three-year period. The success has encouraged them to extend the campaign for another two years.

Celebrity Tie-ups

Bollywood personalities such as Salman Khan, Anil Kapoor, Shilpa Shetty, Bipasha Basu and Sunny Deol have joined hands with the project. For instance, when a campaign was organized to raise awareness among truck drivers, Sunny Deol, their icon, was chosen to address a crowd of 4,000.

Media Tie-ups

The mass media has been a springboard for the project to conduct social events and campaigns. Doctors, writers and even HIV-affected people sitting across the table contributed to message development. HIV-affected people tell their stories and the stigma and discrimination that they suffer; however, they relate this as another person's story. Sometimes, even a touch of humour is added to such messages. Ogilvy airs new advertisements every eight weeks.

Government Tie-ups

The Heroes Project also works closely with government organizations and NGOs, both at the national and the regional level. At the national level, the project works hand-in-hand with the National Aids Control Organisation (NACO) in its innumerable social campaigns. NACO buys huge airtime on Doordarshan and the ads that they air are sometimes those developed by the Heroes Project.

The project also works to spread awareness among local people with the help of the regional branches of NACO, i.e. the State AIDS Control Societies (SACS) and local bodies and organizations. For example, in Tamil Nadu, the project is currently working with local bodies to strategize a media campaign all over the state.

Promotion

The communication campaigns aim at education and involvement of target people.

- *Short messages:* The project collaborated with the STAR network and Ogilvy for an SMS (text messaging) campaign where the viewer could send an SMS to 7827 to get information on HIV/AIDS using a menu. The number was given at the bottom of the screen during advertisements. This interactive campaign was rolled out in two phases and centred on HIV/AIDS and titled "Gain from *Gyaan*." Aptly aimed at 15- to 24-year olds, the contest offered users the facility to access HIV/AIDS information on their cell phones in an exciting format. This medium provided easy access to life-saving information for the younger generation and drew an extraordinary response of approximately 200,000 hits over a three-month period. Ninety thousand of these were unique numbers. The success of this campaign earned a special mention at the XVI International AIDS Conference as an innovative and exemplary paradigm for youth outreach.

- *Specific-query response:* The ongoing initiative enables an individual to seek any information on HIV/AIDS through an SMS from a trained medical counsellor. This initiative has garnered overwhelming response.
- *"Test is Best" campaign:* On World AIDS Day, SACS and the Heroes Project collaborated on a campaign called "Test is Best" where people were educated on the importance of visiting a testing centre. Apart from this, both the organizations also ran a campaign in around 9,500 schools in Tamil Nadu.

Chess grandmaster Vishwanathan Anand was the official ambassador for this campaign.

The Road Ahead

As a part of its advocacy campaigns, the project is also tying up with business houses to conduct workplace programmes. In Tamil Nadu, an event calendar is being formulated with SACS. Events for every month, like blood donation camps and campaigns focusing on specific groups like auto and taxi drivers are being formulated.

DISCUSSION QUESTIONS

1. The key to success in social marketing is tie-ups and partnerships on one side and touch points of target audience on the other. Examine the Heroes initiative in light of the above statement.
2. Suggest some educative and exciting approaches to make the campaign more effective.

Source: Nayantara Som, "Heroes for a Cause," July 2007, available at www.expresshealthcare.in/200707/strategy02.shtml.

CASE 7 MARKETING OF TV CHANNELS

The new reality show on Imagine TV, "*Desi* Girl," will have eight glamorous celebrities milking cows, making cow dung cakes and more in a village. Village-based fiction shows such as "*Bandini*" and "*Kashi*" on Imagine TV and "*Balika Vadhu*" and "*Na Aana Iss Des Laado*" on Colors have already become popular. The abundance of reality shows based on rural life indicates the fact that competition is brewing for rural markets among television channels.

Like FMCGs and consumer durables, television channels have started spreading their wings in the rural markets. The new interest can be attributed to the growth in cable and satellite (C&S) television homes from 40 million to 60 million in the last two years.

Different TV channels have adopted different approaches to create interest in the programmes.

STAR TV

The channel put STAR *Utsav gaddis (*rural vans) into operation. These vans, equipped with 29-inch televisions and a DVD player, show the channel's bestsellers *Kyunki Saas Bhi Kabhi Bahu Thi* and *Kahani Ghar Ghar Ki* as well as popular reality shows such as *Khulja Sim Sim* on the streets of many small towns in Uttar Pradesh, Rajasthan, Maharashtra and Gujarat.

Utsav aims at catering to markets with a population of less than 0.1 million, which can afford only a certain amount towards cable charges. The target market is free-to-air (FTA) homes and the task is to attract them to view pay channels. According to Puneet Johar, Senior Vice-President, STAR India, STAR *Utsav* was launched as a market development channel so that viewers from FTA homes can sample the popular STAR Plus programmes and graduate to other pay channels in the STAR family.

The aggressive marketing strategy comprises interactive events such as contests based on its various shows where prizes are given out. In *Vote Do Show Lo*, people are asked to vote for a show they would like to watch. On-air promos are supported by personal visits. Visits are made to residential colonies, cinemas and colleges and people are encouraged to fill the voting forms.

Advertisers have also contributed to the popularity of the channel. The *Utsav Di Gaddi,* that presents the channel's programmes, is also used by mass marketers. Nokia promotes its dual-language phones and Asian Paints talks about its Tractor emulsion. Hindustan Unilever has sponsored the *Vote Do Show Lo* contest.

SAHARA ONE

This channel has focused its programming to suit the rural markets based on the recognition that 60 per cent of viewership comes from the smaller markets and the return on investment is much higher in these markets. Purnendu Bose, COO, Sahara One says, "It is the smaller markets from which a broadcaster gets its loyal audience." Accordingly, the channel designed on-ground activities to woo audiences in the smaller markets. Bangle carts in village *haats* and umbrellas of street-side *paan* shops are branded to promote its show *Hare Kaanch Ki Choodiyan.*

SAB TV

SAB TV, from the Sony bouquet, is strategically associated with smaller markets as the channel positions itself as a middle-class channel. Such a stand was taken because small towns are viewed as big markets. Vikas Bahl, business head, SAB, said that they get the bulk of their revenue from the advertisers who focus on rural markets. SAB TV is adopting a push strategy. It has made deals with local cable operators to promote its show, *Wah Wah,* in smaller markets.

SONY

Sony is capitalizing on the large distribution network of FMCGs by tying up with them. It tied up with Parachute and the bottles now have the *Indian Idol* branding on them. Sony depends on the trickle-down approach. Its strategy has always been to penetrate the metros first and subsequently reach the smaller markets, where it markets only certain shows.

ZEE NETWORK

A significant percentage of Zee's viewership comes from the smaller markets. According to Ashish Kaul, senior vice-president, Zee, "The Indian heartland is a priority market for us. Some of our recent launches such as *Kam Ya Zyada* anchored by Manoj Bajpai, *Saregamapa Challenge* 2005 and *Saat Phere* have been extensively promoted across the Indian heartland."

Rationale of the Campaigns

The success of FMCGs in the rural markets and the growing popularity of the programmes of different channels indicate that the rural markets are definitely the markets of tomorrow. Channels should focus on developing content relevant to both small towns and the metros.

DISCUSSION QUESTIONS

1. Prepare a comparative analysis of marketing approaches of different TV channels.
2. Develop a comprehensive marketing strategy for STAR TV to reach the rural masses.

Source: Radhika B., "Indian Reality TV Goes Rural with Desi Girl," 14 April 2010, available at http://newshopper.sulekha.com/indian-reality-tv-goes-rural-with-desi-girl_news_1165502.htm; Ajita Shashidhar, "The Big Rural Picture," *The Hindu Business Line*, 16 March 2006, available atwww.thehindubusinessline.com/catalyst/2006/03/16/stories/2006031600270100.htm.

CASE 8 DOCTOR'S CHOICES

According to industry estimates, the rural share in pharma markets is on the rise. In 2007, while metros and cities accounted for nearly 60 per cent of the total pharma market, small towns (20 per cent) and rural markets (21 per cent) accounted for the balance.

The rural market share increased to 18 per cent in 2005 from 16 per cent in 2004 showing an annual rise of 2 per cent. The domestic pharma market is showing double-digit growth and it is primarily driven by new products and market expansion strategies. According to Utkarsh Palnitkar of Ernst & Young, smaller markets in rural areas are driving the Indian growth rates in the region of 20 per cent. The credit for the growth goes to the strong wholesale distribution system.

According to a market analyst, the observation has an important implication for pharmaceutical companies. Sales infrastructure deployed in these markets is inadequate to realize current as well as future market potential. The emerging new segments have increased the potential. Hitesh Gajaria of consulting firm KPMG observed, "Though rural markets are dominated by acute ailments, chronic (lifestyle related) segments have slowly started making inroads. It is found that in an average mass product sales division, only 20–30 per cent of the sales force is deployed in these markets. The number is even lower in case of specialty products divisions.

Focusing on Sales

RAINBOW Pharmaceuticals, a mid-size generic company from India, aims to penetrate up to 1,500 new villages with population below 40,000, 300 villages with population of 40,000 to 100,000 and over 75 peripheral villages and towns around Kolkata Metropolitan region. For this, it decided to boost its current sales force by recruiting around 1,000 sales and marketing professionals. The newly recruited field staff will be mainly deployed to sell drugs in India's fast-emerging rural markets and tier 2 and tier 3 cities across the country.

Knowing the Key

The company has decided to provide information inputs to its sales force about doctors in the rural areas. Doctors play a pivotal role in pharma marketing. They are given utmost respect by patients and are treated like gods. Whatever a doctor prescribes, the patient has to purchase and make use of. He has neither the knowledge to evaluate the prescriptions nor the guts to question the doctor.

The Study

A management trainee was asked to conduct a study with the following objectives.

(*i*) To identify the available facilities for treatment

(*ii*) To find out the inflow of patients and the nature of complaints

(*iii*) To know the type of treatment offered by the doctors, and

(*iv*) To ascertain the extent to which pharma companies are providing services to doctors in terms of information, samples, etc.

A questionnaire was developed (Exhibit 8.1) to elicit the views of doctors.

Exhibit 8.1

Questionnaire Designed for Medical Practitioners

IDENTIFICATION NO. (FOR OFFICE USE ONLY)

Part A: Profile of the Medical Practitioner
(Information to be collected either by personal observation or by interview)

1. Name of the Doctor :
   (Note down the name legibly)

2. Address :
   (Note down the address legibly)

Location	
Vill/Town	
P.O	
District	
State	
Pin No.	
Phone No.	

3. Age : Years
   (Note down the age in complete numbers)

4. Sex : Male [ ] : Female [2]
   (Circle the appropriate box)

5. Degree/Diploma :
   (Note down appropriately)

6. Registration No. :
   (Write the registration number accurately)

7. Practice Type :
(Circle the appropriate entry under Column 2)

Sl No.	Practice Type	Circle Appropriately
(0)	(1)	(2)
1.	Allopathy	A
2.	Homoeopathy	B
3.	Biochemic	C
4.	Ayurvedic	D
5.	Naturopathy	E
6.	Unani	F
7.	Acupuncture	G
8.	Other (state)	H

8. (For non-MBBS practitioners). How did the doctor get inducted in allopathy practice? (Note down in detail.)

____

____

9. Does he/she have any other parallel profession apart from allopathic practice (like agriculture/ compounding /teaching/role of pharmacist/chemist, etc. (Note down in detail.)

____

____

Part B

(Information to be collected primarily by interview supplemented by personal observation.)

1. Doctor, are you a resident of this area? Yes: ☐ No: ☐
(Put a circle in the appropriate box)
2. (If the answer to the above question is "No" then, ask): Do you come from outside to cater to the patients of this area? If so, from where? How far is that place from this area?
(Note down the name of the outside village/town legibly in Column 1. Also, note down the distance of that place, in complete kilometres from this area in Column 2.)
(Also ask) What type of transport service do you normally use for attending to patients of this area?

Sl No.	Name of village/town	Distance (in km)	Transport (use code)
(0)	(1)	(2)	(3)
1.			
2.			

Note: Code of Transport service: (a) through bus, (b) through tram, (c) through other public road transport, (d) through personal two-wheeler, (e) through personal four-wheeler, (f) through cycle, van, rickshaw, bicycle, (g) through country boat (h) through launch steamer waterways (i) combination of public road transport (including bus service) and cycle rickshaw/van, (j) combination of public road transport and walking, (k) combination of tram and cycle rickshaw/van, (l) on foot, (m) others.

3. (*a*) Doctor, how many clinics do you maintain?
   (*b*) Doctor, do you also maintain a roving practice?

0	1		
Yes	Y	No	N

   (*a*) Doctor, could you please give your full address, wherever you are available for consultation. (Note down the full address)
   (*b*) Also, please tell us when you are available at the address we have just noted down (Note down practice time/week approximately).
4. For roving practice: What type of drugs do you carry for patients' treatment?

Sl No.	Drug Type	Sl No.	Drug Type	Sl No.	Drug Type
(0)	(1)	(0)	(1)	(0)	(1)
1		6		11	
2		7		12	
3		8		13	
4		9		14	
5		10		15	

5. (*a*) Doctor, do you normally receive patients from outside villages/towns? Yes: No: (Put a circle in the appropriate box.)
   (*b*) Doctor, what percentage of your patients normally come from each area? (Write percentage figure against each in Column 2.)

Sl No.	Description	Percentage of patients
1.	From this village/town only	
2.	From outside villages	
3.	From outside towns	

   (*c*) Could you please give us the name of other village(s)/town(s) from where the patients normally come to you for consultation?
   - Note down the name of village(s)/town(s) legibly under Column 1.
   - Also, note down the distance of those village(s)/town(s) in complete kilometres under Column 2.

Sl No.	Name of the village(s)/town(s)	Distance (in km)
(0)	(1)	(2)
1.		
2.		
3.		
4.		
5.		
6.		
7.		
8.		
9.		
10.		

6. Doctor, on an average, how many patients do you treat per day?
   (Circle the appropriate entry under Column 2)

Sl No.	Practice type	Circle appropriately
(0)	(1)	(2)
1.	1 to 10	(A)
2.	11 to 20	(B)
3.	21 to 30	(C)
4.	31 to 49	(D)
5.	50 and above	(E)

7. (*a*) Doctor, in a week, out of 100 patients, what percentage of patients come to you for consultation directly?
   (Note down the exact number.) ☐
   (*b*) Doctor, in a week, out of 100 patients, what percentage of patients come to you for your consultation indirectly, through other doctors? (Note down the exact number.) ☐
8. Doctor, can you recall the name(s) of those doctor(s)/expert(s) who often refer their patients to you?
   (Note down the name(s) of the doctor(s) in Column 1. Also, note down the location of their clinic/chamber in Column 2.)

Sl No.	Name(s) of the doctor(s)	Location of clinic/chamber
(0)	(1)	(2)
1.		
2.		
3.		
4.		
5.		

9. Doctor, approximately, what could be your fees per patient? (Note down the fees of the doctor under Column 2.)

Sl No.	Description	Fees (in Rs)
(0)	(1)	(2)
1.	When the patient comes to your clinic	
2.	When you visit the patient in the patient's house	

Note: Fees of the patient at home should not include transportation charges.

10. (*a*) Doctor, during emergency, say, during odd hours or midnight, do the patients of this area have access to your service? Yes ☐ No ☐
(Put a circle the appropriate entry.)
(*b*) Doctor, what kind of emergencies do you face? (Note down the names of complaints in details.)

____

____

____

11. (*i*) Generally speaking, what are the types of complaints with which and for which the patients come to you for treatment?
(Record the response *ad verbatim* in Column 1)

Sl No.	Complaints		Complaints
1.	Feverish	6.	
2.	Vomiting	7.	
3.	Pains	8.	
4.	Stomach ache	9.	
5.	Allergies	10.	

(*ii*) Doctor, do you receive patients with long-term diseases (like diabetes, hypertension, BPH, psoriasis, asthma, arthritis), i.e. out of 100 patients treated by you in a week, how many are of this type? (Note down the percentage.) ☐☐☐
(*iii*) If there are some patients who are on long-term treatment, how regular are they in taking the prescribed therapies? (Note down the response in detail.)

____

____

12. Doctor, one does not obviously expect to get all the different facilities in such a location as one would have otherwise obtained in a city. In this context:
(*i*) In what condition would you possibly refer the patient to some other place or centre or expert? (Note down the conditions legibly *ad verbatim* in Column 1.)
(*ii*) What would you recommend on such occasions?

(Record the response of the doctor covering the location, type of institution, type of expert(s)/professional(s), etc, under Column 2.)

Sl No.	Condition(s)	Recommendations of the doctor
(0)	(1)	(2)
1.		
2.		
3.		
4.		
5.		
6.		
7.		
8.		
9.		
10.		

(If needed, attach extra sheet.)

13. (*a*) Does the patient get the medicines prescribed by you directly from you? (Circle the appropriate entry under Column 2)

Sl No.	Description	Circle appropriately
(0)	(1)	(2)
1.	Fully always	(A)
2.	Partly	(B)
3.	Not at all	(C)

(*b*) If the answer is B, what types of medicines does he personally provide? (Note down the details.)

(*c*) If the answer is not A, ask: From where do your patients procure the medicines prescribed by you? (Note down the location of the store properly.)

Sl No.	Location of the store	Distance (in km)
(0)	(1)	(2)
1.		
2.		
3.		
4.		
5.		

14. (*i*) Doctor, whatever drugs you prescribe, do your patients normally get such drugs in this area?
Yes ☐ No ☐
(Circle appropriately)
(*ii*) If the answer is No, ask what type of drugs are not available in this area?
(Note down the names of the drugs under Column 1 properly. Also, note the comments of the doctor in this respect under Column 2.)

Sl No.	Name of the drugs	Remarks of the doctor
(0)	(1)	(2)
1.		
2.		
3.		
4.		
5.		

15. (*i*) Doctor, do you only use oral therapies or use injectibles/parenteral therapies or both? (Put a tick mark.)
Oral therapies only ☐
Injectibles/Parenteral therapies only ☐
Both oral and injectibles/parenteral ☐
(*ii*) Doctor, do you undertake minor cutting, dressing, stitching and wound healing in your clinic? (Put a tick mark.) Yes ☐ No ☐
(*iii*) When you write the prescriptions which language do you write in?
English only ☐ Vernacular only ☐ Both English and vernacular ☐

16. (*a*) Doctor, do you get the service of the industry? (Wait...then say) In the last 15 days did any medical representative meet you? Yes ☐ No ☐
(*b*) (If the answer is "yes", ask): Doctor, can you recall the names of these companies?
(Write the names of these companies under Column 1.)
(*c*) (For these companies) Can you remember the frequency of visit of MSR (use code)?

Note: Periodicity of visit: (a) Once in a week (b) Twice in a week (c) Once in two weeks (d) Once in three weeks (e) Twice in three weeks (f) Once in a month (g) Once in two months (h) Once in three months (i) Once in six months (j) Once in a year (k) Others.

Company name	Frequency	Company name	Frequency
1.		9.	
2.		10.	
3.		11.	
4.		12.	
5.		13.	
6.		14.	
7.		15.	
8.		16.	

(*d*) Doctor, can you recall the names of other companies who are occasional visitors?

Company name	Company name
1.	9.
2.	10.
3.	11.
4.	12.
5.	13.
6.	14.
7.	15.

(*e*) Doctor, how do MSRs convey their message? In English or in vernacular or in both?
English only ☐ Vernacular only ☐ Both ☐

(*f*) How do you keep yourself informed (*i*) about new medicine(s)? (*ii*) about disease management? (Circle the appropriate entry under Column 2.)

Sl No.	Description	Circle appropriately
(0)	(1)	(2)
1.	Through medical representatives	(A)
2.	Through medical journal	(B)
3.	Through fellow colleagues	(C)
4.	Through medical conferences	(D)
5.	Through agents/distributors/drug suppliers	(E)

Thank you doctor for your cooperation.

Source: Rupali Mukherjee, "Rural India Grows Bigger in Pharma Pie," *The Times of India*, 04 December 2007, available at www.iespanchayat.net.in/pdf/2007-december.pdf.

DISCUSSION QUESTIONS

1. Develop a model that presents the aspects of inquiry.
2. Evaluate the questionnaire design.

CASE 9 NUTRINE—LEADING THE RURAL MARKET

Nutrine Confectionery Company Limited is the flagship company of the Nutrine group of companies, spanning diverse products and services such as confectionery, gums, fruit bars, granites and transportation, etc. The turnover of the group crossed Rs 17.1 billion in 1999. B. Venkatramana Reddy, a graduate from National University, Adyar, established Nutrine Confectionery Company (NCC) in 1952. From a small-scale unit manufacturing only candies in the early 1960s, Nutrine Confectionery has grown to be a multi-market giant and has been the single-largest manufacturer of confectionery and toffees in India since 1980.

Product

Since 1985, Nutrine has diversified into food products such as gums, fruit pulp and dehydrated fruit bars of mango, banana, papaya, guava, pineapple, apple, grape, etc. Being the leader in the industry for more than two decades, Nutrine has always endeavoured to satisfy the wants and desires of customers with special emphasis on quality, range and cost effectiveness. It has more than 70 varieties of candies, toffees, lozenges, etc. Nutrine is the only company in India producing dehydrated fruit bars, using an innovative technology. The company has a well-equipped research and development laboratory where continuous product testing and product development is organized. Exhibit 9.1 shows the product range of Nutrine.

Chocolates: Chocolate Eclairs, Wild Koffy, Superstar Assortment, Nutrine Gold, *Aasay*, *Dishum* Special, *Dishum* Pineapple, Caramella, *Kokanaka* Cookies, *Maha* Lacto, *Aam Ras*, Milk Cream, Bon Bon, Marvel Assortment, *Gulkand*, Ginger Caps, Sunshine Fruits, Orange Candy, Lollipop, Coolers, Fruit Roll.

Bubble gums: Boomer, Big Bubble, Big fun, Funda, Donald, Bunny Bubble Gum, Wrestler.

Chewing gum: Gum Yum, OLE, Juicy fruit, Center Fresh, Double mint, Spear mint, Brooklyn.

Fruit bars—Naturo: Mango, Banana, Guava, Papaya, Grape, Apple.

Exhibit 9.1 Product Range of Nutrine

Manufacturing Process

Nutrine produces its confectionery at its main factory at Chittoor. The packaging of the confectionary is carried out at various centres. Chittoor district lies in an advantageous horticultural belt where tropical fruits such as banana, mango and papaya grow in abundance. Lime, tomatoes, etc are also cultivated in the area. Vegetable and fruit processing are, therefore, natural developments in this region and Nutrine has been in the forefront of these development activities. Their current research extends to the processing of guava pulp and banana pulp and also a host of health and dietary products. The production capacity of Nutrine and its major competitors is given in Exhibit 9.2.

Company	Capacity (in tonnes)
Nutrine	20,000
Parle	20,000
Parrys	15,000
Ravalgaon	10,000

Exhibit 9.2 Production Capacities

Market

The overall industry growth rate is 6 per cent per annum whereas the organized sector exhibits a growth rate of 8–10 per cent. Nutrine enjoys a market share of 34 per cent in the confectionery segment in the organized sector. The company's strength lies not only in its manufacturing capabilities but also its wide marketing reach. Nutrine is available throughout the country through a network of 32 depots-cum-C&Fs, more than 2,210 distributors and 0.4 million retailers. Its main competitors are listed in Exhibit 9.3.

Confectionery	Parrys, Parle, Bakemans, Ravalgaon, Nestlé
Chocolates	Nestle, Cadbury, Campco
Gums	Wrigley, Perfetti Gum (India) Ltd, VM Confectionery
Instant foods	Orkay, Nestlé, MTR
Fruit bars	Sunrays

Exhibit 9.3 Major Competitors of Nutrine

Nutrine has exported confectionery and mango fruit bars to Australia, Bahrain, Bangladesh, Canada, Kenya, Malaysia, Mozambique, New Zealand, Nepal, Norway, Saudi Arabia, Singapore, Sri Lanka, USA, etc. It is aiming at becoming the leader not only in confectionery, but also in vegetable and fruit-processed food products, etc.

Tapping the Rural Market

The company has been highly interested in rural areas right from its inception. It has been focusing more on the untapped areas of rural India because of the growing competition in urban areas. Added to this, the projected market size for chocolates in rural areas is estimated at 20,000 to 22,000 tonnes. It was only 10,000 tonnes three years ago.

The company has received a positive response from the rural markets, especially for its brands such as *Mahalacto*, *Kokanaka*, *Dishum* and *Aasay*. The main competitors of Nutrine confectionery are Parrys, Ravalgaon, Kwality and also the unorganized sector to a large extent. In the highly competitive confectionary market, Nutrine controls 40 per cent of the rural market.

Distribution

The distribution channel is depicted in Exhibit 9.4.

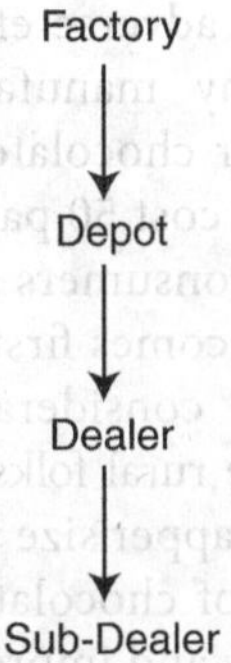

Exhibit 9.4 Distribution Channel of Nutrine

The depot covers 2–3 districts. The sub-dealer employs his own people to distribute chocolates in the interior regions with the help of the company. The company salesman distributes chocolates in areas with a population more than 25,000.

The major areas of operation include Andhra Pradesh, Tamil Nadu, Kerala, Karnataka and some parts of Northern India. The growth rate in this sector is forecast at 5 per cent per year. All distribution activities are coordinated and controlled by the marketing head office situated at Chennai.

The Strategy

Products are developed keeping in mind familiar tastes such as Coconut, Mango, Papaya, etc. Unfamiliar and alien flavours such as strawberry, lime, etc. are not considered.

Products

Thick, attractive and glossy packaging is used to capture the fancy of children. The products are made available in three types of packaging—twist, basket, and pillow. However, consumers seem to favour the pillow type of packaging.

The Price

The government had imposed a 100 per cent excise duty on confectioneries in the last budget.

This has had an adverse effect on the industry compelling many manufacturers to increase the price of their chocolates. The *Aasay* brand, which originally cost 50 paise, is to be priced at 75 paise. Rural consumers are highly price sensitive. The price comes first followed by quality in the purchase consideration process. So in order to keep the rural folks happy, the company increased the wrapper size with a small increase in the quantity of chocolate. They re-launched the brand as new and improved.

The Place

The traditional places include groceries, *paan* shops, platform shops near schools, etc. The company has adopted a strategy of covering "unconventional shops," i.e. shops where one would not normally think of buying chocolates such as hair-style salons, STD booths, coffee centres and other shops where people gather. It also uses vans to distribute products in rural areas. It has a total of 10 vans, of which 2–3 vans are allotted to each state where it has a major market.

The Promotion

School-level promotional activities include wrapper collection, slogan contests and games. For instance, they recently organized a wrapper collection scheme with the following gifts:

- 10 wrappers: Bunny eraser
- 20 wrappers: Bouncing ball
- 30 wrappers: Chinese car
- 40 wrappers: Luxor Papermate pen
- 50 wrappers: Funskool Snakes and Ladders game

The company believes that its name and logo should be focused on in promotional activities and advertising campaigns. At present, Mudra, Lintas and Madison are handling their account. Their ad themes stress the involvement of family and their relatives in the choice and consumption of chocolates.

According to company sources, the print media is not very effective because very few households buy magazines and newspapers in rural areas. The radio has been considered the most effective medium so far. However, with the advent of television and cable, television has become the most preferred channel. Apart from these channels, road shows are also organized to promote the products.

Social Contribution

The company believes in fulfilling its corporate social responsibility obligations. It has been contributing to the society by way of donations and charities, sponsoring different events, working with PHCs to eradicate health issues such as Vitamin A deficiency, organizing blood donation and eye camps, etc.

DISCUSSION QUESTIONS

1. Analyse the competitive situation of Nutrine.
2. Evolve a strategy for Nutrine to win both the rural and urban markets.

Source: Students of TIME (The Management School of Tirupathi) who undertook the survey under the supervision of the authors.

CASE 10 CONCRETE AMBITIONS

Jaypee Rewa Cement (JRC), a division of the construction giant, Jai Prakash Industries, beat the stagnation in the cement market by aggressively pursuing the rural consumer. It was able to create brand equity in the cement market, a segment in which the product had been traditionally perceived as a commodity with no brand preferences.

Sellers' Market

The Indian cement market had always been a classic sellers' market. The Government, which was also the principal buyer consuming an estimated 40 per cent of the industry's output decided not only the manufacturing capacities, but also the quantities to be released to dealers. Things started changing in 1982 when the industry was partially decontrolled. In 1989, controls were removed fully. The effects of decontrol can be understood from the following statistic—between 1985–1986 and 1992–1993, installed capacities went up from around 42 million tonnes to about 65 million tonnes. Then, in 1992, the Government, trying to reduce its spending, cut purchases dramatically from 40 per cent to only around 18 per cent. In the meantime, input costs rose and squeezed profits. Suddenly, there were higher margins. The sellers' market was rapidly dying a messy death.

The Question

Like other companies in the cement industry, Jaypee had been quite content to limit its marketing activity to running jingles on the radio and painting some shops and walls with its name. With the change in the environment, JRC needed new markets. Where were they to go?

The Answer—Go Rural

Jaypee decided to go deep into rural India. The rationale for the decision was:

- Firstly, the number of rural markets far exceeded the number of urban markets in Uttar Pradesh and Bihar.
- Secondly, if a rural buyer does develop brand loyalty, he tends to stick by the brand.
- Thirdly, large cement manufacturers had not made significant efforts to tap the rural market. So, while penetrating rural India would hardly be a cakewalk for JRC, the competition would also face the same degree of difficulty; it was a level playing field. In fact, JRC would have a first-entrant advantage in establishing links with the end consumers and influencers.

JRC decided to increase its share in the two states of UP and Bihar. In India, primary markets for cement makers are within a 250 km radius of the plants, since transporting cement is an expensive proposition. JRC's plant is located at Rewa in Madhya Pradesh. JRC was interested in these two states since Madhya Pradesh is a cement-surplus state and UP and Bihar are cement-deficient ones,

Rural Consumers

The rural market is interestingly different from the urban markets. The challenge lies in adapting to the idiosyncrasies of rural consumers:

1. *Not durable:* In urban markets, cement would be classified as a durable. In the rural market, on the other hand, a buyer purchases cement year after year, because he usually keeps adding a room at a time as he doesn't have the money to complete the desired construction in one go.
2. *Peculiar quality testing:* The rural consumer has his own ways of checking cement quality. He tests the quality by throwing handfuls of cement against the wall to see how it attaches itself to the surface, or by examining the colours (the darker the better) or even tasting it (bitter is preferred). Quality control

executives have no choice but to adapt to the vagaries. Many firms have started adding colour at the grinding stage to darken the cement.

3. *Commodity perception:* The perception of cement as a commodity creates problems in both urban and rural areas. A buyer doesn't ask for a specific brand. He asks for a number of bags of cement. The only brand which had any recognition was ACC.

Market Research

JRC and marketing consultancy firm Gaur and Nagi (G&N) teamed up to make an in-depth study of the target market. Forty-two areas in UP and 35 in Bihar were chosen for the market research. The four-month long exercise involved administering structured questionnaires to 1,200 buyers and 1,100 masons and unstructured interviews with 480 buyers.

The research was an eye opener:

- *Influencers:* It had always been assumed that the *Sarpanch* or village head is the chief influencer in the brand-choice decision. It was now discovered that his influence level was zero. It was the mason and the dealer whose opinion swayed the customer the most. Word-of-mouth recommendations by other users and sheer familiarity had a strong role to play. The research also indicated that masons knew little about the product and wanted to know more. However, no cement maker had addressed the need.
- *Brand identification:* Buyers sometimes brought in an empty bag of cement to indicate the brand they wanted as the brand name was printed in English and, therefore, unfamiliar to them.
- *Promotion:* JRC's original marketing plan consisted of using inoculations at the Public Health Centre (PHC) as a promotional exercise, instituting trophies for rural sports such as wrestling and airing advertisements on television. However, the market research indicated that most functional PHCs exist only on paper. Out of the 77 markets surveyed, only one hosted a wrestling competition during the period of research. TV was just not a viable medium because of the power problems that exist in rural and even in semi-rural areas.
- *Market index:* The consultancy firm, G&N, created a market index for JRC. Most businesses use financial indicators such as sales, order booking, collection, outstanding, inventory, etc. to assess and plan growth. However, the new index measures non-financial business indicators such as market attractiveness, business-development cycles, employee and dealer motivation and customer satisfaction. These soft parameters were converted into hard numbers. G&N set about developing the index with interviews at all levels of the sales and marketing team. Employees were quizzed about what they considered were Jaypee's most attractive markets and why. From these interviews, seven parameters emerged that defined market attractiveness—potential, net cement realization (the earnings after removing freight, excise, commissions, etc.), credit, market share, dealer's strength, inventory movement and premium available. G&N then asked the same people to assign weightages to the parameters. The scale was then applied to all the markets JRC was operating in. The composite score for each was calculated and markets categorized as "good," "bad" and "average." JRC could now decide on the specific markets to concentrate on and develop individual strategies for each market, instead of focusing its efforts across all markets and approaching all of them with the same game plan.

Game Plan

The action plan decided on ranged from mason-contract programmes to advertising media to promotions, keeping the markets in Uttar Pradesh and Bihar in mind.

- *Video vans:* Since TV advertising was not an option, it was decided that video vans would be used. The film developed by the marketing department explained the manufacturing process, composition and other details of cement and highlighted JRC's brand Jaypee. The aim was to make the name Jaypee synonymous with cement in the mind of the audience. The 30-minute film had actor A. K. Hangal as the hero—a mason and songs and dances were thrown in for good measure.
- *Melas and fairs: Melas* or fairs are important vehicles for brand communication in rural India. The usual route taken by marketers is to have stalls and banners in and around the fair. Jaypee's stall, however, offered tea free of charge to all visitors to the *mela*. Paintings were also used.
- *Mason-contact programme:* JRC conducted mason-contact programmes to educate masons about the product. A company spokesperson spoke about Jaypee cement, addressed the mason's problems providing a forum where masons could air their views. Each mason was photographed against a Jaypee banner and received a copy of the photo. This turned out to be an effective relationship builder.

Future Outlook

As a result of the efforts, sales went up and JRC emerged as the market leader in UP with 17.8 per cent share. JRC is planning to increase capacity by 60 per cent, which will make it the largest cement manufacturer in the country. It may seem an optimistic move since cement consumption has been growing only at an average compounded rate of 7–8 per cent since 1982. The outlook may change radically if the Government enters the infrastructural sector.

DISCUSSION QUESTIONS

1. Explain how JRC could convert a crisis into an opportunity.
2. In your view, what are the major factors responsible for the success of Jaypee cement?
3. Can other markets be addressed keeping in mind the marketing programmes in UP and Bihar?

Source: Harveena Herr, "Concrete Ambition," *A & M* (July 1994): 54–56.

Index

Page numbers in italic type refer to tables or boxes.